Says Who?

A Guide to the Quotations of the Century

Says Who?

A Guide to the Quotations of the Century

Jonathon Green

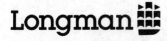

LONGMAN GROUP UK LIMITED
Longman House
Burnt Mill, Harlow, Essex CM20 2JE, England
and Associated Companies throughout the World

© Jonathon Green 1988

First published 1988

British Library Cataloguing in Publication Data

Says who?: guide to the quotations of the
  century.
  I. Green, Jonathon, *1948* –
080

ISBN 0-582-89336-4

Typeset on a Linotron 202,
in Caladonia $9\frac{1}{2}$ on $11\frac{1}{2}$ point

Printed in Great Britain at The Bath Press, Avon

A

ACHARD, MARCEL (1899–1974) French playwright and scriptwriter

Women like silent men. They think they're listening.

A typically mordant comment on the sex war from one of France's leading comedy writers, whose wide variety of works for both stage and screen combined burlesque, pantomime and pathos. Among his plays are *Jean de la Lune* (1929) and a translation of Ben Jonson's *Epicene, or the Silent Woman* (1609), a play based on the impossible search for a woman who will not talk, and one which Dryden characterised as the most perfectly plotted of all comedies. His films include the second 'Clouseau' farce with Peter Sellers, *A Shot in the Dark* (1964).

ACHESON, DEAN (1894–1971) US statesman

Great Britain has lost an Empire and not yet found a role.
speech on December 6, 1962

Speaking to the US army cadets of West Point Military Academy, Acheson was commenting on Britain's decline as a world power, for which, along with the concomitant rise of the US, he was as responsible as anyone. Although many influential Britons resented his opinion, in which he stated that the the once great power could no longer expect to trade either on its leadership of the Commonwealth or on the 'special relationship' with America and should start looking towards greater involvement with Europe, the essential truth could not be denied. The problem, however, was that Europe, personified by General de Gaulle, was not particularly interested.

ACHESON, DEAN

It is worse than immoral, it's a mistake.

Acheson did not take the US into Vietnam, but as one of what David Halberstam called 'the best and the brightest' of America's government officials, he was instrumental in escalating her involvement there. Working on the premise that it was America's destiny to drive out Communism wherever it might be found, he initially saw the war as a moral crusade. Only when the great adventure misfired was he forced, pragmatically, to make the comment above.

1

ACHESON, DEAN
The greatest mistake I made was not to die in office.

Acheson made this remark after listening to the eulogies of his successor as US Secretary of State, John Foster Dulles, at Dulles' funeral on May 27th, 1959. Dulles, who created the nuclear war policy of 'massive retaliation' ('don't challenge us or we'll nuke you off the face of the earth') and coined the term 'brinkmanship', was fortunate to die with his policies relatively unimpaired. Acheson died in 1971, a witness to the utter collapse of his advocacy of the Vietnam war.

ACHESON, DEAN
The first requirement of a statesman is that he be dull. This is not always easy to achieve.
quoted in 1970

Acheson, a man of whom the former Canadian Prime Minister Lester Pearson said in in 1971 'Not only did he not suffer fools gladly, he did not suffer them at all', was serious, but not dull. He led that group of hard-nosed American foreign policy makers, drawn from the East Coast establishment of businessmen, lawyers and financiers, who helped consummate their country's climb to super-power status in the 1950s. Their basic credo was that Communism was bad and Communists understood only force. That way, in a more volatile decade, lay Vietnam and their, and America's, fall from grace.

ACHESON, DEAN
I will undoubtedly have to seek what is happily known as gainful employment, which I am glad to say does not describe holding public office.
on leaving his post as Secretary of State, 1952

Acheson left his post as Truman's Secretary of State on December 22 1952. He was detested by the American right wing, typified by the 'Neanderthal' republican Senator Hugh Butler of Arizona, who loathed Acheson's sophistication, his urbanity and his Anglophilia, declaring that he stood 'for everything that has been wrong with the United States for years' and urging him to 'get out, get out'. Presumably Acheson's advocacy of the war in Vietnam, on his return to power under Kennedy, must have pleased Butler more.

ADAMS, FRANKLIN P. (1881–1960) (F.P.A.) American journalist
The trouble with this country is that there are too many politi-

cians who believe, with a conviction based on experience, that you can fool all of the people all of the time.
Nods and Becks (1944)

President Abraham Lincoln defined the prudent politician's credo in 1862, saying 'You can fool some of the people all of the time, and all of the people some of the time, but you cannot fool all of the people all of the time'. Adams, epitomising the cynical attitudes common to his circle of New York sophisticates, the 'Algonquin Round Table', was suggesting that, given the nature of both 'the people' and the average politician, Lincoln was being over-modest if not downright naive. A contemporary, James Thurber, ran another change on the old line when he suggested in *Fables for Our Time* (1940) that 'You can fool too many of the people too much of the time.'

ADAMS, FRANKLIN P.

When a man you like switches from what he said a year ago, or four years ago, he is a broad-minded person who has courage enough to change his mind with changing conditions. When a man you don't like does it, he is a liar who has broken his promises.
Nods and Becks (1944)

The tolerance of the Algonquinites for each other's behaviour, both in opinion and activity, was extensive. Their intolerance for even the minor peccadilloes of those who fell outside the charmed circle was legendary. Adams, while not writing perhaps of his elite peers, doubtless spoke for them, as well as noting a more general human characteristic.

ADAMS, FRANKLIN P.

When the political columnists say 'Every thinking man' they mean themselves; and when the candidates appeal to 'every intelligent voter', they mean everybody who is going to vote for them.
Nods and Becks (1944)

On the whole the chic writers of 1920s New York were uninterested in politics. They campaigned not, neither did they vote. Or not conspicuously. Their own writing dwelt on the ephemera: wit, and above all performance, both in public and, perhaps more importantly, in private. Broadway and its environs felt nothing but disdain for Foggy Bottom, unless, of course, like George S.

Kaufman, you could pen a box office monster, ridiculing the entire system, such as *Of Thee I Sing* (1932).

ADAMS, HENRY BROOKS (1838–1918) American historian

Politics, as a practice, whatever its professions, has always been the systematic organisation of hatreds.
The Education of Henry Adams (1907)

As the grandson and great-grandson of American presidents (John Quincy Adams and John Adams) Adams may be presumed to have some justification for his opinion. He was a historian himself, teaching at Harvard University after spending some of his youth in England, where his father, Charles Francis Adams (1807–86) had been the American minister during the US Civil War, and where Henry met such luminaries as Gladstone, Lord John Russell and A.C. Swinburne. Adams wrote a number of major works on both American and European history. His autobiography *The Education of Henry Adams* remains his best memorial. This book attempts to deal with the challenge of the new 20th century (only seven years old on its publication). Its main thrust is to point up the uselessness of a contemporary formal education in dealing with the complex 'multiverse' and to expound the author's own 'Dynamic Theory of History' as a possible means of dealing with an increasingly technological world.

ADE, GEORGE (1866–1944) American humourist

Do unto yourself as your neighbours do unto themselves and look pleasant.
Hand Made Fables (1920)

George Ade's work is less popular today than it was at the turn of the century but his *Fables In Slang* (1899) sold 70,000 copies on its first printing, and subsequent collections of his short, highly colloquial fables, first created for his column in the Chicago News-Record, made him for twenty years one of America's foremost humourists. He was fortunate to have at his disposal an America at its most enthusiastically expansive, developing from a relatively backwards, if brash, nation of immigrants and frontiersmen, into the nascent super-power that crossed the Atlantic in 1917 to save the Old World from itself. His writing, capitalising on the social absurdities of the era, depends less on actual slang than on the vernacular traditions of Josh Billings and Finlay Peter Dunne, but his was a crueller wit, more cynical and less folksy than theirs. Among his many fans were Mark Twain, Carl Sandburg and H.L. Mencken.

ADLER, ALFRED (1870–1937) German psychoanalyst

It is easier to fight for one's principles than to live up to them.
quoted in *Alfred Adler* by Phyllis Bottome (1939)

This concept, while couched in lay terms, reflects a central aspect of the psycho-analytic theories espoused by Adler, a contemporary and latterly a rival of Sigmund Freud in Vienna. Unlike Freud, Adler rejected the theory of the libido and of infantile sexuality as the root of neurosis, substituting for them a belief in the vulnerability of the infant and the concomitant feelings of vulnerability. The infant desires to overcome and compensate for these feelings and the way in which he or she attempts to do this is dependant on the inter-personal relationships within the family. The result of this process is that the child develops his or her own lifestyle. If that lifestyle fails to work adequately, the result will be continued feelings of inferiority and thus neurosis.

ADMIRALTY 1939

Winston is back.
signal to the British Fleet, August 1914

At the outbreak of World War II in September 1939 Winston Churchill was still in the political wilderness. A long-term advocate of rearmament and an early opponent of Hitler, he had been shunned by the appeasers who dominated the British government throughout the 1930s. Twenty-five years before, in a previous World War, he had been First Lord of the Admiralty. Now, when Prime Minister Neville Chamberlain, bowing to the demands of a new conflict, reinstated him in his old post an exultant Admiralty cabled this message to its warships.

ADORNO, THEODOR W. (1903–1969) German philosopher, social theorist and music critic

Of the world as it exists, one cannot be enough afraid.

Adorno was born in Germany and taught at the Institut fur Sozialforschung in Frankfurt. In 1934 he was forced to emigrate to America, where the Institut was reconstituted in New York as the New School for Social Research. Here he stayed until it retransferred to Frankfurt in 1960. Adorno is regarded as the most brilliant and versatile, although the least widely known of his peers at the school, whose studies were devoted to the aesthetics of a mass society. He dealt particularly in musicology and the sociology of art, music and mass culture. The main thrust of his work is that reality cannot be confined by any theoretical or ideological strait-jacket, all of which lead inevitably to totalitarian, oppressive systems. Marxism and existentialism were not free of such a taint, but his prime villain is empirical science, which has made itself a willing servant of market forces, rejecting any considerations other than those of the creation of saleable commodities.

ADVERTISEMENT
Roses grow on you
campaign for Cadbury's 'Roses' chocolates

Cadbury's Roses are an assortment of soft and hard centred chocolates. This slogan was adopted in the mid-Sixties and became especially popular as demonstrated by comedian Norman Vaughan who would raise his thumb and watch as 'roses' sprung from it. The gesture, and the choice of Vaughan derived from his current celebrity as compere of television's Sunday Night at the London Palladium, where he had developed his own catchphrase of 'Swinging...' (thumb raised) and 'Dodgy' (thumb down).

ADVERTISEMENT
Does she...or doesn't she? ... Only her hairdresser knows for sure
campaign for Clairol 1955

Shirley Polyakoff, the copywriter who created the question, and its ambiguous answer, claimed in her memoirs, also titled *Does She...or Doesn't She* (1975), that the idea for Clairol's highly successful advertisement came when she quite innocently asked her husband whether he thought that a girl with a particularly vivid shade of red hair dyed it or not. When Polyakoff submitted the line to her boss at Foote Cone and Belding she suggested that the answer to the question should be 'Only her mother knows for sure!' or, alternatively 'So natural, only her mother knows for sure.' Given the sensibilities of America's beauty salon operators, who were after all supposed to know their jobs, this had to be changed to 'Only her hairdresser knows for sure'. There was even a slight hiccup when Life magazine, claiming the line was a double entendre, rejected it. Only when research among Life's female employees failed to find a single woman with a mind as dirty as the men, was the decision reversed.

ADVERTISEMENT
Guinness is good for you
campaign for Guinness 1929–41

Guinness resisted the need to advertise until 1929 when, after 170 years of purveying their popular stout, they turned to the S.H.

Benson agency and asked for a campaign. Bensons undertook some market research, by no means the automatic event that it is today, and discovered that the majority of Guinness drinkers believed that the dark, foamy brew actually benefited their health. On the basis of this their copywriter Oswald Greene created the slogan 'Guinness is good for you'. Initially rejected as being too ordinary, it was adopted and proved massively successful, although it was discontinued around 1941. Certainly Guinness have yet to find an ad campaign to equal Benson's.

ADVERTISEMENT
You don't have to be Jewish to love Levy's Rye Bread
campaign for Levy's Rye Bread, 1959

Rye bread is a staple of New York City in the way that fish and chips go with London. On the other hand, while fish and chips are pretty much a universal, rye bread brings with it automatic Jewish connotations. When Bill Taubin of the agency Doyle Dane and Bernbach wrote this line, he set out deliberately to override that image, setting his caption beneath a variety of individuals, all far from stereotypically Jewish, who were contentedly munching their slice of Levy's. The ad worked well, and the line has stuck for ever, with a variety of 'You don't have to be...to...' spinoffs.

ADVERTISEMENT
I dreamt I was Cleopatra in my Maidenform Bra
campaign for Maidenform foundation garments

The copywriter at agency Norman, Craig and Kummel who thought up this line was tapping into a rich vein of fantasy, although how many potential purchasers of Maidenform's somewhat rugged brassieres even knew who Cleopatra was, let alone imagined themselves as a latterday Queen of the Nile, can only be guessed at.

ADVERTISEMENT
Can you tell Stork from butter?
campaign for Stork margarine

In the days before agencies had discovered the health angle, and could thus promote their margarines as 'polyunsaturates' and claim that eschewing butter would give you a better sex life, career, larger house and similar material appurtenances, they were forced to persuade the shoppers that margarine, a much-despised butter-substitute, was in fact better than the real thing. The most celebrated version of this was the 'Stork Test', a public challenge compered by a suitably oily television 'personality' who would offer

7

supposed housewives pieces of bread, duly buttered or Storked, and ask 'Can you tell Stork from butter?'. Unsurprisingly, none of those who made it to what commercial television still called the 'natural break', ever managed.

ADVERTISEMENT
It cleans your breath while it cleans your teeth
copy for Colgate toothpaste

This copy line for Colgate, written by Madison Avenue's Ted Bates, was one of the earliest examples of what advertising calls the USP or 'unique selling proposition', a concept that works by three rules: it offers specific benefits from the product; the competition don't claim it; it sells. Coined in 1940 it fulfilled all three criteria. The particular beauty, common to many great advertisements, is that while the benefit one claims is not actually unique to your client's product, your campaign is the only one to claim it. Bates was only stating something that must be true of all toothpastes, given the proximity of breath and teeth, but no-one else had bothered to point it out.

ADVERTISEMENT
Beanz Meanz Heinz

Ruth Watson of the advertising agency Young & Rubicam created this slogan for Heinz Baked Beans. It updated, but did not replace, the image of Heinz '57 Varieties', which had hitherto characterised the company and featured chirpy pre-teens slurping down their teatime treat.

ADVERTISEMENT
Body Odour

The concept of 'body odour', or as it became more widely and sinisterly known 'B.O.' was created as the basis of an American advertising campaign for Lifebuoy soap, launched in the 1930s. The grim tones of a chorus intoning the horrors of the unwashed armpit, albeit as nothing in the face of the soapy saviour, imprinted the malodorous plague onto the minds of myriad radio listeners.

ADVERTISEMENT
Drinka Pinta Milka Day

This glibly assonant slogan was designed in 1958 to extol the virtues of milk, and its British Marketing Board. While the creative department at the consulting agency, Mather and Crowther, apparently loathed it; the clients, the executive officer of whose publicity council, one Bertram Whitehead, had actually coined the phrase, were all too keen. Aping the slightly earlier (c.1940) but semantically and phonetically similar 'cuppa' (tea), 'pinta' may now be found in the august pages of the Supplement to the *Oxford English Dictionary*, O-Scz (1982) although citations show that it has gone on to embrace beer as well as milk.

ADVERTISEMENT
Go to work on an egg

Every advertising copywriter proclaims that they have a novel, or these days a film script, right there inside their word processor, just waiting, come the right moment, to burst forth in remunerative but literate and thus acceptable glory. The role model for many such hopefuls may well be the novelist Fay Weldon (1933–), author of such books as *Down Among the Women* (1971), *Praxis* (1978) and *The Life and Loves of a She-Devil* (1983), who was among the creators, if not the sole creator of this slogan for the British Egg Marketing Board when, in 1957, she worked for the agency Mather and Crowther.

ADVERTISEMENT
We're number two. We try harder.

The premise of American advertising was always ballyhoo until this pragmatic but appealling slogan was developed for Avis Rentacar by their agency Doyle Dane & Bernbach. Avis had failed for years to overtake their main and superior rivals Hertz. Their acknowledgement of the rivalry and their secondary status captivated America, a nation not generally known for its espousal of the runner-up.

ADVERTISEMENT
Even Your Best Friends Won't Tell You
campaign for Listerine

This copy line for Listerine Mouth Wash worked for many years by exploiting the perennial fear of social embarrassment. As kissing couples suddenly parted and secretaries shrank from the boss's dictation, millions took to blowing surreptitiously into their own cupped hands, desperate to check for telltale foulness, and possibly to replace it with an even more pungent, if antiseptic odour, that of Listerine.

ADVERTISEMENT
You're never alone with a Strand
campaign for Strand cigarettes, 1960

ADVERTISEMENT

Advertisements usually have to become successful before their copylines infiltrate the national or even international consciousness. Not so copywriter John May's line for Strand, a cigarette launched in 1960 by W.D. and H.O. Wills. In the dim days before health warnings and similar impedimenta to trade, Wills wanted to launch a cheap filter cigarette straight at the youth market. May envisaged associating the new cigarette with the 'young Sinatra'. The aim was to push the alienated lonely youth angle. Benson's found a suitable Sinatra lookalike, one Terence Brook, a 28-year-old actor who fortunately looked somewhat like James Dean as well. They dressed him in a trenchcoat and slouch hat, dumped him on a corner in some atmospheric lighting and a voice-over intoned May's line. And then the campaign failed. The young were unimpressed: 'alone' you might never be, but the image was of a miserable solitary person and no-one wanted to know. Strand was withdrawn, but May's slogan lives on regardless.

ADVERTISEMENT
Tonic water by you-know-who
campaign for Schweppes 1963

The big thing in mass entertainment in 1963 was the spy, especially in the form of James Bond and such cut-rate clones as Danger Man. Royston Taylor and Frank Devlin, respectively copywriter and art director at Mather & Crowther, capitalised on the furore to create a campaign for Schweppes tonic in which they posed actor William Franklyn in a variety of silly spy situations and then had him mouth 'Schhh... you know who'. As Taylor has pointed out, the campaign 'accorded with the old copywriter's dream of not showing or even naming the product if it could possibly be avoided'. Franklyn went on to a few acting roles and Sch... sold a good deal of tonic.

ADVERTISEMENT
Nice one, Cyril
for Wonderloaf bread, 1972

In 1972 there appeared on TV an ad for Wonderloaf, attempting to promote this particular variety of pre-sliced, steamed and polythene enwrapped 'bread' as possessing some quality of individuality over and above its peers. The dialogue, featuring two alleged bakers, congratulated one Cyril on his baking skills, identifiable apparently in the loaves he had created, with the line 'Nice one, Cyril'. This was taken up by the public, especially by supporters of the Tottenham Hotspur footballer, Cyril Knowles. It vanished as suddenly as it had appeared, although the Spurs team made a record featuring the line.

ADVERTISEMENT
Say it with flowers
for American Florists

This popular slogan, since used by florists everywhere and incorporated into a number of song titles, was created in 1917. The chairman of the National Publicity Committee of the Society of American Florists, Henry Penn, had decided that the Society required a snappy line to sell their product. He consulted with advertising agency chief Major Patrick O'Keefe (1872-1934). O'Keefe offered 'Flowers are words that even a babe can understand'. Penn rejected this as over-wordy, at which point O'Keefe came back with 'Why, you can say it with flowers in so many words'. Suitably abbreviated, a slogan was born.

ADVERTISEMENT
Every picture tells a story
for Doane's Backache Kidney Pills

Pictures of suffering humanity, bent double beneath some hideous ailment, accompanied the advertisements that appeared earlier in the century for Doane's Backache Kidney Pills in such popular magazines as The Strand and The Windsor. The origins of the phrase have all but vanished, and the advertisements for such patent remedies, once so commonplace, are quaintly obsolete. The phrase lingers on. Perhaps its most celebrated use of recent years was as the title of the first album (issued 1971) by singer Rod Stewart (1945-), which launched him on his long and successful career.

ADVERTISEMENT
Put a tiger in your tank
for Esso Petroleum, post 1964

Esso, the petroleum distributing side of the Standard Oil (SO) Company of America, had consistently used the image of a tiger in their advertising. In 1964 the tiger became the star of a cartoon ad, which carried the copy line 'Put a tiger in your tank'. This exhortation, with its satisfying sexual double entendre, proved a world-wide winner. Every country, it seemed, had the line translated. Other products, notably Japan's Tiger Beer, accorded the Esso tiger the ultimate accolade, parodying the original line for their own promotions. The campaign ran in Britain for about two years, and the tiger, albeit bereft of his most famous copy, is still to be seen in Esso advertising, in or around the tank.

11

ADVERTISEMENT
It beats as it sweeps as it cleans
for Hoover Vacuum cleaners

Hoover Vacuum Cleaners, invented in 1908 by James Murray Spangler, but marketed and popularised by William H. Hoover, have long been part of that elite vocabulary of eponyms whereby a trademark has become the generic term for a whole range of similar products. Not a little credit must be paid for this to Gerald Page-Wood, a copywriter at the advertising agency Erwin Wasey, of Cleveland, Ohio, who based his famous slogan on the main feature of the machine, a triple action whereby it first beat or tapped the carpet to loosen the dirt, then sucked it up into its bag and finally brushed the now clean carpet. The slogan was written in 1919 and has yet to be abandoned.

ADVERTISEMENT
Fingerlickin' Good
slogan for Kentucky Fried Chicken during 1970s

Kentucky Fried Chicken, one of the first fast-food franchises to take a grip on British eating habits, after a long reign as America's favourite take-out snack, produced this particular slogan in 1975 and ran it for several years on both sides of the Atlantic. The image of greasy chicken, sticky fingers and fat-encoated tongue might appal the gourmet but as Kentucky Fried Chicken sales soared, the company must have felt they were doing something right.

ADVERTISEMENT
'I'm ..... . Fly me'
campaign slogan for National Airlines, 1970s

America's National Airlines titillated their male customers and infuriated feminists when they launched this campaign, in which they accentuated unequivocally the concept of stewardess as sex symbol. The ambiguity of 'Candy' or 'Bobbie' or whoever as she pouted her invitation across the screen left no-one in any doubt as to just what she meant by 'fly'. So popular was the slogan that it formed the title of a hit song by 10cc, 'I'm Mandy, Fly Me', released in March 1976. The unfortunate hostess in this particular tale did not 'fly' anywhere much: her plane crashed.

ADVERTISEMENT
At 60 miles an hour the loudest noise in this new Rolls Royce comes from the electric clock
slogan for Rolls Royce, 1958

This slogan extolling the virtues of Rolls Royce cars was written by David Ogilvy, head of the Ogilvy and Mather advertising agency in 1958. Followed by 607 words of factual copy that simply listed thirteen facts about the car and its manufacturers, the ad exemplified what Ogilvy in his book Ogilvy on Advertising (1983) calls 'doing one's homework': simply learning as much as possible about the product one is advertising. 'I have always found this extremely tedious but there is no substitute for it'.

ADVERTISEMENT
You've come a long way, Baby
for Virginia Slims cigarettes

This advertisement created by the Leo Burnett agency must stand as one of the most unashamedly cynical exploitations of a supposedly sincere movement. The campaign, which pictured sophisticated, svelte and supposedly 'liberated' women, pitched itself at the burgeoning ranks of the American women's movement. The 'long way' that the Slims' putative smokers were supposed to have come was presumably from the restrictions of yesteryear, although the sleek models parading their equally slender cigarettes would have probably stayed well out of the kitchen in any era.

ADVERTISEMENT
Stop me and buy one
for Walls Ice Cream

This slogan, which adorned the tricycles of 8,500 Walls Ice Cream salesmen as they pedalled their wares around Britain, was coined in 1923 by the brothers Lionel and Charles Rodd, both of whom were directors of the T. Wall and Sons ice cream manufacturers. The same slogan can still be seen on the occasional ice cream van, along with more lurid exhortations, but it will probably live far longer rephrased as a graffitto on condom-vending machines: 'Buy me and stop one'.

ADVERTISEMENT
Blondes have more fun
campaign for 'Lady Clairol', 1957

Copywriter Shirley Polyakoff's line for hair-dye 'Lady Clairol' was chosen from a short-list of ten suggestions, among which were the ponderous 'Is it true that blondes are never lonesome?' and 'Is it true blondes marry millionaires?' This celebration of the flaxen doubtless referred back to Anita Loos' best-selling book *Gentlemen Prefer Blondes* (1925), although those seeking social reincarnation through hair colouring would presumably have eschewed her subtitle 'The Illuminating Diary of a Professional Lady'. The agency would have also found the answer to their second, unused question in Loos' sequel: *But Gentlemen Marry Brunettes.*

ADVERTISEMENT
Top People Take The Times
campaign for *The Times*

In 1954 the London Press Exchange, who handled advertising for *The Times*, commissioned a survey to assess how the newspaper's readers felt about it. The survey came up with very little, and the management saw no need to alter the paper, either by taking the advertisements off the front page, giving by-lines to the stories, or any such new-fangled nonsense. Conversely, they could not deny that sales were dropping and they demanded a campaign to boost them. The slogan that satisfied them was created by chance. An unemployed copywriter, G.H. Saxon Mills, happened to meet his acquaintance Stanley Morison, an executive of the paper. As a favour he was asked to prepare a brochure which could be given out to visitors to the Times offices at Printing House Square. The brochure he created had pictures of various supposed opinion-makers, each illustration crowned with the line 'Top People Take The Times'. Thus was born a successful campaign.

AGATE, JAMES (1877–1947) British film and dramatic critic

The English instinctively admire any man who has no talent and is modest about it.
Ego (1935–48)

Agate was born in Lancashire, the son of a cotton merchant. He worked for some years in his father's business but in 1907 began writing theatrical criticism for the *Manchester Guardian*. From 1923 until his death he worked for the *Sunday Times*. His reflection on the essential worry felt by the average English person when faced by an exceptional individual rings as true today as ever. Modest mediocrity remains the most comforting of personas, if only to those whom, to their relief, it cannot threaten.

AGATE, JAMES

Theatre director: a person engaged by the management to conceal the fact that the players cannot act.
Ego (1935–48)

Agate's nine-part autobiography, appearing between 1935–48, was entitled *Ego*. In the main it detailed the critic's life in, and observations on the major figures of the worlds of literary and theatrical London, and took the form of a diary. The remark above may have stemmed from his oft-repeated credo that after seeing Sarah Bernhardt (1845–1923) and Henry Irving (1838-1905), he appreciated that the standards of acting that they had set could never be rivalled, let alone surpassed.

AGEE, JAMES (1909–55) American film critic and novelist

It is a peculiar part of the good photographer's adventure to know where luck is most likely to lie in the stream, to hook it and to bring it in without unfair play, and without too much subduing it.

Agee remains one of America's most respected film critics, whose seminal collection Agee on Film was published posthumously. He also wrote a number of screenplays, including that of *The African Queen* (adapted in 1951 from C.S. Forester's novel) and several novels, the most famous of which was the semi-autobiographical *A Death in the Family* which deals with how a Tennessee family is destroyed after the father is killed in a car accident.

AGNEW, SPIRO T. (1918-) American politician

A spirit of national masochism prevails, encouraged by an effete corps of impudent snobs who characterise themselves as intellectuals.
speaking on October 19, 1969

Vice-President Agnew spoke at a New Orleans dinner on October 19, 1969, ostensibly delivering a relatively unexciting exposition of the current Nixon foreign and economic policy. The guests, the attendant press corps, and soon the entire country – and particularly its liberal intellectuals – were surprised to hear Agnew's opening remarks, in which he attacked what the media soon paraphrased as 'the effete snobs' for their refusal to back the President in Vietnam. The general belief is that presidential speech-writer William Safire penned the offending lines, but Safire himself, now best known for his regular 'On Language' column in the New York Times, claims in his Political Dictionary where he deals with the quote, that the Vice-President composed the introduction himself.

AGNEW, SPIRO T.

Once you've seen one city slum you've seen them all.
comment in October, 1972

It was presumably on the basis of the knowledge that, thanks to

White House 'plumbers', phonetaps, illegal surveillance, slush funds and the rest of the wide-ranging malfeasances that had been mobilised to ensure the re-election of President Richard Nixon in 1972, nothing could hinder the Republican juggernaut, that Spiro Agnew, campaigning as the vice-presidential candidate, was allowed to parade his prejudices so openly. Agnew's disdain for liberals, minorities and a variety of progressive groups was well known; his contemptuous dismissal of America's inner city problems still outraged many, for all that it encapsulated the views of the 'Silent Majority', safely immune in their Mid-Western farmlands. Nemesis did eventually strike, and soon Agnew, like his boss, faced the consequences of the Watergate revelations and resigned one step ahead of impeachment.

AITKIN, DON (1937–) Australian politician
Whatever politicians, activists and manipulators propose, it is the phlegmatic, indifferent, ingrained electorate which disposes.
in *The Bulletin* magazine, 1969

'Nam homo proponit, sed Deus disponit', said Thomas à Kempis (1380–1471) in his book *De Imitatione Christi*, a Latin phrase translated neatly as 'Man proposes, but God disposes'. Thomas' great work traced the gradual progress of a soul to Christian perfection. Whether Aitkin's 'phlegmatic, indifferent, ingrained' voters qualify as earthly Gods may be debated, as may the concept of their ballots leading Australian politicians even as far as parliamentary perfection, but their ability to pour cold water on the most impassioned ideologue is, fortunately, undisputed.

AKINS, ZOE (1865–1958) American playwright
The Greeks had a word for it
play title, 1929

Zoe Akins wrote her play *The Greeks Had a Word for It* in 1929. Writing to Burton Stevenson, an American compiler of two large dictionaries of quotations, she explained that 'the phrase is original and grew out of the dialogue'. However the line does not appear in the text, only as the title. Either way, it caught on with impressive alacrity and by 1930 it was popular throughout the English-speaking world. The 'it' in question is 'love' and the word presumably is 'eros'.

ALAIN, (EMILE CHARTIER) (1868–1951) French writer
Nothing is more dangerous than an idea, when a man has only one idea.'
Propos de la Religion (1938)

Chartier, who chose the pen-name 'Alain' after the 15th century French poet Alain Chenier, was a philosopher, teacher and essayist. This particular aperçu was published in his Propos de la religion, one of the many propos (suggestions or resolutions) on life, art, politics and a variety of allied topics which for many years he had published in his local newspaper, the Dépêche de Rouen.

ALBEE, EDWARD (1928–) American playwright
Who's Afraid of Virginia Woolf?
Who's Afraid of Virginia Woolf? (1964)

This play, produced in 1962, was Albee's third. As his first full-lenght creation, it took him from the 'theatre of the absurd' in which his early works *The Zoo Story* (1959) and *The American Dream* (1961) were positioned to a more naturalistic and accessible style. The title, with its nursery-rhyme parody and its reference to the doyenne of Bloomsbury (and of scores of college theses), evokes an atmosphere of fear and tension, and the constant suggestion of 'something nasty in the woodshed'. Two academic couples dine together, the one pair older, apparently cynical and certainly in increasingly obvious pain. The other, young, naive and vulnerable, find themselves sucked into the sadomasochistic ritual that is the sole sustaining bond in the senior relationship.

ALBEE, EDWARD
The way to a man's heart is through his wife's belly, and don't you forget it.
Who's Afraid of Virginia Woolf? (1964)

Drunkenly extolling the virtues, and necessities, of campus adulteries, George, the older and more raddled of the two academics who, in Albee's play, are dining together with their wives, is using his youthful guest's naivety and growing drunkenness to lure him into the perverse games that dominate his own relationship with his wife Martha. As a supposedly civilised dinner degenerates into games characterised as 'Get the Guests' and 'Hump the Hostess', George parodies the traditional proverb usually offered to young wives: 'The way to a man's heart is through his belly'. Unsuprisingly, when the younger man begins to take him at his word, George, although not Martha, showers him with abuse.

ALDISS, BRIAN (1925–) British science fiction writer
When childhood dies, its corpses are called adults and they enter society, one of the politer names of hell. That is why we dread children, even if we love them. They show us the state of our decay.
in The Guardian, 1971

Aldiss is most popularly known as a prolific science fiction writer. He has published many books, including the Helliconia Trilogy' (1982–85) which details the evolution of a whole planetary system. He is a major historian of the genre, which he dates back to Mary Shelley's *Frankenstein*, and he has written his own tributes both to her in *Frankenstein Unbound* (1973) and to H.G. Wells in *Moreau's Other Island* (1980), as well as a comprehensive history of S-F, *Billion Year Spree* (1973). Aldiss surprised many of his fans, and gained a certain notoriety, with the first volume of his autobiography *The Hand-Reared Boy* (1970) in which he recalled, inter alia, his youthful masturbation.

ALDRICH, THOMAS B. (1836–1907) American poet and editor

Civilisation is the lamb's skin in which barbarism masquerades.
The Ponkapog Papers (1903)

Aldrich was born in Portsmouth, New Hampshire and used it as the setting for his later novel, the semi- autobiographical *The Story of a Bad Boy* (1870). He was never in the forefront of American literature but specialised in producing a quantity of sophisticated, light verse for various periodicals. The above aphorism is a good example of his work, according suitably with the fin de siècle attitudes such writing encouraged. Between 1881–1890 he edited the distinguished American magazine of literature, politics and the arts, the *Atlantic Monthly*, founded in 1857 by J.R. Lowell.

ALEXANDER'S RAGTIME BAND

Come on and hear, come on and hear, Alexander's Ragtime Band
screenplay (1938)

Irving Berlin wrote twenty songs for this schmaltzy story of two songwriters, played by Tyrone Power and Don Ameche, who take the history of the years 1911–1939 as background for their emotional duelling for the hand of Alice Faye. Faye sings the title song as well as the popular 'When That Midnight Choo-Choo Leaves for Alabam'.

ALGREN, NELSON (1909-1981) American novelist

Never play cards with any man named 'Doc'. Never eat at any place called 'Mom's'. And never, ever, no matter what else you do in your whole life, never sleep with anyone whose troubles are worse than your own.
What Every Young Man Should Know

Such streetwise philosophies are typical of Algren, whose books include the best-selling *Man with the Golden Arm* (1949), *A Walk on the Wild Side* (1957), and *Never Come Morning*. Algren's intention to give some form of recognition to the life that 'multitudes of people have been forced into' made him a favourite writer of the non-ideological left. Algren's terse, spare writing transcends its pulp-magazine topics, dealing naturalistically in the mean streets and their junkies, hoods, pimps and whores, and predating and surpassing his many latterday imitators. Writing thirty years later Algren might have been a real success; at the time he received a mere £15,000 for the rights to *Man With the Golden Arm*, and summed up his career: 'There is no way of being a creative writer in America without being a loser'.

ALGREN, NELSON

The avocation of assessing the failures of better men can be turned into a comfortable livelihood, providing you back it up with a Ph.D.
in *Writers at Work* 1st series (1958)

Algren's best books were written in the period immediately following his discharge from the Army in 1945. He lived in a £10 a month room, starved himself in the traditional way of artists in garrets, and produced three novels. The failure of these novels to reach the audience he hoped would understand and appreciate them – the middle-class left-wingers who paraded their sympathies for the American underclass of which he wrote – permanently alienated Algren from the literary establishment. He particularly loathed the critics who, in the late Forties, preferred to tip Norman Mailer, Gore Vidal and Truman Capote for the literary top. Algren would have doubtless agreed with another of the many artists disgusted by those who criticise their work, his fellow writer Whitney Balliett (1926–) who wrote in *Dinosaurs in the Morning* (1962) 'A critic is a bundle of biases held loosely together by a sense of taste.'

ALI, MUHAMMAD   (1942–) American boxer

No Viet Cong ever called me Nigger.
in D. Atyeo & F. Dennis *The Holy Warrior* (1975)

Muhammad Ali was arguably the greatest heavyweight champion the world has seen. In 1964, as Cassius Clay, he had defeated 'the big ugly bear' Sonny Liston to take the title. Superbly outrageous, his arrogance and self-promotion outside the ring was surpassed only by his performances inside it. Clay changed his name later that year, when he joined the militant Black Muslims. To many, this was merely another gloriously infuriating example of the boxer's wilfulness but in 1967, facing compulsory military service in Vietnam, Ali stated that as a Muslim minister 'I find I cannot be true to my belief in religion by accepting such a call.' To the press he put it more succinctly. He was fined £10,000 and sentenced to five years in jail for draft evasion. Far worse, he lost his titles and for three-and-a-half years, when he should have been at his peak, he suffered exile from the ring.

ALINSKY, SAUL (1909–1972) American radical

A racially integrated community is a chronological term timed from the entrance of the first black family to the exit of the last white family.

Alinsky's sour comment on the realities of white liberalism reflects harshly on the grim realities of modern inner city life. The population shifts that have changed once prosperous areas into slums have persisted since the last World War and as black 'block-busting' families have moved in, it has been impossible in many cases for all but the most blinkered to deny the flight of the white middle classes. Alinsky, however, did not live to see the reverse process: the gentrification and embourgeoisement of those same areas, high prices and fashionable developments driving out the blacks in the face of new 'block-busters': the upwardly-mobile young whites.

ALL ABOUT EVE

Fasten your seatbelts, its going to be a bumpy night.
screenplay by Joseph Mankiewicz (1950)

In *All About Eve* Bette Davis plays Margo Channing, a fading but still peppy Broadway star whose laurels are about to be seized by the scheming Eve Harrington (Anne Baxter). In the end the film is Hollywood's sentimental evocation of a legion of theatrical clichés, but Davis' performance is superb and George Sanders, as the waspish critic Addison de Witt, plus protégé Marilyn Monroe in her second proper role, as his pneumatic 'friend', 'a graduate of the Copacabana School of Dramatic Arts', is maliciously alluring. In a performance for which he won an Oscar Sanders defined his calling in lines that could only have been written by someone who had suffered critics himself: 'My native habitat is the theatre, I toil not, neither do I spin. I am a critic and a commentator. I am essential to the theatre – as ants to a picnic, as the boll weevil to a cotton field.' The film, which won a total of six Oscars, sparkles with bitchery and wisecracks; critic Pauline Kael described it as 'ersatz art of a very high grade and one of the most enjoyable movies ever made'.

This particular line comes from Davis, preparing to host a party in her honour, but spying de Witt and Eve and preparing for the worst as her friends buzz around, all trying to pretend that there's nothing to worry about.

ALLEN, FRED (1894–1956) (John F. Sullivan) American comedian

A gentleman is anyone who wouldn't hit a woman with his hat on.

The 'gentleman', usually of the English variety and beset with the social mannerisms that such categorisation implies, has often been found wanting in performance of those charms that he is permitted in image. Fred Allen's witty putdown mocks both the illusion and the affectation. In *The Ipcress File* (1962), Len Deighton offered his own variation: 'Ross was a regular officer; that is to say he didn't drink gin after 7.30 pm or hit ladies without first removing his hat', and HL Mencken categorised the gentleman as one who didn't hit a woman 'without provocation.'

ALLEN, FRED

Television is chewing gum for the eyes.
quoted in Leslie Halliwell *The Filmgoer's Companion* (1985)

Fred Allen's preferred medium was radio, although his droopy-eyed expression could very occasionally be seen in such second-rate films as *Thanks a Million* (1935) and *Love Thy Neighbour* (1941), and he appreciated, as did many radio stars, just how much of a threat television posed. The ironic fact that the new medium was, with certain notable (and short-lived) exceptions, aimed firmly at the lowest common audience denominator merely accentuated its bogeyman status. Allen, who also wisecracked 'Imitation is the sincerest form of television', was only one of many performers who hoped, in vain, that the new monster would simply go away.

ALLEN, STEVE (1921–)

Is it bigger than a breadbox?
on *What's My Line*, US TV show

Steve Allen appeared regularly on the perennial US television show *What's My Line?* through the 1950s. The ever-popular show, which transferred successfully to the British audience, features a panel of 'celebrities' faced with the task of elucidating a visiting individual's occupation, on the basis of a number of yes/no questions. The more amusing, outrageous and witty the question, the better the show, although the panel is by no means invariably successful. Allen, who appeared on radio, TV and occasionally in the movies, where he once played the swing band-leader Benny Goodman, used this as his regular, laugh-provoking catch-phrase.

ALLEN, WOODY (1935–) Allen Konigsberg) American film director and screenwriter

Don't knock it, it's sex with someone you love.
Annie Hall (1977)

Woody Allen's career as a comedian began by writing for what is still considered by many to be US television's greatest comedy programme, Sid Caesar's *Your Show of Shows*, which ran through the 1950s and harnessed America's top writing talents. Allen worked simultaneously as a stand-up comic, offering audiences the life and neuroses of a short, bespectacled Jewish Everyman, before graduating first to other people's films, and thence to his own productions, including *Bananas* (1971) and *Play It Again Sam* (1972). This remark, extolling the virtues to the otherwise paranoid of masturbation, a classic piece of Allen observation, comes in *Annie Hall* (1977), a film that more than any other established Allen both as a major humourist and film director.

ALLEN, WOODY

I am not interested in an inanimate statue of a little bald man, I like something with long, blonde curls.
comment in 1970

Allen refused in 1970 to attend the regular Academy Awards ceremony in Hollywood, a self-congratulatory movieland beano where the industry's elite meet to award its current favourite sons and daughters a golden statuette that has earned its nickname, the Oscar, from the alleged similarity of its features to the uncle of one Margaret Herrick, librarian of the Academy of Motion Picture Arts and Sciences in 1931. In the way of such events, for the more rebellious stars not attending, or sending some show-stopping proxy, has become almost as traditional as turning up.

ALLEN, WOODY

Life is a concentration camp. You're stuck here and there's no way out and you can only rage impotently against your persecutors.
in *Esquire* magazine, 1977

The original title of Allen's film *Annie Hall* was Anhedonia, a psychoanalytic term derived from the Greek, which means inability to experience pleasure. For all of the film's undeniable humour, its attempt to prove just how awful life is takes it far from such slapstick predecessors as *Take the Money and Run* (1969). The film encapsulated Allen's angst in all its glory. For him 'the concentration camp is the real test: There are those who choose to make terrible moral decisions and betray their best friends and do horrible things, and there are others who behave with unbelievable courage. That's exactly what happens in life...'. Of course, there is one 'way out', but as Allen has said elsewhere 'I don't want to achieve immortality through my work. I want to achieve it through not dying.'

ALLEN, WOODY

Art is the artist's false Catholicism, the fake promise of an afterlife and just as fake as heaven and hell.
in Esquire magazine, 1977

Allen stressed that he had no time for the concept of art as a solution to the dread of death: one cannot hope that simply by creating one's creativity will somehow provide a barrier against the inevitable. On the other hand, for a man who has turned everyone's ultimate fear of death into the leitmotif of his own black comedy, he admits that making films is at least a distraction, a way of avoiding 'grimmer thoughts', for all that many of his films seem to dwell, albeit with great humour, on those very thoughts.

ALLEN, WOODY

It seemed the world was divided into good and bad people. The good ones slept better..., while the bad ones seemed to enjoy the waking hours much more.
Side Effects (1981)

Or, as actress Tallulah Bankhead remarked, 'It's the good girls that keep the diaries, the bad ones don't have the time.' The division between the moral and immoral and how the latter always seem to have more fun while the former, while they may be storing up brownie points in heaven, seem to have a less enjoyable time here on earth, is one of Allen's preoccupations. His Jewish guilt urges him to restrain his hedonistic urges; his hedonistic urges urge him to abandon his Jewish guilt.

ALLEN, WOODY

More than any other time in history, mankind faces a crossroads. One path leads to despair and utter hopelessness. The other, to

total extinction. Let us pray we have the wisdom to choose correctly.
Side Effects (1981)

This grim statement begins Woody Allen's 'My Speech to the Graduates', part of this collection of small written pieces. He continues 'I speak, by the way, not with any sense of futility, but with a panicky conviction of the absolute meaninglessness of existence which could easily be misinterpreted as pessimism.' The 'speech', a paranoid's commencement address and too pertinent to be merely a parody, continues to bemoan the failings of all the popular panaceas for the present malaise: science, religion, the government, the very technology that is supposed to ameliorate one's suffering. There remains only the future, which still holds great opportunities, as well as some pitfalls. 'The trick is to avoid the pitfalls, seize the opportunities, and get home by six o'clock.'

ALSOP, JOSEPH (1910-) American political journalist

Gratitude, like love, is never a dependable international emotion.
syndicated column

Joseph Alsop, with his brother Stewart, represented the journalistic arm of the wealthy, East-Coast establishment of lawyers, businessmen and financiers who dominated US politics in the 1950s. Alsop's right-wing, hawkish column provided a lodestone for the vagaries of US policy throughout this period and on to the Vietnam years. He consistently defended the supposed right of the US to combat Communism wherever on earth it appeared, acknowledging, in this remark, that America's pursuit of its manifest destiny, however justified, did not always meet with approval, even from those who were being helped.

ALSOP, JOSEPH AND STEWART

(Joseph) McCarthy is the only major politician in the country who can be labelled liar' without fear of libel.
syndicated column, 1953

The Alsop brothers' newspaper column was generally right-wing, but writing in 1953 of the demagogic, witch-hunting senator from Wisconsin, whose style and name stamped an era in American life, their sympathies, if only on the basis of aristocratic hauteur, decried the vulgarities and excess of 'Tail-Gunner Joe' in his absurd yet terrifying pursuit of the reds beneath America's bed. Ironically McCarthy, whose efforts tainted a generation of American life, was substantially helped, in his crusade against the alleged Communist infiltration of the government, by a series of pieces Joseph Alsop had written in 1950, claiming that the US had in 1949 'allowed' the Maoist revolution in China, and entitled 'Why We Lost China'. By 1953, of course, McCarthy was past his peak, and in 1954 he would fall, but for Establishment figures such as the Alsops to attack him, was still a slight acknowledgement that the mania he personified was not completely beneficial to America.

ALTMAN, ROBERT (1922–) American film director

What's a cult? It just means not enough people to make a minority.

Altman, despite such successes as *M.A.S.H.* (1970) and *McCabe and Mrs. Miller* (1971), has remained a controversial director in Hollywood. Such films as *Nashville, Buffalo Bill and the Indians,* and *A Wedding* have earned him as many brickbats as bouquets and thus, in critical parlance, he can be pigeon-holed as a 'cult' director. Nonetheless this wry self-analysis is perhaps unfair to a career which, if it fails to produce the youth-orientated blockbusters that have become Hollywood's staple product, continues to turn out a regular flow of films.

ALVAREZ, AL (1929–) British writer

Mass democracy, mass morality and the mass media thrive independently of the individual, who joins them at a cost of at least a partial perversion of his instinct and insights. He pays for his social ease with what used to be called his soul, his discriminations, his uniqueness, his psychic energy, his self.
in *The Listener*, 1971

Alvarez, poet, novelist and literary critic is best known for his study of suicide *The Savage God* (1971), which describes a phenomenon that has 'permeated Western culture like a dye that cannot be washed out' and which dealt with the general history of suicide and the detailed consideration of one successful suicide attempt, that of the poet Sylvia Plath (1932–63), and one failure, his own. He has further considered divorce in *Life After Marriage: Scenes from Divorce*; and poker in *The Biggest Game In Town* (1983).

AMALRIK, ANDREI (1938–80) Soviet dissident

Marxism has placed its stake on force – which Marx called the midwife of history. And though the midwife perpetually delivers

monsters... Marxists never tire of promising that the next child will be a splendid one.'
quoted in 1977

It is implicit in any revolution that it cannot be achieved without violence. Karl Marx's belief in continuing class struggle as a basis of historical progress meant that such violent revolutionary upheavals must be the essential adjunct to the appearance of any new historical developments. Since the Russian Revolution of 1917 his theories have been made political flesh, embodied in the world's Communist governments. Amalrik, a long-time critic of such governments, points out that present practice, for all its ideological optimism, has yet to make this past theory even remotely perfect.

AMERY, LEO (1873–1955) British politician

Speak for England.
in the House of Commons, September 1, 1939

In September 1938 Prime Minister Neville Chamberlain had returned from appeasing Hitler at Munich to promise an end to the threat of European war and 'peace in our time'. Twelve months later, on September 1 1939, Hitler invaded Poland. When it appeared the next day in the House of Commons that Chamberlain was again seeking to avoid military commitment the acting leader of the Labour opposition, Arthur Greenwood, rose to speak. Fearing no more than a rote, partisan denunciation of Tory policy, L.S. Amery, a Conservative MP, shouted to Greenwood 'Speak for England!'. Amery always claimed this honour, although diarist Harold Nicolson (1886–1968), who was present, attributed the cry to Lord, then Sir Robert, Boothby (1900–86). The consensus appears to be that Amery shouted first, Boothby echoed him, followed by the remaining Tory members. Either way, the entreaty worked, Chamberlain was swayed and World War II began on the following day, September 3rd.

AMERY, LEO

You have sat too long here for any good you have been doing. Depart, I say, and let us have done with you. In the name of God, go!
speaking in the House of Commons, May 7, 1940

Amery extended his role as Chamberlain's goad on 7 May 1940. After nine months of 'phoney war', during which the Germans occupied much of Scandinavia, the country was becoming increasingly critical of the government's conduct of the hostilities. Amery initially took it upon himself to demand from Chamberlain greater motivation and fighting spirit, choosing a speech made by Oliver Cromwell, rallying his troops in the English Civil War. This speech led to another, delivered when Cromwell dismissed the Rump Parliament in 1653. Thus, reaching the peroration of his own speech, Amery used Cromwell's words not merely to exhort Chamberlain to action, but to demand his resignation. The House was on his side and Chamberlain duly resigned. A National Government, led by Winston Churchill, was formed on May 10.

AMIS, KINGSLEY (1922–) British novelist

More will mean worse.

in *Encounter*, 1960

Kingsley Amis appeared as one of England's first 'angry young men' with the publication of his best-selling campus novel *Lucky Jim* in 1954. The satiric comedy that informed that novel has persisted throughout his work ever since, but his politics, once left-wing and anti-Establishment, have gradually shifted to the right. In 1960 he pointed out that the much-vaunted expansion of higher education, epitomised by the creation of even more of the provincial universities he had satirised in *Lucky Jim*, would not guarantee that merely by increasing the quantity of those able to enjoy such studies so would the quality of their minds be increased as well. Students for students' sake would not work: more, he stated, will mean worse.

AMIS, KINGSLEY

Growing older, I have lost the need to be political, which means, in this country, the need to be left. I am driven into grudging toleration of the Conservative Party because it is the party of non-politics, of resistance to politics.

in the *Sunday Telegraph* on 2 July 1967

Writing at the heart of the liberal, permissive frenzy that typified the 1960s, former enfant terrible Amis was testifying to that affliction so common to those who have been radical in their youth: the shift to the right. Critics of the Amis style, from angry young man to what some would see as a curmudgeonly old one, date his conversion from as early as his fourth novel, *I Like It Here* (1958). Following the three novels that established him as an 'angry', Amis deserted the red bricks of the provincial university to set this book in Portugal. In it, for the purposes of humour, he adopts a deliberately reactionary pose. Over the subsequent years the pose has become practice, and Amis, whose satirical novels remain as popular as ever, has become a champion not of the left, but of the establishment that he once spurned.

AMIS, KINGSLEY

By his station in society a member of the intelligentsia really has no political interests to defend, except the very general one (the one he most forgets) of not finding himself bossed around by a totalitarian government.
Socialism and the Intellectuals (1957)

Intelligentsia derives from its coinage in pre-Revolutionary Russia, and is defined as that part of a nation that aspires to intellectual activity, and was thus originally the class of society that is seen as possessing culture and political initiative. Amis, who might in 1957 still be regarded as of the broad left, excluded the British variety from much interest in politics other than his ensuring that ideology did not interfere with his own pursuits. Perhaps the ideal definition for English purposes is that put forward by H.G. Wells in *Mr Britling Sees It Through* (1916) '...an irresponsible middle class with ideas'.

AMORY, CLEVELAND (1907–) American writer

A 'good' family is one that used to be better.
Who Killed Society (1960)

The whole concept of a 'good' family is rooted in the gentility of a bygone world. It implies obeisance to social norms, to respectability, to rectitude and responsibility. Amory's point is that the implication in defining a family as 'good' is that once upon a time they were more than simply respectable, they were actually smart and fashionable, but at that stage, the type of person who would use these definitions would probably have called them 'too clever by half' or 'getting above themselves'.

ANGELOU, MAYA (1928-) American writer

Most plain girls are virtuous because of the scarcity of opportunity to be otherwise.
I Know Why The Caged Bird Sings (1969)

Angelou has become known as one of the leading black women writers in the US, and her work has been read widely in Britain. Her reputation has sprung mainly from her autobiography, in the first volume of which this comment appears. Angelou's work tends to be praised as 'frank and warm-hearted' but this remark, quite in the mordant tradition of Dorothy Parker or Helen Rowland, shows that her experiences as a young black girl growing up in Alabama left her with a sardonic assessment of the world.

ANIMAL CRACKERS

**My name is Captain Spalding,
The African explorer–
Did anyone say schnorrer?**
screenplay by Bert Kalmar (1930)

Animal Crackers was the Marx Brothers' second film, and like its predecessor *The Coconuts* (1929) it originated as a hit Broadway play. Groucho played Captain Spalding, singing this song, which he would adopt as his theme song throughout his later solo career, written for him by Kalmar and and his partner Harry Ruby, more generally known for penning some of the era's more schmaltzy love lyrics. The Yiddish word 'schnorrer', well enough known on Broadway but presumably mystifying out in the sticks, means 'thief'.

ANKA, PAUL (1941–) American rock singer

I didn't want to find a horse's head in my bed.

Anka, who entered show business aged only 12 and whose biggest hit 'Diana' celebrated the love of a sixteen-year-old for a twenty-year-old girl – 'Oh Diana you're so old!' – and sold nine million copies worldwide, developed into a successful songwriter. Among his major titles was 'My Way', a song that has been popularised by everyone from Sid Vicious to Miss Piggy, but which remains best known as Frank Sinatra's theme song. Anka responded as above when asked why he didn't capitalise on the song himself. Referring tongue-in-cheek to an episode in Mario Puzo's Mafia novel *The Godfather* (1969) in which a figure, allegedly modelled on Sinatra or his friend Dean Martin, has the severed head of a racehorse owned by a producer who has hitherto refused to give him a coveted movie role placed in the executive's bed, and referring by implication to Sinatra's oft-denied association with organised crime bosses, Anka explained the pragmatism he felt lay behind his gift.

ANNE, PRINCESS (1950–) British princess

When I appear in public people expect me to neigh, grind my teeth, paw the ground and swish my tail – none of which is easy.
in the *Observer* May 22, 1977

Princess Anne's love-affair with horses is typical of many women of her background, but her position as one of the Royal Family, not to mention being the daughter of a woman who declared that at the age of six she 'wanted to be a horse', has meant that in the eyes of the popular press and its readership, this accomplished equestrienne has sometimes felt that she would be better off actually hooved and harnessed. Only the advent of her two sisters-in-law, on whom the harsh spotlight of tabloid fascination has more recently been turned, has permitted the Princess to elude the newshounds with whom she has had so many antagonistic encounters.

ANNIE GET YOUR GUN

There's No Business Like Show Business
screenplay by Sindney Sheldon (1952)

Film critic Pauline Kael has called the ten Irving Berlin songs that are featured in this Broadway musical, subsequently filmed by MGM, 'surprisingly exhilarating in their simple crudity' and goes on to classify the whole show by its 'primer mentality'. The real-life Annie Oakley was a sharpshooter, managed by her husband, who left half a million dollars when she died in 1926, after a lifetime of exhibition shooting. In the musical Annie reverses roles, persuading her husband-to-be that he's the star shot and singing 'You can't get a man with a gun'. Judy Garland was supposed to play the lead but after a nervous breakdown she was replaced by Betty Hutton. Howard Keel played Annie's beau Frank Butler. Among the various standards in the making was the duet/duel 'Anything You Can Do I Can Do Better'.

ANNIE HALL

In California they don't throw their garbage away – they make it into television shows.
screenplay by Woody Allen (1977)

Alvy Singer, the Allen character in this film, is a New York Jewish comedian. He loves New York, has no desire to emigrate to Hollywood, and simultaneously despises and fears the whole sun-and-health ethos that he sees as epitomising California. When his girlfriend Annie (Diane Keaton) persuades him to visit Los Angeles, he remains unimpressed. This dismissive remark, delivered as they drive from the airport, is in response to Annie's delighted cry 'God, it's so clean out here.'

ANNIE HALL

Life is divided into the horrible and the miserable.
screenplay by Woody Allen (1977)

The Allen philosophy, which has remained fairly consistent

throughout his writing, is thus expounded. Jewish humour, which has a substantial influence on his style (although his philosophising extends into far more universal applications than the simply ethnic) has always assumed that life is tough and only the distancing that humour helps achieve can make it even partially bearable. And after all, it's the only one we've got. As he puts it in the nightclub monologue that opens this film: '...life: full of loneliness and misery and suffering and unhappiness, and it's all over much too quickly.'

ANONYMOUS

Hollywood buys a good story about a bad girl and changes it to a bad story about a good girl.

This anonymous complaint was presumably authored by one of the New York or Chicago newspapermen who were imported whole-sale into 1930s Hollywood and used en masse to create scripts for the massive output required by the studios at that time. The prudishness of Hollywood's moguls was legendary, almost as much as the amoral off-screen lifestyles of the stars they created, exploited, pampered and sometimes destroyed. Once the Hays Office was established in 1933, an attempt by the producers to censor themselves before the government did it for them, Hollywood scripts, once reasonably racy, concentrated on the so-called family values of chastity, sobriety and law-abiding cosiness. The studios' appetite for material meant that any good story might be bought up for possible filming. The parallel need to attract the mass audience, and leave its supposed moral purity untainted, meant that the story as bought and the story as filmed were often two utterly alien creatures.

ANONYMOUS
I'm Backing Britain

This little piece of British popularism seemed slightly embarassing even amongst the white-hot enthusiasms of Harold Wilson's technological revolution of 1968. Against the assassination of Robert Kennedy and Martin Luther King, the crushing of the Prague Spring in Czechoslovakia and the Tet Offensive in Vietnam, the efforts of a bunch of typists to promote an army of suburban Stakhanovites seemed, and seems quite ludicrous. But the marketing potential was duly expoloited, the girls feted for the obligatory fifteen minutes of celebrity and another episode in the endless 'silly season' that for some was the 1960s, took its place.

ANONYMOUS
Keep on trucking

ANONYMOUS

This hippie slogan springs, as does so much of our slang vocabulary, from black usage. Trucking, or more usually truckin', started life as a fast-tempo dance, favoured by US blacks in the 1930s. By the time it was adopted by the hippies thirty years on, the image was more of steadfast, determined movement, of waging life's struggle against any odds. A famous cartoon by the underground's premier cartoonist Robert Crumb concentrated on this aspect, the outsize sneakers of the central figure forging on down the road.

ANONYMOUS

Careless talk costs lives

This British slogan of the Second World War, rewritten in America as 'Loose talk costs lives', was one of the many exhortations levelled at the 'home front'. It was launched in July 1940, at the nadir of the British war effort, after Churchill had ordered his senior civil servants and military commanders to check the flow of idle gossip and rumour that he felt was undermining morale. The slogan adorned a poster of Hitler and Goebbels (the Nazi Propaganda Minister) sitting on a bus, eavesdropping on the conversation of a pair of chattering housewives. As well as this slogan, the Ministry of Information urged 'Join Britain's Silent Column', 'the great body of sensible men and women who have pledged themselves not to talk rumour and gossip'. The Silent Column, pitted against various tattletales called 'Mr. Secrecy Hush Hush', 'Miss Teacup Whisper' and 'Mr. Pride in Prophecy', proved most unpopular, and was scrapped when the over-patriotic began denouncing their more verbose, but innocent acquaintances to the authorities.

ANONYMOUS

Lousy but Loyal

King George V, grandson of the austere Queen Victoria and son of the flamboyant Edward VIII had ascended to the British throne in 1910. It was not expected that his reign would be particularly glorious nor that he would be conspicuous among Britain's reigning monarchs. His pleasures appeared to be the Navy, shooting and stamp-collecting and as his biographer Harold Nicolson was forced to admit 'He is all right as a gay young midshipman. He may be all right as a wise old King. But the intervening period is... hard to manage or to swallow'. Yet by his Jubilee in 1935 George V had gained a degree of respect and popularity that far exceeded expectations. This slogan, painted on a banner displayed in the

East End during the celebrations, refers to body lice, not simply to human unpleasantness.

ANONYMOUS

Black is beautiful

Every interest group who chose to parade their particular identity in the 1960s had a slogan. Hippies, gays, and above all the blacks. Black power, the creation of Stokely Carmichael and H. Rap Brown, was essentially a response to the fact that while the slaves had been ostensibly freed in the aftermath of the US Civil War, America's black population, a century later, remained almost without exception confined to second-class citizenship. The redefinition of black people that the movement envisaged was summed up in this slogan: an affirmation of black worth, in the face of years of both overt and tacit racism and stereotyping, and a call for the black population to unite, to recognise its heritage and to build a sense of community.

ANONYMOUS

Say it out loud we're black/gay and we're proud

Like Black Power's 'Black is beautiful' slogan, this couplet, initially black and subsequently adopted by the emergent gay rights movement, stated the affirmative, positive image of a hitherto despised minority. Simple, even naive in its all-purpose, all-embracing declaration, it provided an oral banner, offering its message and its proclamation to anyone who wished to enlist beneath it.

ANONYMOUS

Hey, hey LBJ, how many kids did you kill today?

America's involvement in S.E. Asia began in the 1950s, taking up where the French left off, and successive presidents, including the erstwhile golden boy John F. Kennedy, embroiled their country ever deeper in Vietnam. Of all of them, it was with Lyndon Baines Johnson, 'LBJ', that the disasters of that involvement became most intimately and painfully associated. Troop numbers peaked under Johnson, and with them the growing awareness that for the first time, America was mixed up in a war she could not win. 'Ho! Ho! Ho Chi Minh! Viet Cong are going to win!' chanted the demonstrators across America and in Grosvenor Square, London. But the chant that supposedly hurt most was the accusation above. In early 1968 Johnson declared that he would not run, though eligible, in the forthcoming Presidential elections. The lame duck president escaped his responsibilities in January 1969; the lame duck war dragged on until 1972.

ANONYMOUS

The trains run to time

Between them the regimes of Benito Mussolini's Fascist Italy and Adolf Hitler's National Socialist Germany killed millions, tortured many more, dispossessed, robbed, and deformed the morals of both nations and individuals. As the Axis powers they united in plunging Europe and then the rest of the world into six years of global war. In the face of such depredations, one claim was consistently made, especially of Italy, where dedication to efficiency, especially in transport timetables, had hitherto ranked low in the national characteristics: both natives and visitors would report, with a distinct air of congratulation 'The trains run on time!'.

ANONYMOUS

We shall overcome!

The phrase, ever-popular among activists of all sorts, first appeared in the Spanish Civil War in 1936, where it came in Spanish as 'Venceremos!'. The Spanish usage persisted amongst Fidel Castro's guerrillas, struggling through the 1950s, and was then taken up by Che Guevara's band, hoping with less success to revolutionise Bolivia. Imported into America in translation and set to music by folk singers Pete Seeger and Joan Baez as well as impromptu street choirs of protesting civil rights, anti-war, gay, black and women's rights demonstrators all marching together through the Sixties, 'We shall overcome!' became the staple theme tune of all manner of less spectacular but equally heartfelt revolutions.

ANONYMOUS

Though I walk through the Valley of the Shadow of Death I shall fear no evil because I am the baddest motherfucker in the Valley

There were a variety of messages with which the GI serving in Vietnam could inscribe his helmet or poncho cover, among them the ubiquitous peace symbol. Many drew up a short-timer's calendar, listing the days they were destined to serve 'in country'. Among the most popular was this parody of the 23rd Psalm, replacing, as it were, the influence of God with that of the M-16, the Huey helicopter and the awesome firepower of 'Puff the Magic Dragon'.

ANONYMOUS

Overpaid, (overfed), oversexed and over here

The Nazis may have occupied most of Europe during the Second World War, but to many Britons, the Americans had taken over the UK. Of the 1,421,000 allied troops based mainly in Southern England by 1944, awaiting the D-Day invasion, the vast majority were 'Yanks'. Gum-chewing, well-dressed, luxuriating in an abundance of supplies, the GIs (for the legend 'Government Issue' stamped on their kit) were loved, loathed and wholly envied by both the impoverished British troops and civilians, especially the female variety. In 1917 American songwriter George M. Cohan (1878–1942), the celebrated 'Yankee-Doodle-Dandy' himself, had written his hit 'Over There' speeding the doughboys on their way to World War I. Now the 'occupied' British turned his phrase around, apostrophising the Americans with a mixture of fury and fascination.

ANONYMOUS

When the going gets tough the tough get going

Some sources claim that this phrase, the epitome of hard-nosed American macho, was popularised by President Kennedy, who in turn learned it at his father Joe's Boston Irish knee. For most people it gained far greater notoriety under Kennedy's erstwhile rival, Richard Nixon, who offered it as his credo as his adminstration fell apart under the revelations of the Watergate Affair in 1973. Variations on this theme, a natural for graffiti enthusiasts, was writer Hunter S. Thompson's 'When the going gets wierd, the wierd turn pro' (qv) and the anonymous Eighties tribute to yuppiedom: 'When the going gets tough, the tough go shopping'.

ANONYMOUS

Close your eyes and think of England

This injunction to hapless womanhood, fettered by her wedding ring to the regular, and in this context invariably distasteful, submission to her brute spouse's conjugal demands, remains a popular suggestion, even in a post-feminist world. It probably predates the 20th century, stemming in the opinion of lexicographer Eric Partridge from the stiff upper-lip pronouncement of beleaguered Britons suffering untold horrors on the colonial outstations of the late 19th century. It has also been attributed to one of Queen Victoria's ladies in waiting who murmured it to her mistress on her wedding night, and to Lady Hillingdon who in 1912 wrote

35

in her Journal: 'I am happy now that Charles calls in my bed-chamber less frequently than of old. As it is, I endure but two calls a week and when I hear his steps outside my door I lie down on my bed, close my eyes, open my legs and think of England'.

ANONYMOUS

No man is drunk so long as he can lie on the floor without holding on.

The writer and critic H.L. Mencken attributes this line to Anonymous' in his *Dictionary of Quotations* (1942); other sources prefer to cite the film actor Dean Martin (Dino Crocetti, 1917–), whose long career has been based on jokes about his over-drinking and who often plays a drunk in his film roles.

ANONYMOUS

Turn on, tune in, drop out

Among the first of the buttons that served to proclaim one's hippie allegiances in the 1960s was one bearing this slogan. At least as early as 1966 the trickle, and soon the flood of young hopefuls that poured into San Francisco, the LSD capital of the world, were wooed by the seductive come-on. Turning on was to LSD; tuning in was to the wonderful new world revealed on one's 'acid trips' and dropping out was the concomitant rejection of 'straight society' that would often follow. Achieving the nirvana that many assumed lay at the intersection of San Francisco's Haight and Ashbury Streets proved to be a more elusive challenge. Timothy Leary, the guru of lysergic acid, chose the slogan for the title of a lecture given in 1967; his book *The Politics of Ecstasy* (1970) expounds it at length.

ANONYMOUS

Say it ain't so, Joe

In 1919 the Chicago White Sox baseball team reached the World Series, baseball's championship. Owned by the miserly Charles A. Comiskey the Sox were a troubled team. Their opponents in the Series were the Cincinnati Reds, generally considered as the underdogs. So disgruntled were some of the White Sox that eight team members, including Joseph Jefferson 'Shoeless Joe' Jackson, then the greatest hitter in baseball, whose nickname derived from his impoverished youth, arranged with the nation's leading gambler and all-purpose fixer Arnold Rothstein to throw the Series. The players were paid £80,000. Rothstein alone bet £270,000 on the Reds. After the Series was over, blatantly tossed away by Chicago five games to three, the fix was soon revealed. As Joe Jackson, summoned to a grand jury hearing, left the court, a small boy appeared to ask 'It ain't true, is it, Joe?' 'Yes, I'm afraid it is,' he replied. All eight men were banned for life. Only the boy's quote, rewritten by the papers, survived intact.

ANONYMOUS

Anyone for tennis?

In common with so many popular quotations, no researcher has yet been able to find the play, replete with flannelled fool, shrieking flappers, austere elders and french windows upstage centre, in which the young gentleman appears, racket in hand, to ask 'Anyone for tennis?'. It persists, nonetheless, as the shorthand for that particular type of play, the theatrical equivalent of the country-house murder story, so common in the 1920s, and, among actors, for the 'Young Juvenile', who prances through such material. Among those who supposedly uttered the immortal phrase was Humphrey Bogart, whose early stage career belied the tough-guy he would become on film.

ANONYMOUS

Tout psychologizer, c'est tout pardonner

Echoing the more popular 'Tout comprendre, c'est tout pardonner', this revision takes a dig at psychology and perhaps at the liberal consensus that declares the death of absolutes and their replacement by the modulated excuses of Freudian theory.

ANONYMOUS

Obscenity is whatever gives a judge an erection.

The struggle between those who would permit anything to appear in film, on TV or inside a book and those who would censor with equal fervour shows no signs of abating, for all the so-called sophistication of modern society. The great era of obscenity trials in Britain and America stretched from the 1950s to 1970s, but while the major trials seem to have ended, the general shift of both countries to a reactionary mood has given censorship a new impetus. This comment by an angry American lawyer may well be correct but does not, unfortunately, diminish the repressive threat.

ANONYMOUS

A pessimist is just a well-informed optimist.

ANONYMOUS

Alexander Dubcek (1921–), a former resistance fighter and long-time Party apparatchik, became 1st Secretary of the Central Committee of the Czechoslovak Communist Party, the equivalent of Prime Minister. Schooled in government during the 'liberal' era of Khruschev's de-Stalinisation, Dubcek attempted to extend the new, relative freedoms to a hitherto untried extent. Many Czechs, as well as commentators in the West felt most optimistic. But such optimism was ill-informed and the anonymous author of this quotation already sensed problems when he spoke in March 1968. The 'Prague Spring' lasted a scant eight months. 'Socialism with a human face' did not serve Dubcek's ultimate masters, the Politburo in Moscow. In August the Soviet Army invaded, submitting the country to military rule. Dubcek was forced to resign in April 1969 and the traditional hard-liner Gustav Husak took over.

ANONYMOUS

Television is a whore. Any man who wants her full favours can have them in five minutes with a pistol.

The hi-jacking of an aircraft in order to promote one's cause, and the concomitant exploitation of the world's media, is an art that international terrorists have been developing since 1970, when three airliners were hijacked by members of the PLO, flown to Jordan and blown up in the full glare of publicity, though mercifully emptied of their passengers. The media have yet to resolve the basic conflict between their primary role, the dissemination of news, and their obligation to national and international security, which in such circumstances may well run contrary to their news values. Every terrorist group understands and uses the dichotomy and the world's televisions continue to be filled with the images of violence and fear.

ANONYMOUS

I wouldn't tell the people anything until the war was over, and then I'd tell them who won.

To the military mind it is axiomatic in wartime that the less the public know, the better. This anonymous American censor, speaking in 1941 when America was still reeling from the Japanese attack on Pearl Harbour, was merely being more candid than is usual. The concept of the 'big lie' was not restricted to Hitler's Germany; Churchill himself suggested that the only reason to tell people the truth on topics they could check for themselves was to ensure that when one had to dissimulate absolutely, the public would be unable to conceive of such calumny.

ANONYMOUS

It became necessary to destroy the town in order to save it.

Few wars have created such volumes of obfuscatory euphemism as
that waged by America in Vietnam. And amongst that farrago of
deception, the concept of 'pacification' ranks among the most
grotesque. Originally the word meant the establishment of peace.
In Vietnam the idea was the same, except that it was achieved by
choosing an area, removing local people and then destroying their
homes, crops, supplies and anything else deemed potentially
useful to the Viet Cong, or, as Robert MacNamara put it in 1963,
using 'demonstrable retaliatory pressure'. Hence, this remark,
following the razing to the ground of the town of Ben Tre, during a
'pacification' exercise in 1968.

ANONYMOUS

Old soldiers never die, they simply fade away.

This song, popular in the First World War and in some use ever
since, was originally a parody of the song 'Kind Thoughts Can
Never Die' and uses the same tune. It runs
>'Old soldiers never die,
>Never die,
>Never die,
>Old soldiers never die -
>They simply fade away.
>Old soldiers never die,
>Never die,
>Never die,
>Old soldiers never die -
>Young ones wish they would.'

One of the best memoirs of that war, by Frank Richards, took the
song as its title, but the phrase's most well-known use was by
General McArthur in 1952 (qv).

ANONYMOUS

Bombs away with Curt LeMay!

General Curtis LeMay was the first commanding officer of the US
Strategic Air Command. LeMay was a no-nonsense military hard-
charger who saw nuclear weaponry merely as another, more
powerful adjunct to the nation's armoury and one that ought to be
used against the Communists as soon as possible. He was restrained from such strikes in the 1950s but as the Vietnam War
proved increasingly disastrous, suggested that America's optimum

ANONYMOUS

policy would be 'to bomb the Cong back to the Stone Age'. The anti-war protesters, appalled by such hawkishness, offered their own ironic response.

ANONYMOUS

You don't have to be a Marxist to see that history repeats itself, first as tragedy and then as farce.
in the *Sunday Times* on 14 September 1975

Or, as the writer Horace Walpole had put it in a letter to Lord Strafford in 1786 'History makes one shudder and laugh by turns.' The anonymous coiner of this remark was extending not merely Marx, whose theories are based in the concept of historical materialism – whereby 'it is not the consciousness of men which determines their existence; rather, it is their social existence which determines the nature of their consciousness' – but the basic concept that 'History repeats itself' which belief has persisted among writers from Thucydides (in his History c.410 BC) onwards. The idea has lent itself to various reinterpretations, notably that put forward in 1978 in the satirical London magazine *Private Eye* which suggested that History repeats itself – the first time as tragi-comedy, the second time as bedroom farce.'

ANONYMOUS

A good terminology is half the game.
quoted in Arthur Koestler, *Bricks to Babel* (1981)

The need for those in power, or indeed those in any variety of interest group, be it social, professional or occupational, to resort to the linguistic privacy of their own jargon seems to have become a basic human requirement. From the glib euphemisms that are the politician's stock-in-trade to the grim obfuscations of nuclear war planning, jargon is everywhere and touches everything. What they don't know won't hurt them, and if you must communicate, there's no nhur Woodstone (1972)

ANONYMOUS

Fatty ham fried in grease.
quoted in *Nixon's Head* by Arthur Woodstone (1972)

'Anyone who wants to be President', opined one eminent American politician, 'ought to have his head examined'. On the basis of this New York freelance Arthur Woodstone wrote *Nixon's Head*, taking a long hard look at the psychology of just one President, Richard Nixon, whose desire for the office had always been so great as to be nearly tangible. Appearing when the Watergate Affair was yet to emerge, Woodstone's reflections proved uncannily accurate when Nixon came under pressure a year later. The usual put-down of the

40

President concerns the unlikeliness of his being a plausible used-car salesman, but the description above surely rivals it for concise, cruel accuracy.

Anonymous

I don't like the family Stein
There is Gert, there is Ep, there is Ein
Gert's writings are punk
Ep's statues are junk
Nor can anyone understand Ein

quoted in R. Graves & A. Hodge *The Long Weekend* (1940)

This low-brow American limerick current in the Twenties' epitomised the contemporary philistinism that pervaded the middle and lower classes in the US and UK. It referred to three major cultural and intellectual figures, whose 'family' links were strictly cerebral. Gertrude Stein (1874–1946) established in Paris the era's leading salon for the literary and artistic avant-garde from both sides of the Atlantic; her own writing was sufficiently complex and experimental to alienate all but the most dedicated. Jacob Epstein's sculptures were consistently vilified and attacked both by reactionary critics and, physically, by members of the public. Albert Einstein, the mathematician, philosopher and latterly nuclear physicist, simply worked at an intellectual level and in a discipline far removed from ordinary mortals.

Anouolh, Jean (1910–) French playwright

Every man thinks God is on his side. The rich and powerful know he is.

The Lark (1955)

Anouilh's life of Joan of Arc, *L'Alouette (The Lark)* is one of several plays dealing ostensibly with historical figures (Joan, Thomas à Becket, Robespierre in *Poor Bitos*) and like them is informed by far more modern concerns. Like all of his plays, it is the private rather than public that counts and Joan, like the other 'real-life' figures, is considered as much as a human being, with all the concomitant pains and fears, as she is a symbol of French nationalism.

Anouilh, Jean

Oh, love is real enough, you will find it some day, but it has one arch-enemy—and that is life.

Ardele (1948)

The theme of *Ardele*, epitomised by this line, is that common to all of Anouilh's plays: the defeat of high, idealistic hopes by harsh reality. Anouilh's horror at what life is compared with what it could be is reflected in all his work. In this play the plot revolves around the quest for purity and spiritual peace, which quest, with cruel irony, creates only cynical disillusionment and marginal contentment.

ANOUILH, JEAN

Saintliness is also a temptation.
Becket (1959)

Saint Thomas à Becket (1118-70), was the 'turbulent priest' who so angered his monarch Henry II by his insistence on the independence of the Church from the State that on 29 December 1170 the King sent three knights to assassinate him at his own cathedral of Canterbury. The King then claimed that his orders had been misinterpreted by the killers, but only by absolute self-abasement was he able to restore relations with the Pope. Anouilh, Tennyson and T.S. Eliot have all used the story as the basis of a play. In Anouilh's version the facts are less vital to the plot than its true theme: the priest's emotional inability to return the love extended to him by King Henry.

ARAFAT, YASSER   Palestinian leader

Peace for us means Israel's destruction, and nothing else.

The Palestinian Liberation Organisation (PLO) emerged as the mouthpiece for the many political organisations that had developed in the Middle East representing the Arab inhabitants of the former British mandate of Palestine, as of 1948 the State of Israel. The PLO was formed at a meeting of the heads of Arab states in Cairo in 1964 but did not achieve international prominence until after the Six-Day War of 1967, when orthodox Arab military power had most palpably failed. Under its leader Yasser Arafat, the PLO continues to represent, according to one's belief, either a major international terrorist threat or the sole source of hope for a dispossessed nation.

ARAGON, LOUIS (1897-1982) French poet, novelist, essayist and journalist

Life is a traveller who lets his suitcase drag behind him to cover his tracks.
Les Voyageurs de l'imperiale

Aragon began his career as a Dadaist and moved on to become one of the supreme exponents of Surrealist prose. In 1932 he deserted Surrealism for Communism, forsaking experimentation for the disciplines of socialist realism, through which he hoped to sub-merge the individual writer in works that combined social as well as literary progress. During World War II he spearheaded the intellectual resistance to the German occupation. He has been called 'one of the most dazzling comets ever to have crossed our literary sky' and his 65-year-long career produced some 60 books.

ARDEN, ELIZABETH (1884–1966) American cosmetician

Nothing that costs only a dollar is worth having.
quoted in *Fortune* magazine,1973

Elizabeth Arden, whose cosmetics adorn millions of the world's women, laid down this snobbish rule, doubtless tailored to the wealthy readers of *Fortune*. Born Florence Nightingale Graham, Arden was the consummate career woman, whose only interest other than her business was horse-racing. She was a martinet who treated her staff as servants, assuming that they would ask per-mission prior to marrying. At her death she headed an empire that sold a range of 450 products (in 1500 shades) all over the world. She advocated a regime of exercise, massage, diet and good posture, all of which would create beauty. Her cosmetics used as pure as possible ingredients.

ARENDT, HANNAH (1906–1975) American writer

The banality of evil
Eichmann in Jerusalem (1961)

Adolf Eichmann, former commander-in-chief of the Nazi concent-ration camps, was captured in S. America by the Israeli secret service and tried in Jerusalem in 1961. Arendt dealt with the trial and its defendant in *Eichmann in Jerusalem: Report on the Banality of Evil*. This essay caused much controversy, suggesting that not only were Europe's Jews complicit in their own destruc-tion, but that Eichmann, the perfect, robotic bureaucrat, was not an aberrant monster, but simply a mechanical one, unable to interpose a personal morality between the demands of the system and their effects. The phrase became a standard and even merited a varia-tion: during the Watergate Affair in 1973 Richard Nixon's conduct was described as 'not the banality of evil but the evil of banality'.

ARENDT, HANNAH

Nothing and nobody exists on this planet whose very being does not presuppose a spectator. In other words, nothing that is,

insofar as it appears, exists in the singular; everything that is is meant to be perceived by somebody. Not Man but men inhabit the earth. Plurality is the law of the earth.
in the *New Yorker*, 1977

Arendt's last work, *The Life of the Mind* was published posthumously, still in an unfinished state, in 1978. It posited an embracing system, but in common with such previous works as *On Revolution* (1963) which considered the relative importance of the French and American Revolutions, giving the palm to the latter, it was insufficiently worked out to make the implicit theories clear or to attain a major influence.

ARLEN, MICHAEL (1895–1956) (Dikran Kuyumjian) British author

Any man should be happy who is allowed the patience of his wife, the tolerance of his children and the affection of waiters.

Arlen was born in Bulgaria of Armenian parents, but educated at an English public school. His fame rests on his novel *The Green Hat* (1924), a book that both predated and, in its period was considered to rival Evelyn Waugh's treatment of the 1920s and their 'Bright Young People', and which was based on a successful confection of smartly cynical views, leavened with a pinch of romance. In 1928 Ahren moved to the South of France, where he was prominent amongst the sophisticated American and British expatriates and continued to write. Eventually he moved to New York where he died. Arlen was a notably dapper figure, whose amour-propre was punctured severely by the description given him by the feminist writer Rebecca West who named him 'Every other inch a gentleman'.

ARMSTRONG, NEIL (1930–) American astronaut

That's one small step for a man, one giant leap for mankind.
landing on the moon, July 21, 1969

In 1961 President Kennedy, reflecting his country's embarrassment at the Soviets' continuing successes in the space race, committed America to landing a man on the moon by the end of the decade. Just before 4 am BST on Monday 21 July 1969 Neil Armstrong fulfilled Kennedy's promise as he stepped onto the moon's surface. As 500 million TV viewers watched, Armstrong delivered the line he had been preparing throughout the five days' flight of the Apollo XI spacecraft. Close analysis of the transmission momentarily undermined Armstrong's quote: it appeared that he had actually said '...one small step for man' and forgotten the article, thus blowing his nicely balanced line. Back on earth he persisted in attributing the error to a bad recording, and soon, whatever the truth, the amended version passed into history.

ARON, RAYMOND (1905-1983) French sociologist

Racism is the snobbery of the poor.

Aron's dictum points out that if one is beset with grievances, and yet has no economic inferior upon whom to vent them, then it appears that the natural course is to invent a racial inferior and blame that phenomenon for one's troubles. Thus the indigenous underclasses of the world tend to represent the most virulent advocates of racial prejudice, directed against those who have immigrated into their country and who, with their availability for cheap labour and their willingness to work in a desire to drag themselves from the bottom of the heap, represent so potent a threat to the disadvantaged natives.

ARON, RAYMOND

What passes for optimism is most often the effect of an intellectual error.
The Opium of the Intellectuals (1957)

Aron, a leading French academic and political commentator was initially a close associate of Jean-Paul Sartre, but broke with him in 1957 with the writing of *L'Opium des intellectuels*. In this essay, its title punning on Marx's description of religion as the 'opium of the people', Aron claimed that for Sartre and his fellow Marxist intellectuals, an unquestioning adoration of the USSR was their opiate, and that like all addictive drugs, this had undermined their intellectual independence and enslaved them to Moscow's ideological line. He preferred to move right, offering his support to De Gaulle and to the Western alliance as spear-headed by the USA.

ARON, RAYMOND

Man is a reasonable human being, but is mankind?
Dimensions de la Conscience Historique

In 1968 Aron, then a professor at the Sorbonne, resigned his post as a protest against what he saw as the pusillanimous conduct of his academic colleagues in the face of les Événements, in which a panicky French establishment, for a brief moment, saw the alliance of students and workers as the start of a new revolution. His gesture was typical of his continuing intellectual attitude: refusing to kow-tow to the prevailing orthodoxy, whether of left or right, and one that earned him respect for maintaining the courage of his convictions.

ARP, JEAN (1887–1966) French artist

Man declares red what he called green the day before, and what in reality is black. He is forever making definitive statements on life, man and art, and he has no more idea than a mushroom what life, man and art actually are.
Dadaland

Arp began his artistic career in Munich, where he exhibited at the Blaue Reiter exhibition of 1911. Moving to Paris in 1914 he became one of the leading Dadaists, editor of the movement's journal *Die Schammade,* and creating many of its most striking works, notably collages and reliefs made from superimposed pieces of plywood. After meeting André Breton he turned to surrealism and concentrated on whimsical examples of freestanding sculpture. With his wife Sophie he founded the Abstraction-Creation group in 1931. For Arp art was 'a fruit that grows in a man, like a fruit in a plant' and his most mysterious works represent a fusion of human and botanical shapes in a single organism.

ARTAUD, ANTONIN (1896-1948) French theatrical theorist, director and actor

There is in every lunatic a misunderstood genius whose idea, shining in his head, frightened people, and for whom delirium was the only solution to the strangulation that life had prepared for him. And what is an authentic madman? It is a man who preferred to become mad in the socially accepted sense of the word, rather than forfeit a certain superior idea of human honour. So society has strangled in its asylums all those it wanted to get rid of or protect itself from, because they refused to become its accomplices in certain great nastinesses. For a madman is also a man whom society did not want to hear and whom it wanted to prevent from uttering certain intolerable truths.
in *Selected Writings* (1976)

Artaud is remembered in the theatre for his rejection of all its established conventions and forms. In his major work *Le Théâtre et son double* (1938) he defined his concept of 'the theatre of cruelty' which sets out deliberately to provoke the audience as the actors subordinate plot and narrative to harsh physical and sensual rituals, all dedicated to ensuring that all concerned undergo as savage and shocking an experience as possible. Artaud was briefly involved with the Surrealists, but broke with them, expressing his disappointment that they chose to channel their artistic anarchism into the ideological confines of Communism. The personal anarchy which dominated his life gradually overtook him and he spent the last decade of his life in mental homes, in one of which he died.

ARTAUD, ANTONIN

All writing is garbage. People who come out of nowhere to try to put into words any part of what goes on in their minds are pigs.
in *Selected Writings* (1976)

In the anarchic anti-theatre that lay at the heart of Artaud's theories, in which the dramatic form was employed to destroy itself, smashing down the whole concept of the theatre as 'representation', Artaud believed that rational constructs were irrelevant; instead one needed only irrational sounds, formless but meaningful grunts, screams, whispers and exclamations, backed by physical gestures that reinforced their meaning. Only thus, bereft of the intellectual game-playing imposed by rationality, could the theatre attain its ideal form: a primitive rite concerned only with basic human wants.

ASIMOV, ISAAC (1920-) American science fiction writer

When the lay public rallies round to an idea that is denounced by distinguished but elderly scientists and supports that idea with great fervour and emotion, the distinguished but elderly scientists are then, after all, right.
in *Fantasy & Science Fiction* magazine, 1977

Isaac Asimov emigrated from Russia to America and began his professional life as a research chemist, becoming Associate Professor of Biochemistry at Boston University. In this role he has written a number of medical and popular scientific textbooks but it is in his capacity as a leading science fiction writer that he is best known. Eschewing the sword-and-sorcery fashions of science fantasy, Asimov has always reflected his research background, concentrating on his elaborate and scientifically viable studies of a world in which robots are an everyday fact. He has propounded 'Laws of Robotics' and among his major works are *I, Robot* (1952), the *Foundation Trilogy* (1951–53) and the *Caves of Steel* (1954).

ASKEY, ARTHUR (1900-82) British comedian
Hello playmates!
catchphrase

The catchphrase has always been a hallmark of mainstream British comedians, as vital and personal a label as the jaunty little ditty with which, no matter what material had preceded it, he would sing himself from the stage. 'Big-hearted', if diminutive (he was just 5'2") Arthur Askey rose to fame via the radio in the 1940s. His first choice catchphrase 'Hello folks!', used on BBC's *Bandwagon* in 1938, brought him up against fellow radio funster Tommy Handley, who claimed this relatively uninspiring phrase as his own. Askey dropped it, replacing it by 'Hello playmates!'. Askey's other verbal identifier was his strangulated 'Aythangyew' or 'I thank you'.

ASQUITH, H.H. (1852–1928) British prime minister

It is fitting that we should have buried the Unknown Prime Minister by the side of the Unknown Soldier.
speaking on November 5, 1923

Asquith, formerly as H.H. Asquith, England's Liberal Prime Minister, made this cruel if accurate comment when the ashes of Andrew Bonar Law, a Conservative Prime Minister, were interred in Westminster Abbey on November 5, 1923. Asquith had never liked Bonar Law and this lesser political light had few supporters. A Presbyterian from Canada, his conservatism was not rooted in the traditions or symbols of the past, nor in his support for the vested interests of the Establishment but simply from his inherent caution, lack of ideas, and of intellect. His sole interest, in critical assessment, was in success, of no matter what sort.

ASQUITH, H.H.

You had better wait and see
catchphrase, coined spring 1910

Asquith's catchphrase, for which he earned the popular nickname 'Old Wait and See', was probably picked up during his years in the legal chambers of Sir Henry James. His own use came on a number of occasions between March and April 1910, when he was attempting to avoid making a commitment as to the reintroduction of Lloyd George's budget, which at its first appearance had been rejected by the House of Lords. Asquith was not attempting to avoid giving an answer, merely warning his questioners off. So notorious did the phrase become that Punch ran a punningly satirical cartoon and during World War I defective French matches were known as 'wait-and-sees'.

ASQUITH, MARGOT (1864–1945) British aristocrat

He could not see a belt without hitting below it.
Autobiography (1927)

Alice Margaret Tennant became in 1894 the second wife of the liberal politician H.H. Asquith and in due course Countess of Oxford and Asquith. Egocentric, 'unteachable and splendid' she was a great influence on contemporary taste and fashion. Dorothy Parker, reviewing her memoirs in the New Yorker remarked 'The affair between Margot Asquith and Margot Asquith will live as one of the prettiest love stories in all literature'. Margot was not devoid of her own malicious wit. This remark, categorising Prime Minister David Lloyd George, is included in her *Autobiography*. Whether it referred to the 'Welsh Wizard's' alleged propensity for disloyalty, or perhaps, more obliquely, to his womanising, remains moot.

ASTOR, NANCY (1879–1964) American-born British MP

Astor: Winston, if I were married to you, I'd put poison in your coffee. Churchill: Nancy, if you were my wife, I'd drink it.
interchange circa 1912

Nancy Astor, the first woman member of the British House of Commons, although herself a scion of the aristocratic Virginian family, was a combative and witty woman who said of herself when in 1929 she was offered sympathy on her failure to be offered a Cabinet post 'Nobody wants me as a Cabinet Minister and they are perfectly right. I am an agitator, not an administrator'. This exchange with Winston Churchill took place in Blenheim Palace, the Churchill family home. The British voters adopted her as a native Englishwoman, apostrophised by Lord Lothian as Virginia's 'second conquest of Britain'.

ATKINSON, BROOKS (1894–1984) American critic

There is a good deal of solemn cant about the common interests of capital and labour. As matters stand, their only common interest is that of cutting each other's throat.
Once Around the Sun (1951)

Atkinson was the long-time drama critic for the New York Times, pausing only during World War II to work as a journalist in China, for which efforts he won a Pulitzer Prize. This reflection, doubtless based on the bloody struggles between American employers and employees throughout the 1930s and beyond, remains depressingly perceptive.

ATKINSON, BROOKS

Life is seldom as unendurable as, to judge by the facts, it logically ought to be.
Once Around the Sun (1951)

ATKINSON, TI-GRACE American feminist

Love is the victim's response to the rapist.

Grace Atkinson, who embellished her name to give it a suitably threatening and militant flavour, was one of the pioneers of the women's liberation movement in America. This deeply cynical comment, which expresses a feeling consistently held by many feminists who claim that all men in their hearts are rapists, typifies her aggressive stance. More surprising than such rhetoric, however, was her involvement with a leading New York Mafioso, Joey Gallo, who was assassinated, and duly mourned by Ms Atkinson, in 1972.

ATLAS, CHARLES (1894–1972) (Angelo Siciliano) American body builder

You too can have a body like mine
advertisement copy

Angelo Siciliano was born in Sicily and like many compatriots emigrated to America. Here in 1922 he won the title 'The World's Most Perfectly Developed Man'. The basis of his development from the time when 'I was a seven stone weakling' (itself an Atlas catchphrase), was his observation of a lion rippling its muscles, which gave him idea for his technique of 'Dynamic Tension'. Capitalising on his physique and promising 'a body like mine', he began offering mail-order body-building training, using his famous comic-strip advertisement telling 'How Joe's body brought him FAME instead of SHAME' and featuring the hapless Joe's humiliation in front of his girlfriend when the beach bully kicks sand in his face. Still using copywriter Charles Roman's best-known catchphrase, the technique continued to attract 60,000 interested runts a year throughout Siciliano's life.

ATTLEE, CLEMENT (1883–1967) British politician

Democracy means government by discussion but it is only effective if you can stop people talking
quoted in A. Sampson *Anatomy of Britain* (1962)

Attlee was never especially good at stopping people talking, and his administration, like the era it governed, was distinctly austere. The Prime Minister was never very popular, insufficiently left for the left and seen by the defeated Tories and their supporters as the harbinger of revolution. Diarist Harold Nicolson, himself a member of Attlee's Labour party, wrote in November 1947 'Attlee is a charming and intelligent man, but as a public speaker he is, compared to Winston, like a village fiddler after Paganini'.

AUDEN, W.H. (1908–1973) British Poet

British poet Wystan Hugh Auden decided at the age of 15 to become a poet. After reading natural sciences and then English at Oxford, where his poetry was already seen as important, he started working as a schoolmaster, an occupation that provided intermittent employment throughout the 1930s. Using a mixture of post-Freudian imagery, left-wing, near-Marxist politics and a mixture of archaic and modern style, Auden became the foremost poet of his generation. Heavily influenced by Eliot, who in 1930 accepted his first book of poems at Faber and Faber, and by Gerard Manley Hopkins, he has himself influenced virtually every English poet who has followed. As well as many collections of poetry, Auden produced libretti, film scripts, travel books, criticism, anthologies and, with various collaborators, plays. He was awarded many honours and was Oxford's Professor of Poetry from 1956–61.

AUDEN, W.H.

All poets adore explosions, thunderstorms, tornadoes, conflagrations, ruins, scenes of spectacular carnage. The poetic imagination is not at all a desirable quality in a statesman.
The Dyer's Hand (1963)

Discussing the personality of the poet, Auden says that the very nature of the poetic interest and the nature of poetic creativity militate against an understanding of the mass issues that determine politics or economics. The poet deals in the minutiae of individual lives, the politician and economist in great issues in which individuals are reduced to 'the Public', a faceless, passive entity. 'The poet is bored to death by the idea of the Common Man'. The poet cannot understand money: if he is successful then he alone appreciates how a piece of journalism, knocked off in a day, can earn ten times the sum a poem, laboured over for months, will make. If a failure, he will become embittered and revolutionary. 'Society has always to beware of the utopias being planned by artists manqués over cafeteria tables late at night'.

AUDEN, W.H.

In our age, the mere making of a work of art is itself a political act.
The Dyer's Hand (1963)

AUDEN, W.H.

Auden's statement has become increasingly hackneyed in an era devoted to conferring the palms of creativity on every piece of ideologically inspired mediocrity, but his justification for it remains undeniable to any open-minded person. In a society where the trend is constantly towards the mass and away from the individual, any creative act, whether bad or good, of greater or lesser appeal, has to be considered a political statement since it reminds the Establishment that people are not a homogeneous lump, but individuals who, for better or worse, should each be allowed their say.

AUDEN, W.H.

The absolutely banal – my sense of my own uniqueness.
The Dyer's Hand (1963)

Auden dismisses one of our most cherished fantasies in a single statement of ruthless self-knowledge. As a champion of the individual he does not condemn the world to faceless anonymity but goes on to point out that it is the excitement and variety of one's experiences, emotions and ideas, in constant ebb and flow, change and realignment, that create the individual, not the simple fact that one is a solitary body.

AUDEN, W.H.

Man desires to be free and he desires to feel important. This places him in a dilemma, for the more he emancipates himself from necessity the less important he feels.
The Dyer's Hand (1963)

Auden is discussing the problem of reconciling freedom from the constraints of the world in which one lives with gaining the admiration and respect of that world, for which one must adhere to its rules of success, which tend to run against the pursuit of individual freedoms. The result of such a conflict, he suggests, is the criminal *acte gratuite*, often in the form of a bizarre and publicity-generating murder. The individual has rejected society by breaking its laws; by breaking them in a sufficiently spectacular way, he has gained society's attention, albeit for a short time and in anything but an admiring manner.

AUDEN, W.H.

Life is not a game because one cannot say 'I will live on condition that I have a talent for living'.
The Dyer's Hand (1963)

The truth of life, a hard competition in which there can be no spectators, however determined the more reclusive may be to take that position, is as banal as that of the old sporting cliché: nobody's interested in second place. In Auden's view, no-one says 'We almost won the war': one either wins or gains nothing. 'In life the loser's score is always zero'.

AUDEN, W.H.

My duty towards God is to be happy; my duty towards my neighbour is to try my best to give him pleasure and alleviate his pain. No human being can *make* another one happy.
The Dyer's Hand (1963)

Auden's recipe for life: we are all individuals, unique in our way; we are all selfish individuals, out for ourselves, however cunningly we may disguise it to others and to ourselves. Happiness, he believes, is not a right but a duty, a religious duty, and the more we are miserable, the greater is our sin. Given our selfish individuality, we cannot be expected to create happiness for another; given their individuality it would be a presumption to assume knowledge of what makes them happy. The best we can offer, itself a duty, is help in times of trouble, and pleasure rather than cruelty.

AUDEN, W.H.

**Let us honour if we can
The vertical man
Though we value none
But the horizontal one**

'Epigraph'

All statues are to dead heroes. Those who fall in battle are often honoured more enthusiastically than those who survive and come home, often bringing with them unpleasant reminders of a bloody reality that can conveniently be forgotten in the war memorial's granite sanctity. Auden's quatrain suggests that merely staying alive, and he does not specify that this must be in battle, is in itself an achievement worthy of congratulation and even reward.

AUDEN, W.H.

Almost all our relationships begin, and most of them continue as forms of mutual exploitation, a mental or physical barter, to be terminated when one or both parties run out of goods.
The Dyer's Hand (1963)

Auden underlines this cruel analysis by noting that if such a thing as love is to be fostered, then it is essential that we pretend to ourselves both that the love is far stronger and our selfishness far weaker than is the truth. The result of such self-deception can be seen in the paranoid whose fear of indifference is so great that he divides the world into those who love him and those who hate him and acts accordingly.

AUDEN, W. H.

No poet or novelist wishes he was the only one who ever lived, but most of them wish they were the only one alive, and quite a number fondly believe their wish has been granted.
The Dyer's Hand (1963)

Auden's collection of critical essays, *The Dyer's Hand* is prefaced by a prologue divided into sections headed 'Reading' and 'Writing', in which he takes as his own epigraph C.G. Lichtenberg's line 'A book is a mirror: if an ass peers into it, you can't expect an apostle to look out'. This is followed by a number of aphoristic remarks, all tied to the relation of readers to writers and writers to their creations. That cited above deals with the egocentricity of the creative. Others worthy of note include: 'Pleasure is by no means an infallible critical guide, but it is the least fallible.' 'Some writers confuse authenticity, which they ought always to aim at, with originality which they should never bother about.' 'Only a minor talent can be a perfect gentleman; a major talent is always more than a bit of a cad. Hence the importance of minor writers – as teachers of good manners.' Poetry is not magic. In so far as poetry, or any of the other arts can be said to have an ulterior purpose, it is, by telling the truth, to disenchant and intoxicate.'

AUDEN, W.H.

Small tyrants, threatened by big, sincerely believe they love Liberty.
City Without Walls (1969)

In this political gloss of the concept of every flea having another flea upon it, Auden suggests that no-one in a position of power is willing to forfeit it until someone of greater power appears as a more potent threat. At this point the tyrant, who has happily suppressed the liberty that might erode his own status, makes a swift U-turn in the hope of regaining the support of those who he has repressed and using their rekindled affection to stave off his own deposition.

AUDEN, W.H.

To the man-in-the-street, who, I'm sorry to say

Is a keen observer of life
The world intellectual suggests right away
A man who's untrue to his wife.
Notes on Intellectuals from *Collected Shorter Poems* 1927/57 (1966)

There is more irony here than one might suspect and while Auden has composed a wryly pertinent little poem, there is within it a genuine cri-de-coeur. Auden, Isherwood, Spender and Macneice, all the so-called Pylon group, believed that they genuinely could reach the masses with their writing. Taking a whole-heartedly left-wing stance, they saw their task as the exposition of the great events of their time in a way that everyone could understand. But aiming at the mass they hit only the intellectually sophisticated bourgeoisie, their own peer group. The word 'intellectual', and Auden and his fellows were certainly that, held few charms for the man or woman in the street. Writing in Esquire magazine some time later, Auden faced up to the ambiguous status of the 'artist' once more, saying 'In the end art is small beer. The really serious things in life are earning one's living so as not to be a parasite and loving one's neighbour.'

AUDEN, W.H.

The image of myself which I try to create in my own mind in order that I may love myself is very different from the image which I try to create in the minds of others in order that they may love me.
The Dyer's Hand (1963)

Here Auden deals, under the title 'The Well of Narcissus', with image, both as projected on others and perceived in oneself. Quoting Nietzsche's dictum 'He who despises himself nevertheless esteems himself as a self-despiser' he points out that with our infinite capacity for self-delusion we are quite capable of projecting characteristics that we dislike in ourselves in a manner that we feel will appeal to others, in this case, false humility.

AUDEN, W.H.

Some books are undeservedly forgotten, none are undeservedly remembered.
The Dyer's Hand (1963)

Auden here is discussing the role of the critic, and suggests that there is no real need to attack bad art – and all art may become bad as taste alters – because it will simply fade away as time passes; no-one bothers to immortalise such second-rate creativity. Given the vagaries of taste a book that is in fact excellent may be passed over by an unhappy error and thus never achieve the greatness it deserves, but trash, even if it appears, will not last.

AUDEN, W.H.

The supreme masters have one trait in common with the childish scribbling mass, the vulgar curiosity of a police-court reporter.
The Dyer's Hand (1963)

The 'supreme master' of whom Auden was thinking when he put forward this opinion was most probably Charles Dickens (1812–70). Dickens' novels and essays are categorised universally as great literature, but underlying the stylistic brilliance is Dickens' social conscience, a live force that drives the plots and activates his characters in a way that mere literary flourishes could not. Dickens was never a police-court reporter, although his early journalism involved reporting the proceedings of the House of Commons, but in *Sketches by Boz* (1836–37) and such novels as *Oliver Twist* (1837) he showed that he could produce what would today be termed investigative reporting.

AUSCHWITZ CONCENTRATION CAMP

Arbeit Macht Frei. (Work Makes Free)

Possibly the grimmest slogan ever intended to inspire those reading it was this legend, meaning 'Works Makes Free' placed above the entrance of the most notorious of all the concentration camps established for the extermination of Jews, gypsies, homosexuals and any other 'sub-humans'. Like the 'showers' that hid the gas chambers, this blackly ironic exhortation underlined the sadistic humour that many of the administrators gained in the pursuit of the 'Final Solution'.

AUSTIN, J.L. (1911–1960) British philosopher

Fact is richer than diction.
Philosophical Papers (1961)

J.L.(John Langshawe) Austin was professor of Moral Philosophy at Oxford from 1952 until his death, and presided over 'Oxford philosophy' during its most influential years. Austin believed that the clash between philosophical theories and more down-to-earth beliefs is caused by the misunderstanding of a common language. He expounded his theory that all one really believes is based on personal ideas and sensations in *Sense and Sensibilia* (1962), and set out the differences between 'performative' and 'constatative' utterances (the former either promise or do something, the latter simply communicate information) in *How to Do Things with Words* (1962).

AYCKBOURN, ALAN (1939–) British playwright

Comedy is tragedy interrupted.

quoted in the *Penguin Dictionary of Modern Quotations* (1980)

Ayckbourn is without rival amongst contemporary British comic dramatists, analysing with merciless, pertinent humour the vagaries of suburban, middle class life, its vanities, its awful ironies and its obsessive social conventions. As critics have pointed out, echoing Ayckbourn's own comment on his art, while his plots tend almost to farce, with their complex of interwoven actions and chronologies, the themes with which they deal are more akin to tragedy. His first West End hit was *Relatively Speaking* (1967); this was followed by many others. Ayckbourn, for all his success, continues to live and work in Scarborough, Yorkshire, where he has been, since 1971, artistic director of the Theatre-in-the-Round.

AYER, A.J. (1910–) British philosopher

Philosophers are intellectual troublemakers. They are reluctant to take things at their face-value. They set out to disturb complacency. Ignorance is not altogether bliss, and in the field of learning, as in politics, it is only because some people are prepared to make trouble that anything of importance ever gets done.

in *The Guardian*, 1963

Sir Alfred Jules Ayer was educated at Eton and at Oxford where he studied under Gilbert Ryle. In 1936 he proved himself a philosophical wunderkind with the publication of his *Language, Truth and Logic*, which expounded for British readers the doctrines of the Vienna Circle, proponents of logical positivism. Ayer stressed the links between this philosophy and those of Locke, Hume, Russell and G.E. Moore. Subsequent works have included the *Foundations of Empirical Knowledge* (1940), after which he became Professor of Philosophy at University College, London; and then Wykeham Professor of Logic at Oxford from 1959–77. As well as his philosophical ground-breaking, Ayer's libertarian attitude to moral and political issues echoes that of his predecessor Bertrand Russell.

AYER, A. J.

There is then a simple answer to the question 'What is the purpose

of our individual lives?' – they have whatever purpose we succeed in putting into them.
quoted in the *Sunday Times*, 1957

Ayer is the chief modern exponent of the British tradition of
philosophical empiricism, a doctrine that embraces the work of
such philosophers as John Locke (1632–1704), David Hume (1711–
76) and John Stuart Mill (1806–73), as well as the more modern
Bertrand Russell (1872–1970). This philosophical system regards
experience as the only legitimate source of knowledge and takes its
name from the sect of ancient physicists, the Empirici (from the
Greek word for 'experience'). The question and answer sequence
above, dealing with what would on any grounds be accepted as a
major human preoccupation, emerges quite logically from such a
system.

AYME, MARCEL (1902–67) French writer

Life always comes to a bad end.
Les Oiseaux de lune (1955)

Ayme was born the son of a blacksmith and was destined to become
a physician. Instead, hating school and spurning such plans, he
moved from his native Auxerre to Paris where he ran through a
number of miscellaneous jobs, before starting a writing career. His
early works drew upon his own experiences of rural life, but he
developed into a satirical novelist, writing with ironical detachment and showing a quite amoral sense of humour. *Les Oiseaux de
lune* is the story of a character who can change people into birds.

AZNAVOUR, CHARLES (1924–) (Shahnour Aznavurian) French singer

**(Success) is the result of a collective hallucination stimulated by
the artist.**

This reasonably accurate description of contempory popular success is doubtless based in personal experience. The Armenian-
born Aznavour has enjoyed a career of capitalising on his own
looks, mass sentimentality and the seemingly insatiable appetite of
women 'of a certain age' for schmaltzy ballads.

B

BACON, FRANCIS (1909–) British painter

Existence, in a way, is so banal, that you might as well make a kind of grandeur.
quoted in *the Sunday Times*, 1975

Bacon, who started professional life as an interior decorator and furniture designer, is a self-taught painter who has since World War II been a major figure in British art, concentrating almost exclusively on representations of the human figure. The grandeur of which he talks can be found in works that combine modern imagery with a style of painting that in its sensuousness is more reminiscent of the Venetian and Spanish artists of the 17th century. Many of Bacon's works are disturbing in their depiction of the single, usually male figure, isolated in an enclosed space, surely reminiscent of a personal, private nightmare.

BAKER, HYLDA (1909–86) British comedian

She knows, y'know
catchphrase

Hylda Baker is a British radio comedienne, who has also made various 'character' appearances on TV and in films. This catchphrase, delivered in the knowing tones of an inquisitive Lancashire landlady, was first used on the radio show *Just Fancy* in 1959. It was ritually intoned by the tiny comedienne, referring to her gangling stooge Cynthia; on delivering the line she would give Cynthia a sharp nudge in the ribs and shout 'Don't yer?!'

BAKER, RUSSELL (1925–) American humourist

Baker is a syndicated columnist whose columns appear regularly in many of America's newspapers. In 1972, Baker compiled his own collection of aphorisms, *The Sayings of Poor Russell*. These aperçus, which range from the wisecrack to something a little more substantial, take their title from Russell's literary predecessor Benjamin Franklin (1706–90), a printer and inventor, and signatory in 1786 of the US Constitution. Franklin's almanac, Poor Richard's Almanack appeared annually from 1733–58, gaining immense popularity with its amalgamation of practical information, satirical prophecies, aphorisms and proverbs. Among Baker's offerings are:

The dirty work at political conventions is almost always done in the grim hours between midnight and dawn. Hangmen and politicians work best when the human spirit is at its lowest ebb.

Usually, terrible things that are done with the excuse that progress requires them are not really progress at all, but just terrible things.

People who have the power to make things happen don't do the things that people do, so they don't know what needs to happen.

In April if the glands work properly it is possible to see the world as it might be if only it were not the world.

These final quotations come from Baker's *New York Times* columns:

Inanimate objects are classified scientifically into three major categories – those that don't work, those that break down and those that get lost.

People seem to enjoy things more when they know a lot of other people have been left out on the pleasure.

BALANDIER, GEORGES French diplomat

Le Tiers Monde (The Third World)
speech in April 1955

This phrase, describing those nations whose territories, if not their politics, do not form part of the industrially developed world, was coined by Balandier in 1956 and referred specifically to the 29 African and Asian nations who met at the Bandung Conference in April 1955. This conference, despite a number of inevitable differences regarding the various political and cultural groupings, passed a number of motions supporting cultural and economic cooperation, self-determination and opposition to colonialism. Although it has been challenged as a description by the concept of 'developing nations' and the new term 'The South', the phrase is still generally popular.

BALCHIN, NIGEL (1908–70) British writer

Children are cruel, ruthless, cunning and almost incredibly self-centred. Far from cementing a marriage, children more frequently disrupt it. Child-rearing is on the whole an expensive and unrewarding bore, in which more has to be invested both materially and spiritually, than ever comes out in dividends.
quoted in *Sunday Express* (1965)

Balchin was trained as a scientist at Cambridge University and wrote only as a relaxation from his research and from his business interests. He wrote a number of novels before his first best-seller, *The Small Back Room* appeared in 1943. This topical treatment of wartime scientific research with its inevitable frustrations and exciting climax made an equally successful film. Among his later successes were the novels *Mine Own Executioner* (1945) and *The Borgia Testament* (1948).

BALDWIN, JAMES   (1924–1987) American writer

If they take you in the morning, they will be coming for us that night.
If They Come For You In The Morning (1971)

Angela Davis was appointed in 1969 as professor of philosophy at UCLA in California. As a registered Communist, an associate of the Black Panther Party and a vital symbol of black self-determination, she came to stand for everything that the authorities wished to suppress. Urged on by then Governor Ronald Reagan, UCLA fired Davis, citing her politics, notably her involvement with the case of George Jackson, a fellow militant, held in Soledad prison. When an attempt was made to free Jackson during an appearance in court, Davis was placed on the FBI's Most Wanted list and charged with conspiracy, kidnap for ransom and murder. During her imprisonment, which followed an FBI hunt, a book was published by her defence committee. Among the contributors was Baldwin, from whose 'Open Letter to My Sister Angela Y. Davis' this line, the title of the book, was taken. At her trial, in 1971, she was acquitted of all charges.

BALDWIN, JAMES

Children have never been very good at listening to their elders, but they have never failed to imitate them.
in *Esquire* magazine, 1960

Baldwin's autobiographical memoir *Fifth Avenue, Uptown* was written as the result of his discovery that a new housing project had supplanted his childhood home. The Fifth Avenue he describes is not the elegant up-market shopping mall of midtown Manhattan, but 'filthy, hostile Fifth Avenue' in the heart of New York's black ghetto. To him these housing projects epitomise everything that black people hate about the many indignities they are forced to suffer by the dominant white society. The imitations of their elders that black children are forced to perfect are those of 'our immorality, our disrespect for the pain of others'. They must do this, says Baldwin, since the ghetto offers no alternative model.

BALDWIN, JAMES

Be careful what you set your heart upon – for it will surely be yours.
Nobody Knows My Name (1961)

Ambition is one thing, achieved ambition is quite another. What we lack we search for and the search motivates us to action and gives a meaning to our lives. It may be a futile search, it may be grossly misdirected, but so long as we continue aiming for a target, our lives retain a point, however spurious. Once our ambitions are gained, once the target is reached, all that remains is disillusion. Baldwin sees no happy endings, only disappointment. Baldwin has put his pessimism another way, confining his opinion simply to the world of work, saying 'The price one pays for pursuing any profession or calling is an intimate knowledge of its ugly side.'

BALDWIN, JAMES

The real world accomplishes its seductions not by offering you opportunities to be wicked, but by offering opportunities to be good, to be active and effective, to be admired and central and apparently loved.
Nobody Knows My Name (1961)

In Baldwin's view, real problems begin not in what are generally considered varieties of human wickedness, but in its reverse, human goodness. To be sinful brings opprobrium, which he sees as a punishment in itself, but to be good, to be 'admired and central and apparently loved' brings self-delusion. The most foolish thing is to believe not the bad things people say of you, but the good ones.

BALDWIN, JAMES

Nobody is more dangerous than he who imagines himself pure in heart; for his purity, by definition, is unassailable.
Nobody Knows My Name (1961)

Baldwin's point is that those who set themselves on pinnacles have nowhere to look but down and looking downward, they see only the faults in others, and their own perfection reflected in them. To place oneself thus in relation to the rest of the world is dangerous and it denies reality. At the best one is naive, but even that naivety can have serious consequences. As he puts it elsewhere in this collection of essays 'People who shut their eyes to reality simply invite their own destruction. And anyone who insists on remaining in a state of innocence long after the innocence is dead, turns himself into a monster.'

BALDWIN, JAMES

Freedom is not something that anybody can be given, freedom is something people take and people are as free as they want to be.
Nobody Knows My Name (1961)

The paradox of Baldwin's thesis is that while emotionally and intellectually freedom is indeed something one takes and does not wait to be given, politically, economically and socially, freedom is not so easily obtained. The position of blacks in America, of which he was talking, was far from free in 1961, when the great civil rights movements of the Sixties were in their infancy. Twenty years later, while blacks have achieved a far greater degree of self-awareness and cultural identity, which might be construed as mental 'freedom', their economic status is in the main as mediocre as ever and the freedoms of material choice are still frustratingly distant.

BALDWIN, JAMES

Perhaps the whole root of our trouble, the human trouble, is that we will sacrifice all the beauty of our lives, will imprison ourselves on totems, taboos, crosses, blood sacrifices, steeples, mosques, races, armies, flags, nations, in order to deny the fact of death, which is the only fact we have.
The Fire Next Time (1963)

The two essays that comprise this book deal in both the past and the future. The past is a catalogue of racist mistreatment of America's blacks. If the future is to hold any improvement, that past must be rejected completely and if it takes violence and extremism to do it, then Baldwin, heavily influenced by the separatist philosophies of Elijah Muhammad's Black Muslims, accepts such a necessity. But he appreciates that dreams of black power are only dreams, and that the true reality for everyone is death. White America fears death. It hates the blacks because they symbolise the truth: life is tragic. Instead of denying mortality 'one ought to rejoice in the fact of death – ought to decide, indeed, to earn one's death by confronting with passion the conundrum of life'.

BALDWIN, JAMES

If the concept of God has any validity or use, it can only be to make us larger, freer and more loving. If God cannot do this, it is time we got rid of Him.
The Fire Next Time (1963)

Baldwin's study of the black problem in America, one of the earliest essays on the topic from a black writer, derives its title from an old slave song which says
>'God gave Noah the rainbow sign,
>Nor more water, the fire next time!'.

The book is intensively personal, fuelled by Baldwin's own passion and bitterness. This passage sums up his thoughts on religion, which underline the essential hypocrites of white Christianity, whose earnest precepts falter in the face of black demands. The white man's heaven, he quotes a Black Muslim minister, is the black man's hell and he urges that 'whoever wishes to become a truly moral human being...must first divorce himself from all the prohibitions, crimes and hypocrisies of the Christian church'.

BALDWIN, STANLEY (1867–1947) Earl of Bewdley, British Prime Minister

The papers conducted by Lord Rothermere and Lord Beaverbrook are not newspapers in the ordinary acceptance of the term. They are engines of propaganda, for the constantly changing policies, desires, personal wishes, personal likes and dislikes of these two men.... .What the proprietorship of these newspapers is aiming at is power, and power without responsibility – the prerogative of the harlot through the ages.
speech on March 17, 1931

Lords Beaverbrook and Rothermere, proprietors respectively in the 1930s of the Daily Express and the Daily Mail, were as unrestrained in their attempts to influence British politics in pursuit of their personal aims as they were in waging the circulation wars of the era. These incursions into politics climaxed in the by-elections held in 1930–31. Both magnates attempted to impose their ambitions on the democratic process and were united in opposing the current government, although both men denied vociferously any taint of a vendetta against the Prime Minister. Baldwin lost his patience in a speech on March 17, 1931. His speech, which concluded with these final lines penned by his cousin Rudyard Kipling, was widely praised although, for all its rhetorical flourish, it actually said nothing new. The most unlikely response came from the Duke of Devonshire who noted the word 'harlot' and declared 'Good God, that's done it; he's lost us the tarts' vote!'. Tom Stoppard, writing in his novel *Lord Malquist and Mr. Moon* (1965) talked of 'The House of Lords, an illusion to which I have never been able to subscribe – responsibility without power, the prerogative of the eunuch throughout the ages.'

BALDWIN, STANLEY

A platitude is simply a truth repeated till people get tired of hearing it.

quoted in 1924

BALDWIN, STANLEY

There are three groups that no British Prime Minister should provoke: the Vatican, the Treasury and the miners.

This dictum, attributed to Stanley Baldwin who generally managed to steer his political path clear of all three threats, has been used by a variety of politicians. Harold Macmillan used much the same phrase, substituting the 'Roman Catholic church' for the Vatican – although in both cases it might be wondered how that institution, officially the representative of a minority religion since 1536, could be such a threat unless it is a code word for Ireland. The most pithy version was that of R.A. Butler (1902–82), who stated 'Do not run up your nose dead against the Pope and the NUM.'

BALDWIN, STANLEY

You will find in politics that you are much exposed to the attribution of false motives. Never complain and never explain.

political credo, July 21, 1943

Diarist Harold Nicolson breakfasted with Baldwin, now Earl Baldwin of Bewdley, on July 21, 1943. They each ate a kipper and talked of Kipling, Ramsay MacDonald, Winston Churchill and of 'human ambition and endeavour'. Baldwin claimed to believe that in the end people are as good as you think them. In addition he offered Nicolson the warning and suggestion cited above: his own political credo.

BALDWIN, STANLEY

My lips are sealed
speaking in 1936

Faced by a barrage of questions during the Abdication Crisis of 1936, Baldwin refused to be drawn, telling fellow politicians and the press 'My lips are sealed. I am bound to keep silence', and thus ostensibly supporting his king while engineering his removal from the throne. Baldwin's initial use of this phrase, which he used often, came in a speech on the Italian invasion of Abyssinia, in 1935, when he promised that his policy was sound but could not yet be revealed since 'my lips are not yet unsealed.'

BALDWIN, STANLEY

When I was a little boy in Worcestershire reading history books I never thought I should have to interfere between a King and his mistress
speaking on January 20, 1936

The desire of King Edward VIII, formerly a distinctly playboy Prince of Wales, to marry the doubly divorced Mrs. Wallis Simpson, escalated gradually but inevitably from their first chance meeting in the 1920s to the full-blown Abdication Crisis of 1936. What might pass for a Prince would not do for a King and as Prime Minister Stanley Baldwin found himself at the head of those traditionalists who were determined that Edward should renounce either Mrs. Simpson or the throne. Edward was supported by such as Winston Churchill and Sir Henry 'Chips' Channon, but the 'King's Party' for all its chic, lacked the political clout of the Prime Minister. Baldwin may have claimed to find the situation somewhat overawing, but he never faltered and on 11 December 1936, Edward formally abdicated from the throne.

BALFOUR, ARTHUR   (1848–1930) British Prime Minister

Nothing matters very much, and very few things matter at all.

Balfour served as Prime Minister from 1902–05 and later, under Lloyd George, was appointed Foreign Secretary in 1916, but prior to such political eminence he had already established a reputation for his scholarship as a philosopher, notably for his book *A Defence of Philosophic Doubt* (1879) which makes this remark, somewhat inconclusive from prime ministerial lips, rather more understandable.

BALFOUR, ARTHUR

His Majesty's Government looks with favour upon the establishment in Palestine of a national home for the Jewish people, and will use their best endeavours to facilitate the achievement of this object, it being clearly understood that nothing shall be done which may prejudice the civil and religious rights of existing non-Jewish communities in Palestine...

The Balfour Declaration, 1917

In 1917 the British Army in the Middle East was poised to take Jerusalem from its Turkish occupiers. British governments had long been coming under pressure to found some form of nation in which the world's much-diffused Jewish diaspora might come together. Zionist spokesmen, led by Theodor Herzl, and supported by such English Zionists as Lord Rothschild, demanded action. Balfour, appreciating that his capitulation on this issue would not only appear in a humanitarian light, but would also gain the support of America's and Central Europe's increasingly influential Jewish communities, responded to Jewish wishes by writing on 2 November 1917 a letter to Lord Rothschild, affirming their desires: the Balfour Declaration. It led directly to the founding of the state of Israel in 1948, though the lack of attention paid to the final clause has yet to be remedied.

BANKHEAD, TALLULAH (1902–1968) American actress and film star

Daughter of a leading Southern politician, Miss Bankhead rose to become one of America's foremost actresses, her throaty tones and outrageous lifestyle making her a true star. As fellow actress Mrs. Patrick Campbell put it 'Tallulah is always skating on thin ice. Everyone wants to be there when it breaks'. She delighted both New York and London throughout the 1920s, but gradually the intensity of her off-stage antics began inevitably to erode her genuine talents. She was, of course, eminently quotable, the majority of her lines being careless but knowing self-deprecation:

It's the good girls who keep the diaries; the bad girls never have the time.

I'm as pure as the driven slush.

Cocaine isn't habit-forming. I should know – I've been using it for years.

They used to photograph Shirley Temple through gauze. They should photograph me through linoleum.

BANKHEAD, TALLULAH

There is less in this than meets the eye.
circa 1925

As recounted by the US theatre critic Alexander Woollcott (1887–1943) Miss Bankhead, 'a comely young actress', and Woollcott were watching a revival of Maeterlinck's *Aglavine and Selysette* 'a monstrous piece of perfumed posturing, meaning exactly nothing. Two gifted young actresses and a considerable bit of scenery were involved, and much pretentious rumbling of voice and wafting of gesture had gone into the enterprise.' Miss Bankhead, 'fearful, apparently, lest she be struck dead for impiety', became desperate as the play went its dreary way and turning to her companion, whispered none too softly 'There is less in this than meets the eye'.

BARAKA, IMAMU AMIRI (1934–) (Leroi Jones) American playwright

A rich man told me recently that a liberal is a man who tells other people what to do with their money.
in 1966

Baraka, born Jones but like many other militant blacks of the 1960s preferring to take an African name to replace his 'slave name', is one of America's leading black writers. Writing in 1966, he cast this cynical light on the contemporary scene, in which white liberals were ostensibly dedicated, among other fashionable causes, to helping the American black.

BARING, MAURICE (1874–1945) British novelist and critic

There is no amount of praise which a man and an author cannot bear with equanimity. Some authors can even stand flattery.
Dead Letters (1910)

Baring, son of the great banking dynasty and educated at Eton and Cambridge, was the prolific producer of a wide range of articles, plays, biographies, and criticism of literature, art and music, all of which reflected his urbane liberalism and subtle, refined syle. He worked both for the Foreign Office and covered the Russo-Japanese War of 1905 as a journalist. As the author of several volumes on Russian literature, he discovered Chekhov while in Moscow and pioneered his reputation in the West. During the Twenties he wrote a number of successful novels, all reflecting the milieu in which he moved; his best work is generally seen as the novella *The Lonely Lady of Dulwich* (1934).

BARING, MAURICE

If you would know what the Lord God thinks of money, you have only to look at those to whom he gives it.
quoted by Dorothy Parker in *Writers at Work* 1st series (1958)

Baring moved in the world of the rich and powerful, but he was obviously unimpressed by its glamour. This well-known put-down derives from Alexander Pope (1688–1744), who wrote in *Thoughts on Various Subjects* (1727) 'We may see the small value God has for riches by the people he gives them to.'

BARNES, CLIVE (1927–) British dramatic critic

Television is the first truly democratic culture – the first culture available to everybody and entirely governed by what the people want. The most terrifying thing is what the people do want.
in the *New York Times*, 1969

Barnes had already risen to preeminence among British critics, successively theatre critic for the *Daily Express* and *The Times* when, in 1965, amid much ballyhoo, he left Fleet Street for New York. Now, on the *New York Post*, he has one of the most powerful jobs in the American theatre. In England a review can help or hinder, but in America it requires only that Barnes and his few critical peers raise or lower their thumbs on a new production for it to succeed wildly or plummet, within days of the first night, into the abyss. Some might wish that Barnes had similar powers, distinctly undemocratic ones, over television.

BARRETT, WILLIAM (1844–1925) British physicist

It is the familiar that usually eludes us in life. What is before our nose is what we see last.
quoted in the *Listener*, 1978

Barrett was born in Jamaica and was professor of physics at Dublin University from 1873. He was responsible for some of the earliest experiments in the study of telepathy, but his work on magnetic alloys, with its more concrete, demonstrable use, gave him greater intellectual acclaim. This might be termed the scientific version of 'you can't see the wood for the trees'.

BARRIE, JAMES (1860–1937) British dramatist and author
Sir James Barrie was born in Kirriemuir, Scotland and began writing in London in 1885. He gained his first success with his stories of the 'Kailyard School', based on his own and his mother's reminiscences, the most successful of which (although he came to loathe it) was *The Little Minister* published in 1891, the same

year in which his first play *Richard Savage* was performed in London. Barrie's success continued until his death, but despite it, he preferred not to embrace worldly sophistication but to escape from adult preoccupations with such books as *Sentimental Tommy* (1896) *Tommy and Grizel* (1900), and in which the love of childhood was mixed with what later analysis would call 'mother-fixation'. Barrie's greatest achievements were his plays, notably *Peter Pan, The Admirable Crichton* and *What Every Woman Knows*.

BARRIE, JAMES

Death will be an awfully big adventure.
Peter Pan (1904)

Barrie began evolving his character Peter Pan or 'the Boy Who Would Not Grow Up' in stories told to the five sons of his friends Arthur and Sylvia Llewellyn Davies whom he had initially befriended in Kensington Gardens and to whom he latterly gave a home when their parents died. It is unlikely that there was anything overtly sexual in Barrie's relationship with the exceptionally attractive boys, but he unashamedly worshipped them. In 1904 the five-act play *Peter Pan* was performed. Charting the tale of the Darling children, their loving parents, their canine nurse and their adventures in Never Land with the Lost Boys and their leader, the faun-like Peter, it was and has remained massively successful. For many years the role of Peter became a virtual rite of theatrical passage for a succession of young actresses. A statue of Peter was erected in Kensington Gardens in 1912.

BARRIE, JAMES

If you have it, you don't need to have anything else.
What Every Woman Knows (1908)

What 'every woman knows' is the old cliché: behind every great man stands a woman without whose encouragement his efforts would be nothing. Barrie's play concerns the successful rise of one John Shand, a Galashiels ticket-collector turned autodidact who makes his way to political success and, despite an infatuation with a fashionable hostess, realises before it is too late that his true soulmate is not Lady Sybil but plain Maggie Wylie, the faithful typist who has for years transformed his dour, humourless speeches into a pathway to fame. The 'it' referred to here is charm, defined by Maggie as 'a sort of bloom on a woman'.

BARRYMORE, JOHN (1882–1942) American actor

The Barrymores, known as 'the Royal Family of Broadway' have been one of America's greatest theatrical clans, of whom the supreme generation were John and his brother Lionel (1878–1954) and his sister Ethel (1879–1959). Ethel's career began on Broadway and then progressed to Hollywood where she spent her later years epitomising the movie ideal of the gutsy granny with a heart of gold. Lionel was a jack-of-all the acting trades, although he concentrated on film work. He portrayed a variety of ageing characters during a long career with MGM. Most celebrated of them all was John, matinee idol turned romantic movie star who played Sherlock Holmes, Beau Brummell, Arsene Lupin, and many other leads, moving through his films, as Heywood Broun put it 'like an exquisite paper knife'. He squandered his great talent in the obligatory artistic manner, enjoying years of drink, drugs and degeneracy. He was massively egocentric, and a boon for the quote addict:

The good die young – because they see it's no use living if you've got to be good.

Sex: the thing that takes up the least amount of time and causes the most amount of trouble.

I like to be introduced as America's foremost actor. It saves the necessity of further effort.

and on his deathbed: **Die? I should say not, dear fellow. No Barrymore would allow such a conventional thing to happen to him.**

his brother Lionel, asked to suggest his own last words, offered: **Well, I've played everything but a harp.**

BARTH, KARL (1886–1968) Swiss theologian

Men have never been good, they are not good, they never will be good.
quoted in *Time* magazine (1954)

After serving as a pastor in Switzerland before World War I, Barth became an academic theologian and a professor at various German universities. Abandoning his erstwhile liberalism in the face of the jingoism in 1914 of his supposedly peaceful colleagues, he revised his theories, basing them strictly on Biblical texts, although he resisted absolute fundamentalism, and elaborated a system of 'dogmatics', whereby the graciousness of God was revealed through Christ, all were predestined to heaven, and the church represented the community of the faithful. In 1934 he drew up the Barmen Declaration, exposing Nazism's pseudo-religious posture and through his own example helped many believers to see the Bible as their most powerful shield against encroaching disaster. After the war he returned to Basle and remained a major figure until his death.

BARTZ, WAYNE R.

The more ridiculous a belief system, the higher the probability of its success.
Human Behaviour (1975)

Human gullibility is the basis of Bartz' comment. Quite why humanity does fall prey to systems, ideologies and theories that seem patently absurd is arguable, but perhaps the truth is that for most people the grim truths of mundane reality are so unpalatable that any alternative, however bizarre, is an improvement.

BARUCH, BERNARD (1870–1975) American financier and presidential adviser

Let us not be deceived – we are today in the midst of a cold war.
speech at Columbia, S. Carolina on 16 April 1947

Baruch's scriptwriter, the three-time Pulitzer Prize winner Herbert Bayard Swope (1882–1958), coined the idea of a cold war, as opposed to a hot or shooting war, in 1946 when he inserted it in a draft speech on the atomic bomb. At first Baruch dismissed it as overly provocative but a year later, speaking at Columbia, S. Carolina on 16 April 1947, he included it, as above. The phrase was popularised when it was noted by Washington's chief political commentator, Walter Lippmann (1889–1974), reporting on its use in Baruch's statement to the Senate War Investigating Committee on 24 October 1948. When Lippmann himself began to gain credit as the coiner, Swope disabused the public, stressing that he had first used it, in private letters, as early as 1940.

BARZUN, JACQUES (1907–) American literary critic and historian

A tale charms by its ingenuity, by the plausibility with which it overcomes the suspicion that it couldn't happen. That is art.
quoted in *Murder Ink* (1977) ed. Dilys Winn

As well as his more orthodox academic work at Columbia University, Barzun has become one of the world's foremost authorities on the classic detective story. The 'tale' to which he refers above is the detective story, and he has expounded his preference for such material, albeit decried by the modern 'hard-boiled' school, in his essay 'From Phèdre to Sherlock Holmes' (1956), his introduction to *The Delights of Detection* (1961) and in his comprehensive guide to crime literature based on fifty years of reading, *A Catalogue of Crime* (1971).

BARZUN, JACQUES

The young man who is not a radical about something is a pretty poor risk for education.
Teacher in America

Barzun is one of the 20th century's leading historians of culture and ideas, writing extensively on art, music and literature. His comment reflects the hope that any young person with an enquiring mind should automatically be in contention with the current orthodoxies, be they political, cultural, scientific or whatever.

BATTIE, BILL American sports coach

Class: when they're running you out of town, to look like you're leading the parade.
in *Sports Illustrated* magazine (1976)

The fate of the professional sports coach is mercurial: when the pack of athletic individuals for whose fortunes one is responsible are doing well, then the world is one's oyster, not to mention the adulation of the hometown fans. When that same team is failing, then nobody wants to know and the mortality rate of managers, trainers and allied individuals is remarkable. As Battie points out, the only way to go is with head held high so that in the employment stakes one is at least leading the parade into the next job.

BAUM, L. FRANK (1856–1919) American children's author

The road to the City of Emeralds is paved with yellow brick.
The Wonderful Wizard of Oz (1900)

Baum, the son of an early oil millionaire, worked his way through a variety of jobs until he began in 1897 to write successfully for children and, inspired by a cyclone which destroyed two Kansas towns in 1893, wrote in 1900 *The Wonderful Wizard of Oz*. He wrote fourteen Oz books himself; a further nineteen were added posthumously by Ruth Plumley Thompson. The books were massively popular, although modern librarians, bowing perhaps to the Puritan work ethic, have become loath to stock them, fearing that such unashamed fantasy might corrupt the youthful workers. Baum's fame was restricted to America, but MGM's film *The Wizard of Oz* (1939) which turned Baum's line into 'Follow the yellow brick road', remains an international favourite with its score by Harold Arlen and E.Y. 'Yip' Harburg and its performances by Judy Garland, Bert Lahr and others.

BAX, ARNOLD (1883–1953) British composer and writer

One should try everything once, except incest and folk-dancing.
Farewell to My Youth (1943)

Bax's musical career combined a prolific output of symphonic and instrumental music, accepted as his greatest achievement, with settings for a wide range of British writing, from anonymous poetry to the works of Thomas Hardy and A.E. Housman. In parallel to this an early encounter with W.B. Yeats led him towards Celtic influences and he spent much time in Ireland, writing several volumes of poetry, plus novels and stories, all under the pseudonym 'Dermot O'Byrne'. This line has also been attributed to another witty musician, Sir Thomas Beecham.

BEARD, PETER (1903–1985) American photographer

You know what they say: the sweetest word in the English language is revenge.
in *Interview* magazine, 1978

Beard's personalised version of the proverb 'Revenge is sweet' probably reflects the feelings of a great many people. They should be advised however by another proverb, not recorded prior to the 19th century but surely older: 'Vengeance is a dish that should be eaten cold'.

BEATON, CECIL (1904–1980) British photographer

Perhaps the world's second worst crime is boredom. The first is being a bore.

Beaton started his career as a photographer of fashionable 1920s London society after an education that included the same prep school as Cyril Connolly and George Orwell. His first exhibition was held in 1927 and his successful *Book of Beauty* (feteing every contemporary belle) appeared in 1930. Throughout the Thirties he worked for various magazines as well as producing illustrated travel books. As an official war photographer he worked in London and the Far East, managing to confer on his pictures of blitz and battle the same theatricality as epitomised his fashion work and portraiture. Beaton remained a pillar of fashionable society, embracing each new wave of youthful aristocracy, whether of blood, money or talent as it took centre stage. His crowning achievement, the imprimatur of society, was his knighthood.

BEATTY, VICE ADMIRAL SIR DAVID   (1871–1936) British sailor

There seems to be something wrong with our bloody ships today.
May 31, 1916

The battle of Jutland lasted from May 31–June 1, 1916. It was the sole major naval engagement of World War I and proved to be the beginning of the end of German attempts to challenge British naval hegemony. At the time it appeared less clear-cut, with no outright victory for either side. As a succession of British battle-cruisers were destroyed by the German guns, most disastrously in the loss at 4.26 on May 31 of the Queen Mary with 1,266 officers and men, the imperturbable Admiral Beatty turned to his Flag Captain Ernle Chatfield to make this remark. Some versions attribute the additional words 'and with our system' and claim that Beatty then ordered the fleet to move nearer to the enemy, but Chatfield did not back this up.

BEAVERBROOK, LORD   (1879–1964) Canadian-born British press magnate

Buy old masters. They fetch a better price than old mistresses.

William Maxwell 'Max' Aitken, the son of a minister, made his first fortune as a financier in his native Canada, then in 1910 moved to England where he began a career in politics and from 1916, when he bought the *Daily Express*, established himself as the country's most influential and flamboyant press magnate. A dedicated controversialist, his campaign for 'Empire Free Trade' inspired Baldwin's 'prerogative of the harlot' speech (qv) and his campaign against the Common Market thirty years later showed his energies were unabated. During the war he worked in a variety of ministerial posts.

BEAVERBROOK, LORD

Why don't you start a vendetta against someone? That's the way to get people reading your columns.

Beaverbrook's devotion to the progress of his newspapers was legendary and it succeeded: the *Daily Express* (bought in 1916), the *Sunday Express* (founded in 1918) and the *Evening Standard* (bought in 1923) were for many years Fleet Street's most influential publishing unit, serving their owner's whims and obsessions, employing many of the best writers of the time and waging a constant circulation war with the rival publications of 'the Beaver's' opposite number, Lord Rothermere. Waugh denied it, but his fictional press barons Lords Monomark and Copper (appearing respectively in *Vile Bodies* (1930) and *Scoop* (1938)) reflected clearly the style of a man who like to offer this sort of advice to his aspirant writers.

BEAVERBROOK, LORD

You are a great man now. You must talk like a great man, behave like a great man.
November 13, 1911

Beaverbrook prided himself on his own status, which in England in 1911 was still restricted to that of a Canadian millionaire and the representation of Ashton-under-Lyme in Parliament. He directed this comment to the distinctly milk-and-water Andrew Bonar Law who had just been selected as leader of the Conservative party. It is unlikely that Bonar Law, a shadowy figure compared to the robust, idiosyncratic Beaverbrook, came up to the future press magnate's hopes when he replied 'If I am a great man, then a good many great men must have been frauds.'

BECKETT, SAMUEL (1906–) Irish playwright and novelist
Beckett was born in Dublin and in 1928 moved to Paris where he has lived as a teacher and writer ever since. In 1928 he met James Joyce and worked for a while as his secretary. His first published work, in 1929, was an essay on Joyce, and he helped translate part of *Finnegan's Wake* (1939) into French. *Whoroscope*, a volume of poems, appeared in 1930, followed by a monograph on Proust (1931) in which he expounded his personal philosophy, stating that 'the only world that has reality and significance (is) the world of our own latent consciousness' and affirms suffering as 'the main condition of the artistic experience'. Beckett has written a number of novels, loosely allied to French existentialism, but his genius lies in his plays, epitomised by *En attendant Godot* (*Waiting for Godot*, 1952), minimalist, sparse and intellectually challenging, which established him as one of the century's leading literary figures. Perhaps the ultimate exposition of Beckett's style is *Breath* (1969), a thirty-second play consisting of a pile of rubbish, a breath and a cry. Among Beckett's noteworthy

remarks are the following:

That desert of loneliness and recrimination that men call love.

The major sin is the sin of being born.

Our life is a succession of Paradises successively denied ...
the only true Paradise is the Paradise that has been lost.

We are all born mad. Some of us remain so.

BECKETT, SAMUEL

Estragon '...Let's go'
Vladimir 'We can't.'
Estragon 'Why not?'
Vladimir 'We're waiting for Godot'
Waiting for Godot (1952)

Beckett's supreme achievement remains *En attendant Godot*. It deals with individuals who are forced, in the absence of any other succour and however reluctantly, to depend on each other. Estragon and Vladimir are tramp-like figures, working out their dialogue, reminiscent of a pair of music-hall comics, against a stark, featureless background. The eponymous Godot never does appear but the pair meet another incongruous couple: the tyrannical Pozzo, leading his slave Lucky by a rope around his neck. In a monologue Lucky sets out Beckett's basic belief, one that is unpalatable to the two 'tramps', that in the end we die and such is the meaning of life. They are determined that time should be infinite and Beckett leaves them suspended: 'Well? Shall we go?' asks Vladimir. 'Yes, let's go' says Estragon, but the stage direction notes 'They do not move'.

BEECHAM, THOMAS (1879–1961) British conductor

Beecham's father was also Sir Thomas, of the famous patent pills, a patron of music and ballet. The young conductor gained attention with the London opera seasons he conducted from 1909–19, during which he took the opportunity of introducing what were then new works. Throughout his career he devoted his enthusiasm and his personal fortune to encouraging music in England. In 1911 he brought Diaghilev's Russian Ballet to London; he founded the Beecham Opera Company, which became the British National Opera Company; in 1932 he founded the London Philharmonic Orchestra, imposing upon it his own high standards. Although he professed for years to scorn recorded music, his capitulation to the studio made him one of Britain's most popular musical figures. His outspoken wit, of which these are a few examples, also emphasised his larger-than-life personality.

The English may not like music – but they absolutely love the noise it makes.

Criticism of the arts.. taken by and large, ends in a display of suburban omniscience which sees no further than into the next-door garden.

BEERBOHM, MAX (1872–1956) British writer and caricaturist

Anything that is worth doing has been done frequently. Things hitherto undone should be given, I suspect, a wide berth.
Mainly on the Air (1957)

Beerbohm's career as a wit, critic, essayist and cartoonist spanned a period from the 1890s and their Yellow Book preciousness to the 1950s when, in a very different atmosphere, he enjoyed a new career as a broadcaster. The 'incomparable Max' (as Bernard Shaw called him) used his elegant style to point up a variety of ironies, especially when dealing with his contemporaries in art, literature and politics. As stylish in dress as in his prose, his essay on Dandies (1896) persuaded the less discriminating to dismiss him as superficial, but his wide-ranging career belies such analysis. He remains best remembered for *Zuleika Dobson: An Oxford Romance* (1911), an alluring fantasy, set in 1890s Oxford.

BEERBOHM, MAX

> **A swearword in a rustic slum**
> **A simple swearword is to some,**
> **To Masefield something more.**

Fifty Caricatures

John Masefield (1878–1967) followed a brief career in the merchant navy, by a nervous breakdown and then, still only 17, by a variety of odd jobs in America, where he read continually and started writing his own verse. His first published work Salt-Water Ballads, featuring the famous 'I must go down to the sea again' appeared to much acclaim in 1902. For the next thirty years Masefield's reputation grew, although his elevation in 1930 to Poet Laureate, thus recommended by the Labour government, and the revolution in verse pioneered by Auden, Spender and MacNeice made him decreasingly fashionable. His down-to-earth style, backed by a dedication to the poor and needy, is nicely summed up in Beerbohm's own lines, which were the caption to a caricature.

BEERBOHM, MAX

Port: the milk of donhood.
quoted in Geoffrey Madan's *Notebooks* (1981)

Beerbohm's comment on the propensity of Oxbridge dons to consume quantities of vintage port, and presumably, if it equates to milk, to gain (intellectual) nourishment from it, appears in a collection of aphorisms published in 1981 and collected in *Notebooks* throughout his life by Geoffrey Madan (1895–1947), a unique individual whose obligatory career in the City came a poor second to his appreciation of conversation, wit, and their allied pleasures.

BEERBOHM, MAX

The dullard's envy of brilliant men is always assuaged by the suspicion that they will come to a bad end.
Zuleika Dobson (1911)

Beerbohm's novel, subtitled 'An Oxford Romance', is a fantasy set in a highly romanticised Oxford of the 1890s. In keeping with the period, and with the prose style of its author, the book, which tells the story of the ultimate in university femmes most literally fatales, is replete with aphorisms, of which this is but one example. The plot, briefly, concerns the visit of the beautiful Zuleika to her uncle, the warden of Judas College, during one Eights Week. Every undergraduate falls besottedly in love and when she rejects them all, they plunge lemming-like into the River Isis. Only one Noaks, who trips on his way to a watery grave, survives the holocaust.

BEHAN, BRENDAN (1923–1964) Irish playwright

Other people have a nationality. The Irish and the Jews have a psychosis.
Richard's Cork Leg

At fourteen Dublin-born Behan was a member of the Irish Republican Army; two years later, while on 'active service' in England, he was sent to Borstal. Released, he returned home and continued working for the IRA. Jailed again in 1942 he was freed in 1945. Behan lived a brawling, boozy highly public life, interspersed with literary production. He commemorated his Borstal days with *Borstal Boy* (1958) and the IRA with the posthumous *Confessions of an Irish Rebel* (1965). His fame rests on two plays, *The Hostage* (1958), which deals with a British soldier captured by the IRA and held in a Dublin brothel, and

The Quare Fellow (1959), set in an Irish prison the night before a hanging. Both were well-received and have remained popular, although the author remarked 'Critics are like eunuchs in a harem: they know how it's done, they've seen it done every day, but they're unable to do it themselves'. Behan's dedication to his uproarious image eventually killed him, after a mammoth drinking spree in New York. As he lay dying he told a nun 'Thank you sister. May you be the mother of a bishop!'

BELL, MARY   (1957–) British child murderess

Murder isn't that bad. We all die sometime.
statement to police, 1968

Mary Flora Bell was born in 1957; her mother was a mentally unstable Scotswoman and her natural father never appeared. Her stepfather was rarely at home. Mary was an attractive child, if withdrawn, but her playmates found her excessively boisterous. There were a number of incidents, overlooked by all concerned, in which various children had been hurt while playing with Mary. On May 25 1968 the strangled body of four-year-old Martin Brown was discovered in the Scotswood area of Newcastle, near Mary's home. On July 31 another child, Brian Howe, was found, strangled and mutilated with scissors. After police enquiries Mary Bell was questioned and then charged with both murders. Psychological tests, which elicited this remark, proved her severely disordered, but not abnormal. She was jailed for life in 1968 and released in 1980.

BELLOC, HILAIRE   (1870–1953) British writer

I shoot the Hippopotamus
With bullets made of platinum
Because if I use leaden ones
His hide is sure to flatten 'em.
The Bad Child's Book of Beasts (1896) 'The Hippopotamus'

Belloc, born in France but educated in England, combined a career in politics with a prolific output of essays, criticism, travel and biographies. Much of his work reflected his devout Catholicism. His collaborations, both literary and ideological, with G.K. Chesterton created a style of pro-Catholic debunkery known as 'Chesterbelloc'. From 1906–10 he was literary editor of the right-wing Morning Post. Apart from his adult writing, mainly historical biographies, he wrote several books of light verse for children of which this, appearing in 1896, was his first. The bestiary includes the Polar Bear, the Lion, the Tiger and several others, all of an amusing bent and with illustrations by 'B.T.B.'.

BELLOC, HILAIRE

> **And always keep a hold of Nurse**
> **For fear of finding something worse.**

Cautionary Tales (1907) 'Jim'

This was Belloc's second collection of minatory verses for the young. These lines concern 'Jim who ran away from his Nurse and was eaten by a Lion'. Despite his friends who constantly regale him with 'Tea and cakes and jam/and slices of delicious Ham' Jim, on a visit to the Zoo, runs off. He is eaten 'beginning at the feet' by a lion called Ponto. His parents show no surprise, given his refusal to do what he was told, and gather their other offspring to hear this moral.

BELLOC, HILAIRE

> **Sir! you have disappointed us!**
> **We had intended you to be**
> **The next Prime Minister but three,**
> **The stocks were sold; the Press was squared,**
> **The Middle Class was quite prepared.**
> **But as it is!...My language fails!**
> **Go out and govern New South Wales!**

Cautionary Tales (1907) 'Lord Lundy'

Lord Lundy 'from his earliest years/Was far too freely moved to tears' and although his own inclinations lay elsewhere was at the age of twenty-six forced into politics. Here his lachrymosity betrayed him and instead of the glorious career for which he had been destined he was, as stated above, sent out to the disgrace, albeit reasonably grand, of governing a colony.

BELOTTI, ELIANA GIANINI   Italian sociologist

No woman, except for so-called deviants, seriously wishes to be male and have a penis. But most women would like to have the privileges and opportunities that go with it.
Little Girls (1973)

Ms Belotti is the director of the Montessori 'Prenatal' Centre in Rome. In this book she explores the sexual stereotyping which even from before birth assigns traditional, lifetime roles to boys and, as discussed here, little girls. The book exposes the deep-rooted prejudices that lie behind this process and suggests that while girls should not be reared henceforth along male lines, their potential should be recognised and encouraged over and above training as future submissive wives and mothers.

BENCHLEY, ROBERT (1889–1945) American writer, wit and actor

Streets full of water. Please advise.
quoted in *Wit's End* by James R. Gaines (1977)

Benchley, apostrophised by Stephen Leacock as 'the most finished master of the technique of literary fun in America' was one of the founders of that celebrated circle of wit and bitchery, the Algonquin Round Table, where sat such luminaries as Dorothy Parker, George S. Kaufman, Harpo Marx and many others. Benchley specialised in the comic monologue, capitalising on the apparent intractability of so much of modern life. This telegram, sent back to the Algonquin on arriving in Venice, was typical of Benchley's approach to life's little obstacles.

BENCHLEY, ROBERT

Everyone becomes the thing they most despise.
quoted in *Wit's End* by James R. Gaines (1977)

Benchley died in 1945, the glories of the Round Table a distant memory, with many of his contemporaries already victims of a gaudy life. Quite what Benchley despised is debatable. His background was conventional, he graduated from Harvard and balanced his public image with a home life of relative respectability, although he managed the occasional extra-marital affair. He testified, as a liberal, in the trial of the alleged anarchists Sacco and Vanzetti. As the Twenties passed, so did the glamour of the Round Table, and Benchley gradually became disenchanted. His drinking intensified and for all his fame, it may have been that his inability to find the ability to transcend the essential superficiality of the 'Vicious Circle' weighed increasingly heavily.

BENCHLEY, ROBERT

Drinking makes such fools of people, and people are such fools to begin with, that it's compounding a felony.
quoted in *Wit's End* by James R. Gaines (1977)

Benchley's own drinking habits ensured that he knew just what he was talking about. At the outset of his career, as noted by Edmund Wilson, he was a quiet and modest young Harvard graduate, 'with whom it was a pleasure to deal'. Gradually, as he began to believe his own publicity, both as a wit in New York and a comedian in Hollywood, his charm evaporated and in its place came a new persona, 'florid and self-assertive'. Much of this may have been show, designed to offset his conventional, bourgeois family life, but like many successful people, Benchley felt such excesses were necessary to his own image. Drinking heavily was part of this, and it killed him; he died in 1945, aged only 56, of cirrhosis of the liver.

BENJAMIN, WALTER (1892–1940) German writer

Nowhere more naively than in banknotes does capitalism display itself in solemn earnest. The innocent cupids frolicking about numbers, the goddesses holding tablets of the law, the stalwart heroes sheathing their swords before monetary units are a world of their own: ornamenting the facade of hell.
One-Way Street (1925–26)

During a relatively brief but influential career Benjamin combined both traditional and progressive intellectual ideas to produce a wide range of material embracing philology, literary and political criticism and the philosophy of history. He turned increasingly towards Marxism and became one of the first champions of the playwright Bertolt Brecht. After he was forced to flee Germany by the Nazis he moved to Paris, where he produced a massive study of Baudelaire. As the Nazis advanced on Paris he fled again, intending to enter Spain. When the Spanish authorities refused him entry, he committed suicide.

BENN, ANTHONY WEDGEWOOD (1925–) British politician

If I rescued a child from drowning, the press would no doubt headline the story 'Benn Grabs Child'.
quoted in Mark Hollingsworth *The Press and Political Dissent* (1975)

Tony Benn's early political career, as Harold Wilson's Minister of Technology, put him at the heart of the 'white-hot' technological revolution of the Sixties and as such at the top of Fleet Street's popularity polls. Not until Benn supported the workers in the Upper Clyde Shipbuilders dispute of 1971 did the white-haired boy falter. From a 'brilliant' contender for the party leadership, he declined overnight to 'an erratic and power-hungry butterfly'. This campaign intensified throughout the 1970s and Benn, who continued to maintain the same radical posture as had informed all of his career, became a quite satanic figure, red revolution with dripping fangs and the epitome of the 'loony left'. The line above was delivered first in 1975, by a fellow Labour MP, but Benn used it himself later.

BENN, ANTHONY WEDGEWOOD

The House of Lords is the British Outer Mongolia for retired politicians.

Tony Benn, as is his preferred title today, was born the hereditary peer, Viscount Stansgate, the son of a left-wing politician and the inheritor of his father's political values. Peers may not sit in the House of Commons and Benn fought a lengthy battle to renounce his title and assume his responsibilities as an MP. This statement stems from that fight, and was delivered on 11 February 1962, a year before he was finally able to rid himself of the encumbrance. Since then he has held ministerial office in the Labour administrations of Wilson and Callaghan. His role as Fleet Street's leading left-wing bugaboo has been supplanted by a number of subsequent targets since in 1981, amid intense publicity, he stood for the usually unexciting post of Deputy Leader of the Labour Party, a contest which he lost.

BENN, ANTHONY WEDGWOOD

Broadcasting is much too important to be left to the broadcasters.
quoted in 1969

Benn's line echoes that of the French Prime Minister Clemenceau who remarked during World War I that war was far too important to be left to the generals, and Charles de Gaulle who felt politicians were not up to politics. His opinion has certainly not changed in the near twenty years since, as Minister of Technology, he voiced it; no politician is a greater foe of the media, or believes more vehemently, and with some justification, that the massed ranks of broadcasters, plus newspaper journalists, are ranged against him.

BENNETT, ALAN (1934–) British playwright

I have never understood this liking for war, it panders to instincts already catered for within the scope of a respectable domestic establishment.
Forty Years On (1968)

Alan Bennett initially conceived of his first play as a series of sketches collected as a literary revue. As these developed it evolved into a school play, under the direction of a headmaster who embodies the style and attitudes of a traditional public school. It was originally titled 'The Last of England' but took its new title for the first night, on 31 October 1968. John Gielgud played the headmaster, his mind running between memories of the glorious past and the fidgeting schoolboys in front of him. 'Standards are always out of date', he says. 'That's what makes them standards.' Bennett played a junior master.

BENNETT, ALAN

Life is rather like a tin of sardines – we're all of us looking for the key.... We roll back the lid of the sardine tin of life, we reveal the sardines, the riches of life therein, and we get them out, we enjoy them. But, you know, there's always a little piece in the corner you can't get out. I wonder – I wonder, if there's a little piece in the corner of your life? I know there is in mine.
in *Beyond the Fringe* (1960)

Beyond the Fringe, an amateur review in the Cambridge University tradition, started life at the Edinburgh Festival and transferred to London where, on the basis of its enormous success, it provided the foundation for a new tradition – the 'satire boom' – that monopolised fashionable humour in the 1960s and has not fully vanished even today. All of its four performers, Jonathan Miller, Dudley Moore, Peter Cook and Alan Bennett have gone on to other, if not consistently greater things. Of the various sketches, targetting the Macmillan government, nuclear defence, World War II nostalgia, and many other topics, Bennett's immeasurably unctuous vicar, all platitudes and high church vowels, remains among the best-remembered.

BENNETT, ALAN

They are the most embarrassed people in the world, the English. You cannot look each other in the face.... Is there anyone not embarrassed in England? The Queen perhaps. She is not embarrassed. With the rest it's 'I won't make you feel bad as long as you don't make me feel bad'. That is the social contract. Society is making each other feel better.
The Old Country (1977)

Like Bennett's later play *An Englishman Abroad* (1982) which dealt with the 'missing diplomat' Guy Burgess who fled London one step ahead of the police, and his meeting, while resident in Moscow, with the actress Coral Browne, this play deals with the life of one of the 'Cambridge traitors' during his exile in Russia. Unlike Burgess, this spy is fictitious, but his concerns are those which Bennett feels are common to such figures.

BENNETT, ARNOLD   (1867–1931) British writer

Pessimism, when you get used to it, is just as agreeable as optimism. Indeed, I think it must be more agreeable, must have a more real savour than optimism – from the way in which pessimists abandon themselves to it.
Things that Have Interested Me (1921)

Bennett was born the son of a self-educated solicitor in the Potteries town of Hanley, Staffordshire. Aged 21 he moved to London where he worked as a clerk while attempting to promote his writing career. Desperate to shuck off his provincial, pious background, he placed his earliest work in *The Yellow Book* and *Tit-Bits*, both in their way outré publications. His first novel, *A Man from the North* appeared in 1898. Meanwhile he had extended his journalism, working as editor of *Woman* magazine and later, from 1926, as the influential book reviewer for Beaverbrook's *Evening Standard.* He wrote prolifically but his reputation rests on his 'Five Towns' novels, set in the potteries of his youth. These included *Anna of the Five Towns* (1902), *The Old Wives' Tale* (1908) and the 'Clayhanger series' (1910–18).

BENNETT, ARNOLD

What great cause is he identified with? He's identified with the great cause of cheering us all up.
The Card (1911)

Arnold Bennett wrote his satire on upward mobility in provincial Edwardian England in 1911. It was among his lighter works, featuring the go-getting, if sometimes overly ambitious Denry Machin, to whom the line above, the final words of the book, refer. The model for Denry was Henry Hales (1868–1942) who rose from being an apprentice in Burslem to becoming the MP for Hanley. The story follows his career from washerwoman's son to mayor through opportunism and scheming, all based on immeasurable charm.

BENNY, JACK   (1894–1974) (Benjamin Kubelsky) American comedian

Everything is habit. Everything is rhythm.
quoted in *Esquire* magazine 1965

Jack Benny's reproachful look, his ever-present violin, the source of constant jokes, and his overriding pose as the most extreme of misers all combined to endear him to American and worldwide audiences throughout a lengthy career. He began playing the same vaudeville circuits as the Marx Brothers and W.C. Fields, and like them went onto greater things, working consistently on the stage, in films, radio and television. His greatest film was *To Be Or Not To Be* in which he plays a Polish actor who is forced to pose as a Nazi in order to fool the real Nazis. A typical Benny gag: Holdup Man: 'Your money or your life! Come on, hurry up!' Benny: 'I'm thinking it over!'

BENSON, A.C. (1862–1925) British writer

Land of Hope and Glory, Mother of the Free,
How shall we extol thee, who are born of thee?
Wider still and wider shall thy bounds be set
God, who made thee mighty, make thee mightier yet.
Land of Hope and Glory

Benson, the eldest son of the Archbishop of Canterbury, was the brother of E.F. and R.H. Benson, both writers of some acclaim. He was master of Magdalene College Cambridge, and wrote widely, capitalising on his ability to compose for great occasions; his diary alone totals five million words. His reputation failed to survive his lifetime but his lyrics to 'Land of Hope and Glory', designed to be sung as the finale of Elgar's Coronation Ode with music from the first Pomp and Circumstance march have made it into an English patriotic classic.

BENTLEY, EDMUND CLERIHEW (1875–1956) British writer

Sir Christopher Wren
said 'I am going to dine with some men,
If anybody calls
Say I am designing St. Paul's'
Biography for Beginners: Sir Christopher Wren (1905)

Bentley was destined for the law but chose instead to become a journalist and writer, eventually succeeding Harold Nicolson as literary editor of the Daily Telegraph. His mentor and great friend was G.K. Chesterton. In his collection of verses *Biography for Beginners* he created a novel form, which he called the 'clerihew' after his middle name. These epigrammatic verses consist of two rhymed couplets, differing in length, and usually deal with the life or works of a well-known figure. Several further volumes followed. Bentley's other literary contribution was his detective story *Trent's Last Case* (1913) which is considered by afficionados to have set the pattern for the modern 'classical' treatment of the genre.

BENTLEY, ERIC (1916–) American writer and scholar

Ours is the age of substitutes: instead of language we have jargon; instead of principles, slogans; and, instead of genuine ideas, bright ideas.
The Dramatic Event (1954)

Bentley is an author, critic and lecturer on comparative literature. Born in England he has followed an academic career in America since 1952. He has won a number of awards and fellowships. Among his works are *The Life of the Drama* (1964), *The Fall of the Amazons* (1982) and *The Kleist Variations* (1983). His translations of Brecht helped popularise the playwright in America.

BERENSON, BERNARD (1865–1959) American art historian

All we really want is otherness, tossing from side to side, and greeting every toss with shouts of welcome, and of contempt for the previous toss.
The Passionate Sightseer (1960)

Berenson was born in Lithuania and in 1875 his family emigrated to Boston, Mass. After college he settled in Italy, to enjoy further the artistic treasures the appreciation of which formed the basis of his aesthetic and professional life. Prior to Berenson there was only the chaos of 19th century attributions, few of which were authentic. As the world's leading specialist in the Italian Renaissance his 'Lists', which began appearing in the 1920s, remain definitive. His personal philosophy, as stated in this diary entry of 1954, concentrated on the search for 'ideated sensation', based on the belief that the 'tactile values' of a work of art should be capable of inspiring a state of increased awareness in the spectator.

BERGER, JOHN (1926–) British writer and art critic

Art has a significance only insofar as it offers an alternative to what is, an alternative which expresses the potential freedom of man in all his experiences.
in *The Guardian*, 1971

Berger was trained as a painter but preferred to write as an art critic, first making his name in the 1950s when, taking a Marxist view, he advocated the orthodoxies of socialist realism over the experimentation of the American abstract artists. Berger has avoided simple polemic and has made himself the most original British art critic since 1945. His best works underline his attempt to relate art to life and society and to reflect above all the interests of those not immediately involved in the dominant culture. Other works include novels, one of which, *G*, won the Booker Prize in 1972, and *Pig Earth* (1979), a study of the French peasantry.

BERLIN, ISAIAH   (1909–) British philosopher

When a man speaks of the need for realism one may be sure that this is always the prelude to some bloody deed.
quoted in *The Times*, 1981

Berlin was born in Latvia but educated in the UK and has made his career as a philosopher in England. He has also held a number of diplomatic posts. He has been president of the British Academy (1974–78), as well as holding many other honours. The radical pluralism of his philosophical stance means that he consistently casts doubt on those who, claiming their own version of 'realism', tend to suppress the rival 'realisms' of others. Among his major works are *Four Essays on Liberty* (1969) and the essay 'The Hedgehog and the Fox', included in *Russian Thinkers* (1978).

BERLIN, ISAIAH

Life may be seen through many windows, none of them necessarily clear or opaque, less or more distorting than any of the others.
Personal Impressions (1980)

In Berlin's scheme of things there are no final answers to the many questions with which every generation is faced. As a firm believer in liberalism he has refused to espouse the truth of any single ideology, offering instead the opportunity to view life, as this quotation puts it, through many windows. Such pluralism may not offer the simple answers that appeal to the doctrinaire, but they free everyone to examine experience by their own lights and to impose on their life their own moral system. The defined, rigid ideology, he claims, acts in the end to defeat liberty, however much it may state its belief in it.

BERLIN, ISAIAH

Philosophers are adults who persist in asking childish questions.
quoted in the *Listener*, 1978

Berlin's distinguished career as a philosopher and historian of ideas has made him the doyen of the defenders of modern philosophical liberalism. Preferring concepts based on the variety and subtlety of historical precedent, he has rejected the attempt by the logical positivists to find a timeless language that would serve to define one constant reality. To him philosophical investigation, the analysis and evaluation of the way people work, has a definite historical dimension, stemming from a body of ideas first spread through the West in the 1730s by Vico and Herder and still of great relevance.

BERNAL, J.D. (1901–71) British scientist

Life is a partial, continuous, progressive, multiform and conditionally interactive self-realisation of the potentialities of atomic electron states.
The Origin of Life (1967)

Bernal was an X-ray crystallographer and writer on science and society. He has expounded his views in a number of books, claiming, on Marxist lines, that science should be planned and directed. His scientific achievements helped implement the analysis of X-ray diffraction photographs and, through his study of liquid crystals, contributed to the understanding of the mesomorphic state. During World War II he worked in Civil Defence. He was professor of physics at Birkbeck College, London, working on the structure of liquids and the origin of life.

BERNE, ERIC (1910–) American psychiatrist

To say that the bulk of social activity consists of playing games does not mean that it is mostly 'fun', or that the parties are not seriously engaged in the relationship...The essential characteristic of human play is not that the emotions are spurious, but that they are regulated.
Games People Play (1964)

Berne's best-selling handbook, subtitled 'The Psychology of Human Relationships' appeared just in time for the boom in self-analysis that began in the 1960s and has continued, pandering to the fears and fantasies of what Tom Wolfe called the 'Me Generation' ever since. Berne's theories are based on transactional analysis, a concept he has developed in which interpersonal relationships are considered as a series of transactions or ritual social communications between the participants – parents and child, husband and wife, etc. – all of which he calls 'games'.

BERNE, ERIC

We are born princes and the civilising process makes us frogs.
Games People Play (1964)

This aphorism provides the rationale for Berne's manual *Games People Play*. One arrives in the world with all the potential of individual grandeur but as layers of civilisation descend upon us, that potential is eroded and we are left not as individuals but as programmed units, capable only of responding, like frogs in a lab experiment, to a series of predictable stimuli. In his book Berne claims that such programming can be cast aside and that self-actualisation is possible and desirable.

BERNE, ERIC

Human life is mainly a process of filling in time until the arrival of death, or Santa Claus, with very little choice, if any, of what kind of business one is going to transact during the long wait.
Games People Play (1964)

This quotation is taken from the final chapter of Berne's manual of self-realisation in which he asks 'After Games, What?' His answer, given in a single brief paragraph, offers to certain fortunate individuals the possession of 'awareness', which transcends all classifications of behaviour; 'spontaneity', which rises above the programming of the past; and 'intimacy' which is 'even more rewarding than games'. On the other hand, he admits, such things may be too frightening for most people who are better off staying the way they are and seeking salvation in the usual old techniques of social action, such as one or another variety of 'togetherness'. In a final sentence of chilling psychological elitism he states 'There is no hope for the human race, but there is hope for individual members of it.'

BERNHARDT, MICHAEL   American soldier

For a second I said to myself, maybe I screwed up in basic training, missed a couple of days, and maybe this is what war is all about.
testifying at the trial of Lieut. William Calley, 1969

The revelation in 1969 of the massacre on March 16 1968 of 109 Vietnamese men, women and children in the village of My Lai 4 (Song My) by American troops appalled a nation who not only liked to win their wars but assumed they won them clean. The massacre would have gone unnoticed had freelance investigative journalist Seymour Hersh not been tipped off about the forthcoming court-martial of one Lieutenant William Calley (aged 26) for mass murder. Hersh's story was syndicated throughout America to little initial reaction but after one paper unearthed official pictures of the slaughter, the scoop went round the world. The trial centred on Calley, who claimed throughout that he was following orders from above. The Army chose not to investigate further and Calley was sentenced to life imprisonment, reduced to 10 years, in 1971. He was freed in 1974.

BERRIGAN, DANIEL (1921–) American radical

A revolution is interesting insofar as it avoids like the plague the plague it promised to heal.
quoted in *New York Review of Books*, 1971

Berrigan was a Jesuit father who, appalled by the continuing American involvement in Vietnam, took radical action. With fellow protestors he invaded a draft centre and ransacked the files, covering vital papers listing those eligible for call-up with animal blood. With his brother Philip (1923–) Berrigan was the first ever Roman Catholic priest to receive a sentence from a US federal court for radical activism.

BETJEMAN, JOHN (1906–1984) British poet and conservationist

Pam, I adore you, Pam you great big mountainous sportsgirl Whizzing them over the net, full of the strength of five.
Pot-Pourri from a Surrey Garden

Betjeman, British poet laureate from 1972 until his death, had his first book of verse, *Mount Zion*, published in 1931, at which time he was writing for the *Architectural Review*. His first book of architectural criticism was *Ghastly Good Taste* (1933) and poetry and buildings, especially their conservation, remained his twin preoccupations. He produced a number of books of verse, to growing acclaim, until the publication of his *Collected Poems* in 1958 sold 100,000 in its first edition. With his friend John Piper he edited a number of *Shell Guides to England* and in the 1960s made several successful television programmes, usually on architecture. The lines quoted are quintessential Betjeman, the home counties bourgeoisie rendered lyrical.

BETJEMAN, JOHN

**Childhood is measured out by sounds and smells
And sights, before the dark of reason grows.**
Summoned by Bells (1960)

Betjeman wrote no autobiography, although a substantial television series offered many reminiscences near the end of his life, but his lengthy poem *Summoned by Bells* dealt in some detail with his boyhood in Highgate, son of a manufacturer of household goods, and with his education at Marlborough, which he hated, and at Magdalen College Oxford, which he enjoyed and where he met fellow poets W.H. Auden and Louis MacNeice, and Maurice Bowra, already a young don, who encouraged him to write poetry.

BETJEMAN, JOHN

I have a Vision of the Future, chum,
The workers' flats in fields of soya beans
Tower up like silver pencils, score on score:
And Surging Millions hear the challenge come from microphones
in communal canteens
'No Right! No Wrong! All's perfect, evermore'.

The Planster's Vision (1945)

This poem satirising the excessive enthusiasms of state-directed planning was written as the Labour government came to power in 1945, but Betjeman's lines became even more apposite as the Fifties and then the Sixties saw the wholesale destruction of so much of Britain's architectural heritage. His own pleasure, in 'suburbs and gas lights and Pont Street and Gothic revival churches and mineral railways, provincial towns and garden cities', was mocked when he began initially to display it, but as more and more vanished and less and less acceptable replacements were built, the public began to value his campaigning architectural conservatism.

BETJEMAN, JOHN

Sand in the sandwiches, wasps in the tea,
Sun on our bathing dresses heavy with the wet,
Squelch of the bladder-wrack waiting for the sea,
Fleas round the tamarisk, an early cigarette.

Trebetherick (1940)

Betjeman was a lifelong fan of the north Cornwall coast and the area around Padstow is now known as 'Betjeman country'. This poem evokes the typical English picnic, and the adult who remembers it as a childhood pleasure hopes that his children too will be able to enjoy such delights. His popularity waned during the Sixties, when it seemed too simple to be intellectually credible, but it is his ability to touch so delicately on the English middle-class experience that has ensured the renaissance of his appeal.

BEVAN, ANEURIN   (1987–1960) British politician

No attempt at ethical or social seduction can eradicate from my heart a deep and burning hatred of the Tory party.... So far as I am concerned they are lower than vermin.
speaking in 1945

Nye Bevan, as he was universally known, was MP for Ebbw Vale from 1929–60 and the long-term leader of the radical left wing of the British Labour Party. His fame rests on his undaunted championship of the miners, his acerbic opposition to Winston Churchill's wartime ministry and his setting up, despite the frantic opposition of the medical establishment of the National Health Service in 1948. He had no truck with Tory politicians, and his criticisms of Churchill, even when it seemed to many that party prejudices might be abandoned for the duration of the war, proved his dedication to his class. This particular attack was delivered at the height of his struggle for the NHS, and his comment related to the 1930s when Tory policies 'condemned millions of first-class people to semi-starvation'. This provoked near hysterical reaction from the Tories and condemnation from the more temperate Labour members who felt that Bevan's outburst cost them two million votes.

BEVAN, ANEURIN

If you carry this resolution and follow out all its implications and do not run away from it you will send a Foreign Secretary, whoever he may be, naked into the conference chamber.... Able to preach sermons, of course; he could make good sermons. But actions of that sort is not necessarily the way in which you can take away the menace of the bomb from the world.
speech, October 1957

For all Bevan's political ideals, he remained in the most important areas a pragmatist. It was axiomatic on the left wing of the party that if elected to power, they would impose unilateral disarmament on Britain, irrespective of any commitments to the Western alliance and NATO. As leader of the left it was incumbent upon Bevan to share this view, but he did not. Debating the bomb at the Labour conference of 1957 Bevan delivered these words and ran into intense opposition from former supporters who saw his remarks as an outright betrayal. He refused to be swayed and remained unimpressed by woollier optimists such as

J.B. Priestley who suggested that the hard bargaining of international politics would be influenced by 'the force of our example'.

BEVAN, ANEURIN

His ear is so sensitively attuned to the bugle note of history that he is often deaf to the more raucous clamour of contemporary life.

Bevan's attacks on Winston Churchill were frequent and did not cease just because the Prime Minister was generally seen as England's best chance against Hitler. Churchill's feel for the grandeur of history certainly dominated his political style and served admirably as a rallying cry in a time of national crisis. Bevan's own interests lay in the future, one that would ideally be consecrated to his socialist ideals. As the Labour landslide in the 1945 election proved, Churchill's refusal to note the 'clamour of contemporary life' duly cost him dear.

BEVAN, ANEURIN

Stand not too near the rich man lest he destroy thee – and not too far away lest he forget thee.

Bevan's appetite for the company of the rich brought him a degree of opprobrium and the label 'Bollinger Bolshevik'. But his enjoyment of some of wealth's pleasures did not undermine his basic class allegiance and while he was prepared to indulge in what he called 'slumming in the West End', making frequent visits to the home of the arch-capitalist Lord Beaverbrook, he kept his ideological distance. He invented the mock-Biblical injunction cited here to sum up his attitude.

BEVAN, ANEURIN

Political toleration is a by-product of the complacency of the ruling class. When that complacency is disturbed there never was a more bloody-minded set of thugs than the British ruling class.

Representing the left wing of the Labour party Bevan was less impressed by the ostensible toleration of democratic politics than those who felt less commitment to socialist principles. If it were necessary to impose a variety of state controls to wrest control of the nation's power bases, both political and economic, then so be it. The Conservatives might boast that they were, on those terms, the true party of human liberty and tolerance, but Bevan's view was that such liberality came on strictly expedient grounds.

Bevan, Aneurin

The Prime Minister has got very many virtues and when the time comes I hope to pay my tribute to them, but I am bound to say that political honesty and sagacity have never been among them.

While many Labour MPs felt that the exigencies of wartime required that they suspend the normal antagonisms of party politics, Bevan refused to sacrifice the convictions of a lifetime. He found especially intolerable Churchill's realpolitik, taking as allies individuals whose politics Bevan found repellant. In general England, at Churchill's behest, opted for establishment parties, rejecting the many groups of left-wing resistance fighters. Bevan, who understood just what this would imply for the post-war world, made it clear that he deplored Churchill's attitude. Such attacks brought him much opprobrium; A.A. Milne for instance calling Bevan, in the News Chronicle, a bonus for Dr. Goebbels.

Bevan, Aneurin

I read the newspaper avidly. It is my one form of continuous fiction.

Compared with the treatment meted out in recent years to modern radical left-wingers, the British press were reasonably restrained in their dealing with Bevan, who as the most visible left-winger of his time was a potential candidate for such opprobrium. His 'lower than vermin' speech was greeted by the *Sunday Dispatch* with the headline 'The Man Who Hates 8,093,858 People' (the number of Tory voters in 1945), but on the whole Bevan gave as good as, if not better than, he received. He condemned the *Daily Mirror* as 'strip-tease artists' and wrote to Beaverbrook suggesting that the *Daily Express*, if nothing else, would do no good for its proprietor's political ambitions. (Beaverbrook returned the letter, rewritten with the word *Tribune*, the hard-left paper edited by Bevan, substituted for the *Express*).

Bevan, Aneurin

How can wealth persuade poverty to use its political freedom to keep wealth in power? Here lies the whole art of Conservative politics in the 20th century.
In Place of Fear (1952)

In Place of Fear was Bevan's political testimony, published at the height of his fame and at the time creating a great deal of interest. With its call for the implementation of real socialist policies and its insistence on the rights of the working people, the book echoed the Bevan style, described by his biographer Michael Foot as that of an 'outrageous ranter.' While such points as this one remain as true as ever, Bevan's credo, once considered so vital, has long remained unread upon the shelves.

BEVAN, ANEURIN

We know what happens to people who stay in the middle of the road: they get run over.
speaking in 1953

Bevan probably would not have recognised the middle of the road had he ever bothered to move that far to the right of his own aggressively socialist posture. Throughout his lengthy political career he fought ceaselessly for his own class, and in particular for the mining communities of S. Wales. That it cost him the leadership of the Labour party must have hurt, but he resisted any temptation to soften his line. Speaking as he was in 1953, he may have also been reflecting on the Labour government, far less socialist than he would have preferred, which had been trounced in the 1951 election.

BEVAN, ANEURIN

There is no reason to attack the monkey when the organ grinder is present.
speaking in, 1956

This phrase, like its peer 'Why talk to the oily rag when I can talk to the engineer' is in general slang use. Its first use by a politician is usually ascribed to Churchill who was replying to Britain's Ambassador in Rome who had requested whether he should discuss a certain topic with Mussolini or with his Foreign Minister. More celebrated is Bevan's use. In a debate shortly after the Suez debacle, Bevan was questioning the Foriegn Minister, Selwyn Lloyd. On seeing the Prime Minister, Macmillan, enter the House of Commons he abandoned his questions and made this remark.

BEVAN, ANEURIN

A desiccated calculating machine.
speech, September 29, 1954

Bevan's invective was never limited to his party political opponents. He could be as ruthless in his condemnations of Labour politicians whom he felt were insufficiently dedicated to socialism. Responding to Attlee's suggestion that the Party should not react emotionally to the recently announced news of German rearmament, Bevan deplored such disinterest, saying 'I know that the right kind of leader for the Labour Party is a desiccated calculating machine who must not in any way permit himself to be swayed by indignation' and continued in this vein. Critics immediately took this to be an attack on Hugh Gaitskell, who in 1955 beat Bevan in the leadership contest, but Bevan stoutly denied the charge, blaming his opponents in the press for spreading this 'canard'.

BEVAN, ANEURIN

Whereas in Britain we are slaves to the past, in Russia they are slaves to the future.

The 1930s saw a flood of British intellectuals and politicians to Russia, all eager to see the vaunted wonders of the Russian Revolution. None more so than Bevan who naturally believed that in the Soviet Union his own cherished dreams of socialism in action had finally been achieved. That the truth was somewhat different seemed at this juncture not to matter to these visitors. Some did find the reality too threatening to their beliefs and on returning to England recanted their earlier enthusiasm, but the majority, unwilling to see Stalin's dictatorship for what it was, came home to proselytise for the true faith.

BIBESCO, ELIZABETH   (1897–??) British writer

Attributing our own temptations to others, we give them credit for victories they have never won.
Haven (1951)

Elizabeth Bibesco was the daughter of H.H. Asquith and Margot Asquith, married in 1919 to the Rumanian Prince Antoine Bibesco. Lacking traditional disciplines her work, as Elizabeth Bowen has noted, was 'artless... spontaneous, uncalculated, natural and unfeigned'. She wrote a number of novels. *Haven*, published after her death, is a collection of short stories which includes a selection of the Princess' aphorisms, grouped under the headings of Human Relations, Giving and Receiving, Love, Gods and Men, and General. They include:

How many men would recognise a woman undressed of his emotions?

We go through life expecting to be tasted while we are being swallowed.

We are able to behave perfectly to those who have never mattered enough to be a disappointment.

To withhold the unwanted is the supreme test of generosity.

Irony is the hygiene of the mind.

BIBESCO, ELIZABETH

To others we are not ourselves but a performer in their lives cast for a part we do not even know that we are playing.
Haven (1951)

BIBESCO, ELIZABETH

How much easier to make pets of our friends' weaknesses than to put up with their strengths.
Haven (1951)

BIERCE, AMBROSE (1842–1914) American satirist
Bierce, the autodidact son of an Ohio farmer, began his journalistic career in San Francisco, writing from 1868 the satirical 'Town Crier' column for a weekly financial sheet. From 1872–76 he moved to London where he worked for *Fun*, a short-lived rival to *Punch*, writing under the pseudonym Dod Grile. Back in America he returned to full-time journalism and his modern reputation is based on his *Devil's Dictionary*. The *Dictionary* appeared over a number of years, from 1881–1911, but it appears to stem from a short Town Crier piece of 1869, satirising American lexicography. The completed *Dictionary* appeared in 1911, as part of the *Collected Works of Ambrose Bierce*. Bierce's journalistic career climaxed in his employment in 1887 by William Randolph Hearst on the *San Francisco Examiner*. Here he earned a high salary and appears to have enjoyed elite status. In 1913, aged 71, Bierce took a trip to Mexico, then embroiled in a civil war. He never reappeared and his death remains a mystery although it is assumed that he fell foul of one revolutionary faction or another.

BIERCE, AMBROSE

Alliance, n: in international politics, the union of two thieves who have their hands so deeply inserted into each other's pocket that they cannot safely plunder a third.
The Devil's Dictionary (1911)

BIERCE, AMBROSE

Battle, n: a method of untying with the teeth a political knot that will not yield to the tongue.
The Devil's Dictionary (1911)

BIERCE, AMBROSE

Bore, n: a person who talks when you wish him to listen.
The Devil's Dictionary (1911)

BIERCE, AMBROSE

Conservative, n: a statesman who is enamoured of existing evils, as distinguished from the Liberal who wishes to replace them with others.
The Devil's Dictionary (1911)

BIERCE, AMBROSE

Cynic, n: a blackguard whose faulty vision sees things as they are, not as they ought to be.
The Devil's Dictionary (1911)

BIERCE, AMBROSE

Destiny, n: a tyrant's excuse for crime and a fool's excuse for failure.
The Devil's Dictionary (1911)

BIERCE, AMBROSE

History, n: an account mostly false, of events mostly unimportant, which are brought about by rulers, mostly knaves, and soldiers mostly fools.
The Devil's Dictionary (1911)

BIERCE, AMBROSE

Insurrection, n: an unsuccessful revolution.
The Devil's Dictionary (1911)

BIERCE, AMBROSE

Liberty, n: one of imagination's most precious possessions.
The Devil's Dictionary (1911)

BIERCE, AMBROSE

Mythology, n: the body of a primitive people's beliefs, concerning its origin, early history, heroes, deities and so forth, as distinguished from the the true accounts which it invents later.
The Devil's Dictionary (1911)

BIERCE, AMBROSE

Peace, n: in international affairs, a period of cheating between two periods of fighting.
The Devil's Dictionary (1911)

BIERCE, AMBROSE

Politics, n: a strife of interests masquerading as a contest of principles.
The Devil's Dictionary (1911)

BIERCE, AMBROSE

Rebel, n: the proponent of a new misrule who has failed to establish it.
The Devil's Dictionary (1911)

BIERCE, AMBROSE

Revolution, n: in politics, an abrupt change in the form of misgovernment
The Devil's Dictionary (1911)

BIERCE, AMBROSE

Acquaintance, n: a person whom we know well enough to borrow from but not well enough to lend to. A degree of friendship called slight when the object is poor or obscure, and intimate when he is rich or famous.
The Devil's Dictionary (1911)

BIERMANN, WOLF (1936–) German poet

Life goes at such a terrific pace – A few years full of youth and grace and then you fall flat on your face before world history.
Bilanzballade in Breissingsten Jahr

Biermann was born in Hamburg where his father was a member of the Communist resistance until he was detected and sent to Auschwitz. In 1953 Biermann moved to East Germany (DDR) and from 1957–59 he worked with the Berliner Ensemble, founded by the late Bertolt Brecht, before concentrating on poetry from the early Sixties. Biermann's refusal to tailor his verses to the State's demands have brought him into continual conflict with the DDR where the authorities have banned certain works, but their censorship was somewhat relaxed in the Seventies, permitting him to publish *Deutschland, Ein Wintermachen*, an outspoken attack on life on his side of the Berlin Wall.

Biff Kardz

Life is a meaningless comma in the sentence of time.

Biff Kardz, created by illustrators Chris Garratt and Mick Kidd, first appeared in 1980 as a 'non sexist, nonaligned, nondescript multinational corporation' dedicated to providing a new style of postcards. Their products, combining popular images culled from a wide range of popular and academic media, literally cut up and redesign both pictures and words, mixing the banal, the grandiose and the bathetic to create a wittily surrealist satire on the mores of the Eighties.

BIKO, STEVE   (1946–1977) South African radical

The most potent weapon in the hands of the oppressor is the mind of the oppressed.
speech to the Cape Town Conference on Inter-racial Studies, 1971

Biko was a youthful Black nationalist leader, challenging apartheid in South Africa, when his death in police custody brought him from relative obscurity to international importance. As founder of the South African Students Organisation and the Black People's Convention he was banned from political activism in 1973 but his continued work led to his arrest in 1977. Although a subsequent investigation cleared all the officials involved, it was accepted by the Black community and by the world at large that Biko had been beaten to death in the cells of Pretoria's police headquarters. He remains one of South Africa's most potent martyrs, the inspiration of many of those young people who are still fighting for their freedom.

BINSTEAD, ARTHUR   (1861–1914) British journalist

The great secret in life... (is) not to open your letters for a fortnight. At the expiration of that period you will find that nearly all of them have answered themselves.
Pitcher's Proverbs (1909)

Binstead was known to his cronies and the large readership of the *Sporting Times*, otherwise celebrated throughout the messes, clubs, race tracks and similar watering holes of London and the Empire as 'The Pink 'Un', as the Pitcher, an abbreviation of Tale-Pitcher. He was the acknowledged leader of an improvident, raffish group of journalists, few of whom achieved literary eminence but whose joie de vivre made them valued members of the less staid sections of London society in the 1890s. While Wilde stayed in the Cafe Royal, pontificating over art, Binstead, 'the

Dwarf of Blood' (restaurant critic Nathaniel Newnham-Davies), 'Swears' (club owner Ernest Wells), and 'Shifter' (William F. Goldberg) preferred Romanos in the Strand and the Pelican Club in Gerrard Street, mixing with Gaiety girls and guardees.

BINYON, LAWRENCE (1869–1943) British poet

They shall grow not old, as we that are left grow old:
Age shall not weary them, nor the years condemn.
At the going down of the sun and in the morning
We will remember them.

poem in the *Times*, September 21, 1914

Binyon was the assistant keeper of prints and drawings at the British Museum and a prolific writer, both of studies on art and of plays and poems. The poem from which these lines are taken was written early in the First World War and published in the *Times* on 21 September 1914, mourning those who had fallen 'across the sea' in the war's first encounters. They have subsequently been recited, almost as a mourning prayer, at the annual Remembrance Day ceremonies on or around November 11th.

BIRCH, NIGEL British politician

They've shot our fox.

in the House of Commons, 1947

Birch, a Conservative MP, took it upon himself to wage a vendetta against the then Chancellor of the Exchequer Dr. Hugh Dalton, campaigning to undermine Dalton's position in the House of Commons. It is traditional that the Budget must be seen by the members before it is released to the Press (although this seems to be observed less and less today) and in 1947 Dalton foolishly leaked vital sections of his proposals to Fleet Street prior to the usual Budget Day speech. The outcry that followed this blunder forced Dalton's resignation. On hearing the news Birch registered his frustration in these squirearchical terms.

BLACKMUR, R.P. (1904–65) American critic

Criticism, I take it, is the normal discourse of an amateur.
Language as Gesture (1952)

Blackmur was from 1951 Professor of English at Princeton University. He wrote a number of volumes of poetry, but his reputation rests on his work as a critic, and leading proponent of the 'New Criticism', a discipline that concentrated on intense textual scholarship at the expense of purely literary enjoyment or ease of presentation, looking for verbal nuance and thematic organisation rather than dealing with the traditional concerns of the author's background or personality. To Blackmur the text was an object on a page to be considered strictly on its own merits; auctorial motivation was of secondary importance. Despite this disclaimer, such analysis was hardly amateur work.

BLAHA, HENRY American sportsman

Rugby is a beastly game played by gentlemen; soccer is a gentleman's game played by beasts; football is a beastly game played by beasts.

Blaha, speaking in 1972, was embellishing the traditional division between rugby and what most of the world calls football but the Americas differentiate from their own US football as 'soccer'. Like all such generalisations, it rings both true and false, and whereas the rugby/soccer division is based in English class-consciousness and in the preferences of 19th century public schools, his condemnation of the undeniably violent but equally skilful US football seems rather unfair.

BLEASDALE, ALAN British playwright

Gizza job!
Boys from the Black Stuff (1982)

Alan Bleasdale is a Liverpool playwright whose five-part television series based on the experiences of six unemployed builders became an instant classic, among the most important dramatic treatments of one of the central problems of 'Thatcher's Britain'. The series derived from an earlier TV play, of the same name, in which 'the Boys' whose speciality is laying tarmac on roads, hence the black stuff, were attempting in a mixture of black humour and unsentimental pathos to work a 'foreigner', and earn some money to boost their unemployment pay. Each episode of the series centred on one 'boy'. The most impressive was 'Yosser's Story' which charts the breakdown of the team's most unstable member 'Yosser Hughes', who loses his mind and his family as he cracks under the pressure of joblessness. His desperate appeal 'Gizza job!' became a national catchphrase.

BLOCK, HERBERT (1909–) (Herblock) American political cartoonist

If it's good, they'll stop making it.
dictum

Herbert Bloch, who signs his regular works 'Herblock' is one of America's most respected and widely syndicated political cartoonists. His work appears in many newspapers and is occasionally picked up in the UK. This cri-de-coeur in the face of the relentless drive for progress, based on the cherished concept of built-in obsolescence, rings all too true.

BLONDE CRAZY

You dirty rat!
screenplay (1931)

James Cagney (1899–1986) always claimed that he never once muttered his most famous catchphrase on a film set, and *Blonde Crazy*, a pot-boiling B-movie made to capitalise on the success of the star's first big hit, *Public Enemy* (1931) was hardly a film for actors or audiences to remember. But a million impersonators can't be that wrong and somewhere along the way Cagney did call someone 'you dirty, double-crossing rat'. Close, but no cigar.

BOCUSE, PAUL   (1926–) French chef

The so-called nouvelle cuisine usually means not enough on your plate and too much on your bill.
quoted in the *Standard*, 1985

The *nouvelle cuisine*, and its close cousin *cuisine minceur* (cooking for slimmers) appeared in the 1970s as cookery's answer to the small is beautiful philosophy that lies behind the exercise and diet fads of the period. Such French chefs as Bocuse and the Troisgros Brothers jettisoned the creams, liqueurs and animal fats of traditional haute cuisine for a new regime of lighter-than-light, fatless, aesthetic cookery, using the finest ingredients and heavily influenced by the minimalism and artistry of Japanese cooking. Unfortunately this innovatory style has all too frequently paled into the insubstantial, clichéd imitations served up by second-rate artisans in the rash of restaurants capitalising on this new culinary fashion. Bocuse may be mocking himself here, but one should bear in mind an earlier comment, made in 1978, in which he stated that 'Life is a practical joke'.

BOGART, HUMPHREY   (1899–1957) American film star

I should never have switched from Scotch to Martinis.
quoted in L. Halliwell 'The Filmgoers' Companion' (1985)

This terminal wisecrack was attributed to Bogart as his 'famous last words' but like so many such farewells, the truth was probably more banal. They do, on the other hand, point up

105

Bogart's drinking, which he saw as a necessary part of his image, the tough-guy boss of the Holmby Hills Rat Pack, a coterie of pals that pre-dated Frank Sinatra's verminous acolytes. Bogart, who was also credited with remarking 'The trouble with the world is that everybody in it is three drinks behind', was by no means a charming drinker. As restauranteur Dave Chasen put it, commenting on the star who one critic called 'unflinching, cynical and a realist, a tough guy in a trenchcoat, a man's man', 'Bogart's a helluva nice guy until 11.30 pm. After that he thinks he's Bogart'.

BOHR, NIELS (1885–1962) Danish atomic physicist

An expert is a man who has made all the mistakes which can be made, in a very narrow field.

After working with Ernest Rutherford in England on the nuclear atom, Bohr developed in 1912 his quantum theory of atomic structure and founded the Institute of Theoretical Physics in Copenhagen to pursue studies in this area. Bohr won the Nobel Prize for his work in 1922. After a period of research into Heisenberg's uncertainty principle, Bohr turned in 1930 to nuclear physics, specialising in nuclear fission, studies pioneered by Enrico Fermi. Like Fermi, Bohr was enlisted in the Manhattan project, working to create the world's first atomic bomb, and like many of those responsible for the weapon attempted later to restrict its proliferation. Bohr's most important works include *Atomic Theory and the Description of Nature* (1934) and *Atomic Physics and Human Knowledge* (1958).

BOHR, NIELS

A weapon of unparalleled power is being created. Unless, indeed, some international agreement about the control of the use of the new active materials can be obtained, any temporary advantage, however great, may be outweighed by a perpetual menace to human society.
letter, 1944

As Robert Oppenheimer put it, the scientists involved in the development of the atomic bomb had 'known sin'. While their invention would never conveniently vanish, a number of those concerned attempted to expiate their sin by campaigning at the highest level for the control of the bomb's use and, ideally, for the restriction of all atomic power to peaceful uses. In 1944 Bohr wrote the letter from which this warning is taken to President Roosevelt and to Winston Churchill. By the time the first bombs were dropped, neither man was still in power, although it is unlikely that either would have acted on Bohr's plea.

BOHR, NIELS

The opposite of a correct statement is a false statement. But the opposite of a profound truth may well be another profound truth.

Among the distinguishing features of the great scientists, at least if their reported comments are to be believed, is their understanding of the fact that today's incontrovertible theory is tomorrow's exploded fallacy, although both 'facts' will hold true within their own context. Bohr is pointing out the way in which life, as well as science, can produce situations in which absolute opposites do not necessarily cancel each other out, and must each be accepted as truths in their own right.

BOLT, ROBERT   (1924–) British playwright

Morality's not practical. Morality's a gesture. A complicated gesture learnt from books.
A Man for All Seasons (1962)

A Man for All Seasons is Robert Bolt's most successful play, a study of the conflict between King Henry VIII and Sir Thomas More. This play, filmed in 1966 with Paul Scofield as More, Robert Shaw as the King and Orson Welles as the scheming Cardinal Wolsey, deals with Henry's creation of the English Reformation, a religious revolution that stemmed from the King's desire for a divorce. More is an unalloyed hero, a saintly figure who was indeed canonised in 1935, a Tudor intellectual and patron of the arts who embraced the most sophisticated learning but likewise refused to let his monarch destroy his primary allegiance, to the Pope. More was found guilty of high treason and beheaded in 1535.

BONAR LAW, ANDREW   (1858–1923) British prime minister

I must follow them, I am their leader.
speaking in 1922

Bonar Law, apostrophised by his successor H.H. Asquith as 'the Unknown Prime Minister' (qv), lacked many of the forceful, purposive characteristics that fellow politicians and the public prefer to see in their leaders. Lacking in any ideological drive, he was swayed primarily by success, no matter in what field, but as an essentially reticent man, did not display the characteristics that might have brought him his own achievements. According to some sources even this self-deprecatory phrase, offered in 1922 to his secretary, was not his own work: Ledru-Rollin, a left-wing French liberal, surveying the mobs fighting at the barricades during the Revolution of 1848, supposedly said it first.

BONHOEFFER, DIETRICH (1906–45) German theologian

A God who would let us prove his existence would be an idol.
No Rusty Swords

Bonhoeffer was one of Europe's leading theologians in the 1930s. His political consciousness matured alongside his theological pursuits and he came increasingly to see the two strands of thought as indissoluble. Such opinions brought him into conflict with the Nazi regime, which he had attacked from its emergence, especially on the grounds of its anti-semitism. He announced himself as a 'conditional pacifist', becoming increasingly involved in German anti-Nazi movements. Banned in 1939 from speaking or writing publicly, he continued his work underground until he was arrested in 1943. Implicated in the Stauffenberg conspiracy against Hitler, he was hanged on 9 April 1944. His unfinished study *Ethics* (1953) showed him as an advocate of the unification of Christianity and secular humanism, through which the church should affirm 'mankind come of age' and reconnect with its earliest, Jewish roots. His influence remains potent among radical theologians.

BOOKER, CHRISTOPHER (1937–) British writer

The fashionable drawing rooms of London have always been happy to welcome outsiders – if only on their own, albeit undemanding terms. That is to say, artists, so long as they are not too talented, men of humble birth, so long as they have since amassed several million pounds, and socialists so long as they are Tories.
Now magazine 1981

Booker was part of the Shrewsbury School and Oxford University clique who founded the satirical magazine *Private Eye* in 1961. He was the magazine's first editor, simultaneously writing scripts for BBC-TV's *That Was The Week That Was*, and as such a pioneer of the 'satire boom' of the 1960s. Booker broke with *Private Eye* and by the late 1960s was establishing himself as a prototype 'young fogey', a stance epitomised in his book *The Neophiliacs* (1969) in which he lambasted the so-called 'Swinging Sixties' as a form of collective madness, novelty purely for novelty's sake. Since then he has written widely and concerned himself particularly with the conservation of Britain's architectural heritage.

BOORSTIN, DANIEL (1914–) American academic

The celebrity is a person who is well-known for his well-knownness,... celebrities intensify their celebrity images simply by being well-known for relations among themselves. By a kind of symbiosis, celebrities live off each other....A sign of a celebrity is that his name is often worth more than his services.
The Image (1962)

After a career as a leading academic lawyer Boorstin was appointed in 1975 the Librarian of Congress, running America's largest and most prestigious library. As well as a number of historical studies, including *America and the Image of Europe* (1958) and *A History of the United States* (1981), Boorstin's most influential book has been *The Image, or What Happened to the American Dream* (1962). This book, more sociological than historical, deals with the realities, rather than the fantasy of the 'American dream' which had informed the pioneers, but had long since become altered and, in some eyes, debased. Here Boorstin is comparing the artificial media celebrity with the hero, who created himself on the basis of his own achievements.

BOORSTIN, DANIEL

...The messiness of experience. That may be what we mean by life.
New York Post, 1972

Speaking from the marbled fastness of the Library of Congress it may be that Boorstin's own experiences are currently less messy than most, but his summation of the complexities of life seems pertinent. What one does about the mess remains, of course, subject to the wider debate that, among other things, is known as philosophy.

BOORSTIN, DANIEL

A best-seller was a book which somehow sold well simply because it was selling well.
The Image (1962)

The best-selling novel is a phenomenon of the 20th century. Dickens sold substantial quantities, as did many of his contemporaries, but the gaudy extravaganza, seemingly intensified with every new launch, that has become the necessary accompaniment to the appearance of each tinsel-wrapped volume of meretricious wish-fulfilment, is a strictly modern event. When Boorstin made his assessment he was, at least, dealing only with much-touted books. Today's situation, where many so-called novels are in effect no more than a necessary way-station in the triumphant and well-paid progress to a TV mini-series, means that while indeed the book still 'sells well', one wonders whether the sales are to the public, or to the film or television rights departments.

BOREN, JAMES H. (1925–) American bureaucrat

When in doubt, mumble; when in trouble, delegate; when in charge, ponder.
quoted in *The Official Rules* by P. Dickson 1972

Paul Dickson's *The Official Rules* was a collection of those infuriating but seemingly inescapable 'laws' that interpose themselves between what we set out to do and what life permits to happen. The purest example is Murphy's Law: if something can go wrong, it will. Dickson also included some of the more cynical pointers to capitalising on the rules, of which James Boren's directive, culled from years of working in the American bureaucratic system, is one.

BORGES, JORGE LUIS (1899–1986) Argentine writer

We have stopped believing in progress. What progress that is.
quoted in Ibarrai, *Borges et Borges*

As one of Argentina's leading 20th century intellectuals, Borges was heavily influenced by European and in particular English culture. He travelled widely before returning to Buenos Aires where the publication of his first volume of short stories, *The Universal History of Infamy* (1935) established him as a major South American writer. His first international success was *Labyrinths* (1953). From 1938–46 he worked as a librarian, which job he lost for political reasons, but in 1955 he was appointed director of the National Library of Buenos Aires. His writing slowed down as he became totally blind, but he remained an important figure until his death. Ostensibly non-political, he resisted involvement with any ideology, and, as he puts it above, sees no charm in the supposed allure of progress.

BORGES, JORGE LUIS

Writing is nothing more than a guided dream.
Dr Brodie's Report (1971)

This line is taken from Borges' last collection of stories, which appeared a decade after blindness had brought his new writing to a halt. It reflects his own style, an enigmatic, labyrinthine maze of puzzles, philosophies, and other intellectual arcana. Like dreams, Borges' tales often seem cyclical, with no concrete start or finish, dealing in the bizarre and the otherwise unknown, bringing in for no apparent reason the fleeting minutiae of the strange.

BORGES, JORGE LUIS

Democracy is an abuse of statistics.
quoted in Jàcobo Timerman *Prisoner Without a Name, Cell Without a Number* (1981)

Timerman, a liberal newspaper editor and a Jew, whose book describes his own incarceration and torture in 1977 by Argentine's military government, cites Borges' remark as an example of how in his country's multifaceted political make-up, every group (left, right and centre) would agree with the premise, but interpret it in contradictory ways. Borges himself claimed to stand outside politics; the breadth of his learning and the complexities of his prose exceed the 'truths' of party lines. This refusal to espouse the liberation theories of any left-wing guerilla group meant that he became branded, on no grounds other than his disinterest, as a right-winger.

BORGES, JORGE LUIS

Nothing is built on stone; all is built on sand, but we must build as if the sand were stone.
writing in 1972

This aphorism reflects Borges' philosophy and his literary style, which brought the concept of 'Magic Realism', coined by Franz Roh in 1925, from Europe to South America and which has influenced many of the continent's writers. In magic realism the bizarre, the unlikely and the fantastic are described in terms of realism and rationality. The sand, as it were, is made to appear as stone. Borges' combination of folk-tales, myths and a wide range of recondite knowledge, set against a fluctuating, fluid timescale that represents a dream rather than a simple start-to-finish narrative, exemplifies this style of writing.

BOSSIDY, J.C. American writer

> **And this is good old Boston**
> **The home of the bean and the cod**
> **Where the Lowells talk to the Cabots,**
> **And the Cabots talk only to God.**

toast, 1891

Bossidy delivered this toast, which has developed into a popular verse, at a dinner at Harvard University around 1891. It refers both to the staple products of this Puritan city, with its pre-Revolutionary bluebloods and its large Irish immigrant population, and to two of its most important families, both of whom represent America's 'aristocracy'. Among the most famous Lowells is the poet Robert (1917–77) and the Cabots produced America's ill-starred ambassador to S. Vietnam in the 1960s, Henry Cabot Lodge.

BOTTOMLEY, HORATIO (1860–1933) British journalist and fraud

> **'Ah, Bottomley, sewing?' 'No, reaping.'**

conversation between a visitor, seeing him working in the prison garden, and Bottomley.

Bottomley was a larger-than-life 'character' whose topsy-turvy career took him from an orphaned youth to great wealth, greater disgrace, and a pathetic end. A superb publicist, he amassed his first fortune by 1897. Further companies proved less successful: he went bankrupt 67 times between 1900–05. Undaunted he lived as a true robber-baron, mixing daring with disaster. He founded the *Financial Times* and in 1906 the ultra-patriotic *John Bull* magazine. His political career was chequered with his bankruptcies. In 1919 came his greatest adventure: the Victory Bonds, an ultimately fraudulent scheme in which Bottomley, touting himself as 'The Friend of the Poor' systematically robbed them. He was jailed in 1919 – after a trial in which he was permitted an 11.30 am 'medicinal' glass of champagne – and this conversation was recorded during his seven year sentence. He emerged to poverty in 1926 and ended his days appearing, as himself, on the stage of the Windmill Theatre.

BOULESTIN, MARCEL (1878–1943) French chef

Good food is more important than many so-called important things of life. I can imagine no more charming picture than the wife seeing to the perfection of the evening meal, and the husband on his way home from the office looking forward to it. Happiness sits smiling at their table.
Simple French Cooking for English Homes 1923

This idealised picture of culinary and domestic bliss comes from one of the pioneers of decent eating in England. Boulestin's small book revolutionised the eating habits of the discerning in the 1920s in the same way as did Elizabeth David's efforts, reaching a far larger audience, in the 1950s. Contemporary English food tended to offer either the over-elaborate recipes of the rich, prepared by servants and hangovers from Edwardian excess, or the 'plain fare' of the mass. Boulestin responded to the new world of the 1920s, offering fine ingredients and simplicity of cuisine and proclaiming what the French knew but the English, even now, suspect as slightly degenerate: that good food and drink are essential to a civilised life. His restaurant, in name at least, still survives in London.

BOWEN, ELIZABETH (1899–1973) Anglo-Irish writer

Experience isn't interesting till it begins to repeat itself – in fact, till it does that, it hardly is experience.
The Death of the Heart (1938)

Bowen was born into the Anglo-Irish upper classes and in 1930 inherited her father's house, Bowen Court in County Cork. She began writing aged 20, publishing various collections of short stories and several novels, of which the most important are *The Death of the Heart* (1938) and *The Heat of the Day* (1949). Unsurprisingly her best work deals with her own milieu, the cosmopolitan upper classes; inspired by the war, she added to an already accomplished treatment of both people and places (and in particular landscapes and weather) a reputation that places her as one of the best writers of the Blitz. She has also, in *The Cat Jumps*, dealt with the supernatural.

BOWEN, ELIZABETH

The heart may think it knows better but the senses know that absence blots people out. We have really no absent friends.
The Death of the Heart (1938)

Bowen's best known novel deals with the story of Portia, an orphan whose appearance in the sophisticated lives of her half-brother Thomas and his wife Anna threatens to disrupt their existence. In her turn Portia's stability is threatened by her infatuation with the glamorous, youthful Eddy, himself made wretched by his obsession with Anna. Absence in Bowen's view, does not make the heart grow fonder, it merely frees it for other occupations.

BOWEN, ELIZABETH

Happy that few of us are aware of the world until we are already in league with it.
The Death of the Heart (1938)

As she puts it elsewhere, in her novel *The House in Paris* (1935), in Bowen's view 'fate is not an eagle. It creeps like a rat.' Time wreaks changes upon the individual that are beyond the ability or desire of that individual. Here the innocent Portia, besotted with her own infatuation, is almost unaware of the threat she poses to her half-brother and his wife. She appears, a young orphan, in their smart London world and instantly, without malice, finds herself disrupting it. Being aware of her function might have given her pause. In her dangerous naivety she is the proverbial loose cannon on a rolling deck.

BOWEN, ELIZABETH

Jealousy is no more than feeling alone among smiling enemies
The House in Paris (1935)

Bowen's facility for the dissection of her characters' emotional states, and the effect they have upon the relationships in their lives, has made her a highly acclaimed writer. People are not happy in her books: the tensions, disturbed emotions and wretched responses all combine to create pictures of miserably apposite human pain. Such a feeling is no better illustrated than by her terse, aphoristic definition of love's most depressing bedfellow.

BOWIE, DAVID   (1947–) British rock star

I would rather retain the position of being a photo-stat machine with an image, because I think most songwriters are anyway.

Bowie's transmogrifications, from hippie fantasies through Seventies space-age glitter, to the decadent poses of the 'Thin White Duke', and from rock 'n' roll to the movies, have made him the most chameleon-like of today's rock megastars. Born plain

David Jones, he has parlayed undoubted talents into an international career that shows few signs of waning. Flirtations with drugs, bisexuality and similar tricks of the trade seem to have left him unscarred. His albums continue to offer new facets of his personality and a variety of films, from *The Man Who Fell to Earth* (1976) to *Merry Christmas Mr. Lawrence* (1983) simply embellish the Xerox persona, which continues to become as complex as the technology it claims to ape.

BOWRA, SIR MAURICE   (1898–1971) British academic

I'm a man
More dined against than dining.
attributed by Sir John Betjeman

Betjeman's tribute to his mentor and friend Maurice Bowra appears in his poetic memoir *Summoned By Bells* (1960) in which the line is one of Bowra's 'fusillade of phrases'. Bowra was one of the century's leading classical scholars who combined his learning, 'lightly worn' as Betjeman puts it, with elegant and sometimes acerbic wit and a reputation for Lucullan hospitality. While some, like Waugh who vilified him as the proselytising Anglo-Catholic don 'Samgrass' in *Brideshead Revisited* (1945), found him less than appealing, his favourites, who included Cyril Connolly among many others, rejoiced in his company.

BRABEN, EDDIE   British scriptwriter

What do you think of the show so far? Rubbish.
catchphrase

Braben was the long-time scriptwriter for comedians Eric Morecambe (1926–84) and Ernie Wise (1925–) who joined forces on the variety stage in 1943, but whose real fame came with their massively successful Morecambe & Wise television series. This running gag for Morecambe & Wise was the most celebrated of their catchphrases, usually delivered by Morecambe (born Bartholemew and renamed in honour of the town of his birth) and aimed at Wise (born Wiseman, but resisting the town of his birth, Leeds). Others included 'Get out of that!', 'Short, fat, hairy legs' and 'This boy's a fool', and Morecambe's smirking reference to Wise's alleged hairpiece 'You can't see the join!'.

BRADBURY, MALCOLM   (1932–) British academic and novelist

I like the English. They have the most rigid code of immorality in the world.
Eating People Is Wrong (1955)

Bradbury was educated at a variety of English universities before becoming an academic himself and being appointed in 1970 Professor of American Studies at the University of East Anglia. Here he has instituted on American lines one of England's few 'creative writing' courses. He has written a number of critical works, which focus on the experimental work of a variety of American writers, including Thomas Pynchon, William Gass and William Gaddis. His own novels are more conventional, dealing wittily with his own experiences on British and American campuses. The title of *Eating People Is Wrong*, the first of these, is taken from Michael Flanders' song The Reluctant Cannibal, in which the line occurs. Best known is *The History Man* (1975), featuring the campus politicking and sexual frolics of the machiavellian Howard Kirk.

BRADBURY, MALCOLM

Never despise fashion. It's what we have instead of a God.
in *Ins and Out: Debrett 1980–81*, by Neil Mackwood

In his criticism and his fiction, Bradbury is generally recognised to capitalise on fashion and its fluctuations. His analyses of the more progressive of American novelists, for all that these writers go substantially unread outside the campuses on which they are scheduled as set books, are certainly dealing with the forefront of Western fiction. The protagonists of his novels are usually guided by or in opposition to the prevailing socio-politico-academic chic. As Bradbury implies here, in a slight volume that was designed to celebrate the ephemera of smart taste, worship of the potentially successful new has taken over from that of the distinctly debased old.

BRADBURY, MALCOLM

We stay together, but we distrust one another. Ah yes...but isn't that a definition of marriage?
The History Man (1975)

Howard Kirk, protagonist of Bradbury's most successful book (subsequently filmed for TV), is a scheming, politicking figure, who divides his time between his manipulations of the faculty and his seductions of the prettier members of the student body. Kirk exploits everyone, including his hapless wife Barbara with whom the conversation above is held, and everything, notably the fashionable political or intellectual conceits of the moment, in which he has scant belief but which, as a dedicated opportunist, he apppreciates. Kirk is an unsympathetic figure but a succcessful one. As the novel ends he is seducing and plotting as ever; upstairs, as a party swirls around her, Barbara is deliberately slashing her wrists. Kirk is modelled, some claim, on Laurie Taylor, the broadcaster and sociologist. Taylor refutes the claim, the two dons have never even met, but has written a piece on the problems of being thus identified.

BRADLEE, BENJAMIN   (1921–) American journalist

News is the first rough draft of history.

Bradlee was born into one of Boston's aristocratic families and educated at Harvard before joining the *Washington Post* in 1948. Since 1968 he has been the paper's executive editor. Bradlee's fame extended beyond purely professional circles when in 1973 he authorised his reporters Carl Bernstein and Bob Woodward to pursue the investigations that led to the revelations of the Watergate Affair. His book *Conversations with Kennedy* (1975), an intimate memoir of the late President, was a best-seller. This definition has also been attributed to the late owner of the *Post* and thus Bradlee's boss, Philip Graham, whose widow Katherine is now proprietor.

BRADLEY, F.H.   (1846–1924) British philosopher

(Monte Carlo) is the temple of Providence where disciples still hourly mark its ways and note the system of its mysteries. Here is the one God whose worshippers prove their faith by their works, and in their destruction still trust him.
Aphorisms (1930)

Francis Herbert Bradley, brother of the Shakespearian scholar A.C. Bradley (1851–1935), was a leading English exponent of European philosophy, and particularly that of Hegel. His most important works were *Ethical Studies* (1876) and *Appearance and Reality* (1893), a discussion of contemporary metaphysical thought. His personal belief included the demonstration of friendship to others by taking them to see his dog's grave. T.S. Eliot claimed to have been profoundly influenced by Bradley's *Essay on Truth and Reality* (1914). These lines are taken from his book of aphorisms, posthumously published in 1930.

The craving to be understood may in the end be the merest egosim.

There are persons who, when they cease to shock us, cease to interest us.

117

BRADLEY, GENERAL OMAR (1893–1982) American soldier

We have grasped the mystery of the atom and rejected the Sermon on the Mount.

Bradley was one of America's leading generals in World War II, known for the affection he inspired in his troops as 'The Soldiers' General'. He led the invasion of Sicily and was then instrumental in planning Operation Overlord, the D-Day landings of June 1944. After D-Day Bradley was placed in charge of four American armies, some 1.25 million men and the largest single force ever commanded by a US field officer, which fought their way across Europe and into Berlin. Bradley's essential humanity and rejection of the gung-ho postures of many of his peers is reflected in this comment, made in 1948, on the developing arms race. He further amplified his attitude in April 1952 when he said 'The way to win an atomic war is to make certain it never starts'.

BRADLEY, GENERAL OMAR

The wrong war, at the wrong place, at the wrong time and with the wrong enemy.

Unlike General Bradley, America's General Douglas MacArthur exemplified the hard-charging, up-and-at-'em military philosophy that had dominated his campaigns against the Japanese as well as the military strategy, complete with tanks, bayonets and tear gas, that he proposed in dealing with the 15,000 World War I veterans who marched on Washington, demanding a bonus, in 1932. When, in 1950, MacArthur demanded that he be allowed to take US troops over the Yalu River in Korea and into Republican Chinese territory, Bradley testified to the Senate inquiry that was held to consider this wish and summed up his views as above. President Truman agreed with Bradley and instead of backing MacArthur, he dismissed him.

BRAINE, JOHN (1922–) British novelist

Room at the Top
book title, 1957

Braine was born and brought up in Bradford, Yorkshire, where for many years he worked as a librarian. His first novel *Room at the Top* (1957) celebrated the opportunistic rise of Joe Lampton, working class boy on the make, whose ruthless self-promotion cuts a swathe through the settled world of a provincial Northern town. *Room at the Top* was hailed by the Fifties' critics who saw Braine as another angry young man and Lampton as the epitome of the brash proles who were revolutionising staid old English society. The novel was filmed in 1958 with Lawrence Harvey as Joe and Simone Signoret (who won an Oscar) as the older woman from whom he gets sophistication and sex but who has to be rejected in favour of a self-aggrandising wedding to the boss' daughter. Braine's later work has rejected the 'angry young man' tag and his current anger is directed firmly at the radicals.

BRAMAH, ERNEST   (1868–1942) (Ernest Bramah Smith) British writer

The province of philosophy is not so much to prevent calamities befalling as to demonstrate that they are blessings when they have taken place.
Kai Lung Unrolls His Mat (1928)

So reclusive that many people doubted the evidence of his work and claimed that he did not exist, Bramah began working in the provincial press before moving to London as Jerome K. Jerome's secretary and working for his periodical *To-day*. He divided his talents between his fictional detective, the blind Max Carrados who first appeared in 1914, and his supposed Chinese sage Kai Lung who appeared in 1900, the appeal of whom was compounded by the 'Oriental' tinge of his author's surname. Kai Lung liked a good aphorism, of which this is a typical example.

BRAND, STEWART   (1938–) American environmentalist

You can't blame the baby for the afterbirth.

Brand is one of the environmentalists whose interests in the land and its preservation developed from the San Francisco hippie era of the late 1960s. In 1969 Brand published the first edition of the *Whole Earth Catalog*, a guide and mail order catalogue to every available facet of self-help; the L.L. Bean catalogue of the alternative society. As its title implies, the *Catalog* embraced the concept of 'holism', the relationship between psychological and physical well-being, here extended to an environmentalist context, without which no-one and nothing can achieve true fulfilment. Brand's comment, suitably elliptic, supposes that the earth itself cannot be blamed for the way in which it has been exploited.

BRANDO, MARLON   (1924–) American film star

Acting is the expression of a neurotic impulse. It's a bum's life. Quitting acting, that's a sign of maturity.
quoted in L. Halliwell *The Filmgoer's Companion* (1985)

Brando, the son of a mid-West salesman and a mother whose own theatrical ambitions never bore fruit, gained his initial fame as the finest exemplar of the Stanislavskian 'method' acting encouraged by New York's Actor's Studio, although one critic typified his studied mumble as 'a mouth full of wet toilet paper'. His first major role, in Tennessee Williams' *A Streetcar Named Desire* (1947), brought him critical acclaim and he repeated it for Hollywood in 1952, initiating his cinema career. Among his most popular films have been *On The Waterfront* (1954), *The Fugitive Kind* (1962), *The Godfather* (1972), *Last Tango in Paris* (1973) and *Apocalypse Now* (1979). A staunch supporter of racial minorities, in particular the American Indians, he has never chosen to fall into the Hollywood rut, commenting sourly on his peers 'An actor's a guy who, if you ain't talking about him, ain't listening', a line that was echoed by his fellow-actor, the English leading man Michael Wilding (1912–79) who remarked 'You can pick out the actors by the glazed look that comes into their eyes when the conversation wanders away from themselves.'

BRECHT, BERTOLT (1898–1956) German playwright and poet

Brecht was born in Augsburg where he trained briefly as a medical student (and worked as a medical orderly during World War 1) before turning to poetry and play-writing in Weimar Germany. After his play *Drums in the Night* won the Kleist prize in 1922 he was appointed to his first job in the theatre. Although his stance was unashamedly political, the plays he wrote in the Twenties lacked a solid ideological standpoint and can be categorised as anti-Establishement rather than pro-Party. They climaxed with *The Threepenny Opera* (1928), a revised version of Gay's *Beggar's Opera* which remains for most audiences Brecht's major achievement. During the 1930s Brecht joined the Communist party, writing rigorously didactic plays on Party-approved 'social realism' lines. Brecht was forced to flee Nazi Germany in 1933 and settled in America form 1941–48, where he wrote a number of his major works. He returned to East Germany in 1948 and lived there until his death, directing the Berliner Ensemble, the custom-made vehicle of his creativity, and elaborating the particular style of acting embodied in 'the epic theatre', and the 'alienation effect' which became known worldwide as 'Brechtian'.

BRECHT, BERTOLT

Fearful is the seductive power of goodness.
The Causcasian Chalk Circle (1948)

This play within a play takes the form of a parable recounted by a folk-singer who is called upon to adjudicate between the opposing farming schemes proposed by members of two collective farms in Soviet Georgia. The folk-singer tells and sings the story of the chalk circle, and the judgement made within it. Under the direction of judge Azdak, who propounds natural rather than statutory justice, supporting the poor against the powerful, the custody of a child is determined. The baby is placed in the circle and its actual, aristocratic mother and the nurse who has sheltered it are told to drag it from the circle. The mother grabs the child but Azdak awards it to the peasant since she, fearful of harming the baby, has chosen not to pull. Although Brecht offers this 'happy ending', the line quoted refers to the problems that befall the nurse when she decides, to rescue the abandoned child and points out that 'Those who have had no share in the good fortunes of the mighty/Often have a share in their misfortunes.'

BRECHT, BERTOLT

When the leaders speak of peace
The common folk know
That war is coming
When the leaders curse war
The mobilization order is already written out.

From a *German War Primer*

Brecht wrote this bitter poem as one of fifteen that made up his supposed War Primer. He was in exile at the time, forced to flee Germany by the man whom he only ever referred to as The House-Painter, as in another of this group of poems, 1939, *Little News Is Reported from the Reich*: 'The House Painter speaks of great times to come/The forests still grow./The fields still bear./The cities still stand./The people still breathe.' Another, a bitter comment on the futility of protest in the face of totalitarian determination, runs 'On the wall in chalk is written/"They want war."/He who wrote it/Has already fallen.'

BRECHT, BERTOLT

Every day, to earn my daily bread
I go to the market where lies are bought
Hopefully
I take up my place among the sellers.

Hollywood in *Collected Poems* 1913–1956 (1976)

Brecht left Germany in 1933 and took refuge in Denmark. He stayed here until it became clear that Hitler's territorial aims ensured that Europe offered little security to so unpopular an individual. He arrived in Hollywood in 1941, joining a distinguished band of German refugees. Brecht loathed California. He despised the 'cheap prettiness' and noted that brute nature, in the form of the Mohave Desert, was forever poised to take back the land it had lost to the city. Nonetheless he had to work and his miserable sojourn in Tinseltown, where he preferred to hide amongst the refugee community and spurned the synthetic revolution of the fashionable fellow-travellers, is summed up by this harsh, fatalistic self-denunciation.

BRECHT, BERTOLT

War is like love, it finds a way.
Mother Courage (1941)

Mother Courage, the intinerant trader Anna Fierling who sells supplies to both sides in the Thirty Years War, first appeared in a story by the 17th century picaresque writer Grimmelshausen. Brecht borrowed the name but the story, of a woman who lives by the war and must therefore pay the war its due, is his own. One by one Courage's three children, the daring Eiliff, the simple but honest Swiss Cheese and the retarded Katrin have to be sacrificed. Brecht's theory was that Courage deserved her misery: she has sacrificed her children to her lust for profits; modern audiences prefer a sympathetic view and find her fate moving.

BRECHT, BERTOLT

You can only help one of your luckless brothers
By trampling down a dozen others.
The Good Person of Setzuan (1938–41)

A typically cynical Brechtian sentiment, found in this parable play, set in contemporary China. Three gods appear on earth, searching for the perfect human being. The respectable people of Setzuan refuse them hospitality and only the prostitute Shen Te is welcoming. For this she is awarded a small gift of cash. Her fellow citizens hear of her fortune and clamour for a share. Shen Te disguises herself as Shui Ta, a tough young man, ostensibly her cousin. When Shen Te becomes pregnant she realises that only by using her Shui Ta personality can she hope to survive and she duly reincarnates him. As Brecht stresses in these lines, pure goodness cannot hope to defeat the realities of the world, although an epilogue asks, in that case should the world not be changed.

BRECHT, BERTOLT

Pity the country that needs heroes.
The Life of Galileo (1937–39)

Galileo Galilei (1564–1642) was a Venetian astronomer who startled the contemporary world by claiming, accurately but with little initial support, that in defiance of the teachings of the Church, the planets including the Earth revolve around the sun and not vice versa. Galileo is no plaster saint: he states fraudulently that he alone invented the telescope, he shifts allegiances for his own purposes, and when the Church denies his discovery, accepts eight years of self-suppression. When a new Pope, Urban VIII is elected, he hopes at last to speak out, but recants, when shown on 22 June 1633 the instruments of torture. His pupil, Andrea Sarti, denounces him, saying 'Pity the country that has no heroes', but Galileo replies, 'No. Pity the country that needs heroes.' Years later, Galileo gives his pupil his clandestinely rewritten Discorsi, and the truth can be disseminated at last. Andrea claims that he is after all a hero, but Galileo still regrets his cowardice and the setting of an example which will, he fears, render all scientists subservient to the State.

BRECHT, BERTOLT

Eats first, then morals
The Threepenny Opera (1928)

Die Dreigroschenoper, a free adaptation of John Gay's *Beggar's Opera* (1728), with ballads derived from Francois Villon and Rudyard Kipling, remains Brecht's one major popular success. Brecht aimed to create a theatre for the masses but then and now he has attracted mainly intellectuals and even this, his most accessible work, attracts a solid bourgeois following. Brecht's play takes Gay's cast of villains and mountebanks, policemen and whores, featuring the notorious highwayman Captain MacHeath, and sets them in a bizarre 19th century Soho. Interwoven with the picaresque plot Brecht offers his own harsh views on society, of which this line is the most celebrated. Its rejection of ideological promises in favour of material actions rings ironically against his own austere Marxism of the next decade. Other notable lines from *The Threepenny Opera*, all expounding the playwright's disillusioned standpoint include:

What is robbing a bank compared to founding one?

**How does a man live? By resolutely
Ill-treating, beating, cheating, eating his fellow men.**

> A man can only live by absolutely
> Forgetting he is a human being.

BRECHT, BERTOLT

He who laughs has not yet heard the bad news.
To Posterity, in *Svendborg Poems*

Brecht wrote this grim poem 'An die Nachgeborenen' (literally To those born later) that starts 'Truly I live in dark times!' during his exile in Denmark in 1938. It is a poem filled with desperation, with cynicism and despair. Above all the privations, the betrayals, the endless exile 'changing countries more often than our shoes', stands the central defeat: that those involved in this era must accept that for all their hopes, for all their designs for a better world, such goals would now never be achieved and that their lives were being lived out in failure, mere searchers for survival, forced by a cruel era to become cruel themselves.

BREMER, ARTHUR (1950–) American citizen

Today I am one trillionth part of history.
after attempting to assassinate Governor George Wallace, 1972

In 1968 George Wallace, the outspoken segregationist Governor of Georgia, remarked after a stormy campaign meeting 'I suppose one day someone might throw something other than rotten eggs at me'. Four years and a Presidential campaign later, on May 15 1972 Arthur Herman Bremer, an unemployed ex-busboy from Milwaukee, emerged from a group of people in Laurel, Maryland, shaking hands with the Governor to call 'Hey George, over here!' When Wallace turned, Bremer, who had been following him for two months, sprayed him with bullets. Wallace was hit four times and three bystanders were wounded. Wallace survived, but he has been confined to a wheelchair ever since. Bremer was seized and later offered policemen this assessment of his historical role. The mystery of how an unemployed youth managed to finance eight weeks of cross-country travel remains. Revelations during the Watergate Affair linked Bremer with the FBI, but the connection has not been checked out.

BRENAN, GERALD (1894–1987) British writer

The things we are best acquainted with are often the things we lack. This is because we have spent so much time thinking of them.
Thoughts in a Dry Season (1978)

Edward Fitzgerald Brenan was destined for the Army but chose instead to embark on what he intended to be a lifetime of travel. After serving with distinction in World War I he settled in Spain and lived there until he died, but for a brief repatriation during World War II. Aside from two undistinguished novels Brenan's success derived from non fiction: *The Spanish Labyrinth* (1943), a history of the causes of the Spanish Civil War, and *The Literature of the Spanish People* (1951). His autobiographical works, *South From Granada, A Life of One's Own* and *Personal Record*, all confirmed his reputation for craftsmanship and erudition. *Thoughts In A Dry Season* was his last work, a collection of aphorisms on life, death, art, love, nature and similar topics.

BRENAN, GERALD

Intellectuals are people who believe that ideas are of more importance than values. That is to say, their own ideas and other people's values.
Thoughts in a Dry Season (1978)

BRENAN, GERALD

Everyone is a bore to someone. That is unimportant. The thing to avoid is being a bore to someone else.
Thoughts in a Dry Season (1978)

BRENAN, GERALD

Imagination means letting the birds in one's head out of their cages and watching them fly up in the air.
Thoughts in a Dry Season (1978)

BRENAN, GERALD

To a writer or painter creation is the repayment of a debt. He suffers from a perpetual bad conscience until he has done this.
Thoughts in a Dry Season (1978)

BRENAN, GERALD

Works of art and literature are not an entertainment or a diversion to amuse our leisure, but the one serious and enduring achievement of mankind – the notches on the bank of an irrigation channel which record the height to which the water once rose.
Thoughts in a Dry Season (1978)

Brenan, Gerald

The only test of a work of literature is that it shall please other ages than its own.
Thoughts in a Dry Season (1978)

Brenan, Gerald

The new ideas of one age become the ideologies of the next, by which time they will in all probability be out of date and inapplicable.
Thoughts in a Dry Season (1978)

Brenan, Gerald

Religions are kept alive by heresies, which are really sudden explosions of faith. Dead religions do not produce them.
Thoughts in a Dry Season (1978)

Brenan, Gerald

Poets and painters are outside the class system, or rather they constitute a special class of their own like the circus people and the gypsies. For the sake of their moral health they should be relatively poor and should mix mainly with their own kind. When they are short of money it is better for them to practise shop-lifting than to give lectures.
Thoughts in a Dry Season (1978)

Breslin, Jimmy (1930–) American novelist and journalist

Football is a game designed to keep coal miners off the streets.
column in *New York Herald Tribune*

Given Breslin's noisy support for the American working man this somewhat elitist comment seems surprising. Breslin's columns have run in New York newspapers since 1963 when the former sportswriter was hired to write regularly in the now defunct *New York Herald Tribune*. Reading them it would appear that his preferred sport is horse-racing; certainly the majority of his perennial 'characters', the low-life denizens of Queens, appear to support themselves at the track. Other than betting the points spread, football seems to offer little appeal.

Bresslaw, Bernard (1933–) British comedian

I only arsked (asked).
The Army Game TV series 1957–62

Bresslaw is one of that sterling band of second-rank British actors who seem to have appeared in every Carry On... film, not to mention a wide selection of similarly homegrown comedies, heavy on the slap, tickle, smut and puns. He initially made his name as Private 'Popeye' Popplewell, a large and gormless individual, enlisted in the highly successful television series *The Army Game*. Whenever anyone attacked Popeye he responded with his doleful catchphrase, which soon found a million imitators up and down the country. He lacked, as Leslie Halliwell has put it, big screen quality, but manages to keep working.

BRETON, ANDRÉ (1896–1966) French poet, essayist and critic

Breton, like other young French intellectuals such as Louis Aragon and Paul Eluard, felt that World War I had undermined humanity's belief in the charms of progress and its perfectibility, and looked for ways of changing the world. In 1924 Breton issued his first *Manifeste du surréalisme*. The first authentic surrealistic work was *Les Champs magnétiques* (1924) by Breton and Soupault. Willy-nilly the surrealists replaced the Dadaists, taking on their scandalous reputation with gusto, and issuing in 1924 a scurrilous attack – the Corpse – on the recently dead and widely revered writer Anatole France. Breton was acknowledged as the leader, so much that he was nicknamed the 'Surrealist Pope', but after World War II drove him into American exile, his return to Paris proved a farce. Sartre and the existentialists were intellectually dominant and Breton's excesses seemed embarassing and pretentious.

BRETON, ANDRE

Beauty will be convulsive, or it will not be.
Surrealism and Painting (1972)

This line is taken from Breton's Surrealist manifesto, in which he set down Seven Commandments, as follows:

First Commandment: Everything should be capable of being freed from its shell (from its distance, its comparative size, its physical and chemical properties). Never believe in the interior of a cave, always in the surface of an egg.

Second Commandment: Wander, the wings of augury will come and attach themselves to your shoulders.

Third Commandment: Place your desire beyond reach and you will recreate it endlessly.

Fourth Commandment (always promulgated, always valid): Beauty will be convulsive, or it will not be.

Fifth Commandment: Deprive yourself. Revelation is the daughter of refusal.

Sixth Commandment: Whatever happens, never doubt. Love is always before you. Love (Seventh, and, to this day, last commandment).

BRETON, ANDRÉ

The simplest surrealist act would be to go out into the street, revolver in hand, and fire at random into the crowd.
quoted in *Esquire* magazine, 1969

Breton's definition of surrealism was 'pure psychic automatism by which it is intended to express, either verbally or in writing, the prime function of thought. Thought dictated in the absence of all control exerted by reason and outside all aesthetic or moral preoccupations'. On this basis, his 'simple...act' would indeed be murder at random but while the surrealists cheerfully embraced the role of enfants terribles, few wished to take their theories quite so far, although a number, finding the strain of living a suitably surrealist life, were driven to suicide.

BRITISH BROADCASTING CORPORATION

And the next Tonight is tomorrow night. Good night.

The BBC's *Tonight* programme was created in 1957 as a direct counterblast to commercial television's ITN, the efficiency and slickness of which had drastically reduced the ratings of the BBC's staid, restrained news bulletin. Lacking ITN's budget, and tied to the Reithian tenets of state broadcasting, the BBC made a conscious decision that if the news itself could not change radically, then it would make a major commitment to current affairs programmes, still an infant art. Two were launched: the heavyweight *Panorama* and the lighter *Tonight*. *Tonight* ran until 1965 and its presenter, Cliff Michelmore, signed off with this phrase every night.

BRODER, DAVID   (1929–) American journalist

Anybody that wants the presidency so much that he'll spend two years organising and campaigning for it is not to be trusted with the office.
in *Washington Post* 1973

Broder, a respected political reporter on the *Washington Post*, made his comment following the 1972 US presidential election to

Tim Crouse, who was writing his book *The Boys on the Bus*, a study of the press corps who followed that election. The accuracy of Broder's statement, which can be applied to any political office in any country, was borne out as the Watergate Affair, investigated by two junior reporters who were certainly not 'on the bus', revealed just how untrustworthy the current incumbent was.

BROGAN, COLM   (1902–) British writer

There is only one word for aid that is genuinely without strings, and that word is blackmail.

Brogan is the brother of the historian Sir Denis Brogan. After starting his career in his native Glasgow, first in teaching and then in journalism, he moved to London where he continued working as a political journalist. He wrote a number of books, the best known of which take a critical and satirical view of the Welfare State, then in its heady infancy: *Who Are the People* (1943) and *Our New Masters* (1947). He also wrote *The Educational Revolution* (1955) and a number of other works.

BROGAN, DENIS   (1900–74) British historian

The combination of a profound hatred of war and militarism with an innocent delight in playing soldiers is one of those apparent contradictions of American life that one has to accept.

Sir Denis Brogan was born in Scotland and educated both in England and America. He began his career as an academic historian as a lecturer at the University of London before being appointed professor of Political Science at Cambridge in 1939. He wrote a number of books on French, American and English history, including *The Development of Modern France* (1940), *America in the Modern World*, and *The English People*.

BROGAN, DENIS

We all invent ourselves as we go along, and a great man's myths about himself tend to stick better than most.

Traditional history deals in great moments and great men. Kings, generals, prime ministers and similar luminaries. What has become known as the 'Annales' school of history – based on the French journal which pioneered it, and which deals in micro-rather than macro-history – has still not taken over in the classroom, whatever its effect on the university. Society still tends to look to epic figures, heroes and villains, and Brogan suggests that those who rise furthest are those most capable of creating an enduring public image, accurate or otherwise.

BRONOWSKI, JACOB   (1908–1974) British scientist

Among the multitude of animals which scamper, fly, burrow and swim around us, man is the only one who is not locked into his environment. His imagination, his reason, his emotional subtlety and toughness, make it possible for him not to accept the environment but to change it. And that series of inventions, by which man from age to age has remade his environment, is a different kind of evolution not biological but cultural evolution. I call that brilliant sequence of cultural peaks 'The Ascent of Man.'
The Ascent of Man (1975)

Dr. Bronowski, one of the most genuinely popular British scientists of the century was also, along with Lord Clark in his treatment of *Civilisation*, a pioneer of what has now become familiar television material: the lengthy series dealing with a major facet of human life, both written and presented by the same intellectual or authoritative figure. *The Ascent of Man* made Bronowski even more of a household word, and brought the story of human evolution into every amenable sitting room. The chat to camera, the globe-trotting, the complex-made-simple style that has become a regular feature of such programmes was still new and Bronowski's series remains one of the best of the genre. His scripts were often quotable, and a few of the better lines include:

A genius is a man who has two great ideas.

The hand is the cutting edge of the mind.

Revolutions are not made by fate but by men.

That is the essence of science: ask an impertinent question and you are on the way to a pertinent answer.

We are all afraid – for our confidence, for the future, for the world. That is the nature of the human imagination. Yet every man, every civilisation, has gone forward because of its engagement with what it has set itself to do.

BRONOWSKI, JACOB

The wish to hurt, the momentary intoxication with pain, is the loophole through which the pervert climbs into the minds of ordinary men.
The Face of Violence (1954)

130

BROOKE, RUPERT (1887–1915) British poet

> If I should die, think only this of me:
> That there's some corner of a foreign field
> That is forever England. There shall be
> In that rich earth a richer dust concealed.

The Soldier

Immensely charming, strikingly beautiful, the young Rupert Brooke dominated literary life in Cambridge, where he was a scholar of King's College. He began publishing poetry in 1909 and his work was considered outstanding. Brooke was also notably neurotic and in 1913, after winning a fellowship at King's, he suffered a breakdown and attempted to repair his emotions by extensive travel in America, Canada and the Pacific. The poems this trip produced are seen as among his best. In 1914 he joined the RNVR. *The Soldier*, published in 1915, made him the public's chosen war poet. His death, en route to the Dardanelles, for all that it lacked any vestige of glory, merely compounded his reputation and the somewhat mawkish verse, far removed from the harsher views of Sassoon or Owen, remains a patriotic staple.

BROOKE, RUPERT

> And when they get to feeling old,
> They up and shoot themselves, I'm told.

The Old Vicarage, Grantchester (1912)

Brooke visited Germany in 1909, the same year in which he settled in Grantchester, a village near Cambridge. This poem, his home thoughts from abroad, is an amusing and exaggerated discussion of the village. All its inhabitants, he explains, live rectitudinous lives and when they reach an age at which they feel they can offer no further to the community, practice self-euthanasia.

BROOKE, RUPERT

> Stands the church clock at ten to three
> And is there honey still for tea?

The Old Vicarage, Grantchester (1912)

Like Brooke's *The Soldier*, with its lasting, if romantically erroneous image of war, these final lines of his musings on Grantchester, written in Germany but nostalgic for home, have come to evoke a whole world of bucolic peace. The clichéd

nirvana of English rural life rears up, overladen with that extra
fantasy that persists of the 'long, golden summers' of the dead
Edwardian world. The honey came from Brooke's landlord at the
Old Vicarage, where he rented his home and the clock, apparently, was a tease at its timekeeper.

BROOKS, LOUISE   (1906–) American film star

**I never gave anything away without wishing I had kept it, nor
kept it without wishing I had given it away.**
in Ken Tynan, *Show People* 1980

Critic Ken Tynan's essay on Louise Brooks, more a work of
adulation than a dispassionate study, virtually rediscovered this
once brilliant star of the silent screen who offered these words to
Tynan as her possible epitaph. Brooks began her film career in
America but her amazing beauty and acting talent was never fully
exploited until she appeared in two films by the German director
G.W. Pabst (1885–1967), *Pandora's Box* (1928) and *Diary of a
Lost Girl* (1929). Brooks' guiltless amorality conveyed an unrivalled erotic charge and her stardom was guaranteed. Yet her
career never progressed. Her greatest roles were drawn dangerously from life and she was too intelligent and too self-willed to
bend to Hollywood's needs. From 1930, she appeared only in
third-rate work, if at all. She quit Hollywood in 1940 and remains,
reclusive but staunchly free from bitterness, living alone in
Rochester, NY.

BROOKS, LOUISE

**Most beautiful but dumb girls think they are smart and get away
with it, because other people, on the whole, aren't much smarter.**
in *Show People* by Kenneth Tynan 1980

Brooks who was undeniably beautiful but, as her witty perceptions of her Hollywood contemporaries, published in 1982 have
proved, far from dumb, was talking both of such girls in general,
but also of her own role as Lulu, a blissfully amoral creature
whose career progresses, with the inexorability of a Greek
tragedy, to her final, fatal meeting with Jack the Ripper. She
talked to Tynan of the 'beautiful but dumb' label that was slapped
on her when she arrived in New York in 1922, pointing out that
the sufferers are not the average pretty starlet but 'a very small
group of beautiful women who know they're dumb, and this

makes them defenseless and vulnerable. They become the Big Joke'. Such self-knowledge, Brooks believes, killed the exemplar of the type, Marilyn Monroe.

BROOKS, MEL   (1926–) American film director, writer and actor

Bad taste is simply saying the truth before it should be said.

Brooks was born Melvin Kaminsky, the son of Russian immigrants. His first job was a 'tummler' (resident offstage entertainer) at a hotel in the 'Borscht Belt' of the Catskills, preferred holiday resort for New York's Jews. Here he met Sid Caesar, then a saxophonist. After the war Brooks was hired as a writer by Caesar, now a starring comic. From 1950–54 Brooks was part of the team who made Caesar's 'Your Show of Shows' the most popular comedy on US television; he worked with Caesar until 1959. His hit record 'The Two Thousand Year Old Man' (1961) made Brooks a success as an entertainer, but his career foundered until his film *The Producers*, a cult hit, was released in 1968. Brooks followed this with *Blazing Saddles* (1974) and *Young Frankenstein* (1974), the enormous success of which guaranteed him Hollywood acceptance. Since then he has continued to make films, many successful, but nothing has rivalled his annus mirabilis of 1974.

BROOKS, MEL

If Presidents don't do it to their wives, they do it to the country.
as *The Two Thousand Year Old Man*

Brooks invented his character 'The Two Thousand Year Old Man' in 1953, as one of the comic dialogues he and his friend the actor, writer and director Carl Reiner (1922–) performed at parties. Reiner would throw an introduction at Brooks who would then wing it. Thus when one night Reiner announced 'Ladies and gentlemen we are fortunate to have with us tonight a man who was present at the crucifixion of Jesus Christ', Brooks responded with this new figure. Twice as old as Methusaleh and still sprightly, the 'Two Thousand Year Old Man' had not just wit, it seemed that he had beaten mortality too. In 1960, with his career as a TV scriptwriter at an all-time low, Brooks, with Reiner, brought out the 'bit' for a Hollywood party. The resulting LP, inspired by its enormous success, appeared in 1961 and sold a million-plus copies. Successful sequels followed in 1962, 1963 and 1973.

BROOKS, MEL

Why do we have to die? As a kid you get nice little white shoes with white laces and a velvet suit with short pants and a nice collar and you go to college, you meet a nice girl and get married, work a few years and then you have to die! What is that shit? They never wrote that in the contract!
Playboy (1975)

For all his humour Brooks is quite sincerely obsessed with death. In the tradition of Jewish humour Brooks, like Woody Allen, is locked in a constant struggle with the malign forces that govern the universe. Everything relates to survival: the whole world of communication, especially comedy, is merely a magnified version of the playground weakling who survives only by making the bullies laugh. For Brooks, the fear of death is a driving force and if no-one, except perhaps his creation the 'Two Thousand Year Old Man', can hope for immortality, one must leave a memorial. As he said in the same interview 'You can win a conditional victory against death – it all boils down to scratching your name in the bark of a tree. I Was Here.

BROPHY, BRIGID (1929–) British writer

The thriller is the cardinal twentieth century form. All it, like the twentieth century, wants to know is: Who's Guilty?
In Transit (1969)

Brophy is the daughter of the author John Brophy (1899–1965); her first novel, *Hackenfeller's Ape*, appeared in 1953. Others include *The Snow Ball* (1962) and *Flesh* (1962) and she has written biographies of Aubrey Beardsley (1968) and Ronald Firbank (1973). *In Transit*, from which this analysis of one of contemporary writing's dominant forms is taken, is set in an airport transit lounge. The narrator, of indeterminate sex, uses the boredom to look at his/her identity through memories, fantasies and the author's use of experimental typography.

BROUN, HEYWOOD (1888–1939) American journalist

History is largely concerned with arranging good entrances for people and later exits not always quite so good.
Pieces of Hate (1922)

Broun abandoned his wealthy background for journalism. He worked his way up through the sports desk to writing dramatic

criticism and making himself into one of its most respected practitioners. His contentious column 'It Seems To Me' spoke out boldly for his beliefs, notably that in organised labour, his support for which infuriated the various proprietors for whom he worked. Of the Algonquin wits, he was the most overtly political, protesting at the trial of Sacco and Vanzetti in 1926 'We have a right to beat against tight minds with our fists and shout a word into the ears of old men. We want to know, we will know "Why?"'
Broun died in 1939, on the day his first column appeared in a new paper, the *New York Post*. His best pieces had been collected in *Pieces of Hate*, from which these quotations have been taken:

A liberal is a man who leaves a room when the fight begins.

Free speech is about as good a cause as the world has ever known. But it... gets shoved aside in favour of things which seem at a given moment more vital... everybody favours free speech in the slack moments when no axes are being ground.

Just as every conviction begins as a whim, so does every emancipator serve his apprenticeship as a crank. A fanatic is a great leader who is just entering the room.

The most prolific period of pessimism comes at 21, or therabouts, when the first attempt is made to translate dreams into reality.

BROWN, DREW 'BUNDINI'   (1929–) American boxing trainer

Float like a butterfly,
Sting like a bee,
Your hands can't hit
What your eyes can't see!

catchphrase

Brown is an ex-US sailor (joined up at age thirteen, toured the world 27 times, discharged after attacking an officer with a meat cleaver), ex-shoe-shine boy, and all-purpose drifter, who met Cassius Clay, soon to be Mohammad Ali, in 1963. When Brown wandered into former champion Sugar Ray Robinson's Golden Gloves Barbershop in Harlem, NYC and started mixing with the boxing fraternity, his path led inexorably to the sensation of the era: Cassius Clay. Once they met, the two men developed a special relationship. Brown was listed as an 'assistant trainer' but he was much more than that. Ali's loyalest booster, he invented the verse that became the champion's theme.

Brown, Helen Gurley American journalist

Self-help...that is my whole credo. You cannot sit around like a cupcake asking other people to eat you up and discover your great sweetness and charm. You've got to make yourself more cupcakeable all the time, so that you're a better cupcake to be gobbled up.
Esquire 1970

Helen Gurley Brown launched herself into the Western consciousness with the publication in 1965 of her manifesto 'Sex and the Single Girl'. This was hardly a feminist tract, – making oneself 'cupcakeable' is not exactly the stuff of women's liberation – but for many women the book reflected an aspect of female liberation that, while ideologically impure, in its own way helped get the girls out of the kitchen. Helen Gurley Brown's gospel was in the tradition of American self-help gurus: make the most of yourself, assert your best qualities, don't be backward in rushing forward; and that included sex. Like *Cosmopolitan*, the magazine that she created in the 1970s, and its 'Cosmo girl', Brown's self-help stayed strictly within traditional boundaries. Girls were not yet, unless specifically asked, to get on top.

Brown, John Mason (1900–69) American essayist and critic

Some television programmes are so much chewing gum for the eyes.

Brown was the dramatic critic on a number of leading American newspapers and as such highly influential on the theatre of the 1920s and 1930s; he wrote several books on the theatre. In this interview of July 1955, he coined a notable and oft-repeated phrase, stemming from his distaste for a medium that, for a great many people, had displaced the one of his choice and his career.

Brown, Lew American lyricist

Climb upon my knee, Sonny Boy
Though you're only three, Sonny Boy

Sonny Boy (1929)

Show business songwriter Brown wrote this mawkish ballad of paternal affection for the master of such schmaltzy arts, Al Jolson (1886-1950). It featured in his film *Sonny Boy* (1929). Although this film failed to make the impact of its predecessors *The Jazz Singer* (1927), the world's first, if only partially talking film, and *The Singing Fool* (1928), the title reappeared in 1975 to front Jolson's most recent biography.

BROWN, NORMAN O.   (1913–) American cultural critic
There is no death by natural causes.
Life Against Death (1959)

Academic Brown has been variously a professor of classics, comparative literature and of the humanities. After a work on Greek myths, Brown made his name with *Life Against Death*: the Psychoanalytical Meaning of History, a searching re-examination of traditional Freudian theories in which he applied the erotic and destructive forces categorised as the 'id' to the study of history and culture. Claiming that liberal progressivism, whether post-Freudian or Protestant, could only perpetuate negation and sublimation, he stated that only psychoanalysis offered real hope.

BROWN, NORMAN O.

The dynamics of capitalism is postponement of enjoyment to the constantly postponed future.
Love's Body (1966)

Brown's work was taken up during the late 1960s by many of those who proposed the establishment of an 'alternative society'. His association of psychoanalysis with liberation, although not expressed in specifically political terms, used such concepts as this, the traditional assessment of the bourgeois Judaeo-Christian work ethic, to underline his views. They naturally appealed to those who preferred not to postpone their pleasures.

BROWNMILLER, SUSAN   (1935–) American feminist

Rape is ... nothing more or less than a conscious process of intimidation by which all men keep all women in a state of fear.
Against Our Will

Susan Brownmiller's tract on rape was one of the major documents of the feminist movement. The attitude underlining it is that all men wish, subconsciously or otherwise, to rape all women and that the so-called 'sex war', so beloved of comedians, film-makers and the like, is just that: a battle.

BRUCE, LENNY   (1923–66) American comedian

I'll die young, but it's like kissing God.
in A. Goldman *Ladies and Gentlemen: Lenny Bruce* (1975)

Drugs and Lenny Bruce were inseparable. The humour that made him famous sprang from a mind usually twisted out of shape by some cocktail of excess and the same stimulants that gave life to his acerbic mind eventually robbed him of his life. The drugs

137

of choice were usually opiate derivatives: heroin, morphine and the proprietary dilaudid. For Bruce, getting high was a daily, necessary ritual, both an increasingly vital prompt for his performances and an unequivocal statement of the hipster's life that he exemplified. That the drugs became the act and the life was brutally foreshortened was merely the downside of the wager that lies at the heart of addiction.

BRUCE, LENNY

Your kid is better off watching a stag movie than 'King of Kings'... I just don't want my kid to kill Christ when he comes back. Tell me about a stag movie where someone got killed in the end, or slapped in the mouth or heard any Communist propaganda.
How to Talk Dirty And Influence People 1965

Bruce's comment, taken from his alleged autobiography, a factually dubious but amusing essay in image-enhancing disinformation, epitomises the exploitation of paradoxes on which a great deal of his humour was based. Ironically prefiguring those moralists who vow 'It's not the sex, it's the violence' that they deplore, but who would be unlikely to enlist Bruce as an ally, he is pointing out the phenomenon whereby many people would prefer to be entertained by some act of sickening, blood-drenched violence, rather than watch what in one of its most frequent euphemisms is after all termed 'making love'. His use of the crucifixion as the basis of his analogy is, of course, one of the reasons why Bruce continued to infuriate the less scrupulously pure in heart.

BRUCE, LENNY

The what should be never did exist, but people keep trying to live up to it. There is no 'what should be', there is only what is.
How to Talk Dirty And Influence People 1965

Bruce was essentially pragmatic. Every element of his humour was aimed to emphasise the philosophy expounded here: human beings are fallible, weak, prey to all the deadly sins and more. What Bruce was battling against was the belief in ideological purity, whether political, religious or otherwise, that promised a perfection that not only wooed the gullible but simultaneously claimed the right of attacking anyone who chose not to be so suborned. As he put it elsewhere, decrying the attempts of those who hoped to smooth over the unfortunate discrepancies between image and reality: 'You can't get snot off a suede jacket'.

BRUCE, LENNY

A knowledge of syphilis is not an instruction to contract it.
from the LP 'Lenny Bruce at Carnegie Hall'

Bruce's line is surely an indictment of the whole concept of censorship, the belief by a vocal, prurient minority that what frightens them must be denied to everyone, whether or not those whom they claim to protect have chosen such intellectual prophylaxis. To appreciate that something is bad does not mean that one is automatically espousing it; for Bruce the greater sin was foolish self-protection: to pretend that nothing was bad, simply by denying it first to yourself, and then in your fear to others.

BRUCE, LENNY

The whole motivation for any performer: "Look at me, Ma!"
in A. Goldman, *Ladies and gentlemen: Lenny Bruce* (1975)

Bruce was talking from the heart in his analysis of show business motivation. It was an opinion that didn't merely spring from Freudian dogma: his actual mother, Sadie Kitchenberg, was a veteran vaudeville performer, dancing, singing and joking as Sally Marr. Her own career blended the stage-struck fantasies of a young girl who won, in 1919, a beauty competition judged by Rudolph Valentino, and severe stage fright. In the traditional manner, Sally pushed her boy's stage career and Bruce, in this comment, acknowledges just who, in reality or otherwise, was always out there beyond the lights.

BRUCE, LENNY

**Man, we're all the same cats, we're all the same schmuck –
Johnson, me, you, every putz has got that one chick, he's yelling
like a real dum-dum: 'Please touch it once. Touch it once, touch
it once.'**
in *The Essential Lenny Bruce*, ed. J. Cohen (1967)

Male sexual dependency was a running theme of Bruce's work. The obsession of every man, however supposedly blasé or otherwise powerful, with the satisfaction of his lusts. Even the US President, Lyndon Johnson at the time, was a sucker for some girl at some time. For all its humour Bruce's 'bit', as ever, captures the awful self-abasement of sexual desperation.

Bruce, Lenny

Now a Jew, in the dictionary, is one who is descended from the ancient tribes of Judea... but you and I know what a Jew is – one who killed Our Lord... . A lot of people say to me 'Why did you kill Christ?' I dunno, it was one of those parties, got out of hand, you know...'. We killed him because he didn't want to become a doctor, that's why we killed him.

quoted in *The Essential Lenny Bruce*, ed. J. Cohen (1967)

Lenny Bruce would never simply stand on stage and say something was bad. What he created was a mini-drama, what he called a 'bit', a free-form fantasy into which he wove his own opinions interlarded with popular cultural and media references, all blended into an overall humorous effect. Here, dealing with anti-semitism, he offers a little lexicography, some theology, the classic 'my son the doctor' cliché, a tip of the hat to the hipsters with 'one of those parties', all combining to deflate the traditional race libel.

Bruce, Lenny

Satire is tragedy plus time.

quoted in *The Essential Lenny Bruce* ed. J. Cohen (1967)

Bruce came out of what he called 'the toilets', the third-rate nightclubs and burlesque shows where the comic merely gave pause for the appearance of the next tawdry stripper. By the mid-1950s he was attracting an increasingly sophisticated audience who revelled in his particular brand of savage humour. What he purveyed was indeed satire, in the brutal tradition of Swift, tearing apart sensitive issues, to reveal their inner paradoxes and ironies. Among other points, he noted that yesterday's disaster is today's sick joke. After Bruce, whose influence they all acknowledged, the comedians of Britain's 'satire boom' were merely waving slapsticks after his rapier.

Bruce, Lenny

The liberals can understand everything but people who don't understand them.

quoted in *The Essential Lenny Bruce* ed. J. Cohen (1967)

For the extremist, the middle-of-the-road liberal is never a sympathetic figure. However well-intentioned, perhaps indeed because of that vaunted philanthropy, the liberal is reduced merely to a do-gooder, a spineless figure who likes to talk but not to act, whose opinions of the world would be modified by some participation in it and whose open mind is closed to the fact that some benighted individuals might just not be liberals too.

BRUCE, LENNY

If you can take the hot lead enema, then you cast the first stone.
The Essential Lenny Bruce, ed. J. Cohen (1967)

If a single strand runs through Lenny Bruce's humour, touching on all the diverse areas that he chose to probe and anatomise, it is the concept that in the end we are guilty. No-one is so pure that they can stand up, unblemished, and tell the rest of the world how to live. Bruce's philosophy is a rewrite of the Biblical mote and beam colloquy given a new and inevitably scatalogical twist.

BRYANT, ANITA   (1940) American right-winger

If God had meant us to have homosexuals, he would have created Adam and Bruce.

Mrs Bryant has become known over the last decade as one of right-wing America's foremost campaigners for what she calls traditional values and her opponents vilify as reaction and repression. Her campaign against feminism touched a nerve in the American psyche and helped defeat the Equal Rights Amendment, an amendment to the US Constitution designed to recognise the new position of women in America. In an AIDS-conscious nation she has touched another nerve in her unceasing attacks on the gay world, disseminating a range of dubious but popular canards, claiming among other things that 'As a mother, I know that homosexuals cannot biologically reproduce children; therefore, they must recruit our children.'

BUBER, MARTIN   (1878–1965) Israeli theologian

The real struggle is not between East and West, or capitalism and communism, but between education and propaganda.
in *Encounter with Martin Buber* by A. Hodes

Buber was in 1900 a leader of those Zionists who wished not merely a Jewish political renaissance but for a cultural one as well. He edited two major German Jewish papers and in 1926 he started *Die Kreatur*, with gentile collaborators, and thus initiated the major influence he had, greater possibly than on his co-religionists, on Christian culture and theology. He fled Germany in 1938 and was apppointed professor of social philosophy at the Hebrew University in Jerusalem. Buber's magnum opus was *Ich und Du* (1923, I and Thou). In this he drew on the Hasidic tradition to assert that God is encountered in one's soul and in every vestige of daily life. His work has influenced European Catholicism and such secular concerns as psychotherapy and educational theory.

BUCHAN, LORD TWEEDSMUIR, JOHN (1875–1940) British writer and government official

An atheist is a man who has no invisible means of support.

John Buchan combined a career as a writer of successful adventure stories with one in public and diplomatic life, culminating in his appointment as Governor-General of Canada from 1935-40. Buchan's heroes seem unlikely today, although he modelled his greatest figure, 'Sandy Arbuthnot' on a mix of Lawrence of Arabia and Auberon Herbert, but his treatment of natural phenomena, if not that of human relations, has ensured that his work has outlived that of many contemporary best-sellers. His most popular works include *The Thirty-Nine Steps* (1915), *Greenmantle* (1916) and *Mr. Standfast* (1918), all featuring Richard Hannay, like his creator a veteran of South Africa and an increasingly important public figure.

BUCKLEY JR., WILLIAM F. (1925–) American editor and diplomat

Idealism is fine, but as it approaches reality the cost becomes prohibitive.

Buckley has often been proposed as the American right wing's answer to Gore Vidal and in his syndicated column and his books he displays the same informed urbanity, albeit devoted to opposite ends. His first publication *God and Man at Yale: the Superstitions of Academic Freedom* (1951) expounded his conservative faith; *McCarthy and His Enemies* (1954) took it further. In 1955 Buckley founded the *National Review*, a large-circulation right-wing weekly of which he remains editor-in-chief. His column 'A Conservative Voice' appeared in 1962; a syndicated version 'On the Right' is taken by more than 200 papers. In Buckley's television programme, 'Firing Line', he has pitted himself against a number of distinguished opponents.

BUGS BUNNY

What's up, Doc?

Warner Brothers created the world's most popular cartoon rabbit in *Porky's Hare Hunt* in 1937. Bugs' career lasted until 1963 when he 'retired'. True to the traditions of such showbiz farewells, he returned in the 1970s to host a number of compilations of his old hits. Bugs' voice, like that of his eternal pursuer and butt Elmer Fudd, was the responsibility of Mel Blanc (1908–), who has also spoken for Sylvester and Tweetie Pie, and who was responsible for this, the rabbit's long-time catchphrase. Bugs won an Oscar in 1958 for *Knighty Knight Bugs* and in 1972 Peter Bogdanovich directed Ryan O'Neal and Barbra Streisand in the movie farce *What's Up Doc?*.

BUKHARIN, NIKOLAI A. (1888–1938) Russian politician

We might have a two-party system, but one of the two parties would be in office and the other in prison.

Bukharin was one of the earliest Bolsheviks, a supporter of Lenin, whose theories, although diverging from Lenin on several issues, were used by him in his own theoretical works. After 1917 Bukharin abandoned many of what Lenin called his 'semi-anarchist' positions and joined the Party's central committee, although he remained nominal leader of the Party's 'left' wing. Under Stalin Bukharin abandoned his old radicalism and began leading the 'right' and supporting the New Economic Plan. Although he was chairman of the Committee that produced the Stalinist Constitution of 1936, his growing opposition to his master proved a mistake. He was arrested in 1937 and shot, like so many 'old Bolsheviks' in the purges of 1938. He is allegedly the model for Arthur Koestler's Rubashov, the hero of *Darkness at Noon* (1940) and has yet to be officially rehabilitated.

BUKOWKI, CHARLES (1920–) American poet and essayist

The difference between a Democracy and a Dictatorship is that in a Democracy you vote first and take orders later; in a Dictarorship you don't have to waste your time voting.
Erections, Ejaculations, Exhibitions and Tales of Ordinary Madness (1972)

Bukowski was born in Germany in 1920 and emigrated to Los Anglese with his parents. A wretched childhood was followed by a variety of poorly-paid jobs, then by settling down for fourteen years in the US post office, from which he resigned in 1970. He began writing poetry in the 1940s and contributed prose to a variety of the underground paper of the late 1960s. Bukowski works very much the wrong side of the tracks, hymning America's and particularly Los Angeles' low life, writing form experience about a world of three-week drunks and one-night shack jobs, the poor, the dispossessed, the crazy and the outcast and in his case, the undeniably talented. He has written some forty books of prose and poetry and a film, *Tales of Ordinary Madness*, starring Ben Gazzarra as Bukowski, was released in 1983.

BUKOWSKI, CHARLES

That's what friendship means: sharing the prejudice of experience.
Notes of a Dirty Old Man (1969)

BUKOWSKI, CHARLES

What's the difference between a guy in the bighouse and the average guy you pass on the street? The guy in the bighouse is a Loser who has tried.
Notes of a Dirty Old Man (1969)

BUKOWSKI, CHARLES

Nothing was ever promised you. You signed no contract.
Notes of a Dirty Old Man (1969)

BUKOWSKI, CHARLES

Sexual intercourse is kicking death in the ass while singing.
Notes of a Dirty Old Man (1969)

BULMER-THOMAS, MP, IVOR British politician

If ever he went to school without any boots it was because he was too big for them.
commenting on Harold Wilson, 1948

Confronting in the 1964 general election a Tory party which derived its image from the grouse moor and the old school tie, Labour leader Harold Wilson set out to emphasise his own proletarian origins. In 1964 his tactic was a winner, but in 1948 it had proved less successful. Wilson, who had been a brilliant undergraduate at Oxford and who at the age of 32 was already President of the Board of Trade, claimed in a speech 'The school I went to in the north was a school where more than half the children in my class never had any boots or shoes to their feet' and let it be inferred that he was among the hapless half. The press duly reported the youthful Minister's deprivations, but the fantasy was ruined when his former teacher wrote indignantly to assure readers that Mr. Wilson appeared in full uniform. The Tories were suitably amused and Bulmer-Thomas, not Harold Macmillan to whom the line is often attributed, made his remark at their 1949 Conference.

BUNUEL, LUIS (1900–1983) Spanish film-maker

To provoke, or sustain, a reverie in a bar, you have to drink English gin, especially in the form of the dry martini.... Connoisseurs who like their martinis very dry suggest simply allowing a ray of sunlight to shine through a bottle of Noilly Prat before it hits the gin. At a certain period in America it was said that the making of a dry martini should resemble the Immaculate Conception, for, as Saint Thomas Aquinas once noted, the generative power of the Holy Ghost pierced the Virgin's hymen 'like a ray of sunlight through a window – leaving it unbroken'.
My Last Breath (1983)

This elegy to the perfect martini is taken from Bunuel's autobiography, published shortly before his death. Here he looked at the pleasures of his long life, including alcohol (including the 'Bunueloni': a Negroni with Carpano substituted for the Campari), the bars in which he consumed it, and the tobacco he smoked to accompany it. The remainder of the book, written with his long-time collaborator Jean-Claude Carrière, deals variously with his upbringing, his role in the Parisian surrealist movement of the 1920s and the Spanish Civil War of the 1930s, his visits to and film-making in Hollywood and Mexico. He also discusses his ideas on religion, sex, politics and death as well as his greatest films.

BUNUEL, LUIS

In any society, the artist has a responsibility. His effectiveness is certainly limited and a painter or writer cannot change the world. But they can keep an essential margin of non-conformity alive. Thanks to them the powerful can never affirm that everyone agrees with their acts. That small difference is very important.
quoted by Anthony Hill in *Contemporary Artists* (1977)

Bunuel, a Spaniard, emigrated to Paris where with Breton and others he founded the surrealist movement. He made his first international impact when he collaborated with his fellow Spaniard, the artist Salvador Dali, on *Un Chien Andalou* (1928), following this with *L'Age d'Or* (1930), a pair of scandalously shocking films. A brief visit to America proved a mistake for all concerned – intellectually staid Hollywood proved impervious to surrealist humour. The rightist victory in the Spanish Civil War made Spain no place for a man whose films savaged the nation's every value from Catholicism onwards. He returned to America, and moved in 1946 to Mexico where he made his powerful studies of society, ranging from *Los Olvidados* (1950, The Young and the Damned) to *Nazarin* (1959). On his return to Europe he began a new style, sophisticated parodies of bourgeois life, including *Belle de Jour* (1967) and *The Discreet Charm of the Bourgeoisie* (1972); his last film *That Obscure Object of Desire* appeared in 1977.

BURGESS, ANTHONY   (1917–) British author and critic

The possession of a book becomes a substitute for reading it.
in the *New York Times Book Review*, 1966

Burgess is possibly England's leading literary polymath and undoubtedly one of the world's most prolific producers of a wide range of writing, from novels to lexicography to criticism, TV and film scripts, journalism, biography and musical compositions. During an early career as a colonial administrator in Borneo and Malaya he wrote his first novels, a trilogy of Malayan life. A further trilogy, featuring the eccentricities of the poet Enderby, began with *Inside Mr. Enderby* (1963), written under the pseudonym Joseph Kell. Burgess gained international stature, and a substantial advance, for *Earthly Powers* (1980), but his popular reputation may well rest on *A Clockwork Orange* (1962), an awful harbinger of a decaying, violent Britain, filled with rampant psychotic youth, which in 1969 was made into a successful film starring Malcolm McDowell.

BURGESS, ANTHONY

Art is a vision of heaven gratuitously given. Being quasi-divine, it is beyond human concerns.
1985 (1978)

In 1978 Burgess published *1985*, a book which combined a critique of George Orwell's *1984* with a grimly comic novella, which drew on his own *Clockwork Orange* (1962), embellished with knowledge gained from the way Britain had changed in the intervening 16 years. The first portion of the book assumes the reality of Orwell's vision, including a catechistic recital of the politico-social status quo, a veteran of 1948 interviewed, a review of Ingsoc, the national language and so on. In the section 'Cacotopia', named for the description he gives Orwell's new society, Burgess considers other cacotopian books and assesses the role of art in contemporary society. Art, he says, has no moral imperatives, the aesthetic should not be confused with the ethic. Given art's independence of ethics, it is thus rendered suspect to the 'narrower moralist'.

BURGESS, ANTHONY

There is usually something wrong with writers the young like.
in *Playboy*, 1974

While not particularly known as a curmudgeon or a reactionary, Burgess is less than enamoured of the twentieth century, once damning a collection of modern quotations with faint praise, saying that while the quotes were indeed not exceptional, they were an all too accurate representation of the era that had spawned them. Like popular music, the celebration of each new generation's discoveries of teenage angst and expectation, the novels that are popular among the young tend to reflect what appeals to that constituency and are inevitably limited by its perceptions. Only maturity, Burgess is saying, will lead one to better books, with more mature perspectives.

BURGESS, GELETT (1866–1951) American humourist

I don't know much about Art, but I know what I like.

Are You a Bromide (1906)

Burgess was one of America's most popular humourists at the turn of the century. He wrote many books but remains best known for his anathematisation of bromides, ie. banal and overly popular remarks, in *Are You a Bromide*, a down-market version of Flaubert's *Dictionary of Received Ideas* (1857). The phrase had probably originated sometime in the 1890s, certainly it had become widely enough spread for Burgess to strike a sympathetic chord with its inclusion in his book.

BURNETT, W.R. (1899–1982) American writer

Mother of God...is this the end of Rico?
Little Caesar (1929)

Burnett's novel *Little Caesar* ensured him a place among the best American thriller-writers of his era, although his fame is minimal compared to that of Hammett or Chandler. His book is a loose interpretation of the rise of a Capone-like Italian gangster, Cesare Bandello, known as Rico. Burnett knew the milieu well; as a hotel desk clerk in Chicago he had been among the first people to view the still reeking St. Valentine's Day Massacre in 1929. In his book, which takes an epigraph from Machiavelli, he set immemorial power struggles against the realism of the streets and speakeasies. Hollywood grabbed the hit, and its release in 1930 made its lead, Edward G. Robinson (1893–1973), into a major star. As a bullet-riddled Rico dies on the book's final page, he offers this cry to God. In the film, presumably for reasons of taste, it was amended to 'Mother of mercy...'

BURNETT, W.R.

Crime is...a left-handed form of human endeavour.
The Asphalt Jungle (1950)

The Asphalt Jungle was one of Burnett's best books, a story of what seems to be endemically American corruption, prefaced by its minatory epigraph, taken from the philosopher William James: 'Man, biologically considered... is the most formidable of all beasts of prey, and, indeed, the only one that preys systematically on its own species.' Filmed in 1950 by John Huston with Sterling Hayden as Dix, the thug with a yen for the country, Sam Jaffe as the criminal mastermind from Mitteleuropa, and a tiny role for young Marilyn Monroe, it concerns a gang's bungled efforts at pulling off the 'perfect crime'. Like all of Burnett's work, which deals in crime but transcends the simplicities of the 'hard-boiled' label, individuals are finely observed, none more so than Emmerich the lawyer, once rich but now forced into crime by a young girl's demands. This is his definition of crime, offered as he watches the scheme fall horribly to pieces.

GEORGE BURNS AND GRACIE ALLEN (1902/06–1964)

Burns: Say good night, Gracie. Allen: Goodnight, Gracie.
The Burns and Allen Show, 1950s

Although George Burns remains the unassailable Grand Old man of the American comic establishment, a veteran trouper whose career has spanned vaudeville, film, radio, television and back to film again, the peak of his popularity came during the thirty central years of his career when, with his real-life wife Gracie Allen, he worked as a double. The Burns and Allen Show was among America's most popular television comedies in the 1950s, developed from its radio origins, and the pair repeated their roles, he as the long-suffering husband, she as the stereotypically scatter-brained wife, in various undistinguished films. This catchphrase-cum-sign off, echoed by Dick Martin and Dan Rowan as they ended the Sixties' Laugh-In shows, epitomised their relationship.

BURRA, EDWARD (1905–1976) British artist

What a fuss art is sometimes, dearie.
in the *Observer*, 1971

Burra was a British artist whose output, if not perhaps serious enough for certain highbrow critical assessment, provided many enjoyable paintings and drawings. Dealing largely with the low-life world that he characterised as 'tarts and sharks' and taking a deliberately flippant tone towards his own role as what he termed a 'fartist', Burra worked consistently, despite the increasing toll of ill health that often confined him to his bed. His work as a set designer for ballet and opera was especially well regarded. His letters, entitled *Well Dearie...!* appeared in 1985, charting his rackety, and often pain-wracked but always productive life and times.

BURROUGHS, WILLIAM S. (1914–) American writer

A paranoid is a man who knows a little of what's going on.
in *Friends* magazine, 1970

With Allen Ginsberg, Burroughs remains the most productive, the most famous and probably the most talented of the writers, poets and artists who founded what was known as the Beat Movement. With a private income derived from the Burroughs business machine family, the young Burroughs was able to indulge himself, which indulgence led to many years of heroin addiction. In 1953, writing as William Lee, he discussed his addiction in *Junkie,* and his homosexuality in *Queer* (not published until 1986). *The Naked Lunch* (1959), written to exploit the 'cut-up' technique pioneered by his friend Brion Gysin, brought him international notoriety, not least for the book's prosecution for obscenity in America. Burroughs has written consistently since then. With their wild, paranoid fantasies, extensive displays of arcane knowledge, celebration of the crazier sides of sexuality and self-destruction, the Burroughs canon remains quite unique.

BURROUGHS, WILLIAM S.

Nobody owns life, but anyone who can pick up a frying pan owns death.

Burroughs' line, used as an epigraph for the Liverpool poet Adrian Henri's poem 'Adrian Henri's Last Will and Testament' (1967) is a typically terse reflection on the unpleasant vagaries of daily life, its ironies and paradoxes. Henri's verses were a supposed response to his imminently expected death, caused not by age (he was 23) but by 'being the first human being to die of a hangover/dying of over-emotion after seeing 20 schoolgirls waiting at a zebra crossing '. The potential of so many quite unnatural causes fits correctly with the Burroughs premise.

BURROUGHS, WILLIAM S.

The police and so forth only exist insofar as they can demonstrate their authority. They say they're here to preserve order, but in fact they'd go absolutely mad if all the criminals of the world went on strike for a month. They'd be on their knees begging for a crime. That's the only existence they have.
in *The Guardian*, 1969

BUTLER, DAVID (1924–) British psephologist

The function of the expert is not to be more right than other people, but to be wrong for more sophisticated reasons.
in the *Observer* 1969

The false modesty with which many acclaimed experts in a given field decry their own infallibility has yet to extend to their refusing to offer views culled from their chosen expertise. Dr. Butler has been Britain's leading electoral analyst for many years, with or without the ubiquitous Swingometer, computer, on the spot exit poll or panel of self-justifying politicos to assist his deliberations. He does not call them wrong.

BUTLER, R.A. (1902–82) British politician

The Art of the Possible.

In the tradition of attributing otherwise uncertifiable quotations to the most deserving candidate, this phrase, which he used in 1971 as the title of his memoirs, was given to the Tory politician R.A. Butler, quite possibly as a belated consolation for his other award, the nickname of 'the best Prime Minister we never had'. A variety of sources offer an equal variety of previous coiners, the most likely of which, if only for having no predecessor, is the use by Bismarck, the German Chancellor, in conversation (and thus recorded) by Meyer von Waldeck on 11 August 1867.

BUTLER, R.A.

The best Prime Minister we have.

The popular tag, invariably attached to the brisker encapsulations of Butler's role in British politics, of his being 'the best Prime Minister we never had' stemmed both from his being passed over when ailing Harold Macmillan preferred the ineffectual Alec

Douglas-Home as his successor in 1964, and from a brief conversation Butler had in 1955. Butler might have had hopes of succeeding Churchill as the Tory leader but these had foundered when Churchill appointed Anthony Eden. Eden's government lasted only a year, and rumblings of discontent surfaced quickly. Faced with a Press Association reporter who caught him en route to an international meeting, Butler was asked 'Mr. Butler, would you say that this is the best Prime Minister we have?' He replied 'Yes' and, as he put it in his memoirs 'I do not think it did Anthony any good. it did not do me any good either.'

BUTLER, SAMUEL (1835–1902) British writer
Butler, the son of a clergyman and grandson of a bishop, resisted taking holy orders himself when assailed by Doubts. Instead he emigrated in 1859 to New Zealand where he became a successful sheep farmer. He returned home in 1864 and began studying painting. He published his utopian novel *Erewhon* (the reverse of Nowhere) in 1872, a brilliant if brief success, the content of which had in part been inspired by his letters from New Zealand. *The Fair Haven* (1873), his ironic debunking of the Resurrection, was well received by more progressive intellectuals such as Darwin, although Butler's own scientific work often challenged evolutionary theory. For the rest of his life he produced books on a variety of topics: travel, art, Homer, his own grandfather and much more, including a comic pastoral oratorio. His final work, *The Way of All Flesh*, dealt with the descent of family traits, and the adverse effects this has, through four generations.

BUTLER, SAMUEL

Some men love truth so much that they seem to be in continual fear lest she should catch a cold on overexposure.
Notebooks (1912)

BUTLER, SAMUEL

God was satisfied with his own work, and that is fatal.
Notebooks (1912)

BUTLER, SAMUEL

Life is one long process of getting tired.
Notebooks (1912)

BUTLIN, BILLY (1899–1980) British holiday camp pioneer

Holiday with pay! Holiday with play! A week's holiday for a week's wage.

Under a parliamentary act of 1938 every British worker was henceforth legally entitled to one week's paid holiday per annum. Billy, later Sir Billy, Butlin had providentially opened the first of new kind of working class holiday centre during the previous year. Butlin's Holiday Camp at Skegness, for all that the rows of bleak chalets and fenced-in grounds might remind the less charitable of its more sinister cousins in Poland or Germany, appeared to be purpose built for mass aspirations. Flocking to Butlin's slogan, they abandoned such traditional festivals as Wakes Week for the delights of communal feeding, early-morning wake-up calls and the ersatz glamour of the knobbly knees contest. It made a change from hiking and it was still good clean fun.

BUTOR, MICHEL (1926–) French writer

Our daily life is a bad serial by which we let ourselves be bewitched.
Repertoire II

Butor, with Alain Robbe-Grillet, is one of the foremost exponents of the French experimental novel, the nouveau roman. Such writers deliberately exclude the traditional literary devices of plot, narrative, motivation and so on from their writing, substituting the elaborate minutiae of psychological and physical detail. Form equals content for such authors and their basic tenet is that it is the duty of each new generation of artists to create a form that improves upon and displaces that created by their predecessors. In the case of the nouveaux romanciers, their aim is to overthrow the prevailing theory of commitment, espoused by Sartre, which existed in their youth. *Repertoire II* is one of the four volumes of criticism he has published.

BUTZ, EARL (1909–) American politician

Coloureds only want three things: first, a tight pussy; second, loose shoes; and third, a warm place to shit.
quoted in 1977

Butz was Secretary of Agriculture under President Gerald Ford. Like all members of the government, Butz did his bit during the electoral campaign of 1976, in which Ford, who had been pinch-hitting for two years after his predecessor Nixon resigned one step ahead of impeachment proceedings, was pitted against the populist Jimmy Carter. Things looked to be going Ford's way after Carter talked injudiciously to Playboy magazine of 'adultery of the heart', but Butz balanced the scales of incompetence when he offered this comment on Republican racial hiring policies. Sophisticated Washington was less perturbed by the content of Butz's gaffe, than by his ignorance. Asked by a Ford supporter, the ageing pop star Pat Boone, why the Grand Old Party hired so few blacks, Butz made his supposed 'joke' in the hearing of ex-Watergate whistle-blower John Dean, then working for the ostensibly liberal *Rolling Stone* magazine.

BYGRAVES, MAX (1922–) British entertainer

Good idea, ... son.
in *Educating Archie*, BBC radio comedy show

Bygraves, born Walter William Bygraves in London's East End slums, remains one of Britain's leading purveyors of showbiz schmaltz. Taking his stage name from his boyhood idol Max Miller, Bygraves was among those who benefited from the BBC's show *They're Out!*, which was devoted to aspirant ex-servicemen. His real break came in 1950 when he was given a job on Britain's radio ventriloquy show: *Peter Brough and Archie Andrews*. Archie, the wooden one, was a youthful Bertie Wooster clone, a blah youngster who required a series of 'tutors', of whom Bygraves was the first. The fact that radio somewhat masked Brough's ventriloquistic skills (which indeed were less than perfect) did not seem to worry the listening faithful. With his writer Eric Sykes, Bygraves developed a variety of catchphrases, of which the above was most popular. Others included 'I've arrived, and to prove it, I'm here!', 'Big 'Ead' and 'Dollar Lolly'.

C

CAAN, JAMES (1938–) American film actor

Sometimes it seems like that is the choice – either kick ass or kiss ass.
interview in *Playboy*, 1976

Caan is one of Hollywood's persistent leading actors who has never quite made the leap to mega-stardom. After his first part, a small role in *Irma La Douce* (1963), he has worked consistently in a variety of films but other than *The Godfather* (1972), in which he played Marlon Brando's macho eldest son Sonny, nothing has ever really taken off. It's unlikely that Caan coined this slang summation of life's basic choices, but on the evidence of most dictionaries, the phrase is of comparatively recent usage.

CABELL, JAMES BRANCH (1878–1959) American writer

The optimist proclaims we live in the best of all possible worlds; and the pessimist fears this is true.
The Silver Stallion (1926)

Cabell, 'a lingering survivor of the *ancien regime*, a scarlet dragonfly imbedded in opaque amber' was the sole writer whom H.L. Mencken in his condemnation of the American South as 'The Sahara of the Bozart' spared from his disdain. Cabell worked as a journalist and genealogist, and from 1904 began publishing a variety of novels, poetry and essays to increasing acclaim. The high point of his success came with *Jurgen* (1919), set in the imaginary nation of Poictesme. But Cabell's style was somewhat too rarified for mass appeal and even his devotees moved elsewhere. By 1930 his fame was no more.

CALL ME MADAM

The Hostess with the Mostes' On the Ball
screenplay by Howard Lindsay and Russel Crouse (1953)

This movie musical took as its theme the adventures of a wealthy Washington hostess who is appointed by the President (Harry Truman) as ambassador to a conveniently picturesque, if impoverished, European country. Ethel Merman starred and belted out Berlin's songs in her usual manner. Among the standout numbers was 'You're Just In Love' which Merman sings with Donald O'Connor. The film is also notable for George Sanders in one of his rare singing roles.

CALLAGHAN, JAMES (1912–) British prime minister

A lie can be half way round the world before the truth has got its boots on.
speech on November 1, 1976

Callaghan succeeded Harold Wilson as Britain's Labour Prime Minister after Wilson decided, seemingly on the spur of the moment, to resign in 1976. Callaghan was voicing the popular complaint, common to all Prime Ministers and their acolytes, that the media is biased, unfair and determined to do them harm. In this case Callaghan had been misquoted on the state of the British economy but before he was able to issue the necessary correction, the media had already seized upon, published and broadcast the erroneous story.

CALWELL, ARTHUR   (1896–?) Australian politician

Two Wongs don't make a white.
quoted in *The Bulletin*, 1972

Calwell was an old-style Australian with his eye firmly on the interests of those who arrived from Britain and other white countries and with little time for Greeks and Yugoslavs, let alone blacks, browns and yellows. Ostensibly Labour, he was staunchly pro-union, but somewhat short on his party's more socially enlightened theories. This pithy putdown was his reaction to rumours of a possible influx of Asians. As a further personal contribution to the 'White Australia' philosophy, Calwell remarked of Africans and West Indian immigrants: 'No red-blood Australian wants to see a chocolate coloured Australia.'

CAMERON, JAMES (1911–1985) British journalist

The press can only be a mirror – albeit a distorting mirror, according to its politics or the smallness of its purpose – but it rarely lies because it dare not.
the *Listener*, 1979

Cameron was one of England's most celebrated and prolific journalists whose expansion of his talents beyond the world of daily reporting ensured that his reputation transcended that of most of his peers. His career embraced all Fleet Street, where he worked mainly as a foreign correspondent, in particular at the weekly *Picture Post*, for which he wrote some of his most impressive pieces on the Korean war and from which, frustrated by proprietorial censorship, he was forced to resign. Cameron adapted ideally to television, which showed off his idiosyncratic, inconoclastic style to its best advantage.

CAMPBELL, A.B.   British traveller

When I was in Patagonia...
BBC Home Service Brains Trust passim

The Brains Trust, invented for the BBC by Charles Hill, the 'radio doctor' who later became the Corporation's chairman, was a regular programme, designed for the middle- to highbrow, in which a panel of experts debated listeners' questions on the day's great and not so great issues. Among the panellists was Commander A.B. Campbell, an explorer of note. This phrase, after which he titled his autobiography and which must be termed, even in a programme not noted for levity, a catchphrase, stemmed from a *Brains Trust* prototype: *Any Questions*. Donald McCullough, the chairman, asked his team, which was the same as that used on the *Brains Trust*, whether they agreed with 'the practice of sending missionaries to foreign lands'. Professor Joad and Julian Huxley made their comments and Campbell began his with the immortal phrase. He was unable to continue for the gales of laughter although he always claimed himself unable to see the remotest humour in his line.

CAMPBELL, MR. British magistrate

People are entitled to shout when they are drunk. That is not being disorderly.
quoted in *Geoffrey Madan's Notebooks* (1981)

Mr. Campbell, an otherwise un-feted magistrate, was reported as having made this comment when sitting on the bench and judging, with clemency, a case of drunk and disorderliness. Madan, a businessman-aesthete who delighted in such material, duly clipped the story and preserved this choice instance of wisdom in the lower courts.

CAMPBELL, MRS. PATRICK (1865-1940) British actress

It doesn't matter what you do in the bedroom as long as you don't do it in the street and frighten the horses.
quoted in *The Duchess of Jermyn Street* by Daphne Fielding (1964)

Beatrice Stella Tanner took her husband's name for the purposes of her professional career but that was one of her few compromises with propriety. 'Mrs Pat' epitomised the tempestuous actress, brimming with her 'art', a character several times larger than life, with what W.B. Yeats called 'an ego like a raging tooth'. She starred in Pinero's massively successful *The Second Mrs. Tanqueray* (1893) in which, for the first time in British theatre, an actress achieved a realistic portrait of that melodramatic, romantic staple 'the woman fallen into sin'. She was equally triumphant in Shaw, Ibsen and Maeterlinck. Her most celebrated relationship was with Shaw, who wrote the role of Eliza Doolittle in *Pygmalion* (1914) for her, and although it was allegedly quite platonic, they exchanged many luridly passionate letters. Mrs. Pat was beautiful and ostentatiously bohemian, declaring 'How glorious to have £700 one week and nothing the next', and defining the idea of monogamy with the remark: 'Marriage is the result of the longing for the deep, deep bliss of the double-bed after the hurly-burly of the chaise-longue'. In the end Mrs. Pat, who had burnt so brightly, faded sadly away. After World War I her appearances became increasingly rare, and her espousal of socialism did not appeal to her public. She died, a relic of Edwardiana, in poverty.

CAMPBELL-BANNERMAN, HENRY (1836–1908) British prime minister

This is not the end of me.

quoted in *Famous Last Words* by Jonathon Green

Sir Henry Campbell-Bannerman, 'a jolly, lazy sort of man with a good dose of sense' according to Sir Alfred Pease, but 'mildly nefarious, wildly barbarious' if one believes Kipling, was disastrously misinformed in this statement, since it represents his last words. It was also somewhat lacking in prophecy since his brief Liberal ministry has not been counted among the major eras of British political life.

CAMUS, ALBERT (1913–1960) French writer

Camus was born in Algeria, then a French colony, the son of an itinerant agricultural labourer, killed in the War, and an illiterate charwoman. He worked in the theatre until the publication in 1942 of *L'Etranger (The Stranger)* and in 1943 of *Le Mythe de Sisyphe (The Myth of Sisyphus)* brought him instant and enormous fame. Both books appealed to the current mood: the first, with its absurd premise of a man's being executed merely for his failure to weep at his mother's funeral, reflected the general wretchedness of occupied France; the second, celebrating pagan sensuality, offered the hope of some future, post-war regeneration. During the war he was a member of the underground resistance and after the Liberation of 1944 wrote for the left-wing newspaper *Combat*. In 1951 Camus published *L'Homme révolté (The Rebel)*, a study of revolt in which he expressed his own disillusionment with both Christian and communist theology. This latter heresy caused a break with the ideologically committed Sartre, who rejected Camus' loathing of totalitarianism. In 1957 Camus was awarded the Nobel prize for Literature. By 1960 he was fully embroiled in France's war in Algeria. Unlike most French intellectuals, firmly supportive of Arab nationalism, Camus, as a settler himself, refused to ignore what he felt were the legitimate fears of Algeria's European population, a move that further alienated him from the left. Camus died in a car crash in 1960, with personal and national problems still unresolved.

Camus, Albert

There is only one truly philosophical problem - and that is suicide.
Caligula

Camus, Albert

I should like to love my country and still love justice.

Camus, Albert

A man's work is nothing but the long journey to recover, through the detours of art, the two or three simple and great images which first gained access to his heart.
in the *New York Times*, 1960

Camus, Albert

Mother died today. Or, maybe, yesterday: I can't be sure.
L'Etranger (1946)

L'Etranger (The Stranger) is the best known of Camus' novels. This is its first line. It is the most most accessible exposition of his own brand of existentialism, which both preceded that of Sartre and found itself opposed to that of the celebrated philsopher. In it Meursault, 'the outsider', stands outside both society and himself. He rejects the standards of the bourgeois life into which he was born, refusing to show due piety at his mother's funeral, and murdering an Arab, during a fit of heatstroke, on the beach. Even at his trial for the killing he is unable to overcome this division between his cool responses and what is about to happen. At the end of the book he is executed, and goes to the guillotine with as little apparent emotion as he showed at the funeral, noting only the 'howls of execration' that greet his demise.

Camus, Albert

You cannot create experience, you must undergo it.
Notebooks (1962)

CAMUS, ALBERT

Politics and the fate of mankind are shaped by men without ideals and without greatness. Men who have greatness within them don't go in for politics.
Notebooks (1962)

CAMUS, ALBERT

The revolution as myth is the definitive revolution.
Notebooks (1962)

CAMUS, ALBERT

Those who write clearly have readers; those who write obscurely have commentators.
Notebooks (1962)

CAMUS, ALBERT

A single sentence will suffice for modern man: he fornicated and read the papers.
The Fall (1957)

CAMUS, ALBERT

To be happy, we must not be too concerned with others.
The Fall (1957)

CAMUS, ALBERT

Too many people have decided to go without generosity in order to practise charity.
The Fall (1957)

CAMUS, ALBERT

The slave begins by demanding justice and ends by wanting to wear a crown. He must dominate in his turn.
The Rebel (1951)

CAMUS, ALBERT

The future is the only kind of property that the masters willingly concede to slaves.
The Rebel (1951)

CAMUS, ALBERT

Every revolutionary ends up either by becoming an oppressor or a heretic.
The Rebel (1951)

CAMUS, ALBERT

What is a rebel? A man who says no.
The Rebel (1953)

CAMUS, ALBERT

Freedom 'that terrible word inscribed on the chariot of the storm', is the motivating principle of all revolutions. Without it justice seems inconceivable to the rebel's mind. There comes a time, however, when justice demands the suspension of freedom. Then terror, on a grand or small scale, makes its appearance to consummate the revolution.
The Rebel (1953)

CANETTI, ELIAS (1905–) Bulgarian/British novelist and essayist

Canetti's background qualifies him as a classically cosmopolitan European intellectual, writing in German but drawing his influences variously from the Sephardic Jewish world from which he is descended, from the remains of the Austro-Hungarian Empire into which he was born, and from many years spent first in Switzerland and then in England, where he lives now. His reputation is based on two works, one fiction, one non-fiction. *Die Blendung* (1935, *Auto da Fé*) was inspired by the burning of the Palace of Justice in Vienna in 1927. Set in the book-lined, claustrophobic rooms of Peter Kien, a secluded Viennese intellectual, struggling to isolate himself from the horrors of the external world, it has been seen as an allegory of the plight of real European intellectuals, trapped amidst the political demands of the inter-war era. His study of crowd behaviour *Masse und Macht* (1962, *Crowds and Power*) asserts that humanity's driving force is a lust for personal survival, which brooks no opposition. He backs up his theory by comparing political developments to the anthropological and psychoanalytic evidence. He was awarded the Nobel prize for Literature in 1981.

CANETTI, ELIAS

Within the crowd there is equality. This is absolute and indisputable and never questioned by the crowd itself.... All demands for justice and all theories of equality ultimately derive their energy from the actual experience of equality familiar to anyone who has been part of a crowd.
Crowds and Power (1960)

CANETTI, ELIAS

How happy one would be in a world in which one did not exist.
quoted in 1951

CANETTI, ELIAS

People love as self-recognition what they hate as an accusation.
The Human Province (1978)

CANETTI, ELIAS

The name 'moralist' sounds like a perversion, one wouldn't be surprised at finding it suddenly in Krafft-Ebing.
The Human Province (1978)

CANETTI, ELIAS

Success listens only to applause. To all else it is deaf.
The Human Province (1978)

CANNON, GEOFFREY British journalist

Dieting makes you fat.
book title, 1983

Geoffrey Cannon's book appeared in 1983, during the height of the British, originally American, obsession with fitness, health and, as ever, dieting. Cannon's theory was that all the much-touted diets in fact had little long-term effect and were placebos rather than panaceas. Instead, as a disciple of jogging and marathons, he advocated healthy foods and extensive exercise. The book was highly successful but diet sheets, on the other hand, remain consistently popular.

CANNON, JIMMY (1890–1974) American sports writer

We work in the toy department.
quoted in *No Cheering in the Pressbox* ed. Jerome Holtzman 1973

Jimmy Cannon was for many years one of America's leading sportswriters, of the hard-drinking, terse-writing model that seemed to emerge straight from Hollywood's cliché department, working for the *New York Post* and writing pieces in a snappy, rebarbative prose style that manages to combine Damon Runyon and H.L. Mencken. In the end Cannon appreciated that for all the ballyhoo, sports, and thus those who write about them, are not all that important. They make money, even more today, but like toys they remain childish things, and those who write about them, at best, are purveyors of childish delights.

CAPLES, JOHN American advertising copywriter

They laughed when I sat down at the piano – but when I started to play!

Caples was a copywriter at the US agency Ruthrauff and Ryan. When asked to compose an ad for a piano tutor put out by the US School of Music he responded with this immortal boast, and inspired a catchphrase that remains in use. On the same model, commissioned this time by a language school, Caples rewrote his line as 'They Grinned When The Waiter Spoke To Me In French – But Their Laughter Changed To Amazement At My Reply', but the rewrite never caught on.

CAPOTE, TRUMAN (1924–1984) American writer

That's not writing, that's typing.
reviewing Jack Kerouac's *On The Road* (1957)

Capote and Kerouac were contemporaries, and both were young men during the late 1940s, but that was where the similarity stopped. Capote was a Southerner, born in New Orleans, whose childhood had been spent amidst the claustrophobic femininity of a houseful of aunts. He won some acclaim in 1948 with his novel *Other Voices, Other Rooms*, but his major success came in 1958, the light-hearted but tough-minded New York novella *Breakfast at Tiffany's* (filmed in 1961 in a much more romantic light with Audrey Hepburn as the amoral Holly Golightly). Kerouac had meanwhile been front-running in the Beat movement, a crazy netherworld far removed from Capote's more precious pleasures. Kerouac's first book had appeared in 1957 and by 1958 was earning widespread admiration. Capote, never over-generous in his praise, was quick to damn this fellow flavour-of-the-month.

CAPP, AL (1909–1979) American cartoonist

Abstract art? A product of the untalented, sold by the unprincipled to the utterly bewildered.

A solid reactionary remark from the dean of right-wing American cartoonists, the creator of Li'l Abner, the leading citizen of the hillbilly settlement of Dogpatch. Capp started his career as an assistant to Ham Fisher, who created Joe Palooka, a boxing hero. Abner appeared in 1934, and represented the populist point of view, demolishing a variety of cherished American values, notably those of the East coast and Southern political and business establishments. Li'l Abner has entered US folklore, but Capp's populism has turned increasingly towards representing rather than debunking the views of the establishment and, since the Sixties, savaging the left and the liberals. He claims merely to satirise, but his targets find something crankily obsessed about his lines.

CARDUS, NEVILLE (1889–1975) British sports and music journalist

There is one great similarity between music and cricket – there are slow movements in both.
quoted in 1967

Neville Cardus managed with great success to combine impressive erudition in what many people might consider to be quite discrete fields of entertainment, but which, as his remark underlines, have a great deal in common. From his childhood in Manchester, Cardus ran his two great interests in parallel, and managed to parlay them both into a career as one of the country's most respected cricket writers and a major music critic.

CARMICHAEL, STOKELY (1941–) American radical

Violence is American as cherry pie.
Black Power (1967)

Carmichael was one of the founders in 1964 of the Student Non-Violent Co-Ordinating Committee (SNCC). He repudiated its avowed principle of change through peaceful means when it became obvious that the American establishment, to which he claims violence is a part of the national culture as folksy as any other, was unwilling to be swayed by soft words. Instead he turned to a new philosophy, *Black Power*, which he expounded in this eponymous book. As he and his fellow author, political science professor Charles Hamilton, explain in their foreword: 'This book presents a political framework and ideology which represents the last reasonable opportunity for this society to work out its racial problems short of prolonged guerilla warfare'. They hoped to avoid such a racial war, but, in the form of such groups as the Black Panthers pitted against the police, it duly flourished for a while. Carmichael emigrated to Africa; the racial issue in America remains a perennial problem.

CARMICHAEL, STOKELY

The only position for women in SNCC is prone.
quoted in 1965

Hard though it is to envisage after twenty years of militant feminism, the origins of the so-called revolution and the establishment of the 'alternative society' foresaw no worked-out place for women. Carmichael, one of the earliest of Sixties radicals and founder of the SNCC, made it clear that women were to retain their traditional secondary role and, if one takes his line literally, to be available simply to service their exhausted heroes. As another, anonymous, hero of the counter-culture put it: 'Women is for the licking and the sticking'.

CARNE, JUDY (1939–) British comedienne and actress

Sock it to me!
catchphrase on 'Rowan and Martin's Laugh-In', 1960s

Rowan and Martin's Laugh-in was one of the quintessential US television shows of the Sixties. From its title, reminiscent of the hippie 'be-in', its cut-rate 'psychedelic' sets, and its off the wall humour, to the dinner-suited comic duo who fronted the whole free-wheeling if rigourously scripted extravaganza, the entire phenomenon, seen today, is nostalgic at best, banal at worst, and utterly dated on both counts. At the time it was massively successful and threw up a number of catchphrases. For pert Judy Carne, an English actress, the cry 'Sock it to me!' was inevitably followed by her being drenched with water. The term dates from 1880s American slang, used by Mark Twain in 1889, and later black jazz use, from which it proceeded to NBC TV and the *Laugh-In*.

CARNEGIE, DALE (1885–1955) American businessman

How to Win Friends and Influence People
book title, 1934

Carnegie personified the achieved American dream for the generation of the Thirties and Forties. Born a dirt-poor Missouri farm boy, he learnt his first lessons in public speaking at Warrensburg State Teachers College in Missouri. It gave him wonderful confidence and in 1912, capitalising on his own experience, he launched a course in public speaking in New York City. The book derived from these lectures, *Talking To Win*, proved a winner itself, selling massively. In 1934, after researching the works of agony aunt Dorothy Dix and psychologists William James and Alfred Adler, and analysing a large selection of success stories, Carnegie wrote *How To Win Friends and Influence People*. In essence Carnegie told hopefuls: respect the other guy's point of view and indulge his ego. Published in 1936 it was an enormous success, outstripping all previous efforts and contributing a new phrase to the language.

CARTER, HOWARD   British archeologist

Surely never before in the whole history of excavation had such an amazing sight been seen.
The Tomb of Tut-ankh-Amen (1923)

Carter was a leading member of the expedition sent by its sponsor Lord Carnarvon to Egypt in 1922 with the aim of discovering the tomb of the boy-king Tut-ankh-Amen, who had died aged 18 thirty-two centuries before. Searching among a century's worth of archeological debris, Carter almost accidentally discovered the tomb, still bearing the seals that denoted its royal corpse. He telegraphed Carnarvon: 'At Last Have Made Wonderful Discovery in Valley; A Magnificent Tomb With Seals Intact; Recovered Same For Your Arrival; Congratulations.' Carter opened the tomb in Carnarvon's presence on November 25, 1922, revealing a wealth of fabulous treasures. A year later, he wrote the event up in his book *The Tomb of Tut-ankh-Amen*.

CARTER, JAMES EARL (JIMMY)   (1924–) American president

I've looked on a lot of women with lust. I've committed adultery in my heart many times. This is something God recognizes I will do – and I have done it – and God forgives me for it.'
interview in *Playboy*, 1976

The lust evinced by modern politicians for the limelight provided by the attendant media and their firm belief that they can thus best create a sympathetic public image for themselves can sometimes prove disastrous. Self-exposure, as opposed to self-promotion, can come unstuck. Jimmy Carter submitted himself to the *Playboy* interviewers in November 1976. As required by his campaigning stance, he was candour itself. After declaring that 'We should live each day of our lives as if Christ were coming this afternoon', he went on to 'fess up to his roving, if celibate, eye. Whether God noticed Jimmy's peccadillo is debatable, but the public did. Carter won the election, but his honesty remained an embarrassment throughout his presidency.

CASABLANCA

Play it again, Sam.
screenplay by Julius and Philip Epstein and Howard Koch (1941)

A major contender for 'deliberate mistake' in any film buff's questionnaire, 'Play it again, 'Sam', that staple of saloon-bar Bogart imitators, is the most popular of those oft-quoted lines that were neither written in a script nor spoken on a screen. Just as Mae West never suggested to anyone that they might 'Come up and see me some time', Humphrey Bogart wasn't even in the room when Dooley Wilson – 'Sam' – was persuaded to play 'As Time Goes By' by 'Ilsa Lund' (Ingrid Bergman). For the record, the script, ran thus:

Ilsa: Play it once, Sam, for old time's sake.
Sam: Ah don't know what you mean, Miss Ilsa.
Ilsa: Play it, Sam. Play 'As Time Goes By'.
Sam: Oh, Ah can't remember it, Miss Ilsa. Ah'm a little rusty on it.
Ilsa: I'll hum it for you. Hm-hm, hm-hm, hm-hmmmmmm...Sing it Sam.
Sam: You must remember this, a kiss is just a kiss...

CASABLANCA

Here's looking at you, kid.
screenplay by Julius & Philip Epstein and Howard Koch (1941)

Unlike 'Play it again, Sam' (qv), the other alleged quotation from this classic film, winner of two Oscars at the time and still as popular as ever, Bogart, playing saloon-keeper Rick, actually did toast Ingrid Bergman (Ilsa) with these words. Although the line has become a staple of bar-room Bogarts the world over, it was an unexceptional toast, a slightly cleaned up version of 'here's mud in your eye!' and probably predated the film, although never so widely.

CASTLE, BARBARA (1911–) British politician

She is so clearly the best man among them.

Margaret Thatcher was elected as the first female leader of the Conservative Party on February 11, 1975, chosen to succeed Edward Heath, who seemed incapable of winning the party any elections. Labour's Barbara Castle, hardly Mrs. Thatcher's opposite number and never in contention for the Labour leadership, but in her time one of the most powerful women in politics, looked at Mrs. Thatcher's male colleagues and summed the situation up.

CASTRO, FIDEL (1927–) Cuban leader

History will absolve me.
on trial in 1953

Castro's father arrived in Cuba as an impoverished labourer and died as a rich plantation owner. His son refused to exploit his wealth further, preferring to politicise his fellow Cubans and overthrow the oppressive dictatorship of the Trujillo regime. In 1953 he was jailed for two years after an unsuccessful attack on the Moncada Barracks. This promise was made at the trial. Released in 1955 he regrouped his forces in Mexico and in 1956 attacked the Cuban mainland. Only eleven fighters survived the assault and for two years they retreated to the mountains of the Sierra Madre, building up their numbers to some 1000 guerillas. Castro began attacking Trujillo's army in August 1958 and took control of the country on New Year's Day 1959.

CAT ON A HOT TIN ROOF

You don't know what love means. To you it's just another four-letter word.
screenplay by Richard Brooks and James Poe (1958)

Taken from Tennessee Williams' play of the same name, the film, starring Paul Newman and Elizabeth Taylor, concerns the problem that dominates the relationship between the couple whom they play: Newman's lack of interest in making love to Taylor. The play's various set pieces revolve around this situation and in the middle of one of the fierce rows that it provokes, Newman dismisses Taylor's protestations of 'love' as 'a four-letter word'. Williams' play may not have originated this particular piece of wordplay, but the film certainly helped popularise it, and it still recurs reasonably often.

CAVELL, EDITH (1865–1915) British nurse

Patriotism is not enough; I must have no hatred and bitterness towards anyone.
last words, 12 October 1915

Nurse Cavell was the matron of a hospital in Brussels at the outbreak of the First World War. Studiously neutral, as was the country in which she was working, she tended the wounded of both sides during the early fighting. Her error, in the eyes of invading Germans, was to help some wounded French and English soldiers on their way to the safety of the Dutch border.

She was arrested and sentenced to death for aiding the enemy. Despite protests she was executed, offering these, her last words, to the attendant British chaplain. After the war her remains were reinterred in Norwich Cathedral and her monument stands near Trafalgar Square at the confluence of Charing Cross Road and St. Martin's Lane.

CÉLINE, LOUIS-FERDINAND (1894–1961) (Louis-Ferdinand Destouches) French writer

If you aren't rich you should always look useful.
in *Journey to the End of the Night* (1932)

Céline (he took his *nom de plume* from his grandmother's given name) fought in World War I, prior to qualifying in 1924 as a doctor. His first novel, *Journey to the End of the Night*, presented with macabre black humour the peregrinations of a misanthropic, unappetising slum doctor during and after the War. In it Céline combined his own experiences and utterly pessimistic view of the world with a revolutionary prose style. The reactionary opinions of his doctor, reinforced by his own gross anti-semitism and his unashamed collaboration with the occupying Nazis after 1940, brought him much obloquy. He fled to Denmark, where he was interned, in 1944 and returned to Paris in 1951, living out his life in solitude. Céline's reputation has increased since his death; without the living man his opinions can simply be dismissed as aberrant and his prose style declared revolutionary.

CHALMERS, PATRICK British poet

What's lost upon the roundabouts, we pulls up on the swings.
Roundabouts and Swings (1912)

A classic piece of homely philosophy, delivered in Chalmers' poem by a travelling showman. When asked, during a stopover in Framlingham in Norfolk, how the fairground trade is prospering he answers with this simplistic response.

CHAMBERLAIN, NEVILLE (1869–1940) British prime minister

How horrible, fantastic, incredible it is that we should be digging trenches and trying on gas-masks here because of a quarrel in a faraway country between people of whom we know nothing.
radio broadcast, 27 September 1938

The insularity so rampant in this statement by a British prime minister in the Europe of 1938 is as shocking now as it was to a fair number of his contemporaries who found his lust for appeasement morally and patriotically distasteful. As his predecessor Lloyd George allegedly remarked, Chamberlain 'saw foreign policy through the wrong end of a municipal drainpipe', and his apparent inability to perceive the realities of Europe seem more attuned to the mental processes of a provincial mayor than of a supposedly international statesman.

CHAMBERLAIN, NEVILLE

My good friends, this is the second time in our history that there has come back from Germany to Downing Street peace with honour. I believe it is peace for our time. Go home and get a nice quiet sleep.
returning from meeting Hitler at Munich, 30 September 1938

Chamberlain's belief that he could appease Hitler and thus avert British involvement in a second World War seemed momentarily vindicated when he returned to London having promised the Fuhrer that England would not interfere in his plans to re-annex the German speaking Sudetenland region of Czechoslovakia if that truly was Hitler's 'last territorial claim in Europe'. He brandished his piece of paper at Heston airport, telling reporters that the agreement which both leaders had signed was 'symbolic of the desire of our two peoples never to go to war with one another again.' Later that evening, as crowds gathered outside 10 Downing Street, Chamberlain added his 'peace for our time' speech. Six months later, when the Germans marched into Prague, Chamberlain could only tell R.A. Butler and Lord Halifax 'I have decided that I cannot trust the Nazi leaders again'. Even the words of Chamberlain's capitulation were not his own. Disraeli had coined 'peace with honour', and Stanley Baldwin, hoping to avert a general strike, had in 1925 hoped that there might be industrial 'peace in our time, oh Lord.'

CHAMBERS, WHITTAKER   (1901–1961) American bureaucrat

Every man is crucified upon the cross of himself.
Witness (1952)

Whittaker Chambers was one of the most notorious of the professional informers used by the House Un-American Activities Committee in its pursuit of alleged subversives and communists during the late 1940s and early 1950s. Chambers wrote his book *Witness* specifically to justify his own role in the hounding of State Department employee Alger Hiss, a witch hunted with particular venom and in pursuit of his own political advancement by president-to-be Richard Nixon. When the case against Hiss appeared to be faltering Chambers conveniently led two HUAC investigators into a pumpkin field he owned, marched up to a likely vegetable and plucked from its depths the micro-filmed evidence of a 'communist conspiracy', supposedly based on papers smuggled out of the department by Hiss. Hiss denied the charge, but the jury believed Chambers and Hiss was jailed and indirectly branded a Soviet agent.

CHANDLER, RAYMOND (1888–1959) American novelist

Chandler was born in Chicago but educated at Dulwich College, in London. In 1912 he settled in California, where he worked without great pleasure or reward for an oil company. He began writing in the 1930s, submitting his first story to the leading pulp magazines, *Black Mask* (founded by the Smart Set editors H.L. Mencken and George Jean Nathan and edited by the legendary Joseph T. Shaw). The story, 'Blackmailers Don't Shoot', was published in 1933. He wrote twenty more stories for *Black Mask* and other leading pulps before his first novel *The Big Sleep* appeared in 1939. In it he produced the near-perfected version of his hero, Philip Marlowe, who had evolved, under a variety of names, through the pulp stories. Marlowe has been analysed at length but in essence he is the apotheosis of Chandler's ideal fictional detective, as expounded in his 1950 essay 'The Simple Art of Murder'. Chandler continued writing Marlowe books until his death, as well as maintaining a copious correspondence and writing several screenplays.

CHANDLER, RAYMOND

It was a blonde. A blonde to make a bishop kick a hole in a stained-glass window.
Farewell, My Lovely (1940)

Chandler's second novel is often cited as his best, called by connoisseur Jacques Barzun 'a model of complexity kept under control'. In it Marlowe encounters the giant Moose Malloy, suffers forcible drug injections, and is as usual beaten and buffeted both by life and some of its denizens. The blonde in question is one Mrs. Grayle, aka Little Velma, a third-rate hoofer who's gone up in the world and starts killing to cover her tracks. As Marlowe puts it, 'She had a full set of curves nobody had been able to improve on', and she's all over him on their first meeting. But Marlowe isn't fooled, although when she does die it's the police, not him who do the job.

CHANDLER, RAYMOND

I think a man ought to get drunk at least twice a year just on principle, so he won't let himself get snotty about it.
in *Selected Letters* ed. Frank McShane (1981)

Chandler was a consistently hard drinker, like his fictional detective, for most of his life. By the 1950s, his drinking accentuated by the miseries that followed his wife's death in 1954, Chandler was a fully-fledged alcoholic whose illness required regular drying out in a variety of expensive California clinics. He was brutally pragmatic about his position, acknowledging on the one hand that something had to be done about his drinking, but pointing out quite candidly that if he did stop, what could the doctors offer but a world without drink, one that could only be termed 'better' if one subscribed, and Chandler did not, to the cosy 'Pollyanna' view of a seamlessly 'normal' society.

CHANDLER, RAYMOND

To accept a mediocre form and make something like literature out of it is in itself rather an accomplishment.
letter to Helga Greene, 25 May 1957

In this letter to his literary agent Chandler goes on to say that he has been told that 'hundreds of writers today are making some sort of living from the mystery story because I made it respectable and even dignified'. He goes on to claim that he had been lucky and that any decent artist should be more interested in his art than in himself, saying that he and John Steinbeck had agreed that they would prefer that some unknown, who had not had their luck in his lifetime, should eventually be the really important writer of their era.

CHANDLER, RAYMOND

When a book, any sort of book, reaches a certain intensity of artistic performance it becomes literature.
quoted in *Raymond Chandler Speaking* (1962)

Chandler had few illusions about his skills as a writer. He saw himself, with Dashiell Hammett and a few other, inevitably lesser, writers as the creators of new form of detective fiction. That it sold well was testimony to their expertise, but the seriousness with which Chandler takes his art in letters and essays make it obvious that he appreciated his own worth. He was not alone. W.H. Auden, in his essay 'The Guilty Vicarage' (1948), in which he confesses his affection for all sorts of detective fiction, lauds Chandler, saying 'I think Mr. Chandler is interested in writing, not detective stories, but serious studies of a criminal milieu, the Great Wrong Place, and his powerful but extremely depressing books should be read and judged not as escape literature, but as works of art.'

CHANDLER, RAYMOND

If my books had been any worse I would not have been invited to Hollywood, and if they had been any better I would not have come.
quoted in *Raymond Chandler Speaking*, ed D. Gardiner and K.Walker (1962)

Chandler candidly despised Hollywood and all its works. He found its personalities vulgar, its ballyhoo meretricious and its product tawdry. In 1945 he wrote a piece for the *Atlantic* magazine in which he said just that, at somewhat greater length. In reply to his vituperation the screenwriter and director Charles Brackett (1892–1969), a collaborator with Billy Wilder, with whom Chandler was rarely able to get on, said 'Chandler's books are not good enough, nor his pictures bad enough, to justify that article'. Concluding that what Brackett meant was that only Hollywood failures or celebrities who never approached the place were allowed to comment on it, Chandler made the comment quoted above.

CHANDLER, RAYMOND

A city with all the personality of a paper cup.
The Little Sister (1949)

Chandler began by liking Los Angeles but as time passed the British public schoolboy could never be happy with its materialism, its vulgarity and its corruption. He moved out, to La Jolla, in 1946, but left a sour portrait in the novel he wrote, in parts a harsh attack on the movie business of Hollywood, in 1949. 'I used to like this town. A long time ago... Los Angeles was just a big dry sunny place with ugly homes and no style, but good-hearted and peaceful.... (Now) we've got the big money, the sharp-shooters, the percentage workers, the fast dollar boys, the hoodlums out of New York and Chicago and Detroit... the riffraff of a big, hardboiled city with no more personality than a paper cup.'

CHANDLER, RAYMOND

Alcohol is like love: the first kiss is magic, the second is intimate, the third is routine. After that you just take the girl's clothes off.
The Long Goodbye (1953)

Chandler's detective was referring to the Hemingway-esque writer Roger Wade, but by 1953 his own drinking had become a problem. Much of it was accentuated by his wife's lengthy, incurable illness. Chandler's drinking probably peaked in 1955 when he actually attempted suicide, but he was never completely able to give it up for the remainder of his life.

CHANDLER, RAYMOND

Organised crime is just the dirty side of the sharp dollar.
The Long Goodbye (1953)

Written as he helped nurse his wife Cecily through her lengthy final illness, *The Long Goodbye* is Chandler's most negative, embittered book, acting as a vehicle for so many frustrations and sorrows. Like many of his books, the plot meanders and sometimes seems to vanish, but the characters are drawn with merciless detail and Marlowe wanders amongst them, the eternally tarnished knight errant. In 1954 the book won the Edgar (for Edgar Wallace) awarded to that year's outstanding crime fiction by the Mystery Writers of America.

CHANDLER, RAYMOND

In everything that can be called art there is a quality of redemption. It may be pure tragedy, if it is high tragedy, and it may be pity and irony, and it may be the raucous laughter of the strong man. But down these mean streets a man must go who is not himself mean, who is neither tarnished nor afraid. The detective in this kind of story must be such a man.
The Simple Art of Murder (1950)

In Philip Marlowe Raymond Chandler created the paradigm of the tough-guy detective hero: cynical, wisecracking, world-weary and finally romantic, a knight errant pitted against a corrupt, selfish world and searching not for the Grail but for truth. He must be, as Chandler continued, 'a man of honour, by instinct, by inevitability, without thought of it, and certainly without saying it. He must be the best man in his world and a good enough man for any world.' Whether such a figure is any more realistic than the buttonholed, monocled fops of classic detective fiction might be debatable, but as Chandler concludes, in an essay devoted to debunking tradition and boosting his man, 'If there were enough like him, I think the world would be a very safe place to live, and yet not too dull to be worth living in.'

CHANDLER, RAYMOND

The constant yelping about a free press means, with a few honourable exceptions, freedom to peddle scandal, crime, sex, sensationalism, hate, innuendo the political and financial uses of propaganda. A newspaper is a business out to make money through advertising revenue. That is predicated on its circulation and you know what circulation depends on.

The Long Goodbye 1953

CHANDLER, RAYMOND

It is not a very fragrant world, but it is the world you live in, and certain writers with tough minds and a cool spirit of detachment can make very interesting and even amusing patterns out of it. It is not funny that a man should be killed, but it is sometimes funny that he should be killed for so little and that his death should be the coin of what we call civilisation.

The Simple Art of Murder (1950)

In this essay, possibly the only exposition of the art by a practitioner rather than an academic or biographer, Chandler stated unequivocally the case for the realistic style, what came to be known as the hard-boiled style of detective fiction. Its intention, he stressed, was to portray this 'not very fragrant world' warts and all. He wanted to take detective fiction out of the vicarage tea-party and put it back in the real world. As he said of his peer Dashiell Hammett, it was necessary to 'give murder back to the kind of people that commit it for reasons, not just to provide a corpse'. Hammett was one of those with the requisite tough mind and cool spirit and so, undoubtedly, was Chandler himself.

CHANEL, COCO (1883–1971) French dress designer

Nature gives you the face you have at twenty, but it's up to you to merit the face you have at fifty.

quoted in, *Ladies' Home Journal* (1956)

Gabrielle 'Coco' Chanel was abandoned by her widowed father and raised in the austerity of a convent orphanage. In 1903 she was apprenticed to a provincial hat-maker and in 1910, helped by her protector Arthur 'Boy' Capel, she set up as a milliner in 21 Rue Cambon, Paris. Chanel dominated French and then international fashion for the succeeding half century (excluding only the years from 1939–54) in a period when the word of the Paris couturiers was still law. She created the 'little black dress', pioneered 'designer' artefacts with her Chanel No.5 perfume, launched in 1920, and turned a suntan, formerly eschewed as the badge of a peasant, into a smart accessory.

CHAPELAIN, MAURICE (1906–) French writer

The final delusion is the belief that one has lost all delusions.
Main courante

We cannot exist without delusions. They may be absurd, impossible, the stuff of one's wildest dreams; they may be self-aggrandising, they may feature the destruction of all real and imagined enemies; they may even, as Chapelain suggests, embrace the greatest delusion of all, that we have come to terms with real life. But humankind, as Eliot pointed out, cannot bear too much reality, and delusions are common to us all. The idea that one has shucked off all fantasy is in itself the supreme example of the phenomenon.

CHAPLIN, CHARLES (CHARLIE) (1889–1977) British film comedian

All I need to make a comedy is a park, a policeman and a pretty girl.
My Autobiography (1964)

The 'obstinate, suspicious, egocentric, maddening and lovable genius of a problem child', as his friend Mary Pickford put it, was one of the most popular comedians the world has ever seen. Chaplin was the right man at the right time, his pathetic tramp figure epitomising a sentimental view of the masses which they liked, even if more sophisticated critics found his pathos merely mawkish, and which particularly appealed to those who saw themselves as society's underdogs. Chaplin was vain, arrogant, a poor critic of his own and others' work (including Shakespeare's); he had an unfortunate predilection for under-age girls and an inability to decide whether or not it was advantageous to admit to his Jewishness; he gave no credit to the crews who helped make his films and in the end had no sense of humour if the topic was himself. Yet his appeal was enormous and the masses who flocked to see their alter ego triumphant cared nothing for his foibles.

CHASE, ALEXANDER (1926–) American journalist

People, like sheep, tend to follow a leader – occasionally in the right direction.
Perspectives (1966)

175

Chase has offered a variety of sardonic aphorisms on the state of the world and its people. Apart from his comment on the propensity of people to follow where their leader beckons, even when for a change he may actually be taking them where they ought to go, his book includes these comments, none of them very cheering:

For the unhappy man death is the commutation of a sentence of life imprisonment.

The rich man may never get into heaven, but the pauper is already serving his time in hell.

The banalities of a great man pass for wit.

CHAYEVSKY, PADDY   (1923–1981)(Sidney Stuchevsky)American scriptwriter

Television is democracy at its ugliest.
quoted in Leslie Halliwell *Filmgoers' Companion* 8th edn. (1984)

Chayevsky made his name as a scriptwriter in 1955 with *Marty*, a celebration of the charms of the world's ostensibly unimportant people, for which he won an Oscar and the film racked up three more. Essentially a TV writer (Marty started life as a TV play, with Rod Steiger taking the role that Ernest Borgnine had on screen) Chayevsky has a love-hate relationship with the medium that made him famous, epitomised in the verbose script for *Network* (1976), a scathing attack on the modern industry in which Peter Finch plays a newsman turned self-appointed messiah, using his nightly slot to rail against the iniquities of the loveless box.

CHAZAL, MALCOLM DE   (1902–) British Writer

The family is a court of justice which never shuts down for night or day.
Sens plastique (1949)

Chazal lived in semi-isolation on the island of Mauritius where, in his solitude, he was able to devote his energies to initiating himself into what he felt were the occult relations between nature and the senses. He mixed his own intuitions and feelings with a range of baroque images in his major work *Sens plastique*, in which he posits the sexual act as a mediator between the extremes of birth and death. On its original publication in Paris *Sens plastique* caused a sensation, and made its reclusive author famous overnight. Later works, filled with his idiosyncratic mysticism, have never lived up to this promise.

Man looks to himself for what he does not find in others, and to others for what he has too much of in himself.

The idealist walks on his toes, the materialist on his talons.

The egotists's feelings walk in single file.

The freedom to be oneself is the highest form of justice towards others.

A voracious sense of smell leans forward on its nostrils like a glutton eating with his elbows on the table.

Women eat when they talk, men talk when they eat.

CHAZAL, MALCOLM DE

Art is nature speeded up and God slowed down.
Sens plastique (1949)

CHAZAL, MALCOLM DE

A mirror has no heart but plenty of ideas.
Sens plastique (1949)

CHERRY-GERRARD, APSLEY (1886–?) British polar explorer

Polar exploration is at once the cleanest and most isolated way of having a bad time which has been devised.
The Worst Journey in the World (1922)

Cherry-Gerrard was a member of Robert Falcon Scott's polar expedition to the Antarctic between 1910–11. They were racing the Norwegian Roald Amundsen to be first to the Pole, and lost both that race and, as far as Scott and four of his companions were concerned, their lives. Cherry-Gerrard was one of the seven men who returned to the base camp, leaving Scott's party to make the final assault on the Pole in mid-December. From thereon in, everything went wrong. They reached their goal only to find that Amundsen had won. 'Great God', wrote Scott, 'this is an awful place', and prepared to trek home. None of the party survived and Scott's diary bears eloquent testimony to their final agonies.

CHESTERTON, G.K. (1874–1936) British essayist, novelist and critic
Chesterton's literary career began in journalism 'the easiest of all professions' and one which gave him the opportunity to exploit his prolix, wide-ranging facility. He began writing on *The Speaker*, a pro-Boer anti-Imperialist magazine, where he met his

lifelong friend and fellow Catholic convert Hilaire Belloc. So close were their attitudes, although Chesterton's unbuttoned style showed the greater tolerance, that they were christened by Shaw, who was with H.G. Wells the main target of their crusading, as 'Chesterbelloc'. Chesterton wrote essays, literary criticism, and a number of novels. His substantial output of poetry all tended to celebrate a particularly hearty fantasy of Britain, with the accent on beef, beer and 'the rolling English road'. His lasting reputation depends on his fictional detective: Father Brown. Created in 1911 Chesterton's gentle, unassuming Roman Catholic priest sees criminals as souls to be saved rather than as villains to be punished. His cases often depend on the author's own love of paradox and the strange and grotesque, and Father Brown relies on his own deep knowledge of human nature, rather than any great feats of ratiocination.

CHESTERTON, G.K.

The rolling English drunkard made the rolling English road.
The Rolling English Road (1914)

Chesterton's particular fantasy of England emphasised a type of 'Merrie England' that the most banal of Hollywood producers would have loved, with its rustics, its golden acres, its foaming beer and roasted beef. Never was he more self-indulgent than in this poem in which he supposes that the winding English country lanes must, in their random peregrinations, have been created by generations of equally random drunks. He posits various ludicrous byways, prior to that final journey, 'to Paradise by way of Kensal Green.'

CHESTERTON, G.K.

It's not the world that's got so much worse but the news coverage that's got so much better.
attributed

CHESTERTON, G.K.

Democracy means government by the uneducated, while aristocracy means government by the badly educated.
in the *New York Times*, 1931

CHESTERTON, G.K.

There is the great man who makes every man feel small. But the real great man is the man who makes every man feel great.
Charles Dickens (1906)

For Chesterton Dickens was the ideal writer, as English as could be desired and a classic too. As one who liked to place himself as the champion of the trueborn Englishman, Dickens' gallery of Victorian types appealed immeasurably. Chesterton cared less for Dicken's social theorising, but promoted his predecessor as the creator of characters who really were 'characters'. As he put it in the same essay: 'When some English moralists write about the importance of having character, they appear to mean only the importance of having a dull character'

CHESTERTON, G.K.

Every man speaks of public opinion, and means by public opinion, public opinion minus his opinion.
Heretics (1905)

CHESTERTON, G.K.

Bigotry may be roughly defined as the anger of men who have no opinions.
Heretics (1905)

CHESTERTON, G.K.

A man who has faith must be prepared not only to be a martyr, but to be a fool.
Heretics (1905)

CHESTERTON, G.K.

The artistic temperament is a disease that afflicts amateurs.
Heretics (1905)

CHESTERTON, G.K.

The men who really believe in themselves are all in lunatic asylums.
Orthodoxy (1909)

CHESTERTON, G.K.

Am in Market Harborough. Where ought I to be?
quoted in *Maisie Ward*, G.K. Chesterton (1944)

Chesterton was known for his lack of organisation. A busy life with many journeys and public appearances was not enhanced by his lack of planning. On the way to one of these appearances, he

CHESTERTON, G.K.

is reported to have alighted from the train and found himself on what was a strange station. He cabled his wife Frances as above. Realising that the intricacies of railway branch lines would only intensify the confusion she replied with the single word 'Home', and having found him in London, sent him off again, this time in the right direction.

CHESTERTON, G.K.

Very few people in this world would care to listen to the real defence of their own characters. The real defence, the defence which belongs to the Day of Judgement, would make such damaging admissions, would clear away so many artificial virtues, would tell such a tragedy of weakness and failure, that a man would sooner be misunderstood and censured by the world, than exposed to that awful and merciless eulogy.
Robert Browning (1902)

CHESTERTON, G.K.

'My country, right or wrong' is a thing that no patriot would think of saying, except in a desperate case. It is like saying 'My mother, drunk or sober.'
The Defendant (1901)

Chesterton, who was at times obsessively pro-British, or at least pro-British national mythology, was mocking in this deflation of super-patriotism, a toast given in April 1916 by the American Stephen Decatur. Decatur, a naval hero, was a guest at a dinner in Norfolk, Virginia, where among a plethora of grandiose toasts, his won the day. Chesterton was by no means the first person to modify Decatur. American politician John Crittenden told the House of Representatives in 1846 'I hope to find my country in the right; however, I will stand by her, right or wrong.' In 1847 President John Quincy Adams had stated 'And say not thou "My country right or wrong", /Nor shed thy blood for an unhallowed cause.' and on January 17, 1872, Senator Carl Schurz of Missouri paraphrased the line as 'Our country, right or wrong. When right, to be kept right; when wrong to be put right.'

CHESTERTON, G.K.

Literature is a luxury, fiction is a necessity.
The Defendant (1901)

CHESTERTON, G.K.

Thieves respect property. They merely wish the property to become their property that they may more perfectly respect it.
The Man Who Was Thursday (1908)

The Man Who Was Thursday is, as far as its projection of Chesterton's political theses, a continuation of the earlier *Napoleon of Notting Hill*. Subtitled 'a nightmare' it is another fanatasy of London life, this time dominated by an anarchist clique, all named for the days of the week, who are aiming to undermine the fabric of British society but who, unsurprisingly, are put in their place by plucky Britons who have no time for the fashionable pessimism of fin-de-siècle Europe.

CHESTERTON, G.K.

The human race, to which so many of my readers belong.
The Napoleon of Notting Hill (1904)

Chesterton's first novel, *The Napoleon of Notting Hill*, of which this is the first line, is a fantasy set in a future version of London. The capital is prey to a bizarre mixture of medieval nostalgia worthy of Hollywood and street warfare. Chesterton parades his political obsessions: glorifying the 'little man' and lauding the romantic fiction that masquerades as 'Merrie Englande' and is better fitted to tourism than to truth. Conversely he attacks big business, technology, and the monolithic state.

CHESTERTON, G.K.

Journalism largely consists in saying 'Lord Jones Dead' to people who never knew Lord Jones was alive.
The Wisdom of Father Brown (1914) 'The Purple Wig'

The Wisdom of Father Brown was the second appearance in book form of Chesterton's ecclesiastical detective, based originally on his friend Father John OConnor. With his face 'as round and dull as a Norfolk dumpling...eyes as empty as the North Sea...several brown paper parcels which he was incapable of collecting...(and) a large shabby umbrella which constantly fell to the floor', Father Brown is the model of inoffensiveness. Of course, beneath this modest exterior and behind the 'harmless, human name of Brown' the priest has an infinite knowledge of human nature which he uses to solve the problems that come before him. Brown is a New Testament creation, an idealised gentle Jesus rather than an angry Jehovah, preferring to counsel and correct

181

rather than to condemn and punish. His greatest success is in his conversion of Flambeau, a French Moriarty, who reforms and under clerical guidance turns to legal pursuits.

CHOU EN LAI (1898–1976) Chinese politician

All diplomacy is a continuation of war by other means.
quoted in 1954

Chou En Lai, here reversing Clausewitz' famous dictum 'War is a continuation of policy by other means', joined the Chinese Communist party in 1924 and soon became one of Mao Zedong's leading advisers. The ties he formed with the Chairman-to-be meant that he survived the vicissitudes of Chinese politics from the original Revolution of 1949 to the Cultural Revolution of the 1960s, and he served as the nation's Prime Minister from 1949 until his death. Chou's belief was that China should establish itself as a major world power, rather than over-accentuating the tenets of Marxist orthodoxy. To this end he recommended that China maintain as amicable as possible relations with the outside world, although Mao's own policies, the fears of the West, and the ideological split with the USSR meant that his hopes remained largely unfulfilled.

CHRISTGAU, ROBERT (1945–) American rock music critic

The old complaint that mass culture is designed for eleven-year-olds is of course a shameful canard. The key age has traditionally been more like fourteen.
in *Esquire* magazine, 1969

Prior to the rise of the teenager, an essentially post-war phenomenon, there was no mass culture as it is understood today. The masses obviously had always had their entertainments but the disposable incomes, provided by jobs or parents, that teenagers had to spend, and manufacturers to indulge, were unavailable until the 1950s. When Christgau, one of America's more respected rock critics (a job that in itself could not have existed before the teenage purse made rock music into a very big business) made his comment, fourteen may indeed have been the mean; today the former figure is truly nearer the mark. Another commentator on the mass media was W.H. Auden, who suggested in *The Dyer's Hand* (1963) that 'What the mass media offer is not popular art, but entertainment which is intended to be consumed like food, forgotten and replaced by a new dish.'

CHRISTIE, AGATHA (1890–1976) British detective fiction writer

A sausage machine, a perfect sausage machine.
on herself in G.C. Ramsey, *Agatha Christie, Mistress of Mystery*

Agatha Christie was destined to a career in music but abandoned it through extreme shyness. She married Archibald Christie, an RFC officer, in 1914 and became a nurse with the VAD and then a qualified dispenser, working throughout World War I. Her first detective novel, *The Mysterious Affair at Styles*, appeared in 1920. In 1926 she gained national fame through both her mysterious disappearance – suffering a brief nervous breakdown as her marriage collapsed – and the publication of her first major success, the ingenious *Murder of Roger Ackroyd*. Living quietly and comfortably, she believed that 'The best time for planning a book is when you're doing the dishes.' She created two immortal detectives – the vain, moustachioed Belgian Hercule Poirot, devotee of his 'little grey cells', and the country spinster Miss Jane Marple, capable of reducing all human perfidy to the dimensions of a cosy if corrupt English village. Christie's books have consistently sold more copies than those of any rival English language author, some 1.5 million paperbacks per year.

CHRISTIE, AGATHA

So let it be Veronal. But I wish Hercule Poirot had never retired from work and come here to grow vegetable marrows.
The Murder of Roger Ackroyd (1926)

This was the book, Christie's seventh in as many years, that took her from modest if respectable English sales to major success around the world. It deals with Hercule Poirot's investigation of the murder of a doctor in a small English village. Laden with clues, it offers, as do all her works, the opportunity to elucidate the identity of the criminal, but many critics, while delighting in her legerdemain, felt that Miss Christie's variation on the 'least likely person' theme sailed somewhat close to the wind. Like it or not, the author never looked back.

CHURCHILL, WINSTON SPENCER (1874–1965) British statesman

Churchill was the eldest son of Lord Randolph Churchill (1849–95), himself a younger son of the 7th Duke of Marlborough, and thus born into the heart of the British ruling class. After Harrow, where he failed to shine, he entered the army and served in Cuba, India, Egypt and the Sudan before participating as a war correspondent in the Boer War. Entering politics he served in a number of ministerial positions in many administrations. Prior to becoming prime minister in 1940, and earning his reputation as Britain's greatest war leader this century, he had been home secretary from 1919–11, First lord of the admiralty 1911–15, secretary of state for war 1918–21, for the colonies 1921–22, and chancellor of the exchequer 1924–29. The determination he showed in 1940 was revealed in a less acceptable light both in 1911, when he used troops against strikers in South Wales, and in his campaign against the General Strike of 1926. Churchill was always a maverick, in and out of office, and advisedly or otherwise, he championed Edward VIII, possibly to a greater extent than the monarch deserved, during the Abdication Crisis of 1936. He called, presciently and consistently throughout the 1930s, for British rearmament in the face of Hitler's increasing militarism. He foolishly attempted to brand Labour as a totalitarian party in 1945, and suffered a landslide rebuff at the polls. He warned of 'the iron curtain' that divided the post-war world. Above all, and in many eyes pardoning all else, he successfully inspired Britain, and by her example the free world, to resist Nazi Germany from 1940–45. His speeches have the ring of melodrama in today's age of carefully modulated television performances, but at the time they worked, as much as anything in impressing the powerful Americans with the need to help. Churchill's role as war leader did not extend into the peace and in 1945 a Labour government under Atlee was elected by the returning troops. Churchill returned from 1951–55, more an elder statesman than an active prime minister, and spent his last years writing his own views of history, painting and building walls.

Churchill, Winston

I remember, when I was a child, being taken to the celebrated Barnum's Circus, which contained an exhibition of freaks and monstrosities. But the exhibit on the programme that I most desired to see was the one described as 'The Boneless Wonder.' My parents judged that the spectacle would be too revolting and too demoralizing for my youthful eyes, and I waited fifty years to see the Boneless Wonder sitting on the treasury bench.
1933

Churchill sat on the back benches between 1929–40; they provided him with an excellent vantage point for the savaging of errant fellow-members, irrespective of party. He wasted little sympathy on Britain's first Labour prime minister, Ramsay Mac-

Donald, whom he had described in 1921 as 'the greatest living master of falling without hurting himself ', when his government lost a succession of votes but could not be replaced, since no-one else could muster sufficient votes to replace him. This attack came on January 28, 1933 and referred to what he saw as MacDonald's excessive conciliation of his Roman Catholic supporters. Later that year Churchill compounded his attack, saying 'We know that he has, more than any other man, the gift of compressing the largest amount of words into the smallest amount of thought'.

CHURCHILL, WINSTON

There, but for the grace of God, goes God.

Churchill always found the ascetic Labour chancellor of the exchequer Sir Stafford Cripps (1889–1952) a particularly unsympathetic figure. He said of him variously that 'He delivers his speech with an expression of injured guilt', and that 'He has all of the virtues I dislike and none of the vices I admire'; but the above description is the one for which Churchill, and thus Cripps, is most celebrated. The same phrase, surely unheard by Churchill, had been delivered a decade earlier by the Hollywood wit Herman Mankiewicz, referring to Orson Welles, with whom he was then writing the script of 'Citizen Kane'.

CHURCHILL, WINSTON

From Stettin in the Baltic, to Trieste in the Adriatic, an iron curtain has descended across the Continent.
speech on March 5, 1945

The speed with which the Soviet Union, an erstwhile ally, became for America and Western Europe a bogeyman soon to surpass even Hitler's Germany, should have surprised nobody, least of all Hitler himself, who had always counted on the West's dislike of Bolshevik Russia to temper the severity of its dealings with his own machinations. Churchill, lecturing at Fulton College, Missouri, was referring in particular to the Soviets' imperialist takeover of the Baltic, an advance which he had himself condoned, if only by a failure to resist Stalin's plans for the imposition of Communist rule on the states concerned, all occupied by the Red Army in its drive to Berlin. While Churchill has been credited with coining the phrase, and it occurs in a number of letters he wrote to President Truman prior to his speech, its original use as regards the USSR can be found in Mrs. Philip Snowden's *Through Bolshevik Russia* (1920) where she states 'We were behind the "iron curtain" at last!'. Reich Propaganda Minister Joseph Goebbels had also used the term in 1945. The writer St. Vincent Troubridge, writing in the *Sunday Empire News* on October 21, 1945, had also predated Churchill with his remark 'There is an iron curtain across Europe.'

CHURCHILL, WINSTON

I have nothing to offer but blood, toil, tears and sweat.
speech, May 13, 1940

Churchill took over from the disgraced Neville Chamberlain on May 10. Three days later he made his first major speech to the House of Commons. Probably referring back to Garibaldi's words to the legion trapped in Rome in 1849, 'I offer only hunger, thirst, forced marches and death', he called upon the House for unity and steadfastness, and continued 'You ask, what is our aim? I can answer in one word: victory, victory at all costs, victory in spite of all terror, victory however long and hard the road may be; for without victory there is no survival.' As Churchill left the Chamber, eyes brimming with tears and like any successful ham quite aware of his histrionic abilities, he remarked to an aide 'That got the sods, didn't it.'

CHURCHILL, WINSTON

It is a good thing for an uneducated man to read books of quotations.

Churchill's own education, though carried out at one of the country's leading public schools, Harrow, seems to have given him little reward and his teachers less pleasure. Like Ralph Waldo Emerson who saw every man as a quotation from his predecessors, Churchill was a great advocate of the learning that could be gleaned from a selection of the wit and wisdom of others. His own contribution to the books of quotations, as borne out in this volume and so many others, is of course substantial.

CHURCHILL, WINSTON

Give us the tools, and we will finish the job.
broadcast, 9 February 1941

Churchill never wavered in his desire that America should as soon as possible step off its isolationist fence and join what remained of the free world in fighting back against Hitler. In speech after speech he called obliquely or directly upon America and its President Franklin D. Roosevelt to abandon neutrality and declare for the Allies. In this broadcast, early in 1941, he coined the phrase that has come to epitomise all such appeals, but in the event it was the Japanese bombing of the US fleet at Pearl Harbor, Hawaii, ten months later that actually obtained him his wish.

CHURCHILL, WINSTON

The nation had the lion's heart. I had the luck to give the roar.
in 1954

Churchill made this comment about his own wartime role in a speech made on his 80th birthday.

CHURCHILL, WINSTON

An appeaser is one who feeds a crocodile – hoping that it will eat him last.
in 1954

Churchill was never a great one for compromise at any stage of his lengthy career. Often this led him into foolhardy policies or opinions, equally often it underlined his reputation as a man, if not of principle, then at least of principles. His lengthy campaign against the appeasement policies of Baldwin's and especially Chamberlain's governments might be said in the first instance to have failed. Britain did not begin rearming until far too late, and Hitler was in no way restrained from his domination of Europe. But in the long term it succeeded. By 1940, as the public sickened of Chamberlain's vacillations and his lack of strategic initiative, it was to Churchill, who had for years been calling for a stronger nation, that they, and the House of Commons, instinctively turned.

CHURCHILL, WINSTON

I do not see any other way of realising our hopes about World Organisation in five or six days; even the Almighty took seven.
minute to Roosevelt, 21 January 1945

Churchill, Roosevelt and Stalin met to sort out the post-war world at the Yalta Conference of January 1945. Roosevelt was already a very ill man (he died in office on April 12 1945) and hoped to get everything out of the way in five or six days at the most. Unlike Churchill, he had a naive faith in Stalin, and thought that an agreement would be simple and would require minimal controversy. Churchill was less sanguine and more pragmatic, to which end he sent this minute to Roosevelt, warning him of the struggle ahead. In the event the Western Allies were unable to influence

Stalin and such World Organisation as did emerge was very much as the Soviet leader desired it. Churchill's lines are reminiscent of Clemenceau's exasperated comment on President Woodrow Wilson's Fourteen Points, upon which he wished to base the treaty of Versailles in 1919: 'Mr. Wilson bores me with his Fourteen Points. Why, God Almighty has only ten.'

CHURCHILL, WINSTON

He is a sheep in wolf's clothing.
on Attlee

Clement Attlee, who became Britain's Labour prime minister in 1945, had been Churchill's deputy during the wartime coalition government. Churchill was unimpressed by this rather reticent man, who lacked his own flash and fire. 'A modest little man', he called him, 'with much to be modest about', and added that while one could respect him, one could never admire him.

CHURCHILL, WINSTON

The Stone Age may return on the gleaming wings of science.
quoted in 1948

The Manhattan Project, founded in 1939 and geared to developing the researches of the world's top atomic physicists into the awesome weapon that became the atomic, and latterly the nuclear, bomb, produced what the Western leaders required of it when in August 1945 the first bomb exploded the equivalent of 20,000 tons of TNT over the Japanese city of Hiroshima. Churchill, who like the other Western leaders had studiously ignored those scientists who warned of the bomb's hideous potential, was suitably impressed. His remark altered no policies, but it was all too accurate. It also reflected his general suspicion of scientists, resenting their technological mumbo-jumbo, while enthusiastically deploying the fruits of their expertise. As he put it, 'Scientists should be on tap but not on top'.

CHURCHILL, WINSTON

Political skill... the ability to foretell what is going to happen tomorrow, next week, next month and next year. And to have the ability afterwards to explain why it didn't happen.
quoted in 1965

Churchill was always the consummate politician, the more so in an era when political life was conducted to a far greater extent in the House of Commons, where debates could, as Churchill and such adversaries as Aneurin Bevan proved, reach a high and exciting level, rather than in the image-conscious, televised arena of today. His remarks on what makes the good politician have lost none of their relevance, although critics might interpret them as an elaborate euphemism for the ability to cover one's misdirected tracks.

CHURCHILL, WINSTON

When I was younger, I made it a rule never to take strong drink before lunch. It is now my rule never to do so before breakfast.
quoted in L. Harris, *The Fine Art of Political Wit* (1965)

Churchill's appetite for alcohol was well-known and while not an alcoholic, he was far from averse to the more than occasional glass. His contribution to gustatory pleasures was the injunction 'Swill champagne but sip claret', and he joked of his consumption 'I have taken more out of alcohol than alcohol has taken out of me'. He was talking to King George VI on one particularly cold morning when the King suggested that, given the conditions, a preprandial drink might be in order. Churchill was forced to admit that he had already had a nip that morning. The King expressed his surprise, and Churchill replied as above.

CHURCHILL, WINSTON

Mr. Chamberlain loves the working man – he loves to see him work.
speaking in 1904

This attack on Joseph Chamberlain (1836–1914), a precursor of those that Churchill would launch thirty years later on his son Neville, came early in Churchill's political career. It showed his usual lack of fear or favour, since Chamberlain was leader of the Conservative party, and thus his political boss.

CHURCHILL, WINSTON

I cannot forecast to you the action of Russia. It is a riddle wrapped in a mystery inside an enigma; but perhaps there is a key. That key is Russian national interest.
speech, 1 October 1939

Churchill gave this assessment of the Soviet Union's position in a speech early in the war, prior to his becoming prime minister, in which, as first lord of the admiralty, he had been asked to comment on the possible stance Russia would take in the war. He went on to say that although there was no answer, it would all depend on the Russian national interest. He could not envisage just how that interest, currently involved in an allaince with Hitler, would alter when German troops crossed the Russian border in 1941.

CHURCHILL, WINSTON

This is not the end. It is not even the beginning of the end. But it is, perhaps, the end of the beginning.
speech, 10 November 1942

The successful North African campaign of 1941–42 was for the Allies the turning point of the war. Add to that Russia's staunch defence of Stalingrad, which broke Hitler's invasion, and the Japanese attack on Pearl Harbour in December 1941 which forced the Americans into the conflict, and Churchill's statement, made in a speech to celebrate the victory in Egypt, seemed not to be grossly over-optimistic.

CHURCHILL, WINSTON

We must beware of needless innovations, especially when guided by logic.
speech, 17 December 1942

It was suggested in the House of Commons that the titles of minister of defence and the secretary of state for war should both be changed, since in neither case did the name logically fit the job. Replying to this suggestion, Churchill made it clear that in politics, as elsewhere, to be guided by pure logic was not always the optimum way.

CHURCHILL, WINSTON

If Hitler invaded Hell, I should make at least a favourable reference to the Devil in the House of Commons.
speech, 1941

Some of Churchill's finest vituperation was reserved for the Axis leaders. Mussolini was 'a whipped jackal' and Hitler, among other things 'this bloodthirsty guttersnipe', 'Corporal Hitler' and 'a squalid caucus boss and butcher'. Churchill's proposed alliance with the Devil refers to his advocacy of Russia after Hitler decided to repudiate the Nazi-Soviet Pact and invade the USSR on June 22, 1941. Churchill had been a lifelong opponent of Bolshevism, but in this instance he was the first to welcome a new ally, under whatever circumstance.

CHURCHILL, WINSTON

Dictators ride to and fro upon tigers which they dare not dismount. And the tigers are getting hungry.
While England Slept

While England Slept is Churchill's attack on the dalliance of successive governments in the face of the increasingly militant European dicatorships of Nazi Germany and Fascist Italy. His image is one of prowling beasts, unleashed by riders who must go where their mount chooses to take them, and as the Thirties progressed, the tigers were looking further and further afield for their prey.

CHURCHILL, WINSTON S.

It was with a sense of awe that (the Germans) turned upon Russia the most grisly of all weapons. They transported Lenin in a sealed truck like a plague bacillus from Switzerland into Russia.
The World Crisis (1923–29)

Churchill was an avowed supporter of the *ancien régime*, a hereditary aristocrat who espoused democratic forms but looked more to the hierarchical past than to any future of socialist equality. He candidly loathed the leaders of the Russian revolution and all their works. He vilified Lenin as above and added of the Russians that 'their worst misfortune was his birth, their next worst – his death'. The deposed Leon Trotsky was 'a skin of malice... he possessed in his nature all the qualities requisite for the art of civic destruction – the organizing command of a Carnot, the mob oratory of a Cleon, the ferocity of a Jack the Ripper, the toughness of Titus Oates'.

CHURCHILL, WINSTON S.

The battle of France is over. I expect that the Battle of Britain is about to begin... . Let us therefore brace ourselves to our duties, and so bear ourselves that, if the British Empire and its Commonwealth last for a thousand years, men will say 'This was their finest hour.'
broadcast, 18 June 1940

Before the war Churchill had not been seen as a great broadcaster, the problem he had pronouncing his 's' didn't help and his style was seen as too rich for a mass medium. During the war, when Britain required a higher-flown brand of oratory, he proved ideal and a number of his speeches to the Commons were repeated for the radio audience. This speech, on June 18 1940, was interpreted as yet another disguised plea to the United States. Writing his memoirs after the war, he called the pertinent volume 'Their Finest Hour', and wrote of the following year: 'The Battle of Britain was won. The Battle of the Atlantic now had to be fought'

CHURCHILL, WINSTON S.

Never in the field of human conflict was so much owed by so many to so few.
speech, 20 August 1940

Obviously, said one irreverent and possibly apocryphal fighter pilot, 'That must refer to mess bills', but with his undeniable flair for the right words at the right time, Churchill's tribute to the RAF pilots who fought the Battle of Britain against the Luftwaffe during the late summer of 1940 has remained high on any list of great British patriotic quotations. Churchill allegedly worked up the sentence after a personal visit to a Fighter Command operations room in mid-August when, overwhelmed with emotion, he sat silent in his car, before coming out with the line.

CHURCHILL, WINSTON S.

We shall not flag or fail. We shall go on to the end, we shall fight in France, we shall fight on the seas and oceans, we shall fight with growing confidence and growing strength in the air, we shall defend our island, whatever the cost may be, we shall fight on the beaches, we shall fight on the landing grounds, we shall fight in the fields and in the streets, we shall fight in the hills, we shall never surrender.
speech, June 4 1940

Plucking victory from defeat in the traditional manner, the British public, typified by the *Daily Mirror* headline 'Bloody Marvellous', saw the evacuation of the defeated British Expeditionary Force as a national triumph. It had been, of course, a superb rescue act, but as France crumbled and the Germans were left supreme in Europe, it appeared that only time lay between England and an invasion. Speaking to the House on June 4, with 338,226 troops (of which 225,000 were British) safely evacuated, Churchill delivered this speech, and ended this rousing peroration with the hope that, were all else to fail 'in God's good time, the New World, with all its power and might, steps forth to the rescue and liberation of the Old.' 'Until then', he muttered sotto voce amid the cheers, England would have to 'beat the buggers about the head with bottles: that's all we've got'.

CIARDI, JOHN (1916–) American poet and critic

Gentility is what is left over from rich ancestors after the money is gone.
in the *Saturday Review*

Ciardi has combined a career of teaching, at Harvard and Rutgers Universities, with working as the poetry editor of the *Saturday Review* from 1956–72 and producing his own poetry. His earliest collection was *Homeward to America*, which was followed by further volumes of verses, including *In Fact* (1962). His translation of Dante's *Divine Comedy* (1956, 1961) has been widely acclaimed and his critical essays have been published as *Dialog with an Audience* (1963) and *Fast and Slow* (1975).

CIORAN, E.M. (1911–) French philosopher

The history of ideas is the history of the grudges of solitary men.
Syllogismes de l'amertume (1952)

Cioran's thesis is that safe in a community, people tend to carrry on much as before, demanding certain material comforts but deriving their chief happiness from the cosy security of doing what everyone else does and assuming, therefore, that on the whole it is the right thing to do. It is from those who are excluded from the community, or who have chosen to ignore its easy seductions, that ideas that change the world come. There must be, of course, many more 'solitary men' working out their grudges than there are new ideologies, and the line between the lonely crank and the inspiration of a new world, like so many divisions between success and failure, is doubtless thin.

CIORAN, E.M.

Tyrants are always assassinated too late. That is their great excuse.

CIORAN, E.M.

The hour of their crime does not strike simultaneously for all nations. This explains the permanence of history.
quoted in *The Faber Book of Aphorisms* ed. Auden & Kronenberger (1964)

CIORAN, E.M.

No-one recovers from the disease of being born, a deadly wound if ever there was one.
The Fall into Time (1971)

CIORAN, E.M.

One is never so much a man as when one regrets being so.
The Fall into Time (1971)

CIORAN, E.M.

All that shimmers on the surface of the world, all that we call interesting, is the fruit of inebriation and ignorance.
The Fall Into Time (1971)

CITIZEN KANE

It is the only disease you don't look forward to being cured of.
script by Herman Mankiewicz and Orson Welles (1941)

As Thompson, the reporter for 'News on the March', makes his way around Charles Foster Kane's former friends and associates, looking for 'an angle', he meets Bernstein, Kane's former business manager (Everett Sloane). After extracting such reminiscences as the old man has to offer, Thompson is leaving when Bernstein asks about another associate, Jed Leland (Joseph Cotten), Kane's former college classmate and subsequent employee. Thompson gives the address, a hospital, and adds 'Nothing particular the matter with him, they tell me. Just — ' and Bernstein cuts in 'Just old age. (smiles sadly) It's the only disease you don't look forward to being cured of.'

CITIZEN KANE

I think it would be fun to run a newspaper.
script by Herman Mankiewicz & Orson Welles (1941)

The model for Citzen Kane, William Randolph Hearst, began his career as a newspaper owner when at the age of 24 he decided to buy up the debt-ridden *San Francisco Examiner* and, by devoting himself wholeheartedly to the task of offering 90% entertainment to a grudging 10% of news, exceed the success of that other master of what became known as 'yellow journalism', Pulitzer. Whether or not he made the remark that Mankiewicz and Welles gave their fictional media czar is unknown, but Kane, whose purchase, promotion and principles in running his fictional 'New

York Enquirer' mirror almost exactly Hearst's techniques, certainly did. It appears in the form of a letter to the lawyer Thatcher, who has been responsible for the young Charles, but who comes to loathe him and all his works, especially the journalistic ones.

CITIZEN KANE

I guess Rosebud is just a piece in a jigsaw puzzle – a missing piece.
script by Herman Mankiewicz & Orson Welles (1941)

Citizen Kane draws in most respects on the larger-than-life career of William Randolph Hearst (1863–1951), America's foremost newspaper magnate of his era, whose empire dominated contemporary media. In writing the script, however, it was seen as necessary to throw in what Alfred Hitchcock would call a 'MacGuffin', a red herring that acts as a plot device and little more. In Kane's case the device consisted of his alleged last word, 'Rosebud'. The framework of the film is the searching of the film magazine reporter Thompson (William Alland) for the meaning of this final word. As the viewer discovers in the scene where the youthful Kane is plucked from obscurity to enormous wealth, the word is simply the brand-name of the sleigh with which he is playing when the lawyer Thatcher (George Colouris) arrives at his mother's humble cabin. In the film's final scene, as Kane's vast collections are catalogued and burnt, Thompson delivers this line as we watch the sleigh, its trademark shrivelling in the heat, vanish into the flames.

CLARK, KENNETH (1903–83) (Lord Clark) British author, art historian and public official

Television is a form of soliloquy.
quoted in the *Guardian*, 1977

Lord Clark was one of Britain's leading art historians. His first book, *The Gothic Revival* (1928), was influenced heavily by Ruskin and by Bernard Berenson, with whom he worked in both England and Florence, and was widely admired as both original and daring. From 1934–45 he was director of the National Gallery and he held a variety of public offices, including the chairmanship of the Arts Council, throughout his life. Clark was instrumental in the establishment of the English National Opera and of commercial television. He travelled widely. His most important contribution to art history is *The Nude: A Study of Ideal Art* (1953). He wrote two volumes of autobiography.

CLARK, KENNETH

I believe that order is better than chaos, creation better than destruction. I prefer gentleness to violence, forgiveness to vendetta.... . I think knowledge is preferable to ignorance and I am sure that human sympathy is more valuable than ideology... . I believe in courtesy, the ritual by which we avoid hurting other people's feelings by satisfying our own egos. And I think we should remember we are part of a great whole, which for convenience we call nature. All living things are our brothers and sisters. Above all, I believe in the God-given genius of certain individuals, and I value a society that makes their existence possible.
Civilisation – A Personal View (1970)

As one who was intimately involved in the earliest days of commercial television, taking the post of the first chairman of the Independent Television Authority (ITA, now IBA), Clark was committed to this new medium, for all that in so many ways it ran directly counter to the values of the art he loved and understood. His very first TV appearance had been in 1937, on the first arts programme to be screened, and in the 1950s, combining the one interest with the other, he began fronting a variety of arts-related programmes, on topics such as 'What Is Good Taste?'. All in all there were 48 such programmes. *Civilisation*, his multi-part review of the development of the European civilisation from the Dark Ages until 1914, was screened by the BBC to enormous interest and many plaudits in 1969.

CLARKE, ARTHUR C. (1917–) British science writer

When a distinguished but elderly scientist states that something is possible, he is almost certainly right. When he states that something is impossible, he is very probably wrong.
Profile of the Future (1973)

Clarke has been one of the foremost advocates of the potential of space since his article 'Extra-terrestrial relays' (1945) became the basis of the development of communications satellites. His book *The Exploration of Space* (1951) was the first of many which attempted to enthuse a larger public with Clarke's own fascination with space flight. In parallel to his non-fiction works Clarke began establishing himself as one of the world's most popular authors of science fiction. In 1968 he wrote with Stanley Kubrick the script for *2001: A Space Odyssey*. Clarke took up residence in Sri Lanka in 1956, from which base he continues to play an

196

important role in the theoretical side of space travel and to write his science fiction.

CLAUDEL, PAUL (1868–1955) French writer and diplomat

Gentlemen, in the little moment that remains to us between the crisis and the catastrophe, we may as well drink a glass of champagne.
speech 1931

This speech was delivered by Claudel in his role as French ambassador to Washington, a job he combined with the writing of plays and poetry. Claudel had a lengthy and distinguished career in the French diplomatic corps, representing his country all around the world. A convert from atheistic scientific determinism to pious Catholicism in 1886 (a plaque in Notre Dame Cathedral commemorates the instant of revelation), his writing is consistently informed by the presence of divine providence, without which, he asserts, all is meaningless. Claudel created what became known as *verset claudélien*, a mixture of Rimbaud and the Old Testament, which found its form in long, rhythmical, free-form, high-flown language. Claudel was resolutely conservative in politics as in religion and served the Vichy government as minister of propaganda.

CLEAVER, ELDRIDGE (1935–) American activist

Americans think of themselves as a huge rescue squad on twenty-four hour call to any spot on the globe where dispute and conflict may erupt.
Soul on Ice (1968)

Cleaver was born in the black slums of Los Angeles; his youth from the age of twelve was spent in a variety of penal institutions and he was jailed from 1957–66 for rape. During this period he read widely, concentrating on various radical texts. On the basis of this self-education, he wrote the essays that appeared to great acclaim as *Soul On Ice*. They dealt with race relations in America: with white racism and the black anger and self-hatred it generated. Cleaver's work was quickly established as a revolutionary textbook and he became on his release an influential member of the ultra-radical Black Panther Party. Pressure from the authorities drove the Panthers underground and Cleaver left the country. He has since returned, bereft of all radicalism, to join the materialist rat-race of Mr. Reagan's America.

CLEAVER, ELDRIDGE

You're either part of the problem or part of the solution.
Soul on Ice (1968)

Cleaver's line, like the book which contained it, became one of the favourite texts of the revolutionary groups of the late 1960s. The White Panthers, a pale reflection, in every sense, of their Black role models (although they too suffered police attacks and railroading by the US courts) used it constantly, and it has even been attributed to their leader, John Sinclair.

CLEMENCEAU, GEORGES (1841–1929) French statesman

War is too serious a business to be left to the generals.
comment in 1917

As a patriot and a radical, who combined searing attacks on both governmental and military incompetence with the ruthless suppression, as minister for home affairs in 1906, of French strikers, Clemenceau, in a similar way to his English junior Winston Churchill, embodied his nation's dogged determination in the face of foreign attacks. In 1917 Clemenceau, who had already been prime minister from 1906–09, was brought back after other leaders had failed. He reviled the government's defeatism and flayed the army's failings. As he understood it 'War is a series of catastrophes which result in a victory.' Once that victory had been gained he dealt only reluctantly with President Wilson, whose preaching left him cold. American power was vital to France, nonetheless, and in 1920 the refusal of the US Senate to ratify the Treaty of Versailles, which thus destroyed the Anglo-American agreement to guarantee France's eastern borders, led to his defeat in parliament and the end of his career.

CLEMENCEAU, GEORGES

We have won the war: now we have to win the peace.
comment, 11 November 1918

Clemenceau made this comment to General Mordacq on the evening of Armistice Day, 1918. A sense of enormous relief flooded through Europe and America, but for all the optimism, the national leaders knew that any treaty negotiations would involve tough bargaining, and that any satisfactory reorganisation of the world would be very hard to achieve. As events turned out, the botched Treaty of Versailles proved to be little more than a collection of grievances that in a very few years would begin providing justification for another world-wide conflict.

CLEMENCEAU, GEORGES

Mr. Wilson bores me with his Fourteen Points; why, God Almighty only had ten.
quoted in 1919

Woodrow Wilson, very much aware that America's vital incursion into World War I had taken her from the back rooms of international relations and placed her firmly at the top table, came to the peace negotiations held at Versailles in 1918–19 armed with Fourteen Points. Insufferably smug and unjustifiably arrogant, he claimed that America had not fought as an ally, but as an 'associated power', and as such was not party to any agreements that France and England might already have made. Instead he offered his own programme, which replaced political imperialism with a moral brand, based on the destruction of the three defeated empires of Germany, Turkey, and Austria-Hungary and their replacement with autonomous states. There was to be disarmament, arbitration in place of war, and the establishment of a league of nations. Europe was unimpressed by Wilson's preaching. He was forced to make many compromises and the Treaty of Versailles neither satisfied the American public nor, as it proved, set Europe to rights.

CLEMENCEAU, GEORGES

How can I talk to a fellow who thinks himself the first man in two thousand years to know anything about peace on earth?
quoted in Thomas A. Bailey, *Woodrow Wilson and the Lost Peace*

Clemenceau liked England and found himself easily able to communicate with her prime minister, Lloyd George, but the progress of the peace talks at Versailles in 1918–19 was seriously impeded by his inability to deal with the American President Wilson. Clemenceau disliked America, describing it as 'the only nation in history which has miraculously gone directly from barbarism to degeneration, without the usual interval of civilisation'. As the *Morning Post* put it, 'Mr. Wilson's name among the allies is like that of a rich uncle, and they have accepted his manners out of respect for his means', but taking American money did not mean accepting the President's Fourteen Points. Neither European leader was especially charitable to his peers. Clemenceau snorted, 'Lloyd George believes himself to be Napoleon, but President Wilson believes himself to be Jesus Christ', and Lloyd George, challenged later with negotiating an inadequate agreement, responded 'Well, it was the best I could do, seated between Jesus Christ and Napoleon Bonaparte.'

CLITHEROE, JIMMY   (1915–72) British radio comedian

Don't some mothers 'ave 'em?
in *The Clitheroe Kid*, 1950s

The Clitheroe Kid was a British radio comedy which ran from 1958-72, starring the eponymous, squeaky-voiced Lancashire comedian. The show lasted until the 'Kid', now a somewhat aged 57, died. This line, its catchphrase, derived from a popular slang expression used to decry a particularly foolish action or statement. A BBC television series, *Some Mothers Do Ave Em*, starring the comedian Michael Crawford as a particularly stupid and, for those who resisted his charms, irritating young man, ran from 1974–79. Jimmy Clitheroe has been resurrected as a cheeky schoolboy, in a uniform far too traditional for the average comprehensive, as part of the children's TV show *The Crankies*.

COCKBURN, ALEXANDER   (1945–) British journalist

The First Law of Journalism: to confirm existing prejudice, rather than contradict it.
in *More* magazine 1974

Cockburn, the eldest son of the radical journalist Claud Cockburn, began his career as a leader of the New Left movement that emerged in London in the late 1960s. 'New' in that they had abandoned the old-line Communism of the old Left, the radicals of the 1930s, and substituted their own contemporary ideological line. Their main outlet was the *New Left Review*, and Cockburn wrote with Robin Blackburn the important *Student Power* (1969). In the early 1970s he emigrated to America, to write the influential Press Clips column for the soft-left *Village Voice*. Cockburn fell foul of his own law when, criticising Israel in a predominantly Jewish town, he found himself accused of anti-Semitism and lost his job. He remains an influential freelance writer.

THE COCOANUTS

What's a thousand dollars? Mere chicken feed. A poultry matter.
script by George S. Kaufman and Morrie Ryskind (1928)

The Cocoanuts was the first Marx Brothers film, taken directly from their successful Broadway play. The plot is set in contemporary Florida, then enjoying an unprecedented if short-term land boom, pioneered by another set of brothers, the architect Addison Mizner and his rapscallion sibling Wilson. The film is as important for its preservation of the (relatively) young Marx

Brothers as for its intrinsic charms, although Groucho manages a few puns like that above, and Harpo, untrammelled by the problems of sound recording, still in its infancy, rises above it all to carry the show and, incidentally to establish the Marx Brothers as film favourites.

COCTEAU, JEAN (1889–1963) French writer, artist and film maker

Cocteau was a central figure in the modernist movement, although unlike many of his peers, such as Diaghilev, Picasso and Stravinsky who dealt respectively in the ballet, painting and music, he had an artistic facility that made it possible for him to involve himself in not one but several disciplines. As well as creating material he was one of the movement's foremost and most active publicists, bringing the avant-garde to the fashionable world. Cocteau produced work as a poet, painter, novelist, film-maker, playwright, critic and essayist. In all these milieux, his greatest creation was himself and he concentrated as much energy on defining the role of 'the Poet' as he did in pursuit of open homosexual amours, a number of which resulted in his chaperoning some talented but unknown young man into fame and fortune. Heavily influenced by Freud he made a number of films which concentrate on the importance of unconscious inspiration to the creative mind.

COCTEAU, JEAN

The essential tact in daring is to know to what extent one can go too far.
Le Coq et l'Arlequin

COCTEAU, JEAN

The greatest masterpiece in literature is only a dictionary out of order.
Le potomak

COCTEAU, JEAN

What the public like best is fruit that is overripe.
quoted in the *The Faber Book of Aphorisms* (1964)

COHAN, GEORGE M. (1878–1942) American entertainer
　　　　We'll be over, we're coming over
　　And we won't come back till it's over, over there.
Over There (1917)

Cohan was a true Broadway legend, the youngest of a vaudeville quartet, The Four Cohans, who was plucked from obscurity one night in 1904 when the young producer Sam Harris, not much better known than Cohan himself, saw him on stage and offered his life savings to back the boy in his own show. By the time Cohan struck the deal Harris was out of cash and had to borrow the £25,000 from a Philadelphia gambler, but the show *Little Johnny Jones* with its showstopper 'Give my regards to Broadway' made both men. They put on fifty musicals in the next 15 years, many of them massive hits. Cohan's song hits included 'Yankee Doodle Dandy', 'Mary's a Grand Old Name', and the one that sanctified him as America's 'Mr. Stars and Stripes', 'Over There', a patriotic ballad struck hot from the jingoistic fervour that sent the doughboys to Europe. Cohan's refusal to recognise the actors' union, Equity, damned him on Broadway after 1920, but he still worked and his greatest memorial is James Cagney's portrait in the biopic *Yankee Doodle Dandy* (1942).

COHN, NIK (1946–) British writer

Generation to generation, nothing changes in Bohemia.
Awopbopa loobopa lopbamboom (1969)

Cohn's column in *Queen* magazine, running through the mid-Sixties, was possibly the best and most stylish example of the new genre, rock journalism, that emerged like so much else from that era. His dry, terse style, replete with spot-on images, provided Swinging London's own small contribution to the New Journalism. Cohn's book *Awopbopa loobopa lopbamboom*, a title taken from the Little Richard song 'Tutti Frutti' (1957), remains one of the best of its type, preaching Cohn's gospel: Good music stopped when Elvis met the US Army, and after that, what was new? After the Sixties Cohn retired, as was fashionable, to the country. Later he moved to New York and a piece on working class discos, published in *New York* Magazine's June 7 1976 issue as 'Tribal Rites of the New Saturday Night', became the monster movie hit *Saturday Night Fever* (1977).

COHN, NIK

When you've made your million, when you've cut your monsters, when your peak has been passed...what happens next? What about the fifty years before you die?
Awopbopa loobapa lopbamboom (1969)

Cohn's obsession, running through this catalogue of Fifties and early to mid-Sixties rock, and echoed in at least two of his novels, is summed up in the question he asks here. The essence of pop success is make it young, and if you've lived out the dream, what else is there? Either like Cliff Richard you become all-family, all-anodyne entertainment or like Jimi Hendrix, Janis Joplin, Keith Moon and so many more, even including, in his way, Cohn's hero Elvis Presley, you live fast, die young and leave an at least presentable corpse.

COLE, G.D.H.   (1889–1959) British economist and historian

Voting is merely a handy device; it is not to be identified with democracy, which is a mental and moral relation of man to man.
Essays in Social Theory (1950)

George Douglas Howard Cole was a leading theorist of the British Labour movement who combined an academic career at Oxford with a substantial and authoritative output on the intellectual history of the Labour movement. Initially a Fabian, he was converted to socialism after reading William Morris' *News from Nowhere* (1891). He became involved in the Guild Socialist movement from 1913–24, during which time he wrote a number of books which stressed the dangers of an omnipotent state while simultaneously advocating the overthrow of capitalism. He abandoned this relative extremism, although he always advocated the maximum of democracy within industry, calling for nationalisation under parliamentary control and the establishment of democratic socialism. As light relief Cole and his wife Margaret collaborated on a number of detective mysteries, all very popular in their day.

COLETTE   (1873–1954) (Sidonie-Gabrielle Colette) French novelist

The only really masterful noise a man makes in a house is the noise of his key, when he is still on the landing, fumbling for the lock.
quoted in *The Wit of Women*, ed. L. & M. Cowans

Colette began her writing career as unloved wife and barely paid ghost-writer to her husband Henri Gauthiers-Villars, known as Willy. When she wrote her own book, *Claudine à l'école* (1900), in which her own undeniable talent was embellished by the titillating (for the time) details of adolescent sex that her husband persuaded her to add, it was instantly successful. Thus independent, she left her husband in 1906 and spent some years working in the Parisian music halls. In 1920 she published *Chéri*, the story of a gigolo and his ill-fated, passionate entanglement with an older woman, which established her firmly as a literary success. Her most successful book, although not her best, was *Gigi* (1943), which was made into a musical and then a hit film. Colette died in 1945, a respected figure in the French literary establishment and honoured with a state funeral.

COLLINS, JOHN CHURTON   (1848–1908) British lecturer and critic

Never claim as a right what you can ask as a favour.
in the *English Review*, 1914

Collins was one of the pioneers of the academic recognition of the study of English literature in curricula of English universities, which in the 19th century were generally restricted to Latin and Greek classics. Pushing his view in many controversial articles in the *Quarterly Review* and the *Pall Mall Gazette*, he gained the support of such luminaries as Matthew Arnold, T.H. Huxley and A.C. Swinburne. Not until 1893 was he successful, when English literature was established as a final honours school at Oxford. In 1904 Collins was appointed professor of English at Birmingham.

COLLINS, MICHAEL   (–1922) Irish nationalist

I am signing my death warrant.
signing the Irish Treaty, 1921

Collins was one of the most dedicated members of the Irish nationalist movement, Sinn Fein. Unlike the movement's founders, who had preached non-violence, Collins believed in guerrilla warfare, or as his opponents called it, terrorism. For two years from 1919 Collins led members of what was now known as the Irish Republican Army on a series of daring, bloody attacks on the British authorities in Ireland. Despite the efforts of the security services the government seemed powerless to stop the IRA. Not until December 6, 1921, when the Irish Treaty formally established the 26-county Irish Free State, did the terrorism stop. Collins, putting his name to the Treaty, remarked 'I am signing my death warrant'. The signing of Treaty took the immediate pressure off the British government but launched a period of vicious internal strife in Ireland. In August 1922, just as he had predicted, Collins, who was the first chairman of the provisional government, was shot down by his former comrades-in-arms.

COLSON, CHARLES (1931–) American government official

I would walk over my grandmother if necessary to get Nixon re-elected.
quoted in 1972

Colson, on whose office wall was framed the Green Berets' slogan 'If you've got them by the balls their hearts and minds will follow', prided himself on being the hard-assedest player on the Nixon White House team, an all-purpose Mr. Fixit, described in a 1971 news story as 'one of the original backroom boys...the brokers, the guys who fix things when they break down and do the dirty work when necessary'. As special counsel to the President Colson was heavily involved in CREEP, the Committee to Re-elect the President, and as such in the deepest machinations of the government corruption that became known as the Watergate Affair. Indicted for his role in the Affair, Colson plea-bargained his punishment down to a wrist-tapping sentence of 1–3 years of which he served only six-and-a-half months. Now a Born-Again Christian, Colson's exploitation of the lucrative lecture circuit ensures that he is reaping exactly where once he sowed.

COME FILL THE CUP

A lush can always find a reason if he's thirsty. Listen. If he's happy he takes a couple of shots to celebrate his happiness. Sad, he needs them to drown his sorrow. Low, to pick him up, excited, to calm him down. Sick, for his health and healthy, it can't hurt him ... a lush just can't lose.
screenplay (1951)

Even by the self-conscious standards of Hollywood's treatments of social topics, in this case alcoholism, *Come Fill the Cup*, based on the novel by Harlan Ware, was no critical success and far from the same league as the classic *The Lost Weekend* (1945). Cagney plays a newspaperman, on the wagon now, who operates his own in-house AA group, giving jobs to ex-alcoholic newsmen. Cagney, tough but still struggling with the demon drink, is asked by his boss to wean the boss's son off the bottle. Less than keen, he offers this homily but sets to work. The wonderful/awful scene is the exodus of Cagney's hacks to comb the city's low-life bars, once their own nemesis, for the wandering millionaire's boy. A happy ending, of course.

COMFORT, ALEX (1920–) British sexologist

An erection at will is the moral equivalent of a valid credit card.
New York Times, 1978

COMPTON-BURNETT, IVY

Comfort was one of the pioneer sexologists of the 1960s, and one of the few Britons in a profession that remains a particularly American phenomenon. A doctor who, in Gay Talese's words 'brought a bedside manner to an orgy', he wrote one of the most popular of all sex guides 'The Joy of Sex', a no-nonsense sexual DIY manual, which has now marked up millions of world-wide sales. Comfort practised initially as an obstetrician and gained a reputation for his permissive views on sex. In 1970 he moved to California as senior fellow of the Center for the Study of Democratic Institutions and joined in the burgeoning world of sexual experimentation that was developing in the state. Since then he has maintained his varied career as philosopher, physician and active sex researcher.

COMPTON-BURNETT, IVY   (1884–1969) British novelist

Real life seems to have no plots.
in the *Guardian*, 1973

Dame Ivy's personal life suffered badly in the First World War and the protracted mental and physical breakdown she experienced meant that her literary career was postponed until 1925 when her first novel *Pastors and Masters* appeared. She wrote 19 novels in all, usually with the same 'X & Y' title style, all set around 1900 against a background of large, run-down houses with an extended family, almost invariably dominated by a tyrannical parent or grandparent, surrounded by industrious servants. These houses seem almost hermetically sealed off from outside life and within them, as in some sociological hothouse, all manner of luxuriance, both sacred and profane, is allowed to flourish. Believing that 'nothing is so corrupting as power', Dame Ivy's claustrophobic novels, conducted almost completely in dialogue, observe what happens when power is abused and its victims have no escape.

CONDON, RICHARD   (1915–) American novelist

It is the rule, not the exception, that otherwise unemployable public figures inevitably take to writing for publication.
quoted in *Esquire* magazine

Condon's original career was as a film publicist, working for twenty years from 1938 in the American and British film industries. His first novel, *The Oldest Confession*, appeared in 1957, and his first best-seller *The Manchurian Candidate*, which mixed anti-McCarthyism with Communist Chinese brain-washing fantasies, in 1960. Like several other Condon novels, this was made into a successful film. Condon proposes the conspiracy, rather than the cock-up, theory of history and has drawn on a variety of actual political events, notably the assassination of President Kennedy, as well as on his own experiences of many different countries, to create his wide range of stories.

CONNOLLY, BILLY (1942–) Scottish comedian

The door opens...crash! And in he comes. The Big Yin. With the long dress and the casual sandals.
in 1975

Billy Connolly's scabrous evocations of his working-class Glasgow childhood and adolescence, the values and vanities of which he uses to tackle any subject, both sacred and profane, have won him enormous fame as a comedian. The Big Yin is the star of his very personal version of the New Testament: Jesus Christ

CONNOLLY, CYRIL (1903–74) British critic, essayist and connoisseur

Cyril Conolly was born into an upper-class English family, with strong Irish connections, but his appearance in lowly Coventry symbolised a life that for all that it was lived in the haute monde was never, as far as its subjects was concerned, quite sufficiently of it. 'At Eton with Orwell/At Oxford with Waugh/He was nobody afterwards/And nothing before', ran his savage self-appraisal, but he was overly cruel. Always a stylist, a perceptive critic and a pungent aphorist, he remained an integral part of the English literary establishment until his death. He is best known for two collections of essays: *Enemies of Promise* (1938) and *The Unquiet Grave* (1945), as well as for his co-founding with Stephen Spender of the magazine *Horizon*. Connolly began writing criticism for the *New Statesman* in 1927, he was literary editor of the *Observer* from 1942–43 and subsequently reviewed regularly for the *Sunday Times*.

CONNOLLY, CYRIL

Destroy him as you will, the bourgeois always bounces up. Execute him, expropriate him, starve him out en masse, and he reappears in your children.
writing in 1937

In 1937 Connolly visited Spain, still in the throes of its Civil war. Unlike the commitment of his prep school and Eton contemporary George Orwell, who condemned such frolickers as 'the pansy left', his Spanish adventures were merely a stopover in a self-indulgent tour of Europe, accompanied by various smart friends. He was only fashionably left-wing, a devotedly fire-breathing salon Marxist who could savage the bourgeoisie in print but remained their faithful admirer in the flesh. No-one so unashamedly elitist and so driven by the dictates of style could ever really be expected to pay much more than lip-service to the proletariat.

CONNOLLY, CYRIL

Those whom the gods wish to destroy, they first call promising.
Enemies of Promise (1938)

The premise of this book is 'a didactic inquiry into the problem of how to write a book which lasts ten years', but its real subject is the insidious prevalence of factors that militate against that achievement. Among these 'enemies' are domesticity, politics, drink, journalism, conversation and above all, success itself. In his chapter devoted to escapism – 'The Poppies' – he excoriates promise: 'Fatal word, half-bribe and half-threat...the burden of expectation which we can never fulfil'. A paragraph decrying teachers and relations, friends and critics, all vaunting one's alleged promise, ends with this parody of Sophocles' line in Antigone 'Whom Jupiter would destroy he first makes mad', itself transmuted into the popular English proverb.

CONNOLLY, CYRIL

All charming people have something to conceal, usually their total dependence on the appreciation of others.
Enemies of Promise (1938)

After charting the wide variety of temptations lying in wait for the aspirant writer, Connolly asks in a chapter entitled 'Outlook Unsettled': 'What consolations can be offered them?' He analyses the optimum literary form and looks at the novel, at humour, the short and long story, comedy, poetry and the stage and suggests the best relationship with health, sex and money. The great thing to avoid is failure, which is so infectious, and it is the charming failure whom he describes above. The writer, he states, must be totally ruthless with these 'aimiable footlers' unless he is to be dragged down with them.

CONNOLLY, CYRIL

There is no more sombre enemy of good art than the pram in the hall.
Enemies of Promise (1938)

Sex, according to Connolly, is not conducive to creative excellence. Not so much simple sex, and elsewhere he advocates the love affair – both happy and unhappy – as a spur to literary effort, but in its more complex forms. On one hand the homosexual is hamstrung through his inability to portray accurately the relations between men and women; on the other the married man is aesthetically ruined by the demands of family life. While a nagging wife and screaming children may be avoided, economic demands run contrary to creative ones and second-rate work – journalism, broadcasting – will be forced on all but the lucky few who possess a private and substantial income. He can hope only for a sympathetic wife who will appreciate the restrictions of domesticity on art and offer the writer some privacy from the quotidian round.

CONNOLLY, CYRIL

Literature is the art of writing something that will be read twice; journalism what will be grasped at once.
Enemies of Promise (1938)

Journalism was to Connolly essentially second-rate, even at its best. It rejected the luxurious complexities of what he called the 'mandarin style', that of Donne, Addison, Johnson, Gibbon, Ruskin and their peers, replacing it with 'less exacting entertainment', aimed at and demanded by the mass public, literate but hardly literary. It was not confined to the press, where it might have been acceptable, but permeated all writing, creating the 'modern movement'.

CONNOLLY, CYRIL

The bestseller is the golden touch of mediocre talent.
Journal and Memoir, ed. D. Pryce-Jones (1983)

Connolly was employed as a proof-reader and occasional reviewer at the *New Statesman* in 1927. Such relatively minor tasks proved insufficiently satisfying and he used his spare time to write a number of aphorisms, in the manner of *Trivia*, a whole volume of such lines compiled by Logan Pearsall Smith, his former employer. They were not published but included this line, and others such as 'It's a wise worm that knows its own turning' and 'The three vices: meanness, insincerity and meanness'. The success of glittering mediocrity remains a constant sixty years on.

CONNOLLY, CYRIL

Always be nice to those younger than you, because they are the ones who will be writing about you.
Journal and Memoir, ed. D. Pryce-Jones (1983)

David Pryce-Jones wrote his memoir of Connolly, a family friend of long standing, in 1983, as context for Connolly's *Journal*, which he had kept between 1928–37. This remark was 'something...I remember him repeating' and the generally sympathetic tone, albeit critical in parts, of Pryce-Jones' reminiscences, the only attempt at a biography to date, bear out the prudence of its subject's dictum.

CONNOLLY, CYRIL

The greatest problem with women is how to contrive that they should seem our equals.
Journal and Memoir, ed. D. Pryce-Jones (1983)

This ur-sexist remark was doubtless of its era, but Connolly's relations with women do seem to have precluded much equality. There are mistresses, wives, secretaries and assistants and of course a large number of the rich. It is in these latter that he sees some means of achieving the appearance of equality, suggesting that while they cannot manage intellectual parity, their economic independence and social chic offers some form of parallel status. Similarly he acknowledges that 'the depth of experience thrust by life upon the underworld' provides criminals, will-nilly, with an intensity almost equal to 'that which we have chosen for ourselves.'

CONNOLLY, CYRIL

The artist is a member of the leisured classes who cannot pay for his leisure.
Journal and Memoir, ed. D. Pryce-Jones (1983)

In Connolly's ideal world, based on his appreciation of and perhaps fantasies concerning the role of the writer in the 18th century, the artist should be allowed absolute freedom to indulge his aesthetic sense. His creativity excluded him, de facto, from the dull labours of duller men. On a practical level, since few artists enjoyed a private income, this meant a patron. The problem in the 20th century, he felt, was that the leisured classes from whom such patrons were drawn were less generous to the artistic than of old and thus artists were forced, to their detriment, into the ranks of the journalists and the reviewers.

CONNOLLY, CYRIL

The rich, particularly rich women, exist to facilitate things.
Journal and Memoir, ed. D. Pryce-Jones (1983)

Like Zero Mostel in *The Producers* Connolly was an expert manipulator and charmer of rich women, his 'Top Ten Play-Girls'. He saw himself as giving them by his company an intellectual cachet that they otherwise lacked, and felt it only fair that in return he should be given the run of the one thing they had that he lacked: money. As he put it: 'A lot of pain and nuisance might be avoided if the rich would only appreciate the point when love becomes money'.

CONNOLLY, CYRIL

Only two things are worth having – money which you have not had the trouble of earning, and irresponsibility.
Journal and Memoir, ed. D. Pryce-Jones (1983)

The artist, said Connolly, must be in a position of freedom, to afford the pursuit of all possible choices all of the time. There must be no bounds to this freedom, particularly those of insolvency and economic need. Thus the pure artist should be untrammelled by responsibility and garlanded with unearned wealth.

CONNOLLY, CYRIL

English Law: where there are two alternatives: one intelligent, one stupid; one attractive, one vulgar; one noble, one ape-like; one serious and sincere, one undignified and false; one far-sighted, one short; EVERYBODY will INVARIABLY choose the latter.
Journal and Memoir, ed. D. Pryce-Jones (1983)

Like many members of the high Bohemia, where social status

attempts to blend with socialistic theory, Connolly found it in the end impossible genuinely to love the masses. These lines, written during his infatuation with the left, epitomised in various exhortatory pieces in the *New Statesman*, in line with the fashionable left-wing tenets of the era, prove that elitism will always out.

Connolly, Cyril

The only way for writers to meet is to share a quick pee over a common lamp-post.
Journal and Memoir, ed. D. Pryce-Jones (1983)

Writers are surly brutes, solitary individuals who prefer lonely writing to social chat. When they meet, according to Connolly, they are 'truculent, indifferent, or over-polite'. The crux of such encounters is whether or not they have read each other's work and, if so, what they thought of it. Only when allied against a common foe, usually a publisher or a third, absent writer, can they, as far as such pleasures are possible, enjoy themselves.

Connolly, Cyril

He would not blow his nose without moralising on conditions in the handkerchief industry.
The Evening Colonnade (1973)

Connolly knew George Orwell when he was still Eric Blair. They shared the same prep school, St. Cyprian's in Eastbourne, and in twin essays – Orwell's 'Such, Such Were the Joys' and Connolly's 'A Georgian Boyhood' – provided their own versions of its regime. Later they both won scholarships to Eton, but after Eton, when Connolly went on to Oxford and thence to a lifetime in London society, intellectual and social, Orwell chose a harsher route. For him Connolly's fashionable and short-lived Marxist principles were but the 'pansy left'. In turn Connolly remarked on Orwell's obsessively earnest socialism, in itself as far from the working classes it championed as Connolly's own aesthetic preoccupations.

Connolly, Cyril (Palinurus)

The civilised are those who get more out of life than the uncivilised, and for this the uncivilised have not forgiven them.
The Unquiet Grave (1945)

Civilisation, to Connolly, was 'Proust in Venice, Matisse's birdcages overlooking the flower-market at Nice, Gide on the 17th century quais of Toulon, Lorca in Granada, Picasso by Saint-Germain-des-Prés'. The modern world of the 1930s, with its abandonment of the past for the allure of the new, is constitutionally incapable of creating civilisation. Civilisation is an elite pleasure and the masses, with their gross tastes, are not only uninterested in it for themselves, but determined that no-one else shall be allowed to enjoy it.

CONNOLLY, CYRIL (PALINURUS)

The more books we read, the clearer it becomes that the true function of the writer is to produce a masterpiece and that no other task is of any consequence.
The Unquiet Grave (1945)

This is the opening line of the first section of Connolly's collection of essays, aphorisms and celebrations of both literary and sensual pleasures, all denied the inhabitants of wartime London. The dissatisfaction that permeated Connolly's professional career and which left him, in his own assessment, as a poor second to such talented contemporaries as Waugh, Betjeman and Anthony Powell, is well expressed in this sentence. As a professed aesthetic purist, Connolly had no choice but to extol the virtues of the masterpiece, although as a critic he was faced constantly with lesser efforts.

CONNOLLY, CYRIL (PALINURUS)

Our memories are card indexes consulted, and then put back in disorder by authorities whom we do not control.
The Unquiet Grave (1945)

In the passage from depression to suicidal despair and thence to some form of recovery, the third part of Connolly's book, 'La Clé des Chants' (The key to the songs) represents a glimmer of hope, of a possible cure for the pervasive melancholy. These lines come early in the section, where Connolly is mourning his lost love and itemising places and things that still symbolise it to him. He is also paraphrasing Nicolas de Chamfort (1741–94), whose work he quotes extensively. In his *Maximes et Pensées*, Chamfort suggests that 'Society and the World are like a library where at first glance all seems in order, for the books are arranged according to their shapes and sizes, but where, on closer scrutiny, there is seen to be utter confusion...'.

CONNOLLY, CYRIL (PALINURUS)

There is sanctuary in reading, sanctuary in formal society, in the company of old friends, and in the giving of officious help to strangers, but there is no sanctuary in one bed from the memory of another.
The Unquiet Grave (1945)

Among the sub-texts of this collection of aphorisms, quotations and reflections is Connolly's mourning for the decline and failure of his first marriage. Shrinking from 'the ten-year torture of two faces', he finds no solace in parting, in adultery, in the compensations of a new partner. The past 'with its anguish' refuses to go away and only time, if anything, will heal the wound.

CONNOLLY, CYRIL (PALINURUS)

Truth is a river that is always splitting up into arms that reunite. Islanded between the arms the inhabitants argue for a lifetime as to which is the main river.
The Unquiet Grave (1945)

Connolly quotes Aristotle 'The knowledge of opposites is one' to back up his concept of the 'two-faced truth,... the Either, the Or and the Holy Both' as the cornerstone of his philosophical belief. The point of such a truth is the ability to see the dualities of life, the comedy and the tragedy, the mental side of the physical and vice versa. For the artist this means to bring 'imagination to science and science to imagination'.

CONNOLLY, CYRIL (PALINURUS)

We are all serving a life-sentence in the dungeon of time.
The Unquiet Grave (1945)

Part Two of Connolly's second collection of reflections on life is entitled 'Te Palinure Petens' (Looking for you, Palinurus) and, starting with the suicides of four of Connolly's friends, is obsessed with melancholy and the author's own suicidal feelings. In pessimistic, sombre and disenchanted passages, he considers decadence, drugs, civilisation and its discontents, and, as ever, the complex role of the artist. The chapter is filled with the bons mots of the great French aphorists Sainte-Beuve, Chamfort and others, and he deals at length with Chamfort's life.

CONNOLLY, CYRIL (PALINURUS)

Imprisoned in every fat man a thin one is wildly signalling to be let out.

The Unquiet Grave (1945)

'That sentence...had already become an everyday tag, had entered the language, although often misquoted, it was an autobiography.' (David Pryce-Jones *Cyril Connolly: Journal and Memoir* 1983). For Connolly the line epitomises the continuing struggle between the aesthetic and the indulgent within his own life, both in the literal form of his sensual appetites and in the more ephemeral one of putting the fine writing he felt he could achieve against what he saw as the lesser criticism which was his forte. The thin man never managed fully to escape and Connolly remained, for all his achievements, profoundly dissatisfied with his career. As he put it elsewhere, 'Obesity is a mental state, a disease brought on by boredom and disappointment.'

CONNOLLY, CYRIL (PALINURUS)

The dread of loneliness is much greater than the fear of bondage, so we get married.

The Unquiet Grave (1945)

Connolly met his first wife Jean Bakewell in 1929 in Paris where, as an eighteen-year-old American heiress, she was studying art. He became deeply obsessed and despite the difference in their ages they were married in America in spring 1930. His comments on marriage scattered through a variety of essays make it clear that in his view once the romance fades, the ties of matrimony offer little to the creative artist. The first few years remained enjoyable, but his journals reveal a mind oscillating between the demands of art and ostensible wedded bliss. By the late thirties, for all that Jean indulged his egocentricity and set no barrier against his philandering, their relationship was over. They finally divorced in 1945.

CONNOLLY, CYRIL (PALINURUS)

We must select the illusion which appeals to our temperament and embrace it with passion, if we want to be happy.

The Unquiet Grave (1945)

Cynicism pervades *The Unquiet Grave*, a work in which Connolly's exploration of melancholia, fuelled by his own appreciation of the futility of man's search for happiness, plunges ever-deeper into his own disenchantment. Human life is worthless, lovers exist only for mutual torture, 'beneath a mask of selfish tranquillity nothing exists except bitterness and boredom' – these and much more are the conceits of a deeply miserable man and he parades Santayana's and Aristotle's definitions of happiness only to shatter them with his own mordant condemnation. Only the mad, who have given up the struggle with reality and have surrendered to an all-embracing illusion, may possibly be considered happy.

CONNOLLY, CYRIL (PALINURUS)

The civilisation of one epoch becomes the manure of the next.
The Unquiet Grave (1945)

In Connolly's view, emphasised by the cynical pessimism that dominates this book, each civilisation is founded upon the decadence of its predecessor. As a new culture reaches its apogee, decay sets in and luxury, scepticism, weariness and susperstition combine to undermine the once seemingly endless stability. Just as young people seek inevitably to take over from the old, so do thrusting, raw young nations and cultures struggle to displace and replace the old.

CONNOLLY, CYRIL (PALINURUS)

Life is a maze in which we take the wrong turning before we have learnt to walk.
The Unquiet Grave (1945)

This aphorism is among Connolly's own contributions to a section of his book entitled 'The Wisdom of Pascal'. If one agrees with Freud, he suggests, then most of life is devoted to the sublimation of the raw self that the psychoanalysts call the 'Id', the repository of greed, anger, fear, vanity and lust. The problem according to Connolly is that humanity has already blundered disastrously before it has managed to shuck off even a tiny part of that negative baggage.

CONRAN, SHIRLEY   writer and novelist

Our motto: Life is too short to stuff a mushroom.
Superwoman (1978)

Shirley Conran, former wife of Sixties design guru Terence Conran, the founder of the chain of Habitat stores, and mother of

Eighties couturier Jasper Conran, initiated her own media stardom with this massively best-selling guide for the newly liberated woman of the Seventies. Its premise, epitomised above, was that in the brave new world of feminism triumphant, there were better things to do than put together little dinners for hubby's business pals. Subsequently Ms Conran has written a number of highly successful popular novels.

COOK, A.J.   (1885–1931) British trade unionist

Not a penny off the pay, not a minute off the day.
slogan for miners, 1920s

As part of the gradual decline of the British mining industry that followed the return of the mines to private ownership in 1921, after a brief period of nationalisation during the First World War, the miners were faced by attempts by their employers to reduce wages and increase hours of work. The miners held a three-month strike and their leader, Cook, coined this slogan. The government responded by setting up a Royal Commission under Sir Herbert Samuel, but their report, in March 1926, failed to satisfy either party. The impasse resulted in the General Strike of May 4-12, 1926, and while this was short-lived the miners' strike lasted a full seven months. Defeated in the end, they both lost pennies and gained minutes.

COOKE, ALISTAIR   (1908–) British journalist and broadcaster

The most damning epitaph you can compose about Edward - as a prince, as a king, as a man – is one that all comfortable people should cower from deserving: he was at his best only when the going was good.
Six Men (1977)

Cooke, America's favourite professional Englishman, wrote his study of six men he had both known and admired in 1977. They were Charles Chaplin, H.L. Mencken, Humphrey Bogart, Adlai Stevenson, Bertrand Russell and Edward VIII. The essence of this portrait is that while the boy was indeed golden, the man proved sadly dross. In his essay Cooke recalls his own part in the Abdication crisis, while working for the BBC in New York, and looks at the British constitution as regards such problems. In the end he is unable to find much to praise in a monarch who was a victim both of his birth and of what he chose to do with it; these closing lines provide a final condemnation.

COOLIDGE, CALVIN (1872–1933) American president

The chief business of the American people is business.
speech in 1925

'Silent Cal' Coolidge was America's thirtieth president, a Republican, elected in 1924. He looked, as Alice Roosevelt Longworth put it, 'as if he had been weaned on a pickle', but from that pursed personality there came a few quotable lines, of which this is most celebrated. He offered it to a meeting of US newspaper editors in 1925. A man whose own mediocrity was the very source, in cynical eyes, of his great appeal, he had, in the words of H.L. Mencken 'no ideas, but he was not a nuisance'. It was of Coolidge that the dismissive quip, attributed in the way of such otherwise sourceless lines, to one of two wits – Dorothy Parker or Wilson Mizner – was uttered. On hearing of his death in 1933, the wit in question asked 'How can they tell?'

COOPER, DIANA (1892–1986) British aristocrat and socialite

Age wins and one must learn to grow old.
quoted in P. Ziegler, *Diana Cooper* (1981)

Diana Cooper, third daughter of the eighth Duke of Rutland, was both an exceptionally brilliant social figure and a beauty whose charms never faded. She grew up in the last years of Edwardian England, moving as the figurehead of a set whose social and intellectual attainments were cut off by its destruction in the First World War. After the war she appeared memorably, and motionlessly, in Max Reinhardt's *The Miracle*. This role was primarily designed to help finance the career of her husband, the erstwhile playboy and nascent politician Alfred Duff Cooper. She remained a leading socialite throughout her life, and shone as Cooper's wife during his appointment as Ambassador to France after World War II. To many people she is best known as the inspiration for Evelyn Waugh's Mrs. Stitch, who first appears, characteristically conducting her levee, in *Scoop* (1938).

COOPER, GARY (1901–1961) American film star

From what I hear about Communism, I don't like it, because it isn't on the level.
testifying to the House Committee on Un-American Activities, 1947

The anti-Communist furore that became known as McCarthyism, from its major proponent Senator Joseph McCarthy, and witch-hunting from its main characteristic, saw in Hollywood a ripe source of the publicity which, far more than the actual discovery of a genuine 'red' threat, provided the justification for its power and existence. Socialism had been fashionable in the late Thirties, as much a way of justifying Hollywood's vast incomes as a statement of real commitment, and many people had joined the Party, if only briefly. Such associations may have been short-lived, but they were savaged by the Committee's members. The industry's bosses, fearful of their receipts, kow-towed to McCarthyism, and many stars followed suit. Among them was Cooper, described by Carl Sandburg as America's 'most beloved illiterate'.

COOPER, TOMMY (1922–198?) British comedian

Just like that!
catch phrase

Cooper spent seven years in the Horse Guards before turning to comedy. In his first audition he bungled all his prepared magic tricks but the watching agent assumed the fluffs were part of the act: Cooper never looked back. A huge, ungainly figure, Cooper, topped with his scarlet fez, specialised in these supposed disasters, failing in every trick until, ending the act, he carried off one flawless, climactic effect. This catchphrase, delivered with a flourish, accompanied his increasingly futile efforts. He debuted at the London Palladium in 1952, moving steadily up the programme until he first topped the bill in 1971. His success transferred to television and he remained a star attraction until he died, suffering a heart attack in the middle of a performance.

COREN, ALAN (1938–) British humourist

Television is more interesting than people. If it were not, we should have people standing in the corners of our rooms.
quoted in *The Penguin Dictionary of Modern Quotations*, ed. J.& M.Cohen (1981)

Alan Coren was for the ten years until 1987 editor of *Punch*, a magazine he has managed to take as far as possible from its Victorian origins, although not from its role as the comfortable disseminator of quintessentially middle-class humour. His own writing is the reason many people take the magazine, and this example is typical of his gently satirical wit.

CORNFELD, BERNARD (1928–) American businessman

Do you sincerely want to be rich?
slogan of International Overseas Services 1960s

International Overseas Services was established by businessman Bernard Cornfeld in the 1960s as one of the largest ever mutual fund organisations. IOS claimed to offer the best ways of avoiding tax and currency regulations and its salesmen promoted a variety of alluring investment plans. These salesmen were the key to IOS's success, and eventually to its downfall. The essence of the organisation was the sale, not the product, and Cornfeld's team were trained rigorously in the art. Indoctrinated in Cornfeld's European headquarters, they learnt up a catechism of which the most vital question was 'Do you sincerely want to be rich?' The answer was obvious, but the salesmen had created a hollow edifice. IOS grew increasingly unstable and collapsed at the end of the Sixties, and its founder faced a seven year investigation for fraud. He was eventually acquitted and now lives in California. Among his other, less salesworthy bons mots is 'A beautiful woman with a brain is like a beautiful woman with a club foot.'

CORNFORD, FRANCES (1886–1960) British poet

> **Oh why do you walk through the fields in gloves,**
> **Missing so much and so much?**
> **Oh fat white woman whom nobody loves.**

To a Fat Lady Seen from a Train

Cornford was the granddaughter of Charles Darwin and the wife of the Cambridge classics scholar Sir Francis Cornford, whom she married in 1910. Starting in 1910 she wrote many volumes of verse and her *Collected Poems* appeared in 1954. She remains best known for this triolet. Her son John, also a poet and a committed Communist, was the first Englishman to enlist in the Spanish Civil War, during which he died in 1936.

COSTA, SAM British comedian

Good morning sir, was there something?
in *Much Binding in the Marsh*, late 1940s

The concept of *Much Binding in the Marsh*, of which this was one of the standing catchphrases, developed from the wartime BBC services radio show *Merry Go Round*, which featured contributions from forces' entertainers. The RAF section brought together Richard Murdoch, already a star in the prewar *Bandwagon*, and Kenneth Horne, who ran a business career in parallel with his burgeoning radio celebrity. Their fictional RAF station, part of 'Laughter Command' was named Much Binding in the Marsh and when peace ended *Merry Go Round*, the BBC decided to keep the station on the air, in a new, civilian guise. A third star was Sam Costa, subsequently a top BBC disk jockey; he played a variety of parts, but always made his first appearance with this line.

COTTON, BILLY (1900–69) British band leader

Wakey-wakeeeyyy!

On *Billy Cotton's Band Show*, BBC radio and TV, 1949–69 The Billy Cotton Band Show was a staple of Sunday morning listening throughout the Fifties, before it graduated to television. The chubby Cotton, the paradigm of jolly fat men, roared his catchphrase each week with saloon-bar vulgarity, urging on his band, featuring Alan Breeze ('Breezy'), singer Kathy Kay and others. The phrase was redolent of World War II NCOs unceremoniously ushering huts-full of squaddies into a new day, and Cotton's annual Battle of Britain tribute to 'The Few' plumbed depths of cloying kitsch.

COUBERTIN, PIERRE DE (1863–1937) French sports administrator

The most important thing in the Olympic Games is not winning, but taking part.
on the Olympic Games, 1908

The original Olympic Games developed from regular athletic contests that had been held in Greece from as early as 776BC. They lasted until 388, the 291st Olympiad, after which Christian piety and barbarian raiders put paid to the event until attempts to revive the Games began in 1859. Particularly enthusiastic was Baron Pierre de Coubertin, a physical education fanatic who, after his country's disastrous showing in the 1870 war against Prussia, attributed French weakness to a lack of athletic prowess. 13 countries met in 1894 to initiate a revived Olympiad, scheduled for Athens in 1896. De Coubertin associated himself with the Olympics throughout his life, being the prime mover in the fight against the incursions of professional sportsmen into the competitions. His most famous statement, repeated above, typifies the Games at their most idealistic but between massacres, boycotts, political posturing, TV exploitation, crass nationalism and, of course, shamateurism, they ring less true as each Olympiad rolls round.

COUÉ, EMILE (1857–1926) French psychologist

Every day and in every way I am getting better and better.
catchphrase of 'Couéism' (1923-26)

Coué developed his system of psychotherapeutic autosuggestion at his clinic at Nancy, established in 1910. Here patients would attend to absorb the theory, essentially the continual repetition of this phrase. Coué lectured in England and America and popularised his teachings through his book *Self-Mastery Through Conscious Auto-Suggestion*. Couéism was further proclaimed by his disciples Frank Bennett and Cyrus Brooks, both of whom wrote books on the subject in 1922. Until his death in 1926, after which the movement vanished almost instantly, Couéism became a widespread fad, undermined only by the sad fact that its adherents, try as they might, could rarely see any great improvement.

COWARD, NOEL   (1899–1973) British playwright and actor
Urged on by his stage-mad mother Coward made his first appearance in 1911, playing 'a boy with elfin ears and foul temper' in *The Goldfish*. He wrote his first play in 1918 and became a star in his own celebration of hard-boiled cynicism, *The Vortex*, in 1924. Coward's plays appealed to smart London society: they were brittle, cynical, witty and chic. For all his sophistication and, for the era, amorality, Coward nursed a sentimental streak, offering a naive, jingoistic version of British history in *Cavalcade* (1931). The rise of a less saccharine post-war theatre undermined his popularity and shocked by the change he attacked the 'kitchen-sink school' with a vengeance. Constantly rebuffed, and quite unfashionable, he became a cabaret star, entertaining his now ageing former fans in London and Las Vegas. His diaries reveal a self-obsessed man, overly sycophantic to the Royal Family, ostentatiously patriotic, although he chose to live in Jamaica, and unable to come to terms with his homosexuality. His epitaph may rest with John Osborne, a leading if unwitting architect of his decline: 'Mr. Coward, like Miss Dietrich, is his own invention and contribution to this century. Anyone who cannot see that should keep well away from the theatre'.

COWARD, NOEL

Good heavens, television is something you appear on, you don't watch.

COWARD, NOEL

> **Spoil the child**
> **Spare the rod**
> **Open up the caviar and say**
> **Thank God!**

quoted in *Ritz* magazine, 1984

COWARD, NOEL

Don't put your daughter on the stage, Mrs. Worthington.
Mrs. Worthington

This admonitory line comes from the lyrics of 'Mrs. Worthington',
a song written in form of a letter to the parent of a theatrical
hopeful. It is typical Coward, putting over a witty point with a
clever use of language, rhythm and verse.

> The profession is over-crowded
> And the struggle's pretty tough,
> And admitting the fact
> That she's burning to act,
> That isn't quite enough.

COWARD, NOEL

Certain women should be struck regularly, like gongs.
Private Lives (1930)

Attempting a reconciliation despite the divorce that has ostensibly ended their unsatisfactory marriage, Elyot and Amanda are
living in her flat in Paris. Certain habits, notably the bickering
that wrecked their last attempt at togetherness, die hard and a
row develops. Elyot concludes it by slapping Amanda's face.
Next morning she is chilly, he is flippant as ever. When she
remarks that she had been brought up believing that no man
should strike a woman, he replies as glibly as ever.

COWARD, NOEL

Honeymooning is a very over-rated amusement.
Private Lives (1930)

Amanda is having her honeymoon with her second husband; she
has divorced her first, Elyot, after years of mutual incompatibility.
In the nice coincidence of such things, she finds that her ex is also
honeymooning in this same Deauville hotel. They meet, craning
from their respective balconies. It seems that they are still in love
and they escape their new spouses, hoping that a new and illicit
honeymoon will rekindle their past affections.

COWARD, NOEL

Strange how potent cheap music is.
Private Lives (1930)

Private Lives is probably the most celebrated of Coward's works,
although it post-dates his annus mirabilis, 1925, when he had
four hits running simultaneously in the West End, and most of his

most quoted lines come from it. This particular remark, occasionally misquoted as 'Extraordinary...' has the added point of referring to one of his own songs: 'Someday I'll Find You'.

COWARD, NOEL
Very flat, Norfolk.
Private Lives (1930)

COWARD, NOEL
Moonlight can be cruelly deceptive.
Private Lives (1930)

COWARD, NOEL
Mad dogs and Englishmen go out in the midday sun.
Words and Music (1932)

Words and Music was a revue made of songs and sketches, lacking any coherent plot. For this song, designed to satirise, albeit gently, the stereotypical colonial administrator, Coward chose a suitably foreign scene against which an English couple sit drinking the ritual chota peg. It is delivered by a rickshaw-borne missionary who, for no reason other than the theatrical, begins declaiming this, one of Coward's best-loved songs.

COWARD, NOEL
Just know your lines and don't bump into the furniture.
advice to his peers

COWLEY, MALCOLM (1898–) American critic
No complete son of a bitch ever wrote a good sentence.
in *Esquire*, 1977

Writing in a piece entitled 'Can a Complete S.O.B. be a Good Writer' American critic Malcolm Cowley discusses the eternal problem: what is the relation between personality and art and can one forgive a vile character who happens to be an angelic creator? The myth of the amoral artist dies hard, although Cowley suggests that there is something naively charming in the way that certain writers have attempted to create their own fantasy images, most notably that of Ernest Hemingway. This is hardly the sign of a 'complete SOB'. What Cowley suggests is that while character and art are connected, it is a far cry from absolute vileness to mere roguery, and he posits five commandments to be obeyed by any creative person: He must believe in the importance of his work; he must believe in his own talent; he must honestly express his own vision of the world; he must produce grandly to the limit of his powers; the true work of art must transcend and outlast its author. If, Cowley says, the artist does obey this literary pentalog, then, however perverse his character may be, he remains genuine and not a complete villain.

CRANE, HART (1899–1932) American poet and writer

Love... a burnt match skating in a urinal.
The Bridge (1930)

Crane worked briefly and reluctantly in advertising before a patron's help allowed him to travel and to devote himself to poetry. His most important works are two lengthy poems, obscure and initially dismissed as unintelligible by the critics: *White Buildings* (1926) and *The Bridge* (1930). This latter was his most ambitious effort, its central symbol New York's Brooklyn Bridge, an attempt to capture the whole fascinating, terrifying and utterly complex structure of American life. The poem is full of metaphors and fantastic images, gathering up such characters as Rip Van Winkle, Columbus and Pocahontas. Crane was an alcoholic, whose ambivalent sexual identity and constant preoccupation with money drove him further to drink. In 1932 he killed himself by jumping from a Havana-bound steamer. Witnesses claimed that as he sank he gave them one last cheery wave.

CRISP, QUENTIN (1908–) British writer and autobiographer

Quentin Crisp lived an anonymous, if by most standards bizarre, life for some sixty years before in 1968 he published what turned out to be the first volume of his memoirs, entitled *The Naked Civil Servant*. In it he charted his life as a flagrantly, uncompromising camp figure in an era long before gay liberation had made such antics slightly more acceptable to the straight world. It was filled with wry observations, witty stories and some that were far from comforting. The book, originally called *My Reign In Hell*, sold 3500 hardback copies but even then this self-styled doyen of 'the stately homos of England' remained a marginal figure, until in 1977 he was portrayed by John Hurt in a television adaption of the book. This brought him enormous acclaim and, displaying a wealth of aphorisms, many stories and the same open philosophies that informed his book, he became a celebrity. After years of bed-sit life in London he moved to New York where, while showing little desire for the city's material allure, he found himself a cult figure.

CRISP, QUENTIN

The very purpose of existence is to reconcile the glowing opinion we hold of ourselves with the appalling things that other people think about us.
How To Become a Virgin (1981)

CRISP, QUENTIN

Culture...television programmes so boring that they cannot be classified as entertainment.
How To Become a Virgin (1981)

CRISP, QUENTIN

What is privacy, if not for invading.
How To Become a Virgin (1981)

CRISP, QUENTIN

The English think that incompetence is the same thing as sincerity.
in the *New York Times*, 1977

CRISP, QUENTIN

The young always have the same problem – how to rebel and conform at the same time. They have now solved this by defying their parents and copying one another.
The Naked Civil Servant (1968)

CRISP, QUENTIN

There are three reasons for becoming a writer: the first is that you need the money; the second that you have something to say that you think the world should know; the third is that you can't think what to do with the long winter evenings.
The Naked Civil Servant (1968)

CRISP, QUENTIN

To know all is not to forgive all. It is to despise everybody.
The Naked Civil Servant (1968)

CRISP, QUENTIN

The vie de bohème is a way of life that has two formidable enemies – time and marriage. Even hooligans marry, though they know that marriage is but for a little while. It is alimony that is for ever.
The Naked Civil Servant (1968)

CRISP, QUENTIN

Life was a funny thing that happened to me on the way to the grave.
The Naked Civil Servant (1968)

CRISP, QUENTIN

What better proof of love can there be than money? A ten shilling note shows incontrovertibly just how mad about you a man is.
The Naked Civil Servant (1968)

CRISP, QUENTIN

A pessimist is someone who, if he is in the bath, will not get out to answer the telephone.
The Naked Civil Servant (1968)

CRISP, QUENTIN

Even a monotonously undeviating path of self-examination does not necessarily lead to a mountain of self-knowledge.
The Naked Civil Servant (1968)

CROMPTON, RICHMAL (1890–1969) (Richmal Crompton Lamburn) British writer

Violet Elizabeth (Bott) dried her tears. She saw that they were useless and she did not believe in wasting her efforts. 'All right', she said calmly, 'I'll thcream then. I'll thcream, an' thcream an' thcream till I'm thick.'
Just William (1922)

Crompton taught classics in a variety of schools, but the publication of her first book for children, *Just William*, in 1922 soon turned her into a full-time professional writer. William and his gang the Outlaws, his sister Ethel, brother Robert, long-suffering parents and adversary Violet Elizabeth Bott became enormously popular. Some thirty books appeared and William was transmuted to film and television. Crompton's appeal was to adults as well as children, the former enjoying her command of language and of irony, the latter identifying, as she surely did, with the scapegrace heroes. She wrote for her era and on occasion reflects its more unfortunate prejudices. It is this, no doubt, that has made William a prime target for ideological censorship, and many ism-conscious librarians will only stock the expurgated and utterly inferior revisions of Crompton's work.

CRONKITE, WALTER   (1916–) American newscaster

That's the way it is.
regular sign-off line

As anchorman for the nightly CBS news during the Sixties and early Seventies Cronkite was one of the first celebrity newscasters. His journalistic career began with UPI, for whom he reported World War II from London. Hired in 1950 by CBS to cover the Korean war, his personality proved ideal for television; his ability to put over the simple basics of the most complex situation combined with a Jimmy Stewart populist image was exactly what was required. In 1961 he was appointed to anchor the plum CBS nightly news bulletin. As the decade progressed, he became an institution, the most trusted man in America. Thus in 1968 when Cronkite, after visiting Saigon during the Tet offensive, condemned the war in Vietnam, the nation, like him formerly pro-government, began to change too. Four years later, fronting a special on Watergate, the Cronkite imprimatur was similarly influential.

CROSLAND, ANTHONY (1918–1977) British politician

What one generation sees as a luxury, the next sees as a necessity.
in the *Observer*, 1975

Crosland was a Cabinet minister in all the Labour governments from 1964–77. With the publication in 1957 of his book *The Future of Socialism*, he established himself as the ideologist of the party's social democratic wing. Accepting the theory if not the Tory practice of Macmillan's 'never had it so good' promises, he assumed that capitalism had been sufficiently well reformed to guarantee full employment and economic stability. His concern was with the equitable division of what he saw as the continuing fruits of that stability. Circumstances militated increasingly against this view and by the mid-Sixties Britain was beginning its long and accelerating economic downturn. He died prematurely in 1977, his career unfulfilled.

CULBERTSON, ELY (1891–1956) American bridge champion

Power politics is the diplomatic name for the law of the jungle.
Must We Fight Russia? (1946)

Culbertson was born in Rumania, where he learnt bridge, and after the Russian Revolution emigrated to America where, in 1923, he married a wealthy bridge enthusiast, Josephine Dillan. Together they set about promoting the game through a number of well-publicised tournaments. The Culbertsons were the first major players to adopt the newly invented game of contract bridge, which soon replaced the traditional auction version in most schools. As well as acting as the game's leading publicist, Culbertson involved himself heavily in international peace movements and the movement for a World Government. In 1942 he founded World Federation Inc. and in 1946 the Citizens' Committee for United Nations Reform. He continued to succeed in bridge but fail in politics until his death.

CUMMINGS, E.E. (1894–1962) American poet

Take the so called 'standardofliving'. What do most people mean by 'living'? They don't mean living. They mean the latest and closest plural approximation to the singular prenatal passivity which science, in its finite but unbounded wisdom, has succeeded in selling their wives.
Poems (1954)

edward estlin cummings was born in Cambridge, Massachusetts, where his father was the first ever professor of sociology at Harvard University. Cummings was a flamboyant campus aesthete, indulging his tastes in art and literature. He volunteered for a private ambulance service working in Europe in 1917 but the report of some indiscreet comments in a friend's letter, censored by the military authorities, led to his arrest and incarceration in a French concentration camp. The result of his imprisonment was his first book, *The Enormous Room* (1922). His first volume of poetry appeared in 1925 and he wrote eleven more during his lifetime. Heavily influenced by Apollinaire he experimented widely in typography, the most obvious example of which was his abandonment of the capital letters in his own name, and rejected the usual rules of spelling and pronunciation.

CUMMINGS, E.E.

A politician is an arse upon which everyone has sat except a man.
A Politician

CUMMINGS, SAM American arms dealer

The arms business is founded on human folly. That is why its depths will never be plumbed and why it will go on forever. All weapons are defensive and all spare parts are non-lethal. The plainest print cannot be read through a solid gold sovereign, or a ruble or a golden eagle.
quoted 1978

Cummings is among the most successful of the world's arms dealers, and one of the few who is willing make his profession public. For all that such traders claim that they are doing no more than filling a need, the arms business represents a murky world, filled with moral ambiguities and extremes of realpolitik. Cummings' opinion, cynical though it may be, rings depressingly true.

CUMMINGS, FATHER WILLIAM T.   American priest

There are no atheists in the foxholes.

sermon, 1942

Father Cummings was commenting on the propensity for the otherwise godless soldiery to turn to what they feared might well be a final prayer when pinned down in a tiny exposed defensive position by enemy fire.

CURTIS, CHARLES P. (1891–1959) American lawyer

Fraud is the homage that force pays to reason.

A Commonplace Book (1957)

If force has no conscience, then it need pay homage to no-one. If, on the other hand, it chooses to temper its injustice with a modicum of mercy, then the most likely result will be some form of deception. Even the optimist cannot expect force simply to abdicate the power that is its raison d'être, but force can hope, by weaving a sufficiently fraudulent blindfold, to delude the optimist into thinking that there has been, if nothing else, some relaxation of overt power.

CURZON, LORD   (1859–1925) British statesman

I never knew the lower classes had such white skins.

quoted in Ronaldshay, *The Life of Lord Curzon*

George Nathaniel Curzon, 1st Baron and 1st Marquis of Kedleston, viceroy and governor-general of India, chancellor of Oxford University and holder of many great offices of state, epitomised the aloof aristocrat. He hoped to become prime minister, but his seat in the House of Lords made that impossible, although he held Cabinet rank in Asquith's government and in Lloyd George's wartime administration. He remained at the centre of the British establishment until his death. Curzon was a true grandee, whose comment, while insufferably arrogant, was probably genuine enough.

D

DAILY HERALD
I seem to hear a child weeping.
caption to prophetic cartoon after World War I

Will Dyson, whose haunting cartoons were considered by many to be the sole reason for taking the newspaper, drew for the pro-Labour *Daily Herald* a cartoon offering the paper's views on the conclusion of the Versailles Peace Conference in 1919. It is headlined 'Peace and Future Cannon Fodder'. In it are portrayed the 'Big Four' – Woodrow Wilson, Clemenceau, Orlando of Italy and Lloyd George – as they leave the conference hall. They pass a child, labelled '1940 Class' and the caption, attributed to 'The Tiger' (Clemenceau's nickname), says 'Curious! I seem to hear a child weeping.'

DAILY MIRROR
The price of petrol has been increased by one penny – official.
cartoon published on March 3 1942

The wartime *Daily Mirror* was a genuinely left-wing paper, which had taken the lead in attacking Neville Chamberlain's lacklustre conduct of the war and which continued to provide an active counterpoint to the pro-government Tory majority in Fleet Street. In March 1942 came the humiliating loss of Singapore to the Japanese; the *Mirror's* response was to publish a cartoon by Philip Zec in which was pictured a half-drowned sailor, clinging precariously to a raft tossed by oily seas. The caption, written by Cassandra (William Connor), who had gained a reputation as a scourge of the establishment, read as above. The line could be taken two ways: either it was a tribute to the courage of the merchant navy or, alternatively, a suggestion that the government was helping big business to make money out of human risk. The government was furious. 'It makes me spit' said Churchill, and threatened to use defence regulation 2D, prohibiting 'revolutionary defeatism', to suppress the paper. Most of Fleet Street, irrespective of politics, moved to back the *Mirror*, and the authorities contented themselves with a severe warning.

DAILY MIRROR
Whose finger?
election day front page, October 25 1951

The *Mirror*, always an opponent of a Tory government, traditionally reserved its most unequivocal pro-Labour statements for its election day front page. The election of October 1951 proved no exception. The incumbent Labour government had been losing popularity; for many voters its creation of a welfare state was more than balanced by its seeming inability to end a state of austerity that had persisted long after the war had ended. The *Mirror* chose to make its pitch on a single issue: that of the still relatively novel phenomenon of atomic weaponry. 'Whose Finger On The Trigger?' asked its banner headline, and the story that followed branded Churchill, still the Tory leader, as a dangerous warmonger, who must be restrained. Churchill won the election, the *Mirror's* final push notwithstanding, and sued the paper for its implications. The case was settled out of court; the £1500 damages went to charity.

DALADIER, EDUARD   (1884–1970) French politician

It is a phoney war.
speech, December 22 1939

The Second World War began on September 3 1939 when Chamberlain was finally prevailed upon, two days after Hitler had invaded Britain's ally Poland, to set an ultimatum before the German ambassador. France too declared war on the Nazis and on both sides of the Channel the people prepared for battles, invasions, bombing, gas and all manner of horrors. But nothing happened. Hitler chose to consolidate in Europe. Chamberlain thankfully talked of 'The Twilight War'. The French Prime Minister Daladier, whose policies like Chamberlain's were reactive rather than active and advocated prudence rather than planning, remarked 'C'est une drôle de guerre', a line translated as 'It's a phoney war' and echoed, if not fully believed, by many people. The fantasy crumbled in spring 1940: Germany attacked Norway and Denmark, then turned to France. In June the British army was scraped off the beaches of Dunkirk. The real war had arrived.

DALEY, RICHARD M.   (1902–76) American mayor

Gentlemen, get the thing straight for once and for all. The policeman isn't there to create disorder, the policeman is there to preserve disorder.
press conference, 1968

Mayor Richard Daley of Chicago was among the last of the great American 'bosses', near-omnipotent machine politicians, operating vast networks of patronage, who delivered the votes of their city-fief as and when they, and their national political allies, desired. His credo, as offered to those who suggested that he (and they) might take advantage of this remarkable power, was 'Don't take a nickel, just hand them your business card.' Daley was a Democrat and in 1968 the Democratic National Convention, was held in his city. 1968 was the year of growing protest. The youth movement arrived in Chicago in 1968 looking to make itself heard. Daley was determined to silence them. What followed as thousands of Chicago cops beat up young people and national television recorded every grim moment was later described by the official report as 'a police riot'. Daley called a press conference to defend his policemen. His statement, blissfully malapropistic, couldn't have summed events up better.

DALY, DANIEL SERGEANT, USMC American soldier

Come on you sons of bitches! Do you want to live for ever!
at Battle of Belleau Wood, June 1918

Daly's cry to his fellow soldiers, pinned down by German fire, has immortalised him in American history, and placed him among the ranks of the US marines' most gung-ho heroes, but while no-one denies his bravery or foolhardiness, his lines were hardly original. The exhortation 'Come on, my lucky lads!' was the usual shout from the sergeant-major to his men, waiting nervously to scramble out of their trenches and start the terrifying march across no-man's-land. The phrase has been traced much further back: Frederick the Great of Prussia (1712–86) asked his troops, as they hesitated during the battle of Kolin in 1857, 'Rascals, would you live forever?'. World War II's most ironic use was in 1944 when bandleader Glenn Miller, who hated flying, suggested to his pilot Col. Norman Baesell, that there was no need to fly across a foggy Channel. 'What's the matter, Miller,' asked the Colonel, 'do you want to live forever?'. Neither Miller, Baesell nor their plane was ever seen again.

DANIEL, YULIY (1925–) Russian writer

We are doomed to remember everything and to tell others.
Prison Poems

Yuliy Daniel and Andrei Sinyavsky, both young Russian writers, were the defendants in the first literary show trial held in Russia since the death of Stalin. They were arrested in September 1965 and charged with publishing anti-Soviet propaganda abroad. At their trial, in February 1966 – ostensibly open but in fact restricted to selected members of the public – it was alleged that their books had poked fun at Moscow's Establishment and at the press. Former Stalinists were delighted but liberal opinion, still thawing out after long years of repression, was appalled. The two writers claimed that there had been no anti-Soviet content, merely satire. The real argument behind the trial was against the growing trend of progressive Russian writers, over-censored at home, to have their work published abroad. The Union of Soviet Writers justified the trial as a necessary restraint on the trend. Both men were found guilty and sentenced respectively to five and seven years in labour camps.

DARDEN, SEVERN (1937–) American film actor

Death is nature's way of telling you to slow down.

Darden is one of a number of perennial American character actors, in his case one who happens to specialise in comedy. In a twenty year career staring with *Dead Heat on a Merry-go-round* (1967), he has played secondary roles in many major movies, including *The President's Analyst* (1967), *Vanishing Point* (1971), *Cisco Pike* (1971) and many others. Whether he originated this classic piece of late Sixties graffiti, tipping its flower-bedecked hat to the perils of life in 'the fast lane', is unlikely. He merely happens to be the person to whom, at last count, it was attributed.

DARLINGTON, CYRIL DEAN (1903–81) British geneticist and botanist

Mankind... will not willingly admit that its density can be revealed by the breeding of flies or the counting of chiasmata.
Lecture, 1960

Born in England Darlington was destined to become a farmer in Australia until he read a classic work on genetics as part of his farming studies and changed his life. He talked his way into a research fellowship at the John Innes Horticultural Institute in 1923 and rose to head the cytology department. His pioneering work on the role of chromosomes in heredity resulted in his book *Recent Advances in Cytology* (1932), a small volume that revolutionised contemporary cell studies. He developed his theories further in *The Evolution of Genetic Systems* (1939), a book that blended cytology with studies in population and evolutionary genetics. He continued writing important and at times controversial papers and books until his death.

DARROW, CLARENCE   (1857–1938) American lawyer

When I was a boy I was told that anyone could become President. I'm beginning to believe it.

Darrow stands as one of the greatest defenders at the American bar, whose many cases, often against apparently insuperable evidence, won him an international reputation. Avowedly agnostic, and devotedly humanitarian, he advocated his 'philosophy of mechanism', whereby he insisted that there must be a cause for every anti-social act and that if that cause could be found and removed, then the victim of the cause could be restored to social health and equilibrium. Darrow pursued these liberal principles to the best of his ability. The Scopes case, or the Monkey Trial of 1925, in which Darrow fought prosecutor William Jennings Bryan over the constitutionality of the Tennessee anti-evolution law proved his apotheosis. Darrow eviscerated the 'Great Commoner's' fundamentalism, reducing his beliefs to absurdity. Scopes, the teacher who had volunteered as the centre of this test case, was found guilty of teaching evolution but the verdict was overturned on appeal.

DAUGHERTY, HARRY   (1860–1941) American politician

A smoke-filled room
coining a phrase in 1920

Daughtery was a Republican politician and power-broker who had long schemed towards making his crony Warren Gamaliel Harding president of the US. Harding's showing in three primaries was so poor as to render his candidacy a joke, but Daugherty persuaded him to go on. As he had hoped, the convention of 1920 remained deadlocked and neither of the leading contenders could defeat the other. Daugherty promised newsmen 'The convention will be deadlocked and after the other candidates have gone their limit, some twelve or fifteen men, worn out and bleary-eyed for lack of sleep, will sit down about two o'clock in the morning, around a table in a smoke-filled room in some hotel and decide the nomination. When that time comes, Harding will be selected.' Daugherty then denied the quote, but Harding was selected, and then became president. His term of office was inept by any standard, mixing cronyism, womanising, twice weekly poker games and a blissful ignorance of the demands of his office.

Daugherty was tried, and acquitted, in 1927 for attempting to defraud the US government.

DAVID, ELIZABETH   (1913–) British cookery writer

Some sensible person once remarked that you spend the whole of your life either in your bed or in your shoes. Having done the best you can by shoes and bed, devote all the time and resources at your disposal to the building up of a fine kitchen. It will be, as it should be, the most comforting and comfortable room in the house.
French Country Cooking 1951

If any one person might be said to have revolutionised post-war middle-class English cooking, it must be Elizabeth David whose series of epochal cook books, starting in 1950 with her *Book of Mediterranean Food*, set new standards of culinary style. Her work appeared at an opportune moment: after World War II many families who would have automatically employed a cook no longer did so and the 'mistress' now had to learn her way around a kitchen. Responding to (and encouraging) a growing interest in Europe and the knowledge that 'good plain' English cooking, despite the availability of wonderful ingredients, might indeed have been plain but was rarely good, David's books proved exactly what was required. Her *French Provincial Cooking* (1960) transformed the country's upwardly mobile dinner tables and her influence remains paramount.

DAVIS, BETTE   (1908–) American film star

I see – she's the good time that was had by all.
remarking on a passing starlet

Davis, born Ruth Elizabeth Davis, dominated Hollywood for a decade from 1937. No apparant beauty, she arrived in Hollywood in 1931, when the studio's official greeter failed to recognise her, reporting back to his boss 'No-one faintly like an actress got off the train'. Her first film was *Bad Sister* (1931) and her first Oscar came in 1935 with *Dangerous*. From thereon in, even after she had swapped major female roles for unforgettable character parts in films like *Whatever Happened to Baby Jane?* (1962) and *The Anniversary* (1967) she has remained a larger than life Hollywood queen. Her offscreen persona was as cultivatedly frank and scabrous as her fictional roles and this remark, gutting some hapless ingenue, was well in character.

DAY AT THE RACES, A

Send two dozen roses to room 424 and put 'Emily I love you' on the back of the bill

script by Robert Pirosh, George Seaton and George Oppenheimer (1937)

A *Day at the Races* was effectively created to satisfy Irving Thalberg's demand for a sequel to *A Night at the Opera*, a film that made up for its artistic failings in its economic success. Groucho plays Hugo Z. Hackenbush, a throughly fraudulent doctor given to such asides as 'Either he's dead or my watch has stopped'. Margaret Dumont, the Brothers' long-suffering foil, is Emily Standish, the usual society lady; Chico and Harpo play their stock roles and Thalberg, as ever, threw in some romance and a few love duets. This line, a classic example of Groucho as caddish lecher, climaxes his wooing of Mrs. Standish, the occupant, of course, of room 424. The film, interrupted by Thalberg's premature death, is seen by many as the last of their classics.

DAY-LEWIS, CECIL (1904–72) British poet

To interview a writer is like interviewing a haunted house. The characters he invented flitting between me and the creator. They are substantial things, in a sense more real than the man who gave them life. Good novelists are seldom striking 'personalities' – their life is diffused and drained out through their creations.

in the *Daily Telegraph*, 1967

After Oxford, where he edited *Oxford Poetry* (1927), Day-Lewis worked until 1935 as a schoolmaster but then abandoned teaching for poetry and, under the pseudonym Nicholas Blake, successful detective fiction featuring his detective 'Nigel Strangeways'. As the 'day' of the group Roy Campbell nicknamed 'MacSpaunday', Day-Lewis was initially ranked with MacNeice, Spender and Auden as a left-winger, but he gradually moved to more personal and pastoral themes, as well as making his own translations of the works of Virgil. Elected professor of poetry at Oxford in 1951, he became poet laureate in 1968.

DE BEAUVOIR, SIMONE (1908–86) French novelist and feminist

One is not born a woman, one becomes one.

quoted in *Esquire*, 1971

De Beauvoir is most celebrated for her pioneering study of women and their role vis-à-vis men which she published in 1949 as *Le deuxième Sexe* (*The Second Sex*). In it she uses biology, history, myth and contemporary facts to analyse the position of women. Her central thesis is that women have from time immemorial been conditioned into accepting an essentially secondary role to that played by men. As she sees it, men can integrate their sexual and personal drives, the nature of women's biological and sexual makeup militates against her achieving individual identity and freedom. Thus women are forced to accept marriage and the automatic dependence that the institution implies. Later feminists have predictably condemned this 'exaltation of the masculine' but *The Second Sex* is a vital feminist work. De Beauvoir's own life was intimately tied to that of the philosopher Jean-Paul Sartre, whom she had met at university in 1929. Most of her autobiographical works deal with this central relationship, including the account of Sartre's lingering decline, *The Farewell Ceremony* (1981).

DE BEAUVOIR, SIMONE

What is an adult? A child blown up by age.
La Femme Rompue

DE BONO, EDWARD   British academic

Think Sideways.
The Use of Lateral Thinking (1967)

De Bono's concept of lateral thinking, summed up in this slogan, developed in the 1960s. His theory divided thinking into two methods. One he called 'vertical thinking', the traditional-historical method, which depends on the use of logical proceses. The other, the novel 'lateral' method, required the rejection of logical processes and the fostering in their place of conceptual 'sideways' leaps. Lateral thinking was not new, it was in effect a synonym for institution or perception, but De Bono's coinage, and his proselytising of the concept, brought home the idea of non-logical thought, the way in which many important discoveries have certainly been made, to a wider public. And he stressed, even if one failed to produce true novelty 'the exercise in flexibility is its own reward'.

DE BONO, EDWARD

A myth is a fixed way of looking at the world which cannot be destroyed because, looked at through the myth, all evidence supports that myth.
Beyond Yes and No

DE BONO, EDWARD

Man looks to himself for what he does not find in others, and to others for what he has too much of in himself.
in the *Observer*, 1977

DE FLERS, ROBERT (1872–1927) French playwright

Democracy is the name we give to the people each time we need them.
L'Habit vert (1912)

De Flers collaborated with a number of partners in various works, including satirical plays, comedies and travel sketches. *L'Habit vert* is a typically light-weight comedy, in which the humour far outweighs any possibility of telling satire. It deflates the pomposity and pretentions of France's scholarly pantheon, the Académie Française, an august body founded in 1634 under the aegis of Cardinal Richelieu with a limit of forty members, which limit is still in power. The aim of the Académie is to perfect and maintain the purity of the French language and it is from the forty members that the regular attacks on such bastard-isations as 'franglais' tend to come.

DE GAULLE, CHARLES (1890–1970) French statesman

Charles de Gaulle, a brigadier-general in the French army and in 1940 the under-minister for war in the French government, came to prominence when after the fall of France he established himself as the leader of the Free French government in exile in a broadcast on 18 June 1940. After the Liberation of 1944 he was declared France's provisional president. He resigned after only 10 weeks, when his autocratic and rather un-French style of government failed to convince the voters of his appeal. He returned in 1958 as the president of the Fifth Republic and dominated French politics until a second abrupt resignation in 1969. His absolute faith in himself was roundly criticised; he was accused of Napoleonic, even fascistic tendencies. When in 1958 he was compared to Robespierre he remarked ironically 'I always thought I was Jeanne d'Arc and Buonaparte – how little one knows oneself.' If he saw himself as embodying the greatness of France within himself, then he was equally determined to present that greatness to allies and enemies alike, and the 'entente cordiale' with Britain was often stretched by his patriotic intransigence.

DE GAULLE, CHARLES

You do not arrest Voltaire.
answering demands to arrest Jean-Paul Sarte for treason, 1960

By 1960 the war in Algeria, between the nationalist Algerians, desperate to attain their independence, and the right-wing French colonial forces, equally desperate to stand in their way, had reached the height of its long savagery. Opinions throughout France had become polarised, with the intellectual left, unsurprisingly, standing firmly behind the nationalists. Sartre, as a leading figure of the left, was prominent in denouncing the war and went so far as to to call upon French troops to desert rather than serve in Algeria. When members of the government called upon de Gaulle to arrest the philosopher, the President refused their demands, and ironically (and perhaps consciously) in citing Voltaire echoed in his actions that individual's oft-quoted belief that while one might deplore one's opponent's statement, one must fight for his right to make it in freedom.

DE GAULLE, CHARLES

The graveyards are full of indispensable men.
attributed line

DE GAULLE, CHARLES

In order to become the master, the politician poses as the servant.
in 1969

DE GAULLE, CHARLES

How can you govern a country which produces 265 different kinds of cheese?
speaking in 1951

Taken to its logical conclusion one might as well ask as to the feasibility of governing a country that offers any sort of demonstrable statistic, but de Gaulle's comment, delivered after the election of 1951 when his party won most seats but still failed to achieve an overall majority, has been cited as epitomising his own opinion of the French people. French taste was not homogeneous and attempting to unify the people 'other than under the threat of fear' was impossible.

DE GAULLE, CHARLES

If I am not France, what am I doing in your office?
to Churchill, when appealing for aid for the Free French, 1940

As the Vichy government prepared to collaborate with the occupying Germans, de Gaulle, who had been Under-Minister for War prior to the fall of France, hastened to London to begin coordinating the Free French government in exile. He was taken to see Churchill who remarked to his English companion 'Why have you brought this lanky, gloomy brigadier?' The answer, grim but accurate, was 'No-one else would come'. de Gaulle saw himself as France's representative; in the circumstances, he seemed almost its only one. The two men, each as egotistical as the other, never became close, but Churchill recognised de Gaulle's importance as the focus of French hopes, and de Gaulle had no choice but to call upon Churchill, and later Roosevelt, as allies.

DE GOURMONT, RÉMY (1858–1915) French critic

It is absurd to try to make children's games reasonable and a great folly to try to purify religions.
The Cultivation of Ideas (1900)

De Gourmont worked from 1884–91 at the National Library in Paris before becoming one of the founders of the *Mercure de France*. This famous journal provided a medium for such members of the Symbolist movement as Mallarmé, Huysmans and Valéry to expound their theories. De Gourmont provided the movement with its main critical voice. This critical ethos extended to his novels which, while strong on analysis and philosophy, barely acknowledge the more traditional aspects of fiction. In England he was well known as a contributor to *The Egoist*, a London fortnightly which fostered the emergent modernist movement, and where fellow contributors included Ezra Pound and James Joyce.

DE LA MARE, WALTER (1873–1956) British poet

Is there anybody there?
said the Traveller, Knocking on the moonlit door
The Traveller (1946)

De la Mare worked for an oil company for twenty years, but by 1895 he had begun contributing poetry to various magazines, taking the pseudonym Walter Ramal under which his first collection, *Songs of Childhood*, appeared in 1902. Further books followed but real popularity did not come until *The Listeners* (1912). De la Mare wrote both for children and adults. Volumes

241

for the former included *Peaock Pie* (1913) and *Tom Tiddler's Ground* (1932), and two long, visionary poems, *The Traveller* (1946) and *The Winged Chariot* (1951) looked to adult readers. In a prolific career de la Mare also wrote prose, starting with *Henry Brocken* (1914) and including *The Return* (1910) and *The Memoirs of a Midget* (1921), as well as short stories, perennially successful anthologies and a number of critical works, including a study of Rupert Brooke, under whose will he benefited. De la Mare became a British institution and was awarded the CH in 1948 and the OM in 1953.

DE MONTHERLANT, HENRI (1896–1972) French novelist and playwright

The soul's longing for infinity, a longing which proclaims its weakness and impotence, is the surest sign of its unworthiness of infinity, which will be forever denied it.
Explicit Mysterium (1931)

Strongly influenced by the ideas of D'Annunzio and Gide, de Montherlant expounded in his writing his personal philosophy of masculine hauteur and chivalric standards, openly disdaining bourgeois sentiment. Being himself strongly attracted to all forms of exercise, he advocated vigorous action as the best means of overcoming life's problems, and travelled widely, and often under dangerous circumstances, throughout his early life. De Montherlant fought and was badly wounded in World War I and wounded again in World War II although he was branded, erroneously, as a collaborator, whose macho intellectual stance made him 'the one prominent French author who...welcomed and adulated the enemy.' Certainly he stood far to the political right, and never accepted the tenets of democracy.

DE MONTHERLANT, HENRI

A lot of people, on the verge of death, utter famous last words or stiffen into attitudes, as if the final stiffening in three days time were not enough; they will have ceased to exist three days hence, yet they still want to arouse admiration and adopt a pose and tell a lie with their last gasp.
Explicit Mysterium (1931)

DE SICA, VITTORIO (1901–1974) Italian film director

Moral indignation is in most cases two percent moral, forty-eight per cent indignation and fifty per cent envy.
in the *Observer*, 1961

De Sica began his career as a matinee idol and film actor in 1922, but won greater and more lasting fame as a director whose name is synonymous with the Italian neo-realistic movement that, with his inevitable collaborator, the scriptwriter Cesare Zavattini, he helped create. De Sica directed his last film in the year of his death but his most important works came in a single eight year period, starting with *The Children Are Watching Us* (1943) and including *Shoeshine* (1946), *Bicycle Thieves* (1948), *Miracle in Milan* (1950) and *Umberto D* (1951). All these films share similar characteristics – non-professional actors working in real-life locations and portraying topics taken from the less fashionable areas of society.

DE VRIES, PETER   (1910–) American novelist

The value of marriage is not that adults produce children, but that children produce adults.

De Vries was born in Chicago but has made his reputation as the laureate of the fictional community of Decency, Connecticut, one of those dormitory towns for Wall Street and Madison Avenue whose hard-charging commuters, with their fads, fancies, foibles and general idiosyncracy, make perfect targets for his incisive satire. Since 1944 he has been on the editorial staff of the *New Yorker*, where his urbane wit and verbal sophistication have found the perfect home. His first book, *But Who Wakes the Bugler* (1940), was illustrated by *New Yorker* cartoonist Charles Addams. Further titles include *Tunnel of Love* (1954), *Comfort Me With Apples* (1956), *The Tents of Wickedness* (1959) and *Through Fields of Clover* (1961). De Vries changed tack, perhaps feeling that his satirical inventiveness was palling, and began a number of novels which seem obsessed with religion, including *Blood of the Lamb* (1962) and *The Vale of Laughter* (1968). He lives in the Connecticut that has provided him and his readers with so much amusement.

DE VRIES, PETER

Gluttony is an emotional escape, a sign something is eating us.
Comfort Me With Apples (1956)

De Vries' sixth novel is a tale of small-town marriage with its concomitant infidelity, blackmail and petty crime. The plot concerns the life of one Chuck Swallow, a columnist on the local newspaper. Wending his way between the vicissitudes of other people's lives, Swallow gradually comes to terms with his own realities and puts aside the fantasies that had at times seemed more alluring.

DE VRIES, PETER

Man is vile, I know, but people are wonderful.
Let Me Count the Ways (1965)

This novel is essentially a study in self-consciousness and its chaotic tendency to farce. This is the book's first sentence and sets the tone for the rest. The story has two narrators: Tom Waltz, a junior-level academic, provides most of the story, while his father Stan, a blue-collar autodidact, balances Tom's efforts with a supply of regular end-pieces. Stan's wife Elsie is a born-again Christian; Stan, an atheist, chooses to respond to this by lapsing into alcoholism. Tom's tale concerns his own career and the way in which he has moved towards his marriage. By the end of the book Stan and Elsie have been reconciled; Tom has been to Lourdes, where he manages to fall ill, but as he is nurtured by his wife Marion it may be assumed that their marriage too will last.

DE VRIES, PETER

If there's one major cause for the spread of mass illiteracy, it's the fact that everybody can read and write.
The Tents of Wickedness (1959)

The Tents of Wickedness was published three years after *Comfort Me With Apples* and draws on the same background and many of the same characters. It is the story of one 'Sweetie' Appleyard, babysitter to Chuck Swallow and his wife, and follows her efforts to break free from bourgeois life and make the big jump to Bohemian Greenwich Village in New York City. The best way to achieve this transformation, she decides, is to become pregnant, but this is easier said than done. Through the various complications of the plot it transpires that Chuck, an ostensibly married man, must agree to inseminate her. The resulting chaos is duly resolved and de Vries leaves all his characters far more satisfied with their status quo than they were at the novel's beginning.

DE VRIES, PETER

Life is a zoo in a jungle.
The Vale of Laughter

This book, in which de Vries' interest in religion is paramount, has been termed by its author a 'tragi-farce'. In it the reader follows the entanglements of two couples – Joe Sandwich and his wife Naughty, and their friends Wally and Gloria Hines. As the humour becomes progressively blacker Joe is killed in an absurd accident and Wally begins a new relationship with Naughty, thus ending the story. The quotation above is explained by considering that if zoos may be seen as classifications of jungle life, so they also lead to distortions of it: the animals have time to think and thus fall into needless confusion.

DEAN, JOHN (1938–) American government lawyer

We have a cancer within, close to the Presidency, that is growing.
advising President Nixon on Watergate, March 21, 1973

On June 17 1972 five men were arrested while attempting to break into the Democratic National Headquarters at the Watergate Complex in Washington, DC. Two years later the revelations of the Watergate Affair brought down the Nixon administration. John Dean III was a youthful but ambitious special counsel to the President, willing to go to any lengths for his boss. His catharsis came in a meeting with Nixon on March 21, 1973. His intention was to point out that it was time for the truth and that the proposed cover-up of White House involvement was pointless. Using a metaphor suggested by a senior special counsel, Richard Moore, he talked of 'the cancer'. The President, to his horror, was unimpressed and instead demonstrated to Dean, who still preferred to assume Nixon's innocence, that he knew far more about Watergate than anyone had dared consider. Furthermore it appeared that Nixon had Dean slated as the conspiracy's scapegoat. Between June 25–29 Dean testified before the Watergate Committee: his evidence provided the linchpin for everything that followed.

DEBS, EUGENE V. (1855–1926) American socialist

While there is a lower class, I am in it; while there is a criminal element, I am of it; while there is a soul in prison, I am not free.
speech at his trial in 1913

In 1918 Debs was America's leading socialist, attracting a respectable following in a country primarily devoted to laissez-faire capitalism. Among the by-products of the jingoism that trumpeted America's belated entry into World War I was a flood of sedition prosecutions, brought under the Espionage Act of 1917. Debs denounced such specious prosecutions, which used the European war as an excuse for the persecution of native left-wingers. He was promptly arrested under the same act. At the trial, held in

Cleveland, Ohio, Debs defended himself, telling the jury 'I admit being opposed to the present form of government; I admit being opposed to the present social system. I am doing what little I can to do away with the rule of the great body of people by a relatively small class...'. Such beliefs did not impress the burghers of the Mid West; Debs was found guilty and jailed for ten years. He was freed in 1921 after President Harding granted him a pardon, although he had forfeited his citizenship.

DEDERICH, CHARLES   American therapist and cult leader

Today is the first day of the rest of your life.
slogan c.1969

This hippie slogan, beloved of a million flower-bedecked, bead-jangling utopian optimists, was created by Dederich, the founder of the Synanon anti-heroin centres in California. Like Alcoholics Anonymous, Synanon aimed to help narcotic addicts enter a programme of self-help, with massive backup from sympathetic peers, and using the same principle as AA's 'one day at a time' philosophy. Synanon worked on the principle of the encounter group, but raised to the toughest level with participants indulging in what they called 'the Synanon game', mauling each other's sensibilities with absolute abandon. For a while in the early 1970s Synanon fell into disrepute as it attempted to replace simple anti-drug therapy with a whole new 'alternative' way of life, and Dederich was denounced variously as an egomaniac and a fascist. After those dramatic days the movement returned to more normal rehabilitation but failed to survive the decade.

DEMARTINI, HUGO (1931–) Czech artist

People are always talking about tradition, but they forget we have a tradition of a few hundred years of nonsense and stupidity, that there is a tradition of idiocy, incompetence and crudity.
quoted, 1968, in *Contemporary Artists* (1977)

Demartini was neither talking wholly about art nor wholly about his native country when he pointed out the flaw in arguments for the preservation of tradition. Novelty for its own sake has no specific virtues, and in the 20th century has been the excuse for some wide-ranging cultural destruction, but hanging on to the old, and preserving the sins of which Demartini complains, can only be justified by those whose heads are buried particularly deep in the sand.

DEMPSEY, JACK (1895–1983) American boxer

Honey, I forgot to duck.
December 23, 1926

This phrase, which, usually bereft of its opening endearment, has become the automatic response to those who ask 'Where did you get that black eye?' has two linked sources, both of which refer to boxing. The first comes from the fight between the then world heavyweight champion, Jack Dempsey, with his challenger Gene Tunney in September 1926. Dempsey was widely expected to win, but in the event he did not. When asked by his wife Estelle 'What happened?' the ex-champ supposedly excused his defeat with these words. The alternative version goes back to another fighter, Jack Sharkey, also a champion but hardly in the same league as Dempsey. In a music hall sketch, two comics discuss the big fight, in which Comic A claims to have thrashed Sharkey, actually a Lithuanian sailor called John Cocoskey, for 14 rounds. Why then, asks Comic B, did you lose? In the 15th round, comes the reply, I forgot to duck.

DENNIS, NIGEL (1912–) British writer and critic

It is usually a mistake to confuse the author's point of view with the form he has discovered for it. When the second is admirable, we give him the Nobel Prize for the first.
quoted in *New York Review of Books*, 1971

Dennis was born in England but educated abroad and spent many years in America where he set his first novel. His most celebrated work is *Cards of Identity* (1955). This a a satirical fantasy set in a metaphorical English country house, which Dennis uses as a backdrop to his comments on the social changes that followed World War II and the concomitant undermining of the security and autonomy of the individual. Other novels include *A House in Order* (1966), a further study of the human predicament, in which the narrator, trapped inside a greenhouse, tries Candide-like to cultivate his small plot while ignoring a warring world outside.

DIANE, COMTESSE French aphorist

We often make people pay dearly for what we think we give them.
Maximes de la Vie (1908)

Comtesse Diane was one of the French aphorists who flourished at the turn of the century, an exception only in that she was a woman. Her remark stresses the way in which ostensible generosity, like supposed modesty, demands full payment in the gratitude or the praise of others to whom we have supposedly deferred.

DICKSON, PAUL (1939–) American writer and lexicographer

Rowe's Rule: the odds are five to six that the light at the end of the tunnel is the headlight of an oncoming train.
The Official Rules (1978)

American author Paul Dickson has compiled a dozen books on language-related topics, and the *Official Rules* was an attempt to codify the wide selection of popular dicta, of which Murphy's Law is probably the best known, which are regularly invoked as the inevitable regulations of daily existence. Rowe's Rule, cynically refusing to accept optimistic statements, especially when issued by public figures in whose interest the optimism is being touted, was particularly popular during the Vietnam War. It seemed that every major figure wanted to see that elusive light but the troops, more pragmatic, preferred to proclaim Rowe's deflatory line.

DIDDLEY, BO (1928–) (Elias McDaniel) American rock singer

Dont let your mouth write no cheque your tail can't cash.
in *The Book of Rock Quotes* by Jonathon Green (1977)

This popular saying derives from American black slang, circa 1960. A variation on 'Don't let your mouth overload your ass', and 'Don't let your mouth buy what your ass can't pay for', it was offered by rock musician Bo Diddley. The patron of 'jungle-rhythm' rock 'n' roll started off life as a jazz violinist, abandoning jazz and the violin for the electric guitar and his new name, which he had first acquired as a teenage boxing hopeful, in 1955. His first song' Bo Diddley' established him as a major rock figure and he remains a legend, influencing such bands as the Rolling Stones, the Who and the Yardbirds, even if the flow of hit singles that continued through the late Fifties dried up in the face of his youthful successors.

DIDION, JOAN (1934–) American writer

There is one last thing to remember: writers are always selling somebody out.
Slouching Towards Bethlehem (1968)

Joan Didion, who with her husband John Gregory Dunne has written a number of screenplays for Hollywood, has a parallel reputation for her own novels and non-fiction essays. *Slouching Towards Bethlehem* was the first collection of these essays, in which, taking her epigraph 'Things fall apart; the centre cannot hold' from Yeats' 'Second Coming', she considers various phenomena, both personal and public, deriving from the mid-1960s in America. This line concludes the book's introduction, in which she outlines the pieces included, and offers her apologia for her own particular choice and style. Prior to this climactic warning, she points out 'My only advantage as a reporter is that I am so physically small, so temperamentally unobtrusive, and so neurotically inarticulate that people tend to forget that my presence runs counter to their best interests. And it always does.'

DIDION, JOAN

Innocence ends when one is stripped of the delusion that one likes oneself.
On Self Respect (1961)

Didion's essay deals with the importance of self-respect, an emotion that can only be dismissed with intense effort since 'most of our platitudes notwithstanding, self-deception remains the most difficult deception' and, for her at least, makes the difference between whether or not one can get to sleep at night. Self-respect requires a degree of inner toughness, 'a kind of moral nerve...what was once called character'. In the end it is the willingness to accept responsibility for one's own life. She sums the emotion up as 'Self-respect...is a question of recognising that anything worth having has its price'.

DIETZ, HOWARD (1896–1983) American film publicist

More stars than in heaven
slogan for MGM

Dietz worked for Sam Goldwyn's Goldwyn Pictures as a librettist and writer (his most popular score was for *The Band Wagon* in 1953) and later became the studio's chief publicist. Around 1916 he was asked to design a company trademark and used a lion, the symbol of his former alma mater, Columbia University. This beast he embellished with the slogan 'Ars Gratia Artis', a Latin phrase translated as 'Art for Art's sake'. When Goldwyn merged with Louis B. Mayer to form Metro-Goldwyn-Mayer, the slogan was carried over. Fittingly for a company that boasted the services of Greta Garbo, Clark Gable, Wallace Beery, Joan Crawford, Jean Harlow, Spencer Tracy, the Marx brothers and so many more, Dietz created a new slogan: More stars than in heaven.

DILLER, PHYLLIS   (1917–) American comedienne

Never go to bed mad. Stay up and fight.
Phillis Diller's Housekeeping Hints

Phyllis Diller has remained one of America's foremost television comediennes since the 1960s. Her zany, grotesque style has entranced millions of viewers in her two best known shows *The Pruitts of Southampton* and *The Beautiful Phyllis Diller Show*. Her idiosyncratic appeal failed to transfer wholly successfully to the cinema screen, but in keeping with many contemporary humourists, she has exploited her appeal in print as well as in pictures. This piece of homely advice comes from her own, quite unique 'housekeeping hints'. On an ostensibly more serious front, Diller's dictum is echoed by the words of US senator (for Illinois) Everett M. Dirksen (1896–1969) whose basic theory of politics was enunciated 'Don't get mad, get even.'

DIOR, CHRISTIAN   (1905–57) French dress designer

My dream is to save (women) from nature.
quoted in *Collier's*, 1955

Dior began designing women's clothes in 1935 and in 1944 was asked to set up his own couture house by the cotton magnate, Marcel Boussac. His first collection appeared in 1947. Called 'The New Look' it shocked and delighted women who had been suffering the rigours of austerity for eight years. Defying the cloth shortages that were still declared by the British and American governments, Dior offered sumptuous, traditionally feminine garments, emphasising the bosom, taut around the waist and with full, lengthy skirts. The New Look devastated haute couture and copies spilled over into the mass market. Dior's company boomed and he remained at the forefront of international fashion, expanding his interests until his death.

DIPLOCK, LORD   British lawyer

Censorship is about stopping people reading or seeing what we do not want to read or see ourselves.
quoted in 1971

Censorship is ultimately about fear: the fear of the parent that the child will learn of things that may bruise or worse still break the parental omnipotence. That the child will learn that its parents are not all powerful is less disastrous than that the parents, as Lord Diplock's remark points out, are forced to come face to face with the fact themselves. This works in politics, in national security, in literature and the arts. Whether the censor works from a basis of spiritual or secular religion, touting God or ideology as the basis for his action, the fear of gazing down to one's carefully ornamented feet of clay lies foursquare behind every act of excision.

DIRKSEN, EVERETT (1896–1969) American politician

There is no force so powerful as an idea whose time has come.
at the 1964 Republican National Convention

In 1964 Dirksen nominated for the Presidency the hardline Senator for Arizona, Barry Goldwater. His speech quoted, wittingly or not, the French novelist Victor Hugo who ninety years before had written slightly differently 'No army can withstand the strength of an idea whose time has come'. Goldwater, who campaigned under the slogan 'In your heart you know he's right' paraphrased by his opponents 'In your guts you know he's nuts', found himself the unwilling focal point of America's most fanatical right-wingers and was forced to enunciate many of their more extreme views. Johnson gave him sufficient rope and let him destroy himself. Ironically, Goldwater's demands that the US toughen its stance against Communism helped force Johnson, who had no wish to be seen as a peacenik, to intensify the disastrous US involvement in Vietnam and thus, in time, to engineer his own decline.

DIRTY HARRY

Do you feel lucky...go ahead punk, make my day!
screenplay by H. and R.M. Fink, Dean Riesner and John Milius (1971)

This film was the first of a series of right-wing fantasies that pitted the solo tough cop, 'Dirty' Harry Callaghan of the San Francisco P.D., against the nation's enemies, embodied in the hippie bad guy, a combination sniper/rapist/kidnapper with a peace symbol to boot. Callaghan, who earned his nickname from tackling all the department's 'dirty' jobs, was played by Clint Eastwood, formerly of *Rawhide* and spaghetti Westerns. The line is Callaghan's catchphrase, delivered immediately prior to blowing away some evildoer. Harry also likes to give the victim a rundown on his gun, the prodigiously phallic Magnum .44 'the most powerful handgun in the world'. Directed by Don Siegel, one of the best makers of action movies at work, the film was perniciously alluring.

DIXON OF DOCK GREEN
Evening, all
catchphrase

The Blue Lamp (1950) set the tone for the next decade of British television's police procedurals as surely as did *The Naked City* (1948) for their American peers. The difference, of course, was that English viewers were offered an infinitely more genteel product, epitomised in the long-running programme, more a soap opera than a cop show, *Dixon of Dock Green*. In *The Blue Lamp* Jack Warner, the former star of radio's Garrison Theatre, had played P.C. Dixon, the model British bobby. Dixon had been shot down by tearway Dirk Bogarde but he was revived for the TV show, where he played the avuncular Sergeant George Dixon who might not have done much actual crime-fighting but whose cheery catchphrase 'Evening, all' and regular warning 'If you're on your bike at night, wear white' (a line that harked back to Warner's earlier 'Mind my bike' radio catchphrase) became engraved on the English national consciousness.

DJILAS, MILOVAN (1911–) Yugoslav writer
The New Class
book title 1957

As a former activist and one-time senior Party official Djilas has been no happier under the Communist regime than under a bourgeois one; in April 1954 a succession of disputes with President Tito culminated in his expulsion from all official posts and his resignation from the party. In 1956 he was imprisoned for attacking the corruption and compromises of Communist rule but managed to smuggle out of jail the manuscript of his book *The New Class*. In it he stressed his own disillusion with a movement that claimed to override the old class system but in fact had evolved a 'new class' based on the elite Party apparatchiks. He was released in 1961 but returned to jail a year later after his attack on Stalin, *Conversations with Stalin*, was deemed too critical, even though the former dictator had been officially condemned in 1956. Since his release in 1966 Djilas has lived in virtual internal exile under a regime of which he remains a severe and uncompromising critic.

DOBIE, J. FRANK (1888–1964) American educator and author
The average PhD thesis is nothing but the transference of bones from one graveyard to another.
A Texan in England (1945)

Dobie was professor of English at the University of Texas from 1933–47 and as an expert in the folklore and history of the American South-West published many books on the topic. These included *Vaquero of the Bush County* (1929), based on the memoirs of the cattleman James Young, *Coronado's Children* (1931), tales of lost mines and buried treasure, *Apache Gold and Yanqui Silver* (1939), *Cow People* (1964) and a number of other titles. His experiences as a visiting professor at Cambridge University during World War II are described in *A Texan In England*.

DOCTOR STRANGELOVE

I can no longer sit back and allow Communist infiltration, Communist indoctrination, Communist subversion and the international Communist conspiracy to sap and impurify all of our precious bodily fluids.
screenplay by Stanley Kubrick, Terry Southern and Peter George (1963)

Peter George's original novel, *Red Alert*, dealt factually with the grim realities of what might happen were a high-ranking military commander to take it into his head to launch a nuclear attack on the Soviets. Director Stanley Kubrick began by taking the novel as it stood, but the enlistment of Terry Southern, co-author of the notorious porno-spoof *Candy* (1959), turned this relatively sober plot into a superb black comedy in which a brilliant cast (Peter Sellers in three roles, George C. Scott, Slim Pickens, Peter Bull and Sterling Hayden) dissected the realities of nuclear war with devastating humour. Hayden plays General Jack D. Ripper, commander of Burpelson AFB, whose obsession with fluoridation, and its Communist inspiration, delivers the world to its final apocalypse.

DOCTOR STRANGELOVE

Gentlemen you can't fight in here. This is the War Room.
Script by Stanley Kubrick, Terry Southern and Peter George (1963)

Dr. Strangelove, or How I Learned to Stop Worrying and Love the Bomb, was the first and only nuclear comedy. It featured Peter Sellers in three roles, as the US President, as an RAF officer seconded to a Strategic Air Comman base under the direction of the mad Colonel Jack D. Ripper, as the sinister Dr. Strangelove, a wheelchair-bound ex-Nazi, who was modelled in part on a mixture of rocket scientist Werhner von Braun, futurologist Herman Kahn, and perhaps a smidgeon of Henry Kissinger, although he had yet to ascend to real international prominence.

The film was grimly funny, oscillating between the advancing nuclear bomber, Ripper's Burpelson AFB and the Pentagon war room. In the end, as the soundtrack intones 'We'll Meet Again', the world explodes in a nightmare of mushroom clouds.

DONLEAVY, J.P. (1926–) American writer

Writing is turning one's worst moments into money.
quoted in 1968

Donleavy, an American Irishman, went to Trinity College Dublin to finish his education. Initially intending to be a painter he held four exhibitions of paintings in Dublin, but his real success came with his hilarious and to some obscene and blasphemous novel *The Ginger Man* (1955). Since then he has continued to produce a succession of novels, usually dealing with the lives and adventures of more or less eccentric young aristocrats. Donleavy took Irish citizenship in 1967 and has lived there in some splendour, a Brooklyn American version of Anglo-Irish elitism, ever since.

DONLEAVY, J.P.

But Jesus, when you don't have any money the problem is food. When you have money, it's sex. When you have both it's health, you worry about getting ruptured or something. If everything is simply jake you're frightened of death.
The Ginger Man (1955)

Donleavy's first novel, a loosely autobiographical romp through Trinity College Dublin and environs shortly after the Second World War, was the literary succès de scandale of 1955. This comic, bawdy tale has inevitably been compared to Joyce and it is surely not coincidental that Donleavy's hero, Sebastian Dangerfield, shares his initials with Joyce's, Stephen Dedalus. The speaker is Dangerfield's friend Kenneth O'Keefe, eternally pessimistic, impoverished and randy and, like the hero, making his way through college on the GI Bill. The book was initially published by Maurice Gorodias' Olympia Press in Paris. The first English edition of the book was 'abridged' before it could appear (in 1956) and no unexpurgated edition could be published until 1963.

DORGAN, 'TAD' (THOMAS ALOYSIUS) (1877–1929) American humourist and cartoonist

See what the boys in the back room will have.
quoted in *New York Times* April 23, 1978

Dorgan worked both as a satirical cartoonist and, latterly, as a sports commentator, but his most enduring fame is as the coiner of a number of words, phrases and sayings, many of which still endure. As well as inventing the culinary description 'hot dog' (although the item itself, then called a frankfurter or wienie, was first created by Harry Mozeley Stevens, caterer at the New York Polo Grounds in 1900), the phrase 'nobody home' to describe stupidity and 'yes-man' for sycophant, he gave the world such dicta as 'The first hundred years are the hardest', 'half the world are squirrels and the other half are nuts', 'As busy as a one-armed paper-hanger with the hives', and the line lauded by comedian Will Rogers as 'The Greatest Document in American Literature': 'Yes we have no bananas', although the song of the same name was written by Frank Silver and Irving Cohen in 1923.

DOUGLAS, ALFRED (LORD) (1870–1945) British aristocrat

It pays in England to be a revolutionary and a bible-smacker most of one's life, and then come round.
quoted 1938

Douglas was the son of the 8th Marquis of Queensberry (of the boxing rules fame). He had some minor talent for poetry but his place in history dates from his meeting in 1891 with Oscar Wilde. His family abhorred the relationship and in 1895 Wilde brought a libel suit against the Marquis, which the latter won. Douglas's friendship with Wilde survived the playwright's imprisonment and lasted until his death in 1900. In 1907 a wealthy friend bought *The Academy* magazine and made Douglas editor. Never really involved, he lasted until 1910. He published a great deal of verse, some of which was highly praised at the time, and two books, totally contradictory of each other, on his relationship with Wilde. Highly litigious, he was imprisoned in 1923 for a libel on Winston Churchill.

DOUGLAS, JAMES British journalist

I would rather put a phial of prussic acid in the hands of a healthy boy or girl than the book in question.
in the *Sunday Express*, 1928

James Douglas worked as book reviewer for the *Sunday Express* during the 1920s. A man of hysterically intemperate conservative views, he spearheaded every attack on what he categorised as immoral or indecent books, often bringing the alleged obscenity to the notice of the authorities, while simultaneously exciting gullible public opinion. This, Douglas' most notorious attack, was on Radclyffe Hall's *The Well of Loneliness*. Douglas declined Bernard Shaw's offer to produce a child, a phial and the book in question, were the reviwer to carry out his promise to administer the prussic acid as stated. Joyce's *Ulysses* he found equally frightening: 'I say deliberately that it is the most infamously obscene book in ancient or modern literature.... All the secret sewers of vice are canalised in its flood of unimaginable thoughts, images and pornographic words...its unclean lunacies are larded with appalling and revolting blasphemies...hitherto associated with the most degraded orgies of Satanism and the Black Mass'.

DOUGLAS, KIRK (1916–) American film star

Virtue is not photogenic.

Kirk Douglas (born Issu Danielovitch Demsky) made his film debut in *The Strange Love of Martha Ivers* in 1946 and has continued ever since as one of Hollywood's favourite heroic leading men. His initial parts tended to weaklings and gangsters, but maturity brought him star roles in such films as *Ace in the Hole* (1951), *Gunfight at the OK Corral* (1957), *The List of Adrian Messenger* (1963), *Spartacus* (1960) and many more. Douglas is known for bringing his own intelligence and determination to parts that, given the confines of the script, might not seem immediately worthy of it. In a long career he has proved that while virtue may not be photogenic, a dimpled chin is good for substantial mileage.

DOUGLAS, NORMAN (1868–1950) British novelist and essayist

Norman Douglas served in the Foreign Office from 1893-1901. His early attempts at fiction were unsuccessful and he left England, to spend most of the rest of his life living on the island of Capri. In 1911 he published his first travel book *Siren Land*, about Capri, and followed this success with a number of others. His most successful work was his novel *South Wind* (1917), a description of the hedonistic delights of the fictional island of 'Nepenthe'. For much of his life he was a notable figure among the literary expatriates who chose, like him, to live in Italy. Other books include *They Went* (1920), *In the Beginning* (1928) and *London Street Games* (1931). He wrote a cookbook, presumably tongue in cheek, listing supposedly aphrodisiac recipes and foods.

DOUGLAS, NORMAN

To find a friend one must close one eye; to keep him – two.
An Almanac

An Almanac is a selection of aphorisms taken from Douglas' books. One pithy witticism is offered for each day of the year.

DOUGLAS, NORMAN

Education is a state-controlled manufactory of echoes.
How About Europe

DOUGLAS, NORMAN

You can tell the ideals of a nation by its advertisements.
South Wind (1917)

DOUGLAS, NORMAN

All culinary tasks should be performed with reverential love, don't you think so? To say that a cook must possess the requisite outfit of culinary skill – that is hardly more than saying that a soldier must appear in uniform. You can have a bad soldier in uniform. The true cook must have not only those externals, but a large dose of worldly experience. He is the perfect blend, the only perfect blend.
South Wind (1917)

South Wind was Douglas' great success, a novel in name, but in form a collection of numerous short essays and disquisitions on a wide variety of topics, some confined to a single paragraph, others encompassing a whole chapter. The entire work is laced together in a framework of fiction, based on a plot which, Douglas explained, was an exploration of 'how to make murder palatable to a bishop'. The bishop in question is exposed to a variety of influences and arguments, which it is intended should slowly and surely sway him from the paths of righteousness. The novel is set on the mythical island of Nepenthe, which is not unlike Capri, on which Douglas lived for much of his life. A further theme informing the novel is that of the eternal contrast between North and South: physical, emotional and cultural.

DOUGLAS-HOME, ALEC (1903–) British prime minister

As far as the 14th Earl is concerned, I suppose Mr. Wilson, when you come to think of it, is the 14th Mr. Wilson.
interviewed on BBC television October 21, 1963

The main legacy of the Profumo Affair of 1963, in which a Tory government minister lied to the House of Commons concerning his involvement with a call-girl, was the resignation, ostensibly on grounds of ill-health, of the prime minister Harold Macmillan.

Unlike the Labour party, which held elections for its leader, the Tories still preferred to 'take the soundings' of the Party and then announce the new man. Betting favoured R.A. Butler, but true to his nickname 'the best prime minister we never had', he was passed over, as he had been in 1955, and Lord Home, who was forced to relinquish his peerage to take on the job, was made Prime Minister instead. Labour leader Harold Wilson, at pains to emphasise his proletarian origins, made the dismissive comment 'After half a century of democratic process, the whole process has ground to a halt with a 14th Earl.' Interviewed later, Sir Alec, as he had become, gave his own version of heredity. Such repartee failed to impress the voters and in the 1964 election, 'thirteen years of Tory misrule' were terminated by Labour's admittedly narrow victory.

DOUGLAS-HOME, ALEC

There are two problems in my life. The political ones are insoluble and the economic ones are incomprehensible.
speech January 1964

Douglas-Home's tenure of 10 Downing Street was mercifully brief, given that this former member of the House of Lords never seemed wholly at home there. His own diffidence, magnified by his inability to master the increasingly important medium of television, not yet the party political battleground it has become, but already highly influential on the voters, made him seem less than fully competent. He was faced by a rampant Harold Wilson, one of the earliest masters of media self-projection, who combined derision of Home's grouse-moor origins and stick-in-the-mud policies with an emphasis on his own impoverished beginnings and on his commitment to technological progress. There was no contest and in an election where image was already starting to count for far more than hard policy, Home never had a hope.

DOYLE, SIR ARTHUR CONAN (1859–1930) British novelist and short story writer

You know my method. It is founded upon the observance of trifles.
The Boscombe Valley Mystery

Doyle took the most notable characteristic of his great detective, the ability to discern an individual's character from the careful observation of details which, while obvious, might well be overlooked by less finely attuned minds, from Dr. Joseph Bell, the surgeon who taught him medicine at Edinburgh University. Bell, 'the man who suggested Sherlock Holmes to me', was indeed a real-life Holmes, using his powers of observation both to impress his students and to facilitate his diagnoses.

DOYLE, SIR ARTHUR CONAN

It is an old maxim of mine that when you have excluded the impossible, whatever remains, however improbable, must be the truth.
The Beryl Coronet

This classic Holmesian aphorism occurs in the story of one Alexander Holder, a banker who has accepted this priceless treasure, one of the Empire's most fabulous possessions, as collateral for a short-term loan of £50,000 to a customer whose name 'is a household word all over the earth'. Holder foolishly mistrusts his bank's strongroom, preferring to store the coronet at home. Here, to his horror, he finds his improvident son Arthur attempting to destroy it. But the boy is not guilty and Holmes informs the father that he owes 'a humble apology to that noble lad'.

DOYLE, SIR ARTHUR CONAN

Elementary, my dear Watson.

Sherlock Holmes himself would be hard-pressed to find just where his most famous line occurs in the canon of his adventures since his creator never used the phrase as such. It turns up, unsurprisingly, in Hollywood's many treatments of Baker Street's most celebrated, if fictional, resident, initially in *The Return of Sherlock Holmes* (1929). The nearest the literary Holmes came to his catchphrase was in the story *The Crooked Man* (1893). After delivering himself of a typically smug delineation of poor Watson's most recent habits, Holmes replies to the doctor's cry of 'Excellent!' with a dismissive 'Elementary', and goes on to point out that Watson himself can produce similarly 'meretricious' effects in his own story-telling, simply by exercising his own tricks of the trade.

DOYLE, SIR ARTHUR CONAN

'Is there any point to which you would wish to draw my attention?' 'To the curious incident of the dog in the night-time'. 'The dog did nothing in the night-time.' 'That was the curious incident' remarked Sherlock Holmes.
Silver Blaze

One of the most quoted of Sherlock Holmes' opinions is this conversation with Inspector Gregory, taken from the story of the missing racehorse *Silver Blaze* and the murder of its trainer. As an example of the concept that a lack of demonstrable action can be as important as its excess, the idea of the dog that does not bark is used constantly in a variety of situations, of which detective stories are but a single area.

DOYLE, SIR ARTHUR CONAN

It is my belief, Watson, founded upon my experience, that the lowest and vilest alleys of London do not present a more dreadful record of sin than does the smiling and beautiful countryside.
The Copper Beeches

The story of the Copper Beeches, set in Winchester, is one of a number of those in which Holmes and Watson speed away from London in pursuit of some rural adventure. As the pair watch the idyllic spring landscape from their railway carriage, Watson remarks on the charming views of Aldershot. Holmes remains unimpressed, condemning such beauties as a mere mask, and suggesting to Watson that while in a city crime, while possibly condoned, can rarely pass unnoticed, in the country, with its lonely houses and deserted acres, 'deeds of hellish cruelty' can happen quite unknown.

DOYLE, SIR ARTHUR CONAN

He is the Napoleon of crime.
The Final Problem

Conan Doyle provided a black and white world: good struggled with evil and if Holmes, as an earthly deity, chose on occasion to exercise his own variety of mercy which did not require the services of statute or precedent, it was necessary that as the personification of good, he should be pitted against that of evil. The Napoleon of Crime is Professor James Moriarty. Like Holmes, whose goodness is flawed by human weakness, so is Moriarty's evil tempered by his undoubted intelligence. His treatise on the Binomial Theorem 'ascends to (the) rarified heights of pure mathematics' but he remains the most evil man in London.

DOYLE, SIR ARTHUR CONAN

It is quite a three-pipe problem.
The Red-Headed League

Among the ritualised impedimenta of Holmes' rooms at 221B,

Baker Street, and prominent in the classic portrait of the detective, as epitomised by many illustrators and by generations of stage and screen actors, is his pipe, invariably a Meerschaum, with its characteristic curve, although here Watson specifies a black clay. Taking tobacco from the Turkish slipper which served as his pouch, Holmes would relapse into his armchair, smoking his way through the ramifications of a new case. Judging by his comment in this story, three pipes took some fifty minutes to smoke.

DOYLE, SIR ARTHUR CONAN

The unofficial force – The Baker Street irregulars.
The Sign of Four (1890)

The original 'Irregulars' were the motley collection of urchins, employed and otherwise, who provided Sherlock Holmes with an unofficial army of messengers, observers and amateur detectives. Latterly the name has been applied to those American Holmesian obsessives whose eponymous society continues to celebrate their fictional inspiration and whose writings have produced such learned theses as 'Who Was Mrs. Watson's First Husband' (1960), 'On the B in 221B' and similar arcana.

DOYLE, SIR ARTHUR CONAN

The Giant Rat of Sumatra, a story for which the world is not yet prepared.
The Sussex Vampire (1924)

In a story in which Holmes informs Watson 'I never get your limits....There are unexplored possibilities about you', the doctor's suggestions that a vampire may have caused injuries to the baby son of an old, rugby-playing friend are firmly pooh-poohed by the Master. Watson, as ever, must await the correct solution, but this late story cites perhaps the most intriguing of Holmes' unchronicled cases, that of the Giant Rat of Sumatra, and the ship Matilda Briggs. Of the Rat one knows only that *rhizomys sumatrensis*, the great Sumatran bamboo rat, may attain a length of 19 inches, excluding its tail.

DRAGNET

Ladies and gentlemen, the story you are about to hear is true. Only the names have been changed to protect the innocent.
American television show, 1950s

Dragnet was one of the classic American cop shows, running from 1951-58 and revived briefly from 1967–69. It was the brainchild of actor Jack Webb, who produced and directed it, as well as starring as Sgt. Joe Friday, the deadpan hero whose catchphrase 'Just the facts' became a parodist's delight. It drew its inspiration from the flat, documentary style of the film *Naked City* (1948) which set the standard for film and TV police procedurals, as well as from the Dragnet radio show of the late 1940s, which claimed to draw its plots from actual cases. The introduction to each episode went as above, and continued with a hard-edged, no-frills listing of events, culminating 'I'm a cop.... My partner: Frank Smith. The boss is Captain Welch. My name's Friday...' Dragnet spawned a number of imitators, but Webb's devotion to the genre and to real-life policework meant that his series remained pre-eminent.

DRAKE, CHARLIE British comedian

Hello my darlings...
catchphrase, 1960s

Drake, according to John Fisher, the historian of British comedy, writing in his book *Funny Way To Be a Hero* (1973), is 'possibly the first comedian actually reared in British television'. Drake, described by Fisher as 'a cherub with a touch of the hoodlum about him' rose to fame in the 1960s. His catchphrase was delivered in high, fluting tones, which were unmistakably camp. His act capitalised on his own acrobatic abilities. Like a number of his peers, Drake attempted to break into film, but his efforts proved generally unsuccessful.

DRUCKER, PETER (1909–) American management theorist

So much of what we call management consists in making it difficult for people to work.
The Practice of Management (1953)

Drucker is professor of management studies at New York University and remains among the most important theorists of corporate management ever. His work concentrates on large organisations and is based on a belief that the emergence in the first half of the 20th century of such organisations has had a profound effect on society at large. He is responsible for the concept of 'management by objective', a system whereby management efficiency can be maximised by giving the relevant individuals defined goals and measuring their progress towards them. The intention is that by offering these goals 'common people (may) achieve uncommon performance'.

DRUMMOND, HUGH British aristocrat

Ladies and gentlemen, I give you a toast; it is: Absinthe makes the tart grow fonder.
quoted in Seymour Hicks, *The Vintage Years* (1943)

Drummond was a prominent member of that group of dissolute young men and their attendant girls whose gallivanting between Romanos in the Strand, the Cafe Royal, a variety of prize-fight rings, racecourses and casinos both in England and abroad variously delighted or scandalised late Victorian society. Drummond, whose idea of a good time was the provision of general mayhem, was a leading light of the notorious Pelican Club, a collection of impecunious but fast-living aristocrats, leavened with the odd notable sportsman, and charmed by the flower of the Gaiety Theatre chorus, with whom, Drummond informed his less than amused mother, 'a man must be seen about to keep up his credit in the City'. Another version of this phrase can be found in writer Jack Hibberd's *Odyssey of a Prostitute* (1983) in which he stated 'Absinthe makes the parts grow stronger'.

DU MAURIER, DAPHNE (1907–) British writer

Last night I dreamt I went to Manderley again.
Rebecca (1938)

Probably one of the most famous first lines in romantic or any other fiction, this was penned by novelist Daphne Du Maurier at the start of her most celebrated work: *Rebecca*, a huge, boiling novel of elemental passion set in the West Country, where the author lived much of her life. Du Maurier was the granddaughter of George du Maurier (1834–96), the novelist and illustrator, and the daughter of Gerald, the actor manager. She began writing as a girl and published her first novel in 1931. She established herself as a popular 'women's writer' and ensured her lasting success with *Rebecca*. The novel continues to sell well and was made into a TV series and in 1940 a successful Hollywood film, directed by Alfred Hitchcock.

DU MAURIER, GERALD (1873–1934) British actor-manager

Good in parts, like the curate's egg.
popular catchphrase

This catchphrase, usually reduced to its 'curate's egg' component, has remained popular throughout the 20th century, although it owes its origins to the 19th. It was used in a *Punch* cartoon of 1895, where it provided such a punch-line as the magazine's laborious humour could then manage. A nervous curate is breakfasting with his bishop. Bishop: 'I'm afraid you've got a bad egg, Mr. Jones.' 'Oh no, my Lord, I assure you! parts of it are excellent.' The caption was written by Gerald du Maurier, a leading figure of the London stage, and an occasional contributor to the magazine.

DUBCEK, ALEXANDER (1921–) Czech politician

Socialism with a human face
motto of the 'Prague Spring' 1968

In January 1968 Dubcek replaced Antonin Novotny as the First Secretary of the Czechoslovak Party. In April he published 'Czechoslovakia's Road to Socialism', a programme of reforms that aimed to humanize state control by introducing basic civil liberties, press freedom, economic decentralisation and similar democratic practice. The period of liberalism that followed, loosely entitled the 'Prague Spring' evolved the slogan 'Socialism with a human face'. Inevitably the Moscow establishment deplored Dubcek's plans. On the night of 20–21 August the Red Army occupied the country and Dubcek and five other leaders were taken in chains to Moscow where they were forced to make major concessions. The invasion destroyed the reform movement and Dubcek was forced out of office and into obscurity in 1969. Leonid Brezhnev (1906–1982), then Soviet leader, justified the invasion in what was termed the Brezhnev Doctrine: 'When internal and external forces which are hostile to socialism try to turn the development of any socialist country towards the restoration of a capitalist regime... it becomes not only a problem of the people concerned, but a common problem and concern of all socialist countries'.

DUCK SOUP

Remember men, we're fighting for this woman's honour, which is more than she ever did.
script by Bert Kalmar, Harry Ruby, Arthur Sheekman and Nat Perrin (1933)

Generally considered to be the Marx Brothers' greatest movie, *Duck Soup*, scripted mainly by a Kalmar and Ruby who for once managed to avoid their mawkish stocks-in-trade, is the film that has brought them their intellectual following, with its references to surrealism, dissociated thinking, social protest and 'commedia del arte'. It is their most obviously political film, if one discounts the anarchic strains running through all their best work, and is essentially a farce about war. The woman for whom they are fighting is, as ever, Margaret Dumont (Mrs. Teasdale), who also tells Groucho 'My husband is dead', to which he replies 'I'll bet he's just using that as an excuse'. The film also features the sequence in which Groucho, as Rufus T. Firefly, leader of Fredonia, is attempting to make his way through a political report. It confounds him, prompting the comment 'Why, a four-year-old child could understand this report. Run out and find me a four-year-old child. I can't make head or tail out of it.'

DUHAMEL, GEORGES   (1884–1966) French playwright, author and critic

I respect the idea of God too much to hold it responsible for a world as absurd as this one is.
Le Désert de Bièvres (1937)

Duhamel qualified as a doctor and surgeon and served as such during the First World War. His experiences at the front evoked two books, *Vie de Marque* (1917), and *Civilisation* 1914-17 (1918), which was awarded the Prix Goncourt. He devoted most of his time to writing and was among the founders of L'Abbaye, a short-lived community of authors and artists estalished at Creteil, outside Paris. Duhamel was Christian in spirit, humanist in belief and interested primarily in the individual. He produced a large quantity of poetry, memoirs, plays and critical studies as well as two cycles of novels.

DULLES, JOHN FOSTER   (1888–1959) American government official

If you are scared to go to the brink, you are lost.
speech at North Atlantic Council, Paris, December 14 1953

As President Eisenhower's secretary of state Dulles was one of the major influences on post-war American foreign policy. In government he set out to overturn the Truman doctrine of 'containing' the Soviets, replacing it by the far more aggressive policy of 'rolling back' the Communists wherever possible, backing his theories with the strategy of 'massive (nuclear) retaliation'. 'Brinkmanship' epitomised the Dulles style, preferring eye-to-eye bluffing to more sophisticated bargaining; it was termed by one wit 'the most popular game since Monopoly'. A devout, even fundamental Christian, Dulles saw himself as the near-saintly bulwark of right against the evils of Communism. He had many critics, notably the trade union leader Walter Reuther who called him 'The world's longest range misguided missile', and commentator I.F. Stone who remarked in 1953 'Dulles is a wily and subtle man. It is difficult to believe that behind his unctuous manner he does not take a cynical amusement in his own pomposities'.

DULLES, JOHN FOSTER

An obsolete conception, and except under very exceptional circumstances it is an immoral and short-sighted conception.
speech at Iowa State College, June 9 1956

Neutralism, which Dulles was condemning in this speech, was an alien concept to a man whose entire life was grounded on the hard inflexibilities of ideological purity. Echoing the Christ he worshipped, he saw only two sides: those who supported America and those who did not. Non-alignment was merely a fancy synonym for hypocrisy. That this made American allies of some of the world's most corrupt, right-wing dictatorships was irrelevant; they hated Communism and the niceties of civil rights or democracy did not matter. Dulles saw no point in any negotiations with communist governments: their ideology made them de facto liars and cheats. He was almost as contemptuous of Europe, castigating imperialism and assuming that any newly independent nation would turn to the US, one of the earliest post-colonial foundations, as an automatic ally.

DUNNE, FINLAY PETER   (1867–1936) American writer

Vice...is a creature of such heejus mien...that the more ye see it, th' better ye like it.
The Crusade Against Vice

Dunne's creation, the stage Irish saloon keeper 'Mr. Dooley', first appeared in 1898 and remained a popular favourite, conferring on his creator the title of 'the greatest American humourist since Mark Twain'. Mr. Dooley was in the tradition of folksy American humour, offering shrewd, native insights into all manner of human activities and predicaments, in his case delivered in an almost impenetrable brogue. This line relates to the activities of America's supreme anti-vice crusader, Anthony Comstock (1844–1915), the founder of the Society for the Suppression of Vice. Mr. Dooley is making a point that a number of Comstock's critics had noted: Comstock gained such publicity from vice that the last thing he wanted was for it actually to disappear.

DUNSANY, LORD   (1878–1957) Irish poet

Humanity, let us say, is like people packed in an automobile which is travelling downhill without lights at terrific speed and

driven by a small four-year-old child. The signposts along the way are all marked 'Progress'.
quoted in 1954

Edward John Moreton Drax Plunkett, 18th Lord Dunsany, was a leading members of that group of Irish writers whose works were known collectively as the 'Irish revival'. Others included W.B. Yeats (1865–1939), Oliver St. John Gogarty (1878–1957) and Lady Gregory (1852–1932). He produced a number of books dealing with myths and legends, notably *The King of Elfland's Daughter* (1924). His first play, *The Glittering Gate*, was performed at the Abbey Theatre in Dublin in 1909. More realistic work was accomplished in his popular 'Jorkens stories', the first of which was *The Travel Tales of Mr. Joseph Jorkens* (1931). Dunsany's work experienced a brief revival in the late Sixties when his bizarre fantasies found a new audience among the hippies of Britain and America.

DURANT, WILL & ARIEL (1885–1981), (1898–?) American historians

History is mostly guessing, the rest is prejudice.

Will Durant was a major popularizer of the history of ideas who wrote copiously in a lengthy career. He devoted his life to expounding history and philosophy, starting with his first book *The History of Philosophy* (1926). Many volumes have followed, most notably the *Story of Civilisation*, which appeared in ten volumes between 1935–67. Durant wrote the first six volumes alone, but for the last four was joined by his wife Ariel. The last volume, *Rousseau and Revolution* (1967) won the Pulitzer prize for non-fiction.

DURANT, WILL AND ARIEL

Civilisation is a stream with banks. The stream is sometimes filled with blood from people killing, stealing, shouting and doings things historians usually record; while on the banks, unnoticed, people build homes, make love, raise children, sing songs, write poetry and even whittle statues. The story of civilisation is the story of what happened on the banks. Historians are pessimists because they ignore the banks for the river.

DURANTE, JIMMY (1893–1980) American comedian

Goodnight Mrs. Calabash, wherever you are.
catchphrase 1950s

Durante was a gravel-voiced American comedian the size and prominence of whose nose earned him the lifelong nickname 'Schnozzle' and who said of himself 'Dere's a million good-looking guys in the world, but I'm a novelty'. He had a long career in vaudeville, night clubs and the mass media. According to his obituary in *Time* magazine, workaholic Durante only once took time off from performing: to care for his ailing first wife, Jeanne Olsen. Although he subsequently remarried, Durante would regularly invoke his late wife, to whom he had given the nickname Mrs. Calabash, at the end of his television appearances, dropping his comedy for a moment to offer this valedictory line.

DURBIN, KAREN (1944–) American feminist and writer

Marriage is two people agreeing to tell the same lie.
quoted in *The Cynic's Lexicon* by Jonathon Green (1985)

Durbin, one of New York's pioneer feminists in the late 1960s and early 1970s, offered this particular dictum in a column for *Mademoiselle* magazine. An unashamedly cynical appraisal of marriage, put forward at a time when the popularity of the institution was at an all-time low, it seemed to represent a general mood. The author, now a senior editor on the weekly *Village Voice*, remains single.

DUROCHER, LEO (1906–) American baseball coach

Nice guys finish last.
remark in July 1952

The 'Corinthian ideal' of gentlemanly amateurism and 'good sportsmanship', the vaunted bedrock of English sport, has never found much favour in America. The rigorous professionalism of US sport has no time for such niceties. This remark, epitomising the hard-nosed approach, comes from a conversation between Leo Durocher, the long-time manager of the then Brooklyn Dodgers, and newspaper columnist Frank Graham. Durocher was referring to one of his less motivated ball-players when he told Graham 'There's Mellot. Take a good look at him. A nicer sort of guy never put shoes on. Fine fellow, but he didn't come to win, that's the answer. Nice guys finish last.' Durocher played the tough guy through his ten years as boss. Dealing with the fantasy of the 'good loser' he said simply 'Show me a good sportsman and I'll show you a player I'm looking to trade'.

DURRELL, LAWRENCE   (1912–) British writer

History is an endless repetition of the wrong way of living.
in the *Listener*, 1978

Durrell, who describes himself as 'one of the world's expatriates' was born in India, educated in England and since his teens has travelled widely, living for much of his life in the eastern Mediterranean. He began writing both prose and poetry when quite young; his first important novel, *The Black Book* (1938) was banned in England but published in Paris. Durell's greatest achievement in his *Alexandria Quartet*, four novels the central topic of which, he has stated, is 'the exploration of modern love'. The novels bring together a wide variety of characters, all bound within a web of political and sexual intrigue. Each novel tells the same 'truth' from the point of view of one of the leading figures.

DYLAN, BOB   (1941–) American singer and poet

Robert Allen Zimmerman was born in Duluth, Minnesota. A self-taught musician he formed his first rock band aged 14. He also began writing his own songs. Influenced, so he has always claimed, by the Welsh poet Dylan Thomas, he changed his surname to Dylan and moved to New York where he became increasingly pre-eminent among the singers of folk and 'protest' songs in Greenwich Villages cafes. His first album was relatively derivative of traditional folk, but subsequent work concentrated on his own material, anthems for an era that, even in a more cynical world, they still encapsulate. In 1966 Dylan shocked his folk fans, but won over most of the rock audience when he abandoned his acoustic guitar for an electric one and introduced his highly accomplished backup band The Band. This period produced a new style of song, heavily drug influenced, full of elliptical, fantasy-filled lyrics, heavy with contemporary reference and relevance, combining to create a form known simply and widely as 'Dylanseque'. They climaxed in 1966 with the double album *Blonde on Blonde*. A near-fatal motorcycle crash in 1966 halted Dylan's progress. He returned with a new album in 1968 but for many the spark was fading. Since then Dylan has played fast and loose with his fans, flirting with a variety of fundamentalist faiths, both Christian and Jewish, abandoning his political stance, advocating conservatism and so on. His concerts still sell out and he remains an elusive figure, his music the undying epitome of a lost era.

DYLAN, BOB

But to (live outside the law), you must be honest
Absolutely Sweet Marie

DYLAN, BOB

Something is happening here
But you don't know what it is
Do you, Mr Jones?

Ballad of a Thin Man

DYLAN, BOB

He not busy being born
Is busy dying

It's Alright Ma, I'm Only Bleeding

DYLAN, BOB

She knows that there's no success like failure, and that failure's no success at all.
Like a Rolling Stone

DYLAN, BOB

Keep a clean nose
Watch the plain clothes
You don't need a weather man
To know which way the wind blows.

Subterranean Homesick Blues

DYLAN, BOB

Come mothers and fathers
Throughout the land
And don't criticize
What you don't understand

The Times They Are A-Changin

E

EBAN, ABBA (1915–) Israeli diplomat

History teaches us that men and nations behave wisely once they have exhausted all other alternatives.
quoted 1970

Eban, the South African-born former Israeli ambassador to the US, has always received a more sympathetic press than more outpoken or extreme Israeli leaders. As Israel's long-time representative in Washington and the country's permanent representative to the United Nations since 1950, he has managed to distance himself from the excesses forced upon politicians operating in the native arena who are forced to voice less temperate opinions. Immediately prior to the Six Day War of June 1967 Eban launched his own version of shuttle diplomacy, attempting to obtain Western influence in lifting Egypt's blockade of Israel. When this failed he supported his country's military efforts, delivering a notable speech in Israel's defence to the UN. Eban offers a sardonic view of the world, doubtless culled from his particular role within it.

EBAN, ABBA

Propaganda is the art of persuading others of what one does not believe oneself.

EDEN, ANTHONY (1897–1977) British prime minister

We are not at war with Egypt. We are in an armed conflict.
speaking during the Suez crisis, 1956

Sir Anthony Eden, British prime minister from 1955–57, was a notably taciturn figure, who was not prone to offering quotable lines. The few which he did create tend, like the above, to picture him in a poor light. Like the Australians in Vietnam, whose spokesman passed over their setbacks with the line 'This is not a defeat, it is a strategic withdrawal', Eden preferred to mask the Suez debacle in diplomatic euphemism. When the time-tabled collusion between Britain, France and Israel misfired, the subsequent crisis destroyed his government. Its toll was never more apparent than in his wife, Lady Clarissa's, statement halfway through the imbrogolio: 'During the last few weeks I have felt that the Suez Canal was flowing through my drawing room.'

EDWARD VIII (1894–1972) British monarch

Something must be done
Speech in Dowlais, Wales, November 1936

Edward VIII began his reign as an immensely popular king. His father, George V, had gained almost mythical affection and Edward had much to live up to, but at first he seemed more than capable of the task. This promise, delivered at the Bessemer steel works in Dowlais, where some 9000 men had been laid off, was seen as typical of the caring, concerned persona of a monarch who, more than any other, was perceived by ordinary people as their friend. Playboy he might be, but beneath those alarming checks beat a heart of pure gold. Unfortunately the effect of Edward's statement, other than on his own popularity, was equally typical of this dilatory, weak man. After promising 'You may be sure that all I can do for you, I will', Edward did precisely nothing. The fact that he had already decided upon his abdication may well have been something to do with this.

EDWARD VIII

I have found it impossible to carry the heavy burden of responsibility and to discharge my duties as King as I would wish to do without the help and support of the woman I love.
Abdication speech on radio December 11, 1936.

'After I am dead,' said his father George V, 'the boy will ruin himself in twelve months' and his prophecy came melodramatically true. Edward VIII met Mrs. Wallis Simpson, the wife of an American businessman and already divorced from a former husband, while he was still the Prince of Wales in the early 1920s. He became infatuated and she was determined to divorce for a second time and marry him. The public had no inkling of an affair which fascinated high society and alarmed Prime Minister Stanley Baldwin. As what H.L. Mencken called 'The greatest story since the Crucifixion' began to take shape, with the indiscreet US papers revelling in the scandal while Fleet Street, reined in by tradition, was forced to remain mute, Edward proved obdurate. He would not abandon Mrs. Simpson, come what might. Secrecy ended on December 1 1936, when the Bishop of Bradford delivered a thinly veiled attack on royal morals, which the press took as carte blanche. The King refused to budge; Baldwin refused to condone any compromise. On December 10 the instrument of abdication was signed and read to a shell-shocked but relieved House of Commons. The next day Edward made his parting speech by radio to the nation, then left England for the South of France and thirty-six years of life as the Duke of Windsor.

EHRLICH, PAUL (1932–) American scientist

The mother of the year should be a sterilized woman with two adopted children.
quoted in *Equilibrium* (1969)

Ehrlich is an expert in population and ecology who came to prominence as the founder of Zero Population Growth, Inc. in 1968. The goals of this organisation were 'the stabilization of the US population size, followed by reduction to a more reasonable level; the stabilisation of energy and resource consumption; the planning of land use.' Ehrlich's world-view is generally pessimistic and in a variety of public statements he has predicted ecological doom for the earth. That some of his fears have not come to pass must be partly due to efforts that he and other scientist have made since the Sixties to alert the world to its threatened future. His most extreme prediction is that by the year 2800 the entire globe will be covered in 2000-storey high tower-block apartment houses.

EHRLICH, PAUL

The first rule of intelligent tinkering is to save all the parts.
The Saturday Review, 1971

EHRLICHMAN, JOHN (1925–) American government official

Let him twist slowly, slowly in the wind
referring to acting FBI director Patrick Grey, March 7/8 1973

Ehrlichman was Richard Nixon's assistant for Domestic Affairs and as such as key member of the president's White House team. He was among the most prominent victims of the Watergate Affair. This particular sentence comes from a phone conversation with John Dean, special counsel to the President, made on March 8 1973. Ehrlichman explains that the President has decided not to appoint Patrick Grey, then acting head of the FBI, as the Bureau's full-time head. Summing up his image of a hanging corpse, Ehrlichman suggested that Grey, as yet, need not be told the bad news. Consciously or otherwise, the line evokes the final paragraph of Aldous Huxley's Brave New World; 'Slowly, very slowly, like unhurried compass needles, the feet turned towards the right; north, north-east, east, south-east, south-south-west; then paused, and, after a few seconds, turned as unhurriedly back towards the left. South-south-west, south, south-east, east...'

EIKERENKOETER II 'REVEREND IKE', FREDERICK J.
(1935–) American evangelist

Don't wait for pie in the sky when you die! Get yours now, with icecream on the top.

quoted in *Esquire*, 1973

The Reverend Ike has probably done more than any other clergyman to resolve that great ethical problem: the simultaneous service of God and Mammon. This son of a South Carolina Baptist minister who beams out his top-rated 15-minute message from the radio station run by his United Church and Science of Living Institute in New York City, stresses that the deferred gratifications of traditional Christianity need not worry his congregation. The lack of money, not its possession, is the root of all evil and the flamboyant Reverend is the finest argument for his own gospel of conspicuous consumption. Appealing mainly to middle-class blacks, he rejects such concepts as humility or turning the other cheek. 'When you kneel down to pray you put yourself in a good position to get a kick in the behind.' The funding for his lifestyle comes from his 'Blessing Plan': every dollar the truly faithful donate to Reverend Ike will be returned, with interest.

EINSTEIN, ALBERT (1879–1955) German physicist

The most incomprehensible thing about the world is that it is comprehensible.

Einstein's researches into theoretical physics radically altered scientific concepts of time and space and his work is largely responsible for the whole direction of 20th century physics. Einstein concentrated all his efforts on finding simple, general and unifying principles that might be used to describe the objective nature of the world. His work on the photo-electric effect proved the most accessible to his peers and in 1922 it earned him the Nobel prize. His findings as regards relativity proved harder to accept, but gradually won more and more adherents. As his fame grew Einstein became an increasingly important figure in international affairs. His involvement in the development of the atomic bomb led him to join those scientists who attempted to persuade the world leaders of its inherent, long-term dangers. He was a dedicated Zionist and was offered, though he rejected, the Presidency of the State of Israel. Throughout his life he represented to many people the archetypical scientist and the classic portrait with his hair awry and eyes gazing past the onlooker has in its way become an instantly recognisable pop icon.

EINSTEIN, ALBERT

God casts the die, not the dice.

Einstein used this aphorism to sum up his own beliefs in a realist interpretation of science. He repudiated the influences of Ernst Mach (1838–1916), whose 'sensationalist' philosophy demanded that all scientific credentials must provide an empirical proof of their own existence, stating that what is perceived is not physical objects, but sensations. He also rejected the Copenhagen interpretation of quantum mechanics which attributed essential indeterminacy to atomic processes. In his view the discipline was basically a statistical theory that applied to a collection of systems, rather than to each individual event. This belief led to his becoming increasingly cut off from the mainstream of scientific thought but of late many physicists are beginning to feel that he was right.

EINSTEIN, ALBERT

God is subtle, but he is not bloody-minded.
carved above the fireplace of Fine Hall, the Mathematical Institute, University of Princeton

EINSTEIN, ALBERT

If only I had known, I should have become a watchmaker.
on realising implication of atomic research, 1945

Einstein's researches into atomic theory were fundamental to the development of atomic weapons, especially in his early association with the Hungarian physicist Leo Szilard, a member of the Manhattan Project, the US government-funded programme that culminated in the creation of the first atomic bombs in 1945. It was at Szilard's urging that in August 1939 Einstein wrote to President Roosevelt recommending that the US begin the development of such weapons. Roosevelt's response to the letter was to create the Advisory Committee on Uranium which became the S-1 Committee and then the Manhattan Project. After his brainchild was realised and dropped on Hiroshima and Nagasaki in August 1945, Einstein, like many participatory physicists, was profoundly shocked. Expressing his horror at his own responsibility, he made the comment above.

EINSTEIN, ALBERT

Before God we are all equally wise – and equally foolish.
Out Of My Later Years (1950)

In his essay 'Cosmic Religion' Einstein elaborates his belief that 'Science without religion is lame; religion without science is blind' and goes on to make this statement about man's relationship to some higher entity. It is vital, he claims, for the scientist to accept this fact and the kind of reaction that the consideration of religion evokes in a physicist has a definite influence on the quality of his creative powers.

EINSTEIN, ALBERT

Common sense is the deposit of prejudice laid down in the mind before the age of eighteen.
quoted in *Scientific American* magazine, 1976

EINSTEIN, ALBERT

The release of atom power has changed everything except our way of thinking, and thus we are being driven unarmed towards a catastrophe....The solution of this problem lies in the heart of humankind.
speech to National Commission of Nuclear Scientists, May 1946

This speech, which virtually replicated a fund-rasing telegram that Einstein had sent that same month to the Emergency Committee of Atomic Scientists, was one of many attempts by Einstein to reverse what he felt was damage for which he was primarily responsible: the development of atomic and latterly nuclear weaponry. Allying himself to such world-renowned peace campaigners as Bertrand Russell, with whom he issued a manifesto stressing the dangers of the superpower arms race, Einstein campaigned ceaselessly against the weapon he had helped create.

EISENHOWER, DWIGHT D. (1890–1969) American president

The military-industrial complex
farewell address as President, January 17, 1961

In this speech which, inter alia, warned against the unholy alliance of the military and those great industries that both depended on and encouraged its consumption of weaponry and material, Eisenhower shocked many of his capitalist supporters but impressed such critics as the commentator Walter Lippmann, who praised this condemnation of a threat to civilian life that came not from foreign but domestic interests. There had been no permanent armaments industry prior to World War II, Eisenhower stated, but since then the demands of the modern world had caused the creation of a 'permanent armaments industry of vast proportions'. Coupled with 3.5 million people involved in the defence establishment, the retiring President stressed how potentially baneful and widespread such a monolith's influence could be.

EISENHOWER, DWIGHT D.

You have a row of dominoes set up. You knock over the first one, and what will happen to the last one is a certainty that it will go over very quickly. So you have the beginning of a disintegration that would have the most profound influences.
speaking at a press conference, April 7, 1954

Eisenhower used this image, first developed by the columnist Joseph Alsop, at a press conference in which he was explaining his decision to offer economic aid to the government of Ngo Dinh Diem in South Vietnam. This concept of the strategic role of Indochina was essentially a reaction to fears of another Munich: appeasement of the Communists would have no better results than that of the Nazis. Critics claimed that this analogy was fallacious, but to several presidents – although Kennedy had reservations – and the vast majority of the American military, government and people, it appeared watertight and remained the cornerstone of America's policy in South-East Asia.

ELIOT, T.S. (1888–1965) American poet

Thomas Stearns Eliot was born in America but in 1914 was persuaded by Ezra Pound to settle in England. In 1915 he produced his first poem 'The Love-Song of J. Alfred Prufrock'. His first collection of poetry appeared in 1917 and *Poems* (1919) delighted the intellectual elite. He founded *The Criterion* magazine in 1922, putting his new poem *The Waste Land* into its first issue. With this poem, a central text of modernism, Eliot took his place as the voice of the disillusioned post-First World War generation. In 1925 he joined publishers Faber and Faber, where he established their influential poetry list and positioned himself henceforth as a major cultural authority. Eliot became a British citizen in 1927 and joined the Anglican church. His idiosyncratic attitudes to his faith can be seen in his poems: *The Hollow Men* (1925), *The Journey of the Magi* (1927), *Ash Wednesday* (1930) and *Four Quartets* (1935–42). During the Thirties Eliot set out to revive poetic drama, writing a number of plays. He was awarded the Nobel Prize for Literature in 1947 as well as the Order of Merit.

ELIOT, T. S.

Half the harm that is done in this world
Is due to people who want to feel important.

The Cocktail Party (1950)

This verse play, one of Eliot's 'comedies', concerns the disillusion of Celia Coplestone, mistress of her lover Edward, when she discovers that although Edward's wife Lavinia has finally left him, he is unwilling to set up house with her, but instead wants Lavinia back. In turn she appreciates that the love she had assumed for Edward was never what she really wanted. Instead she becomes religious and goes to Africa as a missionary; there she is killed. Edward duly gets Lavinia back and they return to their barren marriage.

ELIOT, T.S.

Human kind
Cannot bear very much reality.

Burnt Norton

Eliot's Four Quartets appeared between 1936–42: all four –*Burnt Norton* (1936), *East Coker* (1940), *The Dry Salvages* (1941) and *Little Gidding* (1942) – were published in one volume in 1944 and were intended by the author to be considered as a single work. The Quartets explore questions of time and incarnation in a manner analogous to chamber music. They are largely concerned with time, its unreality and the unreality of human life that is so governed by time that the present dissolves simultaneously into memories of the past and a basis for the future. The immediate theme of Burnt Norton is the mystical experience in relation to time, and the way in which time can protect humanity from unbearable eternity, whether spent in heaven or in damnation. For many readers the Quartets are impenetrably complex, covering a multitude of themes with enormous erudition; even critics accept that they are susceptible only to the detailed and concentrating reading such a work merits.

ELIOT, T.S.

Here I am, an old man in a dry month, being read to by a boy.
Gerontion (1919)

In the poem Gerontion (the 'little old man') is a former seaman, at the end of his tether. He is blind, he lives in a decayed house that is not his own; as he thinks about his future and his past he realises with despair that he has no genuine life to look back upon, neither faith nor passion to support him.

ELIOT, T.S.

> **The last temptation is the greatest treason:**
> **To do the right deed for the wrong reason.**
>
> *Murder in the Cathedral* (1935)

This verse play concerns the murder in Canterbury cathedral in 1170 of Thomas à Becket, chancellor of England and later Roman Catholic saint. When he refused to allow King Henry II to curtail important Church rights he was exiled for seven years to Europe. Eliot's play begins when, recalled to England by the King, who promises a reconciliation, Becket has returned to his cathedral. Inevitably monarch and prelate fall out again and Becket realises that the king will have him killed. These lines are part of his reflection on death that concludes the play's first act, when the Archbishop has, he hopes, overcome the temptations of wealth, power, friendship and, hardest to resist, of the glory of martyrdom itself. The play's interlude gives the sermon Becket preached on Christmas morning 1170 and its second act features the four knights who debate with and then kill Becket, following their murder with a self-justifying apology, in prose, offered directly to the audience.

ELIOT, T.S.

Macavity's not there!
Old Possum's Book of Practical Cats (1939)

This volume of humorous cat-poems was written by Eliot for private and presumably youthful consumption during the 1930s and first published, with illustrations by Nicolas Bentley, in 1939. Among the various feline characters – Growltiger, Skimbles-hanks and the rest – is Macavity the Mystery Cat, reminscent of

Gay's and Brecht's Captain Macheath and Conan Doyle's arch-villain Moriarty. Some critics, less convinced of the immortality of Eliot's adult verses and plays, believe that of all his work, *Old Possum* may survive longest.

ELIOT, T.S.

Success is relative:
It is what we can make of the mess we have made of things.
The Family Reunion (1939)

The Family Reunion is a tragicomic play in verse in which Harry returns to his family after an absence of eight years, haunted by the desire to kill his wife and believing that he has in fact done so. He is liberated from his nightmare by acquiring an insight into an earlier past which he has never understood. His dead father becomes intelligible to him and his own 'crime' turns out to be simply the present version of a family crime projected through the generations: as his father had once wanted to kill his wife, so had the son wanted to kill his. Harry leaves the reunion, the purpose of his visit accomplished and his demons exorcised.

ELIOT, T.S.

We are the hollow men
We are the stuffed men
Leaning together.
The Hollow Men (1925)

The poem *The Hollow Men* (subtitled A Penny for the Old Guy) has as its theme the concept of debasement through the rejection of good, and of despair through consequent guilt. The scarecrow symbol that is central to the poem designates not only the speaker's own ineffectuality, but also his inability to attain love. The straw dummies of the poem are all but damned and the whole poem is dominated by the horror of an earthly hell where 'hollow men' must wait for death to liberate them. The *Hollow Men* was written two years before Eliot's confirmation into the Anglican faith and must be seen, along with several later poems, as one of the works in which he attempts to come to terms with his own conceptions of religious faith. The poem's final couplet 'This is the way the world ends / Not with a bang but a whimper' seems to denounce the whole futility of the First World War and its legacy to the survivors.

ELIOT, T.S.

In the room the women come and go
talking of Michelangelo
The Love Song of J. Alfred Prufrock (1915)

ELIOT, T.S.

I have measured out my life with coffee spoons.
The Love Song of J. Alfred Prufrock (1915)

This poem, Eliot's first published work, takes the form of a soliloquy in which we see Prufrock, a tragic and ineffectual figure, who dares not risk the disappointment of seeking actual love which, even if he did find it and had energy enough to indulge it, would still not satisfy him. Through timidity he is incapable of action and the plight of this hesitant, inhibited man, an ageing dreamer trapped by his own indecisiveness and mediocrity in decayed shabby-genteel surroundings, is the tragedy of one for whom love is beyond achievement but still within desire. Pound called it a 'truly 20th century poem', dealing as it does with what Bernard Bergonzi has called an unstable consciousness tormented by the problem of identity in 'an unsympathetic social context'.

ELIOT, T.S.

I should have been a pair of ragged claws
Scuttling across the floors of silent seas.
The Love Song of J. Alfred Prufrock (1915)

ELIOT, T.S.

I grow old...I grow old...
I shall wear the bottoms of my trousers rolled
The Love Song of J. Alfred Prufrock (1915)

ELIOT, T.S.

April is the cruellest month, breeding
Lilacs out of the dead land, mixing
Memory and desire, stirring
Dull roots with spring rain.
The Waste Land (1922)

Along with the *Four Quartets The Waste Land* is generally considered to be Eliot's greatest work, the exemplary poem of 1920s disillusionment and the text that established the poet as the authentic voice of a cynical generation. Its 433 lines of mainly free verse, replete with quotations from Italian, French and German, and a wide range of literary references, were widely disparaged in 1922 but intellectuals appreciated it as a landmark in English literature, drawing to a close the romantic period, dating from 1798, and replacing it with a new era of predominantly and consciously intellectual verse. The poem mixes classical elements with the commonplace and sordid, setting a pattern that would be found in many of the poets that Eliot chose for his Faber list. The unrelenting grimness of his landscape reflects a civilisation that he, and many others, could see only as the waste land of his title.

ELIOT, T.S.

> **She smooths her hair with automatic hand**
> **And puts a record on the gramophone.**

The Waste Land (1922)

This episode in *The Waste Land*, where a bored typist is seduced in her seedy bedsitter, amidst dirty underwear and drying washing, typifies the wretchedness of the whole poem. Unlike the heroine of Goldsmith's 18th century lyric, whose seduction leads her to thoughts of suicide, the modern girl merely tidies her hair, barely considering the gesture, let alone the event that preceded it, and selects a musical accompaniment for her post-coital triste.

ELIZABETH II (1926–) British monarch

My husband and I

catchphrase

Whether monarchs may be attributed a catchphrase is possibly debatable, but Queen Elizabeth's line, first delivered in her second Christmas broadcast, made from New Zealand, in 1953, has joined that repertoire of stock phrases, the kneejerk delivery of every parodist. By the Sixties she had refined it down to 'Prince Philip and I' and was sufficiently aware of the amusement derived from the original line to make a joke of it on her Silver Wedding Anniversary in 1972 when she informed banquet guests I think on this occasion I may be forgiven for saying "My husband and I".

ELIZABETH, THE QUEEN MOTHER

My favourite programme is *Mrs. Dale's Diary*. I try never to miss it because it is the only way of knowing what goes on in a middle-class family.

quoted in the *Evening News*, c1955

Throughout the 1950s and into the next decade Britain's favourite radio soap opera was undoubtedly *Mrs. Dale's Diary* the on-going saga of Mary Dale, her doctor husband Jim, her mother Mrs. Freeman (complete with cat), her char Mrs. Maggs, and all the rest. As the Queen Mother, whose benign smile and floppy hats might well have qualified her for a walk-, or rather read-on in the show and who is undoubtedly the star of Britain's royal soap opera, put it quite correctly, it did seem the epitome of the middle-class family of the time. The Queen Mother, of all the royals, has always seemed most conscious of the confines of her aristocratic position.

ELLIS, HAVELOCK   (1859–1939) British psychologist

What we call 'progress' is the exchange of one nuisance for another nuisance.
quoted in P. Grosskurth, *Havelock Ellis* (1980)

Ellis' upbringing had been a model of Victorian propriety – he remained a virgin until the age of 32 when he married a lesbian, Edith Lees (1861-1916) and was rendered in any case virtually impotent through shyness – but despite or perhaps as the inevitable result of such repression, he chose to concentrate his own career on the study of sexual behaviour. He was a leading member of the late-Victorian avant-garde and a member of the Fellowship of the New Life, a forerunner of the Fabian Society. Sexual Inversion, his study of homosexuality, appeared in 1896, the first of seven volumes of his magnum opus, *Studies in the Psychology of Sex* (1896–1928). In 1899 its publisher was tried for 'obscene libel'. Ellis refused to appear in court and the book was condemned. His subsequent researches, uniformly branded as unfit for all but professional, medical readers, were published in America.

ELLSBERG, DANIEL   (1931–) American government official

To act responsibly you have to take leaps without being sure.
quoted in *Esquire*, 1971

Ellsberg was a a former US Deputy Defense Secretary who in 1971 leaked to the *New York Times* what were called 'The Pentagon Papers', the classified history of the war in Vietnam. This 7,000 page document had been commissioned in 1967 by Secretary of Defense Robert MacNamara, and its 2.5 million words took a year to amass. It charted the true history of US involvement in Vietnam until 1968, and when Ellsberg's conscience overrode his official duties the government fought hard to suppress his revelations. The *Times* began publishing excerpts from the Papers on June 13, 1971. On June 16 the Justice Department obtained an order restraining further episodes. The press claimed that the papers were in public domain and on June 30 the Supreme Court upheld their right to publish.

EMPSON, WILLIAM (1906–1984) British literary critic

The object of life, after all, is not to understand things, but to maintain one's defences and equilibrium and live as well as one can.
quoted in *Contemporary Literary Critics*, ed. Elmer Borklund (1977)

Empson began his university career by studying mathematics, but in his final year turned to English, in which he was heavily influenced by the scientific and analytical methods encouraged by the critic I.A. Richards (1893–1979). Empson developed Richards' methods even further, concentrating on poetry, which he subjected to an intense semantic analysis. His first book *Seven Types of Ambiguity* (1930) spelt out his theory that the greatness of a poem stemmed from the multiplicity of meanings, not all of them intended, that might be elicited from its text. His second book, *Some Versions of Pastoral* (1935), added a Marxist interpretation to his theories, while he largely abandoned this in *The Structure of Complex Words* (1951), returning to pure semantics.

EPSTEIN, BRIAN (1934–1967) British rock manager

I want to manage those four boys. It wouldn't take me more than two half days a week.
British record shop owner, seeing the Beatles, 1961

In 1961 Epstein was the manager of Liverpool's leading electrical supplies and record store, North End Road Music Stores, generally known as NEMS. A RADA graduate, and emergent homosexual, Epstein combined artistic ambitions with his more prosaic abilities as a retailer. On October 28 1961 18-year-old Raymond Jones asked Epstein for 'My Bonnie', a record by a band called the Beatles. Epstein prided himself on the range of his stock, but this record was not among it. He determined to check out this band, for whom two further requests had been made. On November 9 he made his first visit to the Cavern, the cellar club in which the band regularly played. Whether he liked their music or whether, as the biographies have it, he fell in love at first sight with John Lennon, remains moot. Either way Epstein realised that managing the Beatles could combine his artistic and his business needs. It took him somewhat more than 'two half days': in the end, in every sense, it took his life.

ERHARD, WERNER (1935–) (John Paul Rosenberg) American self-help guru

What I recognised is that you can't put it together. It's already together and what you have to do is experience it being together.
quoted in *Let's Talk About Me* by A. Clare (1981)

Erhard was born John Rosenberg and worked initially as a second-hand car salesman. In 1960 he left his job and his family and changed his name, first to Jack Frost and then to Werner Erhard, a name taken from those of the two men, so he claimed, who had transformed Germany: Werner von Braun and Chancellor Erhard. Sometime during the Sixties Erhard had 'a peak experience', the nature of which was indescribable but led him inexorably to his role, first proclaimed in 1971, as the guru of EST or Erhard Seminars Training. The essence of this therapy, revealed to Erhard during a car ride, was 'it': the realisation that things are exactly what they are or, as disciples learn through special weekends in which they pay well to experience 48 hours of various deprivations and humiliations, 'what is, is and what is not, is not'. EST has expanded worldwide to become one of the most popular of the quick-and-dirty therapeutic cures.

ERNST, MAX (1891–1976) German painter

Such is the vocation of man: to deliver himself from blindness
quoted in *Beyond Painting* by 'The Artist and His Friends' (1948)

Ernst abandoned his career in philosophy and psychology after meeting the painter August Macke in 1911. This move was underlined by his association from 1914 with the sculptor Jean Arp. Ernst devoted himself to finding in art 'the myth of his time'. He became one of the earliest dadaists, using the techniques of collage and frottage (rubbing texture through or onto paint) to create disturbing, challenging images, and then left Germany for Paris, where he played a prominent role in the new movement, surrealism. Although André Breton called his 'the most magnificently haunted mind in Europe', his inability to embrace surrealism's political philosophies led to a gradual estrangement from the hard core, culminating in Ernst's acceptance of an award at the 1954 Venice Biennale.

ERTZ, SUSAN American writer

Millions long for immortality who do not know what to do with themselves on a rainy Sunday afternoon.
quoted in *Quotations for Speakers and Writers*, ed. A. Andrews

Ertz's oft-quoted comment sums up with depressing accuracy the great malaise that besets contemporary life. The contradiction between the lust for eternal life, or perhaps more honestly the fear of death, and the fact that most people find their lives meaningless, whether or not they are prepared to admit to such emptiness, remains an insoluble conundrum. For all its simplicity, Ertz's comment reveals a terrible bleakness to which humanity has yet, for all its alarms and excursions, to find a positive answer.

ERVIN, SAM   (1896–) American politician

This is not executive privilege. It is executive poppycock.
American senator, during Watergate hearings, 1973

Senator Sam Ervin, personifying for the American people at a time when they needed such reassurance most the very image of the nation's mythical embodiment, 'Uncle Sam', headed the Watergate hearings that commenced on May 17 1973. Ervin and his committee listened to a parade of White House staffers vying with each other in their struggles to avoid complicity in the scandal. In the end some 15 of the President's men were disgraced, dismissed, jailed and/or fined. Only President Nixon himself escaped interrogation. Ervin's comment was addressed to Nixon's efforts to claim that his executive privilege, distancing him by virtue of his office from the sordid probings of the committee, ought to be extended to members of his staff. Ervin, whose no-nonsense 'country boy' image endeared himself to his countrymen, showed time and again that he had no interest in such cavilling.

ETTORE, BARBARA   American writer

The other line always moves faster.
quoted in *The Official Rules* by P. Dickson (1978)

A depressing but nonetheless true dictum culled from the circumstances of everyday life and quoted in Paul Dickson's collection of such quotidian rules. Ettore, obviously a veteran of queues – 'lines' in American – in banks, post offices, supermarkets, and anywhere else where the hapless and hopeful customer is greeted by the dubious choice of checkouts or service windows, notes the awful truth: the one which seems most alluring will inevitably, in the way of such things, prove to be the slowest, whether through a lethargic cashier, an eccentric customer or some other, hitherto unforeseen circumstance.

EVANS, BERGAN   (1904–) American educator

Lying is an indispensable part of making life tolerable.

Bergen's philosophy might not endear itself to the more rigidly moral, but there seems little doubt that in one way and another he's right. The only question one might pose is which lies are the most important: the ones one tells to others, or the ones one tells oneself?

EVANS, EDITH   (1888–1976) British actress

There is no secret. The secret is what is is; and what isn't, isn't.
quoted in the *Sunday Times* obituary, 1976

Edith Evans, here apparently quoting EST's guru Werner Erhard (qv), was throughout a long and distinguished career one of England's leading actresses. Not without success in tragedy, her real forte proved to be in comedy and her reputation rests on her interpretation of some of the theatre's greatest comic roles. She first appeared in 1912 in an amateur production, and initiated her professional successes in 1922 as Cleopatra in Dryden's *All For Love*. In 1923 she confirmed her popularity in the first production of Shaw's *Back To Methusaleh*. She played Portia, Cleopatra, Rosalind, Beatrice and other Shakespearian heroines, as well as most of the important female roles in classic comedy. Her reading of Lady Bracknell in Wilde's *The Importance of Being Earnest* (filmed in 1948) defined the role for all her successors. She was made a Dame in 1946.

EVANS, HAROLD   (1928–) British journalist

The camera cannot lie. But it can be an accessory to untruth.
Pictures on a Page (1978)

Evans was editor of the *Sunday Times* for fourteen years. During his tenure, and that of the Thompson organisation which owned the paper, it became England's leading weekly newspaper, offering a level of campaigning journalism and informed opinion that set it far above any rival and took it from its former position as a nondescript paraphrase of Conservative government policy to that of a journal that stood by its own, independent opinions, whether or, more likely, not they reflected those of the establishment. The line quoted above comes from Evans' introduction to a collection of photo-journalism, not all of it taken from his own paper, in which he goes on to explain that while the instant reportage of a camera shot cannot in itself falsify what it sees, its use by a given editor within a given context can do just that.

EVERYTHING YOU EVER WANTED TO KNOW ABOUT SEX

Is sex dirty? Only if it's done right.
screenplay by Woody Allen (1972)

In 1970 America's number one non-fiction best-seller was *Every-thing You Ever Wanted to Know about Sex (but were afraid to ask)* 'explained' (rather than written) by Dr. David Reuben, MD, (1933–), a Californian psychiatrist. This manual for the middle-aged and distinctly repressed, as Gore Vidal put it, 'a compendium of tribal taboos', advocated, among other things, mass cunnilingus and Coca-Cola douches, all interlarded with a rash of generalisations and dubious, if extensive, statistics. Woody Allen parodied Reuben in 1972. Allen's preoccupation with death is matched only by his fascination with sex; as he remarked to the *New York Herald Tribune* in 1975 'Love is the answer, but while you are waiting for the answer, sex raises some pretty good questions.'

EWART, GAVIN   (1916–) British poet
Bad men do what good men only dream.
The Deceptive Grin of the Gravel Porters (1968)

Ewart showed himself precociously talented when, aged seven-teen, he contributed to the first edition of Geoffrey Grigson's magazine *New Verse* joining such luminaries as Auden, Empson and MacNeice. The first collection of his own verse, *Poems and Songs*, appeared in 1939. After World War II he began working as an advertising copywriter, until he turned to full-time freelance writing in 1971. His second collection, *Londoners*, did not appear until 1964. Ewart's verse tends to the comic, the satiric and erotic, and his publications have been far more prolific since the Sixties.

EWER, W.N.   (1885–1976)
How odd of God to choose the Jews

British journalist W.N. 'Trilby' Ewer was present at the Savage Club in London when he overheard an interchange between the Jewish pianist Benno Moisewitsch and a fellow guest. The latter, who was attempting to ingratiate himself with the musician, asked 'Is there anti-Semitism in the club'. Moisewitsch, less than impressed, replied 'Only amongst the Jews!' Ewer forthwith penned his quatrain. The verse has proved sufficiently long-lived to have inspired a number of corollaries, notably that of Cecil Browne who wrote in 1924 'But not so odd / As those who choose / A Jewish God / Yet spurn the Jews.'

F

FADIMAN, CLIFTON   (1904–) American editor and author

We prefer to believe that the absence of inverted commas guarantees the originality of a thought, whereas it may be merely that the utterer has forgotten its source.
Any Number Can Play

Fadiman worked in publishing until 1935 he joined the *New Yorker* magazine as Book Editor and regular lead reviewer. His technique was to deal with the greatest possible number of books, disposing of each in a brisk, concise and above all witty paragraph. For a decade from 1938 he introduced the popular radio programme *Information Please*. As well as reviewing, Fadiman wrote a number of books. These included *Any Number Can Play* (1957), *Enter Conversing* (1962), *Fifty Years* (1965). He was editor of the ten-colume *Gateway to the Great Books* (1963) and for many years he acted as judge for the Book-of-the-Month Club.

FADIMAN, CLIFTON

For most men life is a search for the proper manila envelope in which to get themselves filed.
1960

FADIMAN, CLIFTON

Experience teaches you that the man who looks you straight in the eye, particularly if he adds a firm handshake, is hiding something.
Enter Conversing (1962)

FANON, FRANTZ (1925–61) Martiniquais writer and revolutionary

Violence is man re-creating himself.
The Wretched of the Earth (1961)

Fanon was a major influence on black and white radicals in the Sixties and Seventies as well as on the revolution in his native Algeria. He had studied medicine and psychiatry and used this knowledge in *Peau noir, masques blancs* (1952, Black Skin,

White Masks, 1967), an influential study of the effect of white colonialism on the psychology of its black subjects. Using a variety of psychoanalytic theories, infused by Sartre's existentialism, Fanon showed that in such a relationship the psychology of both sides suffered. He believed implacably in the need for an Algerian revolution in particular and an uprising in the Third World in general. *Les Damnés de la terre* (1961, The Wretched of the Earth) expounded his revolutionary theories, in which as quoted above he abandoned as futile any concepts of non-violent change. Imperialism had been established through violence and only through counter-violence could it be overthrown.

FAROUK, KING (1920–1965) Egyptian monarch

There will soon be only five kings left – the Kings of England, Diamonds, Hearts, Spades and Clubs.
last monarch of Egypt, 1952

For many Europeans and Americans King Farouk provided the perfect stereotype of the oily, bloated, self-indulgent, corrupt Arab monarch, plucked wholesale from the pages of a thousand pulp magazines. Farouk himself did little to offset so negative an image. He lived the life of an international playboy, showing little concern for the nation he ruled and far more for the satisfying of his various gross appetites. He offered this, his sole aphorism, after he had been deposed by an army revolt led by Colonel Gamel Abdel Nasser. The last of the Mohammad Ali dynasty, Farouk escaped unharmed from Egypt, spending the rest of his life in pampered exile, but leaving behind him a number of treasured possessions: a pile of US comic books, six dozen pairs of binoculars, a thousand neckties and several photos of copulating elephants.

FAULKNER, WILLIAM (1897–1962) American novelist
Faulkner was born in Oxford, Mississippi, a town with which his family had long associations and in which he lived out most of his life, drawing on the history both of the state and of his own relations in much of his work. He created a personal style, which in 1950 gained him the Nobel Prize for Literature, by fusing this Southern regionalism with the new techniques of European modernism. After publishing a collection of verse in 1924 he met Sherwood Anderson (1876–1941), who encouraged him to write prose. His books, in a series of novels extending from *Soldier's Pay* (1926) to *The Reivers* (1962), created the fictional history of Yoknapatawpha County, in which the history of the South, with all its racial and sexual tensions well to the fore, was recounted in

his unique style. Contemporary critics protested that he was obsessed with the darker side of America. In retrospect it has been accepted that Faulkner was only a precursor of writers of even more destructive, pessimistic vision and that for all his apparent dedication to the negative, he offered, above all, an original and fascinating literary imagination.

FAULKNER, WILLIAM

One of the saddest things is that the only thing a man can do for eight hours a day, day after day, is work. You can't eat eight hours a day, nor drink for eight hours a day nor make love for eight hours.
interviewed in *Writers at Work*, 1st series (1958)

FAULKNER, WILLIAM

Art is simpler than people think because there is so little to write about. All the moving things are eternal in man's history and have been written before, and if a man writes hard enough, sincerely enough, humbly enough, and with the unalterable determination never, never to be quite satisfied with it he will repeat them because art, like poverty, takes care of its own, shares its bread.
interviewed in *Writers at Work*, 1st series (1958)

FAULKNER, WILLIAM

An artist is a creature driven by demons. He is completely amoral in that he will rob, borrow, beg or steal from anybody to get the work done. He has no peace until then. Everything goes by the board: honor, pride, decency, security, happiness, all, to get the book written. If a writer has to rob his mother, he will not hesitate; the 'Ode to a Grecian Urn' is worth any number of old ladies.
interviewed in *Writers at Work*, 1st series (1958)

Faulkner's romantic claim that art transcends any other loyalty looked good in print, and has often been quoted as his driving belief, but his own life hardly bears out such bravado. If he spent the first thirty years of his life in relative dissolution, piling up debts, both of cash and of favours, then he spent the last thirty paying back every penny and returning every kindness. His years slaving for Hollywood, the only way he could find enough money to support his family, undoubtedly put paid to a number of thus unwritten books. If writers are amoral, as he claims, then it is the morals of non-artistic society that they eschew; few if any first-class writers have not established some code of morals, albeit idiosyncratic, by which they sustain their own existence.

FAULKNER, WILLIAM

A writer is congenitally unable to tell the truth and that is why we call what he writes fiction.
quoted in his obituary, 1962

FEIFFER, JULES (1929–) American cartoonist

Feiffer began his career in cartooning as an apprentice to comic artist Will Eisner. His syndicated strip has been running since 1955, mocking the great and not so great in American society and taking a satirical look at the fluctuating fashions in American mores. He has written his own study of the genre in which he works: *The Great Comic Book Heroes*. His style, however, depends not on the slapstick of earlier illustrators nor on the super-heroics of such as Superman, but on his own wit, and his cartoons are notably verbal. His work originated in the New York weekly newspaper, the *Village Voice*, but it has since been taken up by a wide variety of magazines and newspapers, all of them keen to capitalise on what has been termed his 'visual editorialising'.

FEIFFER, JULES

Christ died for our sins. Dare we make his martyrdom meaning-less by not committing them?
quoted in *Peter's Quotations* by Lawrence Peter (1977)

FELDMAN, MARTY (1933–1983) British comedian

Comedy, like sodomy, is an unnatural act.
quoted in *The Times*, 1969

Feldman was a veteran comic writer, who had worked on such classic radio shows as *Educating Archie* and *Round the Horne*, as well as trying for his own music-hall career as one third of the less than well-known act Morris, Marty and Mitch. After heading the team of writers on *The Frost Report* in 1965, and making his on-camera debut in *At Last the 1948 Show*, the latest in the seemingly endless succession of 'satire' programmes, the pop-eyed Feldman was given his own show, *Marty*, which ran in 1968 and 1969. His anarchic side was given full rein and the show was highly successful, leading to his moving to Hollywood where, before he died, he made a number of films, usually with Mel Brooks, including *Young Frankenstein* (1973), *Silent Movie* (1976) and *High Anxiety* (1978).

FERBER, EDNA (1887–1968) American writer

A woman can look both moral and exciting – if she also looks as if it were quite a struggle.
quoted in *Reader's Digest*, 1954

Ex-journalist Ferber began with short stories before turning to novels in 1924, finding an appreciative audience for *So Big* (1924, which won a Pulitizer Prize), *Show Boat* (1926), *Cimarron* (1929) and others. Many of her works were filmed and she collaborated with George S. Kaufman on a number of hit plays. Ferber was a noted member of that collection of wits and self-publicists otherwise known as the Algonquin Round Table and was never happier than when delivering a bon mot, preferably at the expense of the Table's supreme prima donna, Alec Woolcott whom she characterised as 'that New Jersey Nero who thinks his pinafore is a toga.' Unlike many friends, who were constantly in and out of marriages, she resisted the altar, remarking 'being an old maid is like death by drowning, a really delightful sensation after you cease to struggle'.

FIELD, ERIC British advertising copywriter

Your King and Country Need You
recruiting slogan, July 1914

During July 1914 one Colonel Strachey contacted Eric Field, a copywriter at the Caxton Advertising Agency. He swore him to secrecy, explained that war with Germany was imminent and ordered him to prepare an advertisement to be used for recruiting the 'New Armies' that Field Marshal Lord Kitchener would soon be engaged in raising. Field created a simple image: the royal coat of arms and the line 'Your King and Country Need You'. This appeared throughout the press on the day following the declaration of war. Kitchener insisted that the line 'God save the King' should be appended to all the ads. When the advertisement was used on the cover of *London Opinion* on September 5th, it was further embellished by the picture of Kitchener that has become synonymous with the copy-line. This version was issued as a poster and occasioned Margot Asquith's remark 'If Kitchener was not a great man, he was, at least, a great poster'.

FIELDS, W.C. (1879–1946) (William Claude Dukinfield) American comedian

On the whole, I'd rather be in Philadelphia.
his own suggestion when asked for possible last words

Fields began, like so many early film comedians, as a stage comedian, creating live the persona that would make him so popular on the screen. His initial act was as a tramp juggler and the drinking that became central to his later image developed during the hard years touring America's variety theatres. Fields moved into silent movies as early as 1915 and worked regularly before he moved over to sound and showed that while many glamorous screen lovers faltered when it came to their voices, as far as comedy was concerned, the orotund Fieldsian tones were ideal. In a variety of hits he managed to make the thoroughly disreputable figures that he played strangely sympathetic. Fields' eccentricities and foibles – intolerant, misogynistic, child-hating, alcoholic – proved the stuff of legend, although he denied prejudices saying 'I hate everyone equally.' Of his many quotable lines, these are a representative few:

I exercise extreme self-control. I never drink anything stronger than gin before breakfast.

I never vote for anyone; I always vote against.

Anyone who hates small dogs and children can't be all bad.

If at first you don't succeed, try again then quit. No use being a damn fool about it.

FIELDS, W.C.

I hate water – fish fuck in it.
qouted in *The Book of Hollywood Quotes* (1979)

FIGES, EVA (1932–) English novelist and feminist

When modern women discovered the orgasm it was, combined with modern birth control, perhaps the biggest single nail in the coffin of male dominance.
quoted in *The Descent of Woman*, by Elaine Morgan (1972)

Figes was born in Germany but came to England in 1939 and was educated at the University of London. She has written a number of novels, most of which explore the uncertainties and fragmentation of identity, often using interior monologue. Figes is equally well-known for her important contributions to feminist social and literary criticism. Her best-known work in this field is *Patriarchal*

Attitudes (1970), a major feminist text, and *Sex and Subterfuge: Women Writers to 1850* (1982).

FIRBANK, RONALD (1886-1926) British novelist

The world is dreadfully managed, one hardly knows to whom to complain.
Vainglory (1915)

Firbank's first book appeared in 1905 and he continued writing until his death. His father was an MP but Firbank's grandfather Joseph Firbank (1819–86) began life as a miner before he ended it as a railway magnate and this juxtaposition of rags and riches permeates his work in its mixture of the delicate and the portentous. Desperately nervous, almost incapable of normal conversation and, in Siegfried Sassoon's words 'as orchidaceous as his fictional fantasies' Firbank created a series of artificial, bizarre fin-de-siécle fantasies, the literary equivalent of Aubrey Beardsley drawings. He was generally ignored, except by the avant-garde, in his lifetime, but his work, with its exotic aesthetic, reflective of the homosexual dandy who created it, has survived long enough for critics to have coined an eponynmous description: Firbankian.

FITZGERALD, F. SCOTT (1896–1940) American novelist
Fitzgerald published his first novel, *This Side of Paradise*, in 1920. It was an enormous success and established Fitzgerald as the voice of what he called 'the jazz age'. Armed with this success he wooed and married the beautiful, volatile and capricious Zelda Sayre whose joie de vivre helped make them role models for young America. In 1922 he followed his best-seller with *The Beautiful and Damned* and he maintained his income with a flow of high-priced short stories. In 1925 Fitzgerald published what he called 'about the best American novel ever written', the book his critics concur in ranking as his finest work: *The Great Gatsby*. After the 1929 Crash the Fitzgeralds' fortunes declined alongside the national economy. Zelda's zany antics declined into real schizophrenia, Fitzgerald drank more than he wrote and his next novel, *Tender Is the Night* (1934), failed to attract his former readers. Fitzgerald died in 1940, an antique, almost unknown, working on his unfinished Hollywood novel, *The Last Tycoon*. His reputation was revived by his friend Edmund Wilson whose publication of *The Crack-Up* (1945) revealed the darker side of Fitzgerald's life. Today he stands as a romantic American hero, the subject of one of the most exhaustive scholarly industries outside the Bloomsbury Group.

FITZGERALD, F. SCOTT

All good writing is swimming under water and holding your breath.
Notebooks (1978)

FITZGERALD, F. SCOTT

An author ought to write for the youth of his own generation, the critics of the next and the schoolmasters of ever afterwards.
Notebooks (1978)

FITZGERALD, F. SCOTT

First you take a drink, then the drink takes a drink, then the drink takes you.
quoted by J. Feiffer, *Ackroyd*

The Fitzgeralds epitomised the Twenties and what the Prohibition-ridden Twenties meant was drink. The drinking was fine when Fitzgerald was young, tough and successful. As the decade passed the volume increased and expanded from the social to the stimulant: by 1930 Fitzgerald believed, correctly or otherwise, that without a drink he could not work. For the rest of his life he was locked in a struggle with liquor. The best and most distressing picture of Fitzgerald and drink comes in Budd Schulberg's *The Disenchanted* (1950), a novel based on the author's experience of a lengthy Fitzgerald jag. Fitzgerald was technically sober when he died, but years of alcohol had weakened his constitution and in the end the drink did indeed take him.

FITZGERALD, F. SCOTT

Three British nannies sat knitting the slow pattern of Victorian England, the pattern of the forties, the sixties and the eighties, into sweaters and socks, to the tune of gossip as formalised as incantation.
Tender Is the Night (1934)

Fitzgerald's own life permeated his books and *Tender Is the Night* is no exception. This story, set among the fashionable expatriates of the French Riviera, records the lives of Dick Diver, a psychiatrist, and Nicole, his schizophrenic wife. It was written with difficulty, and reflects the decline in the Fitzgeralds' lives: his alcoholism, her schizophrenia, his compensatory affair with a young Hollywood actress, the terrible toll their hell-bent lives had taken and, as ever, the rich, to whom such problems never seemed really either to happen or to matter. *Tender Is the Night* failed, with its glitzy background – the nannies above represent the last vestige of the British Empire, giving way to the new, American *arrivistes* – to impress his American audience, whose tastes had turned away from such indulgence, however tainted it might be.

FITZGERALD, F. SCOTT

Show me a hero, and I will write you a tragedy.
The Crack Up (1945)

The Crack Up, in which Fitzgerald charted the collapse of his own life, was published posthumously in *Esquire* magazine in 1945. It was written in spring 1936, when his life, both personal and professional, was at the lowest of ebbs. Fitzgerald, of course, was hardly alone in his despair. The whole gaudy edifice of the Twenties, of which he was so paramount a representative, had crumbled in October 1929. In his delineation of his own descent into hell, he was in his way illustrating the downside of the American psyche. The *Crack Up* was designed as a final analysis of his own impotence. Yet its lucid self-dissection rejects self-pity and in itself shows, as would the unfinished *The Last Tycoon*, that Fitzgerald was far from defeated.

FITZGERALD, F. SCOTT

Optimism is the content of small men in high places.
The Crack Up (1945)

FITZGERALD, F. SCOTT

In a real dark night of the soul it is always three o'clock in the morning, day after day.
The Crack Up (1945)

FITZGERALD, F. SCOTT

There are only the pursued, the pursuing, the busy and the tired.
The Great Gatsby (1925)

The Great Gatsby remains Fitzgerald's peak literary achievement. If his stories of 'flappers and philosophers' established him as the voice of the era's fashionable superficialities, then this novel captures the deeper currents running through the age. In Gatsby, the self-made man, half gangster, half American success story, with his paradoxical capacity for idealistic, romantic love, Fitzgerald sets the romantic fictions of America's myths of itself against the meretricious reality of the rich Buchanans and their hangers on. Gatsby is a fascinating, symbolic invention, a genuine revelation after the endless parade of Fitzgerald's rich boys and their belles. And simultaneously in his alienated role he carries on the thread of autobiography common to all Fitzgerald's stories. As Malcolm Cowley said 'It was as if all his novels described a big dance to which he had taken...the prettiest girl...and as if at the same time he stood outside the ballroom, a little Midwestern boy with his nose to the glass, wondering how much the tickets cost and who paid for the music.'

FITZGERALD, F. SCOTT

Her voice is full of money.
The Great Gatsby (1925)

of Daisy Buchanan

FITZGERALD, F. SCOTT

Gatsby believed in the green light, the orgiastic future that year by year recedes before us. It eluded us then, but that's no matter – tomorrow we will run faster, stretch out our arms further.... And one fine morning – . So we beat on, boats against the current, borne back ceaselessly into the past.
The Great Gatsby (1925)

These are the last words of the book.

FITZGERALD, F. SCOTT

There are no second acts in American lives.
The Last Tycoon (unfinished, 1941)

Fitzgerald died before he was able to finish his own version of the 'Hollywood novel'. He generally hated Hollywood; he loathed the philistinism, the aggression and above all the anonymous writers' buildings, with their teams of writers, all pitted against each other in the writing of the same script, a script that would probably be all but rewritten by the producer, director and any other interested executive. Yet the book's chief character, Monroe Stahr, is modelled on Hollywood's boy wonder, the workaholic Irving Thalberg (1899–1936) who in fact, although Fitzgerald chose to set him in a more heroic mould, was more responsible for what Fitzgerald saw as the mawkishness of contemporary films, than many of those, such as Joe Mankiewicz, whom Fitzgerald slated as villains.

FITZGERALD, F. SCOTT

He differed from the healthy type that was essentially middle-class – he never seemed to perspire.
This Side of Paradise (1920)

This Side of Paradise was Fitzgerald's great hit. With it he won his wife, his reputation as a writer and his role as the poet of the Jazz Age. The book, originally titled 'The Romantic Egoist', deals with the sentimental education and subsequent, necessary disillusion of the youthful Amory Blaine. The book was hugely autobiographical, drawing heavily on Fitzgerald's own experiences at Princeton, but it struck the requisite chord in many contemporary hearts. Reading it now the 'immorality' denounced by the more staid critics is hard to find, and it seems at times quite naive, as in the sentiment expressed here, but it brought Fitzgerald immense success at only twenty-four.

FITZGERALD, F. SCOTT

Let me tell you about the very rich. They are different from you and me...
The Rich Boy (1926)

Fitzgerald's story, 'The Rich Boy', published in his collection *All The Sad Young Men*, is typical of the short stories he was writing in the mid-Twenties. It is the story of Anson Hunter, his wealth, his charm and the sense of superiority that he gains from using both. As ever, in his treatment of the rich, Fitzgerald mixes his envy and admiration with distrust and simple fascination about how it is they do live, and he qualifies his comment by pointing out that having never suffered many of normal people's problems, they are 'soft where we are hard, and cynical where we are trustful...they think, deep in their hearts, that they are better than us.' Ten years later, Fitzgerald's friend and rival Ernest Hemingway wrote in the first version of *The Snows of Kilimanjaro*: 'He remembered poor old Scott Fitzgerald and his romantic awe of (the rich) and how he had started a story once that began "The very rich are different from you and me". And how someone had said to Scott, Yes, they have more money. But that was not humorous to Scott.' Nor was what he saw as Hemingway's slight and Fitzgerald duly complained. The name was changed in later editions to 'Julian', but the legend of the great writers' interchange persisted, erroneously. In fact the reply was made in 1936 to Hemingway himself, while pontificating on the rich to the critic Mary Colum who told him 'The only difference between the rich and other people is that the rich have more money.'

FITZGIBBON, BERNICE (1897–?) American writer

Creativity varies inversely with the number of cooks involved in the broth.
Macy's, Gimbels and Me (1967)

Too many cooks spoil the broth, runs the proverb and for most creative people it's a dictum to live by; the idea of artistry en masse appeals to few of them. There's no actual need for the lonely garret, unless one has no choice, but isolation seems to be among the most important factors in helping many creative people do what they do best. When, willy-nilly, they are forced into situations where team-work can't be avoided, there usually emerges some form of hierarchy and when more than one creative ego is involved, the atmosphere is rarely calm.

FITZSIMMONS, BOB British boxer

The bigger they come, the harder they fall.
quoted in 1902

The boxing world had barely emerged from the days of the illicit but heavily supported bare-knuckle prize fight into the modern era of the Queensberry Rules when England's Bob Fitzsimmons challenged the incumbent champion, the huge Jim Jeffries, for the heavyweight championship of the world. Fitzsimmons was a nippy boxer, whereas the massive Jeffries preferred to use brute force. Cocky Fitzsimmons, giving himself and the fans the sort of pre-fight pep talk that Muhammad Ali turned into an art, promised that the hunk held no fears for him. For a change such hubris was not rewarded with instant disaster, but Fitzsimmons' reign as champion was short and the real honours of the era go to Jack Johnson, the first of many great black heavyweights.

FLECKER, JAMES ELROY (1884–1915) British poet

We take the Golden Road to Samarkand
Hassan (1922)

Flecker, one of the last exponents of the aesthetic movement of the 1890s, cannibalised his 'own poem' The Golden Journey to Samarkand (1913) to create his play, *Hassan*. In the poem, a celebration of the important Mohammedan tradition of taking a pilgrimage from Arabia to Samarkand, near the Russian border with Afghanistan, an Epilogue showed merchants and pilgrims chanting in chorus 'We make the Golden Journey to Samarkand'. Slightly adapted, Flecker put this epilogue into his play, which was published seven years after his death.

FLEMING, IAN (1908–64) British author

'I'd like to start with caviar and then have a plain grilled rognon de veau with "pommes soufflés". And then I'd like to have "fraises des bois" with a lot of cream. Is it very shameless to be so certain and so expensive?' She smiled at him enquiringly. 'It's a virtue, and anyway it's only a good plain wholesome meal.... I myself will accompany Mademoiselle with the caviar, but then I would a very small "tournedos", underdone, with "sauce Bearnaise" and a "coeur dartichaut". While Mademoiselle is enjoying the strawberries, I will have half an avocado pear with a little French dressing. Do you approve?' The maitre d'hotel bowed.
Casino Royale (1953)

Ian Fleming, the second son of a Conservative MP and the brother of the explorer and travel writer Peter Fleming, enjoyed a traditional upper-class education before joining Reuters, followed by the family merchant bank. In 1939 he began working abroad both as a *Times* reporter and as a member of British intelligence. This intelligence work continued throughout the war, when Fleming was personal assistant to the Director of Naval Intelligence. After the war he joined Kemsley Newspapers as foreign manager. In 1953 he wrote his first novel, *Casino Royale*, that introduced James Bond 007, a British secret agent licensed to kill. Bond is Fleming writ large: his tastes in food and drink, his treatment and choice of women, his dress sense and preference in motor-cars. Fleming's experience in intelligence obviously added verisimilitude, as did the detailed researches he put into the planning of each book, but in essence the 14 Bond stories are traditional goodies vs. baddies fare, with a heavy leavening of snobbery, sex, sadism and post-war brand-name consumerism.

FOOT, MICHAEL (1913–) British politician

The members of our Secret Service have apparently spent so much time under the bed looking for Communists that they haven't had the time to look in the bed.
on the Profumo scandal, 1963

The main British event of 1963, which offered inter alia Beatlemania, television satire, prototype Swinging London and climaxed in November with the assassination of President Kennedy, was the Profumo Affair. This sex-in-high-places melodrama centred on the relationship between the then Tory Minister of War, John Profumo, and a call-girl, Christine Keeler. The problem was that Miss Keeler was also rendering her services to

Ivanov, a Soviet Embassy attaché. The Opposition, capitalising on native British prudery and a flurry of recent espionage cases, claimed that Profumo's dalliance was endangering national security. Michael Foot, a leading Labour left-winger, put their case very neatly. The affair might have gone away – the permissive Sixties were after all gearing up for an all-out assault on traditional morality – but Profumo foolishly lied to the House of Commons, denying any such involvement. In due course he resigned and after him went the Prime Minister, although he claimed grounds of ill-health.

FORD, GERALD R. (1913–) American president

I am a Ford, not a Lincoln
on taking office as vice-president, December 6 1973

Among the various casualties of the Watergate Affair of 1973 was Richard Nixon's vice-president Spiro T. Agnew, who while not directly involved in Watergate, had been forced to resign after pleading 'no contest' to felony charges regarding tax evasion. His successor was Gerald Ford, the House Republican leader from Michigan, a man of whom former President Lyndon Johnson had remarked 'Gerry's the only man I knew who can't fart and chew gum at the same time'. Ford greeted his own elevation with this carefully self-deprecating statement. Nine months later, when Nixon's own resignation put him in the hot seat, he kept up the line, saying on his inauguration 'I guess it just proves that in America anyone can be President.'

FORD I, HENRY (1863–1947) American automobile manufacturer

Any colour you like, as long as it's black.
slogan advertising the mass-produced Model-T Ford.

Ford did not invent the motor-car, but he invented the assembly line method of building them and thus revolutionised the availability of what up until 1908, when the first of his Model-T Fords rolled off a Detroit production line, had been a rich man's or an enthusiast's craftsman-built luxury. He combined mass production with aggressive marketing to bring motoring to the millions and sold 15 million Model-Ts by 1927. The one thing he did not bother to offer was a choice of colours. The only Ford on offer until 1925, when the company finally bowed to demand, was black.

FORD I, HENRY

Let a man start out in life to build something better and sell it cheaper than it has been built or sold before, let him have that determination and the money will roll in.

FORD I, HENRY

History is bunk
interviewed on May 25 1916

Ford was no scholar, nor did he claim to be one. His native wit and mechanical genius, coupled with his creation of mass produced motor-cars, provided him with such satisfactions as he required. If anything, he could be deliberately stubborn and 'ornery'. Basing its opinion on such characteristics, the *Chicago Tribune* in 1919 described Ford as an 'anarchist' and an 'ignorant idealist'. The millionaire promptly sued for libel. In court he suffered a lengthy cross-examination, in which defence counsel capitalised on his ignorance of the nation's history. Among the questions was one regarding an interview he had given on May 25 1916, where he had informed the reporter Charles N. Wheeler 'History is more or less bunk. It's tradition'. Ford told the court 'I did not say it was bunk. It was bunk to me.' The original phrase stayed and Ford remains branded with it. The *Tribune* was nevertheless found guilty of the libel, but fined a risible six cents.

FORGY, HOWELL M. (1908–) American chaplain

Praise the Lord and pass the ammunition.
at Pearl Harbor, December 7 1941

The Japanese attack on the American fleet at the base of Pearl Harbor, Hawaii, achieved what the British leader Winston Churchill had failed to do despite months of appeals: it brought a hitherto reluctant America into the Second World War. The Americans had broken the Japanese codes in 1940 and thus their leaders had some warning of Japan's hostile intentions, but preferred to ignore them. They knew an attack was due, but had no idea as to its target. On December 6th an intelligence clerk monitored air traffic specifying Hawaii as that target, but the generals were still unimpressed. When the attack did come 2,008 sailors, 218 soldiers, 109 marines and 68 civilians were killed and large numbers wounded; eighteen ships were sunk. As the Japanese planes strafed the harbour, a chaplain, probably Forgy but possibly a Captain McGuire, rallied the defenders with this exhortation.

FORSTER, E.M. (1879–1970) British novelist, essayist and critic

After Cambridge, where he was elected to the elite intellectual club, The Apostles, and greatly expanded his own intellectual abilities, Forster published his first novel, *Where Angels Fear To Tread*, in 1905. It was followed by *The Longest Journey* (1907), *A Room With A View* (1908), all of which drew on his European travels. *Howards End* (1910) confirmed him as a major novelist. Forster continued writing variously – collections of essays and short stories, a travel guide, *Maurice*, a privately circulated novel on a homosexual theme which was not published until 1971 – before his final novel, *A Passage to India* (1922–24), based on his experiences as the secretary of the Maharajah of Dewas Senior. For the rest of his life Forster indulged in a variety of literary activities – fighting censorship, championing civil liberties, and more writing. His Clark Lectures, delivered in 1927, brought him the offer of a fellowship at King's, Cambridge, where he remained until his death. He was awarded the Order of Merit in 1969.

FORSTER, E.M.

Only connect
Howard's End (1910)

Howard's End was the first of Forster's novels to establish him as a serious novelist. 'Only connect' is both its epigraph and the inspiration of a later passage, which reads 'Only connect! That was the whole of her sermon. Only connect the prose and the passion, and both will be exalted and human love will be seen at its height. Live in fragments no longer. Only connect, and the beast and the monk, robbed of the isolation that is life to either, will die.' Forster's novels constantly deal in the attempt to reconcile all the opposing forces that can be seen as struggling to dominate a single, central character. For Forster, with his distrust of ideology, of established ideas (especially religions) and of all institutions, the aim was to gain harmony by uniting all of the contradictory forces, each with their mutually exclusive barriers, that in contemporary life militate against such harmony.

FORSTER, E.M.

I hate the idea of causes, and if I had to choose between betraying my country and betraying my friend, I hope I should have the guts to betray my country.
What I Believe (1938)

Forster's collection of essays *Two Cheers for Democracy*

appeared in 1951, the same year as the unmasking of the first of the 'Cambridge moles', Burgess and Maclean, but this essay was written thirteen years previously. Nonetheless his studied rejection of patriotism, his homosexuality and his subsequent involvement with King's College have led some theorists to ally him with the members of the 'homintern'. Forster's ideas may well have had an influence on between-the-wars Cambridge undergraduates and theories concerning his possible links to the traitors were hardly dispelled when the 'fourth man' Anthony Blunt used the line in trying to persuade mutual friends not to reveal to British intelligence what they knew about the two defectors. Critics have pointed out that his opposing of a single human individual to an anonymous country is fallacious, since every country is no more than a collection of single individuals, with all their interdependent and personal needs and emotions.

FORSTER, E.M.

'Ulysses' is a dogged attempt to cover the universe with mud.
Aspects of the Novel (1927)

Aspects of the Novel is the published version of Forster's Clark Lectures, delivered in 1927. The young F.R. Leavis (1895–1978) damned them as 'intellectually dull', nonetheless they proved a great popular success and King's College offered Forster a three-year fellowship. In 1946 the college made him an honorary fellow and he stayed their until he died. This comment on *Ulysses*, then still banned in England, flew in the face of fashionable opinion. From a liberal such as Forster professed to be, and especially one who was intimately associated with distinctly pro-*Ulysses* Bloomsbury, it seemed a philistine judgement, but Joyce's book obviously proved too explicit for Forster, whose own marginal dabblings in the recherché, in his case homosexuality, could not be published in his lifetime.

FORSTER, E.M.

There lies at the back of every creed something terrible and hard for which the worshipper may one day be required to suffer.
Two Cheers for Democracy (1951)

Forster remained adamant in his rejection of institutions and the ideologies and isms that sustained them. As he put it in the *Observer* in 1951 'Spoon feeding in the long run teaches us nothing but the shape of the spoon'. Consistent in his position, he acknowledged that even in such rejection there developed an automatic 'line' of one's own and rather than simply say 'No', he looked for alternatives. Distrusting religion, he respected if he did not wholly embrace mysticism; and championing liberalism in an era of its decline, he saw its weaknesses and acknowledged them. But he remained sceptical of the great political or religious movements and by the time he died in 1970, he must have felt, in the face of world events, that such scepticism was more than justified.

FORSTER, E.M.

**Porridge or prunes, sir; these are grim words. It is an epitome –
not, indeed, of English food, but of the forces which drag it into
the dirt. It carries the true spirit of gastronomic joylessness.
Porridge fills the Englishman up, prunes clean him out, so their
functions are opposed. But their spirit is the same: they eschew
pleasure and consider delicacy immoral.**
Wine and Food (1939)

Among the various pieces of general writing that Forster contributed during his life were occasional features for *Wine and Food*, the journal of the Wine and Food Society, itself founded in the 1930s by André Simon and fellow gastronomes. As an experienced traveller Forster had the chance to develop a cosmopolitan palate. He had also found himself more adventurous than the sort of English tourists, highly suspicious of anything foreign (particularly the menus), whom he satirised in such novels as *A Room with a View*. This disquisition on the horrors of English staples rings all too true in an era that had yet to be educated by Elizabeth David et al.

FORSTER, E.M.
Human beings have their great chance in the novel.
in Contemporary Literary Critics, ed. Elmer Borklund.

FORSYTH, BRUCE (1928–) British comedian

Didn't he/she do well!
catchphrase

Among the various examples of televised 'family entertainment' conducted under the genial aegis of comedian Bruce Forsyth with fluctuating degrees of success since his days as compere of *Saturday Night at the London Palladium* in the 1960s, BBC-1 TV's *Generation Game* has probably been the most popular. This show featured 'ordinary families' competing in a selection of games, the point of which, for the family, was to win prizes, and for the audience, to see the contestants humiliate themselves. As the beleaguered couples struggled through their challenge, beaming 'Brucie' would ask the viewers 'Didn't they do well!'. Allegedly coined by a technician watching rehearsals from high up on the lighting grid, the phrase soon entered the language, usually with a facetious, patronising air and the speaker's best attempt at Forsyth's own delivery. Similarly popular was Forsyth's entry-line 'Nice to see you! To see you nice!' (the latter half of which was usually accompanied by the mass studio audience).

FORTY-SECOND STREET

You're going out a youngster – but you've got to come back a star.
screenplay by Rian James and James Seymour

Not for nothing was this celebration of theatrical cliché, a remake of a 1929 movie called *On With The Show*, choreographed by Busby Berkeley, the king of the chorines. Bebe Daniels is a fading star who breaks her ankle on opening night, Ruby Keeler her understudy (Peggy Sawyer), Ginger Rogers a gold-digger, Dick Powell the juvenile lead, Warner Baxter the tough director, Guy Kibbee the sugar daddy. Baxter's keynote speech still enthuses aspirant thespians: 'Miss Sawyer...you listen to me and you listen hard. Two hundred people, two hundred jobs, $200,000, five weeks of grind and blood and sweat depend upon you! It's the lives of all these people who've worked with you. You've got to go on and you've got to give, and give and give! They've got to like you, got to. You understand? You can't fall down, you can't. Because your future's in it, my future and everything all of us have staked is on you. All right now, I'm through. But you keep your feet on the ground and your head on those shoulders of yours and, Sawyer, you're going out a youngster, but you've got to come back a star!'

FOUCAULT, MICHEL (1926–) French philosopher

All modern thought is penetrated by the law of thinking of the unthought of.
Les Mots et les choses (1966)

Foucault, professor of the history of the systems of thought at the Collège de France, is one of France's leading Marxist literary critics. He studied at the elite Ecole Normale Supérieure under Louis Althusser, whose teaching portrayed Marxism less as a political philosophy than as the revolutionary study of history conceived as a class struggle. Foucault's first book, *Histoire de la folie* (1961, Madness and Civilisation 1971), analysed the history of social attitudes to madness to show the way in which society represses its various categories of deviants and to suggest that such repression is primarily a means of maintaining the power of those who claim the right of stating who is deviant or not. This view was extended in two subsequent works.

FOWLER, GENE (1890–1960) American writer

What is success? It is a toy balloon among children armed with pins.
Skyline (1961)

Fowler was a journalist, playwright and scriptwriter whose works include *The Great Mr. McGoo* (1931, with Ben Hecht), *Timberline* (1933) and *The Mighty Barnum* (1935, with Bess Meredyth). *Skyline* is a collection of his prose, published posthumously. Fowler, who was a close friend of the actor John Barrymore, also wrote his biography *Goodnight Sweet Prince* (1944).

FOWLER, GENE

Men are not against you; they are merely for themselves.
Skyline (1961)

FRANCE, ANATOLE (1844–1924) (Jacques Anatole Thibault) French novelist, poet and critic

It is in the ability to deceive oneself that one shows the greatest talent.

France, the son of a Parisian bookseller, published his first successful novel in 1881. As a journalist and editor he built himself a major reputation and from 1890 was counted among the most influential figures in French literary life. In 1893 there appeared two campanion volumes – *La Rôtisserie de la reine Pedauque* and *Les Opinions de M. Jerome Coignard* – which together attempted to recreate the mind and sensibility of 18th century France. Four novels, appearing between 1897–1901, comprise the *Histoire contemporaine* and focusssing on M. Bergeret, a disenchanted but observant provincial professor, offer a satirical fantasy on the evolution of human society and institutions. His most popular work is held by many to be *Les Dieux ont soif* (1912), a study of the excesses of the French Revolution. France was awarded the Nobel Prize for Literature in 1921.

FRANCE, ANATOLE

Justice is the sanction of established injustice.
Crainquebille (1901)

Crainquebille, the lead story in the collection of the same name, is the tale of a costermonger who is unjustly jailed for insulting a police officer. On his release he finds himself unjustly despised and rejected by his neighbours and his customers. The result is his decline into poverty and despair. Finally he is reduced to such misery that his only hope is to assault another police officer, who has called him an addlepate, and hope to find the relative security and absolute irresponsibility of a further jail sentence.

FRANCE, ANATOLE

The vice most fatal to the statesman is virtue.
quoted in *The Times*, 1981

FRANCE, ANATOLE

Of all sexual aberrations, chastity is the strangest.

FRANCE, ANATOLE

Men are given to worshipping malevolent gods, and that which is not cruel seems to them not worthy of adoration.
Crainquebille (1901)

FRANCE, ANATOLE

The average man, who does not know what to do with his life, wants another one which will last forever.
The Revolt of the Angels (1914)

FRASER, GEORGE MACDONALD (1925–) British writer

I have observed, in the course of a dishonest life, that when a rogue is outlining a treacherous plan, he works harder to convince himself than to move his hearers.
Flashman (1969)

Writer George MacDonald Fraser's decision to probe further into the adult career of schoolboy literature's most famous bully, Flashman of *Tom Brown's Schooldays*, was one of the great brainwaves of modern popular story-telling. Fraser was deputy editor of the *Glasgow Herald* when he offered readers the first sample of the 'Flashman Papers' 'discovered by chance in a Leicestershire saleroom' and recounting the further adventures of 'Flashy' after he was expelled from Rugby for drunkenness. To date Fraser has opened some eight packets of the papers, revealing Flashman's involvement in virtually every episode of interest in Victorian history, all replete with extensive and scholarly notes. Inevitably Flashman acts in the worst possible way, and equally inevitably he advances his career as the epitome of an Empire-building hero yet further.

FRAYN, MICHAEL (1933–) British writer

To be absolutely honest, what I feel really bad about is that I don't feel worse. That's the ineffectual liberal's problem in a nutshell.

quoted in the *Observer*, 1965

Frayn begin his literary career writing a humorous column first for the *Manchester Guardian* and then for the *Observer*. He has written a number of novels, including *The Russian Interpreter* (1966), *Towards the End of the Morning* (1967) and *A Very Private Life* (1968). Recently he has become better known for his dramatic work, which started with *Alphabetical Order* (1975), *Donkey's Years* (1976) and *Noises Off* (1982). Frayn's satire looks at middle-class fads and fashions, as well as the world of Fleet Street and the media.

FRAYN, MICHAEL

What deeply affects every aspect of a man's experience of the world is his perception that things could be otherwise.

Constructions (1974)

Constructions is Frayn's book of philosophy; made up of a collection of short statements such as that cited above, its aim is to prove the author's theory that in the end the use of philosophy is to remind us of what we already know. And what we know, by reflecting upon our own experience and by looking at what we can clearly see, may sometimes turn out to be as hauntingly strange in its familiarity as is a dream.

FRAYN, MICHAEL

There is a painful difference, often obscured by popular preju- dice, between reporting something and making it up.

The Clouds

Frayn's play deals with a journalist, Owen Shorter, and a novelist, Mara Hill, both of whom have been sent to Cuba to write pieces for rival Sunday colour supplements. We follow their progress, along with that of their guide Angel and that of Ed, a writer from Illinois, as they make the rounds of the official sights. Frayn shows how their impressions of the country are coloured by their emotional reactions – to the heat, the bad food and the difficulties of writing their stories – but mainly determined in the case of the men by their respective successes with Mara, who plays havoc with their feelings. The relationship between Owen and Mara, at first riddled with rivalry, mellows into an uneasy romance.

FREUD, CLEMENT (1924–) British politician and gastronome

About one thing the Englishman has a particularly strict code. If a bird says "Cluk bik bik bik bik" and "caw" you may kill it, eat it or ask Fortnums to pickle it in Napoleon brandy with wild strawberries. If it says "tweet" it is a dear and precious friend and you'd better lay off it if you want to remain a member of Boodles.
Freud on Food (1978)

Freud has managed to combine two careers, as a Liberal MP and a gastronome and cookery writer of some repute. He has also advertised dog food matching his inimitable voice with the mournful looks of an attendant hound. His comments on the double standards of the English as regards hunting, shooting, fishing and subsequent eating, show that the unspeakable sometimes pursue the eatable too.

FREUD, CLEMENT

If you resolve to give up smoking, drinking and loving, you don't actually live longer, it just seems longer.
quoted in the *Observer*, 1964

FREUD, SIGMUND (1856–1939) Austrian psychoanalyst

The credulity of love is the most fundamental source of authority.
in *Collected Works* (1955)

Freud graduated as a doctor in Vienna and then went on to specialise in neurology before moving to Paris where he studied psychopathology. These studies led him to certain conclusions as regards the normal and abnormal mind. Among his main studies were those of infantile sexuality, the workings of the unconscious mind, the nature of repression and the interpretation of dreams. The pursuit of all these ideas was collectively named 'psychoanalysis'. Inevitably, as his ideas spread beyond the consulting rooms in Vienna where he practised until Hitler's Anschluss forced him into exile in London, they became substantially vulgarised, with the adjective 'Freudian' itself becoming a cliché, as have such theories as 'the Oedipus complex', 'penis envy', 'phallic symbolism' and others. Bruno Bettelheim has further argued that once Freud's work was translated into English, the need to dazzle sceptical Americans with its supposed complexity led to mistranslation and an accretion of unnecessary jargon, thus mystifying what should have been far more simple. Freud's discoveries, a religion to some, a myth and a mistake to others, remain a major influence on every aspect of 20th century life and culture.

FREUD, SIGMUND

We are so made that we can derive intense enjoyment from a contrast and very little from the state of things.
Civilisation and Its Discontents

FREUD, SIGMUND

A religion, even if it calls itself the religion of love, must be hard and unloving to those who do not belong to it.
Group Psychology and the Analysis of the Ego (1921)

FREUD, SIGMUND

The principal task of civilisation, its actual raison d'être, is to defend us against nature.
The Future of an Illusion (1927)

FRIEDAN, BETTY (1921–) American feminist

A mystique does not compel its own acceptance.
The Feminine Mystique (1963)

Friedan, a former journalist who had abandoned her profession to devote herself to family life, coined the term 'feminine mystique' to explain the frustrations that she experienced in attempting to reconcile her own desires with those of the domestic American dream. It represented the idealized image of the female as a subservient, child-centred, isolated housewife - an image quite alien from what real women wanted. In her book *The Feminine Mystique* (1963) Friedan outlined her theories and went on to claim that the persistence of this myth is quite simply a conspiracy by men to keep women from competing with them. As co-founder of the National Organisation for Women in 1966 she was a pioneer feminist but by the Seventies she had been displaced by younger, more radical women. She has written two more books: *It Changed My Life* (1976), reflections on her role as the 'mother of women's lib', and *The Second Stage* (1982) in which she suggests that feminism's advances will never be consolidated until men liberate themselves from their mystique too.

FRIEDENBERG, EDGAR Z. (1921–) American sociologist

Not only do people accept violence if it is perpetuated by legitimate authority, they also regard violence against certain kinds of people as inherently legitimate, no matter who commits it.
quoted in 1966

As tests performed in controlled environments have proved conclusively, most people are quite happy to inflict pain on others as long as a guiding authority orders them to do so and assures them that such cruelty is perfectly permissible. By the same token people feel, often instinctively rather than consciously, that certain groups lie beyond the pale and may be forced to suffer without troubling the consciences of those who persecute them. In this case the authority may be external, but just as often it is the unspoken authority of the peer group who have chosen to establish who is acceptable and who is not.

FRIEDMAN, BRUCE J. (1930–) American writer

A Code of Honour: never approach a friend's girlfriend or wife with mischief as your goal. There are too many women in the world to justify that sort of dishonourable behaviour. Unless she's really attractive.
Sex and the Lonely Guy (1977)

Friedman's piece in *Esquire* from which this excerpt is taken, was one of a number of 'Mister Lonelyhearts' columns, aimed at the solitary male, hoping to help him cook, entertain and seduce. The piece is divided into several sections: basic philosophy, categories of women, stragey and tactics and so on. Among Friedman's discoveries are the New Erogenous Zones 'Once it was thought there were only a handful. Now they are all over the place, with new ones being reported every day'.

FRIEDMAN, MILTON (1912–) American economist

There is no such thing as a free lunch.
popular dictum

Friedman, the 1976 Nobel prize-winner for economics, is the world's foremost proponent of laissez-faire free-market capitalism, and as such the most important economist since Keynes, although he works on very different lines from his predecessor. His views are summed up in the word monetarism, defined as 'the belief that the state of the economy can be decisively manipulated through regulating the flow of money' (OED 1982) and that such phenomena as inflation and unemployment can be directly controlled by such regulation. Friedman has been attacked savagely by many expert critics who point to the state of such countries as Israel, Chile and the UK, all monetarist economies, as proof of the futility of what have been called his 'pathological' beliefs. Friedman's most quoted line appears above. Even this, however, is subject to doubt since at least one authoritative dictionary attributes it to 'an anonymous Italian immigrant'.

FRIEDMAN, MILTON

In a bureaucratic system, useless work drives out useful work.

Friedman's variation on the usual dictum 'bad money drives out good' sums up his attitude to government interference in the economy. His monetarist views are based on the belief that as far as government involvement is concerned, less is undoubtedly more. In other words, he espouses the view that government monetary and fiscal policies have no lasting influence on aggregate output and employment but on the other hand are the sole determinants of the price level of the market and of the share of the national output which the government takes up. This theory is based on classical economics, predating Keynes, and assumes that one most always plan for the long run, since short-term government efforts to right the economy are invariably doomed to failure through the difficulty in tying down the development of such initiatives in the real world.

FRIEDMAN, MILTON

Governments never learn. Only people learn.
quoted in 1980

FRISCH, MAX (1911–) Swiss novelist and playwright

Technology...the knack of so arranging the world that we don't have to experience it.
Sketchbook 1966–1971 (1974)

Frisch intended to become a writer but practised as an architect until 1954, at which point the success of his second novel *Stiller* (1951, *I'm Not Stiller* 1958) gave him the freedom to concentrate on literature. Frisch wrote two more novels – *Homo Faber* (1957) and *A Wilderness of Mirrors* (1965) – but his international fame rests on two plays: *Biedermann und die Brandstifter* (1958, *The Fire-raisers* 1961) and *Andorra* (1961). Both take the form of

Brechtian parables, mocking and satirising the pretentions and hypocrisies of the bourgeoisie. Frisch has produced two volumes of notebooks, covering the years 1946–49 and 1966–71, which combine notes on his working method with his own comments on contemporary life and culture.

FROMM, ERICH (1900–1980) American psychologist and philosopher

In the 19th century the problem was that God is dead; in the 20th century the problem is that man is dead.
To Have or To Be (1976)

A psychoanalyst and sociologist, Fromm has taught widely in the world's universities and written a number of important books, mainly on his major theme: the correction of puritanism and authoritarianism. His first book *Escape to Freedom* (1941, UK: *Fear of Freedom*) is a study of the meaning of freedom and authority and argues that until the Renaissance there was no individual freedom, everyone operated happily as part of a mass. From this premise he goes on to argue that the Nazis were able to find so many supporters through humanity's urge to return to the simplicities of a non-responsible crowd. Fromm wrote further influential works, notably *Man For Himself: An Inquiry into the Psychology of Ethics* (1947), *The Art of Loving* (1956) and *To Have or To Be* (1976).

FROMM, ERICH

Modern man lives under the illusion that he knows what he wants, while he actually wants what he is supposed to want.
Escape from Freedom

FROMM, ERICH

Man's main task is to give birth to himself, to become what he potentially is. The most important product of his effort is his own personality.
Man for Himself (1949)

In *Man for Himself* Fromm developed various personality or character types which he saw as emerging as humanity reacted to social influences and which were related to the methods of escape from the basic problem of individual loneliness. Of these types the undesirable ones are 'receptive', 'hoarding', 'exploitative' and 'marketing'; the desirable one is 'productive'.

FROMM, ERICH

The successful revolutionary is a statesman, the unsuccessful one is a criminal.
The Fear of Freedom (1941)

Fromm described the fear of freedom as part of a broad study concerning the character structure of modern man and the problems of interaction between psychological and sociological factors. *The Fear of Freedom* itself concentrates on one aspect of the broader study: the meaning of freedom for modern man.

FROMM, ERICH

The danger of the past was that men became slaves. The danger of the future is that men may become robots.
The Sane Society (1955)

In *The Sane Society* Fromm envisaged an ideal solution to society's problems in which there is equality for all, where each person has the opportunity of becoming purely human, and where individuals relate to each other in a loving way.

FROMM, ERIC

Since modern man experiences himself both as the seller and as the commodity to be sold on the market, his self-esteem depends on conditions beyond his control. If he is 'successful' he is valuable; if he is not, he is 'worthless.'
Man for Himself (1947)

FROST, DAVID (1939–) British television personality

Television is an invention that permits you to be entertained in your living room by people you wouldn't have in your home.
on the *David Frost Revue*, CBS-TV 1971

Frost, the son of a Methodist minister and a trained lay preacher, abandoned religion for the stage while at Cambridge. In 1963 he was made the linkman for *That Was The Week That Was*, BBC-TV's epochal Saturday night review which delighted half the country with its 'irreverent' humour, appalled the rest and made Frost a star almost literally overnight. If nothing else, people remember his cowlick hairstyle and the deflatory catchphrase 'Seriously though, he's doing a grand job'. Since TW3 Frost has parlayed himself into the television personality par excellence. *The Frost Report, The Frost Programme, The David Frost Revue* and many other shows followed in the UK and America. Initially he managed some genuinely probing interviews but more recently he has taken on the bland pervasiveness of the medium to which he seems so perfectly suited, as his is latterday catch-phrase, ripe with redundant bonhomie: 'Hello, good evening, and welcome'.

FROST, ROBERT (1874–1963) American poet

Frost was born in California but lived most of his life in the New England that provides the subject and background for so much of his verse. In 1912 he moved with his family to England, where he published his first two collections of poetry. His return to America in 1915 was greeted with wide adulation and he remained a pillar of the national culture until his death. In 1961 his invitation to read at President Kennedy's inauguration did as much as anything to confer on Kennedy's administration its 'cultured' image. Frost's poetry is interwoven with the culture and the topography of New Hampshire and Vermont where he lived. Its pastoral tones have been seen as a 'simple woodland philosophy' but there is a questioning, combative spirit underlying it and Lionel Trilling has called him a 'poet of terror'.

FROST, ROBERT

A liberal is a man too broadminded to take his own side in a quarrel.

Frost's put-down of the liberal is just one such dismissal among many. Among those who feel that the hapless middle-of-the-roader merits little respect are American journalist Willis Player (1915–), who said 'A liberal is a person whose interests aren't at stake at the moment' and English writer George Orwell who defined a liberal as 'a power worshipper without power'.

FROST, ROBERT

Home is the place where, when you have to go there, they have to take you in.

FROST, ROBERT

> **My apple trees will never get across**
> **And eat the cones under his pines, I tell him.**
> **He only says, Good fences make good neighbours**
'Mending Wall'

This poem was published in Frost's collection *North of Boston* in 1914. It refers to the traditional New England custom of 'walking the line', the annual springtime repairing of the drystone walls that divide field from field. Frost and his neighbour an 'old-stone savage armed' duly perform the ritual but while Frost's neighbour has no more interest in the task than that it be done, the poet prefers to question the whole event, wondering just why they bother to erect and then strengthen these boundaries. 'Before I built a wall I'd ask to know', says Frost, 'What I was walling in or walling out.' His neighbour, on the other hand, is echoing George Herbert who wrote in 1651 'Love your neighbour, yet pull not down your hedge.'

FROST, ROBERT

The best way out is always through.
A Servant to Servants (1914)

FROST, ROBERT

If society fits you comfortably enough, you call it freedom.
in Esquire magazine, 1965

FRY, CHRISTOPHER (1907–) British playwright

Always fornicate between clean sheets and spit on a well-scrubbed floor.
The Lady's Not for Burning (1949)

Fry worked as a schoolmaster, actor and theatre director before turning to play-writing. His output has mixed religious and mystical works with more boisterous comedies. The Lady's Not for Burning (1949), a play set in the Middle Ages and the title of which inspired Mrs. Thatcher's famous pun (qv), was not only a great stage success but its exuberant language made its script a best-seller too. Nonetheless those critics who acclaimed him as a new Christopher Marlowe were balanced by those who felt his style was too verbose for a world dominated by the restraint and puritanism of Eliot. As well as his own work, which suffered somewhat in the face of the 'kitchen sink' school of the Fifties, Fry has adapted and translated the work of Giraudoux and Anouilh.

FULLER, R. BUCKMINISTER (1895–1983) American engineer and philosopher

The most important thing about Spaceship Earth – an instruction book didn't come with it.
Operating Manual for Spaceship Earth 1969

After World War I Fuller spent some years working in industry before creating the first of many important designs, the Dymaximon before creating the first of many important designs, the Dymaxion house, intended as a high-tech solution to the extreme housing shortages of the depression and designed as a mass production, assembly-line product, the architectual equivalent to the Model-T Ford. Dymaximon housing never took off, but the word, coined from dynamic plus maximum efficiency, has been assoicated with Fuller ever since, and the concept of system building, now very much reviled, was central to much of the high-rise housing of the Sixties. Fuller's other great contribution to building is in his geodesic domes, structures designed to achieve maximum spans with a minimum of material. From his original design there are now more than 100,000 of these structures around the earth.

FULLER, BUCKMINSTER

Faith is much better than belief. Belief is when someone else does the thinking.
in *Playboy* magazine, 1972

FULLER, BUCKMINSTER

Evolution is man, man in his universal aspect, functioning as part of the universe.
in *Playboy*, 1972

FUNKHOUSER, G. RAY American businessman

The quality of legislation passed to deal with a problem is inversely proportional to the volume of media clamour that brought it on.
quoted in *The Official Rules* by P. Dickson (1978)

This 'official rule' reflects the fact that the need for a piece of legislation is rarely central to the interests of those who are concerned in promulgating and then administering it. In a media-dominated world the greater the publicity that can be arranged for a given topic, the more likely it is that it will become subject to some form of legislation, but as Funkhouser points out, the act of passing that legislation is seen as sufficient response to the problem. The quality of the legislation and the extent to which it deals with the problem is of secondary importance: the legislators have responded to public clamour and having thus satisfied their mandate can and will pass on to the next item.

FUNT, ALLEN (1914–) American entertainer

Smile! You're on Candid Camera.
catchphrase on *Candid Camera*

Funt's invention, the TV show *Candid Camera*, capitalises shamelessly on a great human characteristic: the delight everyone has in seeing others in awful, embarrassing, absurd and humiliating (but never physically unpleasant) cirumstances. The show has been a television regular since the 1950s and even spawned one film – *What Would You Say To A Naked Lady* (1970) – in which Funt himself starred. *Candid Camera* appears in a number of countries, no special script is after all necessary, and has also led to a number of lookalike imitators.

G

GAITSKELL, HUGH   (1906–63) British Labour politician

There are some of us, Mr. Chairman, who will fight and fight and fight again to save the Party we love.
speech to the Labour Party Conference, October 3, 1960

After serving in the Attlee government as Chancellor of the Exchequer Gaitskell led the Labour party from 1955 until his premature death in 1963 robbed the party's centre and right of a man many saw as their 'lost leader'. Despite challenges from the ostentatiously proletarian Aneurin Bevan and Harold Wilson, Gaistkell, a Wykhamist and an Oxonian, managed to overcome his initial unpopularity among the unions and for a while managed to represent a relatively united party. Gaitskell's greatest challenge from within came in 1960, when he refused to go along with that year's Conference decision to advocate unilateral nuclear disarmament. Gaitskell and his supporters failed to alter Conference's mind, but he made the greatest speech of his life, from which this line, at the height of his peroration, is taken. Unbiased observers called it 'Gaitskell's finest hour'. His opponents won the vote, but Gaitskell himself gained the plaudits.

GALBRAITH, JOHN KENNETH (1908–) American economist
Galbraith has for many years been one of the world's best known
economists whose series of best-selling, accessible books have
developed his own economic theories and his critque of modern
society. His economic style, while contradicting the methodology
and principles of many more orthodox economists, has brought
him an immense following as one of the greatest popularisers of
an otherwise difficult subject. As well as his books, which appeal
both to the expert and to the general reader, he developed his
own themes in the BBC-TV series *The Age of Uncertainty* (1977).
Galbraith's basic premise is that until the intimate connections
between big business and the capitalist states, in which each
party works to sustain the power and profits of the other, can be
severed, there will be no hope of tackling urgent public problems
and social inequalities. He believes that the government must
create economic plans and must manage the marketplace.

GALBRAITH, JOHN KENNETH

Meetings are indispensable when you don't want to do anything.
Ambassador's Journal (1969)

From 1961–63 Galbraith served as America's ambassador to
India, an appointment made by President Kennedy in the spirit of
cultural eclecticism that permeated his administration. While he
was in India Galbraith wrote a series of letters to Kennedy. They
record a world of crisis, war and social trivia, of imperial
privilege, backstage intrigue and dusty detail. As published in
1969 these letters are framed by Galbraith's notes on the lead-up
to his appointment and by his account of life in Washington in the
aftermath of the President's assassination.

GALBRAITH, JOHN KENNETH

The Affluent Society
book title, 1958

The topic of this, Galbraith's best known book, is what the author
terms 'the conventional wisdom', ie the outworn convictions of
traditional economic beliefs, as well as the malignant effects
these beliefs have when put into practice. In the affluent society-
much of the widespread poverty and want that have been the lot
of mankind through the ages has been replaced by sufficient
abundance to enable the population as a whole to enjoy conventional notions of a reasonably comfortable standard of living. In
such a society the 'conventional wisdom', which is geared specifically to dealing with problems of scarcity, is no longer a useful

GALBRAITH, JOHN KENNETH

tool of economic analysis. However this ideal situation is constrained by the realities of the corporate state in which large private organisations act selfishly and government services fail to distribute benefits equally or efficiently. Citing the discrepancy between 'private affluence' and 'public squalor' he contrasts the aggressive spending of private corporations with the decline in public services and the concomitant problems of the poor.

GALBRAITH, JOHN KENNETH

Men have been swindled by other men on many occasions. The autumn of 1929 was perhaps the first occasion on which men succeeded on a large scale in swindling themselves.
The Great Crash (1955)

The Great Crash is Galbraith's account of the financial events of 1929 that resulted in the depression of the Thirties. In his view the depression had the effect of administering a high-voltage shock to the American public, greater even than that of World War I. The discovery of what went wrong in 1929 was for Galbraith an essential basis on which to begin working out ways of creating a new and improved economy in the Fifties.

GALBRAITH, JOHN KENNETH

There is an insistent tendency among serious social scientists to think of any institution which features rhymed and singing commercials, intense and lachrymose voices urging highly improbable enjoyment, caricatures of the human oesophagus in normal or impaired operation, and which hints implausibly at opportunities for antiseptic seduction as inherently trivial. This is a great mistake. The industrial system is profoundly dependent on commercial television and could not exist in its present formwithout it.
The New Industrial State (1967)

In this book Galbraith continues his examination of the relationship between big business and government and describes what he calls the 'technostructure'. He explains 'Management...includes...only a small proportion of those who...contribute information to group decisions. This...group...extends from the most senior officials of the corporation to...blue-collar workers.... This is the guiding intelligence – the brain – of the enterprise.... I propose to call this organisation the technostructure.' On this chain of experts and specialists all corporate judgements of ultimate feasibility depend. Among them are market analysts, pollsters, chemists and physicists, promoters and designers. They

322

never meet as a group and each has the power of veto. The technostructure does not consider responsibility, only feasibility. Galbraith identifies this new sytle of management and attempts to pinpoint the weakness in society that has let it become so pervasive.

GALBRAITH, JOHN KENNETH

The enemy of conventional wisdom is not ideas but the march of events.
The Affluent Society (1958)

GALBRAITH, JOHN KENNETH

People of privilege will always risk their complete destruction rather than surrender any material part of their advantage.

GALBRAITH, JOHN KENNETH

The decisive economic contribution of women in the developed industrial society is rather simple.... It is, overwhelmingly, to make possible a continuing and more or less unlimited increase in the sale and use of consumer goods.
Annals of an Abiding Liberal (1980)

GALBRAITH, JOHN KENNETH

It is a far, far better thing to have a firm anchor in nonsense than to put out on the troubled seas of thought.
The Affluent Society (1958)

GALBRAITH, JOHN KENNETH

Few things are as immutable as the addiction of political groups to the ideas by which they have once won office.
The Affluent Society (1958)

GALBRAITH, JOHN KENNETH

What is called a high standard of living consists, in considerable measure, in arrangements for avoiding muscular energy, increasing sensual pleasure, enhancing caloric intake beyond any conceivable nutritional requirement. Nonetheless, the belief that increased production is a worthy social goal is very nearly absolute.
The New Industrial State (1967)

GALBRAITH, JOHN KENNETH

Anyone who says he isn't going to resign, four times, definitely will.

GALBRAITH, JOHN KENNETH

Politics is not the art of the possible. It consists in choosing between the disastrous and the unpalatable.

in 1969

GALBRAITH, JOHN KENNETH

In a community where public services have failed to keep abreast of private consumption things are very different. Here in an atmosphere of private affluence and public squalor, the private goods have full sway.

The Affluent Society (1958)

GALBRAITH, JOHN KENNETH

These men of the technostructure are the new and universal priesthood. Their religion is business success; their test of virtue is growth and profit. Their bible is the computer printout; their communion bench is the committee room. The sales force carries their message to the world, and a message is what it is often called.

The Age of Uncertainty

GALBRAITH, JOHN KENNETH

Money is a singular thing. It ranks with love as man's greatest source of joy. And with death as his greatest source of anxiety. Money differs from an automobile, a mistress or cancer in being equally important to those who have it and those who do not.

The Age of Uncertainty (broadcast version)

GALLOIS, PIERRE (1911–) French scientist

If you put tomfoolery into a computer, nothing comes out but tomfoolery. But this tomfoolery, having passed through a very expensive machine, is somehow ennobled and no-one dares criticise it.

quoted in *Readers' Digest*

There are few more alluring myths in contemporary Western society than that of the supposed omnipotence of the computer. The belief, as Gallois illustrates above, that merely by cycling some piece of nonsense through a computer's central processing unit and then printing it out for subsequent consumption manages to confer upon that nonsense a finer sensibility and importance, is very widespread. All too often computer use is fashionable, not functional. Less gullible computer buffs sum it up in a neat acronym: GIGO. Garbage In, Garbage Out.

GALLUP, GEORGE (1901–) American pollster

I could prove God statistically.
The Sophisticated Poll-Watcher's Guide (1976)

Gallup is the pioneer of scientific polling designed to assess public opinion on the basis of statistical surveys. After three years of preliminary experiments, Gallup began producing his sponsored weekly press reports, polling the American people as to their opinion on a variety of national issues and current events. Gallup worked on small samples, scientifically weighted to provide as near as possible a perfect cross-section of the population. Gallup gave such polls legitimacy and they were widely adopted by market researchers, politicians and similar figures. Gallup's testing of public opinion was noted by governments, who used his figures when fine-tuning their own policies. His organisation has been widely imitated and for all that the polls can occasionally be disastrously wrong, they have become, especially in political calculations, a fundamental aspect of life.

GALSWORTHY, JOHN (1867–1933) British writer

Idealism increases in direct proportion to one's distance from the problem.

Galsworthy began writing in 1897, gaining his first success in 1906 when his first play, *The Silver Box*, and the first volume of what would become the *Forsyte Saga*, *A Man of Property*, both appeared to great acclaim. Galsworthy wrote eight Forsyte books, gently satirising the world of the Edwardian upper-middle class. He wrote a number of other plays, usually on themes of social justice, and could claim a good share of responsibility for contemporary prison reforms after the success of his campaigning play *Justice* (1910). Galsworthy won many prizes and awards, including the Nobel Prize for Literature in 1932, but remains to sophisticated readers the quintessential middlebrow, although as Cyril Connolly put it in 1963 'Among literary reputations Galsworthy is a corpse that will not lie down'.

GALTON & ALAN SIMPSON, RAY (1930– ; 1929–) British scriptwriters

I came in here in all good faith to help my country. I don't mind giving a reasonable amount, but a pint...why that's very nearly an armful. I'm sorry. I'm not walking around with an empty arm for anybody.
The Blood Donor

Galton and Simpson have been among Britain's most prolific writers of sophisticated situation comedies, most notably for Tony Hancock and for Harry H. Corbett and Wilfred Brambell in BBC-TV's *Steptoe and Son*. Hancock (1924–1968) was a superb comedian whose finest shows, whether with the *Hancock's Half Hour* radio ensemble or solo in such television tours de force as 'The Blood Donor,' from which this quotation comes, were penned by Galton and Simpson. The aggrieved persona, keen to do his duty but even keener to be noticed doing it, that Hancock presents here was at the heart of the character Galton and Simpson helped Hancock create. Hancock was a comic genius, but it was no coincidence that the quality of his performances dropped when, foolishly, he decided to dispense with his writing team.

GALTON & ALAN SIMPSON, RAY

You dirty old man!
Steptoe and Son, BBC-TV (1964–73)

Galton and Simpson's comedy of a father-and-son pair of East End rag and bone men, starring Harry H. Corbett (1925–82) as the son and Wilfred Brambell (1912–) as his father, was one of the most popular television comedy shows of its time. They pitted boastful, garrulous, socially inept Corbett against the eternally embarrassing but rarely embarrassed Brambell, dressed up like a reject from his own old clothes dump. 'You dirty old man!' was Corbett's catchphrase, delivered with lingering, almost incredulous contempt as he looked aghast at some new example of Brambell's eccentric wilfulness.

GANDHI, MAHATMA (1869–1948) Indian leader

Victory attained by violence is tantamount to a defeat, for it is momentary.
Satyagraha leaflet no.13 (1919)

Gandhi developed his system of non-violent, passive resistance between 1907–14 when campaigning in South Africa against discrimination against Indians. In 1920 he defined 'satyagraha' as quite different from simple passive resistance, calling it a weapon of the strongest and explaining that its literal meaning is 'holding on to truth' and thus 'truth force'. As leader of the National Congress in India from 1915-48 Gandhi campaigned continually for 'swaraj' (Indian independence). Employing his 'satyagraha', living a life of absolute self-denial and simplicity, calling for boycotts of British goods and a return to native, village customs, Gandhi became a major political figure. He was arrested regularly by the British authorities. His problem was that his own example did not always influence his followers and there was much peripheral, religion-inspired violence, coming to a climax when in 1947 independence was finally achieved, although at the cost of partition, and when in 1948 he was assassinated by a Hindu fanatic.

GARBO, GRETA (1905–) (Greta Gustafson) Swedish actress

I want to be alone

Greta Garbo was brought to Hollywood by her director Mauritz Stiller and under the careful grooming of MGM became one of the world's great film goddesses. Capitalising on her Scandinavian origins Garbo was cast as the mysterious ice maiden 'the dream princess of eternity' as *Life* magazine had it, but the elusive, reclusive personality that she adopted later in her career was not there at first. Initially as accessible to interviews and photographers as any other beleaguered star, Garbo gradually withdrew into herself and since she retired from films in 1941, she has remained resolutely hidden. Nowhere in her public statements did she ever make her most famous plea, although she did claim to have asked 'I want to be let alone'. Paradoxically she did use the line in at least one movie, *Grand Hotel* (1932) and a title in the silent film *The Single Standard* (1929) proclaims 'I am walking alone because I want to be alone.

GASELEE, STEPHEN (SIR) (1882–1943) British scholar

On china blue my lobster red
Precedes my cutlet brown,
With which my salad green is sped
By yellow Chablis down.
Lord, if good living be no sin,
But innocent delight,
O polarize these hues within
To one eupeptic white.

'On China Blue' (1938)

This ode to the fate of a good dinner was written for the *Wine and Food* magazine by one of England's leading mid-century bibliographers. Gaselee was educated at Eton and Cambridge and from 1908 was a fellow of Magdalene College. From 1908–19 he served as the college's librarian, a post he held at the Foreign Office from 1920 and, in an honorary capacity, at the Athenaeum club. Gaselee was president of the Bibliographical Society from 1932–33 and of the Classical Association from 1939–40. He wrote a number of books on classical and oriental studies as well as editing the *Oxford Book of Medieval Latin Verse* (1928).

GEDDES, ARTHUR (1875–1937) British politician

They are going to be squeezed as a lemon is squeezed – until the pips squeak.
speech December 9, 1918

Geddes, a former first lord of the Admiralty, was speaking at the Guildhall in London when he made this call for the exaction of the maximum retribution from the defeated Germans. In the way of such mots he found it necessary to revise his original version. The speech ran 'I have personally no doubt that we will get everything out of her that you can squeeze from a lemon and a bit more.... I will squeeze her until you can hear the pips squeak.... I would strip Germany as she has stripped Belgium'. The next night, speaking at the Beaconsfield Club, Geddes produced the popular version, saying 'The Germans, if this government is returned, are going to pay every penny; they are going to be squeezed as a lemon is squeezed – until the pips squeak. My only doubt is not whether we can squeeze hard enough, but whether there is enough juice'.

GELDOF, BOB British rock star

Rock and roll is instant coffee.
Irish rock star

In 1985 Geldof was known only as the leader of the Dublin based rock band The Boomtown Rats, whose personal fame had collapsed some years before. Watching the BBC News' reports on the famine in Ethiopia, Geldof was goaded into action. In a phenomenal display of bravado, chutzpah, hard bargaining and the kind of naivety that simply rides right over the objections of those more used to the evasions of sophisticated verbiage, Geldof persuaded rock 'n' roll's major talents first to release a record 'Feed the World' and then to assemble in two huge stadia on both sides of the Atlantic for the mammoth Live Aid concert. The effect was astounding and tens of millions poured into Live Aid's bank accounts, from where, gradually, they are being used to help the starving of Africa. Geldof was nominated for the Nobel Peace Prize and awarded an honorary knighthood. The press christened him 'Saint Bob' but, tiring of his new role, he has announced his return from the world of dried milk to that of instant coffee.

GENET, JEAN (1910–86) French playwright

Crimes of which a people is ashamed constitute its real history. The same is true of man.
notes for *The Screens* (1963)

Genet was born the illegitimate son of a prostitute and brought up by the State. He entered his first reformatory aged ten and had an extensive career in the prisons of Europe. He wrote his first and still probably most successful book *Our Lady of the Flowers* while serving a sentence, using sheets of brown paper for his manuscript. The novel is a paean to homosexuality, crime and betrayal and as such was deemed too strong for English publication until 1964. Genet wrote four plays, all of which suffered censorship problems. In his essay *Saint-Genet, actor and martyr* (1953), Sartre claimed that the writer was an existentialist rebel who, having failed to achieve absolute evil in his life, managed it in art. The success of his works reflected the increased tolerance in the Sixties of society's former outlaws; it was a tolerance that Genet, predicating his art on society's revulsion, totally deplored.

GEORGE, DANIEL (1890–1967) (Daniel George Bunting) British author and critic

Oh Freedom, what liberties are taken in thy name!
The Perpetual Pessimist (1963)

George, who is here paraphrasing the Frenchwoman Madame Roland, whose last words these were at her execution by the guillotine in 1793, was an essayist, critic and anthologist who produced a great deal of writing during a lengthy career. His works include *Tomorrow Will be Different* (1932), *Lunch* (1933), *A National Gallery* (1933). *Roughage* (1935), *The Anatomy of Love* (1962), *An Eclectic ABC* (1964) and many more.

GEORGE V (1865–1936) British monarch

Wake up England!
speech December 5, 1901

GEORGE V

King George V was still Duke of York when he made the speech from which this slogan was taken. Fresh from a trip around the Empire, he adressed 'the distinguished representatives of the commercial interests of the Empire' at the Guildhall in London. He told his audience of the 'impression which seemed generally to prevail among our brethren overseas, that the old country must wake up if she intends to maintain her position of preeminence in her Colonial trade against foreign competitors'. This was generally summed up in the phrase 'Wake up England!'. This warning against complacency was republished in 1911 when George had become King, although it met with as great an indifference then as it had a decade earlier.

GEORGE V

Never miss an opportunity to relieve yourself; never miss a chance to sit down and rest your feet.
advising fellow royals, c1920

George V, who managed to improve his public image from that of a rather dull, stamp-collecting naval man, to that of the national patriarch, said few memorable things, but this piece of advice given to his son Prince George, the Duke of Kent, has doubtless benefited many public figures. The original proponent of timely urination was possibly the Duke of Wellington, who maintained 'Always make water when you can', but King George, who in many other ways set the style for the modern royal family, is generally credited with the line.

GEORGE V

I can't understand it. I'm really quite an ordinary sort of chap.
at his Jubilee, 1935

For a man who came to throne with apparently little to offer his subjects but a rather undistinguished personality and his experiences as a naval midshipman, George V succeeded beyond the wildest expectation as a British King. He lacked the flamboyance of his father, Edward VII, which would be tragically recreated in his own son, Edward VIII, but his staid reliability appealled to the majority of his subjects. At his jubilee, in 1935, he was quite overwhelmed by the nationwide demonstrations of loyalty. In 1932 he had set up what is now the traditional royal Christmas broadcast and in his lack of ostentation, the near bourgeois stability of his family, and his lack of any outstanding intellectual attainments he set the pattern for British royalty.

GEORGE V

Bugger Bognor!
supposed last words, 1936

Famous last words are inevitably subject to debate, especially when the subject is one whose life and thus death is so carefully cocooned as that of a British monarch. Until 1986 the argument over George V's final statement was generally understood to range between the kingly 'How is the Empire?', as claimed by Stanley Baldwin, 'Gentlemen, I am sorry for keeping you waiting like this, I am unable to concentrate', offered to the members of a final Council of State, and the coarse but human 'Bugger Bognor!', which the King allegedly said to a courtier who assured him that he would soon be well enough to visit his favourite resort. The revelation in late 1986 that George V had been, as it were, 'put to sleep' with due attention to the deadlines of the more prestigious Fleet Street papers, ensures only that previous arguments are further complicated.

GEORGE VI (1895–1952) British monarch

I said to the man who stood at the Gate of the Year, Give me a light that I may tread safely into the unknown.
Christmas broadcast, 1936

Royal favour has always been a guarantee of popular success, and never more so than in the public reaction to a poem quoted by King George VI in his Christmas radio broadcast of 1936. Citing this quasi-religious line from 'The Desert,' a poem by Minnie Louise Haskins (1875–1957), the King captured the public imagination. Miss Haskins did not hear the broadcast herself but found herself immensely popular overnight. Her poem was swiftly reprinted and sold 43,000 copies. Plucked from her former relative obscurity, she was entered in *Who's Who* and received an obituary in *The Times*.

GETTY, J. PAUL (1892–1976) American millionaire

The meek shall inherit the earth, but not its mineral rights.
dictum

Getty died as the world's richest man, but as the son of an Oklahoma oil millionaire he had always been well-off. In 1914 he stated his resolve to make his own first million within two years. By 1916, after trading cleverly in oil leases, he had duly made his money. Pausing for a few years of womanising and high living, he returned to business in 1919 and set out on a life of financial accumulation. He added three further millions to his wealth by 1930 but when his father died Getty's philandering had so upset the old man that John Paul inherited only $500,000 of his father's $10 million. Undismayed, although he mused in 1957 that 'a billion dollars isn't worth what it used to be', Getty continued amassing money, usually derived from oil. His allegiance to oil was summed up in this, his revision of the Sermon on the Mount. Humourist James Thurber wrote his version of Christ's words when he suggested 'Let the meek inherit the earth – they have it coming to them.'

GEYL, PIETER (1887–1966) Dutch historian

History is a drama without a denouement; every decison glides without over into a resumption of the plot.
Encounters in History (1963)

Geyl was one of the most important historians of the mid-20th century, whose reputation is based on his monumental three-volume *History of the Dutch People* (1930–37). He was a devoted Netherlands nationalist, who believed that the division of the Low Countries into Holland and Flemish-speaking Belgium was a disaster. His books developed the then revolutionary theory that far from desiring this split, the areas divided simply because, under constant Spanish attacks, the northern area (Holland) was geographically best placed to carry on resistance. Geyl was similarly fascinated by historiography and maintained that since history is 'an argument without end', and 'truth' varies as to the biases and interests of those that write it, there is no such thing as a 'correct interpretation' of the past.

GIBBONS, STELLA (1902–) English writer

Something nasty in the woodshed
Cold Comfort Farm (1932)

Gibbons had already worked for ten years as a journalist before this, her first novel, became a best-seller. It parodied the tradition of earthy, rural novels which were currently popular. In it the heroine Flora Poste visits her relatives the Starkadders at their farm in Sussex, an environment which she finds replete with gloom, seething emotions and rural machinations. Flora proceeds to reform the entire place. Underlining the parody are a number of lushly written passages which Gibbons conveniently marked with asterisks, following the method, as she puts it, 'perfected by the late Herr Baedeker' (1801–59), the doyen of Victorian travel guides. Gibbons' other books never never achieved the same success.

GIBBS, WOLCOTT (1902–1958) American critic

Generally speaking, the... theatre is the aspirin of the middle classes.
More In Sorrow (1958)

Gibbs was one of the earliest recruits, in 1928, to the New Yorker, where he joined a staff of nascent luminaries in producing America's most sophisticated magazine. He proved himself adept at every department, editing superbly and writing prose, verse, parodies, notes and comments, and reviews. Perhaps his best known line is his parody of the stilted convolutions that passed for writing at *Time* magazine: 'Backward ran sentences until reeled the mind.' Subject to severe depression and a lack of self-confidence after his second wife killed herself, Gibbs masked severe diffidence with aggressive rudeness. He succeeded Robert Benchley as theatre critic and wrote his own play, full of insider references to the magazine. He died in 1958, checking the proofs of his latest collection of pieces *More In Sorrow*.

GIDE, ANDRÉ (1860–1951) French writer, critic and playwright

We wholly conquer only what we assimilate.

Gide's personal and professional life were influenced by the continuing conflict he experienced between his orthodox religious upbringing and an inescapable and powerful streak of unorthodoxy that permeated his existence. The beneficial result was a flow of noteworthy books, in all of which he attempted to resolve ·his own literary, sexual, religious, moral and political conflicts. Gide's books were regularly criticised as immoral, and he made little attempt to modify his themes, celebrating hedonism and sensuality, defending homosexuality and attacking the austerity and hypocrisy of his own upbringing. Other books look critically at colonialism and at Communism, to which he was attracted until he visited Russia in 1935. His *Journals* (1947–49), filled with personal opinions and assessments, are generally regarded as his greatest work. Gide received the Nobel Prize for Literature in 1947.

GILMOUR, IAN (1926–) British politician

The more a regime claims to be the embodiment of liberty the more tyrannical it is likely to be.
Inside Right (1977)

Sir Ian Gilmour is one of the most prominent of those Conservative politicians who has been removed from the front benches to the fringes of politics after Prime Minister Margaret Thatcher considered them to be excessively 'wet'. Gilmour stands for an older, more socially responsive Toryism, a version of the party's programme that has been abandoned under its current leader. His book *Inside Right* put forward his own version of the best way to govern Britain. His remark refers presumably to the world's totalitarian governments, whose alleged espousal of liberty tends, when looked at with unsympathetic eyes, to mean the defence of their own liberty in the face of the desire of those whom they are repressing to remove them from office.

GINSBERG, ALLEN (1926–) American poet

I saw the best minds of my generation destroyed by madness, starving hysterical naked.
Howl (1956)

Allen Ginsberg, celebrated variously in the fiction of his contemporary Jack Kerouac as Irwin Garden, Carlo Marx, Alvah Goldbrook, Leon Levinsky and Adam Moorad, has remained since the Forties one of America's foremost poets and for many people, especially of the 1960s, an important social and cultural guru. Along with Kerouac, William Burroughs, Neal Cassady and other, less well-known figures, Ginsberg helped create the beat myth of the post-war years. His lengthy poem *Howl* appeared in 1956, a year before Kerouac's *On The Road* put the whole beat myth on the map, and established him as a leading critic of both America's traditional culture and its society. Since 1956 Ginsberg has remained in the forefront of American alternative culture, voicing the protests and complaints common to his own and later generations.

GIPP, GEORGE (–1920) American football star

One day, when the going is tough and a big game is hanging in the balance, ask the team to win one for the Gipper. I don't know where I'll be, Rock, but I'll know about it and I'll be happy.
last words, December 14, 1920

George Gipp, one of the greatest football players ever produced by America's top college team, Notre Dame University, arrived there in 1916 intending to play his own favourite sport: baseball. Persuaded by coach Knute Rockne to join the football squad he proved a star. He worked his way through college, combining menial jobs with a profitable pool sharking and poker playing to earn his keep. Gipp's off-the-field activities shocked some alumni but his play delighted them all and he helped Notre Dame to unbeaten seasons in 1919 and 1920. In 1920 he caught pneumonia and died, not before offering these lines, his last, to his coach. Rockne set Gipp's suggestion aside until November 12, 1928. In an appalling season the 'Fighting Irish' were losing consistently until the big game: against the Army, unbeaten that year. Before the kickoff Rockne gathered the team and intoned Gipp's last words. As 75,000 fans watched, an inspired Notre Dame whipped the champs, 12–6. In 1941 the incident was set to celluloid in *Knute Rockne, All American*. Pat O'Brien played 'The Rock', Ronald Reagan 'The Gipper'.

GIRAUDOUX, JEAN (1882–1944) French playwright

Giraudoux had already enjoyed a successful career as a diplomat, novelist and essayist before he turned to playwriting with the successful *Siegfried* (1928), an adaptation of his novel of the same name. Giraudoux specialised in taking biblical or mythological figures out of context in order to set them against contemporary themes. His finest exposition of this technique was *La Guerre de Troie n'aura pas lieu* (1935, Tiger at the Gates). Other plays include *Duel of Angels* (1958) and *The Madwoman of Chaillot* (1947). Giraudoux' exploitation of irony and paradox was popular throughout the 1930s and he championed the dramatic text rather than the play's setting.

GIRAUDOUX, JEAN

Heroes are men who glorify a life which they can't bear any longer.
Duel of Angels (1958)

Duel of Angels, originally *Pour Lucrèce* (1953), is a play about vice in the Aix of the Second Empire. Lucile, a virtuous woman, is tricked into believing that she has been violated. She tells her husband who responds by rejecting her. Faced with his reaction and by the realisation that her own belief in herself has been severely damaged, she commits suicide.

GIRAUDOUX, JEAN

Ask any soldier. To kill a man is to merit a woman.
Tiger at the Gates (1935)

Tiger at the Gates is based on the classical tale of Helen's abduction by Paris and the dire consequences of this act. The paradoxical original title – La Guerre de Troie n'aura pas lieu –

demonstrates the theme: Hector's fierce yet fruitless effort to prevent the Trojan War and the fatal advancement of all concerned towards it. In Giraudoux' play war and destiny combine in a great poem of despair.

GIRAUDOUX, JEAN

One of the privileges of the great is to witness catastrophes from a terrace.
Tiger at the Gates (1935)

GIRAUDOUX, JEAN

There is no better way of exercising the imagination than the study of law. No poet ever interpreted nature as freely as a lawyer interprets truth.
Tiger at the Gates (1935)

GISSING, GEORGE (1857–1903) British writer

When I think of all the sorrow and barrenness that has been wrought in my life by want of a few more pounds per annum than I was able to earn, I stand aghast at money's significance
The Private Papers of Henry Ryecroft (1903)

Gissing was destined for great success until being caught stealing while at college in Manchester wrecked his youthful progress. He was jailed for a month and then, in 1876, spent a year tramping in America. Returning to London he worked as a private tutor, then turned to writing, taking as his his topic the worlds of failure, poverty and despair. His first novel appeared in 1880 and was followed by several similar books before in 1891 he produced his celebrated study of penny-a-line hackery, *New Grub Street*. By 1900 Gissing, while never rich, had become a reasonably successful writer. In 1903 he published *The Private Papers of Henry Ryecroft*. Its narrator, unlike most of Gissing's characters, been made financially secure by a legacy, but, more typically, his past life has been one of 'defeated ambitions,... disillusions of many kinds,...subjection to grim necessity'.

GLYNN, PRUDENCE (1935–1986) British fashion writer

Style is something other people have. The merest inkling that you yourself may be in possession of the commodity is enough to ensure that you are not, for style, like the Victoria Cross, is an accolade which must be bestowed by the recognition of a third party.
The Times, 1980

Style, lusted after by the mass and attained by the very few, is a most delicate and rarified commodity. As pointed out by Prudence Glynn, herself noted as a possessor of great style and for many years the autocratic but by no means unsympathetic fashion editor of the *Times*, its paradox is that the very nature of those who have it is that they must never admit to the fact and that only those who do not possess style may be allowed to notice it in others.

GODARD, JEAN-LUC (1930–) French film-maker

Photography is truth. And cinema is truth 24 times a second.
in *Le Petit Soldat*

Godard began his work in films as a critic before starting to make his own short films. His first successful feature was *Au Bout de Souffle* (1960) and during the next eight years he established himself at the helm of what was known as the New Wave with a number of successes. In 1968 he abruptly abandoned this relatively mainstream work and began making overtly political films, shot on 16mm. Since the mid-Seventies he has concentrated on video productions, made in Switzerland. Although Godard inevitably and deliberately sacrificed the mass of his fans by concentrating on political work, his influence within the film world is extensive and the revolutionary techniques he pioneered have become part of every film-maker's reportoire and even appear in television.

GOEBBELS, JOSEF (1897–1945) German Nazi leader

That was the Angel of History! We felt its wings flutter through the room. Was it not the fortune that we awaited so anxiously?
on President Roosevelt's death, April 12 1945

Goebbels served Hitler as the Nazi Minister of Enlightenment and Propaganda from 1933–45. The most educated of the Nazi leaders, Goebbels ran the Party in Berlin and as its leading orator, played a vital role in the election campaign of 1933. Goebbels was a master of modern propaganda, subverting the media, the arts and the entertainment industry to the service of the state. Until 1943, when Germany began losing the war, he concentrated on suppressing Jews, Communists and other racially or politically unsound figures, but thenceforth he clamped down on any form of publishing, broadcasting or entertainment not specifically designed to strengthen the failing Reich. After Berlin fell and eighteen days later Hitler shot himself, Goebbels followed suit, preferring poison to the gun.

GOERING, HERMANN (1893–1946) German Nazi leader

Guns or butter

or Josef Goebbels (1897–1945) (or possibly Rudolf Hess)

This summation of the Nazi belief that military production, and the aggression it would enable, would be of far more use to the State than the pleasures of the flesh, or even a decent diet, comes from one of two or even three major Party bosses. Generally attributed to Goering, it reveals more of his allegiance to the Fuhrer than his own beliefs, based as they were in self-indulgent, hedonistic display. His statement of 1936, paraphrased as above, declared 'Guns will make us powerful, butter will only make us fat'. His rival for power, the Reich Propaganda Minister Goebbels said, earlier that year, 'We can do without butter but, despite all our love of peace, not without arms. One cannot shoot with butter, but with guns'. The final contestant for the phrase is Rudolf Hess, Hitler's deputy who, according to at least one expert, was foremost in urging the Germans to make sacrifices for the State and first used the phrase 'Guns before butter'.

GOERING, HERMANN

If you really want to do something new, the good won't help you with it. Let me have men about me that are arrant knaves. The wicked, who have something on their conscience, are obliging, quick to hear threats, because they know how it's done, and for booty. You can offer them things because they will take them. Because they have no hesitations. You can hang them if they get out of step. Let me have men about me that are utter villains, provided that I have the power, the absolute power, over life and death.

Goering was one of Germany's World War I fighter aces and his origins in the imperial officer corps made some traditionalists see in him the possibility of leading a conservative opposition to Hitler's Nazis. In the event Goering stood only second to the Fuhrer in the Nazi hierarchy, a position consolidated by his development of the Luftwaffe, the vital agent of Hitler's blitzkrieg tactics. Goering's position was eroded by the Luftwaffe's failure to win the Battle of Britain in 1940 and his enemies in the party played on this failure, compounded by his weakness for high living and hard drugs, to ensure that he never regained his influence. Goering was the senior Nazi to face the Nuremburg war crimes tribunal. He remained unrepentant throughout his testimony and managed to commit suicide, by poison, shortly before he was due to be hanged.

GOERING, HERMANN

Naturally the common people don't want war...but after all it is the leaders of a country who determine policy, and it is always a simple matter to drag the people along, whether it is a democracy, or a fascist dictatorship, or a parliament or a communist dictatorship. All you have to do is tell them they are being attacked, and denounce the pacifists for lack of patriotism and exposing the country to danger. It works the same in every country.

quoted in *The People's Almanac* (1976)

GOLDFINGER

A martini – shaken, not stirred.
screenplay (1964)

Ian Fleming's super-spy, consumer paradigm with a license to kill, had to wait until his adventures appeared on screen before this line, possibly his most famous and certainly the one that fixes his personality for fans and detractors alike, could be uttered. His creator, whose own obsessions were imported wholesale into Britain's premier agent, failed to include the line in the printed version of *Goldfinger* (1959). This adventure, in which Bond is pitted against one 'Auric Goldfinger' and his pet Korean psychotic 'Oddjob', had its obligatory girl, 'Pussy Galore', played by Honor Blackman. It was a far cry from *The Avengers*, her TV vehicle, but at least, like 'John Steed', Oddjob too sported a bowler.

GOLDSTEIN, AL (1937–) American pornographer

There will always be a market for sideshows.
in *Playboy*, 1974

Goldstein, a veteran of innumerable jobs, launched his sex magazine in 1968. *Screw*, which went from a 10,000 to 100,000 circulation in three months, provided New Yorkers with the usual raunchy pictures, lurid tales and otherwise impossible contact ads, but combined these with an anti-establishment political line that came straight from the contemporary 'underground press'. Radical populism met sexual liberation, savaging the hypocrisy of the authorities and offering a range of sexual consumer advocacy worthy of Ralph Nader himself. *Screw* was raided in 1969, after infuriating New York's Mayor, the ostensibly liberal John Lindsay. The editors, Goldstein and his ex-US Navy partner Jim Buckley, were acquitted. Screw's circulation rose to 150,000 and the sideshow, as Goldstein called it, stayed wide open.

GOLDWATER, BARRY (1909–) American politician

I would remind you that extremism in defence of liberty is no vice. And let me remind you also that moderation in the pursuit of justice is no virtue.
speech on July 16 1964

Republican Senator Barry Goldwater was the grandson of a Jewish merchant and as such hardly the natural standard-bearer for the values of the American right. Nonetheless he was a conservative and in his determination to present himself as such, he accepted his party's nomination for the Presidency in 1964. In his acceptance speech he made his celebrated comments on extremism, although he admitted privately that he was not even sure whether he had the brains for the job. Lyndon Johnson, his Democratic rival, countered in kind: 'Extremism in pursuit of the Presidency is an unpardonable vice. Moderation in the affairs of the nation is the highest virtue'. In the election, as only the hard-core Goldwater supporters voted Republican, Johnson won 61.1% of the popular votes, a veritable landslide.

GOLDWATER, BARRY

A government that is big enough to give you all you want is big enough to take it all away.
speech in 1964

As the Senator for the Southern state of Arizona, Goldwater represented an electorate in whom the principle of States Rights ran deep. The fear and dislike of a powerful government was endemic to such principles, believing, as Goldwater put it here, that the last thing a state wanted was a strong, intrusive Federal government. This belief by no means died with Goldwater's defeat. Among the great American myths, particularly prevalent in states such as Arizona, is that local autonomy is infinitely more valuable than central government interference. Such beliefs maintain a constant tension between state and Washington administrations. The remark, with just the same meaning, has also been attributed to Gerald Ford, newly appointed president after the resignation of Richard Nixon in August 1974.

GOLDWYN, SAMUEL (1882–1974)
Goldwyn was, as filmographer Leslie Halliwell puts it, 'the archetypical film mogul: the glove salesman from Minsk who became more American than apple pie and founded his credo on the family audience.' He arrived in America with so unpronounceable a name that the immigration officials of Ellis Island

typically changed it to 'Goldfish'. Changing it once more, to Goldwyn, he realised just what mileage lay in the fledgling entertainment medium, the films. In 1910 he began producing in Hollywood and when *The Squaw Man* (1913) proved a massive hit, the former shtetl merchant had established himself as a 'Hollywood czar'. Like many of his peers, he maintained petit-bourgeois morals, helping establish Hollywood's self-censoring Hays Office and proclaiming 'I seriously object to seeing on the screen what belongs in the bedroom'. As the Hays Code shows, this embraced virtually everything outside of Mom, apple pie and Shirley Temple. The famous Goldwynisms, modern Malapropism with a Mitteleuropa accent, were in part Goldwyn's own but there were many apocryphal ones. Those listed here are, as far as possible, the echt-Goldwyn, but even now, not everyone agrees.

GOLDWYN, SAMUEL

An oral contract is not worth the paper it's written on.

GOLDWYN, SAM

Anyone who goes to a psychiatrist should have his head examined.

GOLDWYN, SAM

It's more than magnificent it's mediocre.

GOLDWYN, SAM

I'll give you a definite maybe.

GOLDWYN, SAM

What we want is a story that starts with an earthquake and works its way up to a climax.

GOLDWYN, SAM

I can answer you in two words – Im Possible.

GOLDWYN, SAM

Let's have some new cliches.
quoted in the *Observer*, 1948

GOLDWYN, SAMUEL

Include me out.

GONE WITH THE WIND

Frankly, my dear, I don't give a damn.
screenplay (1939)

Taken wholesale from Margaret Mitchell's (1900–49) best-selling novel, *Gone With the Wind* remains one of the most popular, if hardly one of the most sophisticated films ever made. For many years GWTW was the longest film ever released in the West, at 220 minutes, but its appeal lay not in its length but in the stars involved and in the story itself. The film won five Oscars and its plot is shamelessly indulgent of the myths of the American South, replete with licentious soldiery, blushing belles, cosy darkies and the burning of Atlanta. Clark Gable (1901–60), played the smooth and sardonic Rhett Butler, who delivers this dismissive line to Scarlett O'Hara (Vivian Leigh) as she watches him leave and asks 'Where shall I go? What shall I do?'. Hollywood's censor, the Hays Office, tried to ban the 'damn', even though Mitchell put it in in the book, but compromised when Selznick paid a technical fine of $5000 and Gable, as instructed, put the emphasis on 'give' rather than, more naturally, on what the dictionary defines not as an oath but as a vulgarism.

GOOD, I.J. (1916–) British scientist

When I hear the word gun, I reach for my culture.
A Scientist Speculates (1962)

Good, who occasionally writes under the pen-name 'Doog', was born in London and educated at Cambridge before moving to America where he is currently professor of statistics at the Virginia Polytechnic Institute and the State University at Blacksburg. Among his various publications are *A Scientist Speculates, An Anthology of Partly Baked Ideas* (1962), *The Estimation of Probabilities* (1965) and others. He is a regular contributor to a number of journals, both scientific and general. His line here is a deliberate reversal of that originated by Hanns Johst (qv): 'When I hear the word "culture" I reach for my gun'.

GOODMAN, PAUL (1911–1972) American psychoanalyst and writer

When there is official censorship it is a sign that speech is serious. When there is none, it is pretty certain that the official spokesmen have all the loudspeakers.
Growing Up Absurd (1960)

Goodman has been writing both fiction and non-fiction works since the late 1940s. Both strains of creativity exhibit the same constants, epitomised by a general refusal to conform to the norms of American society, especially as regards its educative processes. Goodman gained a great following among the anti-establishment youth of the Sixties, after the publication of *Growing Up Absurd,* an intensely personal and sociological attack on American culture, branded by the author as 'eclectic, sensational, phony', and on what he sees as its deleterious effects on the young people who have to grow up absorbing it.

GOODMAN, PAUL
Few great men could pass Personnel.

GOREY, EDWARD (1925–) American illustrator

Mystery in writing is not in what you say but in how you say it, and I do, no matter what you might think, I do consider this the best of all possible worlds. I do think that things turn out for the best in the end.
quoted in *Esquire,* 1976

Gorey began illustrating books in the early 1950s. In all he has created forty-odd small, illustrated picture books, more horrific cautionary tales than merry adventures, for all that many of them start off cheerfully enough. Gorey is a unique artist who calls on the world of the Edwardian penny-dreadful and its predecessor the Gothic novel, with their abandoned waifs, distraught ingenues, sadistic nurses, rapacious vamps, caddish overcoat-swathed villains, and a host of unspeakable acts and sights no white (or any other) man should look upon. Working as himself, or as Regera Dowdy, Ogdred Weary and several more pseudonyms, Gorey evokes a nightmarish world of innocence abused. Among his many titles are *The Fatal Lozenge, The Hapless Child, The Curious Sofa, The Insect God, The Evil Garden* and his pop-up book, *The Disappearing Party.*

GRADE, LORD British entertainment mogal

All my shows are great. Some of them are bad. But they're all great.
quoted in *Esquire,* 1976

Lew Grade, born Winogradsky in Russia, is one of three brothers – Leslie Grade, Lord Delfont and himself – all of whom have played a major role in British popular entertainment this century. As his quotes imply, Grade has been the most flamboyant of the three, something of a British Samuel Goldwyn, brandishing an outsize cigar, affecting a populist philistinism and touting the sacred 'family values'. Like his brothers Grade began as an agent and then graduated to promoting shows and thence to television. His long-time role as head of Associated Television and latterly, although with decreasing success, as the purveyor of mass-market feature films, has made him one of Britain's best-known figures on the business side of the entertainment industry.

GRADE, LORD

The trouble with this business is that the stars keep ninety per cent of my money.
quoted in the *Sunday Times*, 1979

GRADE, LORD

Q: What's two and two? Grade: Buying or selling?
quoted in the *Observer*, 1962

GRAFFITO

If you can keep your head when all about you are losing theirs, perhaps you have misunderstood the situation.

This populist graffito is one of many variations on Rudyard Kipling's poem '*If* '. Published originally as one of the poems in *Rewards and Fairies* (1910), the second of his collections of tales from British history, romanticised for children, the four verses cited the various conditional qualities one required to be 'a Man, my son'. Kipling modelled his ideal on the character of Dr. Jameson, of the disastrous 'Jameson's Raid' in South Africa. The lines, as Kipling said, were 'anthologized into weariness' and translated into 27 languages. At first enormously popular, the lines declined in celebrity as did the fame of their author and by the mid-Sixties, when this graffito first appeared, they had come to symbolise (perhaps erroneously) everything that intelligent opinion found wrong with what was decried as Kipling's mawkish, jingoistic conservatism.

GRAFFITO

We are the writing on your wall.
at 144 Piccadilly, 1969

144 Piccadilly was an enormous mansion near Hyde Park Corner in London. In late summer 1969 it was occupied by the London Street Commune, a group of radicals, backed by a variety of rag-tag allies, who wanted to use the grand house for a massive squat. The occupation lasted several days, with media attention duly focused on the event until the police moved in and with relatively little difficulty emptied and then sealed the building. In due course it was almost entirely demolished making way for an

international tourist hotel. The walls were certainly well-inscribed with the usual variety of slogans, but if society had been weighed in the hippie balances and yet again found wanting, as the biblical tone of this graffito implies, it failed to respond in any real way to the plight of London's squatting homeless.

GRAFFITO

A woman without a man is like a fish without a bicycle.
early feminist

This mixture of feminism and surrealism represents one of the earliest graffiti to emerge from the women's liberation movement of the late Sixties and early Seventies. The implication, of course, is that men are in the end irrelevant to militant or any other womanhood and proclaims, with a wit that was all too often absent from the feminist polemic of the era, what a large number of the more radical women felt.

GRAFFITO

Je suis Marxiste, tendence Groucho
Paris, 1968

'Les Evénements', the popular uprisings in France which convulsed Paris in 1968 and showed that even the autocratic General de Gaulle could momentarily be shaken by an alliance of radical students and trade unionists, threw up a number of graffiti. This is possibly the most celebrated, surpassing simple party-line sloganeering and combining as it does the ironic and humorous with the ideological, and setting the whole situation firmly in its era: the Sixties.

GRAFFITO

We are the unwilling, led by the unqualified, doing the unnecessary for the ungrateful.
on GI helmets during Vietnam War

The Vietnam War produced many slogans, of which a large number could be found adorning the helmets or flak jackets of the US soldiers employed in fighting that war. As incompetence in Vietnam compounded by hostility from their countrymen in opposition to the war at home became more and more obvious to the troops, they revealed their own bitterness. The macho parody of the 23rd Psalm 'Though I walk through the Valley of the Shadow of Death I shall fear no evil – for I am the meanest motherfucker in the Valley' gave way to the carefully inscribed 'short-timer's calendar', marking off the 365 perilous days a man had to serve 'in-country', and such bitter reflections as that cited above.

GRAFFITO

Hey, hey, LBJ, how many kids did you kill today?.
anti-Vietnam movement

The popular movement against the US incursion in Vietnam, starting among the politically radical young but gradually spreading to encompass the majority of the US population (and as such paralleled in many Western countries) created many slogans, often transmuted into graffiti. None, it was said, caused more heartache and fury than this attack on 'LBJ', President Lyndon Baines Johnson, whose administration covered the most intense period of US troop involvement. His decision not to stand for President in the elections of 1968, delivered to the US people early that year, has been traced in part to the President's despair when faced with the constant repetition of this bitter accusation.

GRAHAME, KENNETH (1859–1932) British writer

Grahame was born in Edinburgh, the son of a lawyer and after the death of his mother, brought up at Cookham Dene, a Thames-side village. Although one biographer sees his as an unhappy childhood, further researches have contradicted this, although on both counts, childhood experiences bulk large in his subsequent literary career. Grahame became secretary of the Bank of England in 1988, but he had already begun writing. His greatest achievement is *The Wind in the Willows* (1908) where the adventures of anthropomorphic animals epitomise the dual impulses that dominate Grahame's creative imagination: security, as seen in the depiction of safe, happy childhoods, and the endless search for an undefined Arcadia. The book began as bedtime stories for Graham's son Alistair and was not intended for publication. As analysed later it has little to do with childhood, being more a mix of social parable and Grahame's own opinions on art, life, home and travel, but it has become one of the world's most popular children's books.

GRAHAME, KENNETH

> The clever men at Oxford
> Know all that there is to be knowed
> But they none of them know one half as much
> As intelligent Mr. Toad

The Wind in the Willows (1908)

If one accepts that *The Wind in the Willows* is largely concerned with Grahame's own concerns about the nature of art and the artist, then in Mr. Toad, whose self-deluding bravado is epitomised in this song, sung as he escapes from jail, dressed as a comic washerwoman, the author has shown what happens when the artist refuses to discipline himself. Toad's motor-cars, his caravan, the indolence and self-indulgence of his entire life predate but closely resemble Cyril Connolly's 'enemies of promise', those seductive, deleterious forces that undermine the artist's purity. Possibly modelled on Oscar Wilde, imprisoned in 1895, Toad is above all an awful warning: consumed by hubris he rejects the River, saviour of every other animal, and sets off for the Wide World where he comes spectacularly to grief. Only in returning, probably briefly, to his home and his senses, does he redeem himself.

GRAHAME, KENNETH

...after a short interval (Rat) reappeared, staggering under a fat, wicker luncheon-basket.... 'What's inside it?' asked the Mole, wriggling with curiosity. 'There's cold chicken inside it', replied the Rat briefly, 'coldtonguecoldhamcoldbeefpickledgherkinssaladfrenchrollscresssandwichespottedmeatgingerbeerlemonadesodawater – '
'Oh stop, stop,' cried the Mole in ecstasies: 'This is too much!'
The Wind in the Willows (1908)

In this scene, Mole has been enticed by Rat into leaving his spring-cleaning chores and joining him on a picnic, the splendour of which, though Rat demurs, quite overwhelms the simple subterranean. Mole was seen, it has been suggested, by his creator as representing the artist as a human being, and as such resembles Grahame himself in many ways. Rat, on the other hand, while also an artist, is more the creator, blending in his personality both inspiration and craftsmanship. These complementary sides of the artist meet on the River, the flowing imagination that is vital to the production of art.

GRAHAME, KENNETH

There is nothing – absolutely nothing – half so much worth doing as simply messing about in boats.
The Wind in the Willows (1908)

Rat, whose credo this is, was modelled allegedly on the sculling enthusiast, philologist and barrister Frederick J. Furnivall (1825–1910), who both founded the National Amateur Rowing Association and pioneered the New, later the *Oxford English Diction-ary*. In the book he represents, among other things, that side of Grahame that has been called The Wanderer, and which drove him to seek the lotus-eating delights of the South, the sunny Mediterranean, as opposed to the cosy hearths of home and England.

GRASS, GUNTER (1927–) German writer

History is, to begin with at any rate, an absurd happening into which more or less gifted people attempt to introduce some perspectives.
'Die burger und Seine Stimme' 1974

Grass was born in Danzig, then German now Polish, and lived in Paris for a time after World War II. In 1959 he published *Die Blechtrommel (The Tin Drum)* and catapulted himself to interna-tional celebrity when it sold 300,000 copies in Germany, 500,000 in America and equally widely throughout the world. Since then Grass has written many more books, including *Dog Years* (1966), *Local Anaesthetic* (1971), *From the Diary of a Snail* (1974), *The Flounder* (1978) and others. His involvement with the German Social Democratic Party and the introduction of contemporary polemic into more recent novels, replacing the pre-war and World War II settings of his most successful work, have some-what diminished his popularity, but he remains one of Germany's most important post-war writers.

GRASS, GUNTER

Even bad books are books and therefore sacred.
The Tin Drum (1959)

The Tin Drum is Grass' greatest triumph, the first part of his Danzig trilogy', which continues with the novella *Cat and Mouse* (1963) and *Dog Years* (1965). Its German title *Die Blechtrommel* puns on *Blech*, meaning both tin and rubbish. The novel is arranged as the autobiography of the dwarf Oskar Matzerath whose bodily limits find compensation in his mastery of the tin drum with which he beats a pied piper-like rhythm throughout the 1930s and World War II. Grass deals with the whole Nazi era but prefers satire, albeit savage, to prosaic realism in his treat-ment of that grotesque historical period. Like Walter Matern, the hero of *Dog Years*, which deals with post-war Germany as well as this earlier period, Oskar is a fantastic figure whose diminutive body on its picaresque journeyings encompasses larger than life events.

GRAVES, ROBERT (1895–1986) British poet

There's no money in poetry, but then there's no poetry in money either.
on BBC-TV, 1962

Graves was the son of A.P. Graves, a major figure in the Irish cultural revival of the late 19th century. His memoirs of World War I provided him with what remains probably his best-known book *Goodbye to All That* (1929) but Graves was primarily a poet, first published while still a subaltern. Further volumes appeared throughout his life and he was Professor of Poetry at Oxford from 1961–66. Graves wrote prose only reluctantly but if only for financial reasons, as he points out above, he maintained a prolific output of essays, fiction, biographies, children's books and translations. *His Greek Myths* (1955) gained wide popularity and his fictional history of the Emperor Claudius – *I Claudius* and *Claudius the God* (both 1934) – has been particularly popular. Graves lived from 1926–39 in Majorca, returning to Britain for World War II, and then returned to live the rest of his life on the island.

GREEN, JULIEN (1900–) American writer

Our life is a book that writes itself alone. We are characters in a novel who don't always understand very well what the author wants.
Journal

Green was born in Paris to American parents and while his sister Anne (1899–), also a novelist, wrote in her native language, Green preferred to return to Paris as an adult and has produced most of his work, excluding only the autobiographical *Memories of Happy Days* (1942) in French. With such novels as *Mont-Cinère* (1926), *Le Voyageur sur la terre* (1926) and *Le Visionnaire* (1934), he established himself as a major French novelist, distinguished by a grim, but not morbid style.

GREEN BERETS

If you've got them by the balls, their hearts and minds will follow.

Among the various policies created by the bureaucrats in Washington for the American troops in Vietnam was that of winning the hearts and minds of the Vietnamese people and thus, ideals before violence, winning the war against the Viet Cong. That the people of Vietnam, less impressed by this particular manifestation of America's self-proclaimed destiny as big brother to the world, preferred not to offer either their hearts or their minds to the GIs was something Washington preferred to ignore. The troops were less naive, especially those of the elite Green Berets (who earned both a ballad and a film featuring John Wayne). They coined this grim parody, underlining both their cynicism towards Washington's fantasies and their own brutality towards the Vietnamese.

GREENBERG, CLEMENT (1909–) American art critic

All profoundly original work looks ugly at first.
Art and Culture (1961)

Greenberg is one of New York's foremost art critics and was especially responsible for promoting the work of the abstract expressionists, whose paintings dominated the art world in the Forties and Fifties. Pioneering their works he met the inevitable opposition of those who termed such experimental art 'ugly', but the success of his protégés merely confirms the farsightedness of his assessment. Greenberg supported the decision of many painters to turn to non-representational work, producing art that had be judged on its own merits, rather than on those of what it was portraying.

GREENE, GRAHAM (1904–) British writer

Sentimentality – that's what we call the sentiment we don't share.
quoted in *Quotations for Speakers and Writers*, ed. A. Andrews

Greene worked briefly as a journalist but abandoned it for full-time writing with the publication of his first successful novel *Stamboul Train* (1932). It drew on the contemporary political turmoil, an area from which many subsequent books would take their inspiration. This novel was the first of what Greene calls 'entertainments': ostensibly light-weight thrillers. The most successful was *The Third Man* (1950) derived from his own film script. Greene converted to Catholicism in 1926 and subsequent novels are permeated with religious concepts, although all his work stresses moral dilemmas, personal and political as well as religious. Greene has travelled widely and written a number of travel books but the geography of what has become known as 'Greeneland' with its seedy denizens working out their destinies in a variety of demi-mondes, represents a more cerebral country. His most recent work has taken the form of fables, but many of his usual preoccupations persist.

GREENE, GRAHAM

Heresy is only another word for freedom of thought.
quoted 1981

Greene became a Roman Catholic in 1926 and his choice of the word 'heresy' has undoubted religious overtones. His own version of Catholicism, as seen in such overtly religious books as *The Power and the Glory* (1940) and *The Heart of the Matter* (1948), is hardly mainstream doctrine. Some critics have seen it as blending, if tangentially, Christianity, Marxism and the evolutionary utopianism of Teilhard de Chardin (1881–1955). His 'whiskey priests', replete with doubt and fear, can hardly endear him to the Roman hierarchy, and his Catholic 'heroes' tend to concentrate more on the phenomenon of sin than that of grace. But this is not heresey, and Greene's books are filled with his attempt to distinguish the contrast of 'good and evil' with that of 'right or wrong' and the moral dilemmas that spring from such oppositions.

GREENE, GRAHAM

I didn't invent the world I write about – it's all true.
speaking in 1980

As much as any contemporary novelist, and more than many, Graham Greene has invented a distinctly identifiable country, loosely known as 'Greeneland' in which his characters work out their storm-tossed lives. As he says here, it is drawn from fact, whether as to geography or personality, but his evocations of the world's more arcane locales, peopled by its seedier denizens, have acquired a specific style, one that is definitely of Greene's own creation. His influence can be seen in so many of his successors, not least the many purveyors of supposedly 'realistic' spy fiction, in which moral ambiguities dominate a world which, prior to Greene, was often more simply black and white.

GREENE, GRAHAM

That whiskey priest. I wish we had never had him in the house.
The Power and the Glory (1940)

The 'whiskey priest', sodden with liquor and belaboured by a sense of his own failings, is a a classic Greene figure, and the central one of this novel, in which, like several other of Greene's works, an overtly Christian theme is combined with a thriller format. In it the priest is on the run, an outlaw in his own country, Mexico. Despite his failings he is determined to continue as a priest and as such is compared with a variety of characters, themselves mainly flawed too. His decision to offer the last rites to a 'bad' criminal, thus precipitating his own arrest and execution, gives him the status of a martyr and although the Church authorities privately condemned the book as 'paradoxical', Greene's ultimate thesis is that the faith will survive all persecution.

GREENE, GRAHAM

What a mess those inexperienced years can be! Lust and boredom and sentimentality ... in that twilight world of calf-love any number of girls can rehearse simultaneously a sentimental part which never reaches performance.
Ways of Escape (1980)

This book forms the second part of Greene's autobiography, begun in *A Sort of Life* (1971). In it he describes the sources for many of his novels and explains how in his travels around the world, often deliberately in search of danger, he found literary inspiration, although the hottest spots often failed to inspire, while others, less obviously dramatic, proved more useful. He also describes his early attempts at writing and, as above, muses on youthful infatuations.

GREER, GERMAINE (1939–) Australian feminist

Greer was born in Australia and came to England in 1964 to complete a PhD in Shakespearian studies at Cambridge University. As well as lecturing in English at Warwick University she joined the Australian editors of *Oz* magazine, itself an import from the Antipodes, to contribute a number of pieces to England's 'underground press'. In 1970 she published *The Female Eunuch*, which proved itself a world-wide best-seller, made Greer into one of the best-known spokeswomen for the emergent women's liberation movement and remains a vital feminist text. Using history, literature and popular culture, Greer savaged the patriarchal tradition which had served to 'castrate' women and place them as men's inferiors. She urged women to reject their traditional roles and, with a touch of alternative society idealism, to take up communal living. Further books have been less rapturously received, but Greer will always been linked intimately with the first strivings of mass-accessible feminism.

GREER, GERMAINE

We've been castrated. It's all very well to let a bullock out into the field when you've already cut off his balls because you know he's not going to do anything. That's exactly what's happened to women.

in *Playboy*, 1972

GREER, GERMAINE

Probably the only place where a man can feel really secure is in a maximum security prison, except for the imminent threat of release.

in the *Observer*, 1979

GREER, GERMAINE

Mother is the dead heart of the family, spending father's earnings on consumer goods to enhance the environment in which he eats, sleeps and watches the television.

The Female Eunuch (1970)

GREER, GERMAINE

Love, love, love – all the wretched cant of it, masking egotism, lust, masochism, fantasy under a mythology of sentimental postures, a welter of self-induced miseries and joys, blinding and masking the essential personalities in the frozen gestures of courtship, in the kissing and the dating and the desire, the compliments and the quarrels which vivify its barrenness.

The Female Eunuch (1970)

GREER, GERMAINE

It is known that a father is necessary, but not known how to identify him, except negatively.

The Female Eunuch (1970)

GREGORY, DICK (1932–) American comedian and activist

Hell hath no fury like a liberal scorned.

Gregory has been conspicuous among black American entertainers for his uncompromising espousal of radical causes. While many black entertainers are forced into cosy stereotypes, or if unwilling to bow to such pressure, prefer to mute their concern with causes that might alienate them from their audience, Gregory has always allied himself with the potentially unpopular, campaigning against the war in Vietnam or racism in America. Here he underlines his own stance by paraphrasing the proverbial 'Hell hath no fury like a woman scorned', itself found in William Congreve's *The Mourning Bride* (1697) which says 'Heaven has no rage like love to hatred turned / Nor hell a fury like a woman scorned'. The liberal, a figure who by definition prefers brave words to painful action, is never more infuriated when the harder core reject his or her platitudes.

GRENFELL, JOYCE (1910–79) (Joyce Phipps) British comedian

George, don't do that!
catchphrase

Joyce Grenfell made her name as the supreme purveyor of refined and thus humorous gentility, notably in the radio monologues in which, as an infinitely restrained and utterly optimistic bourgeois Nursery School teacher, she regularly delivered this warning to the unseen 'George'. Quite what George was up to remained unstated, but Grenfell's delivery, carefully modulated tones masking the infinite exasperation of patience under pressure, was enough. As well as her monologues, Grenfell appeared as the teacher of somewhat older pupils in the St. Trinians films (1954–60), where she was actually an undercover policewoman, and, playing much the same part, in *The Happiest Days of Your Life* (1949).

GREY, EDWARD (1862–1933) British Foreign Secretary

The lamps are going out all over Europe; we shall not see them lit again in our lifetime.
speech on August 3, 1914

Sir Edward Grey's evocative phrase, delivered on the evening of Monday August 3rd 1914, the day Great Britain, inspired by Grey's own pro-French advocacy, declared war on Germany, has rarely been surpassed in its feeling of darkness descending on the long, sunny afternoon of Edwardian life. That the pre-war world was no paradise for the vast majority of its occupants and that the economies of Europe might, even without a war, have precipitated some form of disaster before long, make no difference. The image Grey retold in his memoirs – *Twenty Five Years* (1925) – of his standing in the twilight watching lamps being lit outside his Foreign Office room remains as romantically imperishable and as fantastic in its way as the world it was already starting to mourn.

GRIFFITHS-JONES, MERVYN (1909–1979) British lawyer

You may think one of the ways in which you can test this book is to ask yourself the question: would you approve of your own son and daughter, because girls can read as well as boys, reading this book? Is it a book you could have lying in your own house? Is it a book you would wish your wife or your servant to read?
prosecuting *Lady Chatterley's Lover*, 1960

D.H. Lawrence wrote *Lady Chatterley's Lover* in 1928; the manscript ran to three versions, the last of which incorporated a number of 'four-letter words' and could not be published publicly at the time. Not until 1959, when the American Grove Press won a court battle to publish their unexpurgated edition did the novel emerge from the shadows. Penguin Books announced the British 'complete' edition in 1960 and before it could appear it was chosen by the authorities as a test case for the recent revision of the Obscene Publications Act of 1959. As 'expert witnesses' queued to defend Lawrence's book, the prosecuting counsel, Mervyn Griffiths-Jones, probably did more than any of them to free Lady Chatterley. His anachronistic misreading of the current social atmosphere ran counter to Britain's increasing populism. His loving enunciation and enumeration of each and every obscenity merely underlined the farce. Lady Chatterley and her gamekeeper were duly acquitted. Two million people rushed to grab copies. If they were disappointed, few admitted it at the time.

GRIGG, JOHN (1924–) British journalist

The personality conveyed by the utterances which are put into her mouth is that of a priggish schoolgirl captain of the hockey team, a prefect and a recent candidate for confirmation.
The National Review, 1955

Grigg was born Lord Altrincham, although he later renounced this title, and it was while still a peer that he became internationally celebrated as the man who dared criticise Her Majesty the Queen, a piece of lèse majesté even more unthinkable to most of her subjects in the Fifties than it is today. Altrincham's piece, entitled 'The Monarchy Today', scandalised the nation, from the infuriated aristocracy who advocated, like the Duke of Argyll, having him 'hanged, drawn and quartered', to the masses, the more fanatically loyal of whom sent anonymous letters filled with obscenities, excrement or both.

GRISEWOOD, FREDDIE British radio presenter

Carry on, London!
in In Town Tonight

Grisewood was the presenter of the long-running BBC radio weekly magazine programme *In Town Tonight*, which started just prior to World War II. The show was one of the first programmes originated by the Corporation's new Variety Department, created in 1933 as an adjunct to the more regular Light Entertainment Department. It was produced by Eric Maschwitz, composer of the musical *Goodnight Vienna* (1932), and a former editor of Radio Times. He designed *In Town Tonight* as 'a shop window for any topical feature' that could not be included in the BBC's listings magazine. The show's signature tune was Eric Coates' 'Knightsbridge March'. It opened with the sound of London traffic which was cut abruptly as the announcer Freddy Grisewood recited the week's feature topics. Then, at the end of the show, at the order 'Carry on, London!', the traffic noise resumed.

GRISWOLD, WHITNEY (1906–63) American historian and educator

Things have got to be wrong in order that they may be deplored.
quoted in the *New York Times*, 1963

Griswold was one of America's foremost historians who was President of Yale from 1950 until his death. His aphorism appears to acknowledge some form of original sin, transferred from the individual to the general sphere and taking as its assumption the facts that, for all that human beings claim to long for some form of utopia, their desire to criticise and complain runs so deep that a state of perfection would be invidious, and that something, therefore, must fail so that it may be seen as so doing and duly attacked as such.

GROPIUS, WALTER (1883–1969) German architect

The car is the greatest problem for architecture.
quoted in the *Sunday Times*, 1960

Born into a family of artists and architects, Gropius was determined to create a new and better world, in his case through architecture. He lacked the originality of such innovators as Mies van der Rohe and Le Corbusier but as founder of the Bauhaus in 1919 he established himself as the foremost teacher of professional and technical teamwork in modern architecture and industrial design. The Bauhaus attracted an unsurpassed group of like-minded, evangelistic reformers. The former Weimar School of Arts and Crafts encouraged its pupils to think in terms of a total architecture, stressing beauty, imagination and economy of style in its every aspect, from the tiny to the immense. The innate qualities of materials were seen as vital and Gropius himself particularly exploited the properties of glass. The Nazis hated the Bauhaus and Gropius was forced to flee to England in 1934, moving on to America in 1938, where he taught at Harvard and founded the Architects' Collaborative.

GROSZ, GEORGE (1893–1959) German artist and satirist

The best thing for art is for it to be treated as a hobby, an incidental thing. For, after all, what do we artists, we insignificant little ants, have to say? We who are nothing more than blown up frogs? Where is our influence? Where, our significance? Do we change the general picture in the slightest?
A Little Yes and A Big No (1946)

Born in Berlin Grosz emerged from World War I as one of the most important of Germany's post-war radicals, such as John Heartfield, who specialised in collage, the playwright Bertolt Brecht and many others. Grosz specialised in portraying the soldiers, the police, the capitalists, the whores and the hapless proletariat who made up the Weimar Republic. No-one was spared his savage line, which became increasingly political, reflecting his all-encompassing disgust. In 1925 he helped write *Der Kunst ist in Gefahr* (Art in danger), proclaiming that art was useful only as propaganda. In 1933, like so many fellow activists, he fled to America, but unlike them, he abandoned his revolutionary stance, softened his artistic line and rejected his former beliefs. Grosz returned to Berlin in 1959, only to die of a fall, just as his early work was being rediscovered by a new and radical generation.

GUEDALLA, PHILIP (1889–1944) British historian and biographer

Autobiography is an unrivalled vehicle for telling the truth about other people.

Guedalla was educated at Rugby and Oxford before working as a barrister from 1913–23 and then attempting, without success, to win a parliamentary seat. At the same time he began writing a number of historical and general works. After abandoning his legal career and political ambitions he turned to full-time writing, drawing something on the manner of Lytton Strachey (1880–1932), who called him an 'imitator', but offering his own original irreverence and epigrammatic wit. He wrote biographies of Palmerston (1926), Wellington (1931) and Churchill (1941) as well as a variety of other reviews, essays and the like.

GUEDALLA, PHILIP

Just as philosophy is the study of other people's misconceptions, so history is the study of other people's mistakes.
Supers and Supermen (1920)

GUEDALLA, PHILIP

History repeats itself. Historians repeat each other.
Supers and Supermen (1920)

GUEDALLA, PHILIP

The twentieth century is only the nineteenth speaking with a slight American accent.
attributed

GUINAN, TEXAS (1884–1933) American nightclub hostess

Hello sucker!
catchphrase

Marie Louise Guinan was born in Canada and reached her apogee in America when, claiming a spurious Western origin as 'Texas' Guinan, she made herself into the favourite entertainer of the Prohibition era speakeasies. In Broadway's heyday she was one of its most legendary attractions, delighting the famous, the infamous and the mere tourists with her ritual greeting. She appeared in a number of undistinguished movies, including *Queen of the Nightclubs* (1929) and *Broadway Through a Keyhole* (1933), but her best 'film appearance' was probably when she was portrayed in her own biography *Incendiary Blonde* (1945) by Betty Grable.

GUITRY, SACHA (1885–1957) French actor and playwright

Vanity is other people's pride.
Jusqu'à nouvel ordre 1913

Guitry, son of the actor-manager Lucien Guitry, made his first stage appearance in one of his father's productions. He wrote nearly one hundred plays, most of which were light comedies; many of them have been successfully performed in English translations. Guitry worked in England and in Hollywood, coming first to London in 1920 with *Nono*, a play he had written aged only sixteen and which starred Yvonne Printemps, the second of his five wives. He worked in a number of films, both as an actor and as the director. As a major collaborator in World War II, Guitry earnt the contempt of some former fans, but he continued to work up to his death.

GUNTHER, JOHN (1901–70) American writer

Ours is the only country deliberately founded on a good idea.
Inside America (1947)

Gunther graduated from the University of Chicago prior to starting work as a foreign correspondent for the American press and going on to make his name for a series of lively, socio-political surveys, beginning with *Inside Europe* (1936). He dealt similarly with Asia, Latin America, America, Africa and Russia. He wrote a number of other non-fiction books, dealing with iron curtain politics, D-Day, the death of his son, and President Franklin Roosevelt, as well as several novels. His reference to America cited here recalls the ideals and hopes of those who wrote the Declaration of Independence and the Bill of Rights and thus established America as a land designed to offer liberty and fulfil what was known as its 'manifest destiny'.

GUSENBERG, FRANK (–1929) American gangster

Nobody shot me!
statement to the police, February 14, 1929

Gusenberg worked for George 'Bugs' Moran (1893–1957), the Irish boss who ran bootleg liquor to Chicago's tough North Side. Moran's gang infuriated their chief rival, the nationally infamous Al Capone (1889–1947), as they attacked his men, hijacked his liquor supplies and generally paid him little respect. This could not last. On St. Valentine's Day 1929, as Capone partied in his Florida mansion, four of his gang, two dressed as policemen, entered Moran's warehouse on 2122 N. Clark Street where as expected they found seven Moran hoodlums, waiting for their boss. Lining the men up against a wall, the 'coppers' produced machine guns and opened fire. Gusenberg, the sole survivor, was questioned by the police as he lay dying with 14 bullet wounds.

'Nobody shot me', he told them, and then 'It's getting dark, Sarge. So long'. Moran fortuitously arrived late and thus escaped death, but after Prohibition he turned to petty crime, dying of a heart attack in Leavenworth Jail.

GYP (1850–1932) (Comtesse de Martel de Janville) French novelist

We don't ask others to be faultless, we only ask that their faults should not incommode our own.
quoted in *A Cynic's Breviary* by J. R. Solly (1925)

In her creation of the character of *Petit Bob* (1882) the Countess created the impudent scapegrace since known as an enfant terrible and as such guaranteed her place in literary history. Her novels were on the whole light entertainments, sometimes wittily if gently satirical, concentrating on the high society life of which she was a part and, in the way of her era, casting an ironic light on the manners and morals of her time.

H

HABERMAN, JR., PHILIP W.   American writer
A gourmet is just a glutton with brains.
quoted in *Vogue* magazine, 1961

The fine differences between the gourmet, who is supposed to be a connoisseur of food and drink, and the gourmand who is merely a consumer, have always agitated those who like to sit down to a good tuck-in, haute cuisine, nouvelle cuisine, meat and two veg or whatever. According to the Oxford English Dictionary, Haberman is right...and wrong, and the snobbish differentiation between the two French words is more academic than apposite. Gourmand is, on the one hand 'one who is over-fond of eating,... a glutton' but in a further definition he is 'one who is fond of delicate fare... a judge of good eating'. Gourmet, Haberman's clever one, is 'a connoisseur in the delicacies of the table', although originally he was simply a wine-merchant's assistant. The most important point is that the French, who should know, seem to use both words quite interchangeably.

HACKFORTH, NORMAN   British radio presenter
And the next object is ...
Mystery voice on the BBC radio show 'Twenty Questions'

Hackforth's fruity intonation gave the mystery 'objects' that were at the heart of this popular BBC radio quiz game an added allure as, unheard by the panel of minor celebrities, he confided them to the listening millions. Derived from America's 'Animal, Vegetable or Mineral', the point of the show was to permit the panel to elucidate the nature of a given 'object' which might as well be some intangible such as a smell or sound as a solid three-dimensional genuine object. They had twenty questions with which to do this. It was all great fun; or at least highly popular.

HAGERTY, JAMES C. American presidential press secretary

If you lose your temper at a newspaper columnist, he'll get rich, or famous, or both.
quoted in W. Safire, *Safire's Political Dictionary* (1978)

Hagerty, who acted as press secretary to President Eisenhower, hardly the most outgoing of Presidents, recognised instinctively that the press were the government's adversaries, however much both parties pretended otherwise, and conducted his office accordingly. It was of his activities that columnist James Reston coined the phrase 'news management'.

HAIG, EARL (DOUGLAS) (1861–1928) British soldier

Every position must be held to the last man: there must be no retirement. With our backs to the wall, and each believing in the justice of our cause, each one of us must fight to the end.
order to British troops, April 12 1918

It has been said that 'the tragedy of Haig, and of Britain, was that he was the man best fitted for command of the British Army in the First World War'. In other words he had risen to the top of a system that had systematically ignored the technological and tactical advances of the previous quarter-century and, like his peers, had neither the experience nor the vision to create adequate tactics for a war in which static trench warfare, machine-guns and poison gas had taken over from the cavalry charge and the sweeping manoeuvre. His belief in 'the horse – the well-bred horse' remained undented. His apparent indifference to massive losses, and the issuing of orders such as this, have made him appear a callous butcher, as epitomised in the play *Oh What a Lovely War* (1964). With military hindsight one can see that Haig hoped to buy vital time with British bodies, and that British losses were less than half of the German ones, but the nation's war memorials are also those to the commander-in-chief's reputation.

HAILSHAM, LORD (1907–) British lawyer and politician

A great party is not to be brought down because of a squalid affair between a woman of easy virtue and a proven liar.
on the Profumo affair, June 1963

Never one to restrain himself when subjected to what he considers impertinence or media intrusiveness, Lord Hailsham, then a member of Mr. Macmillan's Cabinet, was less than emollient when interviewed on the BBC television programme 'Gallery' on the evening of June 12, 1963. John Profumo, the 'proven liar', after informing the House of Commons on March 22 that he had not had an affair with the 'woman of easy virtue', Christine Keeler, had written to the Prime Minister on June 4, admitting his culpability in 'misleading' the House. As Fleet Street sniffed out and then paraded the story, Macmillan returned from a golfing weekend and on June 12 convened a crisis Cabinet meeting. That evening Hailsham faced Robert Mackenzie, who quoted to him The *Times*' thunderous leader of the previous morning, headed 'It *is* a moral issue', (qv) as well as the letters, universally condemnatory of the government, that followed it. Hailsham exploded. 'The Times is an anti-Conservative newspaper led by an anti-Conservative editor!'. And followed this by the comment cited above.

HAILSHAM, LORD

If the British public falls for this, I say it will be stark, staring bonkers.
speaking in the election campaign of 1964

Following the Profumo Affair of 1963, the Prime Minister, Harold Macmillan, had been forced both by Tory backbench pressure and by the demands of political expediency to resign from his post, on the ostensible grounds of poor health. In his place he had appointed Sir Alec Douglas-Home, who as the hereditary Lord Home had been generally considered more at home on the Scottish moors than in the House of Commons, and who had had to relinquish his title to enter the lower chamber. The five year Tory administration ended in 1964 and an election was scheduled for October. Opposition leader Harold Wilson deliberately flaunted his alleged proletarian origins and promised a world of technological revolution. Lord Hailsham, badly misjudging the popular mood, told the electorate that were they to fall for Wilson's Labourite blandishments they would be 'bonkers'.

HAILSHAM, LORD

The English will never forgive a man for being clever.
Now! 1981

HALBERSTAM, DAVID (1934–) American journalist

Always stay in with the outs.
The Best and the Brightest (1973)

Halberstam is one of America's best known journalists and as author of The Best and the Brightest, both the coiner of a memorable phrase and the compiler of a major study of the political side of the American involvement in Vietnam. The best and brightest in question were the government officials who guided the Kennedy and Johnson administrations of the Sixties. In the event they proved tragically fallible and their guidance only led into a dark tunnel at the end of which each of them was desperate to see the light of victory, or at least, as the war grew increasingly impossible to win, the chance of some disentanglement with honour. Halberstam's dictum relates to success in politics and may be seen as Washington's version of Wilson Mizner's famous advice 'Always be nice to the people you meet on the way up, you may meet them again on the way down'.

HALDANE, J.B.S. (1892–1964) British scientist

My own suspicion is that the universe is not only queerer than we suppose, but queerer than we can suppose.
quoted in Kenneth Clark, *Civilisation*

Haldane's father was a distinguished physiologist and the son first experienced science as a nine-year-old guinea-pig for experiments on mine gases. After World War I he worked on creating a link between Mendelian genetics and Darwinian evolution, resulting in his book *The Causes of Evolution* (1932), a landmark in evolutionary theory. In *New Paths in Genetics* (1941) he married two more disciplines, those of genetics and enzymology. Haldane, who was said to know more science than anyone of his era, was politically a Marxist and wrote extensively in the Daily Worker, popularising otherwise abstruse theories. Only when the Party adopted Lysenko's spurious genetic theories was he forced to abandon it. Believing firmly that science was for use, he campaigned for air raid shelters and against nuclear testing. He emigrated to India in 1957, hoping to establish useful biological work in a country too poor for much scientific research. He died there of cancer.

HALDEMAN, H.R. 'BOB'   (1926–) American Presidential adviser

Once the toothpaste is out of the tube, it's hard to get it back in.
on the Watergate affair, 1973

H.R. 'Bob' Haldeman was Richard Nixon's White House Chief of Staff known along with John Ehrlichman, as one of 'the Germans', a nickname that referred not simply to his surname, but to the absolutist control, smacking of some of dictatorial excess, with which he ran first Nixon's administration and then his 1972 campaign for re-election. Haldeman learnt his politics in state and local campaigns in California, and at the University of California he had enjoyed hard-nosed, no-limits campaigns in which the sabotage of rival candidates for relatively nominal offices was known jovially as 'rat-fucking'. When rat-fucking tactics arrived on the national stage, the next stop was the Watergate Affair, and Haldeman, as a prime mover, duly fell from grace. His remark refers to the gradual exposure of that affair by the media and the futility, as more and more facts emerged, of attempting a cover-up.

HALEY, BILL   (1925–1985) American rock star

See you later, alligator...In a while, crocodile
in *Rock Around the Clock* (1956)

Between 1955–56 Bill Haley was the biggest thing in rock 'n' roll. After an an up and down career playing hillbilly and western swing with his band the Four Aces, Haley recorded 'Rock Around the Clock' in April 1954. It sold well, but not as well as the follow-up, Shake Rattle and Roll, which made the Top Ten in the US and UK. 'When Rock Around the Clock' was re-released and added to the soundtrack of the 1955 movie *Blackboard Jungle*, Haley could do no wrong. See You Later Alligator was one of twelve back to back hits and capitalised on a popular teenage phrase of the era. The phrase barely outlasted Haley, whose success evaporated in the face of a real rock star, Elvis Presley, although it gained some added kudos when Princess Margaret, always the hippest Royal, used it to the media's delight.

HALEY, BILL

Don't knock the rock
film title, 1957

Don't Knock the Rock was the title of the second of Hollywood's attempts to capitalise on the transient fame of Bill Haley, the earliest, if by no means the best or even most authentic, rock 'n' roller. The film did well enough at the box office, but such lasting impact as it had stemmed from its title, a phrase then popular amongst teenagers as a shorthand means of asserting the primacy of rock music and thus, since rock was central to their own discrete lifestyle, of the world of teen. Like rock and roll the phrase has lived on, all part of the glorious myth of youth and soi-disant revolution.

HALSEY, MARGARET (1910–) American writer

The attitude of the English towards English history reminds one a good deal of the attitude of a Hollywood director towards love.
With Malice Toward Some (1938)

Margaret Halsey is an American writer whose malice, as seen in this collection of her opinions, is certainly directed towards the British. What she dislikes is that famed British characteristic – hypocrisy and, in the book she takes pains to excoriate it at length. Those biased towards the Mother Country might be tempted to observe that at least she has managed not to allow Hollywood actors to intrude in history.

HALSEY, MARGARET

The English never smash in a face. They merely refrain from asking it to dinner.
With Malice Toward Some (1938)

HAMILTON, ALEX British journalist

Those who stand for nothing fall for anything.
in the *Listener*, 1978

Hamilton is a left-wing British journalist currently allied to the Socialist Workers Party. His contention here is that unless one has an ideology with which one can identify, and presumably from which one is happy to derive one's opinions on the affairs and issues of the day, one is left hopelessly vulnerable to whatever claptrap is purveyed by whichever interest group one may at the time be hearing. Given the propensity of ideology to dispense, claptrap or otherwise, its own version of events, those less politically orientated than Hamilton might suggest that standing for something might equally well preclude the ability to listen to anything else.

HAMMARSKJOLD, DAG (1905–61) Swedish diplomat

Is life so wretched? Isn't it rather your hands which are too small, your vision which is muddied. You are the one who must grow up.
Markings (1964)

Hammarskjold was appointed the second secretary-general of the United Nations in 1953, the successor to Trygve Lie. During his eight-year career he developed the position, and thus the UN itself, into one of genuine international effectiveness, reaching a peak which neither the organisation nor its secretary-generals have ever surpassed. Working from his theory of having the UN fill diplomatic vacuums, he personally initiated a variety of negotiations, between great and lesser powers, especially in those areas of conflict that involved the Third World. He pioneered the use of UN troops as a physical buffer between enemies, starting with the Suez Crisis of 1956. It was during a flight to inspect troops stationed in the Congo that his plane crashed and he died under circumstances that have never been fully explained.

HAMPTON, CHRISTOPHER (1946–) British playwright

Asking a working writer what he thinks about critics is like asking a lamp-post what it thinks about dogs.
in the *Sunday Times*, 1977

The endless battles between critics and creators are never so painfully fought out as in the theatre. While a book can survive adverse criticism – and a great many mass-market books never even reach the review pages – plays tend to live or die by their reviews. Given the number of people constituting the company, a negative review will generate a collective loathing of the critic that extends, although Hampton is citing the writer alone, far beyond a single individual. Hampton, one of Britain's younger playwrights and a long-time member of the essentially experimental English Stage Company, is doubtless as experienced as any of his peers in such battles.

HANCOCK, TONY (1924–68) British comedian

Flippin' kids!
in *Educating Archie*, BBC radio comedy, 1950s

Comedian Tony Hancock had made his way from the fifteen-year-old 'Confidential Comic', a Max Miller clone who lacked the Master's touch, via the Windmill Theatre and end-of-the-pier shows, to the BBC's *Variety Bandbox* when, in 1951, he took over from Robert Moreton as 'Archie Andrews" tutor, in the successful radio series *Educating Archie*. In the way of such shows everyone needed a catchphrase and so successful was Hancock's derisive reference to the show's wooden-topped lead that it made him a star in his own right. For a while Hancock tolerated the line, even billing himself as 'Tony "Flippin" Kids' Hancock' but he deplored such artificial gimmickry. He left 'Archie' in 1952 and moved on to other and for him far better things

Hand, Learned (1872–1961) American jurist

Liberty is so much latitude as the powerful choose to accord to the weak.
quoted in 1930

Learned Hand was the son and grandson of distinguished judges and after practising in Albany, NY, and in New York City became a judge himself in 1909. He served in the Federal Court of Appeals from 1924, becoming its head in 1939. He retired in 1951 but continued to act on special cases. This opinion is taken from his Holmes Lectures delivered at Harvard in 1958 and published that year as the Bill of Rights. In these addresses he cautioned judges not to extend their powers beyond the limits which are established in the US Constitution and to resist the temptation to legislate from the bench.

Handley, Tommy (1894–1949) British comedian

Don't forget the diver!
in the BBC radio show *ITMA*

ITMA stood for It's That Man Again and 'that man' was Tommy Handley, a Liverpudlian comedian who climaxed a lengthy career as the first of BBC radio's parade of nationally famous comics. The show ran from July 1939 until January 1949, when Handley died suddenly, of a cerebral haemorrhage. It produced dozens of catchphrases. This particular example, in which 'the diver' was played by a lugubrious Horace Percival, was first broadcast in summer 1940. He invariably followed this with an even more soulful 'I'm going down now, sir'. Handley claimed that the line came from his memories of an actual diver, a middle-aged, one-legged casualty of World War I, who dived off New Brighton Pier on the Wirral around 1920. He used the line to entice money from passengers disembarking from the Liverpool ferry.

HARBEN, JOAN British comedian

It's being so cheerful as keeps me going
in *ITMA*

Harben played an endlessly moaning, hypochondriac washerwoman suitably named 'Mona Lott' in BBC radio's comedy series *ITMA*. As they did for every character, the writers ensured that she had a catchphrase, by which her every entrance could be instantly identified. In her case, after she had recounted yet another tale of family disaster, the show's star Tommy Handley would encourage her to 'keep your pecker up'. Indomitable Mona, adding no conviction by her delivery, replied as ever 'I always do sir – It's being so cheerful as keeps me going'.

HARBURG, E.Y. 'YIP' (1896–1981) American song-writer

Buddy, can you spare a dime?
catchphrase from song title, 1932

'Yip' Harburg was a prolific song-writer of the 1930s whose most notable collection of lyrics was sung in the film the *Wizard of Oz* (1939), but who penned around 1932 what has become probably the best-known song of the depression era: 'Brother, can you spare a dime?', a tear-jerking ballad, sung by Harry Richman, concerning the plight of a once-stable man reduced, like so many of his real-life peers, to begging in the streets. Why the change occurred is unknown, but the 'brother' of the song-title became generally altered to 'buddy', perhaps in deference to the language of the streets, and it is in this form that the line is still best-known.

HARDING, WARREN G. (1865–1923) American president

I don't know what to do or where to turn on this taxation matter. Somewhere there must be a book that tells all about it, where I could go to straighten it out in my mind. But I don't know where the book is, and maybe I couldn't read it if I found it. My God, this is a hell of a place for a man like me to be!
quoted in *The People's Almanac II* (1978)

Warren Harding may fairly lay claim to being the least competent of all US Presidents. An undistinguished senator (for Ohio) he was selected early in his career by the corrupt Harry Daugherty as the perfect presidential puppet. Daugherty promoted his protégé all the way to the White House, coining the phrase 'smoke-filled room' (qv) en route. In office Harding promised that 'my prime motive in going to the White House is to bring America back to God', but appointed to office as sleazy a bunch of cronies – the Ohio Gang – as Washington had ever seen. As this quote, agonising over the budget, shows Harding preferred poker, sport and women to governing. He fell in 1923 after the Teapot Dome scandal revealed the extent of corruption in his administration.

HARDY, OLIVER   (1892–1957) American comedian

That's another fine mess you've got me into.
catchphrase

Hardy was the fat one in one of America's favourite comic duos: Laurel and Hardy. The long-suffering chunk went through endless disastrous adventures, barely restraining his fury as his lean partner destroyed his peace of mind and physical security yet again. Tetchy, a mass of genteel pomposity, Hardy was the perfect foil for the skinny Stan Laurel (1890–1965). More slapstick than cerebellum, they delighted film fans in dozens of appearances between 1926-52.

HARDY, THOMAS   (1840–1928) British writer

There are certain questions which are made unimportant by their very magnitude. For example, the question whether we are moving in Space this way or that; the existence of God, etc.
quoted in F.E. Hardy, *The Later Years of Thomas Hardy* (1930)

Hardy was born in Dorset, the heart of what became his fictional 'Wessex', and began life apprenticed to an ecclesiastical architect. Between 1871–95 he wrote the series of novels that have given him the dual reputation as both the last Victorian novelist and the first modern one. Hardy's fame increased in direct proportion to critical attacks on his 'pessimism' and 'immorality', although he saw it as irony and nostalgia, culminating in the savaging of *Tess of the D'Urbervilles* (1891) and *Jude the Obscure* (1895), his last novel. For the remainder of his life he concentrated on poetry, which he saw as superior to prose, and on his epic-drama of the Napoleonic Wars, *The Dynasts* (1904–08). He died as the Grand Old Man of contemporary letters, burdened with honours and buried in Westminster Abbey.

HARRIMAN, AVERIL (1891–1986) American politician and diplomat

Anyone who wants to be President should have his head examined.
quoted 1970

Harriman was one of America's east coast aristocracy, a handful of rich families, involved in banking and the law, who often preferred the broking of power to its actual administration, but who have had so great an influence on American policy. As Governor of New York State from 1954–58, and as an unsuccessful candidate for nomination as the Democratic presidential candidate in 1956, Harriman was an exception to his peers in that he had actually stood for office and thus dirtied his hands in actual politics. His remark combines both aristocratic hauteur and the bitter experience of one who had not only wanted to be President, but had failed to do so. Harriman was used by President Kennedy first as a roving ambassador, and then as the Assistant Secretary of State for Far Eastern Affairs, thus rendering him a vital influence on the President's Vietnam policy.

HARRIS, FRANK (1856–1931) (James Thomas Harris) British editor and adventurer

Red bordeaux is like the lawful wife: an excellent beverage that goes with every dish and enables one to enjoy one's food. But now and then a man wants a change, and champagne is the most complete and exhilarating change...it is like a woman of the streets: everyone that can afford it tries it sooner or later, but it has no real attraction. Moselle is like the girl of fourteen to eighteen: light, quick on the tongue, with an exquisite, evanescent perfume but little body. It may be used constantly and in quantities, but must be taken young.
My Life and Loves (1925)

Harris was born in Galway, Ireland, and moved to America aged 14. He embarked, if he is to be believed, on a life of lurid adventure (much of it sexual) before returning to London sometime around 1880 and devoting himself to journalism. He became successively editor of the *Evening News* (1882–86), the *Fortnightly Review* (1886–94) and the *Saturday Review* (1894–96), in which last organ he published among others Shaw, Beerbohm and H.G. Wells. He was a talented editor but his arrogant manner, defiance of Victorian proprieties, and espousal of the German cause during World War I endeared him to few. *My Life and Loves* is his memoir, a catalogue of sexual excess, name-dropping and self-promotion. It is generally accepted as highly unreliable.

HARRIS, SYDNEY J. (1917–) American journalist

Any philosophy that can be put 'in a nutshell' belongs there.
Leaving the Surface (1968)

Harris' comment may infuriate those who prefer to implement the limitations of their attention spans by assuming that every issue or philosophy, great and small, can be presented, cut, dried and easily digestible, for instant consumption. Contemporary life certainly lends itself to such diminution, and many people might say that we simply don't have the time for what is essentially the self-indulgence of subtlety and reflection. The easy self-help banalities so popular today, and with little bearing on the ideas from which, infinitely diluted, they claim to depend, are just what Harris is decrying. The philosophers who created the original systems in question would doubtless differ.

HARRIS, SYDNEY J.

A cynic is not merely one who reads bitter lessons from the past, he is one who is prematurely disappointed in the future.
On The Contrary (1962)

The cynic, as Wilde put it in *Lady Windermere's Fan* (1892), is one who knows 'the price of everything and the value of nothing'. Extended to embrace Harris' definition it might be assumed that he or she is unwilling even to give the future the benefit of the doubt: the past has been loathsome and at best disappointing; how can the future, humanity being what it is, be expected to show any improvement, let alone possess a value which should, if nothing else, be presumed innocent until proven guilty.

HARRIS, SYDNEY J.

You may be sure that when a man begins to call himself a realist he is preparing to do something that he is secretly ashamed of doing.
On the Contrary (1962)

Harris is referring to the concept whereby those who have decided to do something that flies in the face of the better feelings of most of their peers, prefer to mask their excess, their duplicity or their otherwise unpalatable act in the guise of 'reality'. Why this alleged pragmatism should convince others that an otherwise repellent act gains, from its being 'realistic', some form of absolution is a mystery, but those who claim the support of 'reality' consistently seem to believe in its magic powers. Not for nothing is the jargon term for practical politics, unencumbered by ideological or idealistic restraints, 'realpolitik'.

HART, MOSS (1904–1961) American playwright

One begins with two people on a stage, and one of them had better say something pretty damn quick.
quoted in *Contemporary Dramatists* (1977)

Moss Hart was one of the most prolific and influential American playwrights of the century, both in his own right and with a number of collaborators, notably George S. Kaufman and Morrie Ryskind. Among his greatest hits were *Once in a Lifetime* (1930), *You Can't Take It With You* (1936), and *The Man Who Came to Dinner* (1939). Although this advice for aspirant playwrights is nothing if not terse, it probably makes plenty of sense to anyone faced with a blank sheet and a typewriter or, these days, a yawning VDU.

HARTLEY, L.P. (1895–1972) British novelist

The past is a foreign country: they do things differently there.
The Go-Between (1953)

Hartley began writing after Oxford and his first collection of stories appeared in 1924. The successful *Eustace and Hilda* trilogy appeared between 1944-47, and *The Go-Between*, his most celebrated book, of which this is the first, and oft-quoted line, in 1953. The book is narrated by a now-elderly man, recalling the hot summer of 1900 when, staying in a friend's house in Norfolk (often the scene of Hartley novels) he quite innocently takes on the role of go-between, carrying letters between his friend's sister and the local farmer with whom she is involved. As the story progresses, it becomes obvious that this far-off holiday has changed the narrator's life for ever.

HASKINS, HENRY (1875–?) American writer and businessman

Good behaviour is the last refuge of mediocrity.
Meditations in Wall Street (1940)

Haskins was an American businessman, working among the hurly-burly of the Wall Street banks and brokerage houses, who decided to collect his aphorisms and allied opinions in these 'Meditations'. The book was published anonymously, but Haskins' authorship was revealed and his lines have been included in a variety of anthologies.

HASKINS, HENRY

Hope must feel that the human breast is amazingly tolerant.
Meditations in Wall Street (1940)

HASKINS, HENRY

Only the bravest of stay-at-homes asks the ticklish question 'Did anybody ask where I was?'
Meditations in Wall Street (1940)

HAY, IAN (1876–1952) (Major-General John Hay Beith) British writer

Funny peculiar or funny ha-ha?
The Housemaster (1936)

Hay started his writing career in 1908 but as a serving soldier in World War I he gained lasting literary fame with his description of the first of the 'Kitchener Armies', the conscripts who made up *The First Hundred Thousand* (1915). Further works included *The Middle Watch* (1930) and his play, *The Housemaster*. In this play three girls aged 14-20 are placed, for no apparent reason, in a boys' boarding school. The play deals with their effect on the housemaster responsible for their care and in it the fourteen-year-old, improbably named Button, makes for the first time this now popular distinction between the two uses of the word 'funny' in the English language.

HAYES, J. MILTON British writer

> There's a one-eyed yellow idol to the north of Khatmandu,
> There's a little marble cross below the town.
> **There's a broken-hearted woman tends the grave of Mad Carew,**
> And the Yellow God forever gazes down

The Green Eye of the Yellow God

Much-recited at mess dinners, college smokers and kindred assemblies of red-blooded men, this wonderfully melodramatic poem is one of the staples of British fantasies about the East and its alluring but threatening charms. Often mis-attributed to Kipling, who would on the whole have resisted such excesses, it remains central to the myths of an era when there were still things upon which a white man should not look and the sun never set on the British empire.

HEALEY, DENNIS (1917–) British Labour politician

Like being savaged by a dead sheep.
speaking in 1978

Dennis Healey, distinguished in the non-political world for his photography and his renegade eyebrows, is one of the modern masters of the pungent phrase, an exception in an era when the demands of television's image-makers tend to preclude much in the way of oratorical originality. This particular put-down was delivered in 1978 when, as Chancellor of the Exchequer, he was attacked by the Tory shadow Chancellor, Sir Geoffrey Howe. His belief, voiced in 1976, that Labour left-wingers who rejected his economic plans were 'out of their tiny Chinese minds' was ill-judged and won him few friends in the Chinese community.

HEARST, WILLIAM RANDOLPH (1863–1951) American newspaper magnate

Stop running those dogs on your page. I wouldn't have them peeing on my cheapest rug.
quoted in J. Thurber, *The Years with Ross* (1957)

In a 64-year publishing career Hearst made himself into the most controversial, and for a while the most successful, figure in American newspaper publishing. He revolutionised US journalism, aiming squarely at the new immigrants, abandoning discussion for design and worrying more about headlines than honesty. Hearst's classic manoeuvre came in 1898 when, sensing the circulation bonus of a war, he sent correspondent Frederic T. Remington to Cuba, demanding war reports. When Remington cabled that there was no war to be found, Hearst replied 'You supply the pictures and I'll supply the war'. So powerful was Hearst's 'yellow press' that the US government was driven into war and the Examiner chain duly reaped the benefit. The film *Citzen Kane* (1941) draws heavily on Hearst's career, including his palatial mansion at San Simeon, his mistress, film actress Marion Davies, and his mania for collecting. The comment above refers to the short-lived appearance of cartoonist James Thurber, whose trademark were his drawings of dogs, in the Hearst press. Thurber's dogs delighted readers of the New Yorker, but Hearst was unimpressed and had them dropped.

HEATH, EDWARD (1916–) British prime minister

It is the unpleasant and unacceptable face of capitalism, but one should not suggest that the whole of British industry consists of practices of this kind
speaking in 1973

By the time Edward Heath became the first Tory prime minister since Lord Hume, the economic legacy of the Fifties had long been dissipated and the government found itself concerned above all with inflation. Thus when a former member of the Cabinet, Duncan Sandys, was found to have been paid some £130,000 in compensation for abandoning his £50,000 p.a. job as a consultant to the multinational Lonrho Company, the Labour opposition and those members of the public who were less fortunately placed, were duly enraged. Although Sandys had done nothing illegal, and his 'golden handshake' was an everyday fact in the City, such honoraria were seen as in extremely poor taste by a Government struggling with the economy. Prime Minister Heath condemned the payoff, but the country was not particularly mollified, nor, unsurprisingly, was the City notably abashed.

HEATH, EDWARD

I am not a product of privilege, I am a product of opportunity.
quoted in 1974

Edward Heath was first Conservative leader to emerge from outside the usual enclave of such figures: the inner circle of public schools, usually Eton, and either Oxford or Cambridge. A product of a grammar school, although he had a distinguished career at Oxford, Heath's accent, mannerisms and origins made him something of a rare figure in the party and, from 1970–74, an unlikely Tory prime minister. As subsequent developments have proved, his meritocratic, rather than aristocratic origins were to become the Tory norm. Heath's position was further complicated by his refusal to join the ranks of comfortably married Tory gentlemen. But, as he pointed out to critics of his bachelor life 'Pitt the Younger was a great British Prime Minister. He saved Europe from Napoleon, he was the pilot who weathered the storm. I don't know whether he'd have done it any better or quicker had he been married.'

HEATH, NEVILLE (1918–46) British criminal

You might make that a double.
last words, 1946

Heath was a plausible villain who used his charming, suave manners for a variety of crimes, culminating in the two sadistic murders of Margery Gardner, a 32-year-old divorcee, and 21-year-old Doreen Marshall, both of whom he snared by posing as a military officer. At his trial he pleaded insanity, but he was found guilty of both murders. Heath was hanged on 26 October, 1946. Offered the traditional drink prior to his execution, he stayed well in character to ask the warder 'You might make that a double'.

HEFNER, HUGH (1926–) American magazine publisher

If you don't swing, don't ring.
motto over the door of the Playboy Mansion in Chicago

Failed cartoonist, unenthusiastic magazine promotion man, Hugh Hefner produced the first edition of the world's best-known and best-selling 'men's magazine' from his kitchen table in a Chicago apartment. *Playboy*, as he called it, was an enormous success and over the next few years Hefner went on to found what for a while was an unrivalled and apparently boundless sex empire, with its key clubs, its bunny girls, its hip bachelor lifestyle and above all, the magazine itself, touting unashamed consumerism, of food, drink, technology and, of course, pneumatic girls. Hefner celebrated his success by taking over a forty-eight room mansion and fitting it up as a hedonistic pleasure palace, the epitome of his own 'Playboy Philosophy' and filled to the brim with visiting celebrities and complaisant, resident bunnies. Above the door, in dog-Latin was the message 'Si Non Oscillas, Noli Tintinnare', loosely translated as 'If you don't swing, don't ring'.

HEINLEIN, ROBERT (1907–) American science-fiction writer

Stranger in a Strange Land
book title, 1961

Heinlein is one of America's leading science fiction writers and his most celebrated book is *Stranger in a Strange Land* (1961). Its story is that of a human born of space travellers from Earth who is raised by Martians. He returns to earth to find a totalitarian, post World War III society, marked by repressiveness in sexuality and religion. Heinlein's text was seen by many young people as a satire of contemporary America, and the Stranger's creation of a Utopian society, in which people manage both to preserve their individuality and create fraternal communities, particularly appealed to the hippies. Heinlein's book was also central to the philsophies of a less appetising community: the Manson 'family' whose 1969 murders shocked Hollywood and the world.

HELLER, JOSEPH   (1923–) American writer

There was only one catch and that was Catch-22, which specified that a concern for one's own safety in the face of dangers, that were real and immediate was the process of a rational mind.
Catch-22 (1961)

Joseph Heller has written several subsequent books, all of which were reasonably popular, but his fame remains assured by his first novel, a satire based on his own experiences as a bombadier in the USAF during the Second World War. *Catch-22* took eight years to write but its publication brought him massive fame, upon which the less enthusiastic critics of his later work claim that he has been able to coast ever since. The basis of *Catch-22* is the viciously anomalous law that governs the rights of bomber crews to escape the seemingly endless extension of their tour of duty, flying missions over hostile anti-aircraft emplacements on their way to targets in Italy and beyond. The only way out of a mission was to prove oneself insane; as the definition above points out, merely claiming that continued flying was dangerous and utterly terrifying was quite a rational response. But not one that would keep you grounded.

HELLER, JOSEPH

Some men are born mediocre, some men achieve mediocrity, and some men have mediocrity thrust upon them.
Catch-22 (1961)

Among the various characters whose exploits and absurdities illumine the pages of Heller's great novel - Milo Minderbinder, Captain Yossarian, Hungry Joe and the rest - one of the most pitiful is Major Major Major Major, of whom only the first Major denotes his rank. He had, as Heller points out, been born too late and too mediocre' and goes on to offer this paraphrase of Shakespeare's lines from *Twelfth Night*: 'But be not afraid of greatness: some men are born great, some achieve greatness and some have greatness thrust upon them'. Of all the inadequates and neurotics who people the book, Major Major is the most snivellingly wretched, an officer who 'floundered bewilderedly from one embarassing catastrophe to another'. The epitome of his existence is his determination, rather than to meet those who enter his tent, to avoid them all by jumping through its back window when any visitor approaches.

HELLER, JOSEPH

Success and failure are both difficult to endure. Along with success come drugs, divorce, fornication, bullying, travel, meditation, medication, depression, neurosis and suicide. With failure comes failure.

in *Playboy* magazine, 1975

HELLMAN, LILLIAN (1905–84) American playwright and author

I am most willing to answer all questions about myself...(but) to hurt innocent people whom I knew many years ago in order to save myself is, to me, inhuman, indecent and dishonourable. I cannot and will not cut my conscience to fit this year's fashions, even though I long ago came to the conclusion that I was not a political person and could have no comfortable place in any political group.

testifying to the House Un-American Activities Committee, 1952

Lillian Hellman was one of the more successful American playwrights of the 1930s and 1940s, who eschewed the popular stage to produce a variety of 'legitimate' hits. She was also, from 1930, the friend and companion of the great pioneer of modern detective fiction Dashiell Hammett (1894-1960). With Hammett she supported a great many of the period's radical causes, and with him was interrogated by Senator McCarthy's witch-hunting, anti-Communist House Un-American Activities Committee. Hellman's involvement in Communism, like that of many of her peers, was probably far less intense than McCarthy wished to prove, but unlike many of those questioned, she refused to compromise her values, retorting to the Chairman with these celebrated lines. The Committee was duly impressed, or perhaps preferred to move on to more malleable victims, and left her in peace.

HEMINGWAY, ERNEST (1899–1961) American writer

Hemingway served as a volunteer ambulance driver in World War I and then, like many other Americans in search of a muse, settled in Paris where living was cheap and art plentiful. Here he associated with such notables as Gertrude Stein and Ezra Pound and in 1923 published his first book, followed in 1924 by *In Our Time*, his first real success. Among his greatest celebrants was F. Scott Fitzgerald, with whom he maintained a lengthy, love-hate relationship. His terse descriptions and spare dialogue earned such writing the epithet 'Hemingwayese' and the author's fame increased with his novels and his twin paeans to bullfighting and big game hunting. He covered both the Spanish Civil War and the Second World War as a reporter. His last major novel, *For Whom the Bell Tolls*, appeared in 1940. Hemingway's problem was his increasing belief in his own press cuttings, equating tough prose with the need for a hard-man lifestyle. He turned on former friends, destroyed two marriages and seemed consumed by a death-wish. He wrote nothing after receiving the Nobel Prize in 1954, but merely retreated into his own macho fantasies. He shot himself in July 1961.

HEMINGWAY, ERNEST

Courage is...grace under pressure.

HEMINGWAY, ERNEST

What is moral is what you feel good after.

HEMINGWAY, ERNEST

If you are lucky enough to have lived in Paris as a young man, then wherever you go for the rest of your life, it stays with you, for Paris is a moveable feast.
epigraph to his book *A Moveable Feast*

HEMINGWAY, ERNEST

People who write fiction, if they had not taken it up, might have become very successful liars.
in *This Week*, 1959

HEMINGWAY, ERNEST

All good books are alike in that they are truer than if they really happened and after you are finished reading one you will find that all that happened to you and afterwards it belongs to you.... If you can get so that you can give that to people, then you are a writer.
quoted in Carlos Baker, *Hemingway: The Writer as an Artist*, (1952)

HEMINGWAY, ERNEST

Every man's life ends the same way. It is only the details of how he lived and how he died that distinguish one man from another.
quoted in the *Sunday Times*, 1966

HENAHAN, DONAL   American writer

Next to the writer of real estate advertisements, the autobiographer is the most suspect of prose artists.
New York Times, 1977

Echoing Philip Guedalla's remarks (qv) on the topic, Henahan is equally sceptical of the motivation that persuades many autobiographers to commit their precious memoirs to paper. Even if the writer has resisted the temptation to settle old scores, reveal damning facts about fellow celebrities that have evaded their more favourable critics, or admit to intimacies that would not have been permitted had those concerned still been alive and thus protected by the libel laws, it seems that in all but a few cases, the subject of such books does tend to come off best, if not outrageously so.

HENRI, ADRIAN   (1932–) British poet

Love is a fanclub with only two fans.
Love Is... (1967)

Henri has been both a poet and painter, but he is most celebrated as one of the three Liverpool Poets (the others are Brian Patten and Roger McGough) whose work was anthologised by Penguin Books in 1967 as *The Mersey Sound*. From the title, capitalising on the rock 'n' roll 'Mersey Sound' - the Beatles and their imitators – to the topics it hymned, the volume remains a perfect Sixties artefact. Henri himself lectured at Liverpool College of Art and from 1967-70 led the poets' rock outlet 'The Liverpool Scene'. For a while they were almost as famous as genuine pop stars: people stole their discarded clothes and ran across busy streets to touch them.

HENRI, ADRIAN

Beautiful boys with bright red guitars In the spaces between the stars.
Mrs Albion You've Got a Lovely Daughter (1967)

HENRY, O.   (1862–1910) (W.S. Porter) American humorist

Turn up the lights, I don't want to go home in the dark.
last words, 1910

Porter drifted through a variety of jobs before in 1898 he was jailed for five years after being convicted of embezzling from the bank in which he worked. He was freed in 1901, after making his first efforts at writing in jail, and spent the rest of his life in New York. Living a far from fashionable life, but meeting a vast cross-section of 'characters' he began, consciously or not, to collect the material that he transmuted into the substantial canon of short stories that appeared under his pseudonym O. Henry from 1905 onwards. His work was characterised by its humanity, compassion, humour and gentle irony, and by the surprise ending he gave to every tale.

HENTOFF, MARGOT American journalist

Pop culture is, perhaps most of all, a culture of accessible fantasy.
New York Herald Tribune, 1971

The concept of 'pop culture', alongside that of 'pop art', was coined by Lawrence Alloway. Writing in Lucy Lippard's *Pop Art* (1967), he explained that originally 'I used the term to refer to the products of the mass media' and not, as it had come to mean in 1967, 'works of art that draw upon popular culture'. Today's pop culture, as Hentoff points out, refers to a culture that is based on accessible, consumable products, often those hymned by the mass media or produced in large volume. It does not require a discriminating intelligence, if anything it militates against such elitism. It is in the end the fantasy culture of the mass mind, even if, like all culture, it is provided by a relatively small, directing elite.

HICKS, SEYMOUR (1871–1949) British actor-manager

You will recognize, my boy, the first sign of age: it is when you go out into the streets of London and realize for the first time how young the policemen look.
Between Ourselves (1930)

Hicks built up a reputation as a sophisticated farceur and light comedian, acting extensively in successful plays, many of which he had written himself. The best-known include *The Man In Dress Clothes*, *The Gay Gordons*, and *Vintage Wine*, although there is little doubt that Hicks' analysis of passing time has been quoted to a greater extent than any of his other efforts. *Between Ourselves* is his first volume of autobiography; it was followed by a second, *Me and My Missus*, in 1939.

HILL, BENNY (1925–) British comedian

That's what show business is – sincere insincerity.
quoted in the *Observer*, 1977

A girlie magazine in human form, the epitome of what the British call 'naughty knickers' and the Americans 'tits and ass', Benny Hill must be credited with maximising vulgarity's every potential in a show that comes on like an over-sexed Donald McGill postcard. Hill was born Alfred Hawthorne Hill but changed his name apparently to avoid any Cockney mispronuciations. Hill's career began as a stooge to the name comedian Reg Varney in early Margate summer shows, but found greater fame as one of the many comics who were engaged in the early Fifties to help 'Educating Archie' on BBC Radio. He now concentrates on purveying his 'sincere insincerity' via the television, massively popular both in the UK and America.

HILL, JOE (1879–1915) American labour activist and poet

Work and pray, live on hay
You'll get pie in the sky when you die

The Preacher and the Slave

Hill, a Swedish immigrant born Joel Haagland, joined the labour movement in 1910 and rose to become one of its leaders. This poem was composed in 1906/07 as a rallying cry to the masses, and directly parodied a mawkish hymn - 'In the Sweet Bye and Bye' - which promised a wonderful afterlife so long as one suffered in silence on earth. It was taken up first by the militant Industrial Workers of the World (the IWW or 'Wobblies') and gradually lost its political implications, turning into a still-used catchphrase. Hill so infuriated the bosses that in 1914 he was convicted on the flimsiest of charges of the murder of a business-man in Salt Lake City, Utah. Despite worldwide protests Hill was duly executed by a firing squad on November 19, 1915. His last words were satisfactorily inspirational: 'Don't mourn, organise!'

HILLARY, EDMUND (1919–) British climber

We knocked the bastard off!

on reaching peak of Mount Everest, 1953

In the tradition of celebratory lines that turn out to be coarser than might have been warranted by the occasion, Edmund Hillary's exultant announcement of his and Sherpa Tensing's (1914-86) conquest of Mount Everest did not immediately reach a nation waiting for both his success and the Coronation of Queen Elizabeth II. Nonethless, as Hillary reported in his autobiography *Nothing Venture, Nothing Win* (1975), in a passage redolent with stiffened upper lips: 'George (Lowe) met us with a mug of soup just above camp, and seeing his stalwart frame and cheerful face reminded me of how fond of him I was. My comment was not specially prepared for public consumption but for George.... "Well, we knocked the bastard off!" I told him and he nodded with pleasure... "Thought you might have!" Tensing was also reported as offering his mildly profane comment: 'We done the bugger!'

HILLARY, EDMUND

A few more whacks of the ice axe in the firm snow and we stood on the summit.
interviewed in *Life* magazine, June 13 1953

Hillary's official report on the climb up Everest climaxed with this sentence, delivered to *Life* magazine. Hillary posed Tensing with a string of flags and shot a picture for posterity. Tensing carefully buried a few cermonial gifts for the mountain gods and after 15 minutes the pair began their descent.

HILLS, L. RUST   American journalist

Most people's lives aren't complex - they're just complicated.
in *Esquire* magazine, 1970

According to the *Oxford English Dictionary* these two adjectives mean pretty much the same thing: not easily analysed or disentangled, or tangled up, and given that they share the same Latin root in the verb complicare: to fold together, to entangle, this is not surprising, although it tends to make nonsense of Hills' theory. However, what Hills must be claiming is that while people like to stress their difficulties and claim their problems are infintely complex, and thus of subtle and a difficult nature, they are not. What they actually are is tightly interwoven and entwined and if carefully unravelled, subject to relatively easy solutions.

HILTON, JAMES   (1900–54) British writer

Anno domini – that's the most fatal complaint of all.
Goodbye, Mr. Chips (1933)

Goodbye, Mr. Chips (1933) is an unashamedly sentimental tale of an ageing master at a public school, here bewailing the passage of time, which was published initially as a serial in the magazine *British Weekly*. In the same year Hilton published his fantasy of the mythical Shangri-La, *The Lost Horizon*, an enormous bestseller, which offered the mass market readership a comforting philosophy quite at odds with the realities of contemporary life. Both books have been filmed more than once. Mr Chips did for the English public school what the film *Mrs Miniver* (1942) (on which unsurprisingly he also worked) did for Dunkirk, and Hilton fittingly moved to Hollywood where he lived out his days as a scriptwriter.

HIMMLER, HEINRICH (1900–1945) German Nazi leader

It is the curse of the great that they have to step over corpses to create new life.

As Reichsfuhrer S.S. Himmler was the Nazi party's chief of police, and as such charged with the task of maintaining discipline in Germany and the conquered territories. His devotion to Hitler and enthusiasm for the job were undoubtedly vital to the Fuhrer's successes. Himmler was an early Party member, a veteran of the putsch of 1923 who joined the S.S. ('protective squad') and rose to lead it by 1929. This quasi-military elite, recruited only from racially pure Aryans, was used successfully to crush the rival S.A. (Sturm Abteilung) led by Ernst Rohm, in 1934. As Munich police chief, Himmler set up the Dachau concentration camp and was, after Hitler, solely in charge of the 'Final Solution', a policy he saw as 'a glorious page in our history'. He took poison after being captured, in disguise, by British troops.

HIROHITO (1901–) Japanese emperor

The enemy has begun to employ a new and most cruel bomb, the power of which to do damage is indeed incalculable, taking the toll of many innocent lives. Should we continue to fight, it would not only result in an ultimate collapse and obliteration of the Japanese nation, but it would also lead to the total extinction of human civilisation.

radio announcement of Japanese surrender, August 15, 1945

The Emperor Hirohito, a direct descendant of Jimmu Tenno, the first emperor of Japan, came to the throne in 1926, possessed of the divinity claimed by Tenno's Yamato dynasty. He had little influence on practical politics and his influence on the nationalists who urged Japan towards its involvement in World War II was strictly limited. However, his nominal leadership of the country meant that as the American forces gradually moved towards Japan it was for the Emperor to take ultimate responsibility for the country's pursuit of the war. He had already begun tentative negotiations with President Truman, hoping to avoid the appalling loss of face involved in an unconditional surrender. After the USAF dropped atomic bombs on Hiroshima and Nagasaki, Hirohito's response was swift and pragmatic. Its essence is contained in this radio broadcast. He remains Emperor, although he renounced his divinity in 1946, still specialising in the marine biology that has been his lifetime fascination.

HITCHCOCK, ALFRED (1899–1980) British film director

I have a perfect cure for a sore throat – cut it.
quoted in J. Russell Taylor, *Hitch*

Hitchock made his first film in 1925. As director in 1929 of England's first talkie', he established himself as a leading filmmaker, going on to make a vast number of major movies both in England and Hollywood, where he moved in 1940. Because, as critic Andrew Sarris put it, 'he has given audiences more pleasure than is permissible for serious cinema', his work was initially dismissed as 'mere entertainment', but the French established him as an important figure, claiming portentously that his work expressed a deep, religious moral profundity, and ensuring that it was henceforth taken very seriously. Hitchock's best films show him as the 'master of suspense', using techniques learnt in the silent era to manipulate the audience. Quite conscious of his own image—he included a fleeting shot of his own portly self in every film—he delighted in aphorisms, like that above, that emphasised it. Other one-liners include:

Drama is life with the dull bits left out.

Always make the audience suffer as much as possible.

There is no terror in a bang, only in the anticipation of it.

Actors are cattle.

This line infuriated his current star, Carole Lombard, who walked off the set. Hitchock mollified her, and later told pressmen I didn't say actors are cattle; I said they ought to be treated like cattle'. Whether this line is responsible for Broadway's definition of a mass audition as a 'cattle call' cannot be proved.

HITLER, ADOLF (1889–1945) German dictator
Hitler, the son of an Austrian customs official, was inspired by what he saw as the decadence of his country, with its liberal attitudes, powerful Jewish community, and intellectual freedoms, to join the lower-middle class nationalist movement led by Vienna's anti-Semitic Mayor Karl Lueger. After World War I he joined the National Socialist Party, soon rising to lead it. His first attempt to gain power, the 1923 'beerhall putsch', failed and he

was imprisoned. He used the time to compose his credo: *Mein Kampf* (1925-26, My Struggle). Out of jail he began working more carefully, gathering a mass of like-minded followers, enlisting an army of bully-boys to terrorise street-level opposition and campaigning to enlist powerful supporters in politics, business and the army. The inability of the Weimar republic to deal with the problems of the depression gave the Nazis their chance. They won the election of 1933 and Hitler was made Chancellor. The implementation of Nazi policies began, notably with rearmament, the creation of a New Order in Germany, and the repression of radical and liberal intellectuals, Jews, Communists, homosexuals and other allegedly second-class citizens. Once Hitler had remoulded Germany, he began looking elsewhere. Europe preferred appeasement to attack and his incursions into Austria, the Rheinland and Czechoslovakia were unopposed. In 1939 the invasion of Poland, with whom England and France had a specific defence treaty, elicited a more positive response and launched the Second World War. By 1941, after spectacular successes, Hitler was master of Europe: his dream of a Thousand Year Reich seemingly about to become true. But his failure to invade Britain, his turning on Russia and, above all, the entry into the war of America made defeat only a matter of time. The Thousand Years lasted a mere dozen and Hitler committed suicide in the 'Fuhrerbunker' as Berlin burnt around him.

HITLER, ADOLF

But then, that's what young men are there for.
German dictator

commenting on exceptionally heavy casualty lists...

HITLER, ADOLF

Above all, I enjoin the governments of the nation and the people to uphold the racial laws and to resist mercilessly the poisoner of all nations, international Jewry. Berlin 29 April 1945 0400 hours. My wife and I choose to die in order to escape the shame of overthrow or capitulation. It is our wish for our bodies to be cremated immediately in the place where I have performed the greater part of my daily work, during twelve years of service to my people.
last statement, 29 April 1945

Russian and American troops were already in the outskirts of Berlin when a beleaguered Hitler, trapped in his 'Fuhrerbunker', began dictating his last will and political testament to his secretary Frau Junge. In it he restated his beliefs, both in himself and in Germany. As his biographer Alan Bullock notes, there was nothing in it that could not have been found in his apologia *Mein Kampf* or in even earlier speeches of the 1920s. He defended his career and blamed everything, as ever, on the Jews. In a final orgy of megalomania, even as his enemies triumphed overhead, he made his provisions for the Reich's future, expelling Goering and Himmler from the Party and appointing Admiral Donitz as his successor. The diatribe climaxed with the paragraph cited above. At 3.30 in the afternoon of April 30, Hitler and his wife Eva Braun committed suicide. Their bodies were burnt as allied bombers circled overhead.

HITLER, ADOLF

The art of leadership...consists in consolidating the attention of the people against a single adversary and taking care that nothing will split up that attention.
Mein Kampf (1925-26)

The establishing of a scapegoat upon whom all grievances may conveniently be blamed was hardly an invention of the Nazi Party, but Hitler proved himself a master tactician in his choice of the Jews. Fuelled by his own resentments of the Austrian Jews of his youth, he backed his propaganda with the absolute sincerity of his emotions and brought anti-Semitism to a fine art. Generations of assimilation were powerless in the face of Hitler's appeals, capitalising on the anti-Semitism endemic in Germany and, since few European leaders chose to take notice, throughout the continent. The destruction of the Jews was systematised, codified and taken to its logical conclusion in the gas chambers of Auschwitz, Belsen and the other concentration camps. For all that the 'revisionist' school of historians would like to claim otherwise, some six million Jews, not to mention millions of other 'untermenschen' were exterminated.

HITLER, ADOLF

The Final Solution
Nazi code-word for the extermination of Jews, post 1941

Hitler had loathed the Jews since his own youth in Vienna, when like so many others he blamed the city's sophisticated liberal Jewish community for his own inadequacies. He incorporated the anti-Semitic policies of Mayor Karl Lueger's stridently nationalistic party into his own Nazi organisation. It is clear from *Mein Kampf* that he intended to revenge himself on the Jews; at what stage he envisaged the programme of mass extermination that became known by 1941 as Endlosung (the Final Solution) is unknown. The idea of a 'final solution' certainly stemmed from the Fuhrer, although it was not initially specified as a genocidal one. The Nuremberg Laws, the first systematic 'legal' exclusion of Jews from German society, cited 'The Final Solution of the Jewish Problem' and mentioned such concepts as forced emigration. By 1941, when an order from Goering referring to the concentration camps referred both to a 'total' and a 'final' solution of the 'Jewish question', there was no longer any doubt as to the full import of the phrase.

HITLER, ADOLF

Well, he seemed such a nice old gentleman, I thought I would give him my autograph.
on the Munich agreement, 1938

The nice old gentleman in question was British prime minister Neville Chamberlain; the autograph was Hitler's signature on the Munich Agreement, a document that came to symbolise the futility of appeasement and typified Chamberlain's vacillation and weakness and Hitler's cynicism and cunning. Chamberlain first met Hitler on September 13, 1938 when, perturbed by Hitler's much-publicised claims on the German-speaking Sudeten area of Czechoslovakia, he hoped, with the backing of the equally pusillanimous French prime minister Daladier, to conciliate the Fuhrer and thus avert a situation which might otherwise lead to European war. Chamberlain made it clear to Hitler that his plans were acceptable and that the British and French would ensure Czech compliance. Hitler traded on his adversary's weakness to increase his demands. Chamberlain gave in comprehensively, grateful only to return on September 30th, after a third meeting, clutching his 'piece of paper' and prattling happily of 'peace in our time'.

HITLER, ADOLF

It is the last territorial claim I have to make in Europe
on the invasion of Czechoslovakia, 1938

As far as Hitler was concerned, the population of the Sudetenland, the German speaking area of Czechoslovakia which under the Treaty of Versailles had been annexed to the Czechs after the collapse of the Habsburg monarchy in World War I, ought to be reunited with their fellow Germans. Indeed, in his view, the whole Czech state, 'founded on a lie', was ripe for destruction.

Reclaiming the Sudetenland was thus a lever with which to set the process in motion. On 26 September 1938, at the Sportpalast, he delivered a 'masterpiece of invective', declaring '...now stands before us the last problem that must be solved and will be solved. It is the last territorial claim I have to make in Europe, but it is the claim from which I will not recede and which, God willing, I will make good.... With regard to the problem of the Sudenten Germans, my patience is now at an end.' On October 1 German troops entered the Sudetenland and Hitler's diplomats redrew Czechoslovakia's boundaries.

Hitler, Adolf

I go the way that providence dictates with the assurance of a sleepwalker.
quoted in A. Bullock, *Hitler: A Study in Tyranny* (1952)

As can easily be elicited from *Mein Kampf* and from the 700-odd pages of his *Table Talk*, Hitler was a man of unshakable egocentricity, a self-obsession that he transmuted through his own demagogic powers into the direction of a whole nation's life. At no stage, right up until his last, besieged days in his Berlin bunker, did his self-belief seem to waver. He saw himself as an intuitive leader, guided, as he says here, by providence, but protected by the sort of inspired good fortune that keeps the sleepwalker from coming to grief. Boundlessly self–confident he exploited his undoubted talents to the full, riding with destiny and letting nothing sway him from his chosen path.

Hitler, Adolf

I shall give a propagandist reason for starting the war, no matter whether it is plausible or not. The victor will not be asked afterwards whether he told the truth or not. When starting and waging war it is not right that matters, but victory.
quoted in W. Shirer, *The Rise and Fall of the Third Reich*

Hitler was a master of propaganda, of manipulation and of the policy best summed up as 'the big lie': convince the masses of one enormous untruth and they will cheerfully accept all the smaller lies contingent upon it. As he put it candidly, 'What luck for the rulers that men do not think'. First in Germany and then in the conquered territories, he combined propaganda of word and of deed: national constitutions were rearranged on Nazi models while any opposition was crushed ruthlessly. As he promised here, the reason he gave for starting the war was irrelevant: once started he would unleash forces that would make historical niceties unimportant. Victors do indeed have the choice of writing the history that follows. Fortunately Hitler was not among them. Forty years later, American writer Gary Wills (1934–), one of America's acutest political commentators, echoed Hitler's bravado. Talking of rival interpretations of the Vietnam War, he noted in the *New York Times* 'Only the winners decide what were war crimes.'

HOCHHUTH, ROLF   (1931–) German playwright

Men may be linked in friendship; nations are linked only in interests.
The Soldiers (1967)

The Soldiers was the second of Hochhuth's highly controversial and iconoclastic plays dealing with the conduct by certain of its leaders of the Second World War. In it he assesses the possible culpability of Winston Churchill for the death of General Sikorski, the leader of the Free Poles, and for the decision of the British bomber command to start the terror-bombing of German cities in 1943, after the Luftwaffe had been neutralised and the German population lay vulnerable. The play deals with the role of a leader not as a man but as the human embodiment of a nation's interest, acting not as a human being, but as a pragmatic force of history. This attack on Churchill, undisguised by any theatrical pseudonyms, proved unsupportable. The play was banned and not staged until the office of the Lord Chamberlain, the British censor, had been abolished in 1968. In the event the critics were sympathetic, and Hochhuth's study of Realpolitik vs. human ideals given a fair, if not wholly congratulatory hearing.

HOCHHUTH, ROLF

The man who says what he thinks is finished and the man who thinks what he says is an idiot.
The Representative (1966)

Der Stellvertreter (*The Representative*) was one of the most controversial plays of the 1960s. It was the first published work by Rolf Hochhuth, and dealt with the failure of Pope Pius XII to break the Church's Concordat with Nazi Germany or to condemn publicly Hitler's slaughter of the Jews, even though Pius was in possession of detailed information regarding the death camps. The play caused the inevitable furore, although the theories it put forward were by no means Hochhuth's discovery. Hochhuth compounded the controversy by using the real names of those involved, as here in Act Four, where Pius himself defends his position and that of his Church. Above all the play is about responsibility, about the individual and his freedom of choice. If that freedom is declined, the individual sacrifices his rights to individuality. As one critic pointed out at the time, the play's relevance is not to the image of the Papacy, but to the reaction of single human beings facing intolerable pressures.

HOCKNEY, DAVID (1937–) British artist

It is very good advice to believe only what an artist does, rather than what he says about his work.
David Hockney by David Hockney (1976)

Hockney is probably the most successful and certainly the best known of the generation of British artists whose work was collectively known as British Pop Art. In the personality-conscious Sixties Hockney, with his white-blonde dyed hair and granny glasses, was chosen by the media to represent 'painting' for the purposes of the Swinging London myth. His initial work tended to the autobiographical and elusive but since the mid Sixties it has become more representational. His pictures of swimming pools are particularly well known, and were the basis of a cult film. Hockney has worked extensively in California and takes many of his themes from the lifestyles of that state. He works usually from photographs or drawings and sometimes a combination of the two.

HOFFA, JIMMY (1913–1975) American union leader

I do unto others what they do unto me, only worse.
quoted in D. Moldea, The Hoffa Wars (1978)

If British trade unions might be accused of favouring the political left, their American equivalents seem devoted to maintaining the status quo, establishing cosy but lucrative relationships with the employers. Individual members who attempt to break this mould and alleviate some of the injustices that are regularly sanctified by such agreements get short shrift from union bosses who have no desire to see such deals undermined. Epitome of the tough union boss was the Teamsters (truck-drivers) head, James 'Jimmy' Hoffa, a hard-nosed boss whose links with the Mafia and proven theft of at least £225,000 in union funds, for which he was eventually jailed, did not deter his members from electing him again. Only on his release from prison did Hoffa's power fade, and he was killed, in still mysterious circumstances, after he left his home for a meeting and was never seen again. As Moldea puts it 'Jimmy Hoffa's most valuable contribution to the American labour movement came at the moment he stopped breathing on July 30, 1975.'

HOFFER, ERIC (1902–) American philosopher

When people are free to do as they please, they usually imitate each other.
The Passionate State of Mind (1954)

Born in New York City, Hoffer missed most of his formal schooling after an accident rendered him blind until the age of fifteen. At eighteen he left home and began more than twenty years working at a variety of manual jobs in California. In 1951 The True Believer, his study of fanaticism and mass movements in their various guises, was well received by the critics. He followed this with *The Passionate State of Mind* (1955), a collection of aphorisms on politics and other aspects of the human condition which demonstrates his keen perceptions and mastery of generalisation.

HOFFER, ERIC

To have a grievance is to have a purpose in life. A grievance can almost serve as a substitute for hope; and it not infrequently happens that those who hunger for hope give their allegiance to him who offers them a grievance.
quoted in *The Faber Book of Aphorisms* (1964)

HOFFER, ERIC

You can discover what your enemy fears most by observing the means he uses to frighten you.
quoted in *The Faber Book of Aphorisms* (1964)

HOFFER, ERIC

Rudeness is the weak man's imitation of strength.
The Passionate State of Mind (1954)

HOFFMAN, COL. MAX German soldier

They are lions led by donkeys.
on the British tactics during World War I

Trench warfare, the staple diet of the troops engaged on the western front of World War I, was a novelty to all participants, used as they were to the grand gestures of the cavalry charge, the thin red line and the unbroken square. As the massive casualties bear witness, on neither side did the generals come to grips with the new military status quo, but the British, even if they did win, seemed more pig-headed in their conservatism than all the rest. Hoffman's comment was in reply to that made by General Ludendorff who watched in awestruck horror as thousands upon thousands of English troops, in accordance with the inflexible tactics of the generals who directed the offensives of 1915, advanced on dug-in German machine-guns, only to suffer appalling casualties. Ludendorff told his junior officer 'The British troops fight like lions', and Hoffman made his immortal rejoinder.

HOFFMAN, DUSTIN (1937–) American film star

A good review from the critics is just another stay of execution.
in *Playboy* magazine, 1975

Here voicing the actor's traditional distrust of those who make a living criticising his work is Dustin Hoffman, one of Hollywood's most successful male leads since the 1960s. His career went into something of a decline in the Seventies but he has returned triumphantly more recently. His first major film was *The Graduate* (1967), a film that for many summed up the predicament of the young in that youth-orientated decade and, as well as its youthful star, launched the singers Paul Simon and Art Garfunkel to international fame. Others include *Midnight Cowboy* (1969), *All The President's Men* (1976), *Kramer Versus Kramer* (1980) and *Tootsie* (1983).

HOFSTADTER, RICHARD (1916–1970) American historian

Yesterday's avant-garde experience is today's chic and tomorrow's cliché.
Anti-Intellectualism in American Life (1963)

Hofstadter was one of the major influences on contemporary American historiography, ever since his first book, *Social Darwinism* in American Thought, in which he compared the evolutionary 'survival of the fittest' with the struggles for economic development, appeared in 1944. *Anti-Intellectualism in American Life* (1963) was his personal response to the attack on academic freedom during the McCarthyite era in America, where to be intellectual was often considered tantamount to proclaiming one's allegiance to Moscow. Hofstadter deplored the activities of self-appointed populist 'reformers' of this type, pointing out that their enthusiasms were aroused less by altruism than by xenophobia, anti-Semitism, reaction, and a sense of their own lower-middle class limitations.

HOGGART, RICHARD

HOGGART, RICHARD (1918–) British scholar and writer

Most mass entertainments are in the end . . . 'anti-life'. They are full of a corrupt brightness, or improper appeals and moral evasions . . . they tend towards a view of the world in which progress is conceived as a seeking of material possessions, equality as a moral levelling and freedom as the ground for endless irresponsible pleasure.
The Uses of Literacy (1957)

Educated in Leeds Hoggart was a teacher of adult education at Hull University. During this time he began researching mass popular culture and in 1957 published *The Uses of Literacy: Aspects of working-class life with special reference to publications and entertainments.* This book was hugely successful and although based in the Fifties, remains an important sociological work. Drawing heavily on the experiences of his own boyhood, Hoggart combined a sociological overview of 'the working classes' and Orwellian popular criticism of what they read and enjoyed. He had little time for the new mass entertainments of the Fifties (and has had less for what has followed). Summoning up an idyll of pre-television, and pre-cinema, culture when the masses were self-sufficient in their own amusements, he deplores the meretricious shoddiness of the artificial pleasures that have succeeded them.

HOLIDAY INN

I'm dreaming of a white Christmas, just like the ones I used to know
screenplay (1942)

Bing Crosby starred in this hit film musical which managed to combine the cheery amateur 'let's do the show here/in the barn' ethos with snow-bedecked Christmas card scenery. Irving Berlin's 'White Christmas' is still up among the leaders in overall song sales and, in the same way that Prince Albert brought Germanic Yuletide clichés to Britain, so has Berlin's most well-known song extended American ones to the world.

HONDO

A man ought to do what he thinks is right.
screenplay (1953)

The tragedy of so many of the most popular phrases, especially those allegedly engendered by the films, is that no-one ever said them. None more so than the supposedly immortal macho declaration 'A man's gotta do what a man's gotta do', the staple of so many movie heroes and, so it has always been believed, the copyright of The Duke himself, John Wayne, the toughest hombre never to strike a blow or fire a shot in anger. Although the phrase has become hackneyed over the years, and few would dare use it other than as a joke, it is one of those lines that everyone knows. The line above, which was indeed said by Wayne in this 1953 oater, was written by writer James Edward Grant (1902-66) who took his plot from 'The Gift of Cochise', a short story by Louis L'Amour.

HOOVER, HERBERT (1874–1964) American president

There will be a chicken in every pot.
attributed campaign slogan, 1928

According to William Safire the first national leader to promise his people a chicken in their pot was Henri IV of France (1553–1610). Hoover did not in fact say it; the nearest he came was pointing out on October 22, 1928 that, under the economic boom of the Twenties 'The slogan of progress is changing from the "full dinner pail" to the full garage'. Hoover's personal line was confused with a flier issued by his Republican party which was indeed headed 'A chicken in every pot'. The main appearance of this piece of propaganda, boasting that the Republicans had not just given every citizen a chicken and a car to boot but had 'placed the whole nation in the silk stocking class', was its being ridiculed by Democrat Al Smith who asked an audience to 'picture a man working at $17.50 a week going out to a chicken dinner in his own automobile with silk socks on'.

HOPPER, HEDDA (1890–1966) (Elda Flurry) Hollywood gossip writer

Nobody's interested in sweetness and light.

Hedda Hopper started her career as an all-purpose Hollywood actress, working regularly in stock silent vehicles. She never starred in anything, although towards the end of her life, when she had become famous with her scabrous columns of Hollywood love and life, she regularly played cameo roles in such movies as *Sunset Boulevard* (1950) and *The Oscar* (1966). As Hopper's dictum underlines, nobody was interested in good things about the larger than life screen deities they worshipped. Hopper and her rivals dug the dirt relentlessly, tolerated by the studios both for the publicity they rendered the stars and for the fact that they could make and break an actor or actress and thus could be used to manipulate an errant performer if fed the correct information.

HOUSE, COL. EDWARD   (1858–1938) American diplomat

Saturday was a remarkable day.... We actually got down to work at half past ten and finished remaking the map of the world as we would have it, at half past twelve o'clock
on Versailles negotiations, 1919

House was President Wilson's representative at the negotiations in 1919 that determined the clauses of the Treaty of Versailles, the internationally agreed document, prepared by the victors of World War I to 'remake the map of the world' for future reference. As Wilson's man, House was burdened with the President's 14 Points, a list of ideals that only infuriated those leaders who had been far more intimately and lengthily involved both with the war itself and with the state of Europe in general. The President's naivety certainly slowed negotiations but House, generally acknowledged as his éminence grise, managed to smooth over the problem so that indeed, after months of wrangling, the world, so disorganised by four years of war, was settled in one two-hour burst of organisation.

HOUSMAN, A.E.   (1859–1936) British poet

In summertime on Bredon
The bells they sound so clear;
Round both the shires they ring them
In steeples far and near,
A happy noise to hear.

A Shropshire Lad (1896)

Housman was primarily a classical scholar, the Professor of Latin at Cambridge from 1911 until his death, the excellence of whose meticulous translations was balanced only by the open scorn in which he held the work of those he condemned as lesser intellects. His fame, however, is based in his poetry, notably *A Shropshire Lad*. The Lad was published at Housman's own expense and was received in silence by the recognised critics. It had 63 short verses, usually based on ballad forms, evoking a near-legendary Shropshire, 'a land of lost content'. Only when Richard Le Gallienne attributed an 'exquisite simplicity' to the verses did public interest begin to mount and the poem gained immense popularity, based no doubt on its nostalgic appeal, during World War I.

HOWERD, FRANKIE (1922–) (Francis Alexander Howard) British comedian

And the best of British luck!
catchphrase

Howerd was born Howard, changing his name after the war in the hope that, if nothing else so low on the bill, people might notice it as a possible misprint. After RADA he joined the BBC's Variety Bandbox through which he became a major star of the Fifties. Howerd's career faltered badly during the early 1960s, but he returned with the triumphant *A Funny Thing Happened On the Way To the Forum* in 1963 and has never stopped working. Like most comedians of his generation, Howerd uses various catchphrases, including 'I was amaaazed', 'Not on your nelly!' and this one, which originated during Variety Bandbox. Howerd introduced a regular mock opera into the show, badly sung and an excuse for laughs. Whenever the soprano paused before high C, Howerd could be heard muttering 'And the best of luck!' a phrase that developed into 'The best of British luck' and thus the still popular catchphrase.

HUBBARD, ELBERT (1856–1915) American writer and businessman

The selfish wish to govern is often mistaken for a holy zeal in the cause of humanity.
The Notebook (1927)

After a career as a saleman and the writing of several undistinguished novels, Hubbard dropped out of business to become a full-time Bohemian. From 1895-1915 he edited an 'inspirational' magazine, *The Philistine*, which attained some success, although another venture, *The Era* (1908-17), was less popular. Hubbard was a natural fan and among his many writings is *170 Little Journeys*, a catalogue of pilgrimages to the homes of the great. His best known work is *A Message to Garcia* (1899), a book which appealed so much to a number of business magnates that they each bought large numbers of copies for distribution to their employees in the hope that Hubbard's 'message' might promote greater efficiency. Hubbard died in 1915, aboard the torpedoed Lusitania; *The Notebook* was a posthumous collection of his aphorisms.

HUBBARD, ELBERT

Life is just one damn thing after another.
One Thousand and One Epigrams

HUBBARD, ELBERT

A pessimist is a man who has been compelled to live with an optimist.
The Notebook (1927)

HUBBARD, ELBERT

Heaven: the Coney Island of the Christian imagination.
The Notebook (1927)

HUBBARD, FRANK MCKINNEY 'KIN' (1868–1930) American humourist

The less a statesman amounts to, the more he loves the flag.
Abe Martin's Sayings (1915)

Patriotism, intoned Dr. Johnson, is the last refuge of a scoundrel, and Kin Hubbard's fictional sage Abe Martin put it much the same way a century and a half later. Hubbard gained fame as a nationally syndicated columnist and caricaturist, whose work was originally published in the *Indianapolis News* in 1892. His columns were based upon on the 'sayings' of Abe Martin, a folksily humorous character, of a type especially beloved by American audiences of the time, a collection of which sayings appeared annually. Abe quipped away in what was allegedly Indiana dialect, a corn-belt version of New York's 'Mr. Dooley', and gave his own quirky but apposite views on all varieties of the human condition.

HUMPHRIES, BARRY (1934–) Australian writer and comedian

> Oh, I was down by Manly Pier
> Drinking tubes of ice-cold beer
> With a bucket full of prawns upon me knee.
> But when I'd swallowed the last prawn
> I had a Technicolour yawn
> And I chundered in the old Pacific sea.

Chunder Down Under (1964)

If any individual can credit themselves with the single-handed delineation of a national culture, then it must be Australian humourist Barry Humphries, whose appearances as 'Dame Edna Everage – Housewife Superstar' and 'Sir Les Patterson – Australian cultural attaché' triumphantly confirm all too many people's image of 'Down Under' as a brash, braying mix of the opinionated petit-bourgeoisie and foul-mouthed, beer-swilling ockers. Humphries began his career in Australia in the Fifties, before moving to England just in time for the satire boom' of the Sixties. He wrote the 'Barry Mckenzie' cartoon strip for *Private Eye*, and this song first appeared there, sung with graphically suitable illustrations, by 'Bazza' and a number of his inebriated mates. It is as 'Dame Edna' that he has won most success, portraying this gladioli-wielding, self-opinionated representative of Australian suburbia to the delight of worldwide audiences.

HUMPHRIES, BARRY

To tell the truth, I'm as full as a fairy's phonebook. I'm as full as a state school hatrack. I'm as full as two race trains. I'm as full as a seaside shithouse on Boxing Day. Awh, I'm sorry again, ladies. Please forgive me. That's a rotten thing to say in mixed company. I'm as low as the basic wage for talking like that. That's bloody parliamentary language. I'm that low I could parachute out of a snake's arsehole and still free-fall. Are you with me?
as 'Sir Les Patterson', 1978

The Australian government has yet to comment on how they see their soi-disant 'Cultural Attaché', the country's main overseas representative of the national 'yartz'; but Humphries' second most popular caricature, covered with vomit, food and liquor, making normal vulgarity look like Emily Post, has endeared himself to the comedian's many fans. It might be noted that this speech, in the same way as did many of Barry McKenzie's best lines, shows Humphries' love of language, an area in which he is some expert. All these metaphors for drunkenness can be found in Australian slang.

HUXLEY, ALDOUS (1894–1963) British novelist and essayist

Huxley came from a family of scientists but eye problems which caused him near blindness at 16 precluded any ideas of his joining them. Instead he read English at Oxford and during World War I met Lady Ottoline Morrell, the society hostess and literary lion-hunter. He spent much time at her salon at Garsington and there met many literary celebrities, notably those of the Bloomsbury group. He used Garsington, its denizens and others who peopled London's smart literary world as a background for his own early, satirical books. His most enduring work, *Brave New World*, appeared in 1932. The ironies of his early work gradually turned to mordant bitterness as he became increasingly disenchanted with literary and indeed all human society. In 1937 he left England with his friend Gerald Heard (1899-) and in California, where he lived until his death, began to devote himself to the worlds of spirituality, mysticism, parapsychology and hallucinogenic drugs.

HUXLEY, ALDOUS

There are few who would not rather be taken in adultery than in provincialism.
Antic Hay (1923)

Antic Hay was Huxley's second novel, and is typical of the witty allusive work that represents his early writing. In it Theodore Gumbril, former schoolmaster and now inventor of Gumbril's Patent Small-Clothes (pneumatic, padded trousers), sells his invention to Mr. Boldero, a capitalist. In this passage Boldero explains what to him are the beauties of advertising whereby an increasing number of the gullibly fashionable, dominated by its promises and cajolery, would rather commit a major sin than to be marked down as anything but socially smart.

HUXLEY, ALDOUS

You don't suppose any serious-minded person imagines a revolution is going to bring liberty, do you?
Antic Hay (1923)

After thinking up his Patent Small-Clothes while seated on a hard seat in the chapel of the school where he teaches, Theodore Gumbril approaches his tailor, Mr. Bojanus, with the request that he make him up a pair of trousers with suitably comfort-enhancing embellishments. Mr. Bojanus is happy enough to insert the required inflatable portions and begins talking of his predeliction for change, saying 'I was always one for change and a little excitement'. But he tempers pleasure with pragmatism and points out, as above, that revolution and liberty rarely if ever have anything whatsoever in common.

HUXLEY, ALDOUS

Our Ford...had been the first to reveal the appalling dangers of family life.
Brave New World (1932)

Brave New World remains Huxley's great achievement, a prophetic novel of a psychological and biological dystopia, dominated by calculated social and physiological conditioning. There is no room in Our Ford's universe for the individual or his preoccupations. If such an individual appears he may for a while be an object of interest, even affection, but in the end, if he refuses or is unable to conform, then society has no alternative but to destroy him. Huxley's book is less immediately political than Orwell's *1984* (1948), with which it is often compared, but its satire of technology run riot seems increasingly relevant as time, and that same technology, move on.

HUXLEY, ALDOUS

They'll be safe from books and botany all the rest of their lives.
Brave New World (1932)

In chapter two of Huxley's novel the Director of Hatcheries and Conditioning is taking his students on a tour of London's Hatchery and Conditioning Centre, where test-tube babies are decanted into a new life, and carefully conditioned to accept whatever level of existence has been determined for their future. In the Neo-Pavlovian Conditioning Rooms the party observes a group of Deltas, manual workers of the future, for whom such pleasures as literature and flowers will be irrelevant and counter-productive. Thus they are presented with books and roses and encouraged to crawl towards them. As they reach the objects loudspeakers release a hideous cacophony of frightening sounds and the floor is electrified, sending the babies shrieking with pain and terror. Repeated sufficiently often, says the DHC, this experience will condition them for life and as he says 'They'll be safe from books and botany all the rest of their lives'.

HUXLEY, ALDOUS

The most distressing thing that can happen to a prophet is to be proved wrong. The next most distressing thing is to be proved right.
Brave New World Revisited (1956)

Brave New World Revisited is a short book on the problem of freedom in an age of overpopulation, plus a series of articles on governmental and economic power and all the means employed for the reduction of psychological resistance in the individual, from brainwashing and advertising to drugs and hypnopaedia. Huxley attempts to propose ways in which all these menaces might be opposed, suggesting that humanity must hold on to 'fundamentals' and positing new means of education. As the title and the quotation make clear, he is referring back to and extrapolating from his own prophetic work, *Brave New World* (1932).

HUXLEY, ALDOUS

Like every other instrument man has invented, sport can be used for good and evil purposes. Used badly it can encourage personal vanity and group vanity, greedy desire for victory and even hatred for rivals, an intolerant esprit de corps and contempt for people who are beyond an arbitrarily selected pale.
Ends and Means (1937)

Huxley's comments on sport, taken from his philosophical book *Ends and Means*, predate those of George Orwell who in a later essay also pointed out that such fantasies as 'good sportsmanship' and their like are pure illusion. From its very inception sports have been no more than war without weapons, masks for an aggression which, depending on the sport, and these days the amount of cash at stake, is often revealed in all its primordial excess.

HUXLEY, ALDOUS

As long as men worship the Caesars and Napoleons, the Caesars and Napoleons will duly rise and make them miserable.
Ends and Means (1937)

In *Ends and Means* Huxley attempts to relate all social problems, whether of international politics, of education or of economics to one central system of ethics. He then takes ethics and tries to relate those in turn to his own conception of the nature of reality. In the book he asks, and attempts to answer, such questions as: What is the nature of the world? Does it possess value and meaning? Is there a universal meaning? The philosophies Huxley expounds, reflective of his own preoccupation with the futility of temporal ideologies, attracted much interest and the book was widely read.

HUXLEY, ALDOUS

Every ceiling, when reached, becomes a floor, upon which one walks as a matter of course and prescriptive right.
Letters of Aldous Huxley (1971)

Perhaps singer Paul Simon had this line in mind when, in 1974, he released his song 'One man's ceiling is another man's floor'. However Simon was considering relations between individuals, even literally between those sharing apartment blocks, and attempting to point out that peaceful life can only be obtained by respecting one's neighbours. Huxley is also making clear that human nature is such that what one has striven for one day, however seemingly unattainable and thus alluring it may have been, once attained automatically assumes the proportions of an inalienable right, which one has always had and deserved and for which one need feel in no ways grateful, but which serves merely as a base from which to move on to the next target.

Huxley, Aldous

Either you choose... to be a totalitarian fascist...and you find yourself involved in the most atrocious military tyranny. Or you choose socialism or communism, and call the resulting totalitarianism by the name of 'democracy' and end up, if you are sensitive and honest, by finding yourself horribly disillusioned. Or finally, you cling to democratic capitalism and find yourself forced, by the logic of advanced technology, to embrace some form of totalitarianism.
Letters of Aldous Huxley (1971)

As his move towards the paranormal and the spiritual makes clear, Huxley grew less and less interested in the -isms which dominated the lives and opinions of the majority of his contemporaries. For those not possessed of a guiding ideology, his blanket condemnation of all such political disguises for the drive to power seems powerful and persuasive. Whether the mysticism he offered promised any improvement, especially for those whose intellects were less sophisticated and whose incomes did not permit their quitting the quotidian round, must remain highly debatable.

Huxley, Aldous

Half at least of all morality is negative and consists in keeping out of mischief.
The Doors of Perception (1956)

The Doors of Perception was Huxley's attempt to offer to the general reader some of the experiences he gained through the use of hallucinogenic drugs, notably mescalin and LSD. Ideally, he felt, it would possible for mankind to gain an extended awareness of and harmony with what he called Ultimate Reality. That experience, which experimenters with such drugs have called 'seeing God' or 'the white light', could possibly be found through hallucinogens, and indeed a number of American and South American Indian tribes had always used such drugs, derived from plants rather than chemical processing. Huxley decried the 'morality' that rejected such theories. On his own deathbed, in 1963, as the craze for hallucinogens was expanding throughout the California in which he lived, Huxley took a dose of LSD, presumably to ease his passing.

HUXLEY, ALDOUS

Only one more indispensable massacre of Capitalists or Communists or Fascists or Christians or Heretics and there we are – there we are in the Golden Future.
Time Must Have a Stop (1944)

This novel is set among the English intellectuals living in both London and Florence during the 1920s. The principal comic character dies of a stroke and we follow him into the non-sensual world of the hereafter. We watch as he drifts about the edges of the Divine, existing within its gravitational field. At regular intervals he returns to communicate with his friends through the agency of a particularly stupid medium, who garbles his words. In the end, shrinking from the prospect of being absorbed into God, he manages to get himself born back into humanity via the body of a baby who is expected by the wife of one of the characters. Written in 1944 the book reflects Huxley's interest in the spiritual world coupled with his disenchantment with the warring ideologies, religious or political, of the actual world.

HUXLEY, ALDOUS

That men do not learn much from the lessons of history is the most important of all the lessons that history has to teach.
Collected Essays (1959)

Huxley described the range of his essays himself: 'Essays autobiographical. Essays about things seen and places visited. Essays in criticism of all kinds of works of art, literary, plastic, musical. Essays about philosophy and religion, some of them couched in abstract terms, others in the form of an anthology with comments, others again in which general ideas are approached through the concrete facts of history and biography. Essays, finally, in which I have tried to... say everything at once in as near an approach to contrapuntal simultaneity as the nature of literary art will allow'.

I

IBARRURI, DOLORES (La Pasionaria) (1895–) Spanish politician

It is better to die on your feet than to live on your knees.
Spanish Civil War slogan

La Pasionaria, as Ibarruri was known, addressed the women of Spain in a radio broadcast on September 3, 1936. Ibarruri had been born into the middle class but she sought political 'liberation' by marrying a miner and devoting herself to socialism. In her broadcast she called upon Spanish women to defend the republic against Franco's fascist troops and produced this classically inspiring line. Another of her exhortations, also adopted as a slogan by republican fighters was 'No pasaran!' - They shall not pass. Both slogans were popular but neither was original. 'They shall not pass' was first used by Maréchal Pétain, rallying the French forces during World War I. The refusal to live on one's knees comes from the Mexican revolutionary Emiliano Zapata (18770-1919) who told his followers 'Mejor morir a pie que vivir en rodillas!'

IDLE, ERIC (1945–) British comedian

Nudge, nudge, wink, wink, say no more, know what I mean...
in Monty Python's Flying Circus, BBC-TV 1969

Monty Python's Flying Circus, first transmitted in August 1969, was the most successful version of the apparently endless variety of 'satire' shows that had followed 'Beyond the Fringe' since 1960. In the sketch Idle, the classic saloon-bar loudmouth, all suede shoes and RAF blazer, is pestering a bowler-hatted, business suited city gent (Terry Jones) with leering innuendoes. 'Nudge, nudge, wink, wink...is your wife a goer?...' etc. The phrase entered the language at once. Few recalled the sketch's punchline, revealing Idle's oleaginous suggestions as an empty sham: Idle: 'Well, I mean, you're a man of the world, aren't you, I mean – you've been there, haven't you, I mean you've been around, eh?' Jones: 'What do you mean?' Idle: 'Well, I mean, like – you've done it. With a lady. You've slept with a lady.' Jones: 'Yes.' Idle: 'What's it like?'

ILLICH, IVAN (1926–) Austrian educational and social theorist

Man must choose whether to be rich in things or in the freedom to use them.
Deschooling Society (1971)

Illich was the founder in Mexico of the Center for Intercultural Documentation (CIDOC), which hosted many seminars on the concepts of an 'alternative society'. Deschooling Society concentrated on demystifying education, stripping it of the mystique and professional self-interest that Illich saw as standing in the way of making it useful to the majority of potential students. A similar attempt to deprofessionalise health care, *Limits to Medicine* (1976) appealed to those who felt medicine should abandon its inflexible structures. Illich continues to work for mass involvement in the institutions that control mass life, believing that 'the fraud perpetrated by the salesman of schools' is far worse than that perpetrated by a purely commercial salesman since 'the schoolman hooks his people on a much more demanding drug'.

INGE, WILLIAM R. (1860–1954) British clergyman

Personalize your sympathies, depersonalize your antipathies.
More Lay Thoughts of a Dean (1931)

After being appointed Dean of St. Pauls in 1911, Inge was requested by the man who chose him, H.H. Asquith, to 'restore the traditions of culture and scholarship' associated with the Deanery. This he did in full measure, becoming the most outspoken clergyman of his time. Inge was nicknamed the 'gloomy Dean' by the *Daily Mail* because of what the paper saw as his kneejerk opposition to all forms of progress but he defended himself later saying 'I have tried only to face reality, to be honest, and to refuse to be foolishly optimistic'. Such anti-boosterism did not endear him to the masses but he wrote sincerely and forcefully, and if he was conservative in his public pronouncements, deploring what he saw as an all-embracing decline in spiritual values, he remained at the forefront of theological scholarship.

INGE, WILLIAM R.

The vulgar mind always mistakes the exceptional for the important.
Lay Thoughts of a Dean (1926)

INGE, WILLIAM R.

Many people believe they are attracted by God, or by Nature, when they are only repelled by man.
More Lay Thoughts of a Dean (1931)

INGE, WILLIAM R.

Originality is undetected plagiarism.

INGE, WILLIAM R.

Try to arrange your life in such a way that you can afford to be disinterested. It is the most expensive of all luxuries, and the one best worth having.
More Lay Thoughts of a Dean (1931)

INGE, WILLIAM R.

A nation is a society united by a delusion about its ancestry and by a common hatred of its neighbours.
quoted in *The Perpetual Pessimist*, by Sagittarius & George

INVISIBLE MAN, THE

I meddled in things that man must leave alone.'
screenplay by R.C. Sherriff and Philip Wylie (1933)

H.G. Wells' novel appeared in 1897 and this filmed version was directed by James Whale, who had already done a superb job on Mary Shelley's *Frankenstein* in 1931. The Man in question was played by Claude Rains, whose acting was mainly verbal since for most of the film he was invisible. This is his last line, and reminds fans of Edwardian adventure fiction of that other awful confession: He has looked upon things no white man should ever see....'

IONESCO, EUGENE   (1912–) Rumanian playwright

To think contrary to one's era is heroism. But to speak against it is madness.
quoted in *Esquire* magazine, 1974

Ionesco was born in Rumania and settled in France in 1938. His attempts to learn English using the Assimil method led to his first play, among the most celebrated of French avant-garde productions, *La Cantatrice chauve* (1950, *The Bald Prima Donna*), which has always been in production at some Parisian theatre ever since its first night. It is usually produced as a double-bill with *La Leçon* (1951, *The Lesson*) an experiment in the theatre of cruelty and of the absurd. Ionesco is a consistently avant-garde writer but his views tend to the conservative and in *Rhinoceros* (1960) he savages all forms of totalitarianism, both of left and right. Loathing such ideologies and obsessed with death, Ionesco has attempted to point up the extent to which humanity needs love.

IONESCO, EUGENE

The critic should describe, and not prescribe.
Improvisation, or The Shepherd's Chameleon

Improvisation is a play about the theatre and the writing of plays in which Ionesco himself faces the characters whom he has created in his earlier works. In common with many others connected with the stage, Ionesco loses no love on the professional critic, and suggests that the only task he or she need perform is to inform the reader and potential theatre-goer of what the play under discussion contains. There is no need to embellish such a description with personal opinions, praise or blame.

IONESCO, EUGENE

In the name of religion, one tortures, persecutes, builds pyres. In the guise of ideologies, one massacres, tortures and kills. In the name of justice one punishes...in the name of love of one's country or of one's race one hates other countries, despises them, massacres them. In the name of equality and brotherhood there is suppression and torture. There is nothing in common between the means and the end, the means go far beyond the end...ideologies and religion...are the alibis of the means.
in *Esquire* magazine, 1974

IONESCO, EUGENE

It is the enemies of History that, in the end, make it.
Notes and Counter-Notes (1962)

In these writings on the theatre Ionesco presents a valuable collection of essays, interviews, exchanges and polemics with fellow dramatists and critics. He also includes discussions of his own plays and of the modern theatre in which he works. This line stresses his disdain for any form of totalitarianism. His point is that those who wish to alter the flow of history by diverting its course to one form of extremism or another actually create more history, the sum of their own actions.

ISHERWOOD, CHRISTOPHER   (1904–1986) British writer

I am a camera with its shutter open, quite passive, recording, not thinking.
Goodbye to Berlin (1939)

This line, the most celebrated of all of Isherwood's work, sums up the role he takes as narrator of his various stories of Berlin in the Thirties. Although Isherwood wrote both before and after these fictionalised memoirs of his stay as an English teacher in Berlin immediately prior to the Nazis' seizure of power in 1933, his two novels of this period, *Mr. Norris Changes Trains* (1935) and *Goodbye to Berlin* (1939), remain his most popular work. After Berlin he worked with Auden on *The Ascent of F6* and wrote the semi-autobiographical *Lions and Shadows* (1938), in which such friends as Edward Upward, Auden, Stephen Spender and others appear under pseudonyms. He moved to California in 1939 and, like his neighbour Aldous Huxley, became increasingly involved in mysticism, notably Hindu philosophy.

J

JACKSON, HOLBROOK   (1874–1948) British writer

As soon as an idea is accepted it is time to reject it.
Platitudes in the Making (1911)

Jackson was largely self-educated and began his writing career with A.R. Orage's (1873-1934) socialist magazine *New Age* in 1907. He worked on *T.P's Weekly* (founded in 1902 by T.P. O'Connor) from 1911-16 before founding his own 'little magazine', *Today*, in 1917. Many leading contemporary writers contributed to the magazine until its demise in 1923. An obsessive and informed bibliophile he wrote extensively on the history and technology of printing, as well as on bibliography and other book-related topics. His study of George Bernard Shaw (1907) was the first to appear in Britain, and *The Eighteen-Nineties* (1913) remains an important guide to the period's literary world. *Platitudes in the Making* is a collection of Jackson's aphorisms on a variety of topics.

JACKSON, HOLBROOK

Why did nature create Man? Was it to show that she is big enough to make mistakes, or was it pure ignorance?

JACOBS, JOE (1896–1940) American boxing manager

I should have stood in bed.
in October 1934

Jacobs, as a boxing manager, rarely interested himself in other sporting fixtures, but in 1934 he had attended the World Series of Baseball and foolishly backed the losers. Popular myth, including Bartlett's Quotations, had it that Jacobs came out with this oft-repeated line after losing that bet, but the journalist John Lardner claimes otherwise. In his version it was a particularly chilly day and Jacobs, watching his first and last live ballgame, was unimpressed. When a neighbour in the press box, where both Lardner and Jacobs were seated, asked the manager how he liked baseball, Jacobs replied tersely 'I should have stood in bed'.

JACOBS, JOE

We wuz robbed.'
on June 21, 1932

Jacobs managed, among other top-ranking boxers, the German world heavyweight champion, Max Schmeling. Defending his title in America in 1932, Schmeling systematically destroyed his opponent but was still declared the loser, outpointed by the challenger, local boy Jack Sharkey. Coining a phrase that has been used by countless sporting figures, not the least of them practitioners or managers of 'the noble art', Jacobs exploded with rage at the officials who he felt had 'robbed' his boy.

JAGGER, MICK (1943–) British rock star

For most people the fantasy is driving around in a big car, having all the chicks you want and being able to pay for it. It always has been, still is, and always will be. Anyone who says it isn't is talking bullshit.
quoted in *The Book of Rock Quotes* by Jonathon Green (1977)

Jagger has always been one of the most pragmatic of rock stars. The fact that for all the alleged Rolling Stones excesses he remains alive, still producing rock music even in his forties, is testimony to that. While the Stones, and Jagger, have had their problems, and fallen into the same traps as many of their peers, notably their exploitation by less than sympathetic businessmen, Jagger always seems to have perceived his own position as an embodiment of the fantasy he outlines above. It may lack the finer points of more philosophical dreams, but for the majority, for whom it will always remain strictly off limits, this is indeed the good life.

JAGGER, MICK

As long as my picture is on the front page I don't care what they say about me on page 96.'
quoted in *The Book of Rock Quotes* by Jonathon Green (1977)

Jagger long since transcended the single-issue pages of the rock press, although he still appears there as something of an elder statesman, and moved firmly into the world of the gossip column and the profile, more or less adulatory. Of course, the Rolling Stones were always in the popular press, usually as the objects of jealous loathing, alleged shock and feigned horror, placed there through a financially rewarding collusion between the manipulations of their early manager Andrew Loog Oldham, who set them as the deliberate counterpoint to Brian Epstein's squeaky-clean Beatles, and the love of Fleet Street for 'sexy' copy. One picture, as Jagger makes clear, is worth many thousand record sales.

JAMES, WILLIAM (1842–1910) American philosopher

Our civilisation is founded on the shambles, and every individual existence goes out in a lonely spasm of helpless agony.
Varieties of Religious Experience (1902)

James was the eldest brother of the novelist Henry James. At university he fluctuated between art, medicine and naturalism before joining Harvard as an instructor in anatomy and physiology. He was subsequently professor both of philosophy and of psychology at the university. His work is centred on two important publications: *Varieties of Religious Experience* (1902) contained his Gifford lectures given at Edinburgh in 1901; *Principles of Psychology* (1890) established him as a major thinker, both in his assessment of the current state of psychology and in his suggestions for its possible progress. His philosophy was much influenced by a personal decision to deal with the depressions that recurred in an otherwise ostensibly cheerful life, by exerting his own free will. This led to his espousal and development of both pragmatism and radical empiricism, books on each of which appeared respectively in 1907 and 1912.

JAMES, WILLIAM

The moral flabbiness born of the exclusive worship of the bitch-goddess Success.
in a letter to H.G. Wells

JAMES, WILLIAM

A great many people think they are thinking when they are merely rearranging their prejudices.

JAMES, WILLIAM

There is only one thing a philosopher can be relied on to do, and that is to contradict other philosophers.

JARRELL, RANDALL   (1914–65) American critic and poet

If you have been put in your place long enough, you begin to act like the place.
A Sad Heart in the Supermarket (1965)

Jarrell was one of America's foremost literary critics. He wrote a number of volumes of poetry, starting with *Blood for a Stranger* (1942). His single novel, *Pictures from an Institution* (1952) is a satire on life in a progressive women's college and has been seen as one of the earliest examples of the 'campus novel', a genre that includes the work of Kingsley Amis, David Lodge and Malcolm Bradbury. Jarrell's reference here is to his belief in the formative effects of environment: human beings, whether in offices, prisons, the family unit or whatever world they consistently inhabit, tend willy-nilly to become representatives of that place.

JARRELL, RANDALL

It is not just Mowgli who was raised by a couple of wolves; any child is raised by a couple of grown-ups. Father and Mother may be nearer and dearer than anyone will ever be again - still, they are members of a different species.
The Third Book of Criticism (1969)

Taken from this posthumously published collection of his criticism, Jarrell's remark will not endear itself to proponents of the cheerful, isolated nuclear family, a unit set firmly within the larger world. He points out that for all that the family does, if fortunate, generate a high degree of mutual and supportive affection, the fact remains that the children are 'of a different species' to the parents, a fact that becomes apparent early in life, is accentuated by the so-called 'generation gap' and brought to conclusion by adulthood. The cycle, of course, repeats itself every time a new set of adults become parents in their turn.

JAZZ SINGER, THE
You ain't heard nothin' yet'
screenplay (1927)

Warner Brothers were encouraged by their young executive producer Darryl F. Zanuck (qv) to back this, the first of the talkies. In fact there wasn't that much dialogue, but Jolson, the singing sensation of the era, actually ad-libbed the line that made the film and served as a motto for the sound revolution in Hollywood. Jolson was poised to start singing one of his hits, 'Toot Toot Tootsie'. The camera was rolling and microphones open when he paused and exclaimed 'Wait a minute, wait a minute, you ain't heard nothin' yet. Wait a minute I tell you... you wanna hear Toot Toot Tootsie? All right, hold on...' then launched into the song.

JOAD, C.E.M.   (1891–1953) British academic
It all depends what you mean by...
catchphrase on BBC radio programme *The Brains Trust* (1941–48)

From 1941-49 the weekly programme *The Brains Trust*, a name taken from that given President Roosevelt's New Deal advisers, offered intelligent listeners the chance to 'listen in' on the deliberations of a panel of academics, drawn from various disciplines. So popular did the programme become that the verbal mannerisms of the three regulars, Commander A.B. Campbell, Professor Julian Huxley and Joad himself, attained the status of catchphrases. Joad's line came from his insistence that before answering any of the questions sent in to the panel, it was first necessary to establish as far as possible the precise meaning of the question itself.

JOHNSON, HIRAM   (1866–1945) American politician
The first casualty when war comes is truth.
speech, 1917

Johnson was the Republican Governor of California from 1910-17 and then senator for the State until his death. His posthumous reputation is best enshrined in this, his only notable line, which was delivered as America entered World War I amid a mixture of jingoistic propaganda, paranoiac xenophobia and governmental disinformation. The line was used for the title of Australian journalist Philip Knightly's book on the history of the war corrrespondent, *The First Casualty* (1975).

JOHNSON, LYNDON BAINES (1908–1973) American president

Johnson was born in Stonewall, Texas, a fitting birthplace for a politician who showed himself among the most determined of America's presidents. Kennedy's assassination brought Johnson to the White House in 1963; he was elected, in a landslide, in 1964 and served a single term. Johnson's impoverished youth made his an alluringly rags to riches story and he fought sincerely to improve the lot of the poor and the racial minorities. A master manipulator of the US political system, he combined his native bluntness with an unrivalled knowledge of its workings to persuade Congress to pass his radical programme of civil rights, welfare and education legislation. These successes were offset both by his commitment to the Vietnam War, which he saw as a personal crusade, and by widespread urban disturbances by those who saw his programme as merely cosmetic. In February 1968, after the Viet Cong's Tet Offensive had savaged American optimism, Johnson announced that he would not run for re-election and retired from politics after his term.

JOHNSON, LYNDON BAINES

While you're saving your face, you're losing your ass.
quoted in *The Best and the Brightest by D. Halberstam* (1973)

Johnson's tough-guy image may have been psychologically dubious, motivated by the old cliché of vulnerable fragility girded about by butch exhibitionism, but with very few exceptions he maintained it throughout his career. He was not one to apologise, preferring to use his abrasive style and undoubted political savvy to defeat opposition either through pure fear or through subtle manipulation. As the president whose term of office gave rise to the 'credibility gap', the split between the theory of what he said and the contradictory practise of what he did, his attitude to apologies and face-saving was from his point of view probably right, if not in the long run of much use to the nation he claimed to love.

JOHNSON, LYNDON BAINES

So I ask you tonight to join me and march along the road...that leads to the Great Society, where no child will go unfed...where every human being has dignity and every worker has a job; where education is blind to colour and employment is unaware of race.
campaigning speech, 1964

Johnson's greatest success, his package of social welfare, civil rights and educational legislation that he forced through Congress in the mid-Sixties, was the direct fruit of this dream, proclaimed here and on many other occasions under the title of the 'Great Society'. Franklin Roosevelt had used his 'New Deal' to fight the problems of the Depression of the Thirties; now Johnson took on the challenge of illiteracy, racism and poverty. Although more conservative successors have tried to undermine it, the 36th President's lasting achievement was this legislation. As he put it in his inagural speech on January 20, 1965: 'I do not believe that the Great Society is the ordered, changeless, and sterile battalion of the ants. It is the excitement of becoming, trying, probing, failing, resting and trying again.'

JOHNSON, LYNDON BAINES

It's probably better to have him inside the tent pissing out, than outside pissing in.

on J. Edgar Hoover

J. Edgar Hoover was appointed to head the then relatively new Federal Bureau of Investigation in 1924. Hoover made the FBI a highly publicised crime-busting organisation, which may not have been as successful as its boss claimed, but which took a central place in American law and order mythology. Wielding substantial powers Hoover became an extremely important man, maintaining his office while mere politicians came and went. His files on the nation's notables were supposedly extensive and potentially damaging. A number of presidents considered firing him, but Hoover remained in place. When Johnson won his massive victory in 1964 he too thought about removing Hoover but decided against it, justifying his decision with this pithy line.

JOHNSON, LYNDON BAINES

Boys, I may not know much, but I know chicken shit from chicken salad.

on Richard Nixon's 'Checkers' speech, 1952

Johnson had been elected to the US senate in 1948, after a highly controversial campaign, the nature of which occasioned an investigation into allegations of fraud and vote-rigging which was only stopped when the Supreme Court quashed it. This did not restrain Johnson's denunciation of a former fellow senator, Richard M. Nixon who, similarly accused of political malfeasance, appeared on television to justify his own position with what became known as the 'Checkers speech'. Nixon's unappetisingly unctuous style, his reference to the dog, Checkers, and the general implausibility of his speech managed nonetheless to convince America. They did not, as he puts it here, impress the Senator for Texas.

JOHNSON, LYNDON BAINES.

I don't want loyalty, I want loyalty...I want him to kiss my ass in Macy's window at high noon and tell me it smells like roses
quoted in *The Best and the Brightest* by D. Halberstam (1973)

Johnson took his politics very personally. As his decision to quit the Presidency in 1968 shows, he put heart and soul into his leadership of America and if things went wrong he took it hard. An overprotected boyhood resulted in his lifelong desire to present a macho image, and his tough language, peppered with supposedly Texan homeliness, is a case in point. The comment on loyalty above, and the statement that 'I never trust a man unless I've got his pecker in my pocket', were just two of many such lines.

JOHNSON, LYNDON BAINES

If you have a mother in law with only one eye and she has it in the centre of her forehead, you don't keep her in the living room
quoted in *The Best and the Brightest* by D. Halberstam (1973)

The true story of the American involvement in Vietnam did not surface until the so-called Pentagon Papers, the Pentagon's secret story of that involvement, was leaked to the Press in 1971. Prior to that the real role of the 'American advisors' was given a deliberately low profile. Johnson, like his two predecessors, had no desire to alter this situation. After August 1964 when the 'Tonkin Gulf incident' was played up to justify a far greater American role, Johnson promoted his war, but before that he saw no purpose in letting the public in on what was happening. Speaking to senior aides, he used these metaphorical lines to sum up his policy.

JOHNSTON, ALVA American writer

The title 'Little Napoleon' in Hollywood is equivalent to the title 'Mister' in any other community.
in the *New Yorker*

Johnston was among the most admired and popular of the writers employed by the New Yorker magazine during the Thirties and Forties. Among his many pieces was his book-length study of two of America's most remarkable 'characters', Wilson and Addison

Mizner, *The Fabulous Mizners* (1953). This wry comment on the propensity of Hollywood moguls to take themselves with megalomaniacal seriousness and impose their egos on all who had to meet or work with them is born out in any memoir of the Hollywood of the period.

JOHST, HANNS (1890-1978) German playwright

Whenever I hear the word 'culture' I reach for my gun.
Schlageter (1933)

Among the best known and most commonly misattributed quotations of the century is this remark, usually assumed to have been made by any one of Hitler's inner circle of Nazi leaders, most often Goering. In fact it comes from the play *Schlageter*, written by the medicocre Nazi playwright Hanns Johst in 1933. Its topic was the murder by the French occupying forces of a Rhineland German immediately after World War I. With its shades of another Nazi martyr, the pimp and Party member Horst Wessel, Johst's play appealed to the faithful. The line in question ran 'Wenn ich Kultur hore... entsichere ich meinen Browning', and may be translated as 'When I hear the word culture I take the safety catch off my Browning' (an automatic rifle).

JONES, ELWYN (1904–) British lawyer

Someone has described a technicality as a point of principle which we have forgotten.
quoted in 1966

Sir Elwyn Jones, the son of a Welsh Methodist minister, followed his education at the University of Wales with a career as a solicitor, starting in 1927. He rose through the ranks of local government to become Town Clerk of Bangor in 1939. In 1950 he was elected MP and has served as a Labour Attorney-General. As well his his political and legal work, he has written a number of pieces for the press in both Welsh and English.

JONES, JIM (1931–78) American cult leader

We didn't commit suicide. We committed an act of revolutionary suicide, protesting the conditions of an inhumane world.
last message from The People's Temple, November 1978

Of the many cults spawned by the Sixties' yearning for self-realisation within an 'alternative society', the Reverend Jim Jones' People's Temple seemed initially to have some of the most respectable credentials. Jones had been a youthful prodigy, a 12-

year-old fundamentalist preacher who joined the Methodists and won them many converts before his own theology proved too hot for the church and they ejected him in 1954. He founded the People's Temple in 1957, combining supposed 'miracles' with real concern for the poor. In 1977, after Jones had prophecied the imminent apocalypse, the Temple moved to Guyana, where nearly a thousand followers built their communal home, 'Jonestown'. From idyllic beginnings Jonestown declined into a nightmare of exploitation and cruelty. Faced by investigators from America Jones led 913 followers in an act of 'revolutionary suicide', all swigging cups of cyanide-laced Kool-Aid. Jones left a last testament, of which these lines form the crux.

JONG, ERICA (1942–) American writer

The zipless fuck is absolutely pure. It is free of ulterior motives. There is no power game. The man is not 'taking' and the woman is not 'giving'. No-one is attempting to cuckold a husband or humiliate a wife. No-one is trying to prove anything or get anything out of anyone. The zipless fuck is the purest thing there is. And it is rarer than the unicorn. And I have never had one.
Fear of Flying (1974)

What Germaine Greer did for emergent feminist theory with her non-fiction tract *The Female Eunuch*, Erica Jong, a hitherto minor American writer, did for fiction with her novel *Fear of Flying*. A popularised version of less accessible theory it sold massively and made Jong a star and a spokeswoman for the movement. The book deals with one Isadora Wing, her journey to write a piece on a congress of psychoanalysts in Vienna, her tormented inner life and her search for the mythical zipless fuck, a epochal 'coming together' that, in that happy pre-AIDS world, represented everyone's dream of paradise and was (and is) just about as elusive.

JONG, ERICA

Women are the only exploited group in history who have been idealised into powerlessness.
in *Time* magazine, 1978

JOSEPH, MICHAEL (1897–1958) British publisher

Authors are easy to get on with - if you're fond of children.
quoted in the *Observer* (1949)

After serving in World War I Joseph joined the London literary agency Curtis, Brown. He eventually graduated to running his own publishing house, Michael Joseph, and as well as publishing regular lists of other authors wrote a number of his own books. Their titles, *The Commercial Side of Literature* (1925) and *This Writing Business* (1931) fit well with Joseph's comment.

JOYCE, JAMES (1882–1941) Irish writer

riverrun, past Eve and Adam's, from swerve of shore to bend of bay, brings is by a commodius vicus of recirculation back to Howth Castle and Environs.
Finnegan's Wake (1939)

Joyce's last novel, *Finnegan's Wake*, is undoubtedly one of the least penetrable of works produced in this or any century. It has been variously represented as Joyce's tribute to language and as such his supreme and culminating work, and as the sign that he had lost control of his faculties and descended into self-indulgent trivia. Others claim that the book is a revenge on those who had claimed *Ulysses* (1922) was 'difficult'. The Wake takes the form of a long stream of consciousness, full of puns, literary, geographical and other allusions, and a profusion of invented, portmanteau words, representing the dreams of a Dublin tavern-keeper, one Humphrey Chimpden Earwicker, and a paradigm for all human life, past and present. This line is technically the first of the novel, but like the river it celebrates, Joyce intended his work to flow unchecked and thus the last line of the book 'A way a lone a last a loved a long the' is simultaneously part of the first, and thus links the circle.

JOYCE, JAMES

...and how he kissed me under the Moorish wall and I thought well as well him as another and then I asked him with my eyes to ask again yes and then he asked me would I yes to say yes my mountain flower and first I put my arms around him yes and drew him down to me so he could feel my breasts all perfume yes and his heart was going like mad and yes I said yes I will Yes.
Ulysses (1922)

The 20,000 word soliloquy with which Joyce ends Ulysses comes from one of its three main characters, Leopold Bloom's wife Molly, a singer. In the Homerian scheme that Joyce used for the novel, Molly thus represents Ulysses' wife Penelope, left at home to her suitors (in Molly's case the flamboyant Blazes Boylan) while her husband makes his journeys. Molly's speech, mainly on sexual themes, tumbles out in a 'stream of consciousness', climaxing in the final orgasmic Yes. In a book filled with experimental writing, this is the final set piece and one which, along with the bizarre scenes of Night Town, Dublin's red-light area, helped bring the novel to the attention of censors in Europe and America.

JOYCE, JAMES

Mr Leopold Bloom ate with relish the inner organs of beasts and fowls. He liked thick giblet soup, nutty gizzards, a stuffed roast heart, liver slices fried with crustcrumbs, fried hencod's roes. Most of all he liked grilled mutton kidneys which gave to his palate a fine tang of faintly scented urine.
Ulysses (1922)

Leopold Bloom, the Jewish anti-hero of Joyce's novel and the wandering Ulysses of the title, is an advertisement canvasser who falls in with the book's central character, Stephen Dedalus, as they both, sometimes together, sometimes going their separate ways, wander through Dublin on June 16th, 1904, encountering brothel and maternity ward, seashore and public house. Bloom's predeliction for offal acompanies his first appearance in the book, eating his breakfast while his wife Molly slumbers in their bedroom.

JUNG, CARL GUSTAV (1875–1961) Swiss psychiatrist
Jung, until 1913 a close associate of Freud, broke with him to found the main rival branch of psychoanalysis. Jung doubted Freud's insistence on the sexual basis of neurosis and began developing his own theories under the label Analytical Psychology. While Freud looked to infant experiences, Jung concentrated on the older patient, believing that mental health depends on maintaining the unity of one's personality: if that personality falls into disunity, mental illness results. Jung saw the mind as a self-regulating system, almost like a complex machine, and defined neurosis as 'the suffering of the soul which has not found its meaning'. He set out a number of archetypes, repetitive images that arise time and again in dreams and which spring from the collective unconsciousness. These include the animus and anima, the contra-sexual images in the male and female psyche. The idea of such archetypes led him to explore fairy tales, comparative religion, and similar symbol-filled belief-systems.

JUNG, CARL GUSTAV

As far as we can discern, the sole purpose of human existence is to kindle a light in the darkness of mere being.
Memories, Dreams and Reflections (1963)

This is an autobiographical volume which contains not only Jung's own account of his life and work but also essays on his travels, on Freud, on life after death and other thoughts. Always reticent about himself, Jung collaborated on the book with Aniela Jaffe who recorded much of the reminiscences over a lengthy period of time.

JUNG, CARL GUSTAV

With what pleasure we read newspaper reports of crime! A true criminal becomes a popular figure because he unburdens in no small degree the consciences of his fellow men, for now they know once more where evil is to be found.
Archetypes of the Collective Unconscious (1934)

In this article Jung attempted to expound the theory that 'in addition to our immediate consciousness... there exists a second psychic system of a collective, universal and unconscious nature which is identical in all individuals. This collective unconsciousness does not develop individually but is inherited. It consists of pre-existent forms, the archetypes, which can only become conscious separately, and which give definite form to certain psychic contents'. Archetypes are thus universal, inherited dispositions of the human imaginative faculty which dispose the individual to experience and behave in recurrent situations (eg: birth, death) as his ancestors behaved in them. Some archetypes are so developed that they constitute autonomous personality systems.

JUNG, CARL GUSTAVE

The shoe that fits one person pinches another; there is no receipe for living that suits all cases.
Modern Man in Search of a Soul (1933)

Modern Man... is a volume of essays, most of which had originally been delivered as lectures. It takes in a wide variety of subjects, ranging from dream analysis to psychology and literature.

JUNG, CARL GUSTAV

The educated man tries to repress the inferior one in himself, without realising that by this he forces the latter to become revolutionary.
Psychology and Religion (1940)

In 1937 Jung was asked to give the three annual Terry lectures at Yale. The text of those lectures forms the content of this book. In them Jung explores the relationship between Christianity and

alchemy, a topic that arose directly from his study of the archetypes that form the basis, as he saw it, of religious symbolism of
every variety.

JUNG, CARL GUSTAV

**Where an inferiority complex exists, there is a good reason for it.
There is always something inferior there, although not just where
we persuade ourselves that it is.**
interview, 1943

Of the most important archetypes, representations of aspects of
the collective unconscious, that Jung cited in his theories, one is
the shadow, the inferior part of one's personality. That inferior
part is inescapable, although, as Jung asserts here, what we
choose to see as 'the shadow' may well have no relevance to that
part of us, hidden in the unconscious, that actually is inferior.

K

KAEL, PAULINE   (1919–)

**Being creative is having something to sell, or knowing how to sell
something or having sold something. It has been taken over by
what we used to mean by being 'wised up'; knowing the tricks,
the shortcuts.**
Kiss Kiss Bang Bang (1968)

Pauline Kael has for many years been the respected critic of the
New Yorker magazine. Her many reviews have been collected in
a number of volumes, including *I Lost It at the Movies* (1965),
Kiss Kiss Bang Bang (1968), and *Reeling* (1976). All Kael's titles
tend towards some form of pun or allusion; this one in particular
uses what Kael has claimed was an Italian's summation of the
basic content of all the most popular films. Her dour comment on
creativity, a personal attribute that some might invest with a
greater, more fragile value, doubtless stems from many years
spent in close contact with Hollywood and its inevitable commercial 'bottom line'.

KAFKA, FRANZ   (1883–1924) Czech writer

**The joys of this life are not its own, but our dread of ascending to
a higher life: the torments of this life are not its own, but our self-
torment because of that dread.**
quoted in W.H. Auden, *The Dyer's Hand* (1963)

Kafka was born in Prague, the neurotic, over-sensitive, sporadically tubercular son of a Jewish family whose father was a businesslike, healthy individual about whom, he claimed, all his tortured works were written. Kafka's world is predicated on guilt, fear, worry and a sense of one's own inferiority, and the atmosphere he creates has enabled him to join the elite of writers whose work has created an eponym, in his case 'Kafkaesque'. It denotes a situation in which an individual is powerless, a prisoner of nameless forces and subject to unknown and unreasoned cruelties. As well as his own neurosis and his physical weakness, Kafka's career in the Czech civil service undoubtedly intensified his preoccupation with labyrinthine, anonymous, powerful structures.

KAFKA, FRANZ

Every revolution evaporates and leaves behind only the slime of a new bureaucracy.

The meaning of life is that it stops.
The Great Wall of China: Aphorisms 1917–19 (1931)

KAFKA, FRANZ

It's often safer to be in chains than to be free.
The Trial (1925)

KAHN, E.J. (1884–1972) American writer

Kahn: 'I get out of bed and throw up and take a shower and shave and have breakfast'
Gill: 'You throw up every morning?'
Kahn: 'Of course, doesn't everyone?'
quoted in B. Gill, *Here at the New Yorker* (1975)

In his memoir of his career at the New Yorker Gill recalls how as a 'non-smoking, non-drinking, early-to-bed young man' he found himself forced to curb his college-boy high spirits in the face of the dourness that seemed to pervade the magazine's corridors. One did not speak to the literary stars in the fear of provoking a morose dismissal. One day he did strike up a conversation, with a fellow neophyte, E.J. Kahn. Kahn professed himself less perturbed by the matutinal gloom. But then, as this conversation shows, he probably had little desire himself to be overly jokey that early in the day.

KAUFMAN, GEORGE S.   (1889–1961) American playwright

If you have a message, call for Western Union.
quoted in *Wits End* by J.R. Gaines 1977

Kaufman was one of Broadway's legendary figures whose scripts and lyrics helped create a string of hit plays and musical comedies in a career that stretched for three decades. He collaborated with most of his peers and his plays starred the top actors and actresses in America. He was a man filled with contradictions: he wrote comedy but rarely smiled, had major hits but presumed that every new play would fail; he loathed physical contact but seduced dozens of women and adopted a caustic, wise-cracking exterior but performed secret acts of kindness. His best known lines were his twin theatrical dicta, each conforming to his tough-guy pose, and both were contradicted in several of his plays. *Of Mice and Men*, which admittedly he only directed, certainly had its message and 'Of Thee I Sing' was nothing if not satire: it ran for 441 performances and did not 'close Saturday night'.

KAUFMAN, GEORGE S.
Satire is what closes Saturday night.
quoted in *George S. Kaufman and his Friends*, by Scott Meredith (1974)

KAVANAGH, TED   British scriptwriter

After you Claude' 'No, after you, Cecil'
catchphrase for *ITMA*, BBC radio 1940s

Among the many catchphrases spawned by *ITMA*, this short dialogue between Claude, played by Jack Train, and Cecil, played by Horace Percival, was among the most imitated by the millions of devoted listeners. It is still, occasionally in use, although Claude and Cecil, with their camp overtones, come, like 'Julian' and 'Sandy' from Kenneth Horne's subsequent shows, from an era that for better or worse knew nothing of gay liberation, sexism or sundry modern social niceties.

KAVANAGH, TED

Can I do you now, sir?
ITMA catchphrase

'Mrs. Mopp', *ITMA's* eternally obsequious charlady, first appeared in the show on October 10, 1941. Backed by the sound effects of clattering mops and buckets, actress Dorothy Summers asked Tommy Handley 'Can I do for you now, sir?'. The 'for' was dropped in later episodes, and the phrase, as curtailed above, became the favourite of *ITMA's* many catchphrases. Mrs. Mopp did not survive the war, for all her popularity. Many characters were axed when the show was revamped in 1945 and the nation's favourite domestic went with them, although her catchphrase lingered on.

KEEHNER, JIM American psychologist

No American who works for the CIA is a spy. A spy is a foreign agent who commits treason.
New Times magazine, 1976

Keehner, who works for the CIA as a psychologist, is pronouncing the espionage version of that popular concept 'One man's terrorist is another man's freeeedom fighter' and pointing out that ideological purity, in the world of cloaks and daggers, is very much in the eye of the leader whose press secretary is talking. The concept of spying, for all the fictional glamour of a James Bond or the hard-nosed realpolitik of a George Smiley, remains more or less distasteful to most people. As Keehner puts it, a spy is some wicked foreigner, hell-bent on sabotaging the national interest and as such must be deplored.

KELEN, EMERY (1896–?) American journalist

The interview is an intimate conversation between journalist and politician wherein the journalist seeks to take advantage of the garrulity of the politician and the politician of the credulity of the journalist.
in *The Contemporary Dictionary of Quotations* (1981) by Jonathon Green

Politicians need journalists for publicity and journalists need politicians for copy, but in no way does that mean that they either like each other or feel it necessary to be wholly if even marginally honest. Both parties are intent on promoting their own interest and as Kelen's observation makes clear, like two entwined wrestlers, are looking for the weak point in the other's defence. The situation has always been true, but it has become accentuated in an era when personal image rather than party policies tend more and more to determine the outcome of elections.

KELLEY, STANLEY American academic

Last guys don't finish nice.

Kelley's gloss on one of sport's most famous quotations, makes the point that in a world dedicated to victory, losers are not only dissatisfied with themselves, but make sure that everyone else suffers for their failings. If anything but first place renders one unacceptable, then many of these 'last guys' become embittered and aggressive, and not merely in sport.

KELLY, WALT (1913–73) American cartoonist

We have met the enemy and he (they) is us.
in 'Pogo' strip, passim

At the Battle of Lake Erie, fought against the British on September 10, 1813, American naval hero Captain Oliver Hazard Perry, announced his success with the words 'We have met the enemy and he is ours'. In 1858 President James Buchanan rewrote the line, after an electoral setback, as 'We have met the enemy and we are theirs'. The most recent and best known revision came from cartoonist Kelly whose satirical strip first appeared in 1949 and ran until its creator's death. Pogo is a possum, whose adventures consistently satirised the state of America and the world.

KEMPTON, MURRAY (1917-) American journalist

It is a function of government to invent philosophies to explain the demands of its own convenience.
America Comes of Middle Age (1963)

Which came first, the policy or the pragmatism? Kempton, one of America's most acute journalists, is pointing out the way in which governments always cut their political cloth according to the currently convenient measure. The best political attribute is a short memory, and governments prefer not to dwell on last year's or even yesterday's promises, so volatile are the fluctuations of the current affairs that dictate them. Politics is the seeking after power and government is the maintaining of that power, ostensibly in the public interest. The need in a democracy for a government to keep the public who elected them happy enough to ensure that they can continue to wield this power makes for some interesting 'philosophising'.

KEMPTON, MURRAY

The general law of development for political institutions conceived in revolutionary idealism, which is that they begin as an expression of conscience and become in due course agencies for the issuance of licences and the distribution of patronage.
in *Newsday* magazine, 1981

The further one moves from the revolution, the nearer one comes to bureaucracy. Ideals flourish in adversity but, as Kempton stresses, they tend to wither once they have gained power. One need only look at the constrictions of Soviet bloc bureaucracies, all conceived out of idealistic revolutions, to see that Kempton's thesis is constantly proved. The revolution may see off the old aristocracy and bourgeoisie, but there arises what Milovan Djilas characterised as 'The New Class' (qv), the top-ranking bureaucrats whose appetite for issuing licences and distributing patronage is just as great as that of their ideologically impure predecessors.

KEMPTON, MURRAY

A revolution requires of its leaders a record of unbroken infallibility. If they do not possess it they are expected to invent it.
Part of Our Time (1955)

Those who take power through revolution tend to underline their claim to rule by systematically rewriting history. The first chapter of that history is often the taking upon themselves of what Kempton calls 'a record of unbroken infallibility', a record that, if the leader is strong enough, will be maintained, the facts notwithstanding, throughout his years of authority. For all that such revisions are potentially absurd, running counter to generally known facts, the leader and his people, especially in the heady, optimistic days that follow the revolution, make a voluntary pact to accept the glorious fiction. Only death or deposition changes the text once more, and formerly glorious achievements turn overnight into a reprehensible 'cult of personality'.

KEMPTON, MURRAY

A man can look upon his life and accept it as good or evil; it is far, far harder for him to confess that it has been unimportant in the sum of things.
Part of Our Time (1955)

Most people's lives, when measured in terms of lasting influence or achievement, are of little importance. They matter to themselves and if they are lucky, loved and respected, to their immediate family and friends, but there the matter rests. If one resists the tenets of religion, which attempt to give equal weight to every human being, it is hard to deny Kempton's harsh conclusion. It is equally hard, of course, humanity being what it is, for anyone to come to terms with their own unimportance and that stubbornness, fortunately, keeps the great mass of people struggling on.

KENNEDY, FLORYNCE American feminist

If men could get pregnant, abortion would be a sacrament.
quoted in 1976

Kennedy, a black American feminist, was pointing out yet another example of the double standards of a male-dominated world. While men who sleep around are real men, women who follow their lead are merely sluts; opposed by a sternly religious 'Moral Majority' the idea of legalised abortion has always proved deeply controversial in America. Middle-class, middle-aged affluent men make the laws and impose their own prejudices upon them, but it is often working class, young, poor women who find themselves facing an undesired pregnancy. As Kennedy puts it, were the roles reversed, abortion would not merely be legal, but a religious necessity.

KENNEDY, JACQUELINE BOUVIER (1929–) American first lady

Now he is a legend when he would have preferred to be a man.
on her assassinated husband, 1963

The mythologising that followed close on John Kennedy's assassination has yet fully to die away, although revisionist historians and contemporary tattle-tales have made it clear that America's 35th president was by no means the white-haired boy of lachrymose memory. The first line of fantasy involved the assassination itself, just who did it? In parallel was the glorification of the Kennedy years, the iconic 'Camelot' era, when the world's creative artists mingled with its most astute politicians. It was harder to praise Kennedy's actual achievements but the emphasis, unsurprisingly, was always on the positive. As his widow,

Jackie, herself still garlanded with associated glamour, pointed out, none of this was much use to a dead man.

KENNEDY, JOHN FITZGERALD (1917–63) American president

Kennedy was the second son of Joseph Kennedy, a Boston-Irish millionaire who had founded his own fortunes in bootlegging and who was determined that one of his sons should become president. Despite his father's unsavoury reputation and his own Catholicism, Kennedy won the election of 1960, a contest that was among the first to be determined as much by a candidate's televised image as by his political platform. Kennedy's assassination in 1963 gave an overly rosy hue to his foreshortened administration, but hindsight has been less kind. The Bay of Pigs incursion into Cuba was a disaster, his attempt to create a new relationship with Europe was frustrated by de Gaulle, and his domestic policies, touted as the New Frontier, were cautious and largely ineffectual. Yet he faced down Khruschev in the Cuban missile crisis, rallied German morale and extended American relations in Latin America. As summed up by his mentor Harold Macmillan, he probably concentrated too much on adultery and on the advice of the second-rate, but he remains an urbane, sophisticated figure whose possibilities were unrealised.

KENNEDY, JOHN F.

In the first analysis it is their war. They are the ones who have to win it or lose it. We can help them. We can give them equipment, we can send our men out there as advisors, but they have to win, the people of Vietnam.
speaking in 1963

Compared with the massive American commitment in Vietnam under President Johnson, Kennedy was only marginally involved in South-East Asia, but he still chose to transform what was seen as Eisenhower's 'limited-risk gamble' into a 'broad commitment', believing that through no other means could Communist domination of the area be restrained. And although he maintained that the Vietnamese people alone had the power to determine their destiny, he took a number of actions that significantly expanded American political and military involvement. Using 'only limited means to gain excessive ends' Kennedy gradually raised the stakes, while using statements like this to hide his approach from the American people.

KENNEDY, JOHN F.

If a free country cannot help the many who are poor, it cannot save the few who are rich.

Part of Kennedy's much-vaunted New Frontier was the taking on of the challenge of the poverty endemic to America. As he stated here, in a line that was as much a threat to the rich as a promise to the poor, if the powerful fail to alleviate the lot of the most deprived members of society, they just might take affairs into their own hands, a possibility that was intended to jog the pockets if not the consciences of the nations 'haves'. In the event none of Kennedy's welfare legislation was enacted into law and that particular aspect of the New Frontier was only achieved by Lyndon Johnson's Great Society (qv). As Senator Everett Dirksen put it, Kennedy's plans had 'about as much impact as a snowflake on the bosom of the Potomac'.

KENNEDY, JOHN F.

Victory has a hundred fathers but defeat is an orphan.
after the Bay of Pigs fiasco, April 1961

The attempt by a force of Cuban exiles, trained and recruited by the CIA, to invade their country and overthrow its Communist government had actually been planned under the Eisenhower administration, but was taken over and supported by Kennedy. Thus, when the landing at the Bay of Pigs was comprehensively routed, Kennedy took the full blame, although given the circumstances he could hardly have done otherwise. As he pointed out here, everyone wants in on success but failure attracts few allies. The phrase itself has been attributed variously to the Italian Count Ciano (in 1942), to John Foster Dulles (in 1953) and to the film *The Desert Fox* (1951).

KENNEDY, JOHN F.

We stand today on the edge of a New Frontier – the frontier of the 1960s, a frontier of unknown opportunities and perils, a frontier of unfulfilled hopes and threats.... The New Frontier of which I speak is not a set of promises – it is a set of challenges. It sums up not what I intend to offer the American people, but what I intend to ask of them.
campaign speech, 1960

The concept of the New Frontier was supposedly created for Kennedy by his speechwriter Theodore C. 'Ted' Sorenson, who claimed to have minted the phrase, but it can be found both as the title of a book written in 1934 by the American left-winger Henry Wallace and as a keynote of the campaign speeches of Alf Landon, who failed to beat Franklin Roosevelt in 1936. In both cases it meant much the same as when used by Kennedy, referring to emotional challenges rather than physical phenomena. Undoubtedly the Kennedy use has been the most important, but even here, Sorenson's memory has been challenged by those who attribute it to Walt Rostow, then at MIT, who used it at a cocktail party some weeks before the speech, or Max Freedman, Washington correspondent of the then Manchester Guardian.

KENNEDY, JOHN F.

Let every nation know, whether it wishes us well or ill, that we shall pay any price, bear any burden, meet any hardship, support any friend, oppose any foe to assure the survival and success of liberty.
inaugural speech, January 20 1961

Kennedy used his inaugural speech both to reaffirm America's past and look forward to its future. He stressed the way in which all Americans were the spiritual heirs of the original American revolution and urged his countrymen to 'let the word go forth.-..that the torch has been passed to a new generation of Americans' who had been tempered and disciplined in war and peace and who were no more willing to abandon their revolutionary heritage than any of those who preceded them. He then used the lines above to commit America to the defence of freedom and human rights around the world.

KENNEDY, JOHN F.

Let us never negotiate out of fear, but let us never fear to negotiate.
inaugural speech, January 20 1961

Following his pledges to America's allies, Kennedy turned to those nations who would make themselves our adversary'. To these he offered 'not a pledge, but a request: that both sides begin anew the quest for peace, before the dark powers of destruction unleashed by science engulf all humanity in planned or accidental self-destruction.' Without naming his rival superpower, he called on Russia to begin negotiations towards defusing the Cold War that had persisted through the Fifties and assured the American people that 'civility is not a sign of weakness', before coming to the line above and calling for a 'beach-head of cooperation... (to) push back the jungle of suspicion'.

KENNEDY, JOHN F.

And so, my fellow Americans, ask not what your country can do for you; ask what you can do for your country.
inaugural speech, January 20 1961

As Kennedy reached the climax of his speech he turned from his nation's historic tasks and from America's place in the world, 'to the common enemies of man: tyranny, poverty, disease and war itself '. He stressed that 'in the long history of the world only a few generations have been granted the role of defending freedom in its hour of maximum danger' and told the nation 'I do not shrink from this responsibility; I welcome it'. If Americans devoted themselves to this responsibility, then the success of their efforts would 'truly light the world. And so, my fellow Americans, ask not what your country can do for you; ask what you can do for your country. My fellow citizens of the world, ask not what America will do for you, but what together we can do for the freedom of man'.

KENNEDY, JOHN F.

All this will not be finished in the first hundred days. Nor will it be finished in the first thousand days, nor in the life of this Administration, nor even perhaps in our lifetime on this planet. But let us begin.
inaugural speech, January 20 1961

The idea of the 'thousand days' of the Kennedy presidency, which actually lasted only 1,037 days, was confirmed both by Arthur Schlesinger's memoir 'A Thousand Days' and more immediately by Kennedy's successor, Lyndon Johnson. Five days after the assassination Johnson addressed a joint session of Congress. He quoted these lines from Kennedy's inaugural address and added 'Today, in this moment of new resolve, I would say to all my fellow Americans, let us continue'. Johnson's Texas accent did less than magisterial justice to his speech and it was mocked by the cynical, but the feeling he expressed appealed to many Americans.

KENNEDY, JOHN F.

An idealist without illusions.
on himself, 1960

Kennedy tended towards the rhetorical in much of his public speaking and this self-analysis is appealingly assonant, if euphemistic. Kennedy's death gave his administration an aura of near-sanctity for many years, but in many ways his achievements belie the posthumous canonisation of 'Camelot'. He was as hamstrung by reality as any politician and while his premature death may have denied America and the world unrealised potential, he was in the end no more successful than many other world leaders.

KENNEDY, JOHN F.

Two thousand years ago the proudest boast was 'Civis Romanus Sum'. Today, in the world of freedom, the proudest boast is Ich bin ein Berliner...All free men, wherever they may live, are citizens of Berlin, and therefore as a free man, I take pride in the words Ich bin ein Berliner.
speaking in West Berlin, June 26 1963

Kennedy's speech to the people of West Berlin, a beleaguered and divided city since the end of World War II and a small oasis of Western influence surrounded by the Communist government of East Germany, was recognised as a major boost to their morale. He rejected an earlier speech, written in the State Department, and, after spending some time having himself coached in the correct German pronunciation, created this slogan for delivery to an ecstatic crowd. He remarked later, had he told the crowd to tear down the Berlin Wall they would undoubtedly have done just that, and he told an aide 'We'll never have another day like this one as long as we live'.

KENNEDY, ROBERT (1925–68) American politician

What has violence ever accomplished? What has it ever created? No martyr's cause has ever been stilled by his assassin's bullet. No wrongs have ever been righted by riots and civil disorders. A sniper is only a coward, not a hero. And an uncontrollable mob is only the voice of madness and not the voice of the people.
on the death of Martin Luther King, April 1968

Robert Kennedy had worked in his elder brother's administration as US Attorney-General, and when John Kennedy was assassinated he automatically took on his role as the family's leader and thus destined to return the Kennedy name to the White House. Kennedy delivered these despairing lines after the assassination of the black civil rights leader, Martin Luther King. Apart from the poignancy and pertinence of the lines, they possess an awful irony since Kennedy himself was assassinated, while campaigning in California, just three months later.

433

KENT, FRANK (1907–1978) American journalist

The only way a reporter should look at a politician is down.
quoted in *The Boys on the Bus* by T. Crouse (1973)

The relationship between journalists and politicians is nothing if not spikey, based in mutual dislike tempered by the need of each to exploit certain aspects of the other's profession. In the end, however, animosity rules, and as apostrophised by this member of the press corps, while the journalist's power may be greatly inferior to that of the politician, it is vital that his attitude to the latter be one of disdain and candid contempt. Kent was attributed this phrase in Crouse's book, but he may in fact have been quoting an earlier journalist, Frank Simonds (1887-1936) who has been credited with the line in at least one dictionary.

KEROUAC, JACK (1922–69) American writer

The only people for me are the mad ones, the ones who are mad to live, mad to talk, mad to be saved . . . the ones who never yawn and say a commonplace thing, but burn, burn, burn like fabulous yellow roman candles exploding like spiders across the stars.
On The Road (1957)

With the exception of Neal Cassady, their fired-up Holy Fool, all the founding fathers of the post-war Beat generation were writers and Kerouac was their chronicler. John Clellon Holmes' autobiographical *Go* (1952) predated Kerouac's work, but the publication of *On the Road*, his hymn to 'the mad ones' and his recreation of their escapades as they endlessly crossed and recrossed America, hot-foot after that 'beatitude' from which the word 'beat' is in part derived, proved infinitely more influential. Thousands of America's and then Europe's youth read Kerouac's book and joined the movement. By 1957 the old masters were otherwise occupied, but the beatniks, so called by San Francisco columnist Herb Caen, popularised their creation until they, in turn, were swept away by the hippies that followed.

KESEY, KEN (1935–) American writer

Take what you can use and let the rest go by.
quoted in Tom Wolfe, *The Electric Kool-Aid Acid Test* (1969)

After his novel *One Flew Over the Cuckoo's Nest*, an effervescent allegory of modern life set in a mental home, appeared in 1962, Kesey was cited by knowledgeable critics as a young pretender with real literary potential. Kesey continued playing the role of aspirant literateur for a while but his growing involvement with

Californian bohemian life, fuelled by his discovery of LSD, changed all that. Timothy Leary had proselytised the contemplative virtues of 'acid', but Kesey capitalised on its madness and its pure flamboyance. After travelling through America in a bus named 'Furthur', Kesey and his acolytes 'The Merry Pranksters' settled in California and began spreading the lysergic gospel, mainly via massively popular rock concerts, known as 'Trips Festivals'. Twenty years on, Kesey remains an advocate of psychedelia although for most of its users, acid is less of a sacrament than a teenage rite of passage.

KEYNES, JOHN MAYNARD   (1883–1946) British economist

They are a lot of hard-faced men who look as if they have done well out of the war.
The Economic Consequences of the Peace (1919)

This famous description of the profiteers of World War I, redolent of astrakhan-collared overcoats, outsize cigars and black market liquor, has long been attributed to Keynes, but in his book on the economic implications of the War, he was actually quoting a British politician. Keynes does not identify him, but it is assumed that the originator of the phrase was the future Prime Minister Stanley Baldwin. *The Economic Consequences of the Peace* was not Keynes' first book, but with its impressive portraits of Lloyd George, Clemenceau and Wilson, it brought him public acclaim. It stemmed from his personal involvement in the peace negotiations as a British treasury official and was in essence a major attack on the attitudes and policies of the allies, especially as regarded reparations to be paid by Germany.

KEYNES, JOHN MAYNARD

A 'sound' banker, alas, is not one who sees danger and avoids it, but one who, when he is ruined, is ruined in a conventional and orthodox way along with his fellows, so that no-one can really blame him.
Essays in Persuasion (1933)

Traditionally, banking is a conservative profession, attracting those of supposedly sterling qualities, who neither wish to 'rock the boat' nor make any extravagant move that might be interpreted as alien to the wishes and intentions of their peers. Thus in banking jargon, as Keynes notes, the word 'sound', which might otherwise indicate someone of percipience and intelligence, becomes a synonym for safe, sheeplike and above all constrained by the common standard.

KEYNES, JOHN MAYNARD

Practical men, who believe themselves to be quite exempt from any intellectual influences, are usually the slaves of some defunct economist. Madmen in authority, who hear voices in the air, are distilling their frenzy from some academic scribbler of a few years back.
General Theory of Employment, Interest and Money (1936)

This book confirmed Keynes as the world's most influential economist since Adam Smith, Ricardo and Marx. Prior to Keynes' new thesis, it had never been accepted that in an unregulated market economy there might be 'involuntary' unemployment. Keynes needed look no further than the actual experience of Britain in the 1920s and the whole world after the Crash of 1929 to perceive the absurdity of earlier concepts. The 'Keynesian revolution' created a new area of study: macroeconomics, which concentrated on the economy as an interconnected whole, rather than, as was the previous method, on its various fragments. Western governments adopted Keynesian economic theory for some thirty years after World War II, although neither Keynes nor his followers could solve the problem of the inevitable inflation that was found to accompany all attempts to maintain full employment, the market situation notwithstanding.

KHOMEINI, AYATOLLAH RUHOLLAH (1900–) Iranian leader

The word 'Islam' does not need any such adjectives as 'democratic'. Precisely because Islam is everything, it means everything.
quoted in 1979

The Ayatollah Khomeini, as leader of the fundamentalist Shi'ite Muslims in Iran, was expelled from the country in 1963. Khomeini based himself near Paris and became a vital focus for the aspirations of those who wished to overthrow the Pahlevi dynasty. When, in 1979, the Iranian Revolution removed the Shah, Khomeini returned in triumph. He lost no time in establishing a fundamentalist religious hegemony in Iran, subjecting everyone to the tenets of his harsh variety of Islamic belief. The self-righteousness embodied in these lines extends to every aspect of his rule, including the costly war with Iraq, the suppression of all free speech in his country, and the backing of terrorists in many others.

KHRUSHCHEV, N.S. (1894–1971) Russian leader

Nikita Sergeyevitch Khrushchev rose from obscure origins in the Ukraine to become in 1953 first secretary of the CPSU. He gained worldwide attention in 1956 when he denounced Stalin's 'cult of personality' and in 1958, when he became premier, he removed most of the remaining Stalinist leaders from power. Khruschev appeared a liberal, allowing cultural censorship something of a 'thaw', attempting to increase Soviet production of consumer goods, and involving himself continually with his Western opponents, although these relations were consistent only in the Premier's volatile changes of direction. His fluctuations proved too exciting for the more doctrinaire of the world's Communists and he gradually lost influence, alienating Mao's China and losing the Communist parties of the West. He was deposed in 1964 and lived out his life in relative obscurity. His memoirs, which may have been a KGB fabrication, appeared in 1972-74.

KHRUSHCHEV, N.S.

Politicians are the same all over. They promise to build a bridge even where there is no river.
speaking in 1960

Khrushchev's visit to America in 1960, during which trip he spoke to the assembled United Nations, showed both sides of Russia's leader: the dedicated, even terrifying cold warrior, and the simple man of the people, fresh from his peasant upbringing. He used this line as part of the latter image, exploiting the full 'man of the people' stance replete with self-mockery and an attempt to persuade his audience that all politicians were lying buffoons and that really they should not be taken seriously.

KHRUSHCHEV, N.S.

If you feed people just with revolutionary slogans they will listen today, they will listen tomorrow, they will listen the day after tomorrow, but on the fourth day they will say 'To hell with you'
attributed philosophy

Russia faced chronic food problems in the late 1950s, during Khrushchev's premiership. His desire to solve a situation whereby the world's second superpower might have a nuclear arsenal but was unable to feed its people was central to his domestic policies and he developed a grandiose plan to turn the 'virgin lands' of Soviet Asia into food-producing farms. It was the failure of this plan, exacerbated by the wild variations in his foreign policy, that led to his being deposed in 1964.

KHRUSHCHEV, N.S.

Those who wait for that must wait until a shrimp learns to whistle.
speaking in 1955

By some standards, notably those of Russia's most absolute dictator, Joseph Stalin, Khrushchev represented a distinct shift towards liberalism. He denounced Stalin himself, seemed willing to allow writers, artists and other creative figures a good deal more latitude than they had hitherto enjoyed, and generally seemed a more human figure. But he was also a dedicated Communist. To those who watched his progress and wondered whether he might be about to relax the rigidity of the State's political credo, he offered this earthy, definitive line.

KHRUSHCHEV, N.S.

We will bury you.
speaking in 1956

Khrushchev was attending a reception for Poland's leader Wladislav Gomulka at the Polish Embassy in Moscow on November 18, 1956 when he announced, to the delight of the attendant Communists and the horror of Western diplomats and journalists: 'We say this not only for the socialist states who are more akin to us. We base ourselves on the idea that we must peacefully co-exist. About the capitalist states, it doesn't depend on you whether or not we exist. If you don't like us, don't accept our invitations, and don't ask us to come and see you. Whether you like it or not, history is on our side. We will bury you.' The kindest interpretation of this last line is that the Soviets would overhaul Western economic progress, and in the furore that followed Khrushchev tried to emphasise this. The West, deep in the Cold War, was less amused.

KIFNER, JOHN   American journalist

Any official denial is a de facto confirmation.
in the *New York Times*, 1969

Duplicity is so often the politician's stock-in-trade. The needs of government and those of the news media are so fundamentally opposed that there come situations when the authorities seem to have no choice but to deny what the press knows and the press, for all that it does know, is left impotent and unable to print without a proper confirmation. This situation may seem paradoxical in supposedly democratic societies where politicians are supposedly accountable to the electorate, but Kifner's matter-of-fact statement leaves one in no doubt as to what really happens.

KILLERS, THE

Lady, I don't have the time.
screenplay (1964)

The Killers is the Hemingway story of a man who accepts without demur his own execution. The initial version appeared in 1946. This one, directed by Don Siegel and starring Lee Marvin, Angie Dickinson and Ronald Reagan, who plays a crook, was created for television, but was considered as too tough for the small screen and distributed to the big one. This is the film's curtain line. After Reagan's marksman has shot his partner, Marvin drives to Reagan's home and kills him, taking a suitcase of his money. Dickinson, Reagan's girlfriend, pleads for her life but Marvin, capping one of his most ruthless performances, deals with her too, explaining 'Lady, I don't have the time'. As he leaves the house we see that he too has been fatally wounded and as the case falls open and the money blows away, Marvin dies, still clutching at his silenced gun.

KING, ALEXANDER (1900–1965) American writer

To the majority of (newspapermen) a woman is either somebody's mother or a whore.
Rich Man, Poor Man, Freud and Fruit (1965)

While the 'quality' papers might demur, this is as accurate a summary of the policy pursued by the tabloid press of Britain and America as one might wish to find. Whore, of course, is pitching slightly strong, and no-one implies that the Page Three girls are immoral, but on the other hand the caption-writer tends to imply that 'Saucy Sam' or 'Leggy Linda' wouldn't be averse to a bit of slap and tickle. Conversely the papers are filled with both happy and hapless Mums, either lucky winners of some unlikely competition, or pitiful victims of an equally unlikely disaster.

KING, ALEXANDER

That gentlemen prefer blondes is due to the fact that, apparently, pale hair, delicate skin and an infantile expression represent the very apex of a frailty which every man longs to violate.
Rich Man, Poor Man, Freud and Fruit (1965)

Anita Loos' Twenties best-seller *Gentlemen Prefer Blondes* didn't worry too much about the psychology of the obsession; as in the ad for Clairol that promises 'Blondes have More Fun', it has long been assumed that the blonde is archetype of feminine perfection as far as men are concerned. Doubtless King is correct in his assumption, but setting up these flesh-and-blood Barbie dolls as an object for rape fantasies may be just a little harsh on the run of men. Militant feminists, on the other hand, would applaud his sentiments, and probably throw in brunettes as well.

KING, MARTIN LUTHER   (1929–68) American black preacher and civil rights activist
King emerged in the Fifties in Montgomery, Alabama, where he was a preacher, as one of the first campaigners for black civil rights in America. As early as 1957 he became a target for white extremists, but he consistently defied their efforts until his assassination in 1968. King's movement, the Southern Christian Leadership Conference, secured the franchise for black voters, ended the segregation of public facilities in the South, and changed profoundly the whole basis of race relations in the region. King was by no means the sole inspiration of the campaign but his superb oratory and personal style set him above the other black leaders. By the end of his life, despite winning the Nobel Peace Prize in 1964, he was increasingly assailed by a variety of opponents. More militant black leaders were emerging, and the FBI were continually hounding him obsessively. He was shot down in Memphis on April 4, 1968, the day after giving one of his most momentous speeches.

KING, MARTIN LUTHER

Riots are the voices of the unheard.
speaking in 1968

If one has no other means of making one's voice heard and is unable to change one's circumstances, then, as King puts it here, one starts to smash things up in the hope that the noise of their destruction will reach the ears of those who do have the power to make those changes. In theory a democratic society should not require riots to make such points; a system of one man one vote ought to empower everyone to make themselves audible, but as far as America's blacks were concerned, their votes were meaningless and few even bothered to register. King's civil rights movement undoubtedly changed all that, and many of the cities where the rioting was fiercest are controlled by Black mayors today, even if ghetto life remains impoverished.

KING, MARTIN LUTHER

I don't know what will happen now, we've got some difficult days ahead. It really doesn't matter with me now, because I've been on the mountain top. I won't mind. Like anybody I would like to live a long life. Longevity has its place. But I'm not concerned about that just now. I want to do God's will and he's allowed me to go up to the mountain, and I've looked over and I've seen the Promised Land. I may not get there with you, but I want you to know tonight that we as a people will get to the Promised Land. Well I'm happy tonight. I'm not worried about anything. I'm not fearing any man. Mine eyes have seen the glory of the coming of the Lord!
speech in Memphis, Tennessee, April 3 1968

It is unlikely that King knew that this was the last speech he would ever give, but with hindsight it is hard to deny its frighteningly prophetic tone. In fact it was not the first time he had used the image of Moses leading the Children of Israel up to, but not entering the Promised Land. In 1957, preaching in Montgomery, Alabama hours after he had discovered a primed dynamite bomb on his doorstep, the young King told his congregation 'I'm not afraid of anybody this morning. Tell Montgomery they can keep shooting and I'm going to stand up to them; tell Montgomery they can keep bombing and I'm going to stand up to them. If I had to die tomorrow morning I would die happy because I've been to the mountain top and I've seen the promised land and it's going to be here in Montgomery'.

KING, MARTIN LUTHER

I have a dream.
speech on August 28 1963

The largest protest march ever undertaken in America took place on August 28 1963 when a quarter of a million people made the March on Washington. Martin Luther King addressed this Civil Rights demonstration in a sixteen-minute speech that made clear the extent to which Black Americans and their white supporters deplored the lack of improvement made in US race relations in the century since Lincoln's Emancipation Proclamation ended slavery. Speaking close to the Lincoln Memorial King delivered his greatest speech, combining the superb oratory of a revivalist preacher with a powerful political statement. King's dream was of racial harmony, a dream, as he pointed out, rooted in the original

American dream from which no-one, of whatever race, creed or colour, had been excluded.

KING, MARTIN LUTHER

Judicial decrees may not change the heart, but they can restrain the heartless.
Strength to Love (1963)

King was an idealist, but he had few illusions. This line comes from a speech in which he considered the practical use of legislation designed to curb racism. Obviously, as he points out, a piece of paper cannot change the beliefs and emotions of a committed racist, but it can, fortunately, empower those in authority to use the law in question to stop the racists from carrying out their socially disruptive plans. On the other hand, his faith in the efficacy of laws was limited; he did want to see hearts changed. As he put it in 1963 'I want to be the white man's brother, not his brother-in-law.'

KING, MARTIN LUTHER

Human salvation lies in the hands of the creatively maladjusted.
Strength to Love (1963)

King's point is that when exceptional acts are required, only the exceptional person can rise to the occasion. Creative maladjustment may be a synonym for some degree of genius, certainly King himself was an extraordinary figure. He failed to achieve human salvation, no-one could, but in a scant decade of activism for the civil rights cause he left a mark on American society that will never be eradicated.

KING, MARTIN LUTHER

Philanthropy is commendable, but it must not cause the philanthropist to overlook the circumstances of economic injustice which make philanthropy necessary.
Strength to Love (1963)

Philanthropy has always been the rich man's best hope of staking a claim in heaven and salving his conscience on earth. If one gives away sufficient of one's fortune in charity, this surely justifies one's continuing to amass it. King is pig-headedly refusing to allow the rich to get away with this too easily. Although he extends his own charity by refusing to comment on the exploitative way in which many philanthropists make the money they so publicly give away, he does stress that if the basic economic injustice that renders so many needy of philanthropy was removed, then the whole process could be short-circuited.

KING, MARTIN LUTHER

The long hot summer
speaking in 1967

In 1967 the ghettos exploded all over America, as the black communities of eighteen cities took to the streets to riot, burn and loot and register their protest at the conditions under which, despite all the rhetoric successive white governments had mustered, they were still forced to live. The first riots had come in 1966, when Watts, the Los Angeles ghetto, had gone up in flames. Interviewed in early 1967 Martin Luther King warned America that since no-one in authority seemed to have responded positively to the Watts experience, the cities should look out for more trouble. 'Everyone is worrying about the long hot summer with its threat of riots. We had a long cold winter when little was done about the conditions that create riots.'

KINGSMILL, HUGH   (1889–1949) (Hugh Kingsmill Lunn) British writer and critic

A concern with the perfectibility of mankind is always a symptom of thwarted or perverted development.
quoted in Michael Holroyd, *The Best of Kingsmill* (1970)

Kingsmill was an anthologist, biographer, literary critic, novelist and parodist. Among his biographies were those of Matthew Arnold (1928), Dickens (1938) and D.H. Lawrence (1938), and his less than sycophantic tone gave him a reputation as something of an iconoclast. He also wrote in 1932 the life of Frank Harris, with whom he had worked on Hearth and Home magazine in 1912. Kingsmill was a noted aphorist, and some of his better comments on the human condition are listed below.

KINGSMILL, HUGH

Friends are God's apology for relations.
quoted in M. Holroyd, *The Best of Kingsmill* (1970)

KINGSMILL, HUGH

A nation is only at peace when it's at war.
quoted in M. Holroyd, *The Best of Kingsmill* (1970)

KIPLING, RUDYARD (1865–1936) British writer

The female of the species is more deadly than the male.
The Female of the Species (1911)

Kipling's line is in celebration of the tenacity of the female when compared to the relative malleability of the male. Kipling is seen as primarily a 'man's writer' but in this poem he is at pains to point out, if not the superiority of woman, then certainly her greater emotional toughness. It may be a cliché to say that women work on instinct whereas men bend before logic, but Kipling, who was nothing if not a conservative in such matters, puts it very neatly. 'Man propounds negotiations, Man accepts compromise. / Very rarely will he squarely push the logic of a fact / To its ultimate conclusion in unmitigated act.'

KIPLING, RUDYARD

Watch the wall, my darling, while the Gentlemen go by
A Smuggler's Song (1906)

A Smuggler's Song is one of Kipling's romantic evocations of a completely mythical England, a vision better realised by Hollywood than by any historical reality. Much learned by rote, the whole verse runs 'Them that asks no questions isn't told a lie. / Watch the wall, my darling, while the Gentlemen go by! / Five and twenty ponies / trotting through the dark - / Brandy for the Parson / 'Baccy for the Clerk; / Laces for a lady, letters for a spy, / Watch the wall, my darling, while the Gentlemen go by!'

KIPLING, RUDYARD

Where are you going to, all you Big Steamers
Big Steamers (1910)

One of Kipling's most Empire-minded poems, Big Steamers is a paean to imperial trade, lovingly listing the cargoes of the great ships that ply between the red spaces on the map, carrying 'beef, pork, and mutton, eggs, apples and cheese'. When the narrator pledges himself to build new lighthouses and pray for fine weather he is told that there is no need, lighthouses abound and the Big Steamers can tackle rough weather. Even more important, the Big Steamers have powerful seaborne allies - British warships - that will protect them from any alien attacks.

KIPLING, RUDYARD

If you can keep your head when all about you Are losing theirs and blaming it on you...
If – (1910)

For Kipling's critics his poem *If–* sums up so much of what is wrong with his work. Its pietistic moralising represents the worst side of a writer who could transcend his nationalistic jingoism and loathing of intellectuals to depict genuine depths of character, and who remains an incomparable chronicler of Imperial India. In the climate of the time, with Kipling already revered by the middlebrows as the nation's bard, the poem was hugely successful. It was reprinted in 27 languages, Woodrow Wilson claimed it as an inspiration, Marie Stopes demanded that he write a version for girls, and it was anthologised, as Kipling put it, 'to weariness'. It appeared originally in *Rewards and Fairies* (1910), Kipling's second collection of historical stories, aimed at his younger readers. The author's ideal man, from whom these holier than thou qualities are borrowed, is Dr. Jameson, better known for his 'Raid' on the Boers.

KIPLING, RUDYARD

**Then ye returned to your trinkets
then ye contented your souls
With the flannelled fools at the wickets
or the muddied oafs at the goals**
The Islanders (1903)

The islanders of Kipling's poem are the British people, notably the upper classes, whose complacent Tory insularity blinds them to warnings of the German menace and the need for Imperial unity. While Kipling does not spare the workers, the unions and the commercial middle classes, his fiercest scorn is reserved for the squirearchy and the men of letters, condemning their hunting, shooting and artistic concerns as trivial compared with the defence of the nation. After the scathing lines above, he asks 'Will ye pitch some white pavilion, and lustily even the odds, / With nets and hoops and mallets, and rackets and bats and rods? / Will the rabbit war with your foemen - the red deer horn them for hire? / Your kept cock-pheasant keep you? He is master of many a shire...'

KISSINGER, HENRY   (1923–) American statesman and political scientist

Kissinger, a professor at Harvard, made his initial reputation with the publication of *Nuclear Weapons and Foreign Policy* (1957), challenging the then conventional nuclear strategy of 'massive retaliation' and putting forward the concept of limited nuclear war. His international reputation grew after he became in 1969, despite his well-publicised contempt for his President, Richard Nixon's special adviser on national security. Kissinger's 'shuttle diplomacy' helped extricate America from Vietnam and Israel and Egypt from the Yom Kippur War of 1973. Despite his successes Kissinger's pragmatic acceptance of realpolitik came to worry those who prefer to parade some guise of morality and when Nixon fell so, gradually, did his aide. He remains an influential figure, floating on the periphery of American policy-making and careful, as ever, to avoid identification with any interest group.

KISSINGER, HENRY

The conventional army loses if it does not win. The guerilla wins if he does not lose.

in *Foreign Affairs* magazine, January 1969

Kissinger was commenting on the progress of the war in Vietnam and pointing out quite accurately that America's problems stemmed less from the actual weakness of US troops than from their inability to create a large-scale confrontation with the enemy. As both sides acknowledged, such a pitched battle would inevitably have given the victory to the overwhelming numbers and the sophisticated technology of American forces. The North Vietnamese Army and the Viet Cong ensured that such a battle never happened. Instead they maintained guerilla tactics and wore down both the frustrated troops in Vietnam and the decreasingly supportive public at home.

KISSINGER, HENRY

The absence of alternatives clears the mind marvellously.

in *Time* magazine, 1978

Kissinger was presumably thinking of Samuel Johnson's comment, made in 1777 'Depend upon it, Sir, when a man knows he is to be hanged in a fortnight, it concentrates his mind wonderfully'. In the diplomatic context however, it seems rather simplistic: Kissinger's role in international diplomacy ought to have convinced him that alternatives and the choice between them lie at the heart of all such negotiations. Indeed his own preferred method of conducting such talks was to reconcile the least controversial of those alternatives.

KISSINGER, HENRY

We are all the President's men.
of the invasion of Cambodia in 1970

Bordering Cambodia provided a vital 'sanctuary' for N. Vietnamese forces as they made their way to South Vietnam. Such 'sanctuaries' naturally infuriated the American forces, but they did not cross the border to attack. President Nixon changed the policy: in March 1969 he granted a request from the USAF to carry out a B-52 strike on a Communist base camp inside Cambodia. The next year, on April 30, Nixon announced to America that US and S. Vietnamese forces had crossed into Cambodia. The invasion, which had not been approved by the Cambodian government, lasted until the troops withdrew on June 29. Anti-war groups in America were appalled and Kissinger, as much an architect of the plans as his leader, attempted to distance himself from the controversy, using this statement to blame Nixon. The line was later used by Carl Bernstein and Bob Woodward as the title of their first book on Watergate and has come to sum up the Nixon years, just as Halberstam's ' The Best and the Brightest' sums up Kennedy's and Johnson's.

KISSINGER, HENRY

I don't see why we need to stand by and watch a country go Communist due to the irresponsibility of its own people.
on US destabilisation of Chile, 1973

After years of suffering a succession of right-wing military juntas, Chile elected its first Marxist-led government when Salvador Allende Gossens became President in September 1970. The new government appalled America, whose businesses had invested over £1 billion in the country. The influential International Telephone & Telegraph (ITT) company offered the Chilean Congress £1 million to declare the election void, but their efforts were rejected. America did not give up. Nixon declared an economic blockade of the country and the CIA began a systematic campaign of destabilisation aimed at undermining Allende's government. On September 11 1973 the campaign paid off. Allende was butchered in his presidential palace during a right-wing military coup. Asked to defend America's role, Kissinger made his views crystal clear.

KISSINGER, HENRY

We must learn to distinguish morality from moralising.
quoted in 1976

Morality, even in international politics, presumably has certain definable limits and expectations, drawing lines within which those involved may work. Moralising, on the other hand, is merely talking about morality, a perfectly good excuse for pious words with no concomitant compulsion to piety. However one may view Dr. Kissinger's involvement in world politics, he has consistently resisted moralising. Perhaps, for his continuing career as a major influence on American doctrine, it would have been better had he done so.

KISSINGER, HENRY

The superpowers often behave like two heavily-armed blind men feeling their way around a room, each believing himself in mortal peril from the other, whom he assumes to have perfect vision.
quoted in the *Observer*, September 30 1979

As one who was for several years intimately involved with the negotiations between the two superpowers, Kissinger presumably knows what he is talking about. From his point of view the two powers were very much equal, both in their incompetence and in their potential to destroy each other. As the mastermind of US foreign policy he attempted to stress the concept of linkage - whereby one area of conflict was tied into another - and to persuade the superpower leaders that they could both be best served by limiting the way each pursued its interests - often in the same areas - even if they would not actually abandon such policies.

KISSINGER, HENRY

There cannot be a crisis next week. My schedule is already full.
quoted in *Time* magazine, 1977

Kissinger has never been reticent in promoting his own image. At the height of his powers he was indeed one of the most influential men in world diplomacy, endlessly shuttling from one hot spot to another, seemingly sorting out the problems of half the world, while simultaneously, his critics might claim, creating further problems for the other half. Perhaps his greatest success, given this hubristic statement, is that despite his intimate involvement with US foreign politics at the highest level, he has carefully steered clear of domestic wrangles and thus, however damning a number of studies of his policies may have been, has managed to appear in quite a different league to more fallible figures.

KISSINGER, HENRY

The illegal we do immediately, the unconstitutional takes a little longer.
speaking in 1974

Kissinger, alone of President Nixon's senior advisors, managed to isolate himself from the revelations of widespread corruption that comprised the 'Watergate Affair'. As top aides faced prison sentences and the President himself, one step away from impeachment, was forced to resign, Kissinger blithely rephrased the popular slogan, found on a million office walls The difficult we do immediately, the impossible takes a little longer'.

KISSINGER, HENRY

To have striven so hard, to have moulded a public personality out of so amorphous an identity, to have sustained that superhuman effort only to end with every weakness disclosed and every error compounding the downfall – that was a fate of biblical proportions. Evidently the Deity would not tolerate the presumption that all can be manipulated; an object lesson on the limits of human presumption was necessary.
The Years of Upheaval (1982)

Without Richard Nixon Kissinger would probably have remained a Harvard professor, intimately involved in the military-industrial-academic complex, and a powerful éminence grise of American military planning, but hardly the superstar diplomat that he became. Kissinger was initially unimpressed by the President and sneered openly at his capabilities during the 1968 election campaign. Once elected, Nixon became more alluring and Kissinger accepted the post of special adviser on national security. As the inspiration of Nixon's foreign policy Kissinger was able to make himself into a major figure, and by avoiding the Watergate imbroglio he kept his reputation, if not his job, longer than his boss. Writing his memoir of the Nixon years, Kissinger turned scathing once more, and this excerpt recalls Nixon's nemesis in 1974.

KITAIGORODSKI, ALEXANDER   (1914–) Russian scientist

A first-rate theory predicts, a second-rate theory forbids and a third-rate theory explains after the event.
quoted in 1975

KNOCK ON ANY DOOR

Live fast, die young, and leave a good-looking corpse.
script by Willard Motley (1949)

Nicholas Ray directed Humphrey Bogart in this earnest tale of juvenile delinquency. Bogart plays a lawyer, while John Derek, latterly best known for his exploitation of the physical charms of his wife Bo, plays the delinquent at whom he preaches and who he defends on a charge of killing a policeman. The film takes the sociological view, showing in flashbacks the boy's appalling childhood and 'inevitable' path to crime. The best thing about it was this line, the ideal maxim for succeeding generations of alienated youth.

KNOLL, ERWIN (1931–) American editor

Everything you read in the newspapers is absolutely true, except for that rare story of which you happen to have first-hand knowledge.

Assuming the newspaper in question is not under strict government control, and that its proprietor has managed to restrain his desire to promote the more crackpot of his campaigns, one might assume that its journalists do not deliberately set out to tell lies. Yet as Knoll points out, as soon as one has the slightest knowledge of a given story, let alone if one is its subject, the edifice of apparent accuracy starts to crumble. This stems not, one assumes, from deliberate bias but from what the sub-editors who are responsible for the eventual form of the written story would call the paper's style. No news, as the saying goes, is good news, and for the press sensation, even when tempered by the constraints of 'quality' journalism, is what matters.

KNOX, RONALD (1888–1957) British writer and clergyman

It is so stupid of modern civilisation to have given up believing in the devil when he is the only explanation of it.
Let Dons Delight (1939)

Ronald Knox, 'the wittiest young man in England' joined the Roman Catholic church in 1917 and soon proved himself the most influential of such converts. From 1926-39 he was Catholic chaplain to Oxford University, Domestic Prelate to the Pope from 1936 and a member of the Papal Academy of theology from 1937. Combining theological and wordly sophistication he wrote a new English translation of the Latin vulgate Bible, a number of successful detective stories, and a good deal of popular journalism; he was also a well-known broadcaster. *Let Dons Delight* is set against a dream-like background, in which a series of discussions spaced at 50 year intervals in a supposed Oxford senior common room, reveal the way in which specialisation and fragmentation have gradually eroded a once common culture.

KOESTLER, ARTHUR (1905–83) British writer and philosopher

The progress of science is strewn, like an ancient desert trail, with the bleached skeletons of discarded theories which once seemed to possess eternal life.
address to the PEN Club, 1976

Born in Budapest, Koestler began his career as a journalist, working as a foreign correspondent for the German press. After joining the Communist Party in 1932 he travelled in the USSR. Reporting the Spanish Civil War in 1936 he was arrested and very nearly executed by Franco's troops before his release was secured by the International Red Cross. Disillusioned by his experiences in Spain Koestler left the Party in 1938 and in 1940 settled in England, where he lived for the rest of his life. His best-known book, Darkness at Noon, appeared in 1940 and he wrote two further novels, equally concerned with the fate of revolutions and revolutionaries. After the war he abandoned fiction, turning to his studies of the biological and psychological condition of mankind. Koestler was a firm believer in euthanasia and committed suicide, accompanied by his secretary, in 1983.

KOESTLER, ARTHUR

Two half-truths do not make a truth, and two half cultures do not make a culture.
attacking C.P. Snow's concept of 'The Two Cultures' in *The Ghost in the Machine* (1967)

The Ghost in the Machine is the best known of the scientific works in which Koestler attempted to probe the human condition. In it he refines his general and universally applicable theory of hierarchy. But he adds that man is a biological freak, an evolutionary accident in that at some time in pre-history the neocortex of his brain, the reasoning part, grew both quickly and to a disproportionate size. Thus reason and imagination are dissociated. From this comes man's aggressiveness, unique in animal creation. Since a biological malfunction requires a biological corrective, Koestler's prescription is for man to search within the biological laboratories for some substance that will, when discovered, restore the mental balance.

KOESTLER, ARTHUR

If the creator had a purpose in equipping us with a neck, he surely meant us to stick it out.
in *Encounter*, May 1970

KOESTLER, ARTHUR

A writer's ambition should be to trade a hundred contemporary readers for ten readers in ten years' time and for one reader in a hundred years' time
in *New York Times Book Review*, April 1 1951

When Koestler stated his criterion for literary immortality he was still best known for his novels; his major works of non-fiction had yet to appear, although he had made a start with *The Yogi and the Commissar and Other Essays* (1945). Koestler's three novels, the first two of which are still considered by many critics to represent his most enduring work, are *Darkness at Noon* (1940), *Arrival and Departure* (1943) and *Thieves in the Night* (1946). All deal with the politics of revolution and reflect Koestler's own disillusion with Soviet Russia.

KOESTLER, ARTHUR

If one looks with a cold eye at the mess man has made of his history, it is difficult to avoid the conclusion that he has been afflicted by some built-in mental disorder which drives him towards self-destruction. Murder within the species on an individual or collective scale is a phenomenon unknown in the whole animal kingdom, except for man, and a few varieties of ants and rats.
in the *Observer*, 1968

KOESTLER, ARTHUR

The most persistent sound which reverberates through history is the beating of war drums.
Janus: A Summing Up (1978)

Janus, named for the Roman god whose two faces looked both forwards and backwards, is, as its subtitle explains, the systematic summing up of all the many theories, hypotheses and systems that Koestler had developed over the years since he abandoned novel-writing for exploratory non-fiction with *The Yogi and The*

Commissar (1945). While his own work tended to look at topics that both literally and metaphorically were more cerebral, Koestler is forced to note that taken as a whole, history is concerned more with the pursuit of man's anatagonism towards his fellows than with any more positive emotion or activity.

KOESTLER, ARTHUR

The disastrous history of our species indicates the futility of all attempts at a diagnosis which do not take into account the possibility that homo sapiens is a victim of one of evolution's countless mistakes.
speaking at the Nobel Symposium, 1969

The 1969 Nobel Symposium in Stockholm provided Koestler with an opportunity to summarise some of the more alarming conclusions regarding man's development and his possible fate which he had already drawn up in *The Ghost in the Machine* (1967). Thus he referred back to the central thesis of that work: that man, due to an imbalance in the development of the parts of his brain, is in fact a biological freak and predetermined to excessive aggressiveness.

KOESTLER, ARTHUR

Creativity in science could be described as the act of putting two and two together to make five.
The Act of Creation (1964)

In *The Act of Creation* Koestler ranges freely across virtually every aspect of the knowledge required to construct both a general and a specific theory of scientific discovery and artistic creation, with particular reference to the innovational faculty of genius. It consists of two complementary parts. The first sets out his general theory and the second, much more technical, places his theory in the context of a comprehensive hypothesis which posits a hierarchy extending from the simplest living organism to the most complex neural processes of the human brain.

KOESTLER, ARTHUR

God seems to have left the receiver off the hook and time is running out.
The Ghost in the Machine (1967)

KOJAK

Who loves ya, baby?
American TV show, 1974–77

When it was launched Kojak seemed the best police procedural show American television had managed to produce to date. A far cry from such Fifties throwbacks as *Hawaii 50*, a series mainly distinguished by the fact that its hero neither smiled nor ever unbuttoned his suit jacket, Kojak seemed like a revolution. For a start it was set in New York, even if the sets were actually in Hollywood, and for a change the cops seemed real. They weren't, of course, but in the star, Hollywood tough-guy Telly Savalas (1924–), who mixed the usual detective antics with an eye for the ladies, fancy manners and fancier tailoring, not to mention his omnipresent lollypops, and this, his catchphrase, the network had a real winner.

KORDA, MICHAEL (1933–) British writer and publisher

We live behind our faces, while they front for us.
Power in the Office (1976)

Korda is the son of Britain's greatest pre- and possibly post-war film producer, Sir Alexander Korda (1893-1956). Born in Hungary and knighted in England, Korda revived, if only for a while, the country's flagging film industry, and in his own personality and in the half dozen classic films he created, made it a real rival to Hollywood. His son wrote this best-selling analysis of executive in-fighting on the basis of his own experiences as a publisher in New York. In it he explains the niceties of corner offices, wall-to-wall carpeting and similar exotica, as well as the best way to come out on top of the constant struggle that, in his analysis, is office life.

KOVACS, ERNIE (1919–1962) American comedian

Television - a medium. So called because it is neither rare nor well done.
quoted in *The Filmgoer's Book of Quotes*, ed. L. Halliwell (1973)

Kovacs was one of American television's favourite personalities, a larger-than-life character who brandished outsize cigars and wisecracked his way across the nation's screens. Kovacs' dismissal of the medium that helped make him a star is one of the best of its type, ranking with Fred Allen's 'triumph of equipment over people', Robert Carson's 'The longest amateur night in history' and the anonymous 'the bland leading the bland'.

KRAUS, KARL   (1874–1936) Austrian satirist and critic

A woman occasionally is quite a serviceable substitute for masturbation. It takes an abundance of imagination, to be sure.
quoted in Die Fackel

Kraus was a major figure in the intellectual milieu of turn of the century Vienna, and a contemporary there of Freud, Adler, Kokoschka, Klimt, Adolf Loos, Mahler, Schoenberg and Theodore Herzl. In his magazine *Die Fackel (the Torch)* he attacked every form of hypocrisy: the corruption of public life, the suborning of the liberal press to propagandist purposes, the dual standards of sexuality as regarded men and women, and the dangers of modern militarism. He admired Freud, but deplored what he saw as the ruination of his theories by his disciples. He was born a Jew but mocked Zionism and what he saw as the failings of the influential Viennese Jewish community. His Swiftian writing, which spared neither person nor credo, made him equally admired and detested. Apart from *Die Fackel* (published from 1899–1936) his most important work was *Die letzen Tage der Menschkeit* (1919–22, *The Last Days of Mankind*) a factual catalogue of World War I's cruelty and excess. His many aphorisms were collected in *Half-Truths and One-and-a-Half Truths* (1986):

Sound opinions are valueless. What matters is who holds them.

The real truths are those that can be invented.

Language is the mother of thought, not its handmaiden.

My language is the common prostitute that I turn into a virgin.

Newspapers have roughly the same relationship to life as fortune-tellers to metaphysics.

A historian is often only a journalist facing backwards.

Education is what most people receive, many pass on and few have.

Diplomacy is a game of chess in which nations are checkmated.

Moral responsibility is what is lacking in a man when he demands it of a woman.

Virginity is the ideal of those who wish to deflower.

The conjugal bedroom is the coexistence of brutality and martyrdom.

Democracy means the permission to be everyone's slave.

KRAUS, KARL

Life is an effort that deserves a better cause.

Lord forgive them, for they know what they do!

KRAUS, KARL

How is the world ruled and how do wars start? Diplomats tell lies to journalists, and they believe what they read.
Aphorisms and More Aphorisms (1909)

KRAUS, KARL

Psychoanalysis is that mental illness for which it regards itself as therapy.
Half-Truths and One-and-a-Half Truths (1986)

KRIM, SEYMOUR (1922–) American writer

Isn't that what makes artforms change – when life leaves them in the lurch?
Shake It For The World (1970)

Krim has been working as a writer, editor and teacher since 1940 and has published his work widely throughout the American media. He was tried, and acquitted, after he published the 'Tralala' section of Hubert Selby's *Last Exit to Brooklyn* in 1964. His comment here, referring to the shifting styles of artforms, might be seen as particularly American, assuming that art must keep up with life, rather than stating itself as art in no matter what period it is created, and expecting to be assessed as such, no matter what happens in rest of the world.

KRISHNAMURTI, JIDDU (1895–?) Indian philosopher

Religion is the frozen thought of men out of which they build temples.
quoted in the *Observer*, April 22 1928

Krishnamurti was born in Madras but educated in England where he was influenced by Mrs. Annie Besant (1847-1933), with whose Theosophist ideas, in turn inherited from Madame Blavatsky (1831-1891), he became imbued. In 1925 Mrs. Besant, who was also a firm advocate of Indian nationalism, proclaimed him the Messiah and the leader of her Order of the Star in the East. Krishnamurti dissolved the Order, preferring to travel the world teaching and advocating a way of life and thought unconditioned by what he saw as the restrictive narrowness of nationality, race and, as stated above, religion.

KRISTOFFERSON, KRIS (1936–) American rock musician and actor

Freedom's just another word for nothing left to lose.
Me and Bobby McGee (1970)

Kristofferson wrote *Me and Bobby McGee* but the song gained its success through the interpretation of another singer, the late Janis Joplin (1943-70). A 'road movie' set to music, the song's bitter-sweet lyrics reflect America's prevailing fascination with movement, endlessly travelling the massive continent in search of novelty and nirvana. This line, the most quoted in the song, sums up the illusion of the freedom lusted after by so many young people at the time, stressing that in the end the word becomes no more than a synonym for a lack of anything more important in one's life.

KRISTOL, IRVING (1920–) American writer

Being frustrated is disagreeable, but the real disasters in life begin when you get what you want.
in 1977

In 1953 Irving Kristol was one of the founders, with the British poet Stephen Spender (1909–), of the magazine Encounter. Funded by the Congress of Cultural Freedom, an amorphous American organisation widely assumed to have been a CIA front, Encounter represented the close ties that existed between British and American intellectuals during the Fifties, and attracted many important writers. Kristol remains a major American intellectual, in the vanguard of the new right, who offer conservative attitudes as a rebuttal to what they see as the futile liberalism of the Sixties and early Seventies.

KROC, RAY (–1983) American fast food entrepreneur

It takes a certain kind of mind to see beauty in a hamburger bun. Yet is it any more unusual to find grace in the texture and softly carved silhouette of a bun than to reflect lovingly on the hackles of a fishing fly? Or the arrangements and textures on a butterfly's wing? Not if you are a MacDonald's man.
Grinding It Out (1978)

Kroc was already a late-middle-aged salesman of milk shakes and mixers, peddling his wares on America's West Coast when in 1954 he chanced upon a San Bernadino hamburger stand run by two brothers, Maurice and Richard MacDonald. Kroc understood the potential of fast food and he adopted mass-production methods and high-pressure salesmanship to parlay the MacDonalds' burgers into a nationwide success. He bought them out in 1960 and went on to convert most of the world to the delights of the twin golden arches. Kroc's empire is based in Chicago, at Hamburger Central, and at Hamburger University students can major in Hamburger Sciences, with a minor in French Fries. Kroc died in 1983 but his empire still rules the world of junk food.

KRONENBERGER, LOUIS (1904–1980) American critic and writer

Temperament, like liberty, is important despite how many crimes are committed in its name.
Company Manners (1954)

Kronenberger worked as the drama critic of *Time* magazine between 1938–61 and of the defunct PM from 1940–48. He was latterly Professor of Theatre and librarian at Brandeis University. His books include three novels, all of which satirise the world of the very rich and somewhat eccentric. Kronenberger has also written extensively on American and English culture, including studies of 18th century England, John Wilkes, Oscar Wilde, well known aphorists,and modern American letters and society.

KRUTCH, JOSEPH WOOD (1893–1970) American writer and academic

Logic is the art of going wrong with confidence.
The Modern Temper (1929)

Krutch was both an academic and an influential theatre critic. He has written on the American drama and published his memoirs *More Lives Than One* in 1962. *The Modern Temper* is an important analysis of 'meaninglessness', a pessimistic view of modern life written by a 'modern intellectual' who finds that science has destroyed his faith in a beneficent universe and psychology his belief in his innate nobility. Thus he 'finds only in the pursuit of knowledge that which makes life worth living'.

KUBRICK, STANLEY (1928–) American film director

The destruction of this planet would have no significance on a cosmic scale. To an observer in the Andromeda nebula, the sign of our extinction would be no more than a match flaring for a second in the heavens.
publicising his film *2001*, in 1969

Kubrick is one of the most celebrated of contemporary film directors, something of a maverick in whose psyche, as filmographer Leslie Halliwell puts it 'independence is equated with success'. Among his most important films have been *Dr. Strange-*

love, (1963), his grimly funny look at the the world of nuclear defences, and *2001: A Space Odyssey* (1969), an epic production based on Arthur C. Clarke's writing that married science fiction to mysticism.

KUBRICK, STANLEY

If you can talk brilliantly about a problem, it can create the consoling illusion that it has been mastered.

Like those who prefer to make lengthy and convoluted lists rather than actually take action, those who can 'talk a good game' are more likely than not to create the impression that their actions will be equally impressive. This pattern would be more acceptable were the hiatus between words and deeds not often so dangerously self-deluding.

KUBRICK, STANLEY

The great nations have always acted like gangsters and the small nations like prostitutes.
speaking in 1963

Kubrick's cyncial delineation of the way in which the world's nations either choose or have been forced to act is no less pertinent for its negative approach. One would hardly expect much optimism from the maker and co-writer of Dr. Strangelove, and Kubrick neatly sums up the relations between the super-powers, who act as if the whole world is some kind of fiefdom to be divided up like Prohibition-era New York or Chicago, and their various allies, who attempt, as much like pilot fish as prostitutes, to batten onto whatever the great powers condescend to offer.

L

LAING, R.D.   (1927–) British psychiatrist

Laing published his first major book *The Divided Self* in 1959. In it he used the philosophies of existentialism to point out that while to the outside world the schizophrenic might appear 'mad', there was a positive logic to his actions. It was too easy simply to label as insane those whose activities put them outside the mainstream of society. In *Sanity, Madness and the Family* (1964) he showed how in certain family situations a disturbed individual might actively choose madness as a refuge. This concentration on the aberrant individual as opposed to the 'normal' system, and his

LAING, R.D.

lack of faith in the nuclear family, endeared Laing to the counter-culture; he became the psychiatrist of the Sixties, especially with the publication of *The Politics of Experience* (1967). Laing practised much innovative therapy, but his move towards Zen, his publications of poems and recording of an album have both devalued the real importance of his work and confirmed for establishment psychiatrists their belief that Laingian 'anti-psy-chiatry' was never more than a sham.

LAING, R.D.

Insanity—a perfectly rational adjustment to the insane world.
in the *Guardian*, 1972

LAING, R.D.

The brotherhood of man is evoked by particular men according to their circumstances. But it seldom extends to all men. In the name of our freedom and our brotherhood we are prepared to blow up the other half of the world and to be blown up in our turn.
The Politics of Experience (1967)

LAING, R.D.

Human beings seem to have an almost unlimited capacity to deceive themselves and to deceive themselves into taking their own lies for truth.
The Politics of Experience (1967)

LAING, R.D.

We are all murderers and prostitutes. No matter to what culture, society, class, nation one belongs, no matter how normal, moral or mature one takes oneself to be.
The Politics of Experience (1967)

LAING, R.D.

Society highly values its normal men. It educates children to lose themselves and to become absurd, and thus be normal. Normal men have killed perhaps 100,000,000 of their fellow normal men in the last fifty years.
The Politics of Experience (1967)

460

LAING, R.D.

From the moment of birth, when the Stone Age baby confronts the 20th century mother, the baby is subjected to these forces of violence, called love, as its father and mother, and their parents and their parents before them, have been. These forces are mainly concerned with destroying most of its potential.
The Politics of Experience (1967)

LANDRY, TOM (1924–) American football coach

Will power. Intellect tires, the Will never. The brain needs sleep, the Will none. The whole body is nothing but objectified Will. The whole nervous system constitutes the antennae of the Will. Every act of the body is nothing but the act of Will objectified.
sign posted in locker room of the Dallas Cowboys, 1973

This dictum, with its Nietzschean emphasis on the Will, sums up Landry, one of the most intense of coaches in a sport where eccentricity, egocentricity and all-out competitiveness have been raised beyond art to obsession. It may be hard to associate football with such high-flown philosophising, but anyone who has seen Landry's spare form and unsmiling features patrolling the sidelines as his Dallas Cowboys play, will appreciate that the coach, if not the team, is living right up to his locker-room diktat.

LANG, JULIA British children's broadcaster

Are you sitting comfortably...then we'll begin.
Listen with Mother, BBC Radio programme 1950 onwards

Julia Lang was the first presenter of British radio's best-loved children's programme, Listen with Mother. The show was positioned immediately before the even more popular Woman's Hour and the two offered the image of millions of mothers and pre-school children settling down from 1.45 to 2.00pm, lulled by the strains of the BBC's Home Service. Lang came out 'inadvertently' with the line that became her catchphrase, on the first edition of the programme, in January 1950. When she failed to repeat it on day two, the nation's anguished tinies wrote to complain that without her gentle warning, they couldn't get ready to listen.

LARDNER, RING W. (1885–1933) American writer

You know me, Al
book title, 1916

Lardner began his journalistic career writing baseball coverage for papers in Chicago and Boston. When marriage curtailed his touring with the teams he began writing a daily column. His career blossomed when he created the fictional Jack O'Keefe, otherwise known as The Busher (from bush league, meaning unsophisticated, naive and stupid), whose adventures were retailed in the mixture of everyday slang and baseball terminology that Lardner picked up from the real-life ball-players. The columns took the form of letters from O'Keefe, touring with the team, to his pal, Al and every faux pas was met with the self-justifying phrase 'You know me, Al'. When the first collection of O'Keefe stories was published in 1916, they naturally took the phrase as their title. Lardner was recognised as a master of the short story but he was never able to transcend its limitations and he died relatively young, a victim of his own alcoholism.

LARKIN, PHILIP (1922–1986) British poet

> **They fuck you up, your Mum and Dad.**
> **They may not mean to, but they do.**
> **And give you all the faults they had**
> **And add some extra, just for you.**

This Be The Verse (1974)

Larkin was a poet and the librarian of Hull University, a job he held until his death. As one of the poets categorised as 'the Movement', he joined Kingsley Amis, D.J. Enright, John Wain and others as increasingly well-known Fifties literary figures, although he remained notably reticent, apparently satisfied with provincial life and eschewing London's fashionable literary marketplace. His main collections project the poet as deliberately anti-fashion and obsessed with transcience and death. In this poem he decries the fallacies of 'happy family' life and in the final stanza offers his solution: 'Man hands on misery to man. / It deepens like the coastal shelf. / Get out as early as you can. / And don't have any kids yourself.'

LARKIN, PHILIP

> **Sexual intercourse began**
> **In nineteen sixty-three**
> **(Which was rather late for me) –**
> **Between the end of the Chatterley ban**
> **And the Beatles' first LP.**

Annus Mirabilis (1974)

This is the first verse of Larkin's best-known poem, in which he manages simultaneously to celebrate the freedoms of the Sixties, epitomised by his mention of two contemporary icons, and place himself firmly outside their sway. Larkin ends the poem sardonically 'So life was never better than / In nineteen sixty-three / (Though just too late for me) - / Between the end of the Chatterley ban / And the Beatles' first LP.'

LARKIN, PHILIP

Many of them having a beginning, a muddle and an end.
speech, November 1977

Parading his image as something of a literary conservative, Larkin offered this summation of the modern novel when presenting the Booker Prize in 1977.

LASCH, CHRISTOPHER   (1932–) American academic

Nothing succeeds like the appearance of success.
The Culture of Narcissism (1979)

The Culture of Narcissism is Lasch's counterblast to what he calls 'the creed of self-love' that has, in the absence of traditional religious feelings, come to replace the spiritual needs without which so many people find it impossible to maintain self-supportive lives. Lasch excoriates what Tom Wolfe termed the 'me generation' pointing out the futility of this narcissistic obsession, with its lack of interest in past and future, and shallow fascination with a few shallow strictly egocentric emotions. This aphorism refers to the purveyors of the new therapies that are central to the phenomenon, whose cut-down, easily digested sub-Freudianism promises much but hands over little. But what narcissist will admit that after a weekend's immersion in 'rebirthing' or 'est' they haven't become a better person, more 'in touch with themself '.

LASKI, HAROLD   (1893–1950) British political theorist

De mortuis nil nisi bunkum.
quoted in K. Martin, Harold Laski (1953)

Laski taught political science at the LSE from 1926-50. His earliest beliefs were in political pluralism but the rise of fascism drove him further left, believing that capitalism must inevitably embrace fascist doctrines and that only socialism provided a viable alternative. As well as teaching he was a major figure in the Labour party and its chairman during the landslide election victory of 1945, although the Labour leadership found him too

extreme and excluded him from power. He continued campaigning for real socialism until his death. His paraphrase of the Latin
tag 'De mortuis nil nisi bonum' (Say nothing but good of the
dead) refers to the way in which one only needed to die,
irrespective of one's calumnies in life, to attain instant
respectability.

LASKI, HAROLD

**The meek do not inherit the earth unless they are prepared to
fight for their meekness.**
attributed

Laski's espousal of socialism as the only viable system to stand in
the face of escalating fascism reflected the growing power of the
far right in Europe during the Thirties. Under such misnomers as
'national socialism' the right wing had trampled on human rights
and glorified the primacy of the bully-boy. The only way to
oppose violence, Laski made it clear, was for the oppressed to
fight back. The haves were not about to hand over to the have-
nots and those who desired the benefits of socialism were going
to have to struggle for it.

LASSWELL, HAROLD   (1902–1978) American political econom-
ist

Politics is who gets what, when, how.
Politics: Who Gets What, When, How (1936)

Lasswell was one of the century's leading political scientists who
based his influential theories on the single concept that in the end
all politics is the study of influence. This belief permeates his
researches, in which he collaborated with a wide variety of
figures, and his writing, in which he pioneered communications
theory, content analysis and policy sciences. This book deals with
the way the 'values' or 'goods' of income, safety and respect are
distributed in societies. It soon developed into a classic text of
the developing 'behavioural' approach to political science.

LAST FLIGHT, THE

It seemed like a good idea at the time.
screenplay (1931)

The Last Flight is an otherwise undistinguished film in which a
group of American airmen chose to stay behind in Europe after
the end of World War I, but it has been credited by film expert
Leslie Halliwell as the first place in which this popular phrase

occurs. After he gets carried away at a bullfight, one of them leaps into the ring and is gored to death. When the press ask why he should have done such a foolish thing, a friend explains that 'It seemed like a good idea at the time'.

LAVER, JAMES (1899–1975) British fashion expert

The same dress is indecent ten years before its time, daring one year before its time, chic, being defined as contemporary seductiveness, in its time, dowdy three years after its time, hideous twenty years after its time, amusing thirty years after its time, romantic 100 years after its time and beautiful 150 years after its time.
quoted 1966

The fluctuations of fashion are many and varied and clothes expert James Laver manages to encapsulate the whole ebb and flow of attractiveness by setting a garment's career over a hypothetical 160 year period. Laver's expertise covered the whole history of British costume, and he wrote widely on art (often from the point of view of the fashions included in it).

LAWRENCE, D.H. (1885–1930) British writer

Morality which is based on ideas, or on an ideal, is an unmitigated evil.
Fantasia of the Unconscious (1922)

In a book which throws a good deal of light on Lawrence's personality and writing methods, the author stands clearly for his belief in a morality based on natural, intuitive feelings, rather than on some code of law or religious doctrine. Although Lawrence decries ideals in his condemnation of such bases for morality, it is hard to exclude his own concept of a morality that springs untainted from the human soul as anything more than highly idealistic. His own work is filled with intense moralising, and the fact that the ideas it encompassed sprang from his own beliefs, rather than being imposed by some external agency, does not exclude him from his own charges.

LAWRENCE, D.H.

It's all this cold-hearted fucking that is death and idiocy.
Lady Chatterley's Lover (1929)

Or, as he puts it in 'Bibbles' 'You must always be a-waggle with LOVE.' The problem with Lawrence on sex in general and Lady Chatterley's Lover in particular is that for all his reputation as a pioneer of sexual freedom and openness and a purveyor of blunt facts in blunter language, his writing is itself chillingly cold-hearted. He worshipped nature and the emotions a natural man and woman supposedly feel, but in all of Connie Chatterley's and Mellors' graphic couplings, it is hard to find much flesh and blood.

LAWRENCE, D.H.

Of course Celia shits! Who doesn't? And how much worse if she didn't.
A propos of Lady Chatterley's Lover (1929)

Lawrence's pamphlet 'A propos of Lady Chatterley's Lover' was a rejoinder to the banning of the book by authorities in Europe and America. As far as those authorities were concerned, the frequent use of obscene language rendered the book unacceptable. From Lawrence's point of view, this was what people did and as an advocate of naturalness, in sex as in everything else, there was no possibility that he would mask any human function purely to satisfy the morally squeamish. 'Celia' stands for her namesake, the idealised female as hymned in the poetry of the seventeenth and eighteenth centuries.

LAWRENCE, D.H.

Men and women aren't really dogs: they only look like it and behave like it. Somewhere inside there is a great chagrin and a gnawing discontent.
A propos of Lady Chatterley's Lover (1929)

Lawrence's writing of descriptions of nature is generally acknowledged to be among the best achieved. His difficulties begin when he turns to human relationships, which he claims spring like less complex organisms, from that same nature, and should act according to its dictates but which, quite obviously, refuse to be so convenient. Lawrence, it seems, would like his humans to be as natural as dogs, but wishes simultaneously to confer upon them a great - human - dignity. It is this inner discontent, the chagrin, that creates their humanity, but it was this side of humanity that Lawrence was never fully capable of capturing on paper.

LAWRENCE, D.H.

Pornography is the attempt to insult sex, to do dirt on it.'
Pornography and Obscenity (1930)

LAWRENCE, D.H.

Pornography, when taken back to its roots in classical Greek, means the 'writing of whores'. In modern usage it tends to refer to titillatory material, usually designed to stimulate male masturbation. For Lawrence, who touted the delights of 'natural', untainted sex with the chilly fervour of a hellfire evangelist, pornography was just as dirty as the pious moralists he claimed to oppose always said it was. Setting his own visions of sex on a pedestal he turned it into as much of a holy grail as did the puritans. The only difference between the two was that the puritans preferred not to talk about the subject while Lawrence often appeared incapable of shutting up.

LAWRENCE, D.H.

The dirty little secret is most difficult to kill.
Pornography and Obscenity (1930)

Lawrence's description of sex, or sex as experienced and discussed by apparently everyone else in the world except his enlightened self, became an obsession with him. He first used it in this pamphlet, which followed the banning of his novel *Lady Chatterley's Lover* (1929) and the seizure that same year of some thirteen of his pictures from a London gallery. His attack embraced not merely the puritans and 'the mob of people today'; the intellectuals, 'the Bright Young People', the liberated young, the birth-control advocates and everyone else were allegedly prey to 'the dirty little secret'. The sin of these latter, it might seem, was that unlike Lawrence they preferred simply to enjoy sex, rather than endlessly preaching about it.

LAWRENCE, D.H.

You may know a new utterance by the element of danger in it.
reviewing *A Second Contemporary Verse Anthology*, 1923

The 'element of danger' in the new comes not from those who oppose it but from the threat it should present in itself to the established order. The extent to which Lawrence's own works were either new or 'dangerous' is debatable. The irony is that his reputation as a fighter against censorship and for freedom of speech rests on one of his lesser works. Indeed, the eventual freedoms that the trial of *Lady Chatterley's Lover* in 1960 rendered to writers might well not have pleased Lawrence who would undoubtedly have seen much of their work as no more than pornography.

LAWRENCE, T.E.   (1888–1935) Irish adventurer and soldier

All men dream, but not equally. Those who dream by night in the dusty recesses of their minds wake in the day to find that it was vanity: but the dreamers of the day are dangerous men, for they may act their dream with open eyes, to make it possible.
The Seven Pillars of Wisdom (1926)

Lawrence 'of Arabia' remains one of the more enigmatic figures of the century. After working as an archaeologist he became involved in British intelligence and led the Arabs in a guerilla campaign throughout World War I. His intense Arabism brought him into conflict with the British authorities and Lawrence was forced to accept that for all his mystique, he was still playing a useful role in the era's colonial power games. Deeply neurotic, he sought to bury his fame in obscurity, quitting the Colonial Office and joining the RAF as Aircraftsman John Hume Ross. He was discharged in 1923, after his real identity was discovered, and then joined the tank corps as T.E. Shaw, returning to the RAF as Shaw in 1927, and staying in it until his death in a motor-cycle crash in 1935. The Seven Pillars of Wisdom is his history of the Arab campaign. As a man who chose to 'act his dreams with open eyes', he remains a legend, still impenetrable and attractive.

LE BON, GUSTAVE   (1841–1931) French physician and sociologist

Virtuous people often revenge themselves for the constraints to which they submit by the boredom which they inspire.
Aphorismes du temps présent (1913)

Le Bon's primary career was in medicine and sociology and his book of aphorisms appeared alongside such studies as *La Psychologie des Foules* (1895, *The Psychology of Crowds*) and *Les Lois psychologiques de l'Evolution des peuples* (1894, *The Psychological Laws of Human Evolution*). This remark underlines the inbuilt tedium that the more verbose moralists tend to arouse in their hearers. Le Bon's point is that such people believe that not only must they suffer to be good, but that it is also good for others to suffer.

LE CARRÉ , JOHN   (1931–) (David Cornwell) British novelist

A committee is an animal with four back legs.
Tinker Tailor Soldier Spy (1974)

Le Carré attributes his own version of the many aphorisms coined to describe the failings of the committee system to 'Karla', his KGB villain against whom his secret service hero 'George Smiley' is pitted through a trilogy of best-selling novels. The line occurs as Smiley is on the verge of unmasking Karla's mole, the deep penetration agent who has risen to the heights of 'The Circus', Le Carré's name for his intelligence agency. Smiley is explaining to another agent how the mole has consistently fed Britain with alluring but spurious information, using the clashing personalities of a government committee to ease the forgery's passage. 'I rather like Karla's description of a committee, don't you. Is it Chinese? A committee is an animal with four back legs.'

LE CORBUSIER (1887–1966) (Charles Edouard Jeanneret) Swiss-French architect

The house...a machine for living.
Vers une architecture (1923)

In 1918 Le Corbusier, with the painter Amedée Ozenfant, issued an anti-Cubist manifesto, proclaiming the new theory of purism, based on the architectural equilibrium and the functional simplicity of the machine. In 1923 he produced *Vers une architecture*, in which he developed his revolutionary concepts of mass housing, all based on a ferro-concrete modular skeleton, known as the 'Dom-ino' system. He advocated the use of identical skyscrapers as the basis of new town planning and began a series of private houses, all elevated on stilts. His use of concrete continued throughout his career and the post war 'new brutalism' is based on this material.

LEACH, EDMUND (1910–) British social anthropologist

Far from being the basis of the good society, the family, with its narrow privacy and tawdry secrets, is the source of all our discontents.
Reith lecture, 1967

The nuclear family, with its cosy home, its 2.4 children, its pets and its supposed security has been under assault for many years and never more so than in the Sixties. Leach was summarising the views of many contemporaries, especially among the young, who felt that in the family with its insularity and its constraints there lay nothing but neurosis, unhappiness, frustration and repression. Leach's view seemed particularly feasible at the time, given that the regular desire of the young to break free of their families was for the first time backed up by the economic freedoms that gave substance to the fantasy. Emergent feminism only intensified the atmosphere.

LEACOCK, STEPHEN (1869–1944) Canadian writer and political economist

Advertising may be described as the science of arresting the human intelligence long enough to get money from it.
The Penguin Stephen Leacock (1981)

Leacock combined a lengthy career as a professor of economics at McGill University in Montreal with the writing of a large quantity of humorous essays and stories. J.B. Priestley described his work as 'balanced between cutting satire and sheer absurdity'. When Leacock offered this opinion of advertising the industry was still in its infancy. What he would have made of today's infinitely more sophisticated methods of extracting cash from its owners can only be imagined.

LEARY, TIMOTHY (1920–) American teacher and drug advocate

Turn on, tune in, drop out.
The Politics of Ecstasy (1966)

Leary was a Harvard academic when he discovered the hallucinogenic drugs psilocibin and LSD, which were in use, albeit sparingly, as an aid in dealing with certain varieties of mental illness. Leary was expelled from Harvard when it was discovered that he had been using hallucinogens on himself, on his associates and on hundreds of volunteer subjects. Undeterred he established a centre in upstate New York and began proselytising for the psychedelic revolution, urging the world's youth to Turn on, tune in and drop out'. Leary became a target for the American authorities' fury and after bizarre entanglements with the Black Panthers and other radical groups it transpired that he had been involved for some time with the FBI. Leary is currently advocating other means of self improvement and for some time worked the college lecture circuit in a double-act with Watergate mastermind G. Gordon Liddy.

LEAUTAUD, PAUL (1872–1956) French essayist and man of letters

Love makes fools, marriage cuckolds and patriotism malevolent imbeciles.
Passe-Temps

Leautaud was for many years associated with the journal Mercure de France, for a time writing as its dramatic critic under the name Maurice Boissard. He co-edited the well-known anthology of symbolist verse *Poésie d'aujourd'hui*. His literary journal, covering most of his adult life, is cynical and rancorous (emotions often claimed to stem from his miserable childhood) but is of undoubted interest as a record of literary life and encounters. The line quoted here, sparing neither love, marriage nor the state from his blanket condemnation, is typical.

LEBOWITZ, FRAN   (1946–) American journalist and critic

There is no such thing as inner peace. There is only nervousness or death. Any attempt to prove otherwise constitutes unacceptable behaviour.
Metropolitan Life (1978)

Fran Lebowitz worked as the film critic of Andy Warhol's Interview magazine, writing a witty column which dealt as often with the vicissitudes of her own life as a single woman in New York as with the movies under review. She has written two bestselling books: *Metropolitan Life* (1978) and its successor *Social Studies* (1981). Lebowitz is always unashamedly elitist, unimpressed by the successive fads that make slaves of her fellow New Yorkers, and never boring. Her two books are filled with aphorisms, some samples of which, covering many topics, are included below.

LEBOWITZ, FRAN

The three questions of greatest concern are – 1. Is it attractive? 2. Is it amusing? 3. Does it know its place?
Metropolitan Life (1978)

LEBOWITZ, FRAN

Nothing succeeds like address.
Metropolitan Life (1978)

LEBOWITZ, FRAN

All God's children are not beautiful. Most of God's children are, in fact, barely presentable.
Metropolitan Life (1978)

LEBOWITZ, FRAN

Vegetables are interesting but lack a sense of purpose when unaccompanied by a good cut of meat.
Metropolitan Life (1978)

LEBOWITZ, FRAN

The opposite of talking isn't listening. The opposite of talking is waiting.
Social Studies (1981)

LEBOWITZ, FRAN

Remember that as a teenager you are in the last stage of your life when you will be happy to hear that the 'phone is for you.
Social Studies (1981)

LEBOWITZ, FRAN

Your responsibility as a parent is not as great as you might imagine. You need not supply the world with the next conqueror of disease or major motion picture star. If your child simply grows up to be someone who does not use the word 'collectible' as a noun, you can consider yourself an unqualified success.
Social Studies (1981)

LEBOWITZ, FRAN

Original thought is like original sin: both happened before you were born to people you could not have possibly met.
Social Studies (1981)

LEBOWITZ, FRAN

People (a group that in my opinion has always attracted an undue amount of attention) have often been likened to snowflakes. This analogy is meant to suggest that each is unique – no two alike. This is quite patently not the case. People... are quite simply a dime a dozen. And, I hasten to add, their only similarity to snowflakes resides in their invariable and lamentable tendency to turn, in a few warm days, to slush.
Social Studies (1981)

LEBOWITZ, FRAN

If you are of the opinion that the contemplation of suicide is sufficient evidence of a poetic nature, do not forget that actions speak louder than words.
Metropolitan Life (1978)

LEC, STANISLAW J. (1909–) Polish poet and aphorist

Don't shout for help at night. You might wake your neighbours.
Unkempt Thoughts (1962)

LEC, STANISLAW J.

Is it progress if a cannibal uses a fork?
Unkempt Thoughts (1962)

LEC, STANISLAW J.

All Gods were immortal.
Unkempt Thoughts (1962)

LEC, STANISLAW J.

When you jump for joy, beware that no-one moves the ground from beneath your feet.
Unkempt Thoughts (1962)

LEC, STANISLAW J.

When smashing monuments, save the pedestals – they always come in handy.
Unkempt Thoughts (1962)

LEC, STANISLAW J.

When gossip grows old it becomes myth.
Unkempt Thoughts (1962)

LEE, HARPER (1926–) American writer

Shoot all the bluejays you want, if you can hit 'em, but remember it's a sin to kill a mockingbird.
To Kill a Mockingbird (1960)

Harper Lee's best-selling Pulitzer Prize-winning novel was touted as the best book to come out of the American South since *Gone With The Wind* and in its portrayal of the narrator's liberal lawyer father, fighting for the life of a Black accused of rape, it certainly exploits in its own way myths as powerful, if utterly contrasted, as those of the earlier Southern tale. If GWTW celebrates a Civil War South, then Lee's novel celebrates that of Civil Rights. This line, from which the book's title derives, occurs when her Uncle Jack gives air rifles to her and her brother Jem. Her father, Atticus tells them 'I'd rather you shot at tin cans in the back yard, but I know you'll go after birds', then makes his distinction. As Lee explains in the next paragraph 'Mockingbirds don't do one thing but make music for us to enjoy...they don't do one thing but sing their hearts out for us. That's why it's a sin to kill a mockingbird'.

LEE, GYPSY ROSE   (1914–70) (Rose Louise Hovick) American stripper

God is love, but get it in writing.
catchphrase

Rose Hovick, nicknamed Plug by her family, made her stage debut at a club smoker in West Seattle when, aged only four, she accompanied her sister June, two and a half, in 'I'm a Hard-Boiled Rose'. Their mother was divorced and poor and she toured the girls as 'Dainty June and her Newsboy Songsters', backed by six small boys and a menagerie of guinea-pigs, white mice, a turtle and a monkey. By 1924 Dainty June was a minor star but when June eloped, still only 13, Rose took over and the act was renamed 'Rose Louise and her Hollywood Blondes'. When, in Toledo, the bill-topping stripper was jailed for assault Rose volunteered to replace her. She scored a big success and changed her name to Gypsy Rose Lee. Aged seventeen she was taken up by the racketeer Waxey Gordon who arranged her a part as The Queen of Burlesque in one of Florenz Ziegfield's Follies shows. She continued stripping while her figure held up, and retired a respected star of US entertainment.

LEFEVRE, THEO   (1914–1973) Belgian prime minister

In Western Europe there are now only small countries – those that know it, and those that don't know it yet.
quoted in the *Observer*, 1963

Belgium, usually apostrophised by the historians of World War I as 'plucky little Belgium' is otherwise usually seen as a Catholic offshoot of Protestant Holland, the home of the convoluted bureaucracies of the EEC and the birthplace of Hercule Poirot and the Brussels' sprout. Its Prime Minister Lefevre was surely taking such put-downs into account when he pointed out in 1963 that for all the self-promotion of such former Imperial powers as Britain, Germany and France, the hegemony of the two super-powers had rendered all other countries no more than Belgiums in their own right, like it or not.

LEGMAN, GERSHON   (1917–) American academic

Murder is a crime. Describing murder is not. Sex is not a crime. Describing sex is.
quoted in *Maledicta* magazine, 1977

Legman has for years been a maverick academic who has chosen to concentrate his talents on an area – that of the sexual and erotic

– which is considered by many of his peers as beyond the scholarly pale. As such he has been to a great extent placed at a similar distance by the more orthodox philological and folkloric academic community, and for many years has lived in France, an expatriate from America. His most important books include *Love and Death: A Study in Censorship* (1949), *The Horn Book: Studies in Erotic Folklore and Bibliography* (1964) and his monumental taxonomy of popular humour *The Rationale of the Dirty Joke* (1968, 1975).

LEHMAN, ERNEST   (1920–) American screen writer

The Sweet Smell of Success
film title, 1957

Helped by playwright Clifford Odets (1903–63) Lehman adapted his own short story of megalomania, subservience and self-destruction on Broadway for Hollywood in 1957. The film starred Burt Lancaster as a Walter Winchell-like gossip columnist, dispensing fear and favours from his tables in the Stork Club and 21. Tony Curtis played his fawning sidekick, the appositely named Sidney Falco, victim of Lancaster's famous request 'Match me, Sidney', but preying avidly on anyone weaker than himself. The film proved too grimly cynical for American audiences, but Curtis successfully used the role to move from teenage idol to real actor.

LEMAY, CURTIS E.   (1906–) American soldier

Tell the Vietnamese they've got to draw in their horns and stop their aggression or we're going to bomb them back to the Stone Age
suggesting US air force tactics in Vietnam, 1965

Air Force General Curtis E. LeMay, the possible inspiration for the gung-ho General Jack D. Ripper of the film Dr. Strangelove, was the first head of America's Strategic Air Command, the USAF's elite nuclear bomber strike force. SAC, motto 'Peace Is Our Profession', was established under LeMay in 1946 and developed through the Fifties to encompass computer-guided ballistic missiles as well as the aircraft-carried 'dumb bombs'. LeMay, like many soldiers, felt that the only purpose in possessing weaponry was to use it, and constantly urged President Eisenhower to unleash his 'optimum strike', after which he promised that Russia would, in two hours, be a 'smoking radiated ruin'. Even in retirement LeMay urged aggression, suggesting that nuclear weapons should be used in Vietnam and inspiring the ironic slogan 'Bombs Away with Curt LeMay!'

LENIN, V.I. (1870–1924) Russian leader

It is true that liberty is precious, so precious that it must be rationed

dictum, attributed by Sidney and Beatrice Webb, 1936

Of all those Western socialists who made the pilgrimage to Soviet Russia to see the socialist nirvana in action, the Webbs were probably the most fervent. While others returned sadly chastened by the experience of Stalin's grim society, the Webbs returned declaring their complete satisfaction. Presumably, therefore, they quoted Lenin's dictum with approval, and it is certainly in character. Unlike more liberal, and thus less influential figures, Lenin never pretended that the revolution would bring unfettered freedom. As his imitators all over the world continue to point out, as long as the revolution is opposed even by a tiny minority, the State's first duty is to maintain the most rigid of regimes in its defence.

LENIN, V.I.

Communism is Soviet power plus the electrification of the whole country.

slogan promoting electrification, 1920

Lenin's remark reveals in microcosm the way he saw two aims for the still young Revolution: the establishment of absolute Communist power in Russia and the urgent modernisation of the country. The first part proceeded as planned; Lenin's Bolsheviks gained a stranglehold on the country which they have never relinquished, despite the inevitable fluctuations in personnel and the occasional deviation from the central policy. Modernisation has been less efficient, although both Lenin and Stalin created major plans to boost the nation's industry and Khruschev based his premiership on improving the production not just of consumer goods but also of basic foodstuffs. A general imbalance between the West and the Soviets, other than in weaponry, still persists.

LENIN, V.I.

Democracy is a state which recognises the subordination of the minority to the majority, ie: an organisation for the systematic use of force by one class against another, by one section of the population against another.

The State and Revolution

From the first part of this definition, which in context seems accurate enough, even with the aggressive implication of the word 'subordination', Lenin makes an unnerving leap to what he, anyway, sees as its logical extension – the crushing of that minority by the majority. The concept of democracy as used in the West, of 'one man one vote', has no place in Lenin's definition, although the Revolution duly brought universal suffrage to its people. The paradox of universal suffrage in Soviet Russia is that the vote counts for little if there is only one party represented at the polls, yet the one-party state seems to be a concomitant of Marxist revolutions wherever they occur.

LENNON, JOHN   (1941–1980) British rock star

Will people in the cheaper seats clap your hands? All the rest of you, if you'll just rattle your jewellery...
at the London Palladium, 1963

In October 1963 the Beatles had recorded their third consecutive Number One hit, they had made their first European Tour (five days in Sweden) and were topping the bill at the Royal Command Performance, a 'spectacular' that seemed more devoted to a near-forgotten vaudeville than a venue for 'The Fab Four'. But the Command show was still a vital showcase for stars in the ascendant and their manager Brian Epstein warned them to behave. Lennon was less than enthusiastic: 'I'll just tell 'em to rattle their fucking jewellery'. Epstein was appalled. In the event the Beatles, living right up to their lovably irreverent image, captivated all. And Lennon, introducing their last number (of only four) 'Twist and Shout', managed an expurgated version of his ad lib. The next day the *Daily Mirror* coined its own phrase in a one-word headline: 'Beatlemania!'.

LENNON, JOHN

> I see through junkies, I been through it all
> I seen religion, from Jesus to Paul
> Don't let them fool you, with dope and cocaine
> Can't do you no harm to feel your own pain.

I Found Out

By 1971 John Lennon was less than happy. The Beatles had broken up a year before, the various members of the band were involved in costly lawsuits, Lennon himself was a junkie. In an attempt to exorcise those of these demons that were susceptible to therapy, he began seeing Arthur Janov, a West Coast therapist who specialised in what he called 'primal therapy', a system which encouraged its patients to return to the experience of their birth, known as the primal, and then scream their way through the mental pain that such a return presumably engendered. Lennon duly went through his own primal, the most positive result of which was his own first solo album, filled with songs in which he relived the past and generally aired his agonies.

LENNON, JOHN

Christianity will go. It will vanish and shrink....We're more popular than Jesus now. I don't know which will go first – rock and roll or Christianity.
speaking in March 1966

Watching an Al Jolson concert forty years earlier, Zelda Fitzgerald told Ernest Hemingway that the black-face minstrel was better than Christ. Hemingway decided this confirmed her craziness but the matter stopped there. When Lennon voiced his own opinion of the Beatles and millions upon millions of teenagers seemed to prove him right, if injudicious, his statement produced a massive uproar. No-one had even commented in England, where the line was originally published, but five months later, on the eve of a new American tour, the story was splashed in the US teen magazine *Datebook*. The Bible Belt fundamentalists, presumably deprived up till then of the joys of Beatlemania, gave the term a new meaning as they organised Beatle boycotts and Beatle burnings. The tour was a disaster and the Fabs never returned.

LENNON, JOHN AND McCARTNEY, PAUL

**How does it feel to be one of the beautiful people
Now that you know who you are?**
Baby You're a Rich Man (1967)

The original 'beautiful people' sprang full grown from the media fantasy that was entitled 'Swinging London'. Children, or perhaps younger brothers and sisters, of the aristocratically Bohemian 'Chelsea Set' of the 1950s, they were breathtakingly fashionable and dearly beloved of the gossip columnists: the latest generation of upper-class British youth to go ever so slightly but rarely all that far off the rails. With the mass consumption of hallucinogens, especially LSD, everything became 'beautiful' and with it everyone who could muster a pair of crushed velvet trousers and a 'third-eye' headband.

LENNON, JOHN AND McCARTNEY, PAUL

All the lonely people, where do they all come from?
Eleanor Rigby (1966)

Eleanor Rigby, the reverse track on a double-A sided single that also offered Ringo Starr's merry *Yellow Submarine*, was released in August 1966, went straight to Number One and stayed on the charts for 13 weeks. While ageing hippie disk jockeys tend to tout Lennon's *Imagine* and McCartney's *Yesterday* as their finest work, *Eleanor Rigby* 'keeping her face in a jar by the door' has far better claim to the title. On it they managed to create an elegaic picture of human loneliness without sinking into the banalities that most purveyors of popular song would have found impossible to avoid.

LENNON, JOHN AND MCCARTNEY, PAUL

It's been a hard day's night
song and film title, 1964

A Hard Day's Night was the title of the Beatles' first film, and of the chart-topping title track from that film. Directed by Richard Lester (1932–), for whose reputation the film did wonders, the Beatles were portrayed as the epitome of their 'wacky' selves. The scenario mixed a pastiche of their real-life pop star experiences with a plethora of supposedly characteristic wisecracks, and the sort of camera and editing trickery that Lester brought to perfection in his next film *The Knack* (1966). The title, orginally Beatlemania, was changed at the last minute to one of Ringo's favourite phrases. Made on a mere £200,000 budget, it was an inevitable success.

LENNON, JOHN AND MCCARTNEY, PAUL

All You Need Is Love
song title, 1967

All You Need Is Love spent fourteen weeks high on the British charts, slap-bang in the middle of 1967, the hippy-trippy 'Summer of Love'. A vapid piece of work, only marginally superior to the myriad other hippie anthems spawned by the spread of flowers, beads, bells and hallucinogens, it crooned 'Love, love, love' on and on and on. The one neat trick was the final back-reference to the first of their 'yeah-yeah' hits *She Loves You* in 1963.

LENNON, JOHN AND MCCARTNEY, PAUL

**Will you still need me, will you still feed me
When I'm sixty-four?**
When I'm Sixty-Four (1967)

LENNON, JOHN AND MCCARTNEY, PAUL

When I'm Sixty-Four is just one the tracks from the Beatles' 1967 album *Sergeant Pepper's Lonely Hearts Club Band* which has graduated to a modern standard, still turning up regularly on the world's radio stations. The best track on the album, which with its linked songs and Peter Blake cover was one of the first of a rash of 'unified concept' rock productions, is probably the climactic *Day in the Life*, but this melodic musing on family loyalty among the senior citizenry remains a favourite.

LENNON, JOHN AND MCCARTNEY, PAUL

We all live in a yellow submarine
Yellow Submarine (1966)

Yellow Submarine with its merry lyrics and easy to sing chorus is more a children's song than a piece of rock music. Unsurprisingly it became the title of the lengthy Beatles cartoon, in which their names, songs and animated figures appeared, although the Mop-tops themselves only made a brief and embarrassing appearance as an on-screen epilogue. A replica Yellow Submarine, copied from the film, can now be found at Liverpool's Garden Centre.

LEONARD, JOHN   (1939–) American critic

The rich are different from you and me because they have more credit.
in the *New York Times*

Leonard was paraphrasing the famous, if apocryphal dialogue between F. Scott Fitzgerald and Ernest Hemingway (qv) in which the one supposedly claimed that the rich were different 'from you and me' and the other pointed out that this was simply due to their having more money. Leonard was writing in the Seventies, when plastic cards had largely replaced cash for the well off and one's worth was assessed less on the basis of one's income than on the line of credit one could secure against it.

LEONARD, JOHN

It's a crazy business, anyway, writing, locking yourself in a room and inventing conversations, no way for a grownup to behave. Then your book is published, the sun comes up, as usual, and the sun goes down, as usual, and the world is in no way altered, and it must be someone's fault.
Esquire, 1975

The plaint of the writer who can't find a publisher is known well enough, but Leonard is pointing out that once the aspirant finds someone willing to put his or her prose between hard or even soft covers the problems are only just beginning. Never mind the angst of creation, the real agonies begin when the treasured volume is finally published. And nothing happens. As Leonard says, the planets hold to their appointed course, the world remains as unsympathetic as ever and all the writer can do is wonder whose fault it is. Probably, alas, his own.

LERNER, ALAN JAY (1918–) American lyricist

An Englishman's way of speaking absolutely classifies him. The moment he talks he makes some other Englishman despise him.
My Fair Lady (1964)

My Fair Lady, a Lerner and Loewe musical of 1957 transmuted to the screen with direction from George Cukor and design by Cecil Beaton, was based on George Bernard Shaw's *Pygmalion* (1913), one of Shaw's most popular plays, which describes the transformation of a Cockney flower girl into a surrogate duchess by a dedicated phonetician. The plot revolves around Professor Henry Higgins' attempts to prove, as this couplet points out, that the English class system and the variety of English accents are inextricably entwined. Higgins duly creates a new Eliza but she rebels against his tyranny and the play ends with the pair acknowledging each other's role.

LERNER, MAX (1902–) American social commentator

Human history, if you read it right, is the record of the attempts to tame father
The Unfinished Country (1959)

Lerner was born in Russia but emigrated to America, where he began his career as an editor of the Encyclopedia of Social Sciences. As a self-professed 'neo-Marxian liberal' he has written essays on a variety of subjects. Lerner has taught at several top American universities and for many years wrote a regular column for the *New York Post*. *The Unfinished Country* is a collection of his *Post* columns. If one reads Lerner's comment right, it is to be feared that if 'father' represents the cruel, aggressive and acquisitive side of humanity, as seen in dicatorship, self-promoting capitalism and similar aspects of life, we still have a very long way to go to curb him.

LESTER, JULIUS   (1939–) American radical writer

Black people have never rioted. A riot is what white people think blacks are involved in when they burn stores.
Look Out Whitey! (1968)

Lester's book, subtitled 'Black Power's Gonna Get Your Mama', is an uncompromising statement of black ambitions, notably the destruction of white America's programme for the continued repression of its black population. Lester's premise is that all white people, however liberal and well-meaning, have one essential thing wrong: their presumption that in choosing to side with the black man they know, from their unspoken assumption of patronising white superiority, what is best for him. His nicely sardonic remark on the ghetto uprisings of the mid-Sixties underlines his contention that white people just don't know what's going on.

LESTOCQ, HUMPHREY   British comedian

Oh, I say, I rather care for that
on *Merry Go Round*, BBC radio 1940s

Merry Go Round was a BBC radio show devised as a means of capitalising on those stars who, for the duration of World War II, were in uniform. It survived into the early post-war period, before breaking down into such hit shows as *Much Binding in the Marsh*. Among the characters involved in *Merry Go Round* was 'Flying Officer Kite', played by Humphrey Lestocq. Kite, with his braying laugh and catchphrase 'Oh I say, I rather care for that', was drawn from the many real-life ex-pilots who could be found haunting the nation's saloon bars, talking of 'wizard prangs' and wondering what peacetime life would offer.

LEVANT, OSCAR   (1906–72) American pianist and wit

Strip the phoney tinsel off Hollywood and you'll find the real tinsel underneath
Memoirs of an Amnesiac (1965)

Levant's acerbic denunciation of all and everything around him was equalled only by the loathing with which he regarded himself. A multi-talented individual, but a professional curmudgeon, he managed systematically to wreck every enterprise in which he was involved, be it films, for which he wrote scores and acted, or his own TV show. Just as he seemed to have arrived at success, Levant would upset his own apple cart and vanish, seeking new enemies and new opportunities of self-destruction. Among his recorded comments are:

Marriage is a triumph of habit over hate.

I'm a controversial figure – my friends either dislike me or hate me.

I played an unsympathetic part – myself.

LEVERSON, ADA (1865–1936) British novelist

As a rule the person found out in a betrayal of love holds, all the same, the superior position of the two. It is the betrayed one who is humiliated.
Love's Shadow (1908)

Leverson, born Ada Beddington, compensated for the neglect of her rich, gambler husband Ernest, by establishing friendships with a number of prominent writers, notably Beerbohm, the Sitwells, George Moore and Wilde, who nicknamed her The Sphinx. All six of her novels, including this one, with its mordant comment on adultery, pointing out that the betrayer may feel guilty but it is the betrayed who has been traduced, were set in smart London society. Leverson also contributed to *Punch*, wrote a column under the pseudonym 'Elaine' in a Sunday paper, and wrote for the *Yellow Book* and the *Criterion*.

LEVIN, BERNARD (1928–) British journalist

What has happened to architecture since the second world war that the only passers-by who can contemplate it without pain are those equipped with a white stick and a dog?
in *The Times*, 1983

Bernard Levin's denunciation of the excesses of modern architecture referred directly to property developer Peter Palumbo's abortive attempt to have built what would have been the last office tower designed by the late architect Le Corbusier. His derision extended to many of the buildings built in London since 1945 and he reflects what is admitted by many architects as a commonly found British prejudice. While some claim this is due to the innate national conservatism which would prefer some piece of Victorian mediocrity, more than likely an eyesore when it was erected, to some piece of genuinely innovative construction, others appreciate that many recent buildings are indeed so unattractive that if nothing else the weathering of their predecessors makes them more palatable.

LEVIN, BERNARD

Ask a man which way he is going to vote, and he will probably tell you. Ask him, however, why, and vagueness is all.
in the *Daily Mail*, 1964

Levin, then the enfant terrible of the *Daily Mail* and a regular contributor to BBC-TV's satire show *That was The Week That Was*, here pinpoints the dichotomy between knowing how one will vote and exactly why one does so. The general loathing of party political broadcasts and the reluctance to peruse the party manifestos makes it clear that voters are less and less swayed by the minutiae of party platforms. A large number of people vote for the party their parents preferred, backed up by the fact that that party may be presumed to stand for their own interests too. Even more depend on personalities, however much individual politicians may deplore the fact. As the election of President Reagan has shown, competence is irrelevant, what matters is that a leader must appear to lead.

LEVIN, BERNARD

Whom the mad would destroy they first make Gods.
on Chairman Mao, 1967

In his translation of Sophocles' *Antigone* (450BC) the seventeenth century writer James Dupport (1606–79) coined the Latin phrase 'Quem Juppiter vult perdere dementat prius', which has been generally translated as 'Those whom the Gods would destroy, they first drive mad'. Levin chose to reverse the popular phrase in a piece on China's Chairman Mao, a near deity thanks to his 'cult of personality', and his deliberate encouragement of the excesses of the Cultural Revolution, a social experiment seen even by his own countrymen as quite insane. Aimed at consolidating the 1949 revolution and eliminating 'revisionists', it decimated China's economy, reversed such progress as the nation had made and brutalised millions of people, most especially those who actually possessed genuine talent or ability.

LEVINE, JOSEPH E.   (1905–) American film producer

You can fool all the people all of the time if the advertising is right and the budget is big enough.
quoted in L. Halliwell's *Filmgoer's Companion* 1984, 8th edn.)

As a distributor and producer of both cheap exploitation films and a number of European films that appealed only to the minority who patronised the art houses, Levine presumably drew his dictum from experience. Like everyone else who has come forward with similar phrases, Levine was rephrasing Abraham Lincoln's remark in 1862 'You can fool some of the people all of the time, and all of the people some of the time, but you cannot fool all of the people all of the time.'

LEWIS, ROBERT   American pilot

My God, what have we done?
after bombing Hiroshima, August 6, 1945

Lewis was co-pilot, with Paul Tibbets Jr. of the B-29 aircraft Enola Gay, named for Tibbetts' mother, which at precisely 8.15 on the morning of August 6, 1945 dropped a three metre long, 4,000 kilogram weight atomic bomb, nicknamed Little Boy, on the Japanese city of Hiroshima. The bomb, inscribed with a variety of graffiti ridiculing the Japanese emperor Hirohito, exploded in 510 metres above the city and delivered the equivalent explosive yield of 12,000 tons of TNT. The bomb killed 100,000 people, wounded many more and irradiated thousands of survivors. At least 100,000 more victims died of thermal burns and radiation sickness. Four square miles of ground were levelled. As the sky turned from blue to dark yellow and the mushroom cloud rose 50,000 feet into the air, Lewis asked his question.

LEWIS, C.S.   (1898–1963) British scholar, critic and novelist

The future is something which everyone reaches at the rate of sixty minutes an hour, whatever he does, whoever he is.
The Screwtape Letters (1942)

Lewis was a fellow of Magdalen College, Oxford and a specialist in sixteenth century English literature. Outside Oxford he was better known for a number of works of popular theology, of which this is one. A friend of J.R.R. Tolkien (1892–1973), creator of the Hobbits and Middle Earth, he too produced his fantasy kingdom, created in his seven-book saga of Narnia, beginning with *The Lion, The Witch and The Wardrobe* (1950). Although these books combine the necessary excitement and fantasy of such volumes, the adult, if not the child reader, will soon notice the pervasive religious imagery with which they are filled. *The Screwtape Letters* takes the form of an older devil training his junior in the art of tempting a soul. The devil's plans ultimately fail.

LEWIS, JERRY (1926–) American comedian

Comedy is a man in trouble.
in *Newsweek*, 1972

Lewis, the American answer to Britain's pawky Norman Wisdom, combines slapstick and sentimentality to create a character endearing to some and repellent to just as many. As his remark implies, his own humour derives from the problems of everyday people, suitably magnified for comic effect. For several years he teamed with Dean Martin and made a number of popular films. His subsequent solo career became increasingly self-indulgent, although his appearance in *The King of Comedy* (1983) as a Johnny Carson-like chat show host impressed many who had not previously been fans.

LEWIS, PERCY WYNDHAM (1882–1957) British art critic and writer

It is to what I have called the Apes of God that I am drawing your attention – those preposterous mountebanks who alternately imitate and mock at and traduce those figures they at once admire and hate.
The Apes of God (1930)

Born in America Lewis received an English education and always lived in Britain. Drawn to modernism, but reacting against futurism, he joined Ezra Pound in editing *Blast: Review of the Great English Vortex* (1914–15), thus establishing himself as a leader of the Vorticist movement. Lewis worked as a war artist during World War I but deprived of a permanent studio he turned to writing. All his books are polemics, whether philosophical, literary-critical or satirical. Lewis' work proved inaccessible to most readers and his sympathies with British fascism and open admiration of Hitler made him few friends. His savaging of such influential literary contemporaries as the Bloomsbury Group hardly helped. In the end he characterised himself as the Enemy, a challenging and prophetic social critic whose blasts against the 20th century foresaw many of the social developments of the Sixties and beyond.

LEWIS, ROSA (1867–1952) British cook and hotelier

Some people's food always tastes better than others', even if they are cooking the same dish at the same dinner. Now I will tell you why – because one person has much more life in them – more fire, more vitality, more guts – than others. A person without these things can never make food taste right, no matter what

materials you give them, it is no use. Turn in the whole cow full of cream instead of milk and all the fresh butter and ingredients in the world, and still that cooking will taste dull and flabby –just because they have nothing in themselves to give. You have to throw feeling into your cooking.

quoted in *The Queen of Cooks – and some Kings* by Mary Lawton (1925)

Rosa Lewis began life in service but graduated from cleaning to cooking and went on to make her Cavendish Hotel in Jermyn Street, London, one of the most unique establishments of its kind and its era. In the Cavendish 'the Duchess of Jermyn Street' played hostess to half the impecunious aristocratic young men of the country, charging their 'wine' (invariably champagne) to the bills of richer visitors, indulging their excesses and playing the mother confessor to their problems. Her best known portrait appears in Evelyn Waugh's *Vile Bodies* (1930) where she appears as Lottie Crump, patroness of Shepheard's Hotel. Waugh, and most other writers, were barred from the Cavendish after Lewis read the book.

Lewis, Rosa

I knew him before he was born.

quoted in *The Duchess of Jermyn Street* by Daphne Fielding (1964)

Rosa Lewis' description of a wide variety of smart young men became almost a catchphrase. The implication, of course, was either that the child in question had actually been conceived on the premises, or at least the father, with or without a pregnant wife, had been a regular visitor.

Lewis, Sinclair (1888–1951) American novelist

...a thing called Ethics, whose nature was confusing but if you had it you were a High-Class Realtor and if you hadn't you were a shyster, a piker and a fly-by-night. These virtues awakened Confidence and enabled you to handle Bigger Propositions. But they didn't imply that you were to be impractical and refuse to take twice the value of a house if a buyer was such an idiot that he didn't force you down on the asking price.

Babbitt (1922)

In *Main Street* (1920) and *Babbitt* (1922) Lewis revealed himself as the foremost satirist of America's mid-West, mocking its pretensions, its hypocrisies and the smug self-satisfaction of its small-town boosterism where every businessman struggled eternally between parading his 'Ethics' and making sure no-one 'put anything over' on him. After seeing off the businessmen, Lewis gave the same ironic treatment to the worlds of medicine, in *Arrowsmith* (1925) and evangelical preaching, in *Elmer Gantry* (1927). In 1930 he became the first American to receive the Nobel Prize for Literature.

LEWIS, SINCLAIR

In other countries, art and literature are left to a lot of shabby bums living in attics and feeding on booze and spaghetti, but in America the successful writer or picture-painter is indistinguishable from any other decent businessman.
Babbitt (1922)

Realtor George F. Babbitt knows what's what. And never more so than when in his role as keynote speaker at the Annual Dinner of the Zenith Real Estate Board. As written by Lewis, Babbitt's speech is a masterpiece of absurdity, a monster of small-town boosterism, touting 'our kind of folks!' and offering 'the specifications of the Standardized American Citizen...the new generation of Americans: fellows with hair on their chests and smiles in their eyes and adding-machines in their offices...the Real he-Man, the fellow with Zip and bang'. And, as he puts it above, in Zenith, and in America (except perhaps New York which is insufficiently supplied with 'our kind of folks') even the artists understand what really makes the world go round.

LEY, ROBERT (1890–1945) Nazi leader

Strength through joy. (Kraft durch freude)
slogan

Ley was one of the earliest Nazis, a chemist by profession, an habitual drunkard by choice and the Gauleiter of Cologne when the Party took power. Responsible for the trade unions he established the German Labour Front, an organisation which, while promising the workers its support, effectively emasculated their independence and, through its stringent controls, reduced many to near-poverty. Realising that it was necessary to 'divert the attention of the masses from material to moral values', and that circuses were needed to take their minds off the lack of bread, Ley created the 'Strength Through Joy' movement, designed to control such leisure as the masses enjoyed through all-embracing recreational programmes. The masses suffered the new control but many people's attitude was best summed up in a verse guying the Land Jahr, the German equivalent of the land girls: 'In the fields and on the heath / I lose Strength through Joy'.

LIBERACE (1919–1987) (Wladziu Valentino Liberace) American pianist

What you said hurt me very much. I cried all the way to the bank.
rebutting adverse criticisms, 1954

More furs than a zoo, more jewels than Hatton Garden, Liberace played his candelabra-bedecked, mirrored piano and the world's matrons swooned. More orthodox music fans were less impressed, as were such critics who deigned to visit Liberace's star-studded solo performances. After one such critic delivered a stinging attack on the pianist's programme of rearranged light classics he replied with this telegram. Years later, as gloriously awful as ever, and even richer, he told an audience 'You know that bank I used to cry all the way to? I bought it'. As he remarked to *The Times* in 1981 'Too much of a good thing is simply wonderful'.

LIDDY, G. GORDON (1930–) American secret serviceman

It was just basic politics
quoted in *All the President's Men* by Bob Woodward and Carl Berstein (1974)

Aside from the essentially dull but nonetheless actively corrupt bureaucrats and lawyers whose exploits led to the Watergate scandal of 1973–74, there were involved a number of truly bizarre figures. One was the CIA-man turned spy novelist, Howard Hunt; the other was G. Gordon Liddy, Financial Counsel to the Committee to Re-Elect the President (CREEP). Liddy, another secret serviceman, epitomised the hard-nosed, gung-ho agent. As he explains in his autobiography, *'Will'* (1976), being tough is what life's all about. His favourite party trick was to hold his hand above a candle, not flinching as his skin seared, and explaining that the art was 'not minding'. For a man who admits that he married not for love, but to find a mate suitable for bearing ideologically and physically perfect human specimens, his concept of Watergate as 'just basic politics' comes as no surprise at all.

LIE, TRYGVE (1896–1968) Swedish diplomat

A real diplomat is one who can cut his neighbour's throat without having his neighbour notice it.
In *The Cause of Peace* (1954)

Lie, a Norwegian lawyer who became a Labour member of his country's parliament, was elected the first Secretary General of the United Nations Organisation in 1946. He resigned in 1952, giving way to Dag Hammarskjold, and returned to Norwegian politics, serving in a number of further posts in the 1960s. Given his somewhat anodyne reputation, this definition of the lethally charming duplicity that epitomises the skilful diplomat is surprisingly bloodthirsty.

LIEBLING, A.J.   (1904–63) American journalist

People everywhere confuse what they read in newspapers with news.
in the *New Yorker*, 1956

Abbott Joseph Liebling left the *New York Times* for the *New Yorker*, worked as its Paris correspondent during World War II, and then returned to take up an influential role as a commentator on all aspects of New York, and particularly on events in the newspaper world. He also wrote authoritatively on food. As an expert on the press he had no illusions about its content and was duly cynical of what it offered the public. The question he fails to answer in this condemnation of news reporting is that if what one reads in the press isn't news, where is one going to find it?

LIN PIAO   (1908–1971) Chinese politician

The best weapon is not the aircraft, heavy artillery, tanks or the atom bomb, it is Mao Tse-Tung thought; the greatest fighting force is the man armed with Mao Tse-tung thought.
speech to Chinese army heralding the Cultural Revolution, 1965

Defense Minister Lin Piao was one of the greatest proselytizers of the alleged perfection of Chairman Mao Tse-tung. It was this hero-worship that created the massively circulated *Little Red Book of Mao's Thoughts* that was brandished not merely in China but by self-proclaimed revolutionaries all round the world. And Lin informed the Ninth Party Congress in 1969, at which he was named Mao's constitutional successor, 'whoever opposes Chairman Mao Tse-tung's Thought, at any time or under any circumstances, will be condemned and punished...' Even this vehemence failed to save Lin from the internal power struggles that were reflected in the larger-scale convolutions of the Cultural Revolution. By 1971 he had fallen from grace, and had been branded as a 'counter-revolutionary renegade'. He died on September 12, 1971, supposedly killed in an air crash in Mongolia.

LIPPMANN, WALTER (1889–1974) American political commentator

We must remember that in time of war what is said on the enemy's side of the front is always propaganda and what is said on our side of the front is truth and righteousness, the cause of humanity and a crusade for peace. Is it necessary for us at the height of our power to stoop to such self-deceiving nonsense?
speaking in 1966

Lippmann's sixty-year long journalistic career parallelled almost exactly the emergence of his country through 'the American century' from the fringes of the Western alliance to superpower status. Lippmann's influence was felt as early as 1919, when his columns in the *New Republic*, a magazine that he co-founded, were said to have provided President Wilson with the basis for his 14 Points. From 1921–31 Lippmann wrote for the reformist World, then shifted his column to the New York Herald Tribune, where it appeared for many years under the heading 'Today and Tomorrow'. In columns and books Lippmann attempted to dissect the problems of democratic government in a mass society which was graduating into a world power.

LIPPMANN, WALTER

Unless the reformer can invent something which substitutes attractive virtues for attractive vices, he will fail.
A Preface to Politics (1914)

LIPPMANN, WALTER

Successful democratic politicians are insecure and intimidated men. They advance politically only as they placate, appease, bribe, seduce, bamboozle or otherwise manage to manipulate the demanding and threatening elements in their constituencies.
The Public Philosophy (1955)

LITTLE CAESAR

You can dish it out, but you've got so you can't take it no more.
screenplay by Francis Faragoh (1930)

In this adaptation of writer W.R. Burnett's novel of Twenties gangland, loosely modelled on the rise, if not the fall, of Chicago's Al Capone, Edward G. Robinson (1893–1973) played Rico, who mixed Machiavelli with machine guns in his rise to the top of the heap. While Rico was unlikely to have been the first hard-boiled villain to expose his enemy's weakness in this telling phrase, which in the film usually serves as signal for betrayal, murder or both, the success of *Little Caesar*, one of the top-grossing films of 1930, ensured that it gained widespread currency.

LITVINOV, MAXIM (1876–1951) Russian politician

Peace is indivisible.
speech on February 22, 1920

Litvinov was one of the first Bolsheviks, allied with his friend Lenin early in the century and known by the nickname of 'Papasha'. Lenin described him as 'consistent and firm. But these are the qualities of good speculators and gamblers. They are the virtues of a clever and adroit Jew' and declared that he had no future as a man of action. With the revolution achieved, Litvinov fulfilled Lenin's expectations by becoming the head of Soviet Russia's diplomatic corps, a post he held until dismissed by Stalin in 1939 after the Nazi-Soviet pact with Hitler made it impossible for a Jew to sustain the job.

LLOYD, FRANK American art dealer

If it sells, it's art.
quoted in *The Legacy of Mark Rothko*, by Lee Seldes, 1978

Definitions of art abound: some high flown, some perceptive, some witty and some well off beam. Few, however, come within the scope of art dealer Frank Lloyd's no-frills statement, preferring to take their references from an era when art was art and money was money and if the twain did meet, then it was probably in a saleroom long after the artist was safely dead. Modern art, particularly in the ephemeral manifestations that fill in bewilderingly fast succession the galleries of New York's SoHo and 57th Street, works on somewhat different criteria. Art, as Lloyd points out, is no longer for art's sake, but for profit's.

LLOYD GEORGE, DAVID (1863–1945) British prime minister

What is our task? To make Britain a fit country for heroes to live in.
speech on November 24 1918

Lloyd George had been leading the wartime coalition government since he had inspired the conspiracy which drove his predecessor Asquith from office in 1916. With the war won, he called a snap election for November 1918, which became known as the 'khaki election' from the preponderance of voters still in uniform. Speaking in Wolverhampton he asked and answered his own rhetorical question, coining a phrase that became increasingly tarnished as time passed and it became obvious that whatever might happen to Britain, Lloyd George's pious promise was not part of it.

LLOYD GEORGE, DAVID

He has sat so long upon the fence that the iron has entered into his soul.
on Sir John Simon

Sir John Simon's decision to cross the floor of the House and begin voting with the Tories elicited from Lloyd George one of his most scathing speeches, the body of which went as follows: 'My orthodoxy to Liberalism has been questioned but the right honourable gentleman has been the milk of the gospel to Liberalism and it is as if there are two types of men in this world, those who drink and those who do not, and it is as if the right honourable gentleman has been a total abstainer all his life and has suddenly taken to drink and there he is; he swayed from side to side and landed amidst the Tory drunkards.' Then he decried Simon's fence-sitting and ended his speech by declaring that in many similar crossings of the House never has a... 'right honourable gentleman...left behind him such a slimy trail'.

LLOYD GEORGE, DAVID

It is easy to settle the world upon a soap box.
quoted in L. Harris, *The Fine Art of Political Wit* (1965)

Lloyd George's reputation lies today more in the almost mythical standard of his oratory than in much recollection of his political attainments, and whether he was campaigning or speaking in the House of Commons, his own use of 'the soap box' was unrivalled. Nonetheless as a member of government from 1905 and prime minister from 1916–22, Lloyd George was also capable of more practical measures. His comment was aimed at those who preferred words to action, whereas he, as one of the 'Big Three' whose deliberations in 1919 culminated in the Treaty of Versailles, genuinely had the opportunity, albeit squandered, actually to settle the world.

LLOYD GEORGE, DAVID

How these dukes harass us. They're as expensive to keep up as a dreadnought and not half so useful.
quoted in L. Harris, *The Fine Art of Political Wit* (1965)

Lloyd George's background was hardly that of the landed gentry whose families still dominated the House of Commons when he was first elected an MP, for Caernarvon, in 1890. Born in Manchester, he had been brought up in North Wales and began his adult life articled to a solicitor in Portmadoc. Although he sobered with age, he began his political career as a radical, delivering fiery speeches extolling Welsh nationalism and Welsh nonconformity. His distaste for hereditary privilege never faltered, and many of his speeches attacked those he collectivised as 'the dukes'. His budget of 1909–10, in which he planned to increase income tax and establish a new tax of 20% on the unearned increment gained by owning land, particularly appalled the aristocracy.

Lloyd George, David

Mr. Balfour's poodle

speech on the House of Lords, June 26, 1907

Lloyd George had rarely much time for the House of Lords, which he had characterised as the 'lumber room of musty prejudice' and 'an asylum of hereditary delusions'. Speaking as chancellor of the exchequer in Asquith's Liberal administration, Lloyd George was considering the situation whereby the Tories, led by Arthur Balfour, were using their majority in the Lords to block the progress of important Liberal legislation. Referring to the alleged role of the hereditary peers as the 'watchdog' of the British constitution, Lloyd George said 'This is the loyal and trusty mastiff which is to watch over our interests, but which runs away at the first snarl of the trade unions. A mastiff? It is the right honourable gentleman's poodle. It fetches and carries for him. It barks for him. It bites anybody that he sets it on to'.

Loan, Nguyen   S. Vietnamese police chief

Buddha will understand.

after killing a Vietcong prisoner, 1968

The North Vietnamese offensive that was launched during Tet (the Vietnamese New Year) 1968 devastated the Americans and their South Vietnamese allies. Hindsight has proved that Tet was almost North Vietnam's last throw, but in the event the offensive substantially undermined US confidence. During the fighting in Saigon photographer Eddie Adams was taking a routine set of shots of a bound Vietcong prisoner and his police escort. Then 'all of a sudden, out of nowhere, comes General Loan, the national police chief. I was about five feet away from him, and I see him reach for his pistol. I thought he was going to threaten the prisoner. So as quick as he brought his pistol up I took a picture.' Loan did not threaten, he simply shot the man through the head and Adams' picture captured the bullet before it had passed through the prisoner's skull. The image shocked the world and won him an award. The prisoner, who had supposedly killed one of Loan's friends and knifed his wife and six children, died instantly. Loan, who was branded as a killer by the world's liberals, simply shrugged their criticism off.

LOBEL, ARNOLD   (1933–) American illustrator and writer

Wishes, on their way to coming true, will not be rushed.
Fables (1980)

Arnold Lobel is one of America's most popular illustrators of children's books, and has written a number of his own, including the 'Frog and Toad' books, aimed at younger readers. *Fables* appeared in 1980, with his illustrations. Based on Aesop's original conception, in which the the deeds of anthropomorphic animals stand as metaphors for the lives of their human cousins, Lobel produced a number of new characters and drew his moral conclusions from their activities.

LOBEL, ARNOLD

Too much of anything often leaves one with a feeling of regret.
Fables (1980)

LOBEL, ARNOLD

Without doubt, there is such a thing as too much order.
Fables (1980)

LOCKRIDGE, ROSS   (1914–1948) American writer

We...make the modern error of dignifying the Individual. We do everything we can to butter him up. We give him a name, assure him that he has certain inalienable rights, educate him, let him pass on his name to his brats and when he dies we give him a special hole in the ground.... But after all, he's only a seed, a bloom and a withering stalk among pressing billions. Your Individual is a pretty disgusting, vain, lewd little bastard....By God, he has only one right guaranteed to him in Nature, and that is the right to die and stink to Heaven.
Raintree Country (1948)

Lockridge seemed destined for success. Academically distinguished, he began teaching in 1944 but his real obsession was with his novel, a 600,000 word epic devoted to life in one small town on a single day, July 4, 1892. Lockridge was convinced that his book was a masterpiece and publishers Houghton Mifflin offered him a $3500 advance. They also submitted the novel to an MGM competition, which offered $25,000 to the publisher and $150,000 to the author of the winning book, which would then be made into a movie. Lockridge duly won and Houghton Mifflin demanded 15% of his prize money, citing his contract's small print. The book finally appeared on January 5, 1948. After initially glowing reviews, Lockridge had to face an intemperate piece of religious bigotry in the form of an attack by a Jesuit priest. Other writers might have laughed, Lockridge, already depressed by his publishers' intransigence, was deeply wounded. On March 5, 1948 he killed himself. The next morning his novel appeared as Number One on the New York *Herald Tribune's* best-seller list.

LODGE, DAVID   (1935–) British writer

Literature is mostly about sex and not much about having children and life is the other way round.
The British Museum is Falling Down (1965)

In this, David Lodge's first novel, Adam Appleby is struggling with the twin problems of his thesis, for which he reads assiduously in the British Museum, and with his wife's fecundity, which as a practising Catholic he is unable to restrict other than by the dubious methods of 'Vatican roulette'. His comment is made to two of his fellow-readers, Pond and Camel, both teachers of English to foreign students, as they take time off in the pub across the road. When Pond suggests, after a conversation on the precise importance of Karl Marx's old seat, that Appleby is cracking up, Camel suggests that he's suffering from 'a special form of scholarly neurosis. He's no longer able to distinguish between life and literature'. 'Oh yes I can,' says Adam and replies as quoted.

LODGE, DAVID

Four times under our educational system the human pack is shuffled and cut – at eleven-plus, at sixteen-plus, eighteen-plus and twenty-plus – and happy is he who comes top of the deck on each occasion, but especially the last. This is called Finals, the very name of which implies that nothing of importance can

happen after it. The British post-graduate student is a lonely forlorn soul...for whom nothing has been real since the big push.
Changing Places (1975)

Changing Places is the first of Lodge's pair of Anglo-American campus novels (the second is *Small World*, 1984). The plot revolves around the exchange between two academics, the British Philip Swallow, of Rummidge University, steeped in British traditions, and the feisty American from Euphoric State, up to his eyes in trendy involvement, Morris Zapp. As the two men's planes pass each other 'high, high above the North Pole', Lodge gives a rundown of both characters, and contrasts, as here, the difference between the system that created Swallow and that which dealt out Zapp.

LOIS, GEORGE   (1931–) American advertising executive

The business world worships mediocrity. Officially we revere free enterprise, initiative and individuality. Unofficially we fear it.
The Art of Advertising (1977)

Lois is one of American advertising's great copywriters, the man who coined 'If you've got it, flaunt it' for Braniff Airways, and sold the Japanese as 'those wonderful folks who brought you Pearl Harbor'. As one of the first people to break away from the huge agencies which had achieved a stranglehold on the business and set up the small, specialised operations that became known as 'hot shops', Lois has little time for the constraints of big, unwieldy organisations. They may back enterprise and initiative as public policy, but prefer in fact to make themselves into static monoliths in which bureaucracy rules and promotion relates directly to one's approximation to the ideal 'organization man'.

LOMBARDI, VINCE   (1913–70) American football coach

Winning isn't everything, it's the only thing.
catchphrase

Lombardi came to coach the Green Bay Packers pro football team in 1959, when they were at the bottom of their section of the National Football League. After a few months of Lombardi's training, liberally spiced with inspirational lines like this, repeated so regularly that it became something of a catchphrase, the Packers started moving up the table. During Lombardi's tenure the team picked up the best winning record in the NFL although in more recent years Wisconsin's favourite footballers have fallen behind once more.

LONE RANGER, THE

Hi Ho, Silver!
American radio, then TV, series 1940s–50s

The Lone Ranger, the 'masked rider of the plains', was the greatest of those squeaky-clean Western heroes who stalked the airwaves undaunted but who would certainly have been strung up to the nearest tree had they ventured into the real 'Wild West' of the late 19th century. He wore a mask (which was never shed, save for one prequel in which he revealed his tragic past), used silver bullets when talking wasn't enough, was accompanied by his Indian friend Tonto who called him 'Kemo sabay' which may or may not have meant something, and, most important of all, rode his great white horse Silver. As the William Tell overture crashed out to start and finish the show, The Lone Ranger would urge on his horse with a cry of 'Hi ho, Silver...awaaayyy!!'. Tonto had a horse as well, but all he could manage in the way of encouragement was 'Gettum up, Scout'. Clayton Moore played the Ranger, Jay Silverheels was Tonto.

LONG, HUEY P. (1893–1935) American politician

In a political fight, when you've got nothing in favour of your side, start a row in the opposition camp.
American politician

Huey Long was a unique figure, even by the standards of American politics. He blended a genuine desire to alleviate the lot of the poor whites from whom he had sprung with a racketeering hucksterism that saw nothing wrong in wholesale corruption. With a legislature packed with frightened yes-men, the rich soaked for all he could extract, and the poor indulged as never before, Long made populism a going concern. Lousiana soon seemed too small for his ambitions. In 1932 he went to Washington as the state's senator and began eyeing up the White House, even writing a book *My First Days in the White House* (1935). Long was assassinated, like some latter-day megalomaniac Roman emperor, amid the marble halls of the Louisiana capitol.

Long, Huey P.

I looked around at the little fishes present and said 'I'm the Kingfish'.

H.G. Wells called him 'A Winston Churchill who has never been at Harrow', Rebecca West talked about 'Brer Fox', a New Orleans paper preferred 'The Prince of Piffle' and everyone else opted for 'demagogue', but Huey Long called himself 'The Kingfish'. Long was the populist orator come to power, swimming gaily through the murky waters of Louisiana politics and either suborning or simply gobbling up all the other fishy denizens he encountered. His most successful programme rejoiced in the title Share-the-Wealth, based on Long's belief that 10% of Americans owned 70% of the nation's assets. He coined his campaign slogan 'Everyman a King but no man wears a crown' to accompany the programme.

Longworth, Alice Roosevelt   (1884–1980) American wit and socialite

If you haven't anything nice to say about anyone, come and sit by me.
line embroidered on a favourite cushion

Alice Roosevelt was the daughter of President Theodore Roosevelt (1858–1919). Having no need to work she devoted her life to composing caustic comments about the politicians who she inevitably met. Her remarks were not always original, she attributed that on Coolidge to her dentist, who had had it from the last patient in the chair, and that on Dewey to another socialite Grace Hodgson Flandrau. Either way they were unvariably savage. Among other remarks, she was less than enamoured of her cousin Franklin Delano Roosevelt, whom she called 'one third sap and two thirds Eleanor' (his wife).

Longworth, Alice Roosevelt

Dewey looks like the bridgeroom on the wedding cake
on Thomas Dewey

She added to this in 1948, when Dewey was attempting a comeback 'You can't make a soufflé rise twice', and compounded it further 'You have to know Dewey really well to dislike him thoroughly'.

LOOS, ANITA (1893–1981) American novelist and screenwriter

A leader of public thought in Hollywood wouldn't have sufficient mental acumen anywhere else to hold down a place in the bread line.

Like many of the writers who went to Hollywood to make the kind of money their journalistic careers could never have produced, diminutive Anita Loos had little time for the goose that laid her particular share of the golden eggs. Between the ex-furriers turned movie moguls, mixing 'old country' schmaltz with the morals of a thieves' kitchen, the beefcake hunks and prom queens who made up the stars, Tinseltown certainly offered little in the way of mental challenge. Such public thought that did exist turned on money, muscles, makeup or a combination of the three. Only the visiting writers might have upped the intellectual level, but they were too busy swapping wisecracks and counting out their share of the loot to bother very much.

LOOS, ANITA

Kissing your hand may make you feel very good, but a diamond and sapphire bracelet lasts for ever.
Gentlemen Prefer Blondes (1925)

Anita Loos' most famous book, subtitled 'the Illuminating Diary of a Professional Lady', is the story of two jazz age cuties, notably of one Lorelei Lee, a not so dumb ingenue beneath whose contrivedly foolish showgirl exterior beats a heart wired straight to the platinum wristwatches she collects, among sundry similar gewgaws, from her legions of fashionable admirers. 'A girl like I', as Lorelei typifies herself, can do remarkably well playing the dumb blonde, since this particular hair colouring seems, as Loos' title pointed out, to set the masculine mind stirring. British playwright Joe Orton used Loos' dictum: in his play *Loot* he wrote 'God is a gentleman. He prefers blondes.'

LORANT, STEFAN (1901–) Hungarian photo-journalist

The camera should be like the notebook of a trained reporter, to record events as they happen, without trying to stop them to make a picture.
quoted in *Pictures on a Page*, by Harold Evans 1978

Lorant was the editor of Britain's answer to Life magazine, Picture Post. A refugee from Hungary, where he had been a successful journalist, Lorant had an instinctive grasp of the importance of pictures to a story. *Picture Post* flourished with

Lorant's unerring eye making sure that his photographers provided consistently striking pictures. He left for America in 1940 and has remained there, working mainly on picture books.

LORENZ, KONRAD (1903–) Austrian ethologist

It is a good morning exercise for a research scientist to discard a pet hypothesis every day before breakfast. It keeps him young.
On Aggression (1966)

Lorenz began his career as a specialist on comparative studies of animal behaviour, and as director since 1961 of the Max Planck Institute of Behavioural Psychology he has continued to draw conclusions about the activities of the human species on the basis of his observations of animal ones. His own great discoveries have been those of the 'imprint' mechanism, which orientates an animal towards the beings with which it has spent critical parts of its youth, irrespective of its own species, and the 'releaser' mechanism which unlocks innate perceptional patterns, which are common to members of the same species.

LOSEY, JOSEPH (1909–) American film director

Film is a dog: the head is commerce, the tail is art. And only rarely does the tail wag the dog.

Losey left America, where he was developing his Hollywood career, after an informer had turned his name over to the anti-Communist House UnAmerican Activities Committee. He settled in England where he made a number of successful pictures. Although he has suffered criticism for setting art above more immediate filmic effects, Losey is right as far as the majority of successful films are concerned. Indeed, the craven alliance of most Hollywood producers with the right-wingers of HUAC was based not on any real ideological grounds, but on the simple fear that the only headlines Hollywood required were positive, money-making ones, and not the negative feedback from the Committee's probing.

LOVE STORY

Love means never having to say you're sorry.
script by Erich Segal, 1970

Top of the box-office weepies for 1970 was undoubtedly *Love Story*, a three-hankie confection which starred Ryan O'Neal and Ali McGraw in a preppies' downgrade of *La Dame aux Camélias*. Adapted by Harvard academic Erich Segal from his best-selling book, it concerned McGraw's lingering death and O'Neal's mooning around. A typical O'Neal soliloquy, taken from the beginning of the film, asks 'What can you say about a 25-year-old girl who died? That she was beautiful? And brilliant? That she loved Mozart and Bach? And the Beatles? And me?' The film's most famous line occurs twice. Once when McGraw tells it to O'Neal, who has just apologised for something, and secondly as the movie's curtain line when O'Neal offers it to McGraw's father, played by Ray Milland. Barbra Streisand uses the same line to O'Neal at the end of Peter Bogdanovich's farce, *What's Up Doc?* (1972). O'Neal replies 'That's the dumbest thing I ever heard.' The last recorded public use was by president Gerald Ford, campaigning in 1976, who said 'Trust is not having to guess what a candidate means'.

LOWELL, ROBERT (1917–77) American poet

If we can see the light at the end of the tunnel
It's the light of the oncoming train
Day by Day (1977)

Lowell's college friendships with the pioneers of the New Criticism, Randall Jarrell and John Crowe Ransom, determined the style of his poetry, which, whether before or after his conversion to Catholicism in 1940, and irrespective of the notorious chaos of his private life, depended on his fascination with style, with the past, and with the 'temptations' of other languages. Lowell was a conspicuous fighter against militarism. He was jailed for six months during World War II and was a noted protestor against the Vietnam War. It is especially ironic that the sentiment embodied in the first half of this couplet was used so prominently by every government official who sought to justify America's increasingly pointless involvement in Vietnam. Lowell became a mythical figure, as much for his drinking and his clinically manic behaviour as for his role as the greatest American poet of his time.

LOWRY, MALCOLM (1909–57) British novelist

How alike are the groans of love to those of the dying.
Under the Volcano (1947)

Lowry's book, substantially autobiographical and generally considered to be his masterpiece, recounts, through the mind of the film-maker Jacques Laruelle sitting in Quauhnahuac, Mexico on the Day of the Dead 1939, the events of that same day, exactly a year before. The story is of Geoffrey Firmin, an alcoholic former

British consul, his wife Yvonne, a former film star who has been having an affair with Laruelle, and Firmin's brother Hugh, an anti-fascist journalist. Firmin's own self-destruction echoes Lowry's preoccupation with the collapse of civilisation, and the book grows increasingly sombre. It climaxes with the Consul's death, shot down in a bar, and amidst the drunken memories that precede his death is one of an encounter with a Mexican whore, from which comes this line.

LUCE, CLARE BOOTH (1903–?) American writer and diplomat

A woman's best protection is a little money of her own.
quoted in *The Wit of Women* (1967)

Clare Booth Luce was the wife of Henry Luce, the founder and owner of both *Time* and *Life* magazines. As Clare Booth Brokaw she married Luce in November 23, 1935, just two days after the opening of her first Broadway play. She had no need, however, of her husband's influence, since as an author, playwright, actress, congresswoman and diplomat she cut her own wide swathe through American society. More important than these mainly future successes was her financial independence, to which she alluded here. She had already been married once, and Mr. Brokaw, a clothing millionaire, had settled a $425,000 trust fund on her, as well as an income of $2500 per month.

LUCE, CLARE BOOTH

Much of what Mr. Wallace calls his global thinking is, no matter how you slice it, still globaloney. Mr. Wallace's warp of sense and his woof of nonsense is very tricky cloth out of which to cut the pattern of a post-war world.
speech to American Congress, February 1943

Luce was working as one of *Life's* war correspondents, enjoying her privileged view of World War II when her father, a veteran Connecticut Congressman until his defeat in 1940, died. She was encouraged to stand for the seat as a Republican and duly won the election. She gave her maiden speech on February 9, 1943. Congress expected something out of ordinary and Luce delivered it; a tour de force upon which she had laboured hard. Speaking on the subject of 'America's Destiny In The Air', she demanded that America retain the sovereignty of her own airspace and lambasted Vice-President Henry Wallace for his promise to open the airways to international carriers. Using a piece of pure Timese, she coined the word 'globaloney' and took the Congress and the next day's headlines by storm.

LUEGER, KARL   Austrian local government official

I decide who is a Jew.
quoted in A. Bullock, *Hitler: A Study in Tyranny* (1951)

The avowedly anti-Semitic Lueger, head of the Christian Social Party, became Mayor of Vienna in 1897 despite, or perhaps because of its influential Jewish community. Lueger capitalised on the fears of the small businessmen, the petit-bourgeois, who resented Jewish cosmopolitanism and preferred their own narrow, nationalist beliefs. His most important influence however was not on Vienna, but on one still insignificant member of its electorate: Adolf Hitler. Hitler's *Mein Kampf* shows how intently the house-painter watched Lueger and the great extent to which he drew on Lueger's methods to mobilise his own supporters against the convenient scapegoat, the Jew.

LUXEMBURG, ROSA   (1871–1919) German radical

Freedom is always and exclusively freedom for the one who thinks differently.
Social Reform or Revolution (1899)

Luxembourg rejected her Jewish middle-class background and joined a socialist group soon after finishing school; she rose to become a leader of the Socialist International. In her pamphlet Social Reform and Revolution she summed up the arguments in favour of both forms of change, coming down squarely in favour of revolution. Arrested in Berlin in 1915 for anti-war activities, she spent her time in jail composing the series of revolutionary pamphlets known as the 'Spartacus letters', named for the Spartacus League, which she and her colleague Karl Liebknecht re-created as the German Communist Party on her release in November 1918. The Spartacists took the Russian Revolution as a signal for their own uprising, but unlike Lenin, Luxemburg and Liebknecht failed to instigate a new order. They were both murdered by right-wing Freikorps troops on January 15, 1919.

M

MacArthur, Douglas   (1880–1964) American soldier

Old soldiers never die. They just fade away
address to Congress, April 19 1951

In 1950 General MacArthur, the hero of the Pacific, led a seventeen nation United Nations force, of which 48% were Americans, into North Korea. As he advanced towards the Chinese border MacArthur was asked by President Truman what chances there were of a Chinese intervention. He blithely dismissed the problem. Six weeks later, in late November, 850,000 Chinese crossed the border and threw the UN forces out of North Korea. MacArthur demanded wholesale retaliation but Truman preferred a more immediate form of damage limitation: in February 1951 he fired MacArthur. The public still admired the general and he was given a hero's return and allowed to address Congress for one last time. The line was taken from a popular World War I British troop parody of the song 'Kind Thoughts Can Never Die'. One Congressman called MacArthur 'God in the flesh', Truman called it 'a bunch of bullshit'.

MacArthur, Douglas

I shall return
speech in Australia, March 20 1942

In January 1942 General MacArthur was at the head of the US troops stationed in the Philippines. After overrunning the feeble British defences in Singapore and taking the Dutch East Indies, Java and Rangoon, the Japanese turned to the Philippines. On January 6 MacArthur was forced to abandon his base at Manila and move to the Bataan Peninsula. Crippled by malaria and weakened by their decision to share their dwindling rations with the civilians, the defenders suffered further when MacArthur was ordered to retreat to Australia. They surrendered on April 9; MacArthur spoke emotionally to the Australian parliament, promising that come what may, he would go back. 'Never underestimate a man who overestimates himself' Roosevelt had said of MacArthur, and while 75% of the men he had left in Bataan died at Japanese hands, he did return when the tide of war turned America's way.

MACAULAY, ROSE (1881–1958) British novelist

Behaviour of such cunning cruelty that only a human being could have thought of or contrived we call 'inhuman', revealing thus some pathetic standard for our species that survives all betrayals.
A Casual Commentary (1925)

From her first novel, *Potterism* (1920), Rose Macaulay became both a popular and a critical success for her satirical fiction. Her finest, although by no means her most popular novel was *They Were Defeated* (1932), a historical work which features the poet Robert Herrick (1591–1674). Her unrequited love for a married man had long estranged her from religion but, aided by the Reverend J.H.C. Johnson, she returned to Anglicanism after his death in 1942. *A Casual Commentary* is a collection of essays, and her remark comes unsurprisingly from a woman who could castigate humanity as 'a mass of stupid, huddled, muddled minds'.

MacCARTHY, DESMOND (1877–1952) British critic

A critic is a creature without a spiritual home, and it is his point of honour never to seek one.
Criticism (1932)

MacCarthy worked as what he termed a 'literary journalist', editing first the magazines *New Quarterly* and *Eye Witness* (latterly the *New Witness*). In 1913 he joined the *New Statesman* as dramatic critic and then literary editor. Succeeding Sir John Squire, who wrote as 'Solomon Eagle', he took the pseudonym 'Affable Hawk'. He moved to the *Sunday Times* in 1928 and stayed, reviewing books, until 1952. His criticism has been collected in a variety of works, from one of which this self-description has been taken.

MacEWAN, ARTHUR American journalist

News is anything that makes a reader say "Gee whiz!"....News is whatever a good editor chooses to print.
quoted in D. Boorstin, *The Image*

What exactly makes a reader say 'Gee whiz!' and what, given the various readerships for whom the press must cater, actually makes 'a good editor', must vary according to context. The tabloid press, in Britain at least, seems to have abandoned news, as in the facts to be derived from immediately current affairs, and to presume that its readers are more likely to be expostulating over the adulterous soap opera star on page one, the 'curvy cutie' on page three or the bingo cards wherever space permits. Whether the proverbial 'man bites dog' would still arouse any interest is unlikely.

MacInnes, Colin   (1914–76) British writer

Tradition, if not constantly recreated, can be as much a millstone as a millwheel.
England Half English (1961)

MacInnes, who was describing England's slavery, as he saw it, to tradition for nothing but tradition's sake, was beset by such 'millstones' in his own life. As the son of the novelist Angela Thirkell, and thus related variously to Rudyard Kipling, Burne-Jones and Stanley Baldwin, he chafed constantly against the literary establishment of which found himself a part. His own lifestyle, accentuating his homosexuality, his fascination for (and affairs with) London's blacks, his pursuit of the sociological (and simply social) allure of the teenage world, was an exercise in the destruction of his background.

MacInnes, Colin

A coloured man can tell, in five seconds dead, whether a white man likes him or not. If the white man says he does, he is instantly – and usually quite rightly –mistrusted.
England, Half English (1961)

MacInnes' involvement with the London black community, from the earnest Africans studying their degrees to the West Indian militants of Notting Hill, was intense. Although much of it was dictated by his homosexuality, and his love of black 'rough trade', he was one of the first white writers to consider the role of that community in London and later, he was among the most vocal supporters of British Black Power. This comment comes from one of the essays in his 'polyphoto of the fifties', *England, Half English.* 'A Short Guide for Jumbles to the Life of their Coloured Brethren in England' is a catechistic analysis of black culture for the assistance of 'Jumbles', ie. John Bulls, ie. whites. This line follows a selection of instantly alienating statements, guaranteed to appal any black man, notably 'I like coloured people, myself'.

MACMILLAN, HAROLD   (1894–1986) Earl of Stockton
Macmillan was the grandson of a Scottish crofter but the success of his family's publishing firm ensured that he was born into the heart of the upper classes. In 1924 he entered politics as Tory MP for Stockton-on-Tees. A Keynesian before the economist's views became fashionable, he advocated an unprecedented level of state intervention in the economy. He backed the unpopular Winston Churchill in his campaign for British rearmament. Churchill responded by giving him various minor jobs in his wartime government. Most important was his role as Minister Resident in North Africa, a responsible job that formed the real basis of his subsequent career. After World War II he helped form Tory policies both in opposition and in government. In 1957 he succeeded Eden as Prime Minister. He presided over Britain's post-war boom, the 'never had it so good' era of the late Fifties. Christened 'Supermac' by the press, he enjoyed unrivalled prestige until the Profumo scandal of 1963 led to his resignation 'on health grounds'. For the remainder of his life he became an increasingly respected and increasingly elder statesman, accepting in 1984 the peerage he had so often rejected.

MACMILLAN, HAROLD

The most striking of all impressions I have formed since I left London a month ago is of the strength of this African national consciousness. In different places it may take different forms but it is happening everywhere. The wind of change is blowing through this continent. Whether we like it or not, this growth of political consciousness is a political fact.
addressing the South African Parliament, February 3, 1960

Macmillan's speech was written by the diplomat David Hunt and subjected to several revisions, including one by the Prime Minister himself. His first use of the line came a month earlier, speaking in Accra, Ghana, on January 9th, and stressing that the 'wind' was giving Africa a new importance in the world. It made little impression. His reiteration in apartheid-dominated South Africa had a far more resounding impact. The speech's central image possibly drew on that used by Stanley Baldwin on December 4, 1934, when he said 'There is a wind of nationalism and freedom blowing round the world, and blowing as strongly in Asia as elsewhere'.

MACMILLAN, HAROLD

I'd like that translated if I may.
addressing the United Nations, September 29, 1960

Macmillan addressed the United Nations on September 29, 1960. Among his audience was Nikita Khrushchev, the Soviet premier. Khrushchev was at his most aggressive; his summit conference with President Eisenhower, scheduled for that summer, had been cancelled after his aircraft had shot down an American U-2 spy plane, high over Russian air space. As Macmillan put forward his views on the international situation, the Premier took off his shoe and began pounding the table in front him. Without missing a beat Macmillan requested the UN 'I'd like that translated if I may'.

MACMILLAN, HAROLD

Churchill was fundamentally what the English call unstable – by which they mean anybody who has that touch of genius which is inconvenient in normal times.
commenting on Winston Churchill, *The Blast of War* (1967)

Macmillan supported Churchill throughout that period when their political careers coincided. Like Churchill, although hardly as distinguished, he stood outside the mainstream policies of the Conservative Party between the wars. He joined in Churchill's hatred of first Baldwin's and then Chamberlain's desire to appease Hitler, and with his leader demanded that Britain should rearm. When Churchill came to power, in 1940, Macmillan was given a number of minor offices but received nothing worthwhile until 1942 when he became the Prime Minister's personal representative in North Africa and took his first real steps in international politics. Macmillan remained a staunch ally until Churchill, who called him 'the captain of my Praetorian Guard', retired.

MACMILLAN, HAROLD

It has been said that there is no fool like an old fool, except a young fool. But the young fool has first to grow up to be an old fool to realise what a damn fool he was when he was a young fool.
dictum

Macmillan seemed to many commentators, possibly encouraged by the paucity of modern competition, to improve with age. As the Tory Party's and indeed the nation's eldest statesman, his elevation to the House of Lords in 1984, when he finally accepted a peerage, gave him a new lease of life. He showed in his maiden speech that while he may, as she quickly announced after his death in 1986, have offered his advice to Margaret Thatcher on the conduct of her war against General Galtieri, he was far less impressed by her follow-up versus Arthur Scargill and the NUM in 1984. His speech, without notes and witnessed by a vast television audience, showed that young or old, he was nobody's fool.

MACMILLAN, HAROLD

He enjoys prophesying the imminent fall of the capitalist system and is prepared to play a part, any part, in its burial – except that of a mute.
on Aneurin Bevan

As one of the Labour Party's most outspoken, challenging individuals, Aneurin Bevan evoked almost as many attacks on himself as he made on the Tories whom he loathed. As well as Churchill's dismissal of 'the merchant of discourtesy' and 'a minister of disease', was this, offered by a relatively youthful Macmillan, who was one of Churchill's most devoted followers and who, albeit using more temperate language than many back-bench Conservatives, disliked the incessant attacks Bevan made on the Prime Minister.

MACMILLAN, HAROLD

He is forever poised between a cliché and an indiscretion.
on Sir Anthony Eden

Macmillan was appointed Foreign Secretary by Anthony Eden when the latter became Prime Minister in 1955. Like his previous job as Churchill's Minister of Defence, Macmillan found his role frustrating, since the interest of both Prime Ministers in the job he was supposed to control meant that in effect he was rendered no more than a front man for their policies. He was no longer Foreign Secretary in 1956 when the Suez involvement devastated Eden, and although initially one of the most fervent supporters of the plan, he responded to American hostility and a weakened pound by numbering himself among the earliest critics of both Britain's failure and the uncharacteristic blunder of Eden, who hitherto had been respected as one of the country's best negotiators.

MACMILLAN, HAROLD

Jaw-jaw is better than war-war.
remark at Canberra, January 30 1958

Macmillan's tour of the Commonwealth in early 1958 took him to Australia. Speaking at Canberra he summed up the need for international negotiations, especially in the form of arms talks between the great powers, as being infinitely preferable to risking a Third World War. His line echoed Winston Churchill's comment to President Eisenhower at the White House on January 26, 1954: 'Talking jaw to jaw is better than going to war'.

MACMILLAN, HAROLD

When you're abroad you're a statesman: when you're at home you're just a politician.
in a speech, 1958

Macmillan's comment, in which he opined that the difference between the rival perceptions of the same elected individual is based on his current geographical position, is one of many such comments that seek to draw the line between the distrusted, self-promoting politician and the respected, altruistic statesman. Among the earliest of such remarks are George Hillard's 1852 eulogy for the American Daniel Webster 'A statesman makes the occasion, but the occasion makes the politician' and James Freeman Clarke's (1810–88) line 'A politician thinks of the next election, a statesman of the next generation'.

MACMILLAN, HAROLD

It would have been twice as bad if they'd sent the dog.
remarking on USSR cosmonaut Yuri Gagarin's reception in Britain, 1961

On April 12, 1961 Yuri Gagarin, aged 37, became the first man to orbit the Earth in a spacecraft. The circumnavigation took just 108 minutes. Later that year the Russians sent him to Britain, where he received a rapturous welcome. He had, however, been preceded into earth orbit by Kudryavka, an 11 lb. female Samoyed husky, better known to the dog-loving world as Laika, the first animal ever to encircle the globe. The hapless Laika made a perfect flight but no provision had been made for reentry and she died, when her oxygen ran out, ten days after her launch on November 3, 1957. The world mourned. Macmillan, watching the human cosmonaut take his bows four years later, reflected, probably correctly, that the dog-obsessed British would have made an even greater fuss of the deceased canine.

MACMILLAN, HAROLD

I thought the best thing to do was to settle up these little local difficulties, and then turn to the wider vision of the Commonwealth.
speaking to the press, January 7, 1958

Within a year of Macmillan's becoming Prime Minister he was faced with the resignation of his entire Treasury team, including the Chancellor of the Exchequer, Peter Thorneycroft, over the budget estimates for the year. Macmillan was scheduled to leave the UK for a tour of the Commonwealth. His dismissal of the problem as a 'local difficulty', a typical remark from a man who, first and foremost, was always a consummate actor, won him a good deal of respect, with its inference that the affairs of the Commonwealth were of greater importance.

MACMILLAN, HAROLD
You've never had it so good.
speech in Bedford on July 20, 1957

If Macmillan is remembered for nothing else, then this speech in the Bedford marketplace will ensure him immortality. Although the line was used against him, and rings hollowly today, his full text shows that he was warning the voters, not patting himself on the back. 'Let's be frank about it. Most of our people have never had it so good. Go around the country, go to the industrial towns, go to the farms, and you'll see a state of prosperity such as we have never had in my lifetime – nor indeed ever in the history of this country. What is beginning to worry some of us is "Is it too good to be true?" or perhaps I should say "Is it too good to last?" For amidst all this prosperity, there is one problem that has troubled us, in one way or another, ever since the war. It is the problem of rising prices. Our constant concern is: Can prices be steadied while at the same time we maintain full employment in an expanding economy? Can we control inflation?' Macmillan was not the first politician to use the phrase: American Adlai Stevenson campaigned somewhat reluctantly under the same slogan in the election of 1952.

MACMILLAN, HAROLD
There ain't gonna be no war.
after a summit at Geneva, 1955

Macmillan's visit to the four-power summit at Geneva in July 1955 came at the height of the Cold War which dominated East-West relations in the era. As British Foreign Minister he joined his colleagues in the conference to discuss the possibility of German reunification. Little of concrete use was achieved, and Germany remains divided, but on his return to London Macmillan informed the press jauntily 'There ain't gonna be no war'.

MAETERLINCK, MAURICE (1862–1949) Belgian essayist, poet and playwright

All our knowledge merely helps us to die a more painful death than the animals that know nothing.
The Treasure of the Humble (1897)

Maeterlinck first encountered the Symbolist movement on a short visit to Paris and with his first play *La Princesse Maleine* (1889), established himself alongside such leading members of the movement as Mallarmé, Verlaine and Rimbaud. A subsequent play, *Pelléas et Mélisande* (1892) provided the source for Debussy's opera of the same name which was first performed in 1902. For the next two decades Maeterlinck was lauded as 'the Belgian Shakespeare', although such fame failed to survive World War I.

MAGNUSSON, MAGNUS British television personality

I've started, so I'll finish.
'Mastermind' BBC-TV quiz show

Mastermind, the BBC's up-market quiz show, began in 1972. The show's format isolates the contestant in a forbidding steel-and-leather chair, the tension of the moment exacerbated by the single spotlight that shines down from an otherwise darkened arena. The whole melodrama consistently pulls down top ratings, although the questions, both on the contestants' 'special subject' and on more general knowledge, can be dauntingly tough. Adding to the carefully manipulated atmosphere is the quizmaster Magnus Magnusson who plays the judicious dictator, whose own decisions are final, but who himself is dominated by Mastermind's adamant rules: in this case the fact that once he has begun reading a question he must complete it and offer the contestant a chance to answer, even though the buzzer that denotes the end of the questioning period has already sounded.

MAGRITTE, RENÉ (1898–1967) Belgian painter

We mustn't fear daylight just because it almost always illuminates a miserable world.
Le Surréalisme en Plein Soleil (1946)

Unlike the other Surrealists Magritte saw no need to compound the innate surprises embodied in his paintings by parading a life designed simply to shock. With the exception of a short stay in Paris, Magritte spent all his life in Belgium, and despite this comment on the 'miserable world' his own days were marked mainly by their stability. He and his wife had an apparently ideal marriage; he had a close circle of friends, a loyal dog, a comfortable if modest house where he could work or read his favourite Edgar Allan Poe. His paintings, while undoubtedly bizarre, reflect this stability, representing quite 'normal' subjects – a train, a bowler-hatted man, a tuba – except that they are taken completely out of context, creating a series of visual puns that underline his dictum 'An object never fulfils the same function as its name or its image'.

MAHONEY, DAVID   American businessman

If two people agree all the time, one of them is unnecessary.
quoted in Michael Korda, *Power in the Office* (1976)

This theory, taken from Korda's book on the best means of making one's way to the top of the antheap of office life, seems, if it is true, to promote a situation of endless conflict. Presumably the premise is that if two people of equal rank agree, then they are essentially performing the same job and thus one of them is indeed superfluous. On the other hand, even the most go-ahead hard-charger would probably agree that for his underlings constantly to challenge his decisions in the hope of inspiring the cut and thrust of creative debate, would be nothing if not counter-productive.

MAILER, NORMAN   (1923–) American novelist, writer and essayist

The horror of the Twentieth Century (is) the size of each new event, and the paucity of its reverberation.
A Fire On The Moon (1970)

Mailer's comment, culled from his study of the Apollo 11 moonshot of 1969, came fittingly at the end of a decade which had left the world numbed by race riots, assassinations, a disastrous Far Eastern war and so much more. Specifically he was referring to the 'American cool' that pervaded the whole project, especially when the astronauts confronted the media. What Tom Wolfe would later term 'the Right Stuff' took the place of open emo-

tions, and technological jargon substituted for simple communication. Rather than reflect the enormity of what they were doing,
the astronauts preferred to bury it in the anodyne statements of
Mission Control, even, when they finally landed on the moon,
offering a pre-considered emotional response.

MAILER, NORMAN

Hip is the sophistication of the wise primitive in a giant jungle.
The White Negro (1957)

Mailer's essay, looking back to the Beat movement of his youth
and forward, prophetically, to the counter-culture of the Sixties,
mixes Freud, Marx and his own perceptions to provide one of the
most influential summations of the post-World War II 'hip consciousness'. The spectre of imminent nuclear destruction had
created a new, specifically American existentialist who substituted for French rationalism a sense of religion, not specifically
theological, but of 'energy, life, sex, force...'. The model for such
hipsters is, as the essay's title infers, the Black man, master of
sensuality, pioneer of jazz. The hipster is a 'philosophical psychopath' and as such, along with pursuing the rest of his urge towards
the 'infantile fantasy' (and thus especially appealing to adoles-
cents), any indulgence in personal violence, as a cathartic release, must be condoned – a part of Mailer's own psychopathology which still causes him trouble.

MAILER, NORMAN

**The mass of men must satisfy the needs of the social organism in
which they live far more than the social organism must satisfy
them.**
Advertisements for Myself (1961)

Advertisements for Myself is the first of Mailer's collections of
essays, short stories and other pieces and it is probably the best,
showing a Mailer relatively unconcerned with many of the
distractions that have crowded in on his later years. In it he can
be seen for the first time, at the age of 35, to have established his
own voice, and many of the pieces, flagrantly egotistical as they
are, presage the first-person style that would typify his non-fiction
writing from now on. As Mailer has pointed out, while many
people have claimed the invention of the 'New Journalism' of the
Sixties, *Advertisements...* surely deserves a favourable mention
among the contenders.

MAILER, NORMAN

Women think of being a man as a gift. It is a duty. Even making love can be a duty. A man has always got to get it up and love isn't always enough.
Nova, 1969

For a man whose belief in the orgasm as the ultimate act of self-realization, the need, if one is male, to attain an erection prior to arriving at that orgasm, becomes a paramount concern. What Mailer is saying here was typical of those statements that have infuriated feminists. The idea that he conveys is of woman as sex object who must, if she requires her man, make herself alluring before he can make love, rather than simply be in love. Such a concept did not appeal to women's liberationists, whom he branded as 'enemies of sex', and Mailer soon became one of the movement's most loathed bugbears, a role he refused to eschew and if anything rather enjoyed.

MAILER, NORMAN

Alimony is the curse of the writing classes.
quoted in *The Wit of Women*, by L and M Cowan

Mailer has, at last count, amassed six wives and nine children. His need to write to pay off the alimony involved in this substantial scorecard gave rise to a number of books that otherwise might not have been written and drew from a beleaguered Mailer this heartfelt comment. As late as 1979, when he married his sixth wife, he was still paying out regular weekly sums totalling $93,600 per year to a number of previous wives. In another comment on the agonies of entanglement he has claimed 'There are four stages to a marriage. First there's the affair, then there's the marriage, then children and finally the fourth stage, without which you cannot know a woman, the divorce.'

MAILER, NORMAN

Politics is not an art of principles but of timing. The principles are few and soft enough to curve to political winds. The fundamental action of politics is to gain the most one can from a favourable situation and pay off as little as possible whenever necessity forces an unpopular line.
St George and the Godfather (1972)

Mailer's book on the electoral campaigns of 1972 was the latest in a continuing series of campaign coverage, presented either in book or article form, that had begun with his attendance at the Democratic Convention of 1960. It depends as much on the author's own perceptions as on the actual events portrayed. Mailer made his own essay into politics in the New York mayoral campaign of 1969, in which he was teamed with fellow writer Jimmy Breslin. The campaign was a disaster, prompting journalist Richard Reeves to comment 'All Norman Mailer the politician accomplished was to prove that in New York City almost anyone can get 41,000 votes if a million people go to the polls'.

MAILER, NORMAN

Once a newspaper touches a story, the facts are lost forever, even to the protagonists.
The Presidential Papers (1963)

The Presidential Papers was the first of Mailer's books, other than a small book of poetry, to be published in the Sixties. It was originally titled 'Frankie and Johnny', for Franklin Roosevelt, Frank Sinatra and Frank Costello, all famous Franks connected to the Democratic Party, and for John Kennedy. The book contained all his work since 1959 and was dedicated, as the work of 'a court wit, an amateur advisor', to President Kennedy. Like a true court jester, he set out simultaneously to amuse and to be taken seriously. The role was controversial and dangerous, eliciting a wide variety of reviews, but it placed Mailer firmly at the centre of the Sixties ferment.

MAILER, NORMAN

Sentimentality is the emotional promiscuity of those who have no sentiment.
Cannibals and Christians (1966)

This suggestion that those who are incapable of genuine feeling prefer to substitute safe superficialities comes from Mailer's third collection of essays and ephemera. Running through it is a central theme of the absurd, and Mailer explained it in his introduction: 'We live in a a time which has created the art of the absurd. It is our art.' In such a time there exist only two sorts of people: the Cannibals are rightwingers who feel they can only save the world 'by killing off what is second rate'; the Christians are the liberals or the Communists who 'are utterly opposed to the destruction of human life and succeed within themselves in starting all the wars of our own time'.

MAILER, NORMAN

Totalitarianism is the interruption of mood.

MAJOR AND THE MINOR, THE

I must get out of these wet clothes and into a dry martini.
screenplay by Billy Wilder and Charles Brackett (1942)

This wartime comedy was Billy Wilder's first attempt at directing in America, based on the play 'Connie Goes Home' by E.C. Carpenter. Ginger Rogers plays a New York career girl down on her luck who decides to go home to Iowa, for which journey she dresses as a twelve-year-old and thus saves money on a half-price fare. On the train she meets an Army major (Ray Milland), who finds himself perturbed by the attractions of an ostensible child. She is forced to keep up the act, while Milland's fiancée becomes increasingly suspicious and the boys at the military academy where he teaches make constant passes. Robert Benchley displayed his usual comic persona, delivering this, his best and most pirated line. Some sources claim this was his own wisecrack, used long before the movie (others attribute it to Alexander Woolcott). Benchley's consumption of martinis features in a well-documented anecdote: told by an anxious friend 'Do you realise that those martinis that you keep drinking are slow poison?' Benchley replied 'I'm in no hurry.'

MALAMUD, BERNARD (1914–) American novelist

Life is a tragedy full of joy.
New York Times, 1979

Malamud has been one of America's leading writers since his novel *The Magic Barrel* won a National Book Award in 1958. His most famous work, *The Fixer*, which won a Pulitzer prize in 1966, is based on the case of Mendel Beilis, a Russian Jew who in 1913 was falsely accused of 'ritual murder' and pilloried as a focus for a more general anti-Semitism. Throughout all his 'tragedies full of joy' runs the premise that life requires suffering since only thus can one reach maturity through the recognition of one's involvement with and responsibility for other people. All his 'lead' characters attempt to maximise themselves at the expense of their more general role in the community; only when they understand the need to overcome this egocentricity can they achieve a new life.

MALCOLM X   (1925–65) American radical

It is the hinge that squeaks that gets the grease.
in A. Haley, *Autobiography of Malcolm X* (1965)

Malcolm Little pursued the career of a small-time hoodlum and Harlem racketeer until in 1952, serving a term in prison, he abandoned crime for Black activism and until his assassination became one of America's most effective campaigners for Black rights. Little rejected assimilation, preferring to isolate his Nation of Islam from mainstream white America, and substituted X for his old surname, a relic of slavery. His outspoken demands for an inter-racial civil war in America shocked the white establishment but won a number of militant followers to the Nation of Islam, otherwise known as the Black Muslims. He was expelled from the US in 1963 and made a triumphant tour of African and Arab states, making a pilgrimage to Mecca after which he adopted the new 'Islamic' name of Hajj Malik El-Shabazz. On his return to America in 1965 he was assassinated, allegedly by renegade members of his own Nation of Islam.

MALLET, ROBERT   (1915–) French writer

It is not impossibilities which fill us with deepest despair, but possibilities which we have failed to realise.
Apostilles

Given that few people attain their dreams, the 'what if ' syndrome dominates most lives. Mallet's point is that on the whole we are not so obsessed by fantasy as to set up impossible goals, but find it even more frustrating when, appreciating our own limitations, we still know perfectly well that we have failed to succeed in what we can do. That way, he attests, lies real misery.

MALLET, ROBERT

How many pessimists end up desiring the things they fear, in order to prove they are right.
Apostilles

The paradox of establishing a philosophy in which everything tends to the worst of possible worlds is that one's entire belief system can be wrecked if it becomes impossible to deny that things are simply not that bad. Thus the dedicated pessimist, like his cousin the cynic, finds himself revelling in the wish-fulfilment of worst cases and dreading improvement.

MALLORY, GEORGE LEIGH   (1886–1924) British climber

Because it's there.

replying to questioner in 1923

Mallory, one of Britain's foremost climbers, was asked during a lecture tour of America in 1923 why, as he had often announced, he was so keen to climb the world's highest peak, Mount Everest. He replied succinctly 'Because it is there'. He amplified this later by pointing out that every climber wants to climb every mountain simply to exploit his own abilities, irrespective of the problems involved. Mallory duly made his attack on Everest in 1924 but disappeared during the last stages of the climb. Whether he reached the top remains a mystery.

MALRAUX, ANDRÉ   (1901–75) French novelist, art critic and politician

What is man: a miserable little pile of secrets.

Antimemoires (1968)

Malraux involved himself in archaeology, exploration and the Spanish civil war before turning, after World War II, to his twin preoccupations with the philosophy of art and with Gaullist politics. He began his career as the model of a committed left-wing writer, but like many Communists he lost faith after Stalin allied with Hitler, and after fighting for the French Resistance began his accelerating move to the Right, becoming in the Fifties a committed proponent of the Cold War. De Gaulle, recognising his support, made him minister with special responsibility for cultural affairs from 1958–1969. Malraux's philosophy claimed primarily that man must recognise his own qualities, only through action can he know himself and only through art and myth can he situate himself in the world.

MALRAUX, ANDRÉ

All art is a revolt against man's fate.

Antimemoires (1968)

The purpose of art, Malraux claimed, was to help man find a place amidst the cultural structures that make up the world. It cannot be explained by an ideological system, such as Freudianism or Marxism, but represents a means for man of proving the permanence of his own human spirit by continually questioning the status of the universe. The artist keeps looking at the world in a new way and offers humanity a chance to use his vision.

MAN WHO SHOT LIBERTY VALANCE, THE

When the legend becomes fact, print the legend.
screenplay by James W. Bellah & Willis Goldbeck (1962)

The film, directed by John Ford, starred John Wayne as the good guy, Lee Marvin as the bad Liberty Valance and James Stewart as an idealistic young lawyer from the East, who gets robbed on his way out West and is forced to learn about frontier life as a dishwasher. This line is spoken by Stewart to the newspaper editor (Edmund O'Brien) who is querying whether or not he should print the popularly accepted version of Valance's death, in which the local hero wins out, or tell the less glamorous truth. Stewart tells him to go with glamour. The line possibly stemmed from avant-garde French aesthete Jean Cocteau's remark, in 1957: 'What is history after all? History is facts which become legend in the end; legends are lies which become history in the end.'

MANKIEWICZ, HERMAN (1897–1953) American writer and film producer

It's all right, Arthur: the white wine came up with the fish.
to producer Arthur Hornblow, 1953

Mankiewicz, elder brother of the producer/director Joseph and best known for his co-authorship of Citizen Kane (1941) with Orson Welles, was one of Hollywood's more flamboyant characters, a former New York journalist who like so many talented writers, came West for a share of the movies' rich pickings. He was also a notorious drunk who died relatively young after years of excess. Mankiewicz managed to combine both wit and alcoholism in this vignette. Dining one evening in 1935 at the home of Arthur Hornblow (1893–1976), a producer who fancied himself as something of a gourmet, Mankiewicz, who had come on from another party, found it all too much and vomitted across the table. As his fellow guests stared and Hornblow began to protest, Mankiewicz looked across the table and offered this immmaculate response.

MANKIEWICZ, HERMAN

In a novel the hero can lay ten girls and marry a virgin for the finish. In a movie that is not allowed. The villain can lay anybody he wants, have as much fun as he wants cheating and stealing, getting rich and whipping the servants. But you have to shoot him in the end. When he falls with a bullet in the forehead it is

advisable that he clutch at the Gobelin tapestry on the wall and bring it down over his head like a symbolic shroud. Also, covered by such a tapestry, the actor does not have to hold his breath while being photographed as a dead man.

quoted in Pauline Kael, *The Citizen Kane Book* (1971)

In 1926 Mankiewicz cabled an old friend and fellow reporter, Ben Hecht, 'Will you accept $300 a week to work for Paramount Pictures? All expenses paid. The three hundred is peanuts. Millions are to be grabbed out here and your only competition is idiots. Don't let this get around.' Hecht grabbed the chance and became one of Hollywood's leading writers. Mankiewicz's point was that El Dorado did exist and that it lay 3000 miles west of New York City. As this plot summary shows, Mankiewicz, like most of his ex-journalist pals, both despised and exulted in Hollywood. Money for nothing – it was just too much fun to miss.

MANKIEWICZ, HERMAN

There, but for the grace of God, goes God.
on Orson Welles

Although Orson Welles has been given the credit for the film *Citizen Kane* the script itself was originally written by Herman Mankiewicz. Welles' influence was substantial but for all his creativity there would have been no movie without 'Mank'. Unsurprisingly the two men, each a sacred monster in his own right, had a prickly relationship: Welles the youthful genius who had shocked half America with his 'War of the Worlds' broadcast; Mankiewicz older and infinitely more cynical. On one occasion Mankiewicz called the collaboration 'our long conspiracy of love and hate for Maestro, the Dog-Faced Boy', but this comment, which presaged that of Winston Churchill on Stafford Cripps, has lasted longer.

MANSON, CHARLES (1934–) American murderer

Death is psychosomatic.
quoted in *Esquire* magazine, 1971

Manson was one of America's drifters, with no real education and a criminal record, who drifted to California in the mid-Sixties, hoping to capitalise on the innocence and gullibility of the hippie masses. Unlike most of his peers, Manson had a vision. Using his immense personal magnetism he recruited a dedicated band of followers, mostly runaway teenage girls, with a smattering of devoted youths. They lived in the desert outside Los Angeles, indulged in drugs and sex and, with a plan supposedly revealed to Manson by the Beatles' White Album of 1968, prepared for the coming apocalypse. On August 8 1969 four of Manson's followers went to 10050 Cielo Drive, the house of Sharon Tate, wife of director Roman Polanski and one of Hollywood's up-and-comers. There they killed the heavily pregnant Tate and four others. The following night they killed a businessman Leno LaBianca and his wife Rosemary. Jailed for the murders, Manson offered his chillingly disinterested assessment of death.

MAO ZEDONG   (1893–1976) (Mao Tse Tung) Chinese leader

In order to get rid of the gun, it is necessary to take up the gun.
Quotations from Chairman Mao (1966)

A Marxist since 1919, Mao understood that for rural China the hope of revolution lay in the millions of peasants, rather than in the urban proletariat. He established a short-lived revolutionary republic in Kiangsi province but after Chiang Kai-shek's Kuomintang troops dismantled this, Mao and his followers were forced to embark on the famous Long March to North-West China. Mao joined Chiang to fight against the Japanese in 1937 and capitalised on the successes of his guerillas to establish a substantial power base on China. He also used the period to elaborate his plans for the post-Revolutionary state which was established in 1949. Mao followed the Soviet line until 1955 when he began a series of homegrown strategies. After the liberal 'hundred flowers movement' of 1956, and the repressive 'great leap forward' in 1958 came the 'Cultural Revolution' of 1966–69, designed to foster youthful radicalism and purge the Party of backsliders. This last was economically disastrous and when 'The Great Helmsman' died in 1976 the country had yet to recover.

MAO ZEDONG

We must let a hundred flowers bloom and a hundred schools of thought contend and see which flowers are the best and which school of thought is best expressed, and we shall applaud the best blooms and the best thoughts.
launching the Hundred Flowers Movement, 1956

The aim of the Hundred Flowers Movement was to unleash the energies of China's intellectuals which since the Revolution in 1949 had been strictly controlled by a series of repressive measures designed to eradicate counter-revolutionary thought. Mao believed that by enlisting the intellectuals he could now boost the revolution. His hopes proved naive: the intellectuals were no more willing to accept unconditional Maoism than they had been to offer uncritical support to Chiang Kai-shek. Frustrated by their criticisms, he returned to repression and sought, in the Great Leap Forward, the help of the rural masses.

MAO ZEDONG

All reactionaries are paper tigers. In appearance the reactionaries are terrifying, but in reality they are not so powerful. From a long-term point of view it is not the reactionaries but the people who are really powerful.
Quotations from Chairman Mao Tse Tung (1966)

MAO ZEDONG

The peaceful population is the sea in which the guerilla swims like a fish.
Quotations from Chairman Mao Tse Tung (1966)

MAO ZEDONG

Political power grows out of the barrel of a gun
Quotations from Chairman Mao Tse tung (1966)

MARCUSE, HERBERT (1898–1979) German social philosopher

Art is the great refusal of the world as it is.
quoted in *New Society*, 1969

Marcuse was a member of the Institut fur Sozialforschung in Frankfurt before he was forced to flee the Nazis in 1934. He continued working with the Institut when it was re-established in New York, but unlike many colleagues remained in America when it returned to Germany after World War II. Marcuse wrote two of the counter-culture's favourite books: *Eros and Civilisation* (1955) and *One-Dimensional Man* (1964). In the first of these he attempted to combine the erotic liberation of the mind from its repression and the economic liberation of the masses from theirs. The second claims that capitalism, by its use of the mass media to inculcate essentially trivial material desires, can thus use 'repressive tolerance' to maintain its own position by aneasthetising the revolutionary desires of the masses. Only an alliance of students, untainted by such manipulation, and the revolutionary sections of the working class could reverse this position.

MARKHAM, DEWEY 'PIGMEAT' American entertainer

Here come de judge.
in Rowan and Martin's Laugh-In, 1960s

Like British radio's ITMA twenty years earlier, American television's Laugh-In created a number of popular catchphrases. Among these was 'Here come de Judge', intoned by heavyweight Pigmeat Markham, a popular Black ex-vaudevillian, who had little to do on the show other than to deliver, dressed in judicial robes as expected by the weekly audience, his regular line. The phrase was often preceded by the cry of 'Order in de court...'. In summer 1968 Markham released an eponymously titled record which managed eight weeks in the British charts, as did one *Shorty Long*, with about the same degree of success.

MARQUIS, DON (1878–1937) American humourist, novelist and playwright

A man who is so dull that he can learn only by personal experience is too dull to learn anything important by this experience.
Archy Does His Part (1935)

Marquis was a popular newspaper columnist whose best-known work is the series of books which begins with *archy and mehitabel* (1927) and which features the comic prose and verse of archy, a cockroach who has a former existence as a bard. Since archy types with his head, his work is filled with typographical oddities, notably its lack of capitals – since archy cannot reach the shift key. mehitabel is is an alley cat.

MARQUIS, DON

If you want to get rich from writing, write the sort of thing that's read by persons who move their lips when they're reading to themselves.

MARSHALL, THOMAS R. (1854–1925) American vice-president

What this country needs is a good five-cent cigar.
in the US Senate, 1917

As America's Vice-President it was incumbent upon Marshall to preside over debates in the US Senate, irrespective of their innate tedium. Marshall was a cheerful fellow, although the prospect of taking on real power appalled him and he visibly wilted when the President, Woodrow Wilson, appeared dangerously ill after a stroke. During one such epic of boredom, Marshall turned to the chief clerk, John Crockett and commented, a propos of nothing in particular, 'What this country needs is a good five-cent cigar'.

MARTIN, DEAN (1917–) American film star

You're not drunk if you can lie on the floor without holding on.
quoted in *The Official Rules* by Paul Dickson (1978)

Martin, born Dino Crocetti, began life as a singer, a cut-rate Sinatra who was always prominent in his fellow Italian-American's much publicised 'Rat Pack'. Moving to Hollywood from New York in the Forties he starred in a number of movies with comic Jerry Lewis before they split up in 1956. Martin went on to make a number of reasonably successful films during the Sixties. His main image has been that of the roaring drunk, as evinced in this comment and in another line 'I'd hate to be a teetotaller. Imagine, getting up in the morning and knowing that's as good as you're going to feel all day'.

MARX, GROUCHO (1897–1977) American comedian

Time wounds all heels.
quoted in the *Sunday Telegraph* obituary, August 21 1977

The four Marx brothers were described thus by their one time scriptwriter S.J. Perelman: 'The leader wore a large painted moustache and affected a cigar, and his three henchmen impersonated respectively a mute harpist afflicted with satyriasis, a larcenous Italian and a jaunty coxcomb who carried the love interest'. Perelman omitted to add that 'the leader' Groucho, born Julius, was capable of being witty in his own right, even when his lines had not been prepared by a scriptwriter. This reverse of the usual, cosy proverb is one example. Others include:

Military intelligence is a contradiction in terms.

No-one is entirely unhappy at the failure of his greatest friend, a remark surely derived from Confucius' earlier suggestion that 'Life's greatest pleasure is watching one's best friend fall off a roof'.

Any club that would have me as a member, I don't want to belong to, taken from a letter to the committee of the Friars Club, whose members come from America's theatre, and from which Groucho, who rarely attended, wished to resign. The line has been quoted variously as 'Please accept my resignation, I don't care to belong to any club that will have me as a member'; and 'I don't care to belong to any social organisation that will accept me as a member' and, whatever the correct line, it inspired London's Groucho Club, one of the media's favourite watering holes of the mid-Eighties.

MASARYCK, TOMAS (1850–1937) Czech politician

Dictators always look good until the last minutes.

Masaryck rose through the politics of the Hapsburg Empire to become his country's first president in 1918, a post which he held until 1935. Unlike many Czech nationalists, he rejected the prevailing Pan-Slav sentiments, which would have allied the Czechs to Russia, preferring a truly independent nation. He chose to seek an alliance with Britain and France, whom he saw as more democratic. His reliance on Britain and France proved misplaced. Hitler still looked sufficiently 'good' throughout the Thirties for them to prefer appeasing his desire to restore the Sudetenland, ceded to Czechoslovakia in 1919, to Germany rather than stand by their supposed ally.

MASEFIELD, JOHN (1878–1967) British poet

I must go down to the seas again, to the lonely sea and the sky
All I ask is a tall ship and a star to steer her by,
And the wheel's kick and the wind's song and the white sail's
** shaking,**
And a grey mist on the sea's face and a grey dawn breaking.
Sea Fever (1902)

Included in his first successful collection, *Salt-Water Ballads*, Masefield's poem draws on his own experience as an apprentice merchant seaman from the age of thirteen. He had longed for a career at sea and in 1894 sailed with his ship, the Conway, for Chile via Cape Horn. The voyage proved a nightmare, plagued with seasickness, and forced Masefield into some form of nervous breakdown. He returned home, tried the sea again, sailing the Atlantic in 1895, but realised that the ocean held no happy future. Instead he accompanied a succession of odd jobs with an intense programme of reading, the long term fruits of which were a career as, until the Thirties, one of Britain's favourite poets.

MASEFIELD, JOHN

Dirty British coaster with a salt-caked smoke stack,
Butting through the Channel in the mad March days,
With a cargo of Tyne coal,
Road-rail, pig-lead,
Firewood, iron-ware and cheap tin trays
Cargoes (1910)

Cargoes is taken from Masefield's second collection of poetry, published as *Ballads and Poems* in 1910, three years after he had begun building a firm literary reputation as a regular contributor to a number of London journals, and as a member of the staff of the Manchester Guardian. His first prose work, a collection of short pieces called *A Mainsail Haul* had appeared in 1905. His own ambitions for a life as a merchant seaman had collapsed more than a decade before, but the flavour of the ships he might have captained is captured vividly in this verse with its rhythmic evocation of a merchant ship's churning piston engine.

MASTROIANNI, MARCELLO (1923–) Italian actor

Modern man isn't as virile as he used to be. Instead of making things happen, he waits for things to happen to him. He goes with the current. Something...has led him to stop swimming upstream.
quoted in *Playboy*, 1965

Mastroianni was a former clerk who managed his break into the movies with a small part in the film *I Miserabili* (1947). Since then he has become one of his country's most successful and respected leading men. In this section of his *Playboy* interview, Mastroianni, whose films have often cast him as just such an individual, was complaining that man is no longer master of his own fate. Of his own personality, as opaque as that of many actors, he remarks only that 'I only really exist when I am working on a film'.

MATTHAU, WALTER (1920–) American actor

The Jews invented guilt and the Irish turned it into an artform.
interview, August 2 1986

Matthau, born the near-unpronounceable Matasschanskayasky, is probably America's best character actor, a man best summed up, at least visually, by Alan Brien in the *Sunday Times*: 'Once seen, that antique-mapped face is never forgotten – a bloodhound with a headcold, a man who is simultaneously biting on a bad oyster and caught by the neck in lift-doors, a mad scientist's amalgam of Wallace Beery and Yogi Bear'. Among his best films are several in tandem with Jack Lemmon, most notably *The Odd Couple* (1968), and he has often interpreted playwright Neil Simon's work for the screen.

MAUGHAM, W. SOMERSET (1874–1965) British writer

Maugham, the orphaned son of a British lawyer, qualified as a doctor and used his experiences in the East End as the basis for his first novel, *Liza of Lambeth* (1897). His fame grew slowly until his sophisticated comedy *Lady Frederick* (1907) delighted London audiences. In 1908 he had four plays running simultaneously. He married Syrie Wellcome, the daughter of Doctor Barnardo (of the Homes) in 1911 but they lived separate lives. She preferred interior design and London society while he preferred to travel, before in 1926 settling down in Cap Ferrat in the South of France, with his long-time companion and secretary Gerald Haxton. Maugham was a prolific writer, turning out many novels, plays and short stories, notably the Ashenden series. Based loosely on his own experiences working for British intelligence in World War I, he created the disinterested, pragmatic secret agent, a far cry from the gung-ho antics of the James Bond clones, whose type would flower most fully in the work of John le Carré.

MAUGHAM, W. SOMERSET

Love is only the dirty trick played on us to achieve continuation of the species.
A Writer's Notebook (1949)

Maugham began keeping a notebook in 1892 and by 1941 had compiled 'fifteen stoutish volumes', all designed as a 'storehouse of materials for future use and nothing else'. In the event, after concentrating all fifteen volumes in one, and nearly losing the typescript when the Germans overran France in 1940, he did publish the notebooks 'because I am interested in the techniques of literary production and in the process of creation, and if such a volume as this by some other author came into my hands I should turn to it with avidity.' The *Notebooks* combine detailed preparatory work with quite polished and literary descriptions, as well as Maugham's philosophical animadversions on life.

MAUGHAM, W. SOMERSET

From the earliest times the old have rubbed it into the young that they are wiser than they, and before the young had discovered what nonsense this was they were old too, and it profited them to carry on the imposture.
Cakes and Ale (1930)

Cakes and Ale is Maugham's best novel, based on the idea for an unpublished short story parodying the contemporary London literary scene and creating in Rosie Driffield his finest portrait. The narrator Ashenden (Maugham) a novelist, is pumped by a younger novelist Alroy Kear (Hugh Walpole) for the facts on a third literary man, Edward Driffield (Thomas Hardy), whose biography he is writing. The plot is provided by the book's subtitle 'The Skeleton in the Cupboard'. The skeleton in question is Driffield's former wife, the ex-barmaid and enchantress Rosie, herself a former mistress of Ashenden, who since leaving her husband has prospered but whose knowledge of Driffield's less respectable youth threatens the image of the impeccable 'Grand Old Man' that his second wife, who has commissioned Kear's book, wishes to preserve.

MAUGHAM, W. SOMERSET

Some of my best friends are Jews
in letter of May 1946

The great self-exculpation, generally uttered immediately prior to some statement of gross racial prejudice, since the 'but' is always implied. Maugham can hardly be blamed for coining this particular example of mealy-mouthed racism, but he used it, quite sincerely one may presume, in a letter in which he answered charges of being anti-Semitic, writing in full 'God knows I have never been that; some of my best friends both in England and America are Jews...'

MAUGHAM, W. SOMERSET

Dying is a very dull, dreary affair. My advice to you is to have nothing whatever to do with it.
last words, 1965

It is the duty of the witty in life to remain witty at death's door, and Maugham's last words, admirably world-weary and insouciant, are eminently satisfying. It is worth noting, in contrast, some remarks he made on his 90th birthday, which are rather less defiant: 'I am sick of this way of life. The weariness and sadness of old age make it intolerable. I have walked with death hand in hand, and death's own hand is warmer than my own. I don't wish to live any longer'.

MAUGHAM, W. SOMERSET

You can't learn too soon that the most useful thing about a principle is that it can always be sacrificed to expediency.
The Circle (1921)

The Circle is considered by many to be Maugham's best play. The plot is centred on two young people who choose to sacrifice the world for love, even though they have before them the example, in two older people Lord Porteous and Lady Kitty, of just what happens to those who attempt so romantic a step. Maugham almost lets the youngsters get away with it, but everyone's life is upset for love. It is the older people who have the best lines, like this one. In the end Maugham lets sentiment prevail. The old warn the heedless young and these latter, still determined, are helped by the old to escape.

MAUGHAM, W. SOMERSET

We have long since passed the Victorian era when asterisks were followed after a certain interval by a baby.
The Constant Wife (1926)

The Constant Wife was not one of Maugham's most successful plays, full as it is of trivial people whose values come across as unsympathetic. The husband, John, is infatuated with the wife Constance's best friend Marie-Louise. Constance knows but is determined not to acknowledge the fact. Instead she permits herself an affair with her admirer Bernard. In the end John asks Constance to save him from Marie-Louise, who has in any case found a new lover, and is forced in return to watch his wife decamp with Bernard, although she has made the latter promise to bring her back to her husband. The play failed in London, although it was more popular in America. Audiences, it appeared, found the characters both ridiculous and embarrassing.

MAUGHAM, W. SOMERSET

The world is quickly bored by the recital of misfortunes, and willingly avoids the sight of distress.
The Moon and Sixpence (1919)

Maugham's novel of the 'good, dull, honest, plain' middle-aged stockbroker, Charles Strickland, who after seventeen uneventful years of marriage deserts his family, crying 'I've got to paint' and moves first to Paris where he struggles and thence to Tahiti where he triumphs, is based on the story of Paul Gauguin. Strickland's story is that of natural genius, whose efforts are at first decried by fashionable critics but in the end whose daemon rides over all opposition. Maugham creates an alluring picture of middle-class Edwardian London, the world in which he had lived himself, before moving onto the wilder shores of garrets in Paris, the waterfront of Marseilles and the sun-drenched paradise of Tahiti.

MAULDIN, WILLIAM H. 'BILL' (1921–) American cartoonist

Look in an infantryman's eyes and you can tell how much war he has seen.
reporting from World War II, 1944

Depending on the war in question it's a phenomenon known as shell shock, battle fatigue, post-traumatic neurosis and a variety of allied euphemisms, but at the bottom is a simple phenomenon: the destructive effects on the mind of a soldier who can no longer deal with the intense stress of fighting. Mauldin, an American Bruce Bairnsfather one World War later, was dealing with the soldiers of 1944. Twenty-five years later on reporters following the troops in Vietnam saw just the same thing in men, often near boys, who had seen too much for too long; they called it the 'thousand yard stare'.

MAULDIN, WILLIAM H. 'BILL'

'Peace' is when nobody's shooting. A 'just peace' is when our side gets what it wants.
quoted in *Loose Talk*, ed. L. Botts (1980)

The capacity of nations and individuals to delude themselves is never so pronounced as during or after a war. Propaganda flourishes and language degenerates into a convenient, malleable slavey, available in whatever guise and with whatever interpretation its user requires. Qualitative adjectives like 'just' when used with emotive nouns like 'peace' take concepts of absolute truth into hitherto uncharted areas. As Mauldin says, in this context 'just' no longer means 'fair', but 'fair to us'. But as many people have pointed out, it's the victors who get to write history.

MAUROIS, ANDRÉ (1885–1967) (Emile Herzog) French writer and biographer

The only thing experience teaches us is that experience teaches us nothing.

A variation on the running theme of one's inability to learn from history, most notably stated by Santayana (qv), Maurois' comment underlines the unfortunate truth that we never seem to benefit, either as individuals, generations or nations from what has gone before. Everyone, it appears, has to learn afresh what his or her predecessors have found out; each new generation determines to change the world, only to find, as many have done already, that the world changes them.

MAUROIS, ANDRÉ

In literature as in love, we are astonished at what is chosen by others.
in the *New York Times*, 1963

Maurois began his writing career with a novel, *The Silence of Colonel Bramble* (1918), sketches of a British officers' mess that stemmed from his experiences as a liaison officer with the British Army during World War I. He turned to biography in 1923 with *Ariel*, a study of Shelley which appeared in a sixpenny paperback edition in 1935 as the first Penguin book. Other biographies included those of Disraeli (1927), Byron (1930), Proust (1949) and George Sand (1952).

MAXTON, JAMES (1885–1946) British politician

Sit down man, you're a bloody tragedy.
to Ramsay MacDonald

Maxton, one of Parliament's more popular figures, was the Labour member for the poverty-stricken Glasgow constituency of Bridgeton. As chairman of the Independent Labour Party he was a vocal campaigner for every member of what he saw as an oppressed working class. He was unimpressed by Ramsay MacDonald, the Labour party leader and first Labour Prime Minister. In 1937, as MacDonald blundered through what would be his final speech in the House of Commons, Maxton expostulated 'Sit down man, you're a bloody tragedy'. The ILP leader continued his own fight up to the General Election of 1945, when shortly prior to his own death he told his constituents 'Twenty years ago you sent me to parliament to protest and I will protest for you until I die'.

MAXWELL, ELSA (1883–1963) American hostess

Someone said that life is a party. You join after it's started and you leave before it's finished.
How To Do It (1957)

In her prime Elsa Maxwell was renowned as the world's leading professional party giver. As a Washington hostess she used her influence to gather the great and the good and the interesting in massive assemblies, often with a theme, such as the Pet Hate Party of the mid-Thirties when everyone was told to come as the person or object they loathed most. In this instance many of the smart guests, who generally loathed President Roosevelt's New Deal, dressed as the President himself, with cigarette holder and silk hat. Her definition of life, unsurprisingly, sets it firmly in her own milieu.

MAYAKOVSKY, VLADIMIR   (1893–1930) Russian poet

Art is not a mirror to shape the world, but a hammer with which to shape it.
quoted in the *Guardian*, December 11 1974

Mayakovsky was the son of an impoverished nobleman but he joined the Bolshevik party aged only fifteen and was imprisoned three times for revolutionary activity. He began writing poetry in jail, and his first publication appeared in a futurist symposium 'A slap in the face of public taste' (1912). His first book *Ya (I)* appeared in 1913 and he began publishing a series of poems, both revolutionary and, stemming from his triangular affair with Lili Brik and her husband the critic Osip Brik, concerned with the problems of fate and love. His work combined his desire to see the Revolution succeed and the need to express his own, often contradictory, artistic emotions. Despite such poems as the valedictory 'Vladimir Ilich Lenin' (1924) Mayakovsky was not considered truly acceptable and after publishing a last poem 'At the top of my voice', he shot himself on April 14, 1930. Stalin, persuaded by Lili Brik, rehabilitated him fully and he became touted as Russia's ideal poet.

MAYER, LOUIS B.   (1885–1957) American film magnate

Look out for yourself – or they'll pee on your grave.
quoted in L. Halliwell, *The Filmgoer's Companion* (1985)

Mayer started life as a scrap merchant and like a number of other far-sighted immigrants saw the potential of the movies. Allied with Samuel Goldwyn they formed Metro-Goldwyn-Mayer in 1924 and after Goldwyn bought him out, Mayer became one of Hollywood's leading tycoons, an archetype for everyone's idea of the outrageous, flamboyant, egocentric, ruthless, puritanical money-making movie mogul. With his white-haired boy Irving Thalberg, Mayer helped ensure that American films were aimed straight at the family, most notably the fictional Hardy Family, whose filmic adventures provided the cash basis for many grander productions. Mayer was obsessed with detail, called by producer B.P. Schulberg (1892–1957) 'Czar of all the rushes'. Mayer inspired love and hate, mainly the latter, but as a dictator who liked to come on as a star's second father, he inadvertently summed himself up when amending a plotline: 'A boy may hate his father, but he will still respect him'.

MAYER, LOUIS B.

The number one book of the ages was written by a committee, and it was called the Bible.
commenting on mass scriptwriting techniques, 1930s

Although Hollywood had on tap some of the world's major writers, journalists, novelists and playwrights, many of them with strings of published successes to their names, the studios of the Thirties rarely allowed any one to work alone. Every studio had its Writers' Building, where creative talent worked to create the required script. Sometimes they worked alone, sometimes in teams but it was an accepted, though by the writers loathed fact that somewhere just down the corridor another writer or team would be putting out their version of the same story. When all the versions were in they might be amalgamated, but then again, the director might equally impose his own version on the lot. Mayer, who was committed to such seemingly wasteful methods, was wont to justify the system with this classically sanctimonious rebuttal.

MAZRUI, ALI A. (1933–) Asian political scientist

A people denied history is a people deprived of dignity.
in *The Listener*, 1978

Mazrui is referring to a constant factor that recurs amongst those nations only recently emerged from the colonial experience: the fact that their own history had been, until the moment of independence, consistently overlooked. The European colonisers were keen to establish schools, often run by missionaries, and prided themselves on their teaching of the native population, but the syllabus they taught was essentially that of the 'mother country'. This deliberate failure to acknowledge a colony's indigenous history appears today as one more way of confirming the white man's supremacy and, as Mazrui puts it, denying dignity to those he ruled.

MCADOO, WILLIAM (1863–1941) American politician

His speeches leave the impression of an army of pompous phrases moving over the landscape in search of an idea. Sometimes these meandering words would actually capture a straggling thought and bear it triumphantly a prisoner in their midst until it died of servitude and overwork.
on Warren G Harding

McAdoo, Woodrow Wilson's son-in-law and Secretary of the

Treasury, and Philadelphia's one-time Commissioner of Police, was no supporter of Warren Gamaliel Harding, arguably America's least competent President. His description seems apt enough for the hapless Harding whose real forte was for golf and poker and certainly not for rousing, or even comprehensible oratory.

MCAULIFFE, ANTHONY (1898–1975) American soldier

Nuts!
at the Battle of the Bulge, December 23 1944

Faced by the initial success of the Allies' D-Day landings in June 1944, the Germans mounted a counter-offensive that December. In what became known as the Battle of the Bulge, the American 101st Airborne Division, under their commander General Anthony McAuliffe, were defending the town of Bastogne, a strategic point in the Ardennes Forest through which the German armies had to pass if their offensive was to succeed. The 101st stood fast in Bastogne as the Germans pushed forward to encircle them 'like the hole in a doughnut'. After seven days of impasse the Germans offered to accept McAuliffe's surrender. McAuliffe's reply was terse and vulgar and it inspired his men to hold on.

MCCARTHY, EUGENE (1916–) American politician

Being in politics is like being a football coach. You have to be smart enough to understand the game, and dumb enough to think it's important.
campaigning in 1968

Senator McCarthy stood in 1968 for the liberal wing of the democratic party, for what Norman Mailer called 'the academy and suburbs' and for the faith that 'a man must be allowed to lead a modest and respectable life without interference by large force'. McCarthy's supporters were the middle-class Left, soft-core socialists and back to nature idealists, peace and love hippies too spaced out to join the hard-core radicals of SDS and the Yippies, and those of the solid bourgeoisie who had come to hate the war in Vietnam. As his comment makes clear, he was too urbane and too sophisticated to win his party's nomination.

MCCARTHY, EUGENE

We have a three-to-one advantage over the Russians, which I understand means that we have the potential to kill all the Russians twice, and they have the potential to kill us one and a quarter times.
on the nuclear balance of terror, 1968

The concept of 'overkill' is central to nuclear planning. In effect it denotes a nation's power to destroy its enemy 'more than once'. By simply counting warheads and bombs and comparing them to the targets deemed necessary to be destroyed, the planner can work out just how great an overkill factor his side can establish. As McCarthy pointed out during his electoral campaign in 1968, the whole concept is ludicrous, but then, as anyone will find who starts to probe the bizarre world of apocalyptic planning, much of the nuclear stalemate is, apart, unfortunately, from the deadly efficiency of the weapons.

McCARTHY, JOSEPH (1908–57) American politician and witch-hunter

I have here in my hand a list of 205, a list of names that were known to the Secretary of State as being members of the Communist Party and who are nevertheless working and shaping the policy in the State Department.
speaking to the Republican Club in Wheeling, W. Virginia,

Joseph 'Tailgunner' McCarthy, the Junior Senator from Wisconsin, remains the embodiment of the anti-Communist witch-hunting paranoia that ran through America in the late 1940s and early 1950s. While he was by no means the only energiser of the trend, he came to typify its worst excesses and an era and its style is summed up by the eponymous 'McCarthyism'. Although he himself defined the word as 'Americanism with its sleeves rolled' the era has become known as 'The Great Fear'. McCarthy specialised in brandishing lists of alleged Communist sympathisers in the State Department, a technique first exhibited in this speech, given in 1950. That his facts were hearsay and his figures wildly incorrect, his evidence tendentious and his claims absurd mattered not at all. He was a supreme huckster, a cheapjack showman who entranced his audience and sold them his own brand of poisonous political cure-all.

McCARTHY, MARY (1912–) American writer and critic

It may be that the whims of chance are really the importunities of design. But if there is a Design, it aims to look natural and fortuitous; that is how it gets us into its web.
On the Contrary (1962)

McCarthy, who has gained an equal reputation as a satirical novelist and an acerbic critic of American mores, is attempting to link what appear to be the random vicissitudes of one's fate to the belief that perhaps there is a grand design. In this it would seem

537

that she is debating the atheistic view, whereby things 'happen', and the theological one, whereby God has ordained a great plan. If this is so, she is suggesting that God is not only wrathful (Old Testament) and merciful (New Testament) but cunning too.

McCARTHY, MARY

The happy ending is our national belief.
On The Contrary (1962)

The American national psyche, at the risk of stereotyping two hundred-odd million people, does not enjoy failure. Most of those gung-ho quotations that condemn losers irrespective of their fate and extol the winner, no matter by what means he may have won, come from American sources. Thus the unhappy ending, in which the hero does not ride off, as it were, into the sunset, wealth in one hand and the girl in the other, tends to fail both in the real and the metaphorical box office.

McCARTHY, MARY

If someone tells you he is going to make a realistic decision, you immediately understand that he has resolved to do something bad.
On the Contrary (1962)

McCARTNEY, PAUL (1942–) British pop singer

You can't reheat a soufflé.
discounting rumours of a Beatles reunion, 1977

The lust among the press and large sections of the public, not to mention the lucky promoter who would pick up the package, to see a Beatles reunion was for many years a perennial phenomenon. Occasionally the collective mouth would water as two or even three of the 'Fab Four' met for a jam session, a charity concert or some form of one-off. It was in answer to one of these repetitive demands for a reunion that McCartney gave this reply. He was, one presumes, only unconsciously echoing Alice Roosevelt Longworth's comment on US politician Thomas Dewey's attempt at an electoral comeback in 1948: 'You can't make a soufflé rise twice'.

McCOUGHEY, J.D. Australian theologian

God is dead, but fifty thousand social workers have risen to take his place.
in *The Bulletin* magazine, 1974

McCoughey's complaint is that no sooner have the mass of people decided that they have no need for formal religion and thus abandoned God, than they choose to ally themselves with a whole procession of mini-deities, rejoicing in the name of social workers or, as the jargon has it, the 'caring professions'. Whether he is strictly right in claiming that social workers are simply surrogate gods may well be debated, but there is an argument that says that not only do many people feel the desperate need to cry on some sympathetic shoulder, particularly one that, unlike traditional religion, eschews the concept of guilt, but that some social workers, if viewed with a less than sympathetic eye, do appear to conduct themselves like the Almighty.

McCULLIN, DON   (1935–) British photographer

What's the point of getting killed if you've got the wrong exposure.
The Destruction Business (1971)

McCullin is Britain's leading combat photographer, a veteran of more wars than most soldiers, and the creator of more telling images of those wars than any of his rivals. Well known for his courage and his seeming carelessness of his own life in pursuit of the ideal picture, McCullin's comment, taken from one of his collections of pictures, stresses that if one is going to take these risks, then it's vital to make sure that the picture in question is worth the effort.

McGOUGH, ROGER   (1937–) British poet

> **Let me die a youngman's death**
> **not a clean and inbetween**
> **the sheets holy-water death**
> **not a famous-last-words**
> **peaceful out of breath death**

Let me die a youngman's death (1967)

Like Adrian Henri (qv) and Brian Patten, McGough was featured in the Penguin Modern Poets series as one of the highly popular Liverpool Poets. McGough's wish for a dramatic death echoes the 'live fast, die young and leave a good looking corpse' philosophy, but although he wants to die well, he doesn't want to die young. Thus subsequent verses cite possible scenes at the ages of 73 ('mown down by a bright red sports car on my way home from an all night party'), 91 (...'sitting in a barber's chair, may rival gansters with hamfisted tommyguns burst in & give me a short back and insides') or 104 ('may my mistress catch me in bed with her daughter...').

MCINDOE, ARCHIBALD   (1900–1960) British plastic surgeon

Skill is fine, and genius is splendid, but the right contacts are more valuable than either.
quoted in *The Wit of Medicine*, ed. L.& M. Cowan (1972)

McIndoe was born in New Zealand and trained there, in America and in London. As the most eminent pupil of plastic surgeon Sir Harold Gillies he won fame during World War II as surgeon-in-charge at the Queen Victoria Hospital in East Grinstead, where the faces and limbs of wounded men, especially those fighter pilots who had suffered terrifying burns, were remodelled with unparallelled skill. McIndoe was knighted in 1947 and from 1957–59 was vice-president of the Royal College of Surgeons.

MCLACHLAN, DONALD   British journalist

Most Conservatives, and almost certainly some of the wiser Trade Union leaders, are waiting to feel the smack of firm government.
in the *Daily Telegraph*, January 3 1956

McLachlan was the deputy editor of the *Daily Telegraph* in early 1956. Although Anthony Eden had been Prime Minister less than a year there was already emerging a groundswell of discontent with his government. McLachlan's attack, couched in an unsigned editorial in the newspaper, assessed Eden's performance to date and speculated on the new year. He might have been less wounding had he realised that this attack, and similar goads, may well have helped push Eden into the debacle of Suez later that year.

MCLAUGHLIN, MIGNON   American journalist

Every society honours its live conformists and its dead trouble-makers.
The Neurotic's Notebook (1963)

If one accepts one broad definition of society as a group of reasonably like-minded individuals, McLaughlin's aphorism reflects the distaste such individuals have for those who flout their laws, unwritten as well as codified. The young, short-term nonconformists themselves, may find rebels appealing, but the bulk of their elders will not. Once conveniently dead, the nonconformist, in life so tiresome, becaomes a 'character' whose exploits are embellished in every lovingly crafted, relieved obituary.

McLAUGHLIN, MIGNON

Many are saved from sin by being so inept at it.
The Neurotic's Notebook (1963)

Given the extent to which people break one or more of the Ten Commandments, and are often willing prey to a whole run of the Seven Deadly Sins, McLaughlin obviously views the real sinner and his sins as something out of the ordinary. Yet given the passage of the 20th century, with its particularly spectacular abominations, many of which, even the worst, seem all too accessible to the most commonplace of sinners, it is hard not to feel that she is choosing to be perversely optimistic.

McLUHAN, MARSHALL (1911–80) Canadian academic and communications theorist

The new electronic interdependence recreates the world in the image of a global village.
The Gutenberg Galaxy (1962)

The concept of the 'global village' was central to McLuhan's thesis and to the appeal he had to many people, especially the television-saturated young, in the 1960s. McLuhan held that communications technology was no more than an extension of the human nervous system and that technological changes, by making scarcely perceptible changes in the way one sees things, create new sensual and emotional environments. The proliferation of electronic communications around the world had, he claimed, created a degree of instant awareness for everyone with access to them that instantly invalidated all the old rules of perspective space and sequential time. The concept was appealing but had its flaws, notably that given the vast discrepancies between one person's and another's access to the technology, the 'villagers' tended to a single privileged type.

McLUHAN, MARSHALL

If it works it's obsolete.
quoted in *The Listener*, 1971

Society, if one accepts this premise, ought to be in a process of continual flux, eternally searching for new developments and casting aside the old as soon as it has been proven to work. McLuhan's rousing dictum smacks of the Sixties, a period rife with such calls to technological arms. And like so many slogans it looks good, sounds good but fails in the real world to do anyone much good. In company with so many futuristic theories of the era, McLuhan's beliefs depended for their full realisation on continuing economic stability.

MCLUHAN, MARSHALL

Television brought the brutality of war into the comfort of the living room. Vietnam was lost in the living rooms of America – not on the battlefields of Vietnam.
quoted in the *Montreal Gazette*, 16 May 1975

Fitting conveniently into McLuhan's theory of the global village and its instant mass communication, the belief that America lost its war in Vietnam back home on the TV screens of what the fighting troops called 'The World' has remained popular, if not wholly accurate. Initially it was seen by the media as a source of self-congratulation, peaking with their next great triumph, the investigation of the Watergate Affair. Since then the burden of the theory has taken a new twist. America's turn to the right, coupled with the national revulsion towards such exhibitions of failure, has meant that if the war was lost on television it was television's fault. Neither version is truly correct, but the myth is pervasive and both Israel in Lebanon and the British in the Falklands ensured that in their war the cameras stayed as far away as possible.

MCLUHAN, MARSHALL

People don't actually read newspapers. They get into them every morning like a hot bath.
quoted in Tom Wolfe, *The New Life Out There* (1965)

One's daily newspaper summons up a ritualised allegiance that may last a lifetime. Only when some seismic change overtakes one's morning medium will the ritual be shattered and the observance neglected. McLuhan, of course, was attempting to show how newspapers may be paper but they don't purvey news to most readers, who prefer to massage their prejudices, as they would sponge themselves with the waters of a soothing bath, by checking their favourite sections and simply absorbing their morning imput. Unfortunately for his televisual preferences, the messages purveyed by the small screen are if possible even less closely observed. Not for nothing is one of the many descriptions used to denigrate its programmes that of 'wallpaper'.

McLuhan, Marshall

One matter Englishmen don't think in the least funny is their happy consciousness of possessing a deep sense of humour.
The Mechanical Bride (1951)

The Mechanical Bride is McLuhan's first book, and compared with his later works a positive hymn to the glories of the literary standpoint. But in its exploration of what McLuhan called 'industrial folklore', his own version of the semiologists' 'close reading' of advertisements, comic strips and other mass consumption media, it pointed him in the direction of his wider theories. The sense of humour, when taken in nationalistic terms, is a most peculiar and specific phenomenon. In other words, no one nation seems capable of understanding what reduces the next to paroxysms. The British, as McLuhan points out, are never more serious than when boosting the charms of their own variety.

McLuhan, Marshall

The medium is the message. This is merely to say that the personal and social consequences of any medium ... result from the new scale that is introduced into our affairs by each extension of ourselves or by any new technology.
Understanding Media (1964)

McLuhan's theory posited that society has always been 'shaped more by the nature of the media by which men communicate than by the nature of the communication', another way of saying that style is more important than content. In his view, just as the alphabet, with its inbuilt rules, forces the child who learns it to view the world in a specific way, so does electronic technology influence the views of those it touches. The difference is that whereas the print technology led to specialisation and detachment, the alleged universality of electronic technology 'fosters and encourages unification and involvement'.

McMahon, Ed   (1923–) American entertainer

Heeeeeeere's Johnny!
catchphrase on the Johnny Carson TV show

McMahon is the resident greeter on America's most popular late night show, NBC's Tonight show, a staple of the small screen since 1961. This introduction, with the accent on the first word, signals the appearance of the doyen of American chat shows, Johnny Carson. Carson has set the style for every imitator, dispensing the traditional monologue, followed by a succession of guests, usually plugging their latest book, film or similar artefact and always peddling their ego, interspersed with various guest performers. The ill-fated Simon Dee programme showed what happens when you tamper with a master. Dee's audience dutifully intoned 'It's Simon Dee!!!' but the TV's best forgotten one-hit wonder lacked Carson's staying power. The most bizarre use of the line came on film in *The Shining* (1981) when psychopath Jack Nicholson axes his way through a door to announce with glinting eyes 'Here's Johnny!!'

MCSHANE, DENIS   (1948–) British trades union leader

Industrial action is merely the continuation of negotiation by other means.
quoted in 1978

McShane, who as a former leader of the National Union of Journalists has had his own bruising run-ins with management, is echoing and rephrasing the better known line, originated by the military theorist Karl von Clausewitz in *On War* (1832) 'War is nothing but a duel on a larger scale'. He has also chosen to sanctify the popular euphemism 'industrial action', a term that infuriates a number of conservatives who feel that the whole import of such a phrase is that it actually precludes both industry and action.

MEAD, MARGARET   (1901–78) American anthropologist

For the first time the young are seeing history being made before it is censored by their elders.
quoted in *Time* magazine, 1978

Mead was fascinated by anthropology from an early age and published her first book, *Coming of Age in Samoa*, in 1928. Focussing on the fashionable area of adolescence, she contrasted the entrance into maturity of Samoan girls and those in her own country. Continuing to work in the Pacific, Mead published a number of subsequent works. By popularising her discipline, without sacrificing her own standards, she became the world's best known anthropologist and she was among the first to make clear to the developed world the extent to which it could learn from less 'advanced' peoples, and to point out just what was being lost in the gradual erosion of older cultures by the advance of 'progress'.

MEDAWAR, PETER   (1915–) British scientist

If politics is the art of the possible, research is surely the art of the soluble.... Good scientists study the most important problems they think they can solve. It is, after all, their professional business to solve problems, not merely to grapple with them.
The Art of the Soluble (1967)

Medawar trained as a zoologist, but when dealing with serious burn victims during World War II turned to the researches into skin grafts that in 1960 won him a share in the Nobel Prize. His work in immunology, which showed that under the right circumstances it was possible for the body to accept foreign tissue, lies behind many of the recent successful organ transplants. Medawar has also been able to combine his own researches with an ability to make their results accessible to less expert individuals. *The Art of the Soluble*, his collection of essays on scientific and philosophical themes, is widely admired as a model of clarity. As this excerpt indicates, he believes that every solution, however small, that contributes to the lessening of human misery, is worthwhile. Grappling with the huge problems is vital, but so is solving the lesser ones.

MEDAWAR, PETER

I cannot give any scientist of any age better advice than this: the intensity of a conviction that a hypothesis is true has no bearing over whether it is true or not.
Advice to a Young Scientist (1979)

The art of science is to ask questions and having answered them, to ask further questions of those answers. That way, Medawar indicates, lies real discovery. Merely coming up with a satisfactory solution is not enough, since the most satisfactory solution, especially when applauded by one's peers and published in the learned magazines, may well be nothing but a way-station on the way to a better solution and, at worst, be an utter fallacy.

MELLY, GEORGE   (1926–) British critic, journalist and jazz singer

Pop culture is for the most part non-reflective, non-didactic, dedicated only to pleasure. It changes constantly because it is sensitive to change, indeed it could be said that it is sensitive to nothing else. Its principle faculty is to catch the spirit of its time

and translate this spirit into objects or music or fashion or behaviour. It could be said to offer a comic strip which compresses and caricatures the social and economic forces at work within our society. It draws no conclusions. It makes no comments. It admits to neither past nor future, not even its own.

Revolt Into Style (1970)

Among the multifarious pronouncements, quickly dumped between hard or soft covers and promoted as the latest thing in hip philosophy, criticism or self-improvement, George Melly's analysis of the post-war youth culture stands as an exemplary guide to how these things should be done. Taking as his epigraph Thom Gunn's description of Elvis Presley – 'He turns revolt into style' – Melly set about defining British pop art and the culture it spawned. Although nearly twenty years have passed since Melly's work, and society and its concerns have changed radically, his assessment seems as pertinent as ever.

MENCKEN, H.L. (1880–1956) American editor, essayist and philologist

Henry Lewis Mencken, 'The Sage of Baltimore', wrote his first newspaper story in 1899; it ran to five lines and presaged a career of 49 years of massively prolific journalism. While contributing his regular columns to at least one of the four Baltimore papers, he moved into magazine writing and co-edited the *Smart Set* (1914–23) and the *American Mercury* (1924–33). The editors of the Mercury declared their intention to be 'committed to nothing save this: to keep common sense as fast as they can, to belabor sham as agreeably as possible, to give civilized entertainment'. Mencken's whole career was predicated on these simple principles, although they infuriated his many targets. In 1919 he produced the first volume of *The American Language* (two more followed), a substantially influential philological work, perhaps the first fully to establish the autonomy of American from English English. In 1948, with awful irony, he suffered a near-fatal stroke, which robbed him of the power of reading and writing. He survived until 1956, a tragically diminished figure, and died peacefully in his sleep.

MENCKEN, H.L.

Democracy is the theory that the common people know what they want, and deserve to get it good and hard.

A Book of Burlesques (1920)

MENCKEN, H.L.

Puritanism – the haunting fear that someone, somewhere, may be happy.
A Book of Burlesques (1920)

MENCKEN, H.L.

The most popular man under a democracy is not the most democratic man, but the most despotic man. The common folk delight in the exactions of such a man. They like him to boss them. Their natural gait is the goosestep.
A Carnival of Buncombe (1956)

MENCKEN, H.L.

Conscience is the inner voice that warns us that someone might be looking.
A Mencken Chrestomathy (1949)

MENCKEN, H.L.

The urge to save humanity is almost always a false front for the urge to rule.
Minority Report (1956)

MENCKEN, H.L.

Voting is simply a way of determining which side is the stronger without putting it to the test of fighting.
Minority Report (1956)

MENCKEN, H.L.

When I hear a man applauded by the mob I always feel a pang of pity for him. All he has to do to be hissed is to live long enough.
Minority Report (1956)

MENCKEN, H.L.

Under democracy, one party always devotes its chief energies to trying to prove that the other party is unfit to rule – and both commonly succeed, and are right.
Minority Report (1956)

MENCKEN, H.L.

What men value in this world is not rights, but privileges.
Minority Report (1956)

MENCKEN, H.L.

Most people want security in this world, not liberty.
Minority Report (1956)

MENCKEN, H.L.

God is the immemorial refuge of the incompetent, the helpless, the miserable. They find not only sanctuary in His arms, but also a kind of superiority, soothing to their macerated egos; He will set them above their betters.
Minority Report (1956)

MENCKEN, H.L.

A sense of humour always withers in the presence of the messianic delusion, like justice and truth in front of patriotic passion.
Prejudices (1919–27)

MENCKEN, H.L.

The chief business of the nation, as a nation, is the setting up of heroes, mostly bogus.
Prejudices 3rd series (1922)

MENCKEN, H.L.

Unionism seldom, if ever, uses such power as it has to ensure better work – almost always it devotes a large part of that power to safeguarding bad work.
Prejudices 3rd series (1922)

MENCKEN, H.L.

Politics, as hopeful men practise it in the world, consists mainly of the delusion that a change in form is a change in substance.
Prejudices 4th series (1924)

MENCKEN, H.L.

To die for an idea – it is unquestionably noble. But how much nobler it would be if men died for ideas that were true.
Prejudices (1919–27)

MENCKEN, H.L.

Democracy is a form of religion. It is the worship of jackals by jackasses.
Sententiae (1916)

MENCKEN, H.L.

Say what you like about the Ten Commandments, you must always come back to the pleasant fact that there are only ten of them.
Sententiae (1916)

MENCKEN, H.L.

The demagogue is one who preaches doctrines he knows to be untrue to men he knows to be idiots.
Sententiae (1912–1916)

MENCKEN, H.L.

Theology – an effort to explain the unknowable by putting it into the terms of the not worth knowing.
Sententiae (1916)

MENCKEN, H.L.

Husbands never become good. They merely become proficient.
Sententiae (1916)

MENCKEN, H.L.

Love is the delusion that one woman differs from another.
Sententiae (1916)

MENCKEN, H.L.

Truth – something somehow discreditable to someone.
Sententiae (1916)

MENCKEN, H.L.

Self-respect – the secure feeling that no-one, as yet, is suspicious.
Sententiae (1916)

MENCKEN, H.L.

Remorse – regret that one waited so long to do it.
Sententiae (1916)

MENCKEN, H.L.

The difference betwen a moral man and a man of honour is that the latter regrets a discreditable act, even when it has worked and he has not been caught.
Sententiae (1916)

MENCKEN, H.L.

An idealist is one who, on noticing that a rose smells better than a cabbage, concludes that it will also make better soup.
Sententiae (1916)

MENCKEN, H.L.

Immorality is the morality of those who are having a better time.
Sententiae (1916)

MENCKEN, H.L.

Men are the only animals that devote themselves, day in and day out, to making one another unhappy. It is an art like any other. Its virtuosi are called altruists.
Sententiae (1916)

MENCKEN, H.L.

Evil is that which one believes of others. It is a sin to believe evil of others, but it is seldom a mistake.
Sententiae (1916)

MENCKEN, H.L.

Whenever you hear a man speak of his love for his country, it is a sign that he expects to be paid for it.
Sententiae (1916)

MENCKEN, H.L.

Friendship is a common belief in the same fallacies, mountebanks and hobgoblins.
Sententiae (1916)

MENCKEN, H.L.

When a man laughs at his troubles he loses a great many friends. They never forgive the loss of their prerogative.
Sententiae (1916)

MICHAELS, LEONARD (1933–) American writer and academic

Reasons are whores.
in the *New York Times*, 1971

Michaels is professor of English at the University of California at Berkeley and has combined his teaching with writing his own fiction. He has written two collections of short stories and his one novel, *The Men's Club* (1981) centres on a rambunctious night out spent by a group of unregenerately chauvinist Californian males. Michaels' remark stresses that 'reasons', cited without reference to the beliefs or needs upon which they are based, are meaningless as justification for any act, however admirable or repellent, since each individual will tailor his reasons to his own needs.

MIES VAN DER ROHE, LUDWIG   (1886–1969) American-Dutch architect

God is in the details.

quoted in his obituary in the *New York Times*, 1969

The work of Mies van der Rohe epitomises modern architecture at its most ideal. It is to him that building owes its most clean-cut edifices of glass and steel, glass skyscrapers, strip-windowed office blocks, lengthy brick houses with long bare walls penetrating the landscape and other characteristic forms. His architectural principles were supposedly drawn from St. Thomas Aquinas' dictum 'Reason is the first principle of all human work' and his buildings remain models of clean cut, geometrical lines. He gained many ideas during his experience as a practical craftsman, and offered as a working dictum 'It is better to be good than to be original.' He began designing buildings in the Twenties and in 1930 was appointed head of the Bauhaus, then emigrated to America in 1938, where he remained.

MIES VAN DER ROHE, LUDWIG

Less is more.

Given Mies van der Rohe's dedication to clean lines and minimal ornamentation his maxim 'less is more' is a logical extension of his ideals. Not every architect agreed with him, and Frank Lloyd Wright, writing in *The Future of Architecture* (1953), offered his own refutation of Mies' line: 'Less is only more where more is no good.'

MIKES, GEORGE   (1912–1987) British writer

Continental people have sex-lives. The English have hot water bottles.

How to Be An Alien

Mikes emigrated to England before World War II and used his experiences to write *How to be an Alien*, the first of many successful books in which he takes a wry look at the more amusing characteristics of a variety of nations. This line reflects the common belief, from the perspective of a European culture, that the English, unlike more imaginative races, fail to see much beyond the procreative aspects of sex.

MILES, RUFUS American administrator

How you stand depends on where you sit.

quoted in Safire's *Political Dictionary* (1978)

Miles was an employee of the US Bureau of the Budget. His line refers not to physical stance or sitting but to political metaphor. Assuming one is an elected member of a representative body, the likelihood is that your party will occupy one part of its debating chamber, while each opposition party will have their allotted seat. As a party member you will sit with your group and vote with them, often over and above your own feelings on an issue. Were you sitting elsewhere, literally and metaphorically, you might well 'stand' quite differently.

MILLAY, EDNA ST. VINCENT (1892–1950) American poet

> **My candle burns at both ends;**
> **It will not last the night;**
> **But, ah, my foes, and oh, my friends –**
> **It gives a lovely light.**

My Candle Burns at Both Ends (1920)

Millay published her first poem, 'Renascence', when she was just 20 and still studying at Vassar. The poem was much admired and reappeared in her first collection *Renascence and Other Poems* (1917). Her next collection, *A Few Figs from Thistles* (1920) established her firmly as the epitome of the intelligent, sexy, cynical, liberated Twenties woman and her 'double-burning candles', as Dorothy Parker put it, were highly influential, both on progressive girls and on nascent poetesses.

MILLER, ARTHUR (1915–) American playwright

An era can be said to end when its basic illusions are exhausted.

Miller first came to critical attention with his play *All My Sons* (1947), but gained his first hit with *Death of a Salesman* (1949), still the best-known of his work. *The Crucible* (1952) uses the 17th century Salem witch trials as a parable for Senator McCarthy's modern version. Miller himself was subpoenaed by HUAC but declined to name names as required. Further successes followed but his more recent work is less fashionable. The 'basic illusions' that made Miller's early work so popular – his studies of the realities of human relationships within the environment of the American dream – ask too many questions of a generation dominated by Yuppie concerns.

MILLER, ARTHUR

Willy Loman never made a lot of money. His name was never in the paper. He's not the finest character that ever lived. But he's a human being and a terrible thing is happening to him. So attention must be paid.
Death of a Salesman (1949)

Death of a Salesman, Miller's most successful play, concerns the life of one Willy Loman, apostrophised in this prologue to his story. Loman is the salesman of the title and his seduction and eventual rejection by the ultimately false lure of contemporary American life is what brings about his death. Miller uses Loman's experience to portray a whole world of Americans, trapped between the bleak realities of their existence and the demands of the endlessly touted American dream. The solution for Loman is self-deception, and when that self-deception lies revealed, the salesman is destroyed.

MILLER, ARTHUR

Part of knowing who we are is knowing we are not someone else. And Jew is only the name we give to that stranger, the agony we cannot feel, the death we look at like a cold abstraction. Each man has his Jew; it is the other.
Incident at Vichy (1964)

Miller's play deals with the arrest at Vichy in 1942 of a number of men by the Germans. They represent all classes and races; among them is Leduc, both a French officer and a psychiatrist, himself a Jew, who has studied in Vienna. The purpose of the interrogation is to determine who is a Jew and must therefore be deported to the concentration camps. As the arrestees discuss their situation, Leduc suggests that he has yet to analyse a gentile who was not, somewhere in his soul, anti-Semitic. When his opinion is rebuffed, he offers this speech.

MILLER, ARTHUR

A good newspaper is a nation talking to itself.
in the *Observer*, 1961

The appeal of Miller's definition is that the newspaper does not need to be good, by which, given Miller's own work, one may assume him to mean tolerant, liberal, balanced and intelligent, to be seen as the nation's voice. One need only consider the papers that sell the most, invariably the lowest common denominator of their type, to feel that goodness in this context has no bearing whatsoever and that if such papers are a nation deep in self-communication, one is best advised not to listen.

MILLER JONATHAN (1936–) British physician, writer, theatre and opera director

The human body is private property. We have to have a search warrant to look inside, and even then an investigator is confined to a few experimental tappings here and there, some gropings on the party wall, a torch flashed rather hesitantly into some of the dark corners.
The Body in Question (1979)

Jonathan Miller went to university to read medicine and while he is still associated with his role in the satirical *Beyond the Fringe* he remained involved in medicine throughout. His televison series *The Body in Question* was in the tradition of Kenneth Clark's *Civilisation* and Jacob Bronowski's *The Ascent of Man*: a multi-part exploration of an interesting if complex topic narrated and written by an expert with a flair for popularisation. Miller's programmes undoubtedly benefited as much from his own enthusiasm, wildy gesticulating hands threatening at any moment to flythrough the screen, as from his undoubted expertise.

MILLER, JONATHAN

Censorship is nothing more than a legal corollary of public modesty.
in the *Guardian*, 1967

From the point of view of those who enforce this 'legal corollary' Miller may well be right: people do not want kiddie porn or sadistic violence thrust, as it were, into their homes, and thus a law making sure this does not happen ought to be justified. The argument becomes specious, however, when one observes the censor in action. What happens is that it is not public modesty that is being protected, but individual private prudery which, given the attitudes of many pro-censorship campaigners, is no more representative of the public view than is the hard-core pornography they condemn.

MILLER, JONATHAN

There is a particular sort of shrieking hatred which the non-creative have for the half-creative and, equally, an exorbitant admiration that the non-creative have for the very fully-fledged creative. So, therefore, what you get from critics is the exorbitant admiration of the great and the shrieking hatred of those who interpret the fully great.
in the *Listener*, 1978

Miller, as an intellectual and a director or producer rather than an actual performer, is able to phrase more elegantly than most the traditional dislike that people who work in the theatre feel towards those who only arrive to criticise. His assumption, however, is the usual one: critics are not creative; he merely differentiates between the sycophancy they exhibit towards those they see as great and the venom with which they deal with anyone else.

MILLER, JONATHAN

I'm not really a Jew, just Jewish, not the whole hog.
Beyond the Fringe (1961)

Before *Beyond the Fringe* came down from Edinburgh to the West End, the review format was on its last legs, a hangover from Noel Coward's 'sophistication' and more often than not going back even further, to Gilbert and Sullivan. So many spinoffs, developments and plagiarisms of *Beyond the Fringe* have followed, dominating the next twenty years of British humour, that the impact of the original has become hard to recall. The show coincided with its moment. It was characterised as satire, and it did satirise certain topics, notably Mr. Macmillan, the myths of World War II and the possibility of World War III, but as Miller has explained, the intention was to lampoon, to bring out the humour of a topic, rather than to decry it. Either way, the critics raved and the show, brought into London as a stopgap while another review rehearsed, ran for five and a half years.

MILLER, HENRY   (1891–1980) American writer

Writing, like life itself, is a voyage of discovery.
in *Playboy*, 1968

Miller was born in New York and destined for bourgeois respectability but chose instead to reject college and spend the next twenty years enjoying a wide variety of adventures in America, and from 1930 in Paris. His first novel *Tropic of Cancer* dealt frankly with his *wanderjahre*, sparing the reader few sexual escapades. Further adventures continued to detail his own voyage of discovery. Miller's frankness met inevitable censorship and the literary qualities of his books went generally unrecognised. In 1944 Miller returned to America, settling in California. As the moral climate changed, so did Miller's reputation and his books were reassessed favourably, although feminists found him antagonistically chauvinist and even the most charitable found it hard to term them literature. Miller's writing has contributed greatly to the expansion of naturalistic self-expression and the acceptance of his books helped substantially to weaken the censor's grip.

MILLER, HENRY

The history of the world is the history of a privileged few.
Sunday After the War (1944)

Until very recently Miller's statement was correct: winners make the rules and rulers make history. The trend towards a more realistic view of history has developed since 1945, notably in France where the historians associated with the magazine *Annales* have pioneered the attempt to look more closely at the less privileged parts of society. Such efforts are inevitably hampered by the sheer lack of records, but gradually there are emerging some of the answers to Brecht's poem A Worker Reads History in which he asks 'Young Alexander conquered India. / He alone? / Caesar beat the Gauls. /Was there not even a cook in his army?...'

MILLER, HENRY

The democratic disease which expresses its tyranny by reducing everything to the level of the herd.
The Wisdom of the Heart (1941)

Both Miller's life and his books make it clear that he refused to espouse an ideology, of left or right, As a solo performer he rejected any such blandishments, preferring to make his own way. Society, on the other hand, did not leave him alone and the ideologues who maintain the world's censorship made sure that Miller was high on their list of targets. In their eyes it was necessary to reduce everything to the pawky level of the family audience, or as Miller put it 'the herd'.

MILLER, MAX (1895–1963) British comedian

I like the girls who do,
I like the girls who don't;
I hate the girl who says she will
And then she says she won't.

But the girl that I like best of all
And I think you'll say I'm right –
Is the girl who says she never has
But looks as if she.... 'Ere, listen... !!

The Max Miller Blue Book

Miller was born in Brighton, ran away to the circus aged 14 and worked his way through 'concert parties' and the music hall to become the Cheeky Chappie, resplendent in suits of very many colours, and armed with a tongue to rival their brilliance. For his adoring audiences Miller, his innuendoes seeming to keep him just this side of the law courts, nudging them along with his unfinished risqué songs, brandishing his catchphrase 'Now here's a funny thing...', provided what John Osborne has called 'a sense of danger. You thought this is somebody who is dicing, gambling and is going to get away with it'. The embodiment of saucy wickedness, a successful subversive, he intoned his classic poem, to gasps of delighted horror: 'When roses are red, / They're ready for plucking. / When a girl is sixteen, / She's ready for....' but never made the rhyme. No-one surpassed Miller, who could command £1,500 plus a percentage every week and filled theatres on his name alone. When he died, semi-retired in 1963, Fleet Street called him 'The Pure Gold'.

MILLER, VAUGHAN American lyricist

There ain't gonna be no whiskey;
there ain't gonna be no gin;
There ain't gonna be no highball, to put the whiskey in;
There ain't gonna be no cigarettes to make folks pale and thin;
But you can't take away that tendency to sin, sin sin.

'There Ain't Gonna Be No Whiskey' (1919)

Miller wrote his song, almost a theme tune of the thirteen dry years that would follow, as America's days of legal drinking ran out in the face of the Volstead Act which brought Prohibition into law, and became law in 1920. America had always been a hard-drinking country but its religious fervour proved even tougher. Fifty per cent of Americans, concentrated in the fundamentalist states of the 'Bible Belt', were already on the wagon; now, spearheaded by the National Anti-Saloon League, they had outlawed liquor across the country. As hindsight has shown, there was plenty of whiskey, gin, highballs and pretty much everything else, even if some of the liquor should have stayed in the bathtubs from whence it came and the real effect of Prohibition was to foster organised crime.

MILLETT, KATE (1934–) American feminist

Aren't women prudes if they don't and prostitutes if they do.
speech in 1975

Millett's involvement in the civil rights movement of the Sixties led her towards feminism when her commitment cost her her teaching job at Columbia University. Rather than accept dismissal, she chose to use her PhD thesis as a basis for the rebuttal of what she saw as discrimination on the grounds of her sex. In 1969 she published *Sexual Politics*, an enlarged version of that thesis, arguing that in a patriarchal society sex is used as a caste system and that while such restrictions were being undermined between 1830–1930, a counter-revolution had set in after 1930. This was best demonstrated in the ostentatiously pro-male superiority that pervades the works of D.H. Lawrence, Henry Miller and Norman Mailer. *Sexual Politics* became a basic feminist text.

MILNE, A.A. (1882–1956) British writer and playwright

When you are a Bear of Very Little Brain, and you Think of Things, you find sometimes that a Thing which seemed very Thingish inside you is quite different when it gets out into the open and has other people looking at it.
The House at Pooh Corner (1928)

Milne wrote a number of adult books and successful plays, but his fame rests on his children's books, particularly in his creation of Winnie-the-Pooh, 'a Bear of Very Little Brain' who first appeared in *Winnie-the-Pooh* (1926). Featuring Milne's own son, Christopher Robin, accompanied by a cast drawn from his own toys, the books became hugely popular. Almost as important as Milne's writing are the illustrations by E.H. Shepherd. One either likes or loathes Pooh, who has been translated widely, including into a Latin version; there would appear to be no middle ground. Either he conjures up the delights of secure childhood or reduces one to cringing embarrassment.

MILNE, A.A.

James James
Morrison Morrison
Weatherby George Dupree
Took great
Care of his Mother
Though he was only three.
When We Were Very Young: Disobedience (1924)

As well as his Pooh books, Milne wrote two volumes of verse, *When We Were Very Young* and *Now We Are Six* (1927), that were rivalled only by the bear in contemporary popularity. As in his prose, Milne concentrated on whimsy and left readers either delighted or appalled. In retrospect his best work, or at least his most generally acceptable, is probably *Toad of Toad Hall*, his adaptation of Kenneth Grahame's *Wind in the Willows* (1908) which was first staged in 1929 and has proved a staple of Christmas entertainment ever since.

MITCHISON, NAOMI (1897–) British writer

Being married is a value: it is bread and butter, but it may make one less able to provide the cake.
in *The Times*, 1979

Mitchison, the sister of the scientist J.B.S. Haldane, married G.R. Mitchison, a barrister and future Labour politician, in 1916. She has written prolifically throughout her life, and at her peak was considered the outstanding historical novelist of her generation. Her non-fiction works, which reflect and chart her long-term commitment to progressive political and social causes, include her autobiography *Small Talk* (1973), *All Change Here* (1975) and *You May Well Ask* (1979). Her pragmatic view of marriage suggests that what one gains in security one loses, over the years, in excitement.

MITFORD, JESSICA (1917–) British writer

Hons and Rebels
book title, 1960

Of the Mitford sisters, who included a socialite novelist, the wife of Britain's fascist leader, the Duchess of Devonshire, and a fanatical follower of Adolf Hitler, Jessica is the sole representative of the activist Left. She is best-known for her book *Hons and Rebels*, in which she retails her own childhood and that of her sisters and brother in frank and often hilarious detail. Although, as daughters of a lord all the children were indeed 'Hons', as in Honourables, the word derives from 'the Hens which played so large a part in our lives'. Educated at home, the Mitfords were intensely clannish, creating their own language, which they called Boudledidge, destroying a succession of governesses and growing up strangely isolated, even by the standards of their class and era.

MITFORD, NANCY   (1904–1973) British writer

An aristocracy in a republic is like a chicken whose head has been cut off. It may run about in a lovely way, but in fact it's dead.
quoted in *The Wit of Women*, ed L and M Cowan (1969)

Nancy Mitford was the eldest daughter of the celebrated Mitford family, daughters and son of the second Lord Redesdale. She was a leading figure of Twenties' society, but after the collapse of her first marriage moved permanently to France. Her first successful novel was *The Pursuit of Love* (1945), which fictionalised her own family as the 'Radletts', most notably capturing her father's eccentricities as 'Uncle Matthew'. Once in France, the 'republic' she mentions above, she embraced its culture wholeheartedly, writing a number of historical biographies and living there until her death. Apart from the novels, her one specifically 'English' book is *Noblesse Oblige: an enquiry into the identifiable characteristics of the English aristocracy* (1956, with A.S.C. Ross) which coined the terms 'U' and 'Non-U'. Mitford never remarried, although she remained devoted to her distinguished, married French lover, and had no children. As she remarked 'I love children. Especially when they cry – for then someone takes them away.'

MIZNER, ADDISON   (1872–1933) American architect

Absinthe makes the heart grow fonder.
The Cynic's Calendar (1901)

Addison Mizner, elder brother of the scapegrace younger Wilson (qv), was rather more restrained but equally famous, and eccentric, in his own way. He trained initially as an architect but after two years adventuring in the Pacific he returned to compile, with writer Oliver Herford (1863-1935), *The Cynic's Calendar*, a collection of suitably twisted proverbs, including 'The wages of gin is breath', 'Many are called but few get up' and 'Where there's a will there's a lawsuit'. In 1901 it delighted America as the last word in sophisticated wit. Returning to architecture he became one of America's leading designers of houses for the very rich, first in Palm Beach and later in Florida where he engineered the short-lived, hysterical land boom of 1924–25. He delighted the wealthy with his idiosyncratic, grandiose designs, filling his houses with treasures bought cheaply from Latin America's impoverished churches. After the Boom failed, so did Mizner. At his death his estate was proved insolvent.

MIZNER, WILSON (1876–1933) American wit, gambler and writer

I respect faith, but doubt is what gets you an education.
quoted in *The Incredible Mizners* by A. Johnson (1953)

Mizner was born in Benicia, California, a city that was destined to be San Francisco had San Francisco not taken the job, and his life seems to reflect this aura of the greatness that got away. Mizner's career was, as his biographer puts it 'incredible'. He ran a saloon during the Klondyke Gold Rush, helped his brother Addison manipulate the Florida land boom, managed the world heavyweight champion, wrote plays for Broadway, films for Hollywood, and knew everybody worth knowing. Utterly amoral, he seemed impervious to the restraints that fetter lesser men; what in others would be corruption, in Mizner was pure style. Naturally, he wisecracked his way through life: there follows a variety of examples:

Some of the greatest love affairs I've known involved one actor, unassisted.

A fellow who's always declaring that he's no fool usually has his suspicions.

Be nice to people on the way up, because you'll meet them on your way down.

A drama critic is a person who surprises the playwright by informing him what he meant.

Insanity is considered a ground for divorce, though by the very same token it's the shortest mental detour to marriage.

I've had several years in Hollywood and I still think the movie heroes are in the audience.

If you steal from one author it's plagiarism; if you steal from many it's research.

MOLA, EMILIO (1887–1937) Spanish soldier
The Fifth column
quoted in C. Cockburn, *The Devil's Decade* (1973)

Mola was one of Franco's Loyalist generals fighting against the republican government in the Spanish Civil War in 1936. He coined what Cockburn has called 'an international description of the Fascist traitor within the gates' when he stated during his advance on Madrid, that not only did his army have four columns, but that there was within the city a 'quinta columna', a fifth column of people who would join the invaders as soon as they entered the capital. The truth of this statement was less important than was its effect on the defenders' morale. Republican authorities, who heard his statement on Loyalist radio, began house-to-house searches for suspected Fascists, arresting and even shooting large numbers of otherwise innocent people.

MONDALE, WALTER   (1928–) American politician

If you are sure you understand everything that is going on, you are hopelessly confused.
speaking in 1978

Mondale, a Minnesota Senator, was chosen by Jimmy Carter as his running mate in 1976 after the Democratic candidate found himself forced to choose between the national hero, former astronaut John Glenn, and the popular liberal Mondale, as a potential vice-president. The fears were that Mondale would prove overly affable, but in a televised debate between the two vice-presidential nominees, Carter's man showed himself the master of the Republican Robert Dole. Nonetheless Mondale's candour, like that of his President, typified the naivety of the Carter years and his use of this particular line, rather than endearing him to the American people, seemed only to emphasise the administration's incompetence.

MONKEY BUSINESS

I've worked myself up from nothing to a state of extreme poverty.
script by S.J. Perelman, Will B. Johnstone and Arthur Sheekman (1931)

Monkey Business was the first of the Marx Brothers' films to be written as a film rather than as a Broadway show. It was also the first film to be written, even in part, by the renowned humourist S.J. Perelman. The plot deposits the Brothers on an ocean liner, wherein they have stowed away, and follows their manic escapades as they manage to get involved with one Alky Briggs, a bootlegger who is also on the boat. It is one of the most unrestrainedly anarchic of the films, even though it lacks Margaret Dumont and Zeppo is launched as a singer of romantic interludes. Typical is Groucho's complaint 'Do you know who sneaked into my room at three o'clock this morning?' 'Who?' 'Nobody, and that's my complaint'.

MONROE, MARILYN (1926–62) American actress and sex symbol

I had the radio on.
on being asked about her famous calendar spread in 1947

Monroe was born Norma Jean Baker, and baptised personally by the evangelist Aimee Semple Macpherson. After posing for a photographer who had discovered her working in a Los Angeles factory, she graduated from teenage model to Hollywood starlet, at which time she posed for a nude calendar. Her career improved, her name changed to Marilyn Monroe, and she abandoned such sessions, but when in 1953 Hugh Hefner, who paid a Chicago publisher $500 for the picture, republished it in the first edition of Playboy, the media were inevitably fascinated. Monroe, who had just starred in *Gentlemen Prefer Blondes*, had developed a passable line in wisecracks. Given that her resplendent nakedness, posed alluringly on a red velvet drape, really made an answer superfluous, she replied to the question 'What did you have on?' with the line 'I had the radio on', often rephrased as 'Nothing but the radio'.

MONTAGUE, C.E. (1867–1928) British journalist

War has no fury like a non-combatant.
Disenchantment (1922)

Montague joined the staff of the then *Manchester Guardian* in 1890 and rose to become the paper's assistant editor and to marry the daughter of C.P. Scott, who doubled as editor and proprietor. He was officially too old to serve in World War I but his enthusiasm led him to dye his hair and thus cheat his way into the ranks. His wartime experiences so destroyed that enthusiasm that, despite his own courageous conduct, his book *Disenchantment* stands as one of the first to demystify and demythologise the official version of the conflict. As his remark emphasises, his scorn was particularly directed at those who, relatively snug at home, were most desperate to urge the troops to death and glory.

MONTY PYTHON'S FLYING CIRCUS

And now for something completely different!
BBC TV show, 1969

This catchphrase, which was used for the Monty Python compilation film, released in 1971, developed as the easiest method of linking the show's fast-moving combination of live sketches and animation. It originated when read by John Cleese, as a 'BBC newsreader', who would utter the phrase while seated at his desk. As the series progressed a variety of other characters found themselves using it when necessary.

MONTY PYTHON'S FLYING CIRCUS

It's not pining, it's passed on. This parrot is no more. It's ceased to be. This is a late parrot. It's a stiff. Bereft of life it rests in peace. It would be pushing up the daisies if you hadn't nailed it to the perch. It's rung down the curtain and joined the choir invisible. It's an ex-parrot.
programme of December 14, 1969

The ever-popular 'Dead Parrot Sketch', of which this is the climax, was first broadcast on Monty Python's Flying Circus in December 1969. It combined Michael Palin as a shifty pet-shop proprietor and John Cleese, who described the sketch as illustrative of 'the impossibility of getting service', as an obdurately dissatisfied customer, whose parrot, purchased 'not half an hour ago from this very boutique' is dead. The original sketch was well enough received by the studio audience, but over years it has become, along with 'Nudge nudge, wink wink' (qv) the most famous of the Python repertoire.

MOORE, GEORGE   (1852–1933) Anglo-Irish novelist

To be aristocratic in art one must avoid polite society.
quoted in C. Connolly, *Enemies of Promise* (1938)

Moore was the son of an Irish MP who ran a racing stable. Destined for the army he preferred his own interests: spending a decade mixing in Parisian artistic and literary circles. He abandoned painting for a full-time writing career, setting his most successful novel *Esther Waters* (1894) in a racing background. Heavily influenced by Zola, Balzac and Dostoevsky, Moore used both naturalistic and realistic techniques in his own work. Like some of Zola's novels, Moore's *A Modern Lover* (1883), was banned by the influential Mudie's circulating library, a snub that encouraged Moore to initiate a lifelong battle against such prudery. Apart from his fiction, Moore was also largely responsible for the planning of the Irish National Theatre.

MORAVIA, ALBERTO (1907–) (Alberto Pincherle) Italian writer

Modern man – whether in the womb of the masses, or with his workmates or family, or alone – can never for a moment forget that he is living in a world in which he is a means and whose end is not his business.
Man at an End (1964)

Moravia, a longtime correspondent of the Corriere della Sera, established himself, after Italo Svevo, as Italy's leading neo-realistic novelist with his first book *Gli indifferenti* (1929, *The Time of Indifference*), in which he portrays the self-satisfied amoralism of a bourgeois family under Mussolini. Although he has been variously criticised as creating 'grim, hopeless realism' and 'a constantly sombre and haggard atmosphere' and characterised as having 'a morbid love of the sadistic and the grotesque', Moravia has had a substantial influence on modern writing both in Italy and abroad.

MORAVIA, ALBERTO

The ratio of literacy to illiteracy is constant, but nowadays the illiterates can read.
in the *Observer*, 1979

MORGAN, ROBIN (1941–) American feminist

Woman is: finally screwing and your groin and buttocks and thighs ache like hell and you're all wet and bloody and it wasn't like a Hollywood movie at all but Jesus, at least you're not a virgin anymore but is this what it's all about? And meanwhile he's asking 'Did you come?'
Sisterhood is Powerful

Morgan was among the first of the new wave of American feminists. These lines are taken from *Sisterhood is Powerful*, an anthology of contemporary feminist polemic which she edited. The collection advanced on the works of such predecessors as Kate Millett in its greater militancy and in its general condemnation of men as an alien species. Among Seventies' feminism's most widely popular texts, Morgan's book spearheaded an era in which the truly committed feminist rejected men and all their works.

MORLEY, ROBERT (1908–) British actor and wit

Show me a man who has enjoyed his schooldays and I'll show you a bully and a bore.

Morley, whose portly form and orotund tones have long seemed synonymous with the words 'bon viveur', is one of Britain's favourite character actors whose theatrical career began in 1929 and who started making films, which have included *Beat the Devil (1953) and Oscar Wilde* (1960) as well as many cameos. Morley, who has pointed out 'Anyone who works is a fool. I don't work, I merely inflict myself on the public', epitomises to many hedonism's more appealing side. This comment on the horrors of a public school education also underlines the satisfying notion that acting like a gentleman does not automatically mean one has to have fallen prey to a gentleman's less attractive delusions.

MORRIS, DESMOND (1928–) British anthropologist and zoologist

There are one hundred and ninety-three living species of monkeys and apes. One hundred and ninety-two of them are covered with hair. The exception is a naked ape called *homo sapiens*.
The Naked Ape (1967)

Morris gained his PhD for work on animal behaviour and then became famous in the late 1950s as presenter of the television series *Zoo Time*. For some years he was curator of mammals at London Zoo and published a number of academic studies of primate ethology. In 1967 his most celebrated book appeared: *The Naked Ape*, a study of mankind with direct reference to his animal parallels. The book sold eight million copies and coined a phrase.

MORRIS, DESMOND

Clearly, then, the city is not a concrete jungle, it is a human zoo.
The Human Zoo

The Human Zoo was Morris' follow-up to the best-selling *Naked Ape* and like its predecessor attempted to analyse humanity in animal terms. Whereas *The Naked Ape* concentrated on human characteristics, the next book looked at the environment in which the human animal lives. The concept of life as a jungle, with social Darwinism as its determining factor, is well known. Morris attempted to civilise the jungle, seeing the supposedly most intelligent species as a variety of specimens within a global zoo.

MORRISON, JIM (1943–1971) American rock musician and poet

The old get old, the young get younger
They got the guns, but we got the numbers.
Five to One (1968)

Jim Morrison's band, The Doors, took their name from William
Blake's lines 'If the doors of perception were cleansed / All things
would appear infinite', a couplet that had also served for the title
of Aldous Huxley's 1954 study of hallucinogenic drugs. Morrison
took his band above the 'June-Moon', teenage angst banalities of
most rock lyrics, acting out the obsessions and images of his own
intense poetry. The Doors' greatest numbers included 'Light My
Fire', a simple erotic invitation, 'The End', with its heavy
Freudian overtones, intermingled with cathartic shrieks reminscent of primal therapy, and 'Five to One,' which reflects the
prevalent mood of the late Sixties with its messianic belief in the
'youth culture' and 'the revolution'.

MORTIMER, JOHN (1923–) British playwright, novelist and
barrister

No brilliance is needed in the law. Nothing but common sense,
and relatively clean fingernails.
Voyage Round My Father (1970)

John Mortimer is both a leading defence Queen's Counsel, who
has featured in many of the most sensational civil rights and
censorship cases of recent decades, and a successful playwright,
scriptwriter and novelist, creator of the enduring and endearing
barrister 'Rumpole of the Bailey'. Mortimer's father provides the
subject of one of his best plays, *Voyage Round My Father*, from
which this line, advice to the young John, is taken. His father,
who was totally blind, managed nonetheless to pursue a successful career at the bar, helped by his having Mortimer's long-
suffering mother read the depositions of the most sordid of
divorce cases out loud on the morning commuter train into
London.

MORTIMER, RAYMOND (1895–1980) British critic

Conversation is anecdote tempered by interruption.

Mortimer worked briefly at the Foreign Office before becoming a
full-time reviewer in 1919. He wrote for the *New Statesman,* the
Nation, of which he was literary editor, and the *Sunday Times,* as
well as contributing to many other newspapers and journals. This

remark sums up the egocentricity, admitted or otherwise, of many so-called conversationalists who really see all speech as a chance to display their talents and their experiences, and any response as no more than an irritating caesura in their flow.

MORTON, J.B.   British humorous columnist

Justice must not only be done, it must be seen to be believed.
as 'Beachcomber' in the *Daily Express*

The original 'Beachcomber' was D.B. Wyndham Lewis (1894–1969), who wrote the humorous column from 1919–24, but the man who made it his own was J.B. Morton, who for several decades created a cast of bizarre characters such as Mr. Justice Cocklecarrot, Dr. Smart-Allick of Narkover School and Dr. Strabismus (Whom God Preserve) of Utrecht. Their exploits and eccentricities delighted his readers. Morton's wit was often surreal, but he was equally capable of making a telling point, as in this revision of the popular phrase 'Justice must not merely be done, but it must be seen to be done'. Other Beachcomber favourites include:

> **Hush, hush,**
> **Nobody cares!**
> **Christopher Robin**
> **Has**
> **Fallen**
> **Down-**
> **Stairs.**

(from the 'book' 'Now We Are Sick')

Gone to that country from whose Bourne no Hollingsworth returns.

Sixty Horses Wedged In A Chimney: The story to fit this sensational headline has not yet turned up.

MOSLEY, OSWALD   (1896–1980) British politician

The only methods we shall employ will be English ones. We shall rely on the good old English fist.
speaking on May 16, 1931

Mosley appeared to be the coming man of British politics. Attractive, well-born, a good orator, he joined the Labour party in 1924 and was given Cabinet rank. His future seemed assured until in 1929 he resigned from the party as a protest against the government's failure to deal with unemployment. He chose instead to found his own New Party which began propitiously enough but turned, in 1932, into the British Union of Fascists, complete with black shirts, anti-Semitic rhetoric, a private army of thugs, and Mosley's open admiration for Hitler. His comment regarding the 'good old English fist' referred to his attempts to recruit a youth wing for the BUF. The Fascists fought pitched battles in the East End with their left-wing and Jewish opponents until they were banned by the Public Order Act (1936). Mosley was interned under section 18b during World War II and left England to live out his life in France.

Moss, Stirling (1929–) British racing driver

There are two things no man will admit he can't do well: drive and make love.
interview, 1963

Moss' father, a dentist, had raced at Indianapolis in 1924 and while his son made a token attempt at the hotel trade, his move to motor-racing was inevitable. He was successful from his first season, in 1948, and in a fifteen year racing career won every major Grand Prix, although he never became World Champion. A fierce patriot, who would rather lose in an English car than win in a foreign one, Moss became a popular hero. On Easter Monday 1962 he crashed at Goodwood and barely survived, falling into a coma for 28 days. Unlike the macho characters he teases in this remark, Moss realised that by his standards he no longer could drive well and decided to retire.

Mostel, Zero (1915–77) American film actor

Q: You are ... known by 'Zero' as a nickname? Mostel: Yes sir, after my financial standing in the community – sir.
answering Congressional investigators, 1955

Zero Mostel is best known to British film fans for his performance as Max Bialystock in Mel Brooks' *The Producers* (1968), but he had already established himself as a leading Broadway actor when in 1955 he faced the interrogators of the House Un-American Activities Committee (HUAC). The questioning began as cited above, with the Committee Chairman Donald Jackson asking the actor why he was called 'Zero' and receiving a suitable reply. Then Mostel, questioned as to a benefit performance for the left-wing magazine *Mainstream*, claimed that he simply offered his 'imitation of a butterfly at rest', adding 'There is no crime in making people laugh'. He was blacklisted nonetheless. Mostel eventually found employment again, notably in Brooks' film, and gained some small revenge in *The Front* (1975), a film about the blacklist written, produced and largely acted by its victims.

MUGGERIDGE, KITTY British writer

Frost has risen without trace.

in *Now!* magazine, 1981

Malcolm Muggeridge's wife, Kitty, made this comment on TV personality David Frost, neatly skewering him in a phrase that has since been used of a variety of unfortunate celebrities. Her point was that although Frost had undoubtedly become an international superstar, a far cry from his origins on *That Was The Week That Was*, the nature of his rise, and of the programmes from which he drew his fame, was ephemeral and so lacking in worthwhile substance as to render it quite invisible.

MUGGERIDGE, MALCOLM (1903–) British journalist

There is no surer way of preserving the worst aspects of the bourgeois style than liquidating the bourgeoisie. Whatever else Stalin may, or may not have done, he assuredly made Russia safe for the Forsyte Saga.

Chronicles of Wasted Time vol. i (1978)

Malcolm Muggeridge, in common with most intellectuals of his generation, began as a fervent supporter of Soviet Russia but, unlike the more self-deluding, he abandoned his enthusiasms after actually visiting the country. In this, the first volume of his autobiography, he recalled his visit and the way in which the Revolution, however radical its politics, seemed dedicated to preserving the worst aspects of that style of interior decoration beloved of middle-class Edwardians.

MUGGERIDGE, MALCOLM

Never...was any generation of men intent upon the pursuit of happiness more advantageously placed to attain it who yet, with seeming deliberation, took the opposite course – towards chaos, not order, towards breakdown, not stability, towards death, destruction and darkness, not life, creativity and light.

in *Esquire* magazine, 1970

Muggeridge was devoted to his new role as Britain's Jeremiah when he wrote this piece in *Esquire*, summing up what he considered to be the disastrous, Godless decade of the Sixties. From his point of view those responsible for this course had been offered only the best opportunities, and had deliberately and maliciously thrown them away in pursuit of hedonistic pleasures. In his blanket condemnation, Muggeridge refused to accept the value of any advances, such as those in civil rights, freedom of speech and similar developments, seeing them all as no more than the world's accelerating decline into the Pit.

MUGGERIDGE, MALCOLM

Good taste and humour are a contradiction in terms, like a chaste whore.
in *Time* magazine, September 14 1953

The precise nature of the sense of humour can be debated ad nauseam, suffice it to say that everyone has their own and while certain things seem to amuse large numbers of people there is no guarantee that something quite different, while appealing to some of them, will still amuse them all. On the other hand, Muggeridge's statement seems to bear out the belief that humour is always finally seditious, running contrary to good taste, waving its pig's bladder in the face of the earnest and correct.

MUGGERIDGE, MALCOLM

The orgasm has replaced the cross as the focus of longing and the image of fulfilment.
'Down with Sex'

Just as Muggeridge chose to reject his former allegiance to socialism after a visit to Soviet Russia, so, thirty years later did he turn against his role as atheistic iconoclast after experiencing, albeit as an observer, the 'permissive society' of the Sixties. With the ardour of a convert, and the undoubted talent of one of the country's leading journalists, Muggeridge set about savaging the libertarian gospel. This was acceptable in itself, since the glib philosophies of the Sixties were sometimes embarrassingly utopian, but his association with the cranks of The Festival of Light and with Lord Longford's anti-pornography Report tended to diminish his reputation.

MUGGERIDGE, MALCOLM

He was not only a bore, he bored for England.
on Sir Anthony Eden

Muggeridge was still sustaining his role as anti-Establishment critic when he ventured this remark on Britain's former Prime Minister, Anthony Eden, who held office from 1955-57. Eden's reputation has been marred for ever through his participation in the Suez imbroglio and even his former image as a staunch opponent of appeasement has been subjected to detailed analysis, revealing that while he did oppose any compromise with Fascist Italy, he was less adamant when it came to Nazi Germany.

MUHLSTEIN, ANKA   French writer

The parvenu is always someone else.
The Rothschilds (1984)

Muhlstein, in her discussion of the fabulously wealthy Rothschild family, was pointing out one of snobbery's basic tenets: first come, first to put down those who follow. Some might say such snobbery doesn't matter, and others, facing the reality of human arrogance, might note that the real point is not that the parvenu is always someone else but in fact, if one goes back far enough in even the grandest families, everyone, at some stage, has been a parvenu.

MUIR, FRANK   (1920–) British scriptwriter

Wake up at the back there!
catchphrase for Jimmy Edwards in Take It from Here

Frank Muir was Jimmy Edwards' scriptwriter during his early years at the Windmill Theatre and later during his BBC career. Thus when the comedian graduated from the wartime *Navy Mixture* to starring in his own show *Take It From Here* in March 1948, Muir helped develop his character and the vital catchphrase. He punctuated Edwards' speeches with this admonition, a natural progression from his stage act, in which he had roundly insulted the audience, not one of whom ever dared answer back. The show was moderately successful, but when Tommy Handley died suddenly it was promoted, as a gamble, to take the place of the now beleaguered *ITMA*. The gamble paid off and *Take It From Here* soon established itself.

MURCHISON, CLINT   American businessman

Money is like manure. If you spread it around it does a lot of good, but if you pile it up in one place it stinks like hell.
in *Time* magazine, 1971

Murchison, one of Texas' richest men, whose family money comes from oil and who owns vast portions of the state, claimed that he was repeating his own father's advice, but actually he was consciously or otherwise quoting the 16th century scientist, philosopher and politician Francis Bacon (1561-1626) who said in an Essay published in 1625: 'Money is like muck, not good unless spread'. Another rich man to whom this line has been attributed is John Paul Getty I.

MURDOCH, IRIS (1919–) British novelist

Literature could be said to be a sort of disciplined technique for arousing certain emotions.
in the *Listener*, 1978

Murdoch began her career working in the civil service, prior to lecturing in philosophy at Oxford and London. Her wider fame is based on her writing, some twenty novels, as well as plays and poetry. Her fiction is an extension of her philosophical work, with its discussion of the nature of good and evil, religion, taboo, truth and freedom. Above all is the constant lesson: individuals can only learn to appreciate their own reality by defining themselves in the context of their relationship with others.

MURDOCH, RUPERT (1931–) Australian newspaper proprietor

We have to compete with newspapers which have double-page spreads on pubic hairs.
justifying pinups in his papers, 1969

Murdoch's newspaper career began in 1952 when his father, owner of the *Adelaide News*, died. Since then he has built up a substantial media empire in Australia, the US and Britain. Murdoch has some respect, but little affection. Claiming to offer his editors their freedom, he still maintains that 'The buck stops with the guy who signs the cheques.' Many would claim that once Murdoch obtains a paper its only route is downmarket. This comment was used to justify his glorification of the *Sun's* 'Page Three' pinups, and the decline of the paper's news coverage, but given what many people see as the tragic decline of his two quality London papers, that policy, in one form or another, seems to spread right across the board.

MURPHY'S LAW

Anything that can go wrong will go wrong.
popular maxim

Murphy's Law is the principal example of what might be called 'life laws', a truly natural law that has no grounding in statute, merely in constant human experience. The most interesting thing about Murphy's Law, and its many corollaries such as Murphy's Law of Research 'Enough research will tend to support your theory', Murphy's Law of Priorities 'Whatever you want to do, you have to do something else first', Murphy's Law of Thermodynamics 'Things get worse under pressure' and many, many more, is who is 'Murphy'? In his book *The Official Rules* (1978) Paul Dickson cites a number of popular theories, opting, with reservations, for this: In 1949 one Captain Ed Murphy, a USAF development engineer from the Wright Field Aircraft Laboratory in Ohio, was in charge of USAF Project MX981, held at Edwards Air Force Base in California and designed to 'study the factors in human tolerance to high decelerative forces of short duration in order to determine criteria for design of aircraft and protective equipment'. Faced with the incompetence of a technician who had consistently mis-wired a vital strain gauge bridge, Murphy remarked 'If there is any way to do it wrong, he will'. This comment snowballed into Murphy's Law.

MURROW, EDWARD R.   (1908–1965) American broadcaster

Never sound excited. Imagine yourself at a dinner table back in the United States with the local editor, a banker and a professor talking over coffee. You try and tell what it was like, while the maid's boyfriend, a truck driver, listens from the kitchen. Try to be understood by the truck driver while not insulting the professor's intelligence.
advice to aspirant war correspondents, 1944

Murrow remains for many people, both professional and otherwise, the paradigm of a modern reporter. He never worked for a newspaper but as a broadcaster on both radio and television wielded an unrivalled influence through a calm, authoritative style that he summed up in this piece of advice to other, younger reporters. His broadcasts from Blitz-battered London, with their regular sign-off 'Good night and good luck', helped both to forge the myths of an indomitable populace laughing off the Luftwaffe and, more importantly, to persuade America to join World War II. After the war he moved to television where his regular discussion of important current affairs carried the same authority. His refusal to abandon chain-smoking ensured that he died of lung cancer, and his last years were spent as Director of US Information Services.

MURROW, EDWARD R.

We will not walk in fear of one another, we will not be driven by fear into an age of unreason. If we dig deep in our history and our doctrine, and remember that we are not descended from fearful men, not from men who feared to write, to speak, to associate and to defend causes which were for the moment unpopular.
concluding CBS-TV's See It Now special on McCarthy, 1954

Apart from his series of broadcasts from the Blitz, Murrow's most famous broadcast was the special, aired on his regular programme *See It Now*, in which he took on the witch-hunting Senator Joseph McCarthy. In 1954 McCarthy was at the height of his powers and few outside the small radical press had dared challenge him openly. Least of all such media monoliths as CBS, who had preferred to conduct their own 'loyalty tests' rather than risk alienating the advertisers. Murrow kept the show secret from CBS management and it was screened without an in-house preview. The show, which revealed McCarthy's posturing demagoguery simply for what it was, and simply let him hang himself on his own footage, began the Senator's decline. Ironically, despite promises of company support, it also signalled the gradual ending of Murrow's relations with CBS. Such controversy, in 1954, was too hot to handle.

MUSIL, ROBERT (1880–1942) Austrian writer

One does what one is; one becomes what one does.
Kleine prosa (c1930)

Musil's first novel appeared in 1906. Heavily influenced by Nietzsche, Musil made himself into a gifted, perceptive cultural and social critic. His major work began after World War I. *Der Mann ohne Eigenshaften* (1920–32), *The Man Without Qualities)* occupied the rest of his life, and he died without finishing it. Its premise, illustrated here, is that one's qualities are determined by every aspect of one's social environment: relationships, job, ambitions and so on. However, Musil asks, if one removes these layers, what is left? Set in Vienna in 1913, the book uses Musil's own experiences to create a deeply ironic portrait of an era marked only by empty sham and hollow philosophising, in which function is all, but substance, after which Musil chases unavailingly, seems impossible to pin down.

MUSSOLINI, BENITO (1883–1945) Italian dictator

Fascism, the more it considers and observes the future and development of humanity, quite apart from political considerations of the moment, believes neither in the possibility nor the utility of perpetual peace
The Political and Social Doctrine of Fascism (1932)

Mussolini, a former socialist leader, mixed socialism with enthusiastic nationalism to found the Italian Fascist movement. After his strong-arm squads marched on Rome in 1922, he intimidated King Victor Emmanuel III into appointing him Prime Minister, a post he held until 1943. Using propaganda rather than violence, although Fascist thugs were always in evidence, Mussolini gradually consolidated his dictatorship, turning Italy into a one-party state, parading himself as Il Duce, embarking on grandiose programmes of public works and venturing into Albania and Abyssinia, on campaigns combining the maximum of vainglory with the minimum of risk. Italy stayed neutral in 1939 but Hitler seemed so successful that Mussolini chose to back him. In 1943 the defeat of Italy led to his removal by his own Grand Council, and after establishing the pro-German Republic of Salo, he was killed in 1945 by anti-Fascist partisans.

MY LITTLE CHICKADEE

Come up and see me some time.
script by W.C. Fields and Mae West (1940)

As opposed to the many lines which Mae West (qv) definitely did say, this one, perhaps the most famous, eluded her. It is not a complete fabrication but goes back to West's stage hit, *Diamond Lil*, of 1928. In the movie version, *She Done Him Wrong* (1933), West appraises a very young Cary Grant and tells him 'You know I always did like a man in uniform. And that one fits you grand. Why don't you come up some time and see me? I'm home every evening.' The public, who loved the line, found it too tongue-twisting for easy imitation and duly revised it. By the time West starred with W.C. Fields in *My Little Chickadee* the new version was general currency. But West still resisted it: in the film it is Fields who says it to West.

N

NABOKOV, VLADIMIR   (1899–1977) Russian novelist and teacher

Human life is but a series of footnotes to a vast, obscure unfinished masterpiece.

Commentary in *Pale Fire* (1962)

Nabokov's family fled Russia in 1919 and lived until 1940 in first Berlin and then Paris. He moved to America in 1940 working both as an academic and as a novelist, writing in English. This comment comes from the novel *Pale Fire*, as does a further reflection on man's existence 'Our existence is but a brief crack of light between two eternities of darkness.' If they both appear to err towards the pessimistic, Nabokov's immense fluency, his ability as one critic put it, to do anything, apparently, which can be done with words alone' has made his work far from negative. His aim is aesthetic bliss and he pursues it in writing of allusive complexity, filled with linguistic trickery and subtle images.

NABOKOV, VLADIMIR

One of those 'Two Cultures' is really nothing but utilitarian technology; the other is B-grade novels, ideological fiction, popular art. Who cares if there exists a gap between such 'physics' and such 'humanities'? Those Eggheads are terrible Philistines. A real good head is not oval but round.

C.P. Snow's Rede Lectures, entitled 'The Two Cultures and the Scientific Revolution,' were published in 1959. Their premise was that between science and the humanities there existed a gulf, exemplified in the way in which traditional, arts-based culture had failed to accommodate itself to a world in which science and technology were changing civilisation. Nabokov, with the aristocratic disdain of one whose preoccupations concern the higher aesthetics, dismisses Snow's theory. From his point of view neither of the two possesses true culture, any more than the 'Eggheads' understand the meaning of the word. Real culture, he implies, transcends such simple definitions.

NABOKOV, VLADIMIR

The truth is that the great novels are fairy tales.... Literature was born on the day when a boy came crying 'Wolf, wolf!' and there was no wolf behind him.

lecturing at Cornell University, 1958

As well as writing his novels Nabokov was professor of Russian literature at Cornell University. His own work, which concentrates on the themes of loss, exile and nostalgia which derive from his own role as an émigré from Russia, was influenced by such writers as Dickens, Robert Louis Stevenson and James Joyce and in his lectures, expounding a personal theory of the novel, he deals with these writers, and others, both liked and disliked. Unlike many contemporaries Nabokov rejected Freud, 'the Viennese witch-doctor', preferring to look at the novel, as he points out here, as a species of infinitely sophisticated fairy-tale.

NABOKOV, VLADIMIR

Lolita, light of my life, fire of my loins. My sin, my soul. Lo-lee-ta: the tip of the tongue taking a trip of three steps down the palate to tap, at three, on the teeth.
Lolita (1958)

For the public at large, many of whom had not read the book, the main result of the publicity that surrounded the appearance of Nabokov's third English-language novel, was to popularise the word 'nymphet', coined by the author, as the narrator Humbert Humbert, to describe 'between the age limits of nine and fourteen... maidens who, to certain bewitched travellers, twice or many times older than they, reveal their true nature which is not human but nymphic (that is demoniac)...' For intellectuals the book was more important for its exploration of the potentialities of language. An obscenity trial in America and concomitant fuss in the UK, fuelled by passages such as this evocation of the narrator's pre-pubescent goddess, ensured that the book has retained its 'naughty' reputation and that the names of its two main characters have become synonyms for precocious sexuality and the 'dirty old man'.

NAIPAUL, V.S.   (1932–) Indian writer

A writer is in the end not his books, but his myth – and that myth is in the keeping of others.
Steinbeck in Monterey (1970)

V.S. Naipaul combines fiction with a number of travel books, which are in effect sociological discussions of the countries in question, usually of the Third World. Naipaul's views are essentially pessimistic. In fiction and reportage Naipaul's writing bears an air of sadness, of hopes betrayed and ideals rendered hollow by reality. This refusal to go along with the pronouncements of optimistic Third World governments, despite his own origins as an Indian born in Trinidad, has laid him open to charges of racism. His comment on the writer and his myth comes from a piece on the late John Steinbeck and Monterey's Cannery Row, celebrated in his eponymous novel of 1944. Naipaul points out that the realities of Cannery Row differ harshly from Steinbeck's fantasies and the people who live there have a less charitable view of his social concerns, launched from a comfortable apartment in Manhattan.

NAKED CITY, THE

There are eight million stories in the Naked City. This has been one of them.
American TV show, 1950s.

The first version of *The Naked City* was as a film, created in 1948 by producer Marc Hellinger and director Jules Dassin. The film was a mock documentary, with Hellinger narrating, a police procedural featuring the New York Homicide Squad, headed by crusty Barry Fitzgerald, set in a superbly shot Manhattan. Like Britain's *The Blue Lamp* (1950) which dominated UK television's treatment of police shows for a decade, *The Naked City* set the style for American network cop shows. The first example was the movie's own spinoff, which ended every episode with this terse epilogue, as the city spread out beneath the camera.

NAMATH, JOE (1943–) American pro football star

I don't know, I never smoked Astroturf.
asked whether he preferred Astroturf to grass, 1969

Namath was a major US football star of the Sixties. A Southerner, he followed an exceptional college career by migrating North to play quarterback for the unfancied New York Jets. He was the perfect player for the city and the times, exhibiting an arrogance that would have infuriated and certainly angered anyone but New Yorkers, had it not been balanced by his on-field excellence. As this comment implies, 'Broadway Joe', enjoyed off-field antics too, and his club, Bachelors Three, was among the city's favourite singles' bars. His greatest moment came in 1969 when the Jets, unfancied underdogs, met the Baltimore Colts in Superbowl III. Namath promised a victory. The press howled but on the day, to their mingled fury and delight, he duly delivered, trouncing the Colts 16–7.

NAMIER, LEWIS (1888–1960) British historian

Religion: a sixteenth century word for nationalism.
attributed definition

Namier supported himself in business while amassing the research for his two most important books: *The Structure of Politics at the Accession of George III* (1929) and *England in the Age of the American Revolution* (1930). Their publication earned him the chair of history at Manchester University in 1931 and he remained among England's most influential historians until his death. He also wrote on the revolutions of the 19th and 20th centuries, notably on those of 1848. Namier's technique, which changed the way in which history was written, consisted in abandoning the broad interpretation of 18th century history as a struggle between two parties, preferring to emphasize the vital role of patronage and family connections and showing the influence of the country gentry.

NAPPER, GEORGE American policeman

When you're up to your ass in alligators, it's hard to remember that your purpose is draining the swamp.
quoted in *Time* magazine, 1981

Napper was interviewed by *Time* reporters putting together a story on the growing incidence of inner city crime. Like many policemen whose beats encompass the toughest sections of America's cities, Napper had discovered that however idealistic and liberal one might be at the outset, the day to day realities simply eroded one's more optimistic hopes. Instead of helping improve the environment in which criminals were bred, the policeman found that the best he could do was to eliminate some of the criminals themselves, no matter how little that effort, in the long run, really helped.

NASH, OGDEN (1902–71) American poet

> **Candy is dandy**
> **But liquor is quicker.**

Reflections on Ice-breaking

Nash has been on of the century's most prolific and most popular producers of light verse. He enjoys playing with the language, indulging in puns, epigrams, such as this one, and all the games that can be played with rhyme. This poem, a neatly constructed piece of black humour, typifies his sophisticated style.

NASH, OGDEN

In real life it only takes one to make a quarrel.
The Ogden Nash Pocket Book

Nash's territory centred on the sophisticates of New York, for whom the cultivation and display of their neuroses was as much a part of living as drawing breath. His comment aims straight at those whose inner turmoils are such that simply brooding on ambitions, inadequacies or allied detriments of character and achievement are enough to drive the ego into headlong struggles with itself.

NASH, OGDEN

People who work sitting down get paid more than people who work standing up.
Will Consider Situation

The premise here is that those who work in white collar jobs do better than those who work in blue collar ones. Whether that is still true might be debatable, given that a typist is unlikely to earn more than a skilled factory worker, but as far as status is concerned, the differentials seem destined, in class-conscious England at least, to remain.

NATHAN, GEORGE JEAN (1882–1958) American critic and essayist

What passes for woman's intuition is often nothing more than man's transparency.
The Smart Set

Nathan was the influential drama critic for the *American Mercury*, edited by his friend H.L. Mencken, with whom he founded *The Smart Set* magazine and the first and most successful of the detective pulps *Black Mask*. Nathan was irascible and argumentative, blasting the second-rate with the absolute confidence of his acidulous tongue. He had savaged the successful too, if like George S. Kaufman, whom he described as a 'gag man, a slick contriver of stage comedies', they failed to satisfy his criteria of excellence. Perhaps the best testament to his influence comes in Budd Schulberg's *The Disenchanted* (1950) when he wrote of a once successful playwright 'Bane had two hits running on Broadway at the same time. Even Nathan liked 'em. Popular 'n' satirical. Like Barrie only better.'

NATHAN, GEORGE JEAN

Politics is the diversion of trivial men who, when they succeed at it, become important in the eyes of more trivial men.

NAVASKY, VICTOR S. (1932–) American writer

Manners are the lowest common denominator of ethical experience.
Naming Names (1980)

Navasky is a New York journalist who since 1978 has edited the journal *The Nation*. His book *Naming Names* is a meticulously researched record of the McCarthy era, dealing centrally with the role of the 'namers', the voluntary and professional informers without whose testimony, often fraudulent, biased, self-promoting or a combination of all three, the witch-hunt could not have sustained its momentum. The book deals primarily with ethics: of the informer, of the witnesses, of those who chose to defy the Committee and of the Committee itself. As Navasky points out, if one reduces ethics to its most simple form, it may be seen as another variety of good manners. HUAC, and its informers, as far as he is concerned, lacked such manners and as such were similarly devoid of ethical propriety.

NEHRU, JAWAHARLAL (1889–1964) Indian prime minister

You don't change the course of history by turning the faces of portraits to the wall.
maxim

Nehru's father had been an early proponent of Indian nationalism and after an education in England, Nehru returned to India to join Gandhi in fighting the British Raj. He became General Secretary of the All India Congress Committee in 1929 and held the post a total of five times. Imprisoned for his views, which echoed Gandhi's civil disobedience campaign, he served nine years in jail. As prime minister, from Independence in 1947 to his death in 1964, he worked towards the creation of India as a major Asian power, combining neutralism and sensible treaties with a degree of territorial nationalism which brought India into conflict with neighbouring Pakistan. His relations with Britain remained cordial, and he chose to remain within the Commonwealth, observing in this remark that one cannot change the past merely by pretending it has never happened.

NEHRU, JAWAHARLAL

Life is like a game of cards. The hand that is dealt you represents determinism. The way you play it is free will.

NEW YORKER MAGAZINE

Back to the drawing board.
cartoon caption, c1943

This phrase, denoting the need to return to basics after the collapse of one's cherished hopes, comes from the caption beneath a cartoon published in the *New Yorker* by Peter Arno (1904–68). Arno, real name Curtis Arnoux Peters, was among the most dashing and stylish of the New Yorker staff. His fame grew from his creation of the Whoops Sisters, two fast-living harridans whose pictured adventures, tame by today's standards, shocked the staid and titillated those who liked to see themselves as sophisticated. He was especially keen on depicting the breakdown of technology, hence this famous caption, and was the first cartoonist to note that drunkenness, while quite unlike its natural state, could best be represented by drawing the subjects's eyes as crosses.

NEWLEY, ANTHONY (1931–) British actor, composer and singer

Stop the world, I want to get off.
musical show title, 1961

Newley, who had appeared in such films as *Oliver Twist* (1948) and *Cockleshell Heroes* (1956), paraded his versatility in the stage show he wrote with lyricist Leslie Bricusse (1931–) in 1961: *Stop The World I Want to Get Off*. He also performed in it. The phrase, denoting an urgent desire to escape the horrors of responsibility in an inimical world, soon became a popular catchphrase, although it seems to be confined to memory and to the occasional punning headline today.

NEWNHAM-DAVIES, NATHANIEL (1854–1917) British restaurant critic

We all know that in spring a young man's fancy lightly turns to thoughts of love, but it is not such common knowledge that in the early summer the thoughts of a man of mature age turn with equal agility to duckling and green peas.
The Gourmet's Guide to London (1914)

Newnham-Davies, a former Lieutenant-Colonel of the Indian

Army, was gastronomic critic for the *Pall Mall Gazette*, writing his influential appraisals of London restaurants in an era when a dozen courses and as many varied wines were the norm for even an average meal. He also wrote for the raffish, hedonistic *Sporting Times*, otherwise known as the 'Pink 'Un', and dined at Romanos in the Strand. It was with a party of 'Pink 'Uns', led by the music hall star Bessie Bellwood, that Newnham-Davies received the pen-name by which he was known to his faithful readers. After an evening's drinking, Bellwood organised an impromptu pantomime. She distributed parts all round until Newnham-Davies, still unassigned, asked for his role. 'Oh', she replied, 'You can be the Dwarf of Blood', and he signed it to his pieces thereafter.

NEWTON, HUEY P. (1942–) American radical

I suggest we use the panther as our symbol and call our political vehicle the Black Panther Party. The panther is a fierce animal, but he will not attack until he is backed into a corner, then he will strike out.
Revolutionary Suicide (1973)

Martin Luther King consistently advocated non-violence as the best means of destroying America's inherent racism, but many blacks found his ideas too tame, especially after King's assassination, presumably by a racist, in April 1968. Leading hard-liner was Huey P. Newton, whose founding of the militant, weapon-carrying Black Panther Party, based in Oakland, California, is recorded here. Newton, Minister of Defence for the BPP, became as much a target of Establishment attacks as a hero to many blacks, whose homes sported his iconic portrait, beret on head, African spear in hand, erect in a throne-like cane chair. The Party was decimated by police attacks, with violent shoot-outs in Detroit and Oakland, but time, as much as the FBI, wore them down. Newton's book proclaimed his credo 'Reactionary suicide...is a spiritual death that has been the experience of millions of black people in the United States' but he was no more able to eradicate racism than was King.

NICHOLLS, JANICE British pop critic

I'll give it foive!
Thank Your Lucky Stars, TV show 1970

Janice Nicholls was a Birmingham girl, with accent to match, who was recruited by ABC television's pop programme *Thank Your Lucky Stars*, the independent TV answer to the BBC's creaking *Juke Box Jury.* Along with more obviously famous figures she represented the great British public, marking records on a scale of 0–5. When a record delighted her she announced in tones one could cut with a knife, 'I'll give it foive!'. Inevitably, even in the relatively early days of pop packaging, Janice was constrained to exploit her own mini-celebrity with a record, titled with her favourite phrase. The public were unimpressed.

NICHOLSON, VIVIAN   (1936–) British housewife
I'm going to spend, spend, spend!
interviewed after her pools win in September 1961

By contemporary standards the £152,000 won by Vivian Nicholson and her husband Keith on the football pools in September 1961 seems relatively restrained, but for Keith, who made just £7.00 a week as a trainee miner, and Vivian who was struggling to bring up three children in their Castleford, Yorkshire home, it was the stuff of dreams. Interviewed by Fleet Street when they came to collect their cheque, Vivian remarked offhandedly, 'I'm going to spend, spend, spend.' The press loved the line, but it proved her nemesis. Her husband died in a car crash, his successors failed to make Vivian happy. She did spend, on and on, until the cash ran out. Her autobiography and the TV play based on her life, were both unsurprisingly called 'Spend, Spend, Spend'.

NICOLSON, HAROLD   (1886–1968) British politician and diarist
I feel I am getting a down on George V just now. He is all right as a gay young midshipman. He may be all right as a wise old king. But the intervening period when he was just shooting at Sandringham is hard to manage or to swallow. For seventeen years he did nothing at all but kill animals and stick in stamps.
diaries, August 17, 1949

Nicolson, a diplomat, politician, and husband of Vita Sackville-West, set out to write the authorised biography of George V in June 1948. He had been invited to write the book by King George VI, and decided, after weighing up the pros and cons, that in the end it could only benefit him. In the event the work proved tedious. As he confided to his diary, George V may have ended up one of the most beloved of 20th century British monarchs, but his life hardly abounded in excitement. Perhaps he should have noted the comment of Labour politician James Keir Hardie who remarked on George's accession in 1910: 'Born into the ranks of the working class, the new king's most likely fate would have been that of a street corner loafer.'

NICOLSON, HAROLD

We are all inclined to judge ourselves by our ideals; others by their acts.

diaries

Nicolson was born the son of the diplomat Sir Arthur Nicolson, and served himself in various embassies until 1929. From 1935–45 he was MP for West Leicester and a junior minister in Churchill's wartime cabinet. He wrote prolifically, as well as broadcasting on the radio. He remains best known for his diaries, in which he charted the course of his life, in and out of politics, as well as his opinions of his many eminent friends, and for his unconventional marriage to the writer Vita Sackville-West. They created a famous garden at Sissinghurst Castle together, and remained good friends, but each chose to indulge their own homosexual preferences rather than suffer an unhappy sham heterosexuality.

NIEBUHR, REINHOLD   (1892–1971) American theologian

Man's capacity for evil makes democracy necessary and man's capacity for good makes democracy possible.

quoted in *The Times*, July 18, 1977

Niebuhr held only one ministry after receiving his degree from Yale, but his experiences between 1914–27 among the impoverished factory-workers of Detroit's automobile factories affected his thinking deeply. He expressed them in his first book *Does Civilisation Need Religion* (1927). His answer, naturally, was 'yes', but the religion he proposed was hardly the utopian gospel of man's natural goodness as preached by less motivated ministers. Niebuhr has been labelled 'the number one theologian of U.S. Protestantism' and a proponent of 'neo-orthodoxy', in his espousal of Lutheran and Calvinist concepts. Niebuhr simply defined his concerns as with 'the defense and justification of the Christian faith in a secular age'.

NIEMOLLER, MARTIN   (1892–1984) German theologian

In Germany the Nazis came for the Communists and I didn't speak up because I was not a Communist. Then they came for the Jews and I didn't speak up because I was not a Jew. Then they came for the trades unionists and I didn't speak up because I was not a trades unionist. Then they came for the Catholics and I was

a Protestant so I didn't speak up. Then they came for me....By that time there was no-one to speak up for anyone.
quoted in W. Neil, *The Concise Dictionary of Religious* Quotations

Niemoller served in the German Navy from 1910–19 before being ordained a Protestant pastor. His campaign against the Nazis won him much international acclaim, and he was imprisoned in a concentration camp from 1937–45. Quoted after his release, when he was appointed President of the Office of Foreign Affairs of the Evangelical Church in Germany, Niemoller was expressing the guilt felt by many Germans who had not initially been threatened by the Nazis and found, when they did come into conflict with the Party, that having failed to oppose Hitler when there was time, they were now unable to make an adequate defence of their interests.

NIGHT AT THE OPERA, A

You can't fool me, there ain't no Sanity Clause
script by George S. Kaufman, Morrie Ryskind and Al Boasberg

A Night at the Opera was the first film the Marx Brothers made for MGM. It was less anarchic than its Paramount predecessors, influenced as it was by Hollywood's premier wunderkind, Irving Thalberg, a man whose talents were plugged directly into the Middle American psyche. Like all their films the plot revolved around juxtaposing their craziness with a formal environment, in this case the New York Opera. Groucho, as Otis B. Driftwood, is conducting contractual negotiations with Chico. They soon vanish into a morass of legalistic jargon as Groucho intones 'The party of the first part shall be known in this contract as the party of the first part'. When Groucho reaches the 'sanity clause', Chico replies in his glorious, punning cod-Italian 'You can't fool me, there ain't no Sanity Clause'.

NIXON, RICHARD   (1913–) American President

I gave them a sword. And they stuck it in and they twisted it with relish. And I guess if I'd been in their position I'd have done the same thing.
interviewed on TV, 1977

After the humiliation of his resignation from the Presidency in 1974 Nixon lay low for some time. Various rumours, each more lurid than the last, cast no light on the truth. In 1977 he decided to give his version of the Watergate Affair. Interviewed by David Frost, he produced a rerun of that mix of self-justification and self-laceration that seemed to have typified most of the public pronouncements he had offered when his career had come under pressure. His references to swords and the violence of their use, in this case with him as the victim, reflects his statements to Congressmen who questioned as to the validity of the invasion of Cambodia in April 1970: 'Don't worry about divisiveness. Having drawn the sword, don't take it out. Stick it in hard. Hit 'em in the gut. No defensiveness'.

NIXON, RICHARD

You see these bums, you know, blowing up the campuses. Listen, the boys on the college campuses today are the luckiest people in the world – going to the greatest universities – and there they are burning the books. I mean storming around about this issue. You name it. Get rid of this war, there'll be another one.

speech in 1970

Nixon gave the go-ahead to American troops in Vietnam to invade the North Vietnamese 'sanctuaries' in Cambodia on April 30, 1970. On May 4, in common with the students on many other campuses, those at Kent State in Ohio demonstrated against the invasion. Governor James Rhodes, comparing the students to 'the Brown Shirts and the Communist element', sent in the National Guard: when they panicked, four students were shot dead. The following day students boycotted classes at 448 American universities. Nixon claimed to sympathise, but this outburst made his real feelings clear. It has been claimed that he was suffering from a nervous breakdown; certainly his response to the shooting on May 14 of two more students, at the all-black Jackson State College in Mississippi seems a little odd. Looking through photographs of the event, the President contacted the college's head to ask 'What are we going to do to get more respect for the police from our young people'.

NIXON, RICHARD M.

I should say this: Pat doesn't have a mink coat, but she does have a respectable Republican cloth coat....One other thing I should probably tell you, because if I don't they'll be saying this about me too. We did get something, a gift, after the election...a little cocker spaniel in a crate, all the way from Texas....And our little girl, Trisha, the six-year-old, named it Checkers. And you know, the kids love that dog, and I just want to say this right now, that regardless of what they say about it, we're gonna keep it!

the 'Checkers' speech, September 23,1952

In the election of 1952 General Eisenhower chose Nixon, who had made a name for himself as the vehemently anti-Communist senator for California, as his vice-presidential running-mate. In September Nixon was accused of diverting an $18,000 'slush fund' to his own use. After failing to gain Eisenhower's support, despite his plea 'General, there comes a time when you have to piss or get off the pot!', Nixon elected to appeal direct to the nation. He appeared on NBC, with its more than 800 local affiliates. The speech, of which the crux is excerpted above, was described by *Variety* magazine, which knew showbiz when it saw it, as 'Just Plain Dick', punning on the popular radio soap opera 'Just Plain Bill'. The public, soap opera lovers all, loved the speech, and Nixon was exonerated. He was not the first politician to exploit a dog. Franklin Roosevelt's 1944 'Fala speech', arguably his greatest performance and the keynote of his campaign for a fourth term as President, exploited his Scottie, Fala, claiming straight-facedly that 'These Republican leaders have not been content with attacks on me, or on my wife, or on my sons. No, not content with that, they now include my little dog, Fala. Well of course I don't resent attacks, and my family doesn't resent attacks, but Fala does resent them'...

NIXON, RICHARD M.

You know very well that whether you are on page one or page thirty depends on whether they fear you. It is just as simple as that.

Nixon's relationship with the media has always been fraught with difficulty, even though in recent years they seem to be happy to participate in what must be his final political incarnation, as a more or less respected elder statesman. His tortured interpretation of just why one gets in the headlines or lost among the chip-wrapping, is typical of his talent for giving the facts a whole new and hitherto unsuspected slant. Given those periods in which Mr. Nixon has occupied the front page – the Checkers speech, his defeats in 1960 and 1962, the invasion of Cambodia, and finally and most damningly the Watergate Affair – it is hard for the uncommitted to see just in what way the press have 'feared' Nixon. It would surely be more understandable were he to have revised his theory and substituted the word 'hate'.

NIXON, RICHARD M.

This is the greatest week in the history of the world since the Creation.

greeting the astronauts on USS Hornet, July 24, 1969

Never a man to resist hyperbole when a mere superlative would do, Nixon, exercising his prerogative as US President to milk such favourable publicity as he could from the return of the first men on the moon, went to the US navy ship Hornet to greet them in person and deliver this effusive welcome. Later, evangelist Billy Graham, usually a staunch Nixonite, told him 'Mr. President, I know exactly how you felt, and I understand exactly what you meant, but, even so, I think you may have been a little excessive'. Graham forbore to comment on the President's subsequent comment 'For years politicians have promised the moon. I'm the first one to be able to deliver it.'

NIXON, RICHARD M.

You won't have Nixon to kick around any more.
losing gubernatorial election in California, November 7, 1962

After failing to defeat John F. Kennedy and become President in 1960, Nixon tried his luck again in 1962, challenging the Democratic incumbent, Edmund 'Pat' Brown, in the race to become Governor of California. Nixon lost again, and this time, feeling hard done to by the press, refused for some time to appear and make the traditional speech conceding the election. Finally, in a gesture that President Kennedy called 'mentally unsound' and aide John Erlichman attributed twenty years later to a severe hangover, Nixon addressed the media: 'I leave you gentlemen now, and you will now write it. You will interpret it. That's your right. But as I leave you, I want you to know – just think how much you're going to be missing. You won't have Nixon to kick around any more, because, gentlemen, this is my last press conference.' Then he added 'I hope that what I've said today will at least make the TV, radio and press recognize the great responsibility that they have to report all the news and, second, to recognize that they have the right and the responsibility, if they're against a candidate, to give him the shaft, but also recognise if they give him the shaft, put one lonely reporter on the campaign who will report what the candidate says now and then'.

NIXON, RICHARD M.

No television performance takes as much preparation as an off-the-cuff talk.
quoted in *The Making of the President*, by Joe McGinniss (1969)

McGinniss' book took the lid off the elaborate preparations that go into making a political candidate presentable to the electorate.

Not the policies or the platform, but the make-up, the TV lighting, the clothes and all of the rest of the cunningly contrived image that has conspired to render today's elections little more than a contest of two sophisticated packages. In 1960 Nixon had lost to Kennedy as much through his inability to master television as through his failure to capture votes. Ever since, he had been obsessed with perfecting his image and in 1968, groomed to perfection, he certainly dealt satisfactorily with Hubert Humphrey.

Nixon, Richard M.

If some of my judgements were wrong, and some were wrong, they were made in what I believed at the time to be in the best interest of the nation.
resignation speech, August 8, 1974

In a career marred by reverses that would have turned most politicians off their profession for ever, Nixon never displayed the thickness of his skin to such an extent as on August 8, 1974, when, facing the threat of the extreme humiliation – impeachment by Congress for his involvement in Watergate – he chose instead to resign the Presidency. First, he delivered an emotional farewell to the White House staff, extolling every worker, including the 'good plumbers', an unfortunate reference given that 'Plumbers' was the nickname given to the squad who, by their various break-ins and burglaries, had initiated the whole imbroglio. Nixon then addressed the nation in a speech characterised, as this short excerpt shows, less by contrition than by an attempt, even so late in the day, to justify his own position.

Nixon, Richard M.

There will be no whitewash at the White House.
speech on April 30, 1973

Like many recent conservative presidents, Nixon preferred as little contact as possible with the press, eschewing the traditional press conferences of more open men. Instead he preferred to appear occasionally on television, delivering his statements from the safety of a studio. Nonetheless his appearance on the evening of April 30, 1973 cannot have been easy. As the investigations into the Watergate break-in drew increasingly near to implicating the White House, Nixon was forced to sack his two top aides, H.R. 'Bob' Haldeman and John Erlichman. He characterised them as 'two of the finest public servants it has been my privilege to know' and promised America, assonant even as the noose

591

tightened around his own neck 'There will be no whitewash at the White House'.

NIXON, RICHARD M.

It is time for the great silent majority of Americans to stand up and be counted.
speech, November 3, 1969

The phrase 'silent majority' had been a euphemism for 'the dead' since at least the mid-19th century but in this speech, President Nixon gave the phrase a new meaning. As far as the conservative Nixon was concerned the Sixties were an aberration; the best thing his own election could do would be to reverse the liberal trend and reimpose traditional American values. His speech called upon Middle America, the great reservoir of voters who had not been swayed by the oratory of the new gurus, to rise up and make themselves felt.

NOBBS, DAVID   British writer

I didn't get where I am today...
catchphrase in 'Reggie Perrin' books

Nobbs began his career as a contributor to television's early Sixties satire show, and has worked on a variety of comedy shows. He is best known for his trilogy of novels, and the television series he adapted from them, all dealing with businessman and fantasist Reggie Perrin. As played by the late Leonard Rossiter, the stories feature Reginald Iolanthe Perrin (intials R.I.P.), his wife Elizabeth, his son and daughter and the staff of Sunshine Desserts where he reluctantly works. Perrin lacks a particular catchphrase but his boss, C.J., whose conversation manages to encompass a vast range of cliché, intones this self-congratulatory line on all possible occasions.

NORDEN, DENNIS   (1922–) British scriptwriter

We don't want it good – we want it Tuesday.
quoted in the *Guardian*, 1969

Norden, a friend of Frank Muir, who started his career writing routines for the comedian Jimmy Edwards, was able to join him writing the scripts when Edwards graduated to stardom on BBC radio's *Take It From Here*. Together they created one of the country's most beloved comedy families: The Glums, gormless Ron, vacuous Eth and drunken, bigoted, rascally, Cockney Mr, Glum, played by Edwards, a prototype, perhaps, of Johnny Speight's 'Alf Garnett'. Muir and Norden dominated Fifties comedy, as Ray Galton and Alan Simpson would in the Sixties. Norden's comment refers to the demands of those for whom they wrote, more interested in deadlines than excellence.

NORMAN, FRANK (1930–1981) British writer

Fings Ain't Wot They Used T'Be
play title (1961)

Norman, the illegitimate son of parents who abandoned him to the Church of England Adoption Society, was brought up in Dr. Barnardo's Homes. After leaving Barnardo's in 1946 he gravitated to London where he lived mainly on his wits and as a juvenile thief served a number of prison sentences. After the last of these ended in 1957 he began writing. His first piece was published in May 1958 and his prison reminiscences, *Bang To Rights*, appeared the same year. He wrote ten books, three more of which were highly acclaimed autobiographies. Norman's greatest success was his musical, *Fings Ain't Wot They Used T'Be*, which delighted the West End with its nostalgia for the 'good old days' of post-war Soho.

NORTHCLIFFE, LORD (1865–1922) British newspaper magnate

Never put on the table of Demos what you would not have on your own table.

In his era Northcliffe, born Alfred Harmsworth, was the nonpareil of British newspaper proprietors. He capitalised on the new literacy of the late 19th century to bring news to the masses in a format they could enjoy; he also acquired *The Times*. His first venture was *Answers* (founded 1888), a popular journal upon which all his subsequent successes were based. With his brother Harold he bought the *Evening News* in 1894 and founded the *Daily Mail* in 1896. The *Daily Mirror* began in 1903 and, as its name suggested, was promoted as the first British paper ever dedicated unreservedly to women's interests. Like many fellow proprietors, he saw himself at the nation's helm, but Northcliffe always proved most capable when dealing with his newspapers.

NORTHCLIFFE, LORD

I wish to be laid as near Mother as possible at North Finchley. I do not wish anything erect from the ground or any words except my name, the year I was born and this year on the stone. In *The Times* I should like a page reviewing my life by someone who really knows, and a leading article by the best man available on the night.

memorandum issued on his deathbed, 1922

Like the American circus proprietor Phineas T. Barnum, whose last words were to ask about the night's gross at Madison Square Garden, Northcliffe's mind stayed on business to the end. This memorandum was issued from his deathbed. His mental health had been deteriorating for some time and he had been becoming noticeably more eccentric, but after consultations with some thirty specialists in February 1922, Northcliffe was told that his physical health had broken down. He died, with his affairs as far as possible in order, on August 14. The cause of death was variously attributed, by all those specialists, to ulcerative endocarditis, syphilis, Indian jungle fever and a delayed reaction to poisoned ice cream.

O

O'CASEY, SEAN (1880–1964) Irish playwright

English literature's performing flea.
on P.G. Wodehouse, 1941

O'Casey, one of Ireland's most popular and at times controversial playwrights, disliked the work of his fellow-writer, the English humourist P.G. Wodehouse. In 1940, at the fall of France, Wodehouse had been interned by the invading Germans. In 1941, more in naivety than malice, he had been manipulated by the Nazis into making a number of broadcasts to America. This caused a furore in England, where such rabble-rousers as 'Cassandra' of the *Daily Mirror* immediately screamed 'Traitor!'. O'Casey joined in, writing to the *Daily Telegraph* on July 8, 'If England has any dignity left in the way of literature, she will forget forever the antics of English literature's performing flea. If Berlin thinks the poor fish great so much the better for us'. Wodehouse was unable to comment, but in 1953, in a letter included in an autobiographical volume he titled 'Performing Flea', he wrote ingenuously, 'With Sean O'Casey's statement... I scarcely know how to deal. Thinking it over, I believe he meant to be complimentary, for all the performing fleas I have met impressed me with their sterling artistry and that indefinable something which makes the good trouper'.

O'NOLAN, BRIAN (1910–1966) (Myles na gCopaleen) Irish writer

Do engine drivers, I wonder, eternally wish they were small boys.
The Best of Myles (1968)

O'Nolan worked for the Irish civil service until his retirement through ill health in 1953, combining his job with a regular satirical column, 'The Cruiskeen Lawn', in the *Irish Times*, under the pseudonym Myles na gCopaleen. He also wrote novels as Flann O'Brien. The first and best known of these is *At Swim Two Birds* (1939), a complex and fascinating work, combining realism and fantasy, the past and present, where humans, fairies and legendary Irish heroes intermingle in a picaresque tale heavily influenced by and often compared to the work of James Joyce. This remark stems from the asssumed preoccupation, if it still exists in today's world of hi-tech toys, of small boys with becoming engine drivers.

O'NOLAN, BRIAN

What is important is food, money and opportunities for scoring off one's enemies. Give a man these three things and you won't hear much squawking out of him.
The Best of Myles (1968)

Hardly the most idealistic view of humanity, but as near the truth as any other. O'Nolan's grim pragmatism misses out only sex, but then that particular commodity could, if one chose to particularly cynical, be included in the last part of his list.

O'NOLAN, BRIAN

A thing of duty is a boy forever.
as Flann O'Brien, on the perennial youth of policemen

As the actor-manager Seymour Hicks observed, the sure sign of one's own ageing is the way in which the policemen keep getting younger. By the same token, O'Brien's reference, punning on the popular line 'A thing of beauty is a joy forever', points out that, Dorian Gray-like, the police seem eternally youthful while we the public are doomed to grow ever older.

OATES, LAWRENCE 'TITUS' (1880–1912) British explorer

I am just going outside, and I may be some time.
entry in Captain Scott's Last Journal, March 16/17, 1912

Scott's expedition to the Antarctic in 1912 reached the Pole but of the four men who joined Robert Falcon Scott at the bottom of the world, none returned. Scott's journal records the inexorable decline of their strength, immortalising all five as British heroes, none more so than Lawrence 'Titus' Oates, whose feet were so crippled by frostbite that he could not walk and had thus become an additional burden on his companions. According to Scott, Oates decided to ease their journey by leaving their tent and walking off into a raging blizzard. Walking painfully in stockinged feet he vanished into the snow, allegedly offering this exemplary farewell. Less reverent researchers claim that he added the words 'for a pee' after 'outside'.

ODD COUPLE, THE

I've got brown sandwiches and green sandwiches...it's either very new cheese or very old meat.
script by Neil Simon (1968)

Neil Simon (1927–) is one of the American theatre's most prolific and successful playwrights, whose Broadway hits have transferred almost invariably to Hollywood's sound stages. Simon's work is hardly revolutionary, but like England's Alan Ayckbourn he purveys subtle, witty middle of the road fare, devoid of a message, but high on humour. *The Odd Couple* was one of his most popular plays, and as a film starring Jack Lemmon (1925–) and Walter Matthau (1920–) both delighted audiences and launched a successful screen partnership. In Simon's plot, bachelors Matthau and Lemmon live together. Matthau is a slob, Lemmon a nag. This unappetising line comes early in story, when Matthau is entertaining his friends to poker and, asked for food, produces the sandwiches he describes above.

OGILVY, DAVID (1911–) British advertising agent

The consumer is not a moron. She is your wife. And she is grown up.
New York Herald Tribune, 1956

Ogilvy, variously described as 'the most sought-after wizard in the advertising business' and 'the Pope of modern advertising', began work as a chef in Paris, sold Aga cookers in Scotland, worked for Gallup Polls in America and farmed in Pennsylvania. After working for British intelligence during World War II he returned to America and founded the advertising agency Ogilvy and Mather. He had £6000 of capital and no clients, but built up the business into the world's fourth largest agency, with 141 offices in 40 countries.

OLDENBERG, CLAES (1929–) Swedish artist

I am for an art that is political-erotical-mystical, that does something other than sit on its arse in a museum. I'm for an art that grows up, not knowing it's art at all. An art given the chance of having a starting point of zero. I'm for an art that embroils itself with the everyday crap and still comes out on top. An art that imitates the human, that is comic if necessary, or violent, whatever is necessary. I am for art you can sit on, for art you can pick your nose with or stub your toes on. I am in favour of art that is put on and taken off, like pants, that develops holes, like socks, is eaten like a piece of pie or abandoned with great contempt like shit.
Manifesto (1961)

Launching his artistic career in 1956 Oldenberg rejected the prevailing artistic orthodoxy of 'abstract expressionism' in favour of making three-dimensional objects, based on those in the real world but, influenced by the world of 'pop art', created in very different ways. Small objects would be magnified many times, hard ones rendered soft and so on. Typical were Oldenberg's creations Giant Ice Cream Cone (1962) and Giant Hamburger (1962). In 1965 he offered his grand design for huge public monuments: a half-peeled banana in Times Square, a monstrous electric fan replacing the Statue of Liberty. The scheme was rejected, although Yale University backed one project, a giant lipstick mounted on a moveable tractor.

OLDHAM, ANDREW LOOG (1942–) British rock manager

Pop music is sex and you have to hit them in the face with it.
quoted in the *Book of Rock Quotes* by Jonathon Green (1977)

Oldham failed in his own efforts at rock stardom but as manager of the Rolling Stones he did for them, somewhat differently, what Brian Epstein had done for the Beatles. As Nick Cohn put it in 1971 'In high-heeled boots, trousers, puff-sleeved pink shirts and tinted glasses, jewellery and make-up, he was the campest and most vicious and most exhibitionist figure imaginable, and the Stones followed on from him'. Oldham was saying nothing new, but unlike the staid old men who still dominated the rock business, he was saying it. The Beatles were the sort of boys you would love your daughter to marry; nobody ever said that about the Rolling Stones, and their fame as anti-heroes was assiduously promoted by Oldham, whose own style was derived from America's 'Tycoon of Teen', Phil Spector.

OLIVIER, LORD (1907–) British actor

Acting is a masochistic form of exhibitionism. It is not quite the occupation of an adult.
in *Time* magazine, 1978

For all that he chooses to mock his profession, Olivier has been considered Britain's leading actor for fifty years. After the obligatory spell in repertory he scored his first success in 1930 in Noel Coward's *Private Lives*. After a brief spell in Hollywood he joined the Old Vic in 1937, playing a number of major Shakespearian roles, and his films of Shakespeare plays won wide acclaim. Established as one of the world's foremost interpreters of Shakespeare he broke the mould with his performance as the seedy comic Archie Rice in John Osborne's *The Entertainer* (1957). More recent work has been limited by recurring ill-health mainly to roles in films and on television.

ON THE WATERFRONT

I coulda had class! I coulda been a contender! I coulda been somebody! Instead of a bum which is what I am!
screenplay by Budd Schulberg (1954)

Budd Schulberg's script for *On The Waterfront* ostensibly set out to expose corruption in the dockyard unions. With director Elia Kazan, Schulberg fashioned one of the Fifties' most popular films, winner of eight Oscars, and an outstanding vehicle for Marlon Brando as Terry Malloy, an inarticulate, alienated layabout. What audiences chose to ignore was the underlying ethos of the movie: that informing is a positive, praiseworthy act, and one which the church, the family and the authorities are right to encourage. Both Kazan and Schulberg had been co-operative 'friendly' witnesses for the House Un-American Activities Committee and for those who refused to kow-tow to McCarthy, this film, in which the 'bum' finds himself only in betrayal, was their apotheosis.

ONASSIS, ARISTOTLE (1906–1975) Greek shipping magnate

If women didn't exist all the money in the world would have no meaning.

Onassis was one of the most flamboyant of the Greek shipping millionaires whose exploits delighted the gossip columnists of the Fifties and Sixties. Onassis based his career on the timely purchase of six derelict ships when, in 1930, the trade was in a slump. He mothballed the ships until the market picked up and then sent them off to make money. From this base Onassis created a fortune in excess of £500 million, controlling all major decisions himself and proving himself a far-sighted and unconventional entrepreneur. Enthusiastically fulfilling the stereotype of the macho Greek, Onassis had many well publicised affairs. These were topped off by his marriage to Jackie Kennedy, the widow of President Kennedy, in 1968.

OPHULS, MARCEL   (1902–57) French film director

Puritanism... helps us enjoy our misery while we are inflicting it on others.
in the *Listener*, 1978

Ophuls, born Max Oppenheimer in Germany, was a director of lushly romantic films of whom critic Andrew Sarris has written 'If all the dollies and cranes in the world snap to attention when his name is mentioned, it is because he gave camera movement its finest hours in the history of the cinema'. His remark underlines the essential phenomenon of the Puritan who, unsatisfied by his own choice of suffering, must compound his self-denial with ensuring that the unconverted must suffer too. As Thomas Macaulay summed it up in his *History of England* (1848) 'The Puritan hated bear-baiting, not because it gave pain to the bear, but because it gave pleasure to the spectators'.

OPPENHEIMER, ROBERT   (1904–1967) American nuclear physicist

The physicists have known sin; and this is a knowledge which they cannot lose.
lecturing at Massachusetts Institute of Technology, November 25, 1947

The first reaction of the Manhattan Project physicists at the successful testing of their bomb in July 1945 was one of satisfaction, tempered with awe. When the same bomb was exploded over Japan a month later, that reaction changed to one of horror and in some cases of guilt. Even Enrico Fermi, who had always brushed aside ethical questions with an impatient 'Don't bother me with your conscientious scruples. After all, the thing's superb physics!' was impressed and shocked. Oppenheimer's comment to the future scientists and engineers of MIT conveyed, with its mention of 'sin', the sense of religious wonder that pervaded the experience. Those who had invented the bomb had known the greatest sin: the power, attributed by the religious only to a god or a devil, of destroying the world.

OPPENHEIMER, ROBERT

When you see something that is technically sweet, you go ahead and do it.
quoted in Robert Jungk, *Brighter Than A Thousand Suns* (1956)

Looking back on the role he and other physicists played in the creation of the atomic and hydrogen bombs, Oppenheimer undoubtedly regretted what had turned out to be the terrifying results of their work, but equally, he appreciated that as scientists they had no option but to follow to their logical conclusion researches which were both exciting and, as science, highly successful. As he put it 'It is my judgement in these things that when you see something that is technically sweet you go ahead and do it and you argue about what to do about it only after you have had your technical success. That is the way it was with the atom bomb. I do not think anybody opposed making it; there were some debates about what to do with it after it was made.'

OPPENHEIMER, ROBERT

I am become Death – the Shatterer of Worlds
on July 16, 1945

The world's first atomic bomb, code-name Trinity, was detonated at 5:30am, July 16th, 1945, at Almogordo, New Mexico. Equivalent to an explosion of 20,000 tons of TNT, the blast was seen for 250 miles, the sound reverberated over fifty. J. Robert Oppenheimer, the US physicist chosen in 1939 to run the Manhattan Project that developed atomic weapons, who had already used John Donne's *Holy Sonnets* for the name 'Trinity' now turned to the *Bhagavad-Gita* to sum up his own emotions. Kenneth Bainbridge, who was supervising the test, chose a more prosaic remark: 'Now,' he said 'we are all sons of bitches'. Returning home Oppenheimer told one of his daughters that Bainbridge's line was 'the best thing anyone said after the test'.

ORBACH, SUSIE   (1946–) American psychotherapist

Fat Is A Feminist Issue.
book title, 1977

Orbach's book was subtitled 'the anti-diet guide to permanent weight loss' and it challenged the endless dependence of overweight women on one after another of the 'miracle cure' diets that never really cure anything. Orbach's premise was that those diets and the dieticians who created them were looking at fat in the wrong way. As she puts it 'Fat is not about lack of self-control or will power. Fat is about protection, sex, nurturance, mothering, strength and assertion. Fat is a social disease. It is expressive of the modern woman in ways that are seldom examined and even less often treated.' Her book was designed as a self-help manual, with the emphasis on demystifying just why it is women are obsessed with body size and offering them, from a therapeutic viewpoint, a way out of food addiction.

ORTEGA Y GASSET, JOSE   (1883–1955) Spanish philosopher, social critic and essayist

I am I plus my circumstances.
The Revolt of the Masses (1930)

Ortega was professor of metaphysics at Madrid University. A liberal, he opposed the dictatorship of Primo de Rivera and was elected a member of the Republican Constituent Assembly between 1931–33. Unwilling to support either side in the Civil War, he left Spain and lived abroad, teaching in Peru until 1945. After his return he founded, in 1948, the Instituto de Humanidades in Madrid but refused to take up any academic post while Franco still ruled. Ortega's philosophy was based on the concept of each life as a finite 'vital project' which must be lived out in the current historical circumstances. When the individual meets culture, seen as an independent reality, he is faced with its challenge, which he may or may not solve, but which recurs, varying with the current situation, to be faced by each successive generation.

ORTON, JOE   (1933–1967) British playwright

Fay: The British police force used to be run by men of integrity. Truscott: That is a mistake which has been rectified.
Loot (1966)

Orton's second play, *Loot*, was his greatest success. Loot is essentially about police corruption, although Orton drew on his own father's death to provide a subplot, involving money, coffins and a mislaid glass eye, of the blackest of black humour. Inspector Truscott, the representative of law and order, is every bit as corrupt as the thieves he pursues. His every line seems to mock the whole idea of the friendly British Bobby. Echoing the dialogue above, he tells one character who protests against his unfair arrest saying 'You can't do this. I've always been a law-abiding citizen. The police are for the protection of law-abiding people', 'I don't know where you pick up these slogans, sir. You must read them on the hoardings'.

ORTON, JOE

Kath: Can he be present at the birth of his child?
Ed: It's all any reasonable child can expect if the dad is present at the conception.
Entertaining Mr. Sloane (1964)

Kath and Ed are brother and sister. He is a gay businessman, she is a nymphomaniac housewife and between them stands the vaguely androgyne thug, the object of both their lusts, 'Mr. Sloane'. To one side, but intimately involved with all three is the siblings' father. Orton planned 'Sloane' as a reworking of the Oedipus legend, but its eventual climax, the murder of the old man by Sloane and his surrender, as a price of their not telling the police, to both Ed and Kath, rejects the original plan. Kath seduces Sloane at the end of Act One. In Act Three, with their father dead, they decide to share Sloane on a six monthly basis. As the play ends, Kath asks her brother if Sloane can watch his child born. Ed rejects her out of hand and leaves with his prize.

ORTON, JOE

I'd the upbringing a nun would envy and that's the truth. Until I was fifteen I was more familiar with Africa than with my own body.
Entertaining Mr. Sloane (1964)

Orton, once called the 'Oscar Wilde of Welfare State gentility' had a superb ear for the niceties of speech, especially that of the 'genteel' lower middle classes who people his dramas. His dramas combine a formal structure, emphasised by the stereotypical figures – widower, nurse, policeman – who play them out, with alarming excesses of what many saw as depravity (although Orton drew some of the most bizarre incidents from his own family's life), all couched in net-curtained cliché. Kath, the sister in *Entertaining Mr. Sloane*, is a classic Orton type, masking her passions in the language of soap opera and romance fiction.

ORWELL, GEORGE   (1903–50) (Eric Blair) British essayist and novelist

Orwell, the son of an official in the Indian civil service was an Eton scholar but, rejecting privilege, chose a lifetime of advocating the rights and interests of Britain's workers. He changed his name, taking his surname from a Suffolk river, and began courting poverty. His first important book, *Down and Out in Paris and London* (1933), detailed his experiences as a washer-up in Paris and a tramp, albeit with the option of escape, in England. He followed this with *The Road to Wigan Pier* (1937), which dealt with the industrial north of England. His experiences in the Spanish Civil War are recalled in *Homage to Catalonia* (1938). Throughout his career he wrote a continuous stream of penetrating essays, notable for his investigations of popular culture. His reputation as a major political writer came with his two post-war novels: *Animal Farm* (1945) and *1984* (1948). If the former is reasonably light-hearted, the latter is unredeemedly grim, and both books chart his disillusion with the Marxist revolution.

ORWELL, GEORGE

All animals are created equal, but some are more equal than others
Animal Farm (1945)

By the final chapter of *Animal Farm*, Orwell's satire on Stalin's subversion of the Russian Revolution, the revolution at Manor Farm, which once promised the animals so much, has become thoroughly corrupted. The pigs, to whom the others turned for leadership, have consolidated their power, helped by the dogs, their police force. They produce nothing, and consume much, concerning themselves only with bureaucracy. The other animals labour for the leadership, comparing their barren lives with the pigs' constant assurances, backed by statistics, that everything is constantly improving. The final disillusion comes when the animals find that the old Seven Commandments, the basis of the Farm's constitution, have been replaced by a single one: 'All animals are created equal, but some are more equal than others'. To compound the betrayal, the pigs begin negotiating with the once-hated men, and as they sit arguing in the farmhouse, 'The creatures outside looked from pig to man, and from man to pig, and from pig to man again; but already it was impossible to say which was which'.

ORWELL, GEORGE

If you want a picture of the future, imagine a boot stamping on the human face – forever....And remember that is forever.
Nineteen Eighty-Four (1948)

As the novel draws to its close, Winston Smith is being gradually purged of his anti-Party beliefs by the sinister, pragmatic O'Brien. O'Brien combines all the contrivances of modern torture with constant lectures on the futility of Winston's rebellion. In the midst of one such talk, O'Brien explains the basis of the new order: 'It is the exact opposite of the stupid hedonistic Utopias that the old reformers imagined. A world of fear and treachery and torment, a world of trampling and being trampled upon, a world which will not grow less but more merciless as it refines itself. Progress in our world will be progress towards more pain....In our world there will be no emotions except fear, rage, triumph and self-abasement.' All that remains will be 'the intoxication of power.... If you want a picture of the future, imagine a boot stamping on the human face – forever....And remember that is forever.'

ORWELL, GEORGE

Political language... is designed to make lies sound truthful and murder respectable and to give an appearance of solidarity to pure wind.
Politics and the English Language (1946)

In this essay Orwell suggests that English is 'in a bad way' and lays the blame for this decline on political and economic causes. After selecting and analysing a number of passages, he suggests that deliberately political writing is inevitably stale, lacking in precision and, as the lines cited above point out, filled with 'swindles and perversions'. Such writing, he adds, is 'largely the defence of the indefensible'. He offers his own six-point list of methods in which such writing can be avoided and suggests that we consign all 'verbal refuse...into the dustbin where it belongs'.

ORWELL, GEORGE

History is full of ignominious getaways by the great and famous.
Who Are the War Criminals (1943)

Orwell wrote this review of 'The Trial of Mussolini' by the pseudonymous 'Cassius' for Tribune in October 1943. The book's author assembles a selection of witnesses, drawn from the British Establishment, whose words are used to prove that they condoned the rise of the Italian dictator, consistently justifying his worst excesses. Orwell agrees, but takes his study of political hypocrisy one step further. It is not merely Tories who are capable of such deliberate self-delusion: the left had shown equally wilful blindness when refusing to look too closely at the realities of Stalin's Russia. He cannot, in any case, envisage a genuine trial, of Mussolini or any other leader, whether allegedly bad or good.

ORWELL, GEORGE

Four legs good, two legs bad.
Animal Farm (1945)

Once the animals' revolution has turned Mr. Jones' Manor Farm into their own Animal Farm, they turn their attention to creating a new world based on revolutionary ideals. At first things go 'like clockwork. The animals were as happy as they had never conceived it possible to be'. At first the Farm was run by Seven Commandments, notably '1. Whatever goes upon two legs is an enemy. 2. Whatever goes upon four legs, or has wings, is a friend'. With the revolution established, Snowball, the ideologue of the pigs who have been accepted as leaders, argues that seven commandments are excessive. 'After much thought (he) declared that the Seven Commandments could in effect be reduced to a single maxim, namely "Four legs good, two legs bad". This, he said, contained the essential principle of Animalism'.

ORWELL, GEORGE

On the whole human beings want to be good, but not too good and not quite all the time.
in *Collected Essays*

Orwell's remark on the gap between humanity's desire to be good and the more honest feeling that such self-denial can usually be put off to another day, is reminiscent of the prayer offered up by St. Augustine of Hippo (354–430): 'Da mihi castitatem et continentiam, sed noli modo' (Give me chastity and continency, but do not give it yet).

ORWELL, GEORGE

Big Brother is Watching You.
Nineteen Eighty-Four (1948)

Orwell's phrase, which captured the concept of omnipresent totalitarian control so effectively and which has lasted as a popular catchphrase ever since, appears on the novel's first page. Winston Smith, the book's central character, returning to his flat in Victory Mansions sees at one end of a corridor 'a coloured poster, too large for indoor display.... It depicted simply an enormous face, more than a metre wide: the face of a man of about forty-five, with a heavy black moustache and ruggedly handsome features.... It was one of those pictures which are so contrived that the eyes follow you about when you move. BIG BROTHER IS WATCHING YOU, the caption beneath it ran'.

ORWELL, GEORGE

Who controls the past controls the future. Who controls the present controls the past.

Nineteen Eighty-Four (1948)

This line emphasises Orwell's premise, put into practice by Winston Smith and his fellow workers at the Ministry of Truth, that history can be rewritten. Orwell's fictional Ministry takes its central task from the true-life endless revisions of the Great Soviet Encyclopedia, which changes its entries, adding some, deleting others and rewriting many, according to the current political situation. In Airstrip One, as England has been renamed, the Party is constantly rewriting history in order to condition the masses: not only has nothing ever been different, but in the future nothing will ever change. Facts are relative, they can be called up or dismissed at will.

ORWELL, GEORGE

Nationalism is power hunger tempered by self-deception.

Notes on Nationalism (1945)

Orwell's essay differentiates nationalism from patriotism, which he accepts as 'an innoculation against nationalism', and offers a detailed definition of nationalism, summed up in the line above. He divides nationalism into Positive Nationalism (Neo-Toryism, Celtic Nationalism and Zionism), Transferred Nationalism (Communism, Political Catholicism and 'Colour Feeling') and Negative Nationalism (Anglophobia, Anti-Semitism and Trotskyism). In conclusion he suggests that nationalistic feelings are 'part of the make up of most of us, whether we like it or not. Whether it is possible to get rid of them, I do not know, but I do believe that it is possible to struggle against them...and prevent them from contaminating your mental processes'.

ORWELL, GEORGE

The quickest way of ending a war is to lose it.

Second Thoughts on James Burnham (1946)

This essay deals with Burnham's book, The Managerial Revolution (1940), in which the American business expert predicted that the successor to 19th century capitalism would not be socialism but a 'new kind of planned, centralised society which will neither be capitalist nor...democratic'. This society would be controlled by business executives, technicians, bureaucrats and soldiers, all of whom Burnham lumps together as 'managers'. Burnham assumes that Germany will win the war and Nazism will institute a managerial society. Orwell counters his theories. As part of his argument he posits a poll, taken in 1940, as to whether Germany would win and claims that the bulk of those who would have said 'yes' would have been the intelligentsia who loathed the idea of a protracted struggle and thus preferred a quick defeat to a lengthy, if victorious struggle.

ORWELL, GEORGE

The high sentiments always win in the end, the leaders who offer blood, toil, tears and sweat always get more out of their followers than those who offer safety and a good time. When it comes to the pinch, human beings are heroic.
The Art of Donald McGill (1941)

Orwell's essay on the doyen of the 'naughty seaside postcards' appeared in *Horizon* in September 1941. Such investigations are common, almost mandatory today, but at the time it was quite novel, a pioneering form of sociological investigation that had not been attempted, or certainly not with such 'down-market' phenomena as Donald McGill's cast of grotesques. As Orwell pointed out, his art was scarcely aesthetic, but as a staple of British life it was worthy of note. In his analysis he points out that McGill's feckless characters represent the important side of humanity that officialdom, with its constant demands for more than people really want to give, likes to ignore. Surprisingly, the 'high sentiments' do win most of the time, but as Orwell stresses, our McGill side, the 'lazy, cowardly, debt-bilking adulterer' 'needs a hearing occasionally'.

ORWELL, GEORGE

Probably the battle of Waterloo was won on the playing fields of Eton, but all the opening battles of all subsequent wars have been lost there.
The Lion and the Unicorn: England, Your England

The Lion and the Unicorn was cited by Arthur Koestler as 'one of the most moving and yet incisive portraits of the English character, and a minor classic in itself'. This passage prefaces a section in which Orwell discusses the decline of the English moneyed classes between the two world wars. Such a class, he claimed could no longer justify its existence and only hung to power by a steadfast refusal to acknowledge that change was even possible, let alone a good idea. They are not intrinsically evil, but possess an infallible instinct for doing the wrong thing; and

Orwell looks forward to a post-war world in which they no longer matter.

ORWELL, GEORGE

A family with the wrong members in control – that, perhaps, is as near as one can come to describing England in a phrase.
The Lion and the Unicorn: England, Your England

England, Orwell states 'is the most class-ridden country under the sun. It is a land of snobbery and privilege, ruled largely by the old and silly'. Yet he tempers his criticism with the fact that one has to take into account 'its emotional unity, the tendency of nearly all its inhabitants to feel alike and act together in moments of supreme crisis'. He goes on to say 'More than ever it resembles a family, a rather stuffy Victorian family, with not many black sheep in it but with all its cupboards bursting with skeletons. It has rich relations who have to be kow-towed to and poor relations who are horribly sat upon, and there is a deep conspiracy of silence about the source of the family income. It is a family in which the young are generally thwarted and most of the power is in the hands of irresponsible uncles and bedridden aunts. Still, it is a family. It has its private language and its common memories and at the approach of an enemy it closes its ranks. A family with the wrong members in control – that, perhaps, is as near as one can come to describing England in a phrase'.

ORWELL, GEORGE

The typical socialist...a prim little man with a white-collar job, usually a secret teetotaller and often with vegetarian leanings.
The Road to Wigan Pier (1937)

Orwell's first-hand study of the poor in the industrial towns of Northern England falls into two parts. The first is based on his own visits to the North, a factual account of what he saw and who he met. The second part is a discussion of Socialism 'a theory confined entirely to the middle class'. So contentious was his role as what his publisher Victor Gollancz called 'the devil's advocate for the case against socialism' that it was deemed necessary, in what after all was a publication of the Left Book Club, for Gollancz to preface the book with an ideological disclaimer. Orwell's categorization of middle-class socialists as cranks points out to 'tremulous old ladies' that the typical socialist is not 'a ferocious-looking working man with greasy overalls and a raucous voice.' He is either the prim vegetarian or 'a youthful snob-Bolshevik who in five years time will quite probably have made a wealthy marriage and been converted to Roman Catholicism'.

Orwell, George

To the ordinary working man, the sort you would meet in any pub on Saturday night, Socialism does not mean much more than better wages and shorter hours and nobody bossing you about.
The Road to Wigan Pier (1937)

After scourging the fruit-juice drinkers, nudists, sandal-wearers, sex-maniacs, Quakers, 'Nature Cure' quacks, pacifists and feminists, the 'mingy little beasts' who represent bourgeois socialism in England, Orwell points out that for the average member of the working classes, such interests have nothing to do with what he expects if he chooses to vote socialist. The 'more revolutionary type' might see the word as shorthand for some form of rallying-cry against the forces of oppression, but Orwell is convinced that the masses cannot grasp, nor would they truly desire, the sort of wide-ranging upheaval in society that the imposition of real socialism would bring. Some workers have graduated to the theoretical side of Marxism, but in so doing they have abandoned their roots in physical labour.

Orwell, George

Serious sport has nothing to do with fair play. It is bound up with hatred, jealously, boastfulness, disregard of all rules and sadistic pleasure in witnessing violence: in other words, it is war minus the shooting.
The Sporting Spirit (1945)

Orwell's essay on the close relation between sport and the worst excesses of nationalistic fervour was inspired by the visit of the Moscow Dynamo soccer team to England in autumn 1945. He cites a number of examples, both from the tour and from previous sporting encounters, in which the supposed good will of the occasion has been submerged in 'savage combative instincts' that make sport 'frankly mimic warfare'. He scorns the 'blah-blah about...clean, healthy rivalry' and speculates as to the origins of the sporting cult. He rejects the whole exercise and suggests that 'There are quite enough causes of trouble already, and we need not add to them by encouraging young men to kick each other on the shins amid the roars of infuriated spectators'.

ORWELL, GEORGE

Saints should always be judged guilty until they are proved innocent.
Reflections on Gandhi (1949)

Gandhi, the champion of Indian independence, had been dead a year when Orwell wrote this essay, based around a review of his book *The Story of My Experiments with Truth*, covering Gandhi's life until the 1920s. He begins by asking to what extent the alleged saint was moved by vanity and how far he compromised his ideals by involving himself in politics 'which of their nature are inseparable from coercion and fraud'. In the end Orwell cannot like Gandhi, feeling for him a 'sort of aesthetic distaste', and refuses to find much justification for the canonisation of a man whose 'basic aims were anti-human and reactionary'. Nonetheless he accepts that 'compared with the other leading figures of our time, how clean a smell he has managed to leave behind!'.

ORWELL, GEORGE

Most people get a fair amount of fun out of their lives, but on balance life is suffering and only the very young or the very foolish imagine otherwise.
Shooting an Elephant (1950)

Orwell is not, on the whole, a pessimist, rather a realist, and this comment should not be taken as a statement of despair. Unfortunately, in offering the wisdom of anyone who has experienced more than just childhood, (and there is no guarantee of happiness there, one need only look at his ironically titled essay *Such, Such Were the Joys*, in which he recalls the privations of his prep school days), Orwell can sensibly offer no other conclusion.

ORWELL, GEORGE
For the ordinary man is passive. Within a narrow circle...he feels himself master of his fate, but against major events he is as helpless as against the elements. So far from endeavouring to influence the future, he simply lies down and lets things happen to him.

OSBORNE, JOHN (1929–) British playwright

Damn you, England
letter in *Tribune*, August 1961

As befits the playwright whose earliest success was entitled *Look Back In Anger* (1956) and whose attitudes and opinions became synonymous with those of the 'Angry Young Men' of the Fifties,

Osborne's expostulation forms part of a letter in which he savaged the land of his birth. Temporarily based in France, he wrote to the left-wing magazine *Tribune* to tell the Establishment 'This is a letter of hate. It is for you my countrymen – I mean those men of my country who have defiled it. The men with manic fingers leading the sightless, feeble, betrayed body of my country to its death.... There is murder in my brain, and I carry a knife in my heart for every one of you. Macmillan, and you, Gaitskell, you particularly.... I only hope (my hate) will keep me going. I think it will. I think it may sustain me in the last few months. Till then, Damn you England. You're rotting now, and quite soon you'll disappear. My hate will outrun you yet if only for a few seconds. I wish it could be eternal'.

OWEN, WILFRED (1893–1918) British poet

What passing-bells for those who die as cattle.
Anthem for Doomed Youth (1917)

Owen, one of the best poets of World War I, was invalided out of the Front in 1917 to the same hospital to which Siegfried Sassoon, another poet, had been sent by the Army. Sassoon encouraged the younger man's work and was responsible for the posthumous publication of *Poems* (1920) upon which his reputation is based. Like Sassoon, although with a greater use of religious symbolism. Owen wrote poems to express his hatred fo the war, intending that they should in some way help warn those yet to suffer its horrors. Awarded the Military Cross, he was killed seven days before the Armistice. In this poem he contrasts the relative tranquillity and dignity of a peacetime burial wth the minimal rites accorded those slaughtered in battle.

OWEN, WILFRED

**The old Lie: Dulce et decorum est
Pro patria mori.**
Dulce et decorum est (1920)

Owen's poem, probably his best known, scourges the sentimental glorification of World War I, in verses that spell out how far from 'sweet and fitting it is to die for one's country' in a gas attack: 'If in some smothering dream you too could pace / Behind the wagon that we flung him in, / And watch the white eyes writhing in his face, / His hanging face, like a devil's sick of sin; / If you could hear, at every jolt, the blood / Come gargling from the froth-corrupted lungs, / Bitter as the cud / Of vile, incurable sores on innocent tongues, / My friend you would not tell with such high

zest / To children ardent for some desperate glory, / The old Lie.
Dulce et decorum est / pro patria mori'.

Oxford Union

That this House will in no circumstances fight for King and Country
motion in a debate, February 1933

In this debate, held by the undergraduate members of the Oxford University Union, it was resolved by 275 votes to 153 that they would not, if called upon, fight for their country. This excited the contemporary press, who assailed it as a sign of the moral degeneracy of the young. To such Establishment figures as Churchill, the debate provided a clear signal to Hitler that England was no longer to be seen as an important nation and established 'the idea of a decadent, degenerate Britain'. Whether Hitler even knew about the debate is in itself debatable and as contemporaries have pointed out, the pusillanimity of the British government was obvious enough already without needing to take note of a few students.

P

PADDICK, HUGH   British comedian

Hello, I'm Julian, and this is my friend Sandy.
catchphrase in *Round the Horne*, BBC radio 1950s

Round the Horne was one of BBC Radio's most popular comedy shows in the 1950s. Starring Kenneth Horne, who had begun his career on the wartime forces show Merry Go Round, it was full of bizarre characters such as Seamus Android, Daphne Whitethigh, Charles and Fiona, and Rambling Sid Rumpo, many of whom were played by Kenneth Williams, as well as broadcasting's campest duo, Julian and Sandy, played by Hugh Paddick and Williams. Julian and Sandy were 'resting' thespians, their dialogues interlarded with theatrical parlyaree, a language descended directly from 17th century Italian commedia del arte performers, in which man was 'omee', woman 'palome' and 'vardo the riah' meant 'look at her hair'.

PAIGE, LEROY 'SATCHELL' (1906–) American baseball player

Don't look back – something might be gaining on you.
maxim, from Six Rules for a Long Life

Paige was one of the stars of the Negro League in the days, prior to World War II, when American baseball was strictly segregated. Playing for the Pittsburgh Crawfords, Paige was one of a team whose exploits equalled and often surpassed those of their white peers. In July 1948 he joined the white Cleveland Indians to become the first black pitcher in baseball history. His oft-quoted maxim comes from a list of six tips for keeping young; the others are: 1. Avoid fried meats which angry up the blood. 2. If your stomach disputes you, lie down and pacify it with cool thoughts. 3. Keep the juices flowing by jangling around gently as you move. 4. Go very lightly on the vices, such as carrying on in society. The social ramble ain't restful. 5. Avoid running at all times.

PANKHURST, EMMELINE (1858–1928) British suffragette

The argument of the broken pane of glass is the most valuable argument in modern politics.
speech in 1912

Born Emmeline Goulden, she married in 1879 the left-wing barrister Richard Pankhurst. Among her four children were her cohorts Christabel and Sylvia, who with their mother began their campaign for women's suffrage in 1903 when Mrs. Pankhurst founded the Women's Social and Political Union, demanding, quite simply, 'Votes for Women'. The Pankhursts campaigned unceasingly, turning the idea of women voters from a joke into what the government saw as a threat to established order. The suffragettes, as her supporters became known, mixed oratory and direct action, what Mrs. Pankhurst called the 'argument of the stone' or, 'of the broken pane of glass' to keep their cause in the headlines, suffering a great deal of vilification and physical abuse for their pains. After 1914, she turned her enthusiasms to the War, and ended her days by standing as a Conservative candidate for Parliament.

PARKER, BONNIE (1911–1934) American criminal

> Some day they will go down together
> And they will bury them side by side.
> To a few it means grief
> To the law a relief
> But it's death to Bonnie and Clyde.

The Story of Suicide Sal (1934)

Parker, with her boyfriend and fellow criminal Clyde Barrow (1909–34), was representative of the small-time villains, thrown up by the Depression years, who terrorised their peers, the dirt-poor 'Okies', with a series of pointless killings and low-yield robberies. Unlike their filmed image, in *Bonnie and Clyde* (1967), they were far from Robin Hoods, merely vicious and generally incompetent, but sufficiently active to make themselves a reputation: Barrow became known as The Texas Rattlesnake while Parker was christened Suicide Sal. For recreation they took photographs and Parker wrote doggerel verses, such as this one. On May 23, 1934 their careers stopped dead. Betrayed to the Texas Rangers by a friend, Barrow was driving in his socks and Parker munching a peanut butter sandwich when a posse pumped 187 bullets into their bodies.

PARKER, DOROTHY   (1893–1967) American poet, writer and wit

Parker began her journalistic career in 1916 on *Vogue*, moving to become drama critic of *Vanity Fair* in 1917. Here she met Robert Benchley and Robert Sherwood and between them there developed the germ of that collection of self-promoting wits and raconteurs known as the Algonquin Round Table. Parker epitomised the 'new woman' of the Twenties, both in her own wisecracking effervescence and in her writing, reflecting the bitter-sweet preoccupations of the era. For a while she was among the most celebrated wits in America, trading on her reputation to take $5000 a week for Hollywood scriptwriting. After the war the critics turned against her and she wrote much less, although her work for the *New Yorker*, which she had helped establish, continued, as did her reviewing, now for *Esquire*. She died in 1967, a solitary figure in a New York residential hotel, after a life that seemed to have gone on too long for one whose best poems dealt so candidly with early death.

PARKER, DOROTHY

If you get through the twilight, you'll live through the night.
Esquire, 1964

Parker's line, mixing fear with hope, comes from one of her rare art reviews, written for *Esquire* about John Koch's paintings of New York. This short piece uses the paintings as the basis for a brief elegy on a passed, golden era of fading afternoons in 'rooms of lovely lights and lovelier shadows and loveliest people', but with typical Parker honesty, she cannot resist admitting 'I really have no room for the sweet, soft feeling... the sort of nostalgia that is only a dreamy longing for some places where you never were'.

And she ends her reflections 'And I never will be there. There is no such hour on the present clock as six-thirty, New York time. Yet, as only New Yorkers know, if you get through the twilight, you'll live through the night'.

PARKER, DOROTHY

One more drink and I'll be under the host.
quoted in *You Might As Well Live* by John Keats (1970)

Parker's wisecracks were her trademark. As Brendan Gill puts it in his introduction to *The Penguin Dorothy Parker* (1973) 'She made wisecracks – often quite admirable wisecracks – as easily as most people say "Is it hot enough for you?" or "Please pass the bread" '. So did many of her fellow Algonquinites, but on the whole it is Parker's which have lasted. In the end, as time has proved, few of 'The Vicious Circle' were truly first-class talents, concentrating their efforts on self-advertisement. Parker has lasted because she deserved to. Among her better lines are these:

A girl's best friend is her mutter.

The two most beautiful words in the English language are 'Cheque Enclosed'.

If all the young ladies who attended the Yale promenande dance were laid end to end, no-one would be the least surprised.

The only 'ism' Hollywood believes in is plagiarism.

Brevity is the soul of lingerie.

(to a friend who had been making much of her pregancy:) 'Dear Mary, we all knew you had it in you.'

PARKER, DOROTHY

If you're going to write, don't pretend to write down. It's going to be the best you can do, and it's the fact that it's the best you can do that kills you.
quoted in *You Might As Well Live* by J. Keats (1978)

Parker's writing experienced the extremes of critical opinion in a relatively brief period. In the Twenties she was one of the most feted of American wits, and her terse poems summed up an era in which their subject, 'the new woman', was endlessly fascinating to the press and its readers. Early fame in New York brought, as it did for many of her peers, subsequent high earnings in Hollywood. Through the Thirties she mixed scriptwriting with left-wing activism but by the time *The Portable Dorothy Parker* appeared in 1944, her reputation was in eclipse. The critics had turned and although she remained the epitome of the Twenties, her last years were bleak; like so many youthful stars, her physical death came far later than that of her celebrity.

PARKER, DOROTHY

> Razors pain you;
> Rivers are damp;
> Acids stain you;
> And drugs cause cramp.
> Guns aren't lawful;
> Nooses give;
> Gas smells awful;
> You might as well live.

Resume (1927)

Parker's attitude to life was that in the end it was tough and that the best way to deal with the pain was probably suicide. When she did die it was of natural causes and she was seventy-three: for all the angst, she had chosen to heed the resigned advice of her own poem. The poem reflects a similar verse by Parker's friend (and perhaps one-time lover) the writer Ring Lardner, who wrote these lines as the refrain for an unpublished song lyric: 'But cynaide it gripes inside; / Bichloride blights the liver; / And I am told, one catches cold / When one jumps in the river. / To cut my throat would stain my coat / And make my valet furious. / Death beckons me, but it must be / A death that ain't injurious'.

PARKER, DOROTHY

Excuse my dust
self-proposed epitaph

Parker was asked, as were a number of Hollywood stars, for her own suggestion for an epitaph. She came up with this one, but, if one can trust the lexicographers, the phrase was not an original but a common catchphrase in the American west since the early Twenties. Nonetheless, while the catchphrase tends to mean 'I'm way ahead of you and you're not very bright', Parker's self-deprecation is evident in her plea for understanding, even in death.

PARKER, DOROTHY

> Drink and dance and laugh and lie
> Love, the reeling midnight through
> For tomorrow we shall die!
> (But, alas, we never do.)

The Flaw in Paganism (1931)

PARKER, DOROTHY

> Where's the man could ease a heart
> Like a satin gown.

The Satin Dress (1927)

PARKER, DOROTHY

Tonstant Weader Fwowed Up.

review on the New Yorker, 20 October 1928

Parker started writing a book review column 'Constant Reader' in Harold Ross' still fledging *New Yorker* magazine (founded 1925) in 1927. Her column epitomised the style that went down so well at the regular Algonquin lunches – short on praise, long, and incisively brutal when it comes to denunciation. Reviewing A.A. Milne's best-selling children's book The House at Pooh Corner, Parker cited a particularly sickly specimen of Milne's prose, ending her piece with a quote: ' "Pom," said Pooh. "I put that in to make it more hummy." ' And is it that word "hummy", my darlings, that marks the first place in The House at Pooh Corner where Tonstant Weader Fwowed up.'

PARKER, TOM (1909–) (Andreas Cornelius van Kuijk) American rock manager

When I first knew Elvis he had a million dollars worth of talent. Now he has a million dollars.

quoted in *Elvis and Gladys* by Elaine Dundy (1985)

Looking at Parker's past it is hard to disentangle fact from carefully contrived fiction, but it appears that he was born in Holland, rather than in West Virginia as he claims, and emigrated to America in 1929. Here he worked in carnivals, gradually improving his status until he was able to persuade two of America's leading Country and Western singers, Eddy Arnold and Hank Snow, to accept him as their manager. In 1955 he began managing Elvis Presley. Parker swallowed up Presley with the skill and charisma of the practised carny, and never abandoned his property until Presley died, twenty-two years almost to the day after signing his first contract with 'Colonel' Tom. Parker undoubtedly helped make Presley into one of the world's best-selling artists but as the subtext of his boast makes clear, when Elvis had his million dollars he no longer had the full glory of his talent.

PARKINSON, C. NORTHCOTE (1909–) British economist

It is a commonplace observation that work expands so as to fill the time available for its completion.
establishing 'Parkinson's Law' in the Economist, November 19 1955

Parkinson established the law for which he became instantly known in a piece that dealt with the way in which most bureaucratic structures take on the form of a pyramid. His idea appealed immensely at time when the 'managerial' state was developing fast and multinational companies were proliferating. The Law was used as the first line of a book *Parkinson's Law or the Pursuit of Progress* (1957), where it was given two corollaries 'A perfection of planned layout is achieved only by institutions on the verge of collapse' and 'Subordinates multiply at a fixed rate regardless of the amount of work produced.' The book also offered Parkinson's Second Law: 'The Law of Triviality: time spent on any item in the agenda will be in inverse proportion to the sum involved'.

PATCHEN, KENNETH (1911–72) American poet

God must have loved the People in Power, for he made them so very like their own image of him.
quoted in the *Guardian*, February 1 1972

Patchen was born in Ohio and has lived in New York and California. His poetry, marked by religious symbols and intricate figures which recall the Metaphysical poets of the 17th century, is also free in structure and association. As well as poetry his prose includes *The Journal of Albion Moonlight* (1941) and *Memoirs of a Shy Pornographer* (1948). This line echoes that of President Abraham Lincoln who observed 'The Lord prefers common-looking people; that is the reason he makes so many of them'.

PAUL, LESLIE (1905–) British social philosopher

Angry young man/men
title of autobiography, 1951

The Angry Young Men, notably John Osborne, Kingsley Amis, John Wain and Colin Wilson (most of whom have drifted to the political right), were the authorised rebels of the Fifties. The 'Angries' scorned conventional values, seeking to overturn the class-ridden British establishment. Given that the critics tended to praise their work, that same Establishment dealt with them in its traditional manner: extending its approval and licensing them until such time as they settled down, inevitably, as somewhat rebarbative jesters. The phrase itself, although allied to Osborne's play *Look Back In Anger* (1956), was coined by Leslie Paul as the title of his autobiography some five years before Osborne's play appeared. Paul had exchanged his devotion to Russia for what Kenneth Tynan in *Curtains* (1961) called a 'vague Christian humanism'. This was hardly Wilson's or Wain's belief, but the phrase suited the times and it remains convenient shorthand.

PAVESE, CESARE (1908–1950) Italian poet and novelist

The art of living is the art of knowing how to believe lies.
The Burning Brand (1961)

Pavese was a poet and novelist who established himself alongside Alberto Moravia as Italy's major proponent of realistic writing. As his diaries, published as Il mestiere di vivere (1961, *This Business of Living*), make clear, he found it increasingly hard to reconcile himself to what he saw as the duplicities and disappointments of the post-World War II world, and he killed himself in 1950. His final diary entry concluded 'The thing most feared in secret always happens; all it needs is a little courage. The more pain grows clearer and definite, the more the instinct for life reasserts itself and the thought of suicide recedes. It seemed easy when I thought of it. Weak women have done it. It needs humility, not pride. I am sickened by all this. No words. Action. I shall write no more'.

PAVESE, CESARE

Many men on the point of an edifying death would be furious if they were suddenly restored to health.
quoted in *The Faber Book of Aphorisms* ed. Auden & Kronenberger (1964)

PAVESE, CESARE

Mistakes are always initial.
quoted in *The Faber Book of Aphorisms* ed. Auden & Kronenberger (1964)

PAVESE, CESARE

We hate the thing we fear, the thing we know may be true and may have a certain affinity with ourselves, for each man hates himself.
This Business of Living: Diaries 1935–50 (1961)

PAVESE, CESARE

If only we could treat ourselves as we treat other men, looking at their withdrawn faces and crediting them with some mysterious, irresistible power. Instead, we know all our faults, our misgivings, and are reduced to hoping for some unconscious force to surge up from our innermost being and act with a subtlety all its own.
This Business of Living: Diaries 1935–50 (1961)

PEARCE, DONN American writer and seaman

Sometimes nothing is a real cool hand.
Cool Hand Luke (1965)

Cool Hand Luke, made into a successful film starring Paul Newman in 1967, is the story of Lloyd Jackson, otherwise known as Luke, the ex-war hero who finds peacetime life too tame and ends up on a Florida chain-gang. In jail Luke demonstrates his seemingly effortless superiority to his surroundings. As required in such stories of macho resilience, Luke has to prove himself to his companions; this he does in a various ways, notably by eating a vast quantity of hard-boiled eggs at one sitting, by working harder than everyone else on the gang and by playing a devastating game of poker. His philosophising follows one game, in which he bluffs out the opposition with a hand that contains absolutely nothing. The authorities systematically set out to break him and finally shoot him dead but his legend, which is recounted as the novel's plot, lives on.

PEARSON, HESKETH (1887–1964) British biographer

There is no stronger craving in the world than that of the rich for titles, except that of the titled for riches.
The Marrying Americans (1961)

Pearson established himself as one of Britain's most widely read popular biographers with a number of studies beginning in 1921 with *Modern Men and Mummers*, a collection of portraits of the leading actors and theatrical personalities of the time. His biographies were always lively and interesting, although in the light of more modern techniques they seem to lack the element of real inquisitiveness into their subject, often preferring celebration to analysis. *The Marrying Americans*, one of his later works, looked at the propensity of American heiresses to find their husbands among the English aristocracy, who in turn were perfectly happy to restore their fortunes with an infusion from the nouveaux riches.

PEARSON, LESTER (1897–1972) Canadian prime minister

Diplomacy is letting someone else have your way.
quoted in the Observer, March 18, 1965

Pearson was president of the United Nations General Assembly from 1952-53 and in 1957 was awarded the Nobel Peace Prize for his involvement in the unravelling of the Suez Crisis of the previous year, in which, as his remark shows, he proved himself a subtle but persuasive negotiator. He became leader of the Canadian opposition in 1958 and Prime Minister in 1963, retaining power with a minority government in 1965. He resigned in 1968.

PEGLER, WESTBROOK (1894–1969) American journalist

He will go from resort to resort, getting more tanned and more tired.
after Edward VIII's Abdication, 1936

Pegler, who wrote this poignantly prophetic line on the probable future of the Duke of Windsor, formerly King Edward VIII, was one of America's leading journalists of the Thirties. If not its originator, he was certainly most responsible for popularising the derisive concept of the 'bleeding-heart liberal' and among his better known descriptions were those of gossip columnists as 'gents-room journalists', intellectuals as 'double domes' and FBI director J. Edgar Hoover as 'a Stork Club detective'. Pegler gained many enemies, notably President Truman who termed him a 'guttersnipe'.

PERELMAN, S.J. (1904–1979) American humourist
Perelman 'the supreme lunatic humourist in the language' was celebrated as America's foremost humourist who combined wondrous fantasy, malicious humour and biting satire with a phenomenal vocabulary and a style that has influenced such successors as Woody Allen. The success of his first novel, *Dawn Ginsbergh's Revenge* (1929) brought him an offer to write scripts for the Marx Brothers. He wrote *Monkey Business* (1931) and *Horse Feathers*

(1932). Perelman was among the most popular of the distinguished stable of New Yorker writers, and altogether published twenty books, including the records of many adventurous travels. His sixty-year career produced many quotable lines, among which are:

For years I have let dentists ride roughshod over my teeth; I have been sawed, hacked, chopped, whittled, bewitched, bewildered, tattooed and signed on again; but this is cuspid's last stand. *Crazy Like a Fox*

No country home is complete without a surly figure seated in the kitchen like Rodin's thinker, wishing she was back in a hot little room under the Third Avenue Elevated.
Acres and Pains

Love is not the dying moan of a distant violin – it's the triumphant twang of a bedspring.

PÉTAIN, HENRI   (1856–1951) French soldier

They shall not pass.
used at Verdun on February 26, 1916

In 1914 Pétain was a fifty-eight-year-old Colonel, two years from retirement. Four years later he was a Marshal of France, celebrated for his inspiration of the defence of Verdun, during which he gave the French troops their famous injunction 'Ils ne passeront pas' (They shall not pass). In 1940 he negotiated the Armistice with Germany and was appointed head of the collaborationist Vichy Government by the triumphant Nazis. At first Pétain was seen by the occupied French as doing his best, but by 1942 he seemed excessively pro-German and in 1945 he was tried and convicted as a traitor. His comment in 1946 that 'to write one's memoirs is to speak ill of everybody except oneself' was fuelled by more than average bitterness. He may not have even been responsible for his most famous phrase, which has been traced back to the Order of the Day for June 23, 1916 by General Robert de Nivelle (1856–1924), who stated 'Vous ne les laissez pas passer' (You will not let them pass).

PETER, LAURENCE J.   (1919–) Canadian academic

In a hierarchy every employee tends to rise to his level of incompetence...in time every post tends to be occupied by an employee who is incompetent to carry out its duties.... Work is accomplished by those employees who have not yet reached their level of incompetence.
The Peter Principle (1969)

Peter taught education at the University of Southern California before retiring in 1970 to concentrate on lecturing and writing on the best ways of avoiding incompetence and improving life. He is best known for his 'law' – The Peter Principle – which defines the way in which organisations first assess a person as competent to perform one job and use this as a basis for pushing them onto the next work level, at which point they have exhausted that competence. The law was enshrined in Peter's book, written with Raymond Hull: *The Peter Principle, or Why Things Go Wrong*. Dr. Peter has also noted that 'Originality is the fine art of remembering what you hear but forgetting where you heard it.'

PHILBY, ST JOHN   (–1960) British explorer and Arabist

God, I'm bored.
last words, 1960

Harry St. John Philby, the father of Britain's most successful traitor, the 'Third Man' Kim Philby, was a true eccentric, who combined a T.E. Lawrence-like fascination with the East with the manners and tastes of a traditional English gentleman. A dedicated Arabist, he converted to Islam, married a Saudi slave-girl, lived in Mecca and ate camel-meat. Simultaneously he maintained his membership of the Atheneum, wrote for and read *The Times* and attempted never to miss a Test Match. He stood twice for Parliament without success and announced his pro-Hitler sympathies so loudly that in 1940 he was interned under Regulation 18b. He died in Saudi Arabia, offering these last words.

PHILBY, HAROLD 'KIM'   (1912–1988) British Communist spy

To betray, you must first belong.
in Eleanor Philby, *Kim Philby: The Spy I Loved* (1968)

During a career that lasted thirty years from his recruitment while still at Cambridge in 1933, Philby proved himself to be the most successful of those 'moles' whom the Russians infiltrated into the upper echelons of the British intelligence establishment. Of the four men to have been cited as Russian agents – Guy Burgess and Donald Maclean, who defected in 1951, Anthony Blunt who was unmasked in 1964 and himself – Philby was by far the most useful to his Soviet masters. Appointed to establish Britain's counter-espionage system in 1944, he was, in effect, ordered to catch himself. When Burgess and Maclean deflected in 1951 suspicion did fall on Philby but he managed to bluff his way out, although his role within intelligence was severely curtailed. Still mingling with the secret world, he worked as a journalist until January 1963 when he decided to leave for Moscow, where he still lives.

PHILIP, DUKE OF EDINBURGH (1921–) British royal consort

Just at this moment we are suffering a national defeat comparable to any lost military campaign, and what is more it is self-inflicted...I think it is about time we pulled our finger out.
speech on October 17, 1961

Prince Philip, long established as the most outspoken of the Royal Family, made this, his most famous suggestion, in a speech to an assembly of businessmen in 1961. Given that Harold Macmillan had promised quite the opposite of defeat only four years before, Philip's outburst excited much comment. So, naturally, did his colloquialism, reminscent of the lower rather than of the quarter-deck.

PICASSO, PABLO (1881–1973) Spanish artist

You invent something, and then someone else comes along and does it pretty.

Picasso stands as the most inventive of 20th century artists, whose massive output, not to mention his own personality, profoundly influenced every aspect of modern art. Picasso originated many styles, a number of which, as he puts it, were later done 'pretty' by his imitators, but it was his belief that an artist has no business other than to be creating masterpieces, fuelled by his own charismatic appeal to public attention that put him in a league of his own. Picasso is best known to the lay public for the visual distortions that typify the work that followed 'The Three Dancers' of 1925, combining expressionism with surrealism to create a unique style which, for the great mass of non-experts equates with 'modern art'.

PICASSO, PABLO

Art is the lie that makes us realize the truth.
quoted in 1958

PICKLES, WILFRED (1904–1978) British entertainer

What's on the table, Mabel?
catchphrase in *Have A Go*, BBC radio, 1950s

As compere of *Have A Go*, the show that 'brought the people to the people', Pickles, master of the folksy banality, epitome to a twenty million strong audience of the 'common man', was one of British radio's first real superstars. The Pickles magic was based on a set of beliefs much beloved by those to whom it gave an otherwise unavailable moment of celebrity – 'ordinary folk' were the salt of the earth, everyone had a story to tell, old age was an achievement and suffering was good for you. Add to that the opportunity of winning a small cash prize and the BBC found it had an enormous hit. Pickles, who had been the Corporation's first newsreader with a Northern accent, dominated the show. With his wife Mabel 'at the table', Violet Carson on the piano, and producer Barney Colehan (later replaced by Mabel) to 'give him the money, Barney', Pickles bestrode popular broadcasting, the plain man's Colossus.

PINTER, HAROLD   (1930–) British playwright

The more acute an experience the less articulate its expression.
programme note to a double bill of *The Room* and *The Dumb Waiter*

Pinter's first writing was poetry, his first contact with the stage as a repertory company actor and his first play, *The Room* (1957) was written almost by accident on the invitation of a friend in Bristol. His first London play, *The Birthday Party* (1958) ran only five nights, but critic Harold Hobson praised it vigorously and Pinter's reputation grew, fuelled by many subsequent successes. His work, with its brooding menace, its obsessiveness and its strange, unstable characters, has inspired the eponym 'Pinteresque', especially referring to his dialogue, which reflects his dictum in its stuttering inarticulacy and faithful reproduction of the hesitant difficulties of evoking deep experience through colloquial speech.

PITKIN, WILLIAM B.   (1878–1953) American academic

Life begins at forty
book title, 1932

In the tradition of America's self-help evangelists, Pitkin, otherwise the professor of journalism at Columbia University, created a best-seller and coined a phrase with his study of 'life reorientation': *Life Begins At Forty*. The book was based on a series of lectures he had given on the best way of dealing with what would now be called a 'mid-life crisis'. It was cosily uplifting, with such inspirational passages as this: 'Every day brings forth some new thing that adds to the joy of life after forty. Work becomes easy and brief. Play grows richer and longer. Leisure lengthens. Life's afternoon is brighter, warmer, fuller of song; and long before shadows stretch, every fruit grows ripe....Life begins at forty.'

PLATH, SYLVIA (1932–63) American poet

> Dying
> **Is an art, like everything else.**
> **I do it exceptionally well.**

Lady Lazarus (1965)

Plath was educated in America and England and married the English poet Ted Hughes (1930–) in 1956. Her first book of poetry, *The Colossus*, appeared in 1960 and, writing as 'Victoria Lucas', she published her only novel, *The Bell Jar* in January 1963. A month later Plath committed suicide. Her most successful poems appeared in *Ariel* (1965). Among them is *Lady Lazarus*, which deals, as the excerpt infers, with two previous attempts at suicide, and reveals the extent to which Plath's art taxed her emotions to the point of hysteria.

PLATH, SYLVIA

> **Every woman adores a Fascist**
> **The boot in the face, the brute**
> **Brute heart of a brute like you.**

Daddy (1965)

Plath's father was a German professor and entomologist, an emigrant to America who had died in 1940 when she was only eight. This poem, from the posthumous collection *Ariel* (1965), deals with the early loss of her parent in a work that reveals painfully the extent of Plath's inner torments. As one who was called by critics a 'confessional poet', Plath chose to stretch her emotions up to, and finally beyond their limits, in poetry that spared neither reader nor writer in its delvings into an individual psyche.

POLLOCK, CHANNING (1880–1946) American dramatist

A critic is a legless man who teaches running.

Pollock's first play apeared in 1900 and was followed by a long series of farces, melodramas and musical comedy libretto before Pollock turned to serious drama with *The Fool* (1922), the story of a modern churchman who attempts to emulate the life of Christ. Much of Pollock's work was allegorical, notably *Mr. Moneypenny* (1928) in which a wage slave chooses to sell his soul to a modern devil, Mr. Moneypenny, before returning, a wiser man, to his original honest poverty. But the allegories bored the critics and even if Pollock affected to despise their opinions, as quoted here, their condemnation was sufficient to force him to quit the stage.

POPPER, KARL (1902–) British philosopher

We may become the makers of our fate when we have ceased to pose as its prophets.
quoted in the *Observer*, December 28 1975

Popper's great contribution to modern philosophy is his theory, expounded in *The Logic of Scientific Discovery* (1934), that scientific knowledge is derived from a mechanical procedure of scientific generalisation, itself based on absolute certainties that we sense or experience. This knowledge survives only insofar as it can overturn every attempt to prove it false. What distinguishes scientific knowledge from such abstract non-science as metaphysics is that it it deals with concepts sufficiently concrete to be proved false or upheld as truths. He sees Marxism and psychoanalysis, neither of which can be proved in this way, as the great intellectual superstitions of our time.

PORTER, COLE (1891–1964) American lyricist

All the inspiration I ever needed was a phonecall from a producer.
quoted in 1955

Porter started writing song lyrics as a boy, improving his art at the same time as studying both law and music at Harvard. His first attempt to conquer Broadway failed badly and he went to live in Paris where he briefly joined the Foreign Legion, met and married his wife and settled to a life of sophisticated party-giving and going. An American Noel Coward, with the same ability to turn chic into commercial stage success, he became one of the American theatre's most important figures. A solo writer in a era of partnerships, he created a legion of song standards. *Kiss Me Kate* (1948), based on Shakespeare's *Taming of the Shrew*, is still considered the 'perfect musical'.

POTTER, BEATRIX (1866–1943) British children's writer

Madam, I beg you not to trouble yourself with a bag; I will provide oats. But before you commence your tedious sitting, I intend to give you a treat. Let us have a dinner-party all to ourselves! May I ask you to bring up some herbs from the farm-garden to make a savoury omelette? Sage and thyme, mint and

two onions, and some parsley. I will provide lard for the stuff -
lard for the omelette,'
The Tale of Jemima Puddle-Duck (1908)

Beatrix Potter grew up, a privileged but lonely child, privately
educated in a large Kensington house where her wealthy parents
indulged their own adult preoccupations. The high points of her
year were the regular country holidays and she taught herself to
draw and paint the natural world she observed around her. Her
work in classifying fungi, complete with her detailed drawings,
gained serious respect but an illustrated letter sent in 1893 to the
son of her former governess changed her life. The letter developed into the first of her children's stories: *The Tale of Peter
Rabbit*, which she had privately published in 1901. In 1902 she
published *The Tailor of Gloucester*, also privately, but thenceforth her work went through Frederick Warne, which firm
published twenty-four titles before, in 1913, she married a
Lakeland solicitor, William Heelis, and abandoned writing for
her farm in the Lake District. Her books continue to delight
children and their parents; a few favourite passages follow:

POTTER, BEATRIX

I am undone and worn to a threadpaper for I have **NO MORE
TWIST.**
The Tailor of Gloucester (1903)

POTTER, BEATRIX

Peter was ill during the evening, in consequence of overeating
himself. His mother put him to bed and gave him a dose of
camomile tea, but Flopsy, Mopsy and Cottontail had bread and
milk and blackberries for supper.

First he ate some lettuce and some broad beans, then some
radishes, and then, feeling rather sick, he went to look for some
parsley.
The Tale of Peter Rabbit (1902)

POTTER, BEATRIX

It is said that the effect of eating too much lettuce is 'soporific'.
The Tale of the Flopsy Bunnies (1909)

POTTER, STEPHEN (1900–69) British writer, editor and radio producer

Winemanship... remember your mainstay is hypnotic suggestion. Suggest that some rubbishy sherry... is your special pride, and has a tremendously individual taste. Insist on getting it yourself 'from the cellar'. Take about four minutes uncorking it. Say 'I think decanting destroys it', if you have forgotten, or are too bored, to decant it. Keep staring at the bottle before you pour it. When you have drawn the cork, look particularly hard at the cork, and, of course, smell it.
One-Upmanship (1952)

One-Upmanship was the third of Potter's four '-manship' books, designed to offer a witty, satirical guide to making one's way, skating resolutely on the thinnest of social and ethical ice, through the problems and challenges of life. Potter was particularly good at deflating the precious and the pretentious, never more so than in his analysis of 'Winemanship', otherwise known as the snobbery of the self-proclaimed connoisseur.

POTTER, STEPHEN

The Theory and Practise of Gamesmanship, or the Art of Winning Games without Actually Cheating.
book title, 1947

Potter's theory of gamesmanship gave a new word to the language and codified with blissfully satirical humour the charms of what the unamused would term 'bad sportsmanship'. Potter's four volumes – *Gamesmanship, Lifemanship, One-upmanship* and *Supermanship* – were based, according to his introductory note in the first one, on a game of tennis he played with the editor and publisher Francis Meynell in 1933, in which, faced by infinitely superior opponents, Potter suggested that they 'employ gamesmanship'. What is gamesmanship, Potter asks rhetorically, and goes on to use the definition that stands as the work's subtitle. As he points out 'There have been five hundred books written on the subject of games. Five hundred books on play and the tactics of play. Not one on the art of winning.'

POUND, EZRA (1885–1972) American poet

Real education must ultimately be limited to men who insist on knowing; the rest is mere sheep-herding.
The ABC of Reading

POUND, EZRA

Pound was the great theoretician and publicist for Modernism, championing the work of Joyce, Eliot and others. Seeking to escape the sentimentality of Romanticism he founded his own movement, Imagism, advocating free rhythms and concreteness of image. His interest in Imagism waned as he experienced a wider variety of writing, including Latin and Chinese texts, as well as making his own translations from Provencal and early Italian. This cross-cultural reading resulted in his major works: *The Cantos* (the first of which appeared in 1917, the last, posthumously in 1970), *Hugh Selwyn Mauberley* (1920) and the translation *Homage to Sextus Propertius*. Subordinating every consideration to aesthetics, Pound found himself seduced by Mussolini's fascism. After his broadcasts on Italian radio during World War II he was arrested and taken to Washington where, instead of facing a trial for treason, he was placed in a mental hospital. Here he continued to work while the literary world debated the line between artistic style and content in his work.

POUND, EZRA

Literature is news that stays news.
The ABC of Reading

POWELL, ANTHONY   (1905–) British novelist
Powell's first novels dealt with the same milieux as did those of Waugh and Huxley, but his light, satirical tone lacked the harder edge of his two contemporaries and he abandoned such books for his major work, the twelve volumes of *A Dance to the Music of Time* (the title of a Poussin painting), termed by its author a 'consideration of the way in which the upper and middle classes live in England', which relies for its effect on his acute portrayal of 'the interrelations of individuals'. The books are obviously drawn in some part from his own life, which has blended both the social and literary establishments, but the narrator Nicholas Jenkins is not Powell and for all the parallels, the odd proof of which can be found in his four-volume memoirs *To Keep The Ball Rolling* (1976–82), he has always been at pains to warn readers off making simple connections.

POWELL, ANTHONY

All men are brothers, but, thank God, they aren't all brothers -in-law.
At Lady Molly's (1957)

'Lady Molly' is Molly Jeavons, the widow of a Lord and now living in straitened circumstances with her husband Ted, a former 'adventurer' who has been tamed, but for the odd drunken escapade, by his wife. She is also the aunt of Isobel Tolland, who the narrator meets 'at Lady Molly's' and eventually marries at the start of the following book, *Casanova's Chinese Restaurant.* This line is spoken by Jenkins' erstwhile friend and Eton contemporary, Peter Templer, now a stockbroker, whom he encounters on a visit to a nightclub, and who is discussing with him the current marital status of his younger sister Jean and her conspicuously unfaithful husband Bob Duport.

POWELL, ANTHONY

Parents – especially step-parents – are sometimes a bit of a disappointment to their children. They don't fulfil the promise of their earlier years.
A Buyer's Market (1952)

A Buyer's Market is the second of Powell's series, concentrating on Nicholas Jenkins' emergence from Eton and Oxford into the larger world of London society and his first job. The book sets him in a constant whirl of socialising and as the critic James Tucker has pointed out 'when Nicholas is not at a party he is at a dance'. After a lengthy first chapter in which Nicholas attends a smart ball, the second one takes him to a more raffish assembly, 'a low party' in the house of Mrs. Andriadis, purportedly a former mistress of King Edward VII. The speaker is Charles Stringham, an old Etonian friend whose decline from public school glory to wretched, alcohol ridden death, runs through the first half of the series. He is referring to the absence from the party, despite promises to the contrary, of his mother's second husband, 'Buster' Foxe.

POWELL, ANTHONY

People think that because a novel's invented, it isn't true. Exactly the reverse is the case. Biography and memoirs can never be wholly true, since they cannot include every conceivable circumstance of what happened. The novel can do that.
Hearing Secret Harmonies (1975)

Although Powell claims steadfastly that his novels cannot be traced simply to his own experiences, there seems little doubt that he is expounding, through the opinions of Francis Xavier 'X' Trapnel (a figure generally considered to have been modelled on the writer and man-about-Fitzrovia Julian McLaren-Ross, 1912–

64), his own view of the way life can be transmuted into art. Only the novel, continues Trapnel, 'can imply certain truths impossible to state by exact definition'. This is where pure biography fails, since it is forced to attempt that exact definition.

POWELL, ANTHONY

Growing old is like being increasingly penalised for a crime you haven't committed.
Temporary Kings (1973)

Temporary Kings is the penultimate novel in *A Dance to the Music of Time*. As with its successor, 'growing old' is a major concern. Those characters destined to succeed have done so, although their 'kingship' is indeed temporary, restricted by time's inexorable passage. Visiting Venice for a literary conference, Jenkins watches a decrepit old man singing below his hotel window and thinks of the self-described 'professional cad' R.H.J. 'Dicky' Umfraville, and recalls his musings on age, of which this maxim is the central tenet.

POWELL, ANTHONY

Self-love seems so often unrequited.
The Acceptance World (1955)

Powell's comment on the way in which even egocentrics find some depths within themselves that reject their unswerving devotion to their own personalities, comes in the third novel of the series, in which a political element enters the lives of many of his characters. Among the important figures who appear is J.G. Quiggin, the talented working-class intellectual who, at this stage of the books, is a Marxist. The book as whole satirises the salon Left, especially in the person of the ageing grand old literary man St. John Clarke, who takes to Marxism in the same way as he has involved himself in a variety of earlier smart fads.

POWELL, ANTHONY

Erridge, a rebel whose life had been exasperatingly lacking in persecution, had enjoyed independence of parental control, plenty of money, assured social position, early in life. Since leaving school he had been deprived all the typical grudges within the grasp of most young men. Some of these grudges, it was true, he had later developed with fair success by artificial means.
The Kindly Ones (1962)

The Kindly Ones (a translation of the Greek 'Eumenides', a euphemism for the Furies) is the first the three novels that deal with Nicholas Jenkins' experiences in World War II. Erridge, the privileged rebel, is Isobel Jenkins' elder brother in whose house, Thrubworth, troops have been stationed at the outbreak of the war. For all his much-voiced espousal of the masses and their problems, Erridge, never happier than when left alone to his various scholarly devices, is less than pleased with such an invasion. Paradoxically, however, the presence of the troops acts as a tonic to Erridge's 'inner well-being' since the appalling inconvenience of their presence finally gives him a real source of annoyance against which to pit his otherwise underexploited antagonisms.

POWELL, ELLIS British actress

I'm worried about Jim.
in *Mrs Dale's Diary*, BBC radio 1950s

Mrs Dale's Diary was Britain's most popular daytime radio soap opera in the Fifties. Rivalled only by the bucolic *Archers*, which was aired in the early evening, the fantasy world of this middle-class doctor's wife, her husband Jim, about whom, despite his medical qualifications, she was endlessly concerned, her children Bob and Jenny, her mother Mrs. Freeman (and her cat Captain), her comic charlady Mrs. Maggs and the rest of the cast fascinated the country's listeners. Only when, in the democratic Sixties, Mrs. Dale was sent down-market under what the BBC presumably saw as the pacey new title of *The Dales*, did she falter and start her long decline.

POWELL, ENOCH (1912–) British politician

As I look ahead, I am filled with foreboding. Like the Roman, I seem to see 'the River Tiber foaming with much blood'.
speech on April 20, 1968

In 1968 Powell was the Conservative shadow spokesman on defence. Speaking in Birmingham, he dealt with the subject of immigration, a topic that had lain largely dormant since the Notting Dale riots of the late 1950s. Claiming to quote the views of a white constituent, Powell cited statistics based on the black birthrate to promise his audience that 'in this country in fifteen or twenty years the black man will have the whip hand over the white man'. In a speech of startling irresponsibility he went on to promise not only the blood-drenched Tiber (a phrase that he later regretted translating from the Latin, citing it as a classical prophecy rather than a promise of carnage) but a spate of race riots that would rival those consuming American cities that year. Tory leader Edward Heath sacked Powell that same day, but many white voters sympathised with his views and there was revealed a depth of racist xenophobia that continues to bedevil British society.

POWELL, ENOCH

History is littered with wars which everybody knew would never happen.
in 1967

POWELL, SANDY (1900–) British comedian

Can you hear me, mother?
catchphrase

Powell, born in Rotherham and one of many comedians who made their career out of entertaining a strictly Northern audience, created the first ever radio catchphrase. The line was first broadcast in 1932, as part of his radio show 'Sandy at the North Pole'. Powell was supposedly broadcasting from the Pole to his mother and thus forced to make sure that his supposed mother could hear him. According to Powell, when he reached the phrase, which was only scheduled for a single appearance, he dropped his script. The show was live and as he was scrabbling for the scattered pages, he covered his blunder by repeating the line several times. Performing a week later at the Hippodrome Theatre in Coventry, he was asked by the manager to do 'that line'. Bemused, Powell asked for an explanation and was told that his radio fluff had turned into a hugely popular catchphrase. From then on he was never able to abandon it.

POWELL JR., ADAM CLAYTON (1908–1972) American politician

Beware of Greeks bearing gifts, coloured men looking for loans, and whites who understand the Negro.
maxim

Powell succeeded his father as a pastor in New York's black ghetto and built on a large fund of goodwill to establish himself as one of Harlem's most influential religious and political leaders. In 1944 he was elected to the US House of Representatives where he took his seat as an active and visible leader in the fight for black civil rights. Powell never bothered to restrain his flamboyant lifestyle, which appealed to his constituents but alienated many whites. In 1966 his opponents managed to have him barred from his seat in Congress when he was accused of misusing public funds. He returned from 1968 to 1970 but after a defeat in the Democratic primary (which selects the party's candidate for the election) he resigned his ministry and went to live in the Bahamas.

PRIESTLEY, J.B. (1894–) British writer

Marriage is like paying an endless visit in your worst clothes.
quoted in *Frank Muir Goes Into*, by F. Muir (1979)

Like his predecessor G.K. Chesterton, Priestley's writing covers a wide range of interests, both creating entertainment and criticising the quality of life. His most successful novels include *The Good Companions* (1929) and *Angel Pavement* (1930). He also wrote the perennially successful whodunnit *An Inspector Calls* (1947) an analysis of Depression-era Britain, *English Journey* (1934), and many other titles, often dealing with Britain and its people. He became a national figure with his broadcasts during the London Blitz. After the war his continuing concern with the human condition led him to his involvement with the founding of the Campaign for Nuclear Disarmament.

PRISONER, THE

I am not a number – I am a free man!
script by George Markstein & David Tomblin (1967)

The Prisoner, starring Patrick McGoohan (1928–), was one of the classic pieces of off-the-wall creativity to emerge through television in the Sixties. Released in 1967, it featured McGoohan as a man mysteriously transported to a strange isolated community where everyone has their own number (his is Six) and appears to have been brainwashed into a state of happy disinterest. The plot featured McGoohan's weekly efforts to escape his involuntary incarceration, endlessly foiled until the final episode. The series achieved cult status, as much from its sets, which mixed the excesses of pop art decor with the real-life Welsh village of Portmeiron, itself a pastiche of the pink and white Italian towns near Naples, created by the designer Clough Williams-Ellis.

PRITCHETT, V.S. (1900–) British critic

The detective novel is the art-for-art's-sake of yawning Philistinism
Books In General (1953)

PRITCHETT, V.S.

Pritchett is generally accepted as the greatest living British critic. Starting his journalistic career in 1920, he has worked in France and America as well as in England. Pritchett's criticism has been collected in a variety of volumes, including *Books in General*, taken from his *New Statesman* columns published under that headline, and *In My Good Books* (1942). He has also written a number of novels and an autobiography.

PRITCHETT, V.S.

The principle of procrastinated rape is said to be the ruling one in all the great bestsellers.
The Living Novel and Later Appreciations (1964)

PRODUCERS, THE

Leo, he who hesitates is poor.
screenplay by Mel Brooks (1968)

Max Bialystock (Zero Mostel), failed Broadway producer, is overseeing his tax accountant, Leo Bloom (Gene Wilder). Bloom is appalled by the state of Max's books, but the Macchiavellian Bialystock soon convinces him of the joys of a little gentle fraud, or as he calls it 'creative accounting'. As he works Bloom notices that the financing of a Broadway play is so arranged that if it flops, no-one gets their money back. Thus, he hypothesises, one could raise a fortune, ensure the play flopped and walk off with the loot. Max seizes on this idea while the hopelessly twitchy Bloom reminds him that such a scheme would be criminal. Max takes no arguments and half bullies and half sweet-talks Bloom into helping him, conquering his last faltering excuses with a cajoling 'Leo, he who hesitates is poor', and pleads with him 'Bloom, Bloom, I'm drowning. Other men have sailed through life. Bialystock has struck a reef. Bloom, I'm going under. I'm being sunk by a society that demands success when all I can offer is failure.'

PRODUCERS, THE

That's it baby, if you've got it, flaunt it!
screenplay by Mel Brooks (1968)

One of the great cult films of its era, *The Producers* gave Mel Brooks his first big success since the end of Sid Caesar's *Your Show of Shows*. It is the story of an attempt to produce the greatest Broadway flop of all time: *Springtime for Hitler*. Zero Mostel, as the failing producer Max Bialystok, and Gene Wilder, as his neurotic specialist in 'creative accountancy' plan to sell 25,000% interest in the play, assuming that it will inevitably flop and that the cash thus gained will never need to be repaid. In the event all goes wrong and the pair are jailed. This exhortation comes early in the film. Mostel gazes from his fly-specked window to the street below, where a fur-coated success story is ushering his pneumatic girlfriend out of his white Rolls Royce. The line draws on advertising copywriter George Lois' slogan for Braniff Airways.

PROUST, MARCEL   (1871–1922) French novelist
Proust suffered from asthma from the age of nine, a disease which forced him into becoming a solitary writer. The publication of a volume of his verse in 1896, with a preface by Anatole France, brought him some celebrity and he found himself accepted, despite his Jewishness and his homosexuality, in the fashionable world. After several years in smart Parisian society Proust retired in 1902 from public life and spent his last 19 years isolated in a fumigated cork-lined room, creating his great novel *A la recherche du temps perdu (Remembrance of Things Past)* which appeared in seven parts between 1917 and 1927. *Remembrance...* was not particularly popular at first, but sixty years later it is accepted as one of the century's masterpieces, for its literary skill, its analyses of sexual relations, both hetero- and homosexual, and its portrait of a society in flux.

PROUST, MARCEL

It seems that in our social life, a minor echo of what occurs in love, the best way to get oneself sought after is to withhold oneself.
Remembrance of Things Past: The Captive (1923)

PROUST, MARCEL

It is seldom that one parts on good terms, because if one were on good terms one would not part.
Remembrance of Things Past: The Fugitive (1925)

PROUST, MARCEL

The taste was that of the little crumb of madeleine which on Sunday mornings at Combray..., when I used to say good-day to her in her bedroom, my aunt Leonie used to give me, dipping it first in her own cup of real or limeflower tea.
Swann's Way

PROUST, MARCEL

The purely fortuitous incident in which the narrator recalls, through the flavour of a crumb of biscuit, a happy circumstance of his past convinces him that the past never really dies and that it is the task of art to recreate it through writing. This conception is the launching pad for Proust's magnum opus, in which the narrator 'Marcel' (who resembles but is not a facsimile of the author) recalls his life from idyllic childhood to the middle age from which he writes. The novel works on two levels: one is the simple recounting of chronological incidents, with no weight attached to any one; the other is that of the narrator, observing events with the two-edged sword of hindsight. In the final volume, the two strands are woven together to reveal a further, inner plot: the gradual development of Marcel's vocation as an artist.

PROUST, MARCEL

It is a terrible deception of love that it begins by engaging us in play not with a woman of the external world but with a doll fashioned in our brain – the only woman moreover that we have always at our disposal, the only one we shall ever possess.
The Guermantes Way

PROUST, MARCEL

Neurosis has an absolute genius for malingering. There is no illness which it cannot counterfeit perfectly.... If it is capable of deceiving the doctor, how should it fail to deceive the patient?
The Guermantes Way: My Grandmother's Illness

PROUST, MARCEL

Happiness is beneficial for the body, but it is grief that develops the powers of the mind.
Time Regained

PROUST, MARCEL

As soon as one is unhappy one becomes moral.
Within A Budding Grove: Madame Swann at Home

PUTNEY, SNELL   American writer

If the people of a democracy are allowed to do so, they will vote away the freedoms which are essential to that democracy.
The Conquest of Society (1972)

Putney's complaint refers to the apparent propensity of the voters to accept and even encourage the election of a party and the passage of laws which will, sooner or later, erode the freedom that permitted them to cast their vote in the first place. And while the voters may not always opt for their dictators, they certainly accept a large number of laws which, since they are passed by an elected assembly, are considered 'democratic' though in fact they may well be quite restrictive of freedom.

PUZO, MARIO   (1920–) American writer

I'll make him an offer he can't refuse
The Godfather (1969)

Puzo's novel turned the Mafia into a soap opera, with added blood, and made its author a very rich man. The 450-page blockbuster also added a new quotation to the anthologies. When Johnny Fontane, a singer whose career has been hitting some lows, is desperate for a big movie role, he finds that the producer doesn't want him. He turns, as everyone may, to his Godfather, Don Corleone. Taking advantage of the wedding of the Don's daughter, when it is traditional for the Don to grant special favours, he asks for help. Don Corleone lectures him a little then agrees: 'He's a businessman. I'll make him an offer he can't refuse'. The initial offer is refused, but the Don takes no arguments and the deal is duly struck when the producer finds the head of his favourite stallion tucked up gorily in his own bed.

PYKE, MAGNUS   (1908–) British nutritionist

Meat is a status dish in which the sizzle counts for more than the intrinsic nutritional worth.
quoted in 1978

Pyke is one of Britain's leading nutritionists, whose own beliefs have made him something of a Jeremiah as regards the nation's eating habits. It is his contention that we are wasteful of our resources, refusing to regard many healthy comestibles, notably the ubiquitous soya bean, as fit for consumption. If we continue to see meat as a vital dish, not only will we ruin our health, however alluring may be the image of British roast beef, but as resources of livestock dwindle due to ecological degeneration, we will actually find ourselves eating less and less. The advertising men may talk about selling the sizzle and not the steak, but we cannot afford such delusions. As he put it in 1975 'If we don't eat dog biscuits, we could end up eating our dog.'

PYKE, MAGNUS

The trouble is, that science is neutral. It allows us to achieve all the technical triumphs... but it gives us no guidance on how best to use these marvels when we have them.
The Listener, 1962

Pyke's point is that science, and the knowledge we glean from its researches, is an abstract. There is no good science and no bad science. A nerve gas, a chain reaction, a rocket propulsion system are simply the fruits of scientific learning. They have no moral status until the human who created them, and those who wish to employ them, take over. Once science falls into the realm of politics it loses its neutrality and the neutrality of research vanishes.

Q

QADHAFI, MUAMMAR AL   (1938–) Libyan leader

Representation is fraud.
The Green Book (1976–9)

Qadhafi has been Prime Minister of Libya since he engineered the coup which overthrew King Idris in 1969. He believes in a fundamentalist version of Islam and in the need for all Arabs to unite against both the West and Russia. *The Green Book*, named for Islam's sacred colour, is Qadhafi's version of the *Thoughts of Chairman Mao*. As a fundamentalist Muslim he believes, like that other bugbear Ayatollah Khomeini, that all laws, secular and spiritual, can be found in the Koran. Thus the idea of 'democracy' as touted by the West becomes irrelevant. Political representation, as achieved by elections, simply does not count.

QUAIL, JOHN   British writer

It is an unfortunate fact that political theory, no matter how worthy or perceptive, is curiously disembodied; it gives no clues to the passions, the heroisms or the squalid conflicts that it inspired.
The Slow Burning Fuse (1978)

Quail's book, 'a lost history of the British Anarchists', detailed a generally overlooked area of British history. The British anarchists, while borrowing substantially from their European cousins, had their own identity and operated largely in independence from the European movement. They lasted a mere fifty years, from 1880–1930, after which the triumph of Bolshevism in Russia ensured that Communism rather than anarchism would dictate the politics of the radical Left. As Quail points out, dry theory, whether of left or right, has no romance. The historian, of anarchism or any other ideology, must add the flesh of action to the bones of thought.

QUENEAU, RAYMOND (1903–1976) French poet and novelist

History is the study of man's unhappiness.
A Model History

Queneau was a member of the surrealist movement but his work was not widely recognised until after World War II. His fascination was with the mechanics of language rather than art, and he revelled in wordplay and the creation of neologisms. In Queneau's view everyone has the right to do with language whatever he wants. *In Exercices de style* (1947, *Exercises in Style*) he takes the same rather unimportant anecdote and offers it in some 99 different versions, each one revealing the potential of altering the language.

R

RANSOME, ARTHUR (1884–1967) British writer

Better drowned than duffers if not duffers won't drown
Swallows and Amazons (1930)

Ransome, a journalist on the *Manchester Guardian*, became successful with his collection of Russian folk and fairy tales *Old Peter's Russian Tales* (1916), but his reputation remains tied to his series of children's books, featuring two sailing families, the Walkers, known as the Swallows, and the Blacketts, known as the Amazons. In his massively popular books Ransome exploited his own love of the British countryside and his enthusiasms for sailing and fishing. This telegram is received by the three Walkers who have asked their father, a permanently absent figure, for permission to spend their holiday sailing. Its tone of hearty adult disinterest is typical of the books.

RAPHAEL, FREDERIC (1931–) British writer

The Glittering Prizes
title of television screenplay, 1976

Raphael's first novel appeared in 1956 and he has remained one of Britain's more prolific novelists ever since. His main reputation rests, however, on his writing for the screen, both large and small. His second screenplay, *Darling* (1965) won him an Oscar, and he has written a number of others. *The Glittering Prizes* was the title of his sequence of television plays which were broadcast in 1976. They follow the progress of a generation of Cambridge undergraduates from their college days in the early Sixties through their careers, mainly in the media, their entanglements, their failures and their successes. The prizes, so obvious at university, seem decreasingly alluring as one by one they are gained.

RAPHAEL, FREDERIC

Truth may be stranger than fiction, but fiction is truer.
quoted in *Contemporary Novelists* (1976)

Asked for his views on the novel for his entry in this large compendium of literary reference, Raphael was pointing out that in the area of the bizarre, while art tends to come out second in any competition with nature, it is only through art, in his case fiction-writing, that one can hope to convey the feel of that strangeness. The good novelist can select and refine his material, which may indeed be based on real experience, and create a 'truth' that will help the reader understand that experience with much greater clarity than if the natural facts were simply listed as they happened.

RATTIGAN, TERENCE (1911–77) British playwright

A nice, respectable, middle-class, middle-aged maiden lady, with time on her hands and the money to help her pass it....Let us call her Aunt Edna....Aunt Edna is universal, and to those who may feel that all the problems of the modern theatre might be solved by her liquidation, let me add that...she is also immortal.
preface to *Collected Plays vol. 2* (1953)

For the 'kitchen sink dramatists' and the 'angry young men' of the Fifties, Rattigan, his works and above all his audience symbolised exactly what they were struggling to overturn – the comfortable, self-satisfied world of the leisured middle classes. Rattigan himself was a consummate theatrical craftsman, and he stated unashamedly that he preferred 'plays of character and narrative over plays of ideas'. His defence of his own position, in this preface to the second volume of his *Collected Plays*, identified his regular audience in the person of 'Aunt Edna', a figure whom Rattigan created as a joking aside, but who came to epitomise everything the new, determinedly proletarian theatre came to loathe.

RAVERAT, GWEN   (1885–1957) British writer

I have defined Ladies as people who did not do things themselves.
Period Piece (1952)

Period Piece is Gwen Raverat's memoir of her youth before World War I. The 'golden afternoon' of Edwardian England may be nothing but a myth, but for a granddaughter of Charles Darwin life seemed pleasant and undemanding enough. In her book she looks through a child's eyes at what was going on, noting various adult entanglements, suitors calling on elder sisters and so on. Her definition of 'Ladies' as living in pampered idleness is both accurate and nicely reflective of the way a child undoubtedly assessed these grown-ups who never seemed to raise a hand but to summon a servant or sip at a cup of tea.

RAWSON, HUGH   American editor and lexicographer

A basic rule of bureaucracies: the longer the title, the lower the rank.
A Dictionary of Euphemisms (1983)

In his dictionary Rawson divides euphemisms into positive and negative areas. The negative concentrate on means of discussing the otherwise unpalatable in terms that, while spurious, set out to help their squeamish user. The positive 'inflate and magnify, making the euphemized items seem altogether grander and more important than they are'. Nowhere are positive euphemisms more in use than in job titles, especially in bureaucracies and other publicly funded professions. Modern society's desire to mask career and thus personal inequalities with linguistic artifice is typical of a world in which language has been made the stalking horse for those who would render style utopian even if content remains grimly mundane.

Ray's A Laugh

Ee, it was agony, Ivy
BBC radio comedy, 1950s

Ray's A Laugh was first broadcast on April 4, 1949 and lasted until January 1961, starring comedian Ted Ray, who had first broadcast for the BBC ten years previously but had not been re-employed. Ray had been born Charlie Olden in Wigan. A self-taught violinist he was spotted by an agent and sent out touring as 'Nedlo the Gypsy Violinist'. By 1930 he had abandoned the violin for stand-up comedy, and 'Nedlo' for 'Ted Ray'. By the time *Ray's A Laugh* began, he was a major comedy star. The show featured Ray, his 'wife' Kitty Bluett, Fred Yule (from *ITMA*) and, later on, Peter Sellers, Kenneth Connor, Graham Stark and other future comedy stars. It had stock characters and stock catchphrases. 'Ivy' was played by Ray; 'Mrs. Hoskin', who regularly mourned her 'agony', by Bob Pearson.

RAYBURN, SAM (1882–1961) American politician

If you want to get along, go along.
maxim

Rayburn, known to all as 'Mr. Sam', was the long-time Speaker of the US House of Representatives. This, his celebrated maxim, may well have been a traditional political philosophy, but all his own work was 'Rayburn's Law', evolved when he was having problems holding the Democrats together during Franklin Roosevelt's second term. 'When you get too big a majority you're immediately in trouble'; ie. too comfortable a majority encourages party members to forget government and lose themselves in factions. So too was his policy of saying nothing superfluous, since 'You don't have to explain what you don't say'. Journalist Arthur Krock underlined his power in *'Wisdom of a House Freshman'* (1958): 'I love Speaker Rayburn, / His heart is so warm, / And if I obey him / He'll do me no harm. / So I shan't sass the Speaker / One least little bitty / And then I'll wind up / On a major committee.' Rayburn himself claimed that when he did give out a job he made 'nine enemies and one ingrate'.

READY STEADY GO

The weekend begins here!
catchphrase on British TV show, 1965

Ready Steady Go was British television's most popular rock show during the mid-Sixties. Compered by the disk jockey Pete Murray, whose less than up-to-the-minute image was balanced by the amateur but utterly 'with-it' Cathy McGowan, a gushing fashion-plate for Mod fashions, the show went out every Friday evening. 'The weekend begins here!' exulted a voice-over as the titles rolled across dancing teenagers, and for the young fans, taking their role models from the rock bands who played and the super-mod dancers who gyrated around them, it seemed that it really did.

REAGAN, RONALD (1911–) American president

I used to say that politics was the second oldest profession, and I have come to know that it bears a gross similarity to the first.
speaking in 1979

The 'oldest profession' has been one of the favourite euphemisms for prostitution for centuries. By the time Reagan offered his view on politics, which he claimed to see as remarkably similar to whoring, he was sufficiently well-versed in its practice to be speaking from experience. Reagan has proved a bafflingly successful President to those who expect something more in the way of political acumen than policies based on the values of 1940s B-movies. Yet the 'Teflon President' the man to whom nothing negative sticks, has exhibited a remarkable ability to steer around faux pas, scandals and similar problems that would have destroyed another politician. And while critics carp, he remains the man who, for eight years, most of his countrymen chose to lead them.

REAGAN, RONALD

Win this one for the Gipper.
campaign slogan in 1966

Reagan's first 'political' appointment was as president of the Screen Actors' Guild, but his first run for elected office came in 1966 when he stood successfully for the Governorship of California. Of Reagan's fifty Hollywood films only a handful rise above the mundane, but many people remember *Knute Rockne: All American* (1941). In this biopic of Notre Dame University's famous football coach, Pat O'Brien, Hollywood's favourite priest, put 'The Rock' on screen. Reagan played George Gipp, whose death-bed rallying cry supposedly inspired 'the Fighting Irish'. Reagan remembered his role twenty-five years later and used Gipp's parting words as the slogan for his gubernatorial campaign. Reagan's other big movie role, as an amputee in *King's Row* (1941) gave him another quote. When he wakes up, bereft of his limbs, he asks his nurse 'Where's the rest of me?', a line that inspired the title of his autobiography.

REAGAN, RONALD

We could pave the whole country and put parking stripes on it and still be home for Christmas.
speaking on the Vietnam War, 1967

Reagan has always been interested in politics. He had involved himself even when a performer, backing the McCarthyite investigations into the supposed Communist infiltration of the film business and when his acting career was over, he turned to politics full-time. Unsurprisingly, Reagan was a conservative Governor whose constituency was based in the Californian heartland of right-wing, wealthy industrialists, the same men whom he would import to Washington when he became president. This comment on Vietnam was typical of his attitude to the war: Unleash the bombs, flatten the Commies and let's get the boys back home.

REICH, CHARLES A. (1928–) American academic

The Greening of America
book title, 1970

Reich's book was a brief but dramatic sensation, a book that capitalised on the interests of its time, proposed a far reaching, generalised theory and then vanished almost as soon as it had appeared. Reich looked at the Sixties counter-culture and believed every word of its utopian propaganda. He divided the contemporary world into three levels of consciousness: Consciousness I, the self-made man with the 'traditional', pioneer American values of self-reliance and individual freedom; Consciousness II, the verbal, college-educated media man, representing the values of the 20th century; Consciousness III, the 'alternative society', which would create a new, better world. Reich proselytised Consciousness III with all the enthusiasm of an ageing convert, but time has proved him sadly wrong.

REID, BERYL (1918–) British actress

Jolly hockey sticks!
catchphrase in *Educating Archie*, BBC radio show 1950s

Reid started her career in revue, and has since become one of Britain's favourite character actresses, acting variously in the film version of the play *The Killing of Sister George* (1968) and on television as 'Connie Sachs', the ageing intelligence analyst of John le Carré's spy novels. She also made her mark in the popular radio comedy show, *Educating Archie*, the only ventriloquist act ever to make a hit on radio. She joined the show in its third series, playing 'Monica' and shrilling her schoolgirlish catchphrase. Monica was one of Archie's supposed girlfriends; the other was played by a very young Julie Andrews.

REISZ, KAREL (1926–) Czech director

If you can't laugh at a madman for his madness, or a Jew for his Jewishness, you deny these people their humanity. The moment you express what you think you ought to feel, you start to say phoney things. If you demand sympathy for a man by simply showing him as a problem, you reduce him to a beetle in a bottle.
quoted in the *Daily Mail*, 1966

Reisz was referring to his film *Morgan: A Suitable Case for Treatment* (1966), which features a tragi-comic madman, fond of dressing up as and eventually taking on the characteristics of a gorilla. Criticised for making fun of the mad, Reisz pointed out that if one carefully avoids any forms of humour which deal with people as they are, preferring to extend only the sympathy of the supposed 'caring professions', one actually denies people their rights to individuality, reducing them to a thing and not a flesh-and-blood individual.

REITH, LORD (1889–1971) British broadcasting administrator

Despotism tempered by assassination.
proposing his ideal form of government

Informed by a rigorously Presbyterian conscience, Reith, first general manager, then director-general of the British Broadcasting Company (from 1927 Corporation), established a set of standards and values that have yet completely to fade. Churchill dismissed him as 'that Wuthering Height', but Reith saw his job as a mission and set out to ensure that British radio would never fall into the cash-dominated degeneracy of its American counterpart but would fulfil its brief: to inform, educate and entertain. His tastes were austere and he accepted the growth of more demotic programming only reluctantly. Conversely, the BBC brought a new appreciation of the arts, particularly music, to many of its listeners and established a standard of impartiality and accuracy in its news broadcasting, especially in the international World Service.

RENARD, JULES (1864–1910) French novelist

There is false modesty, but there is no false pride.
Journal, 1909

Renard was a French novelist whose most abiding work is his *Journal inédit*, which was written over the years 1887–1910. The Journal contains many notes on contemporary literary events and personalities, and interesting but at times painful accounts of Renard's own family life. Renard was a fascinating chronicler of his times, but as these aphorisms show, he was often unable to conceal his essential pessimism and disillusion with life.

RENARD, JULES

The danger of success is that it makes us forget the world's dreadful injustice.
Journal, 1908

RENDALL, M.J. British broadcasting adminstrator

Nation shall speak peace unto nation
motto of the BBC

Dr. Montague Rendall was one of the first five governors of the BBC, after its incorporation in 1927. It was decided that the broadcasters should have their own coat of arms, for which some form of motto was necessary. Rendall looked to the Bible and paraphrased Micah 4:3 which states 'Nation shall not lift up a sword against nation'. The motto was duly inscribed and lasted without comment until 1932 when, after a policy decision which confined the Corporation's main task to home broadcasting, the line was replaced by the single Latin word 'Quaecunque' (whatsoever). In 1948, after BBC broadcasts during World War II had shown how vital were its international services, the original motto was returned to use.

RENOIR, JEAN (1894–1979) French film director

Masterpieces are made by artisans, not artists.
My Life and My Films (1963)

Son of the painter Auguste Renoir (1841–1919), Renoir was thirty before he made his first film. Enormously influenced by art, and in particular landscapes, Renoir emerged as a popular and influential director in the thirties, with such films as *Les Bas Fonds* (1936), *Une Partie de campagne* (1936), *La Grande Illusion* (1937), *La Bête Humaine* (1938) and *Les règles du Jeu* (1939). Renoir was an extremely modest man who believed that films were made by a team, not one genius, a concept summed up in this remark, in which he saw himself as simply one more artisan.

RESTON, JAMES   (1909–) American journalist

This is the devilish thing about foreign affairs: they are foreign and will not always conform to our whim.
in 1964

Reston is a distinguished senior journalist on the *New York Times*, the London bureau of which he joined in 1939. He moved to the Washington bureau during World War II and there, seven months after Pearl Harbor, wrote his polemical *Prelude To Victory* (1942), a work in which he urged his fellow-Americans to make an all-out effort to defeat fascism. After setting up and briefly heading the Office of War Information in 1942 he returned to national news reporting, for which he earned a Pulitzer Prize in 1945. Since the war he has written a regular column on national affairs and risen to become vice-president of the *New York Times*.

RESTON, JAMES

If it's far away, it's news, but if it's close to home, it's sociology.
Wall Street Journal, 1963

REVERDY, PIERRE   (1889–1960) French poet

One is vain by nature, modest by necessity.
En Vrac

Called by André Breton 'the greatest of living poets', Reverdy was a leading member of the Parisian avant-garde from 1910–26, when he quit Paris, suffering a personal and spiritual crisis and went to live in the country. With Braque and Leger he founded the short-lived review *Nord-Sud*, a platform for both cubists and surrealists. Reverdy's poetry aimed to break traditional patterns, rejecting punctuation, avoiding all superfluous linguistic ornamentation and experimenting with typography. After 1926 Reverdy went to live in the village of Solesmes, where he converted to Catholicism, which new-found religious fervour can be seen in the themes that took over his later poetry.

REVSON, CHARLES   American cosmetics magnate

In the factory we make cosmetics. In the store we sell hope.

Revson was the head of the massive Revlon cosmetics company and his remark shows the fine difference between the prosaic world of manufacturing, no matter what the product may be, and the illusory world of packaging, marketing and promotion. If one doubts the wisdom of his line one need only observe the seemingly constant flow of advertising that is designed to create an aura of glamour around a selection of items that at best gild the lily and at worst disguise a varying multitude of sins.

RICE-DAVIES, MANDY   (1944–) British courtesan

Well, he would, wouldn't he?
giving evidence in court, June 28, 1963

As the Profumo Scandal gathered momentum through the summer of 1963, as *The Times* told its readers 'It Is A Moral Issue' and Harold Macmillan determined that 'no British government should be brought down by the action of two tarts', one of those 'tarts', Marilyn, better known as Mandy Rice-Davies gave evidence in the trial of one Stephen Ward. Ward, whose ostensible occupation for a while gave the profession of 'osteopath' the same connotation as that of 'masseur', was accused of procuring various girls, including Rice-Davies, for paid sex. Ward's defence counsel read out a list of men allegedly using his services and stated that one, Lord Astor, categorically denied having sex with Mandy. To which she replied with a grin 'Well he would, wouldn't he?'

RICHARDS, FRANK   (1876–1961) (Charles Hamilton) British boys' writer

'My esteemed chums', murmered Hurree Jamset Ram Singh. 'This is not an occasion for looking the gift horse in the mouthfulness.'
Billy Bunter's Last Fling

Frank Richards was the more famous of the two pseudonyms under which for fifty years Charles Hamilton wrote some of the world's most popular stories for boys. As 'Martin Clifford' he created Tom Merry for one boys' magazine, the *Gem*, and as

Richards he wrote stories of Billy Bunter, the 'Fat Owl' of the Remove at Greyfriars for another, the *Magnet*. Bunter, with his endless cries of 'Yaroo!!' and 'Leggo', his constant eating and his rarely achieved postal orders remains a classic figure. In his famous essay 'Boys' Weeklies', (1939), George Orwell attempted to explode the Richards world, branding it snobbish, xenophobic if not actually racist, and anachronistic. 'Richards' fought back unabashed and, surprisingly, honours were approximately even. Hamilton died in 1961. An obsessive gambler he whittled away his enormous income, gleaned from a lifetime output of 10,000 stories, the equivalent of 800 novels, leaving only £11,317.

RICHARDSON, RALPH   (1902–1983) British actor

The art of acting consists in keeping people from coughing.
in the *Observer*, 1947

This typically self-deprecating comment comes from one of Britain's favourite theatrical knights, whose career spanned some sixty years and encompassed theatre, television and film work, taking in roles written by playwrights from Shakespeare to Pinter. At the Old Vic he played the full range of classical roles, as well as establishing himself in a number of modern works. His wartime reading of *Peer Gynt* confirmed him as a great actor on a level with Olivier and Gielgud, and he was knighted in 1947. He played a wide variety of roles for the rest of his life, lending his own slightly eccentric, absent minded style to them all; typical were his film cameos, often as God or some similarly authoritative, though distant figure.

RICHTER, HANS   (1843–1916) Hungarian conductor

Your damned nonsense can I stand twice or once, but sometimes always, by God, never!
attributed rebuke to an incompetent second flute at Covent Garden

Richter was the court opera conductor in Vienna from 1875–1900. As one of the chief conductors of the Bayreuth Festspiele he conducted the first nights of his friend Wagner's *Ring der Nibelungen* in Bayreuth in 1876. From 1900–11 he came to England to conduct the Hallé Orchestra in Manchester and simultaneously directed the productions of the Royal Opera House, Covent Garden. He returned to Bayreuth in 1912 and died four years later.

RIESMAN, DAVID (1909–) American sociologist

The media, far from being a conspiracy to dull the political sense of the people, could be viewed as a conspiracy to disguise the extent of political indifference.

Riesman, professor of social science at Harvard, published his major work, *The Lonely Crowd: a Study of the Changing American Character*, in 1950. Taking America as the front-runner of modern society, Riesman observed that a new world of stability and abundance, with relatively small families, had replaced the old competitive world of high population and economic growth. The typical individuals in the new society looked to their peer-group for behaviour models, rather than to their parents as had their predecessors.

RIVERS, JOAN (1935–) American comedienne

Can we talk...?

catchphrase

Rivers, as filmographer Leslie Halliwell puts it, is 'an American cabaret comedienne with a strong line in smut'. She comes on like a raffish aunt, slightly tipsy and keen to regale her listeners with some of the coarser chats she and the 'girls' have over the bridge table. Her conspiratorial catchphrase should probably be rephrased 'I'm going to talk', since it heralds a monologue of scatalogical intent. Rivers has had to tone down her cabaret act for her TV show, in which she seems pretty much as bland as the next Johnny Carson chat-alike, but off screen her savaging of such celebrities as Elizabeth Taylor and Nancy Reagan can cut satisfyingly deep.

ROAD TO UTOPIA, THE

I'll take a lemonade. In a dirty glass.

script by Norman Panama and Melvin Frank (1946)

Bob Hope, Bing Crosby and Dorothy Lamour teamed up for their series of 'Road...' pictures between 1942-52. Their paths led to Morocco, Utopia, Rio and Bali and the films were much the same: Crosby and Hope duelled with each other and for the girl; neither of them ever seemed to get her for long. The pictures aimed to satirise adventure yarns where men were men and women wore sarongs. None of them were great hits, and they dated fast, but Crosby and Hope were consistently enjoyable and Lamour, recruited from the films they were teasing, played up as earnestly as Margaret Dumont with the Marx Brothers. In this particular scene Hope, an unashamed tenderfoot, is standing in a Yukon bar in farthest Alaska. Hoping to impress, but terrified of rotgut whiskey, he asks the bartender for 'a lemonade. In a dirty glass.'

RODEN, CLAUDIA British cooking writer

Everything tastes better outdoors.
Picnic (1981)

After Elizabeth David and Jane Grigson, Claudia Roden is probably the most influential of contemporary cooking writers. Her *Middle Eastern Cookery* (1968, revised and substantially expanded in 1985) has done for that area what the others have done for England, France and Southern Europe. Even *Picnic*, her celebration of al fresco consumption, owes as much to her upbringing in Egypt as to her subsequent life in picnic-addicted England.

ROGERS, WILL (1879–1935) American humorist

You can't say civilisation don't advance...for in every war they kill you a new way.
Autobiography

Rogers is one of the best-known of that particular genre of homespun, folksy American comedians who balance the slick sophistication of New York humour with their hayseed wisdom. Lacking formal education he preferred to travel. He visited Argentina, then Africa, and joined a Wild West Show which took him to Australia and thence back to the States. Rogers performed tricks with a lariat while giving a humorous monologue on current events. In 1913 he took his act to the Ziegfeld Follies where he rivalled the chorus girls as a main attraction, and moved on to Hollywood in 1919. As a popular entertainer he began a widely syndicated newspaper column in which he dispensed a constant flow of crackerbarrel philosophy, although when asked for his sources he responded 'All I know is just what I read in the papers'.

ROGERS, WILL

Any nation is heathen that ain't strong enough to punch you in the jaw.
A Rogers Thesaurus (1962)

ROGERS, WILL

The movies are the only business where you can go out front and applaud yourself.

ROHM, ERNST (1887–1934) German Nazi leader

Brutality is respected. The people need wholesome fear. They want to fear something. They want someone to frighten them and make them shudderingly submissive.... Why babble about brutality and get indignant about tortures. The masses want them. They need something that will give them a thrill of horror.

Rohm was one of the most important of Hitler's early supporters. A career soldier, Rohm combined his increasingly notorious homosexuality with a taste for violence and was one of those whom Hitler described as 'just overgrown children... such elements are unusable in times of peace, but in turbulent periods it's quite different...'. In 1931 Rohm's 'army' was established as the SA (Sturm Abteilung: storm troopers). When Hitler became chancellor in 1933 the SA hoped for unlimited opportunities to extend and legitimise their violence, but the Fuhrer, having used them so effectively, now had no time for such an organisation. After failing to convince Rohm of the need to restrain his troops, Hitler sent the SS against him. On the night of June 29–30 at least one hundred SA leaders and perhaps 300 other supposed supporters, including Rohm himself, were seized and executed.

ROMAN SPRING OF MRS STONE, THE

People who are very beautiful make their own laws.
Warner Bros screenplay, 1961

Tennessee Williams' novella, which was adapted for the screen by Gavin Lambert, is a portrait of an ageing, rich, egocentric widow who, realising that sex is all that keeps her interested in life, decides to ensure herself a regular supply simply by using her money to purchase lovers. Vivien Leigh plays Mrs. Stone and it is of the most prominent of her toy-boy gigolos, played by a young Warren Beatty, that she makes this comment. His laws, of course, exclude her, and while he retains his youth, she is left with nothing but bitterness.

ROMANOFF, MIKE (1890–1972) American restauranteur
Work is the curse of the drinking classes.

Romanoff's real name was Harry Gerguson but he posed for years as a Russian Prince and even when he announced in 1958 that he had chosen as a democratic American to 'renounce' his title, he still promised that 'No-one has ever discovered the truth about me – not even myself '. He played a number of small film parts but his main role was that of proprietor of Hollywood's most famous and expensive restaurant. This reversal of the pious reminder that 'Drink is the curse of the working classes' was suitably amended to reflect the preoccupations and pleasures of his wealthy customers.

ROONEY, MICKEY & JUDY GARLAND (1920–); 1922–69)
American film actors

Let's do it right here in the barn.
apocryphal line

Rooney (born Joe Yule, Jr.) and Garland (Frances Gumm) were both products of America's most exclusive school, the class MGM ran in the 1930s for their youngest contract players. They were groomed for stardom according to production-line principles and when the image-makers had done with them, turned over to the studios to earn their keep. They starred together in various films, simple stories in which the teenage duo usually saved the day. Neither performer ever actually voiced this most self-indulgent of theatrical clichés, but it presumably derives from the plot of *Babes in Arms* (1939) where Rooney and Garland, playing the children of retired vaudevillians, decide to 'put on a show'. Lacking a big city theatre, they are forced on their own resources. A line, as it were, was born.

ROOSEVELT, FRANKLIN D. (1882–1945) American president

I pledge you, I pledge myself to a New Deal for the American people. Let us all here assembled constitute ourselves prophets of a new order of competence and of courage. This is more than a political campaign; it is a call to arms. Give me your help, not to win votes alone, but to win this crusade to restore America to its own people.
speech accepting his nomination as the Democratic candidate, 1932

Roosevelt's New Deal was his shorthand for a wide-ranging programme of measures designed to combat the Depression. It was fought bitterly by Republicans and conservatives, but its relative success won Roosevelt three more elections. The term, like so many made famous by a single speaker, had neither been coined by Roosevelt nor his speechwriters, and researchers have found it recurring throughout American political history, as well as in Lloyd George's 1919 slogan 'A New Deal for Everyone', but Roosevelt's use of the phrase and his espousal of the programmes it encompassed have made it all his own.

ROOSEVELT, FRANKLIN D.

The only thing we have to fear is fear itself.
inaugural address, March 4 1933

This typically uplifting line came from Roosevelt's first inaugural address. Elected on his promise to tackle the problems of the depression, the new President said 'This is preeminently the time to speak the truth, the whole truth, frankly and boldly. Nor need we shrink from honestly facing conditions in our country today. This great nation will endure as it has endured, will revive and will prosper. So, first of all, let me assert my firm belief that the only thing we have to fear is fear itself – nameless, unreasoning, unjustified terror which paralyzes needed efforts to convert retreat into advance'.

ROOSEVELT, FRANKLIN D.

Yesterday, December 7th, 1941, a date which will live in infamy, the United States of America was suddenly and deliberately attacked by the naval and air forces of the empire of Japan.
declaration of war on Japan, December 8 1941

On December 7 1941 a Japanese strike force attacked the US forces based at Pearl Harbor, Hawaii. 368 bombers and fighters, launched from a flotilla of six carriers backed by battleships and cruisers, attacked the 94-strong US fleet. In two hours the Japanese sunk or disabled 19 ships, killing 3457 soldiers, sailors and civilians. The attackers lost only 19 planes. It was America's greatest military disaster, compounded by the fact that US cryptographers had broken the Japanese codes. Roosevelt, who declared war on Japan the next day, was blamed by rival critics both for failing to spot Japanese intentions and letting his troops be surprised, and for spotting them but deliberately letting the attack go ahead and forcing a basically isolationist America into World War II.

ROOSEVELT, FRANKLIN D.

He may be a son of a bitch, but he's our son of a bitch.
on Nicaraguan dictator 'Tacho' Somoza, 1938

As opposed to domestic policy, where the pragmatic demands of realpolitik must be somewhat muted to avoid bruising too openly the voters' sensibilities, foreign policy, which after all is only dealing with foreigners, needs less restraint. Yesterday's enemy is today's cherished ally and vice versa. Roosevelt's comment sums this philosophy up. Talking about the brutal and corrupt Nicaraguan dictator, 'Tacho' Somoza, whose son would be overthrown by the Sandinista rebels fifty years later, Roosevelt made the point that for all his excesses, he remained pro-American and as such must be regarded as a 'good guy'.

ROOSEVELT, FRANKLIN D.

We must be the great arsenal of democracy.
radio broadcast, December 29 1940

Roosevelt's wish to communicate his policies directly to the public was helped by his regular radio broadcasts, which began on March 12, 1933. He used this phrase in his broadcast of December 29, 1940, calling upon America to support the Allies in Europe. Roosevelt did not coin the phrase but heard it indirectly from its originator Jean Monnet, the French ambassador. When Monnet used it in conversation with Justice Felix Frankfurter, the judge suggested that Roosevelt could use it profitably in a speech and asked Monnet not to use it again. The line was passed to Roosevelt's speechwriter Samuel Rosenman who duly inserted into the President's broadcast.

ROOSEVELT, FRANKLIN D.

The only limit to our realization of tomorrow will be our doubts of today.
speech scheduled for April 13, 1945

By 1945 World War II had aged an already sick Roosevelt. He had already had a strenuous first three months of the year. Inaugurated for an unprecedented fourth term on January 20th, he had flown just two weeks later on a 14,000-mile round trip to Yalta where he met Churchill and Stalin. His palpable weakness during this meeting undoubtedly helped Stalin make territorial gains that would have otherwise been denied him and in the long term helped fuel the Cold War. On his return Roosevelt addressed Congress from a chair, an acknowledgement of his illness that he had never previously made. He was scheduled to make a speech on Jefferson Day, April 13. In it he looked to the future, speculating on a world after the war in which America would be playing a prominent place. The speech was never given. On April 12 Roosevelt died after 12 years and 39 days as President.

ROOSEVELT, FRANKLIN D.

A world founded upon four essential freedoms. The first is freedom of speech and expression – everywhere in the world. The second is freedom of every person to worship God in his own way – everywhere in the world. The third is freedom from want...everywhere in the world. The fourth is freedom from fear – anywhere in the world.
speech to Congress, January 6 1941

America was ostensibly neutral up until she entered World War II on December 8, 1941 but Roosevelt, defying the isolationism of many of his countrymen, had always made it clear which side he supported in Europe. In this State of the Union message to Congress he both suggested the Lend-Lease programme, under which the US would 'lend' beleaguered Britain the weapons required to continue fighting and in return Britain would lease America bases in the colonies, and outlined what he termed 'the four essential human freedoms'. These were freedom of speech and expression, freedom of every person to worship God in his own way, freedom from want and freedom from fear, by which latter he meant 'a worldwide reduction in armaments'. These freedoms were later incorporated into the Atlantic Charter.

ROOSEVELT, THEODORE   (1858–1919) American president

Speak softly and carry a big stick – you will go far.
speech 1901

Speaking at the Minnesota State Fair in early September 1901, Roosevelt, then Vice-President, answered those who had questioned the idea of backing one's foreign policy aims with a threat of military force, with a speech in which he included this passage: 'There is a homely adage which runs "Speak softly and carry a big stick – you will go far". If the American nation will speak softly and yet keep at a pitch of the highest training a thoroughly efficient navy, the Monroe Doctrine will go far'. The Monroe Doctrine, originated by President James Monroe in 1823 said simply 'The American continents are henceforth not to be considered as subjects for future colonization by any European powers.' Roosevelt became president after President McKinley was assassinated. His own foreign policy, as his phrase implies, was bullying and jingoist and did little for America's international relations.

ROOSEVELT, THEODORE

My hat is in the ring.
speaking to the press, 1912

Roosevelt retired from the Presidency in 1909, and concentrated on shooting big game, but in 1912, encouraged by a group of Republican governors and fuelled by his own enthusiasm for power, he decided to run again. He had not announced his candidacy when, questioned one night in Cleveland, Ohio, he chose to let the secret out. Using a popular Western phrase, generally equivalent to 'throwing down the gauntlet', he told the press 'My hat's in the ring. The fight is on, and I'm stripped to the buff.' Roosevelt won the nomination but lost the election to Woodrow Wilson.

ROOSEVELT, THEODORE

The men with the muckrakes.
speech on April 14, 1906

Roosevelt played the reformer, but he was as keen to avoid being branded as anti-business as he was to convince the greater public that he was their honest representative. Between 1903–09 there emerged a number of journals, all dedicated to exposing the corruption of an unrestrainedly profiteering business community. Roosevelt decried rampant capitalism when it served, but there were too many businessmen in his own party for him to repudiate it with any real fervour. Speaking in 1906 he warned that such campaigning journalism could go too far. Taking his text from a passage in Bunyan's *Pilgrim's Progress* (1678), concerning the man who could look no way but down and preferred to rake filth on the floor than accept a celestial crown, he said 'The men with the muckrakes are often indispensable to the well-being of society; but only if they know when to stop raking the muck and to look upward to the celestial crown above them, to the crown of worthy endeavour'.

ROOSEVELT, THEODORE

Every reform movement has a lunatic fringe.
speech, 1913

Roosevelt may not have coined the phrase 'lunatic fringe' but his speech in 1913 certainly gave it wide currency. Roosevelt himself was a dedicated reformer, who masked his intellect under a cowboy pose, and had been central to the camapign against the

Rockefeller oil monopoly, but he had no time for what he called 'the votaries of any forward movement'. Talking of the more fanatical socialists he explained 'I am always having to fight the silly reactionaries and the inert, fatuous creatures who will not think seriously; and on the other hand to try to exercise some control over the lunatic fringe among the reformers'.

ROSE, BILLY (1899–1966) theatrical producer

Never put your money into anything that eats or needs re-painting.
in the *New York Post* 1957

Rose was one of Broadway's leading figures in its heyday between the two world wars. His comment, which precludes a large variety of investment in either people, animals or real estate, was borne out in the wrangles over his will. He left $30 million to the Billy Rose Foundation, his own charity, but his two ex-wives claimed that the Foundation was derelict and had themselves declared co-heirs. Rose was not even able to be buried in peace. He had wished to be buried among the large collection of futuristic sculpture he had donated to the Israeli National Museum, but its curator refused permission. After lying for two years in a temporary vault in New York, the body was buried in its own mausoleum in Westchester County.

ROSEN, R.D. American writer

In America where movements spring up overnight like fastfood outlets, all God's children gotta have ideology.
Psychobabble (1977)

Rosen's book deals with the proliferation of a wide selection of allegedly therapeutic cults all dedicated to promoting the concept of self-realisation. They are culled in the main from Freudian analysis, but reduced to sufficiently simple elements so that, unlike the long years of orthodox analysis, a 'cure' may be achieved reasonably quickly and the patients, as contemporary in therapy as they are outside it, can gain value for their money. These offshoots of what the Sixties called 'the human potential movement' have provided for many young people a substitute interest for no longer fashionable political involvement. With their shallow analyses and reliance on the jargon vocabularies that Rosen calls 'psychobabble', these new therapies have, as he puts it, turned 'confession into the new handshake'.

ROSENBERG, ETHEL (1916–53) American housewife

We are the first victims of American fascism.
last letter, 1953

Whether Ethel and Julius Rosenberg, the Jewish husband and wife who were accused of betraying America's atomic bomb secrets to the Russians, were guilty will remain a subject for debate. The evidence against them was by no means watertight, but the times required scapegoats. What is incontrovertible is that their executions in the electric chair on June 19, 1953 made them the first ever American civilians to be sentenced to death for treasonous espionage. They spent just over two years in Sing Sing jail, New York State, after their sentencing on April 5 1951. They died after they had failed in every appeal for clemency. In a final letter to their lawyer Julius Rosenberg (1918–53) wrote 'Ethel wants it made known that we are the first victims of American fascism', and his own last petition to President Eisenhower climaxed: 'We are innocent. That is the whole truth. To forsake this truth is to pay too high a price even for the priceless gift of life. For life thus purchased we could not live out in dignity.'

ROSS, ALAN S.C. (1907–) British academic

U and Non-U.
Noblesse Oblige (1956)

Writing in *Encounter* in September 1955 the writer Nancy Mitford had opened a discussion on the way in which English class was as discernible from the actual vocabulary used as from the accent in which the speaker used it. She based her piece, The English Aristocracy, on the researches by the philologist Alan Ross, but the coinage of 'U' and 'Non-U' (as in 'you' and 'upper') words was all Mitford. She suggested that the upper classes and the less privileged used different terms to describe the same object. This was further elaborated in the book *Noblesse Oblige* (1956) by Mitford and Ross which for a while caused great excitement among those whose class-consciousness was pricked by Mitford's theories.

ROSS, HAROLD (1892–1951) American editor

I understand the hero keeps getting in bed with women, and the war wasn't fought that way.
quoted in James Thurber, *The Years with Ross* (1959)

The *New Yorker* was aimed at a sophisticated audience, but as this comment on Hemingway's *A Farewell to Arms* (1929) reveals, Ross brooked no 'smut'. His staff may sometimes have led bizarre private lives, and their office conversation, on occasions when they chose to rise above the usual sepulchrally gloomy reticence that seems paradoxical for such prodigious wits, may occasionally have been profane and indeed vulgar, but such excesses were strictly barred from the magazine. The comment also underlines Ross' desire to ensure that any fact printed in the *New Yorker* was absolutely correct, a system that has been perpetuated in the magazine's legendary checking department.

ROSS, HAROLD

The *New Yorker* will not be edited for the old lady from Dubuque.
launching his new magazine, 1925

After spending World War I editing the US forces newspaper *Stars and Stripes*, Ross returned to America intending to launch his own magazine. Calling upon the talents of such of his fellow soldiers as Alexander Woollcott and such popular wits as Robert Benchley and Dorothy Parker, and backed by the New York millionaire Raoul Fleischman, Ross produced the first issue of the *New Yorker* in 1925. The prospectus with which he wooed investors made its purpose clear: 'The *New Yorker* will not be edited for the old lady from Dubuque'. Parker and Benchley proved short-term contributors but Ross recruited an unrivalled team, bringing together writers E.B. White, James Thurber and Wolcott Gibbs, the poet Ogden Nash and cartoonists Peter Arno and Charles Addams. He was a punctilious editor, obsessed with perfect punctuation and factual accuracy, and created one of the world's unique magazines.

ROSTAND, JEAN (1894–1977) French biologist and man of letters

Literature: proclaiming in front of everyone what one is careful to conceal from one's immediate circle.
Journal d'un caractère (1931)

Rostand was the son of the dramatist Eduard Rostand. He was a member of the intellectually elite French Academy and author of several works on both the nature and the moral significance of modern biological studies. In books such as *A Biologist's Notebook* (1955) and *Journal d'un caractère* (1931) he offered a variety of aphorisms on man's relations to other men, to religion and to the world in which he lives. They include:

ROSTAND, JEAN

God, that dumping ground of our dreams.
A Biologist's Notebook (1955)

ROSTAND, JEAN

Certitude is servitude.
A Biologist's Notebook (1955)

ROSTAND, JEAN

Kill one man and you are a murderer. Kill millions and you are a conqueror. Kill all and you are a God.
A Biologist's Notebook (1955)

ROSTAND, JEAN

Why long for glory, which one despises as soon as one has it? But that is precisely what the ambitious man wants: having it in order to be able to despise it.
De la vanité (1925)

ROSTAND, JEAN

Merit envies success, and success takes itself for merit.
De la vanité (1925)

ROSTAND, JEAN

We spend our time envying people we wouldn't wish to be.
Journal d'un caractère (1931)

ROSTEN, LEO   (1908–) American writer

Anyone who hates dogs and babies can't be all bad.
after-dinner speech, February 17, 1939

Rosten is best known both as the creator of H*Y*M*A*N K*A*P-*L*A*N and more academically as the American doyen of Yiddish, whose books have helped explain this language of Jewish colloquialisms to an English-speaking readership. Rosten was also responsible for a phrase that is consistently and erroneously attributed to the film comedian W.C. Fields. Speaking at a show business dinner, the Masquers' Club Banquet held in Hollywood on February 17, 1939 to celebrate Fields' twenty-five years in entertainment, Rosten referred to the guest of honour with, among others, this quotable phrase. It has been a by-word for cynical misanthropy ever since. The word 'children' is often substituted for 'babies' and 'small' occasionally placed before 'dogs'.

ROTH, PHILIP (1933–) American novelist

Let the goyim sink their teeth into whatever lowly creature crawls and grunts across the face of the dirty earth, we will not contaminate our humanity thus. Let them...gorge themselves upon anything and everything that moves, no matter how odious and abject the animal, no matter how grotesque or shmutzig or dumb....Let them eat eels and frogs and pigs and crabs and lobsters; let them eat vulture, let them eat ape-meat and skunk if they like – a diet of abominable creatures well befits a breed of mankind so hopelessly shallow and empty-headed as to drink, to divorce and to fight with their fists.... Thus saith the kosher laws, and whom am I to argue that they're wrong. For look at Alex himself... sucks one night at a lobster's claw and within the hour his cock is out and aimed at a shikse on a Public Service bus. And his superior Jewish brain might as well be made of matzoh brei!
Portnoy's Complaint (1969)

Portnoy's Complaint was the literary succès de scandale of 1969, arriving at the end of a decade when literary censorship had been eroded by a revolution in public attitudes. The book is written as its hero Alex Portnoy's 'confession' to his psychoanalyst of the angsts and agonies of a prototypically nice Jewish boy who, among other neuroses, is a slave both to his mother and to masturbation. Roth had already written a number of reasonably successful books but Portnoy took him into a new world of controversy, hate-mail and enormous success. With lines such as 'let's put the oy back in goy and the id back in yid' and 'A Jewish man with parents alive is a fifteen-year-old boy, and will remain a fifteen-year-old boy till they die', both Jews and gentiles weren't sure whether the book was quite marvellous or utterly loathsome.

ROTHKO, MARK (1903–70) American artist

The unfriendliness of society to his activity is difficult for the artist to accept. Yet this very hostility can act as a lever for true liberation.

Rothko began painting in 1925 and in 1935 helped found a group of expressionist artists known as 'The Ten'. His paintings, exploring a world of surrealist fantasy, took up larger and larger canvases, and grew increasingly abstract. Aiming to create universal symbols of 'man's primitive fears and motivations' Rothko sought to paint the 'elemental truth' in the 'simple expression of a complex thought'. His work, which he saw not as objects of decoration but as a subject for contemplation, became increasingly sombre, with the brighter colours of the Fifties giving way to darker tones in the Sixties. Rothko committed suicide in 1970 and the disposition of his works, haggled over by lawyers and dealers, formed a sad postscript to his life.

ROTHSCHILD, LORD (1910–) British businessman, scientist and administrator

There is no point getting into a panic about the risks of life until you have compared the risks that worry you with those that do not.
Dimbleby Lecture, 1978

Lord Rothschild is the third Baron Rothschild and the current head of the English branch of the great Jewish banking family. He has worked in a wide variety of occupations, including British intelligence, Shell Oil, Edward Heath's 'think tank' the Central Policy Review Staff and the family bank. He has written a number of books, usually based on his current employment.

ROWAN AND DICK MARTIN, DAN (1922– ; 1922–) American entertainers

Rowan: Say Goodnight Dick.
Martin: Goodnight Dick.
Catchphrase from the *Rowan and Martin Laugh-In,* 1968-72

Rowan and Martin's Laugh-In was the favourite TV comedy show of the late Sixties. Beamed from 'sunny downtown Burbank' it was pure froth, a blend of corny jokes, sight gags and soft-pedalled digs at American society, set against a 'hippie' backdrop. It caused little pain, made plenty of people laugh, and assembled a number of energetic performers of whom some, like Lily Tomlin, would became famous and others, like Judy Carne, would never find another satisfactory niche. The show spawned a number of catchphrases, including this sign-off from the two linkmen, a straight copy of the similar farewell that for years had concluded the *Burns and Allen show.*

ROWLAND, HELEN (1875–1950) American journalist

When you see what some girls marry, you realise how much they must hate to work for a living.
Reflections of a Bachelor Girl (1903)

665

Helen Rowland, best described as a prototype Dorothy Parker, and indeed Fran Lebowitz, was a woman journalist writing at a time when most middle-class American women were still confined to the home and the children. Rowland has never achieved the sort of reputation that her successors gained in a more liberated world, but her collection of aphorisms, *Reflections of a Bachelor Girl*, provides as witty and cynical a view of women's lives as that offered by anyone who came later.

ROWLAND, HELEN

The follies which a man most regrets in his life are those which he didn't commit when he had the opportunity.
Reflections of a Bachelor Girl (1903)

ROWLAND, RICHARD American film-maker

The lunatics have taken over the asylum.
comment in 1919

By the end of World War I Charlie Chaplin, Mary Pickford and Douglas Fairbanks were Hollywood's hottest properties. They were all rich and destined to become richer but they realised that with such box-office appeal, their best ploy would be to cut out the studios and start making their own films. In 1919, allied with director D.W. Griffith, another major Hollywood figure, they established the United Artists company. On hearing this, one Hollywood executive, generally thought to be Rowland, who worked for Metro, remarked on their move 'The lunatics have taken over the asylum', and the phrase passed into the language.

RUBIN, JERRY (1938–) American activist and stockbroker

Never trust anyone over thirty.
slogan, c.1966

Rubin, with his ally Abbie Hoffman, was for a while one of the loudest, best publicised voices in the political wing of the American counter-culture. He rejected the ideological constraints of the New Left, but chose instead to combine hippie fantasy with political activism and promote the 'revolution' as a phenomenon that was best accompanied by sex and rock 'n' roll and strictly off-limits to the oldies. Rubin's revolutionary apotheosis came at the stormy Chicago Eight trial in 1969, which followed the clashes between Chicago police and the demonstrating youth during the Democratic Convention of 1968. After that Rubin gradually drifted away from 'the Movement'. After dabbling in the 'human potential movement' he moved on, ironically for one who once showered its floor with fake money to watch the brokers scrabble, to make money on the New York Stock Exchange. Jerry Rubin is 50.

RUDE PRAVO

Those who lie on the rails of history must expect to have their legs chopped off.
quoted in the *Listener*, 1979

Rude Pravo is the Czech communist party newspaper. Its blunt image was commenting on the fate of those who attempt to stand in the way of the revolution. The assumption is that the great engine of revolutionary Marxism moves inexorably onwards and that puny mortals who attempt to challenge the juggernaut must expect to be crushed.

RUNYON, DAMON (1884–1946) American journalist

In fact, Sam the Gonoph says, I long ago came to the conclusion that all life is six to five against.
A Nice Price

It may well be that nobody on the Broadway of the Thirties and Forties ever really spoke quite the way Damon Runyon put it down in his best-selling short stories, but few of them were about to quibble. Runyon took the dialect tradition of American humour away from such folksy, ethnic characters as 'Mr. Dooley', and gave it to the 'guys' and 'dolls' of New York's 'Great White Way'. He peopled his stories with gentrified versions of the mobsters, con-men, chorines, whores and assorted villains and down-and-outs who plied their trade in the midtown reaches of New York's famous thoroughfare. They spoke in a language that most Americans had never heard but few could resist. Runyon was already one of America's favourite reporters, and his fame was enormously compounded when he began turning out the tales of what his friend Walter Winchell called 'the Hardened Artery'.

RUSK, DEAN (1909–) American statesman

We're eyeball to eyeball and the other fellow just blinked.
comment on the Cuba crisis, October 24, 1962

After the abortive 'Bay of Pigs' fiasco of April 1961, in which CIA-trained Cuban exiles had failed completely to overthrow Fidel Castro, tension between America and Russia, for whom Cuba was a client state, escalated. On October 23 1962, the US announced that its spy planes had obtained photographs of Russian nuclear missile bases sited on the island. Such missiles could penetrate to targets 1000 miles within the US. American forces instituted a blockade of Cuba and President Kennedy threatened a full-scale invasion if the missiles were not dismantled. The Russians offered a trade-off – their Cuban bases for American installations in Turkey. Kennedy refused and Premier Khrushchev threatened nuclear war and dispatched a ship carrying more missiles for Cuba. On October 28, as the world watched this apocalyptic poker game, the Russians decided not to run the blockade and agreed to dismantle the bases. Secretary of State Dean Rusk remarked to ABC-TV 'Remember when you report this – that eyeball to eyeball, they blinked first', a phrase more generally quoted as above.

RUSSELL, BERTRAND (1872–1970) British essayist and philosopher

As well as the synonym for libertarian protest Russell was Britain's most productive and influential 20th century philosopher. Russell's first, and possibly greatest work, *The Principles of Mathematics* (1903) successfully challenged the mathematical orthodoxies of the period. In the three-volume *Principia Mathematica* (1910–13 with A.N. Whitehead) he explained how all mathematics can be proved from the self-evident truths of formal logic. With his pupil Ludwig Wittgenstein he proposed the theory of 'logical atomism', which posits the task of philosophy as being the analysis of knowledge into its basic and least arguable elements. His first clash with the authorities came when his unequivocal pacifism during World War I earned him a prison sentence in 1918. Between the wars, with his wife Dora (Black) he ran a progressive school, and spent World War II in America, where he wrote his *History of Western Philosophy* (1945), although he was banned from teaching by the puritan lobby. From 1950 he spearheaded the campaign against nuclear weapons and established his own Peace Foundation, which considered, inter alia, Americans' conduct in Vietnam.

RUSSELL, BERTRAND

The average man's opinions are much less foolish than they would be if he thought for himself.

For an intellectual of Russell's calibre, the idea of simply accepting the received wisdom that one's self-proclaimed leaders and superiors choose to apportion out, was inconceivable. His own life, both as mathematician and philosopher and as a campaigner for a variety of liberal and libertarian causes, was dedicated to rejecting opinions that were laid down as incontrovertible facts by others. Russell was exceptional, but he displays his typical humanity by refusing simply to brand the average person as foolish for their acceptance, but only for ignoring their own great potential.

RUSSELL, BERTRAND

Fear is the main source of superstition and one of the main sources of cruelty. To conquer fear is the beginning of wisdom.
An Outline of Intellectual Rubbish (1950)

This essay is an attack on the growth of dogmatism. Intellectual rubbish, as far as Russell was concerned, was epitomised in the way those seeking to promote their own interests masked them in the florid verbiage of ideological argument. Unless that ideology was based in facts, he could see no cause for it, other than to blind those who were subjected to it, to the essential hollowness of the theory.

RUSSELL, BERTRAND

The boa constrictor, when he has had an adequate meal, goes to sleep, and does not wake until he needs another meal. Human beings, for the most part, are not like this.
Human Society in Ethics and Politics (1954)

Russell embarked upon this book with the purpose, to some extent, of re-examining the subjects contained in *New Hopes for a Changing World* (1951). Its purposes are two-fold: in the first place he attempted to set out an un-dogmatic ethic; in the second he tried to see how that ethic could be applied to various contemporary political problems. This comment refers to the human propensity for wars and destruction, almost, it seems, for nothing more than the sake of the violence and aggression involved.

RUSSELL, BERTRAND

The more you are talked about, the more you wish to be talked about.
Human Society in Ethics and Politics (1954)

Russell expanded his theory of what less elegant writers might call 'All publicity is good publicity' as follows: 'The condemned murderer who is allowed to see the account of his trial in the Press is indignant if he finds a newspaper which has reported it inadequately. And the more he finds about himself in other newspapers, the more indignant he will be with the one whose reports are meagre. Politicians and literary men are in the same case'.

RUSSELL, BERTRAND

All movements go too far.
in 1960

Russell was answering those critics who, like so many liberals, were very happy to accompany his protests up to the point at which they actually started to disturb those against whose activities they were protesting. In 1960, against the wishes of many of those who had been, like him, involved with the movement since its inception, Russell founded the militant Committee of 100, a hard-line breakaway group that cut itself adrift from the less aggressive, but original Campaign for Nuclear Disarmament (CND). To those who accused him of 'going too far', he could only point out that that was the purpose of protest.

RUSSELL, BERTRAND

It seems to be the fate of idealists to obtain what they have struggled for in a form which destroys their ideals.
Marriage and Morals (1929)

In 1940, seeking refuge from the European war, Russell went to New York. Here he was allowed to live, but forbidden to engage in any teaching, despite his intellectual attainments, since the city's puritan governors felt that his libertarian views on sex and marriage, as detailed in *Marriage and Morals*, would corrupt the American young. The book is hardly revolutionary but Russell has no time for artificial codes of morality. He discusses the origins and the subsequent failings of the contemporary sexual codes, and possible improvements for the sake of human happiness and well-being.

RUSSELL, BERTRAND

The fact that an opinion has been widely held is no evidence whatsoever that it is not utterly absurd. Indeed, in view of the silliness of the majority of mankind, a widespread belief is more likely to be foolish than sensible.
Marriage and Morals (1929)

RUSSELL, BERTRAND

The more we realise our minuteness and our impotence in the face of cosmic forces, the more amazing becomes what human beings have achieved.
New Hopes for a Changing World (1951)

Russell's book appeared only six years after World War II had bequeathed post-war civilisation a very different world to the one that had initiated the conflict, and as its title suggests, his book attempts to maximise the positive aspects of the contemporary world. He discusses the various international disputes but, rather than reiterate the grim warnings that he had been accustomed to offer, he attempted to see what could best be achieved by treating them sensibly. The book ends with an optimistic picture of what the world could become if its inhabitants chose wisely.

RUSSELL, BERTRAND

Truth is what one is obliged to tell policemen.
quoted in 1984

As a philosopher Russell was well aware of how fluid a word truth may often be. The pursuit of a philosophical definition of truth, as well as of falsehood and meaninglessness, had been central to his study of mathematics, but this particular definition, infinitely more light-hearted, poked fun at his own entanglements with the authorities and with their attempts to keep him under control.

RUSSELL, BERTRAND

We have, in fact, two kinds of morality side by side; one which we preach but do not practise, and another which we practise but seldom preach.
Sceptical Essays (1928)

This collection assembles the essays written during the middle period of Russell's life, in which he examines such questions as the influence of psychoanalysis, the theory of relativity, the decline of the scientific impulse in the West and what he calls the wicked persistence of puritanism. There is also an important discussion of the nature of freedom. As he picks his way among the confusion of ideas that agitate the times, Russell maintains throughout that it is still possible to remain a rational human being, even as he stresses his famous scepticism.

RUSSELL, BERTRAND

The infliction of cruelty with a good conscience is a delight to moralists – that is why they invented hell.
Selected Papers

Russell, who was sternly moral as far as his respect for the sanctity of individual human beings was concerned, was dismissive of artificial moral systems and the puritan or repressive forces who set them up purely to force their own views on unwilling others. As he points out, from the puritan's point of view, the beauty of setting up such systems is that one invariably claims that those who must suffer them are doing it 'for their own good' and thus sustains the necessary coercion with 'a good conscience'.

RUSSELL, BERTRAND

There are two motives for reading a book: one, that you enjoy it, the other than you can boast about it.
The Conquest of Happiness (1930)

This book is a discussion of exactly what, in Russell's conception, makes people happy or unhappy and an attempt to suggest ways of overcoming unhappiness and preserving happiness. It demonstrates Russell's belief that many people who consider themselves unhappy could improve their lot and become relatively happy through a process of sustained, well-directed effort.

RUSSELL, BERTRAND

Man is a credulous animal and must believe something. In the absence of good grounds for belief, he will be satisfied with bad ones.
Unpopular Essays (1950)

In his preface to this collection of essays, Russell explains that most of them, written at various times during the previous fifteen years, are concerned to combat in one way or another the growth of dogmatism, whether of the Right or of the Left, that has characterised the 20th century. He goes on to say that some of the essays, given such momentous topics, may seem flippant, but people who are always solemn and pontifical may not be fought successfully by those who set themselves up as even more solemn and more pontifical. More of his lines follow:

There is no nonsense so arrant that it cannot be made the creed of the vast majority by adequate governmental action.
Unpopular Essays (1950)

People who are vigorous and brutal often find war enjoyable, provided that it is a victorious war and that there is not too much interference with rape and plunder. This is a great help in persuading people that wars are righteous.
Unpopular Essays (1950)

One should respect public opinion insofar as is necessary to avoid starvation and keep out of prison, but anything that goes beyond this is voluntary submission to an unnecessary tyranny.
The Conquest of Happiness (1930)

Obscenity is what happens to shock some elderly and ignorant magistrate.
quoted in *Look* magazine, 1954

The fundamental defect of fathers is that they want their children to be a credit to them.
quoted in the *New York Times*, 1963

Work is of two kinds: first, altering the position of matter at or near the earth's surface relatively to other matter; second, telling other people to do so. The first kind is unpleasant and ill-paid; the second is pleasant and highly paid.
quoted in *The Faber Book of Aphorisms* (1964)

A fanatical belief in democracy makes democratic institutions impossible.
quoted in *The Faber Book of Aphorisms* (1964)

What men really want is not knowledge but certainty.
quoted in the *Listener*, 1964

RYLE, GILBERT (1890–1976) British philosopher

Blast any words that end in 'ist' or 'ism'. They always interfere with any serious discussion of any subject.'
in the *Listener*, 1971

As Oxford's professor of metaphysical philosophy Ryle helped make the university an important centre of philosophy. His best-known book, *The Concept of Mind*, appeared in 1949. Its essential argument is that the traditional view of mind and body as two distinct and puzzling entities is simply wrong and confusing. In *Dilemmas* (1954) he overturned another dualist view, arguing that there is far less of a gap between scientific findings and one's everyday beliefs than traditional opinion maintained.

S

SACKS, OLIVER (1933–) British neurologist

Health is infinite and expansive in mode, and reaches out to be filled with the fullness of the world; whereas disease is finite and reductive in mode and endeavours to reduce the world to itself.
Awakenings (1973)

Sacks is professor of clinical neurology at the Albert Einstein College of Medicine in New York, where he specialises in migraine, mental illness and behavioural development and disorder in children. He has also studied, as detailed in his book *Awakenings*, sufferers from encephalitis largica, patients who were caught up in the sleeping-sickness epidemic of the 1920s. These patients have been virtual zombies ever since then, and in his book Sacks explains the effect of the drug L-dopa on their minds. For a while its use appeared to bring them back to life, offering the 'awakenings' of the book's title. Sacks also deals with sufferers from 'Gilles de la Tourette's syndrome', otherwise known as 'Tourettism': constant physical 'tics, jerks, mannerisms, grimaces, noises, curses, involuntary imitations and compulsions of all sorts'. He has written about tics, among other forms of neurological aberration, in *The Man Who Mistook His Wife for a Hat* (1985).

SAHL, MORT (1926–) American comedian

Would you buy a used car from this man?
attributed remark on Richard Nixon

Richard Nixon has often been characterised by opponents as a somewhat dubious figure. Helen Gahagan Douglas, whom he had defeated in a California election in 1950, effectively smearing her as a Communist, christened him 'Tricky Dicky'. In 1952, when Nixon was standing as vice-presidential candidate and extricating himself with difficulty from allegations of financial finagling, this line became widespread. Traditionally attributed to the comedian Mort Sahl, the line plays upon Nixon's invariably shifty appearance, which only seemed to grow worse the more he attempted to smarten up, and the poor image associated with second-hand car salesmen.

SAKI   (1870–1916) British writer
Hector Hugh Monro began a career as a journalist and writer in 1896. After his first book, *The Rise of the Russian Empire* (1899), he began writing political satire for the Westminster Gazette and from 1902-08 worked as foreign correspondent for the *Morning Post*. He took the pseudonym Saki, taken from the *Rubaiyat of Omar Khayyam*, for his first volume of short stories, *Reginald* (1904) set in the smart world of London society and mixing aphoristic observation and chic satire with a constant edge of the macabre and even tragic. Several more collections followed; a novel, *The Unbearable Bassington* (1912) was set in the same milieu. Munro enlisted in the Royal Fuseliers in 1914. He was killed two years later; his last words were 'Put that bloody cigarette out!'

SAKI

The young have aspirations that never come to pass, the old have reminiscences of what never happened.
Reginald at the Carlton (1904)

SAKI

Scandal is merely the compassionate allowance which the gay make to the humdrum.
Reginald at the Carlton (1904)

SAKI

The cook was a good cook, as cooks go and as cooks go, she went.
Reginald on Besetting Sins (1904)

SAKI

I always say beauty is only sin deep.
Reginald's Choir Treat (1904)

SAKI

A little innacuracy sometimes saves tons of explanation.
The Comments of Moung Ka (1924)

SAKI

All decent people live beyond their incomes nowadays, and those who aren't respectable live beyond other people's. A few gifted individuals manage to do both.
The Match-maker (1911)

SAKI

Every profession has its secrets...if it hadn't it wouldn't be a profession.
The Story of St. Vespalius (1911)

SAKI

Every reformation must have its victims. You can't expect the fatted calf to share the enthusiasm of the angels over the prodigal's return.
Reginald on the Academy (1904)

SAKI

To have reached thirty is to have failed in life.
Reginald on the Academy (1904)

SALINGER, J.D. (1919–) American novelist

Sex is something I don't really understand too hot. You never know where you are. I keep making up these sex rules for myself, and then I break them right away.
The Catcher in the Rye (1951)

Jerome David Salinger is among the most celebrated of modern novelists, although his fame rests basically on a single book and he has published nothing since 1965. That book, *Catcher In The Rye*, created in his teenage, preppie hero Holden Caulfield a symbol of the uncertainties of the generation who were coming of age in the Fifties. Alienation was a keyword in that decade and Caulfield, loathing his contemporaries and dreading immersion in the 'phoney' world of adults, is an exemplar of the emotion. For a while Caulfield represented a modern Huckleberry Finn, a seminal figure in American literature with whom a whole (young) generation seemed to identify. After *Catcher...*, Salinger wrote three books about the fictional 'Glass' family, books that critic Martin Green has called 'baroque extravaganzas', in which the participants' dangerously beautiful minds leave them dissociated from the real world and, in the end, from the reader too.

SALISBURY, LORD   (1893–1972) British statesman

Too clever by half.
comment, 1951

Salisbury was one of the Conservative party's elder statesmen when he made this comment on the young Iain MacLeod and a number of other MPs who had recently arrived in the House of Commons for the first time. Although the Tory party did not exclude intellectuals, the traditional members, recruited from the rural squirearchy, had an equally traditional distrust of those whom they considered overly academic. Salisbury himself was no backwoodsman. His most noteworthy actions were his resignation with his then chief Anthony Eden in protest against appeasement, and his advising the Queen, in partnership with Churchill, to appoint Macmillan rather than Butler to succeed Eden as prime minister in 1957.

SAMUEL, LORD   (1870–1963) British politician

A difficulty for every solution.
commenting on the Civil Service

Herbert Samuel, latterly Lord Samuel, was one of the leading Liberal members of Parliament both under Lloyd George and during the period of the party's decline once the 'Welsh Wizard' had relinquished its leadership. After serving as the Home Secretary during World War I, during which time he implemented daylight saving time, Samuel, a Jew, was sent as the High Commissioner to Palestine in 1920, following the pro-Zionist Balfour Declaration. Lloyd George was less than enthusiastic about him, remarking on one occasion that 'when they circumcised him they threw the wrong part away' and referring to his appointment in Palestine as being 'the first proconsul since Pontius Pilate'.

SANDBURG, CARL   (1878–1967) American poet

Slang is a language that rolls up its sleeves, spits on its hands and goes to work.
in the *New York Times*, 1959

Sandburg's first collection of verse, *Chicago Poems* (1916) established him as a new and important voice in American poetry, challenging contemporary tastes with his use of colloquialisms and devotion to free verse forms. Sandburg represented the romantically liberal tradition of American history, espousing slang as the language of the poor, and creating as his major work a hagiographical study of Abraham Lincoln (1926–39).

SANDERS, GEORGE (1906–72) British actor

An actor is not quite a human being – but then, who is?

Sanders personified the urbane, suave bounder in dozens of movies, many of which were saved from their intrinsic mediocrity only by his performance. His autobiography was called *Memoirs of a Professional Cad* (1960) and nobody played one better. Sanders extended his screen persona into his private life, enjoying such dryly cynical aphorisms as this one, and deprecating his profession as being 'like roller skating – once you know how to do it, it is neither stimulating nor exciting.' His studied world-weariness reached its apotheosis in his death in 1972. Swallowing an overdose of sleeping pills he stayed in character for his suicide note which read 'Dear World, I am leaving you because I am bored. I am leaving you with your worries. Good luck.'

SANTAYANA, GEORGE (1863–1952) American philosopher

Fanaticism consists in redoubling your effort when you have forgotten your aim.
The Life of Reason (1905–06)

Santayana, a Spaniard educated in America, was professor of philosophy at Harvard between 1889–1912, before returning to Europe. As well as his philosophies, which asserted that human ideas, although originating as part of the functions of the human organism, exist on a higher, non-material plane than more mundane activities, he wrote poetry, criticism, memoirs, and one novel, a best-seller, *The Last Puritan* (1935). Appreciative of the mental strength and serenity that can come from religion, but sceptical of the actual dogma, he lived from 1945 as the guest of a community of nuns.

SANTAYANA, GEORGE

The young man who has not wept is a savage, and the old man who will not laugh is a fool.
Dialogues in Limbo (1925)

With *Dialogues in Limbo* Santayana takes up one of the most hallowed of those literary forms devoted to philosophy: the Socratic dialogue. In it he uses the traditional characters in their true representation, and 'Socrates' asks his interlocutors a number of questions, using their own answers to trap them into self-contradiction. The book contains ten dialogues, some of which are virtual soliloquies. Their titles include 'The Secret of Aristotle', 'Homesickness of the World' and 'Normal Madness', from which this line is taken.

SANTAYANA, GEORGE

Why shouldn't things be largely absurd, futile and transitory? They are so, and we are so, and they and we go very well together.
Letters (1918)

This extract is taken from a letter Santayana wrote to Logan Pearsall Smith, aphorist, aesthete and brother of Bertrand Russell's first wife Alys. Smith was the first person to collect Santayana's short essays into book form. The 'things' to which he is referring are Smith's own collection of even shorter pieces: *Trivia*, published in 1903.

SANTAYANA, GEORGE

Progress, far from consisting in change, depends on retentiveness...Those who do not remember the past are condemned to repeat it.
The Life of Reason (1905–06)

The Life of Reason is considered as Santayana's major work. It appeared originally in five volumes, dealing successively with reason in common sense, in society, in religion, in art and in science. As an analysis of the various aspects, historical manifestations and possible ideal values of institutions such as society, religion, art and science, the book, when taken as a whole, constitutes a philosophy of history and civilisation. Santayana's most famous line, a warning to those who refuse to learn from the past, has often been rephrased. Among the more interesting variations was that written in 1976 by Charles Wolf Jr. in the *Wall Street Journal:* 'Those who don't study the past will repeat its errors; those who do study it will find other ways to err.'

SANTAYANA, GEORGE

Intolerance itself is a form of egoism, and to condemn egoism intolerantly is to share it.
Winds of Doctrine (1913)

Winds of Doctrine came at a vital period in both the world's and Santayana's own history. It appeared on the eve of World War I and at the time when Santayana had decided to leave Harvard.

The book unsurprisingly reflects the feeling of an era coming to its close, of its author's emergence from the academic cloister into the world, and of a degree of prophetic intent. In it he looks out on the waters of philosophy, which he sees as muddied and troubled, and attempts to discern and define the individual cross-currents that run through it.

SARRAUTE, NATHALIE (1902–) French writer

Television has lifted the manufacture of banality out of the sphere of handicraft and placed it in that of a major industry.

Sarraute is one of the pioneers of the French 'nouveau roman' (new novel), whose exponents believe that the novel should be primarily about things, and not about characters, plot, ideas or action. The traditional emphasis, with its omnipotent narrator, posits a false situation. The logical, ordered world that such a narrator offers the novel does not exist anywhere but in such books. If the novel is to be true to life, it should concentrate on a systematised and analytical record of objects.

SARTRE, JEAN-PAUL (1905–1980) French philosopher, writer and activist

Man can will nothing unless he has first understood that he must count on no-one but himself; that he is alone, abandoned on earth in the midst of his infinite responsibilities, without help, with no other aim than the one he sets himself, with no other destiny than the one he forges for himself on this earth.
The Words (1964)

Sartre, the nephew of Albert Schweitzer, drew many of his ideas from German thinkers, but his intellectual kingdom was undoubtedly Paris, where his concepts of existentialism dominated intellectual life in the late Forties and the Fifties. Sartre claimed that man, abandoned in a godless world, had no option but to use his own freedom and responsibility to invent his own values. By 1960 he had espoused Marxism and attempted, in a devastatingly complex fusion of theories, to reconcile the absolute individualism of the existentialist with the collectivist stance of the Marxist. This led to the belief that if a man is attempting to assert his individuality in the face of economic repression, he is fully justified in using violence. This attitude, combined with his belief in the duty of a writer to be politically committed, led to his support of the Algerian nationalists and the North Vietnamese.

SARTRE, JEAN-PAUL

Man is a useless passion.
Being and Nothingness (1943)

Being and Nothingness is a philosophical work in which Sartre attempts to account for the whole of reality. His aim is to describe 'the world and consciousness as they appear', with the basic idea that it is in the apparition (and not appearance, which would imply the existence of something 'underneath') that reality must lie. A thing is that which appears to me and nothing else. This philosophy became known as 'existentialism', a belief system which is concerned with existence in an active sense rather than with the abstract nature of existence or of the universe.

SARTRE, JEAN-PAUL

Man is condemned to be free.
Existentialism is a Humanism (1946)

Sartre argues that man can and does emerge from the state of indetermination into which he is born (the freedom to chose any way of thought or life). People, by a sheer act of will, commit themselves to a positive part in social and political affairs, and thus to an awareness of others as well as themselves. And by the fact of their commitment they provide shape for their existence and a common, integrating purpose for humanity.

SARTRE, JEAN-PAUL

Hell is other people.
Huis clos (1943)

In his play *Huis clos* Satre places his three main characters in a hot and ugly room, in which it is impossible for them to escape from one another, and despite their initial attempts, they soon realise that they have lost their freedom and are powerless to change what others have created for them. For Sartre, the concept of traditional, religious hell does not exist and in this play he is describing the torment of the beings who, on earth, live in self deception, or who have chosen to live a life contrary to the general welfare. Their punishment is not in the supposed 'here-after' but here and now.

SARTRE, JEAN-PAUL

Like all dreamers I mistook disenchantment for truth.
The Words (1964)

SARTRE, JEAN-PAUL

I confused things with their names: that is belief.
The Words (1964)

Sartre wrote *The Words* when he came to realize that he could no longer believe in the ideas which for thirty years had formed the basis of his life and work: that writing was the highest and finest human activity and that the writer's job was to write lasting books and win a kind of immortality. It is not a chronological autobiography but a presentation and analysis of certain key attitudes, together with the time and circumstances in which they were formed.

SASSOON, SIEGFRIED   (1886–1967) British poet

I am making this statement as a wilful defiance of military authority because I believe that the War is being deliberately prolonged by those who have the power to end it.
quoted in *Memoirs of an Infantry Officer* (1930)

Sassoon began writing poetry in the trenches of World War I and his work illuminates the futility of the war, the mediocrity of many of those entrusted with its direction, and the bravery, despite all odds, of the average soldier. He received the Military Cross but found the war so painful that he threw away his medal and in 1916 published an anti-war statement, prefaced by the lines quoted above, in the press. The Army preferred not to shoot an officer for treason, as they might a private soldier, but listed him as shell-shocked and dispatched him to a military hospital. After the war he became better known for his three volumes of fictionalised autobiography and began writing poetry with religious themes.

SASSOON, SIEGFRIED

> **If I were fierce and bald and short of breath.**
> **I'd live with scarlet Majors at the Base,**
> **And speed glum heroes up the line to death**

Base Details

Taken from one of Sassoon's most bitter poems, these lines, and those that follow are an evocation of the staff officers, ageing, bombastic and careless of their juniors, safe and fire-breathing far behind the front line. The brief poem—ten lines – concludes 'And when the war is done and youth stone dead, / I'd toddle safely home and die – in bed.'

SASSOON, SIEGFRIED

Soldiers are citizens of death's grey land
Drawing no dividend from time's tomorrows.
Dreamers (1917)

Dreamers was written during Sassoon's stay at the Craiglockhart Hospital and published in the hospital paper. The poem points out that soldiers, even 'in the great hour of destiny', are more concerned with a world beyond the war. The dreams they have are of 'firelit homes, clean beds and wives' and of their peacetime enjoyment of sport and 'picture shows'. Sassoon, safe in his hospital confinement, dreams of them. His dreams are of 'foul dugouts, gnawed by rats, / And in the ruined trenches, lashed with rain / Dreaming of things they did...'

SASSOON, SIEGFRIED

'He's a cheerful old card', grunted Harry to Jack
As they slogged up to Arras with rifle and pack
. . .
But he did for them both with his plan of attack.
The General (1917)

Just seven lines and the ellipsis long, this is as bitter an attack on the war as any in its understated black humour. A general passes troops on their way to the line, cheerily calling 'Good-morning' to the faceless column plodding through the mud. Charitable Harry and Jack, who unlike the general, have names, consider that for an officer he's not so bad. But his bonhomie masks his tragic incompetence and 'the soldiers he smiled at are most of them dead, / And we're cursing his staff for incompetent swine'.

SATIE, ERIC (1866–1925) French composer

We must believe in luck. For how else can we explain the success of those we don't like.
quoted by Jean Cocteau in *Writers at Work*, 3rd series (1967)

Satie revealed his undoubted talent as relatively young man when he composed his *Gymnopédies* in 1888. For the next decade he sustained himself working as a café pianist, but after 1898 retired to an industrial suburb of Paris where he lived out his life in a state of self-imposed poverty. Using the same childlike simplicity and purity of form that had distinguished his earlier work, he began composing a number of strange pieces with stranger titles. In 1911 his work was discovered by Debussy and Ravel and, when he came to dominate the French avant-garde, by Jean Cocteau.

SATURDAY NIGHT AND SUNDAY MORNING

What I'm out for's a good time. All the rest is propaganda.
screenplay by Alan Sillitoe (1960)

Saturday Night and Sunday Morning was one of a crop of English films that jettisoned the middle-class respectability of such social drama as the British industry could manage in the Fifties for a plunge into the world of the hitherto, other than as stock comic figures, neglected working class. Albert Finney and Rachel Roberts starred, Karel Reisz directed, and Alan Sillitoe adapted his own novel of a Nottinghamshire factory worker who decides that if people really have never 'had it so good', then he's out for a piece of the action.

SAVIO, MARIO   American radical

There's a time when the operation of the machine becomes so odious, makes you so sick at heart, that you can't take part, that you can't even tacitly take part. And you've got to put your bodies upon the gears, and upon the wheels, upon the levers, upon all the apparatus, and you've got to make it stop. And you've got to indicate to the people who run it that unless you're free, the machine will be prevented from working at all.
speech to the Berkeley Free Speech Movement, 1964

The student rebellions of the Sixties began on the Berkeley campus of the University of California, near San Francisco. Here in 1964 began the Free Speech Movement, promoting student demands to engage in on-campus political activities. Among its leaders was Mario Savio, whose speech motivated many more towards the students' cause. By 1965, after someone had been arrested for spraying the word 'Fuck' on the steps of the Berkeley students union, free speech had turned, as far as its opponents were concerned, into filthy speech. As the decade proceeded the FSM merged into the larger struggle against the war in Vietnam, and Savio was overtaken by other, even more vocal activists.

SAYERS, DOROTHY L.   (1893–1957) British detective story writer

> As I grow older and older
> And totter towards the tomb
> I find that I care less and less
> Who goes to bed with whom.

quoted in *Such a Strange Lady* by Janet Hitchman (1975)

This neat reflection on the way age can erode one's capacity to summon up interest in the affairs of others comes from one of the century's favourite detective story writers, the creator of Lord Peter Wimsey. Sayers was an outstanding undergraduate at Oxford, devoting herself to studies of religious literature, an interest that she sustained until her death. The need to make a living forced her into working as an advertising copywriter and, in 1923, into writing the first of her Wimsey novels. Sayers' output established her at the heart of the 'Golden Age of detective fiction' and she has been called 'the greatest of living writers in the form'.

SCARGILL, ARTHUR   (1938–) British trades unionist

An idealist—that implies you aren't going to achieve something.
speaking in 1974

Scargill's pugnacious championship of the National Union of Miners, of which he is president for life, have made him simultaneously one of the best known of Britain's heroes or villains, depending on one's political stance. Appearing in the 1970s as a hard-nosed representative of the militant Yorkshire miners, Scargill built up a vocal, energetic following. Despite this support, his attempts to gamble his reputation against that of Prime Minister Margaret Thatcher were repudiated several times by the membership, who had no desire for the strike he demanded. When he did eventually persuade the faint-hearted, the union and the nation were plunged into what many saw as a battle to the death between two dogmatic individuals and one which neither could truly win.

SCHLESINGER JR., ARTHUR   (1917–) American academic

All wars are popular for the first thirty days.

Schlesinger was one of the liberal, East Coast intellectuals who President Kennedy had attracted to his team of advisors and who, among other tasks, helped write a number of Kennedy's speeches. Schlesinger, a historian, was typical of the men who found Kennedy appealing, seeing him as the first 'cerebral' president; in turn he found that they provided him with a veneer of intellectual sophistication. When commentators used the term 'Camelot' to describe the Kennedy years it was of men like Schlesinger, as well as the musicians and poets whom Kennedy liked to parade as his intimates, that they spoke.

SCHNITZLER, ARTHUR (1862–1931) Austrian writer

When we speak of the artistic temperament, we are usually referring to the sum of qualities which hinder the artist in producing.
Work and Echo

Living at the heart of the Viennese cultural and social worlds that dictated European culture prior to World War I, Schnitzler offered in his novels the most acutely observant chronicle of his times. The dominant concerns of the era were the position of the influential but unpopular Jewish bourgeoisie, ambivalent sexual standards, and the role of the army. Schnitzler's books dealt with them all, notably in *Professor Bernhardi* (1912), which dealt with the Jews, *Leutnant Gustl* (1901) which poked fun at the self-righteous military authorities, and above all *Reigen* (1903, *Merry Go Round*), a play that showed, in ten short scenes, a variety of sexual encounters that encompassed individuals taken from every level of Viennese society.

SCHULBERG, BUDD (1914–) American writer

It was right in the groove that Hollywood has been geared for, slick, swift and clever. What Kit calls the Golden Rut.
What Makes Sammy Run? (1941)

Schulberg was born a Hollywood prince, son of the producer B.P. Schulberg (1892–1957). This line comes from the story of Sammy Glick, the quintessential sharp New York Jewish boy who takes the fast track to Hollywood, riding selfishly over every obstacle, human and otherwise, and declaring vaingloriously that 'Living with a conscience is like driving a car with the brakes on.' The book's narrator, another stereotype, this one the journalist whose literary ambitions lead only to Hollywood hackery, is here criticising the latest Glick blockbuster. In 1976 actor Gene Barry, of the TV series *Burke's Law*, commented 'A year in TV is a lifetime in movies... it's the golden rut, a repetition exercise.'

SCHULTZ, CHARLES (1922–) American cartoonist

Happiness is...
catchphrase

Schultz is the inventor of Peanuts, a strip that combines a strain of 'aren't children cute' observation with a strong if never actually stated religious element, stemming from its creator's own conservative beliefs, culled from his status as a lay preacher for the fundamentalist 'Church of God' sect. *Peanuts*, for all this, is a phenomenally successful enterprise, and its Walter Mittyesque beagle Snoopy has become an iconic image as widely merchandised as Mickey Mouse. Schultz created the strip's most enduring catchphrase in 1957 when one of the characters was pictured hugging Snoopy and declaring 'Happiness is a warm puppy', a line that in itself has only intensified the merchandising.

SCHULTZ, DUTCH (1902–35) (Arthur Fliegenheimer) American gangster

Turn your back to me, please Henry, I am so sick now. The police are getting many complaints. Look out. I want that G-note. Look out for Jimmy Valentine, for he's a friend of mine. Come on, come on, Jim. OK. OK. I am all through. I can't do another thing. Look out mamma. Look out for her. Helen please take me out. I will settle the incident. Come on, open the soak duckets; the chimney sweeps. Talk to the sword. Shut up, you got a big mouth! Please help me to get up! Henry! Max! Come over here. French Canadian bean soup. I want to pay. Let them leave me alone.

quoted in *The Directory of Infamy* (1981) by Jonathon Green

Schultz, born Arthur Fliegenheimer, had in 1930 the reputation for purveying the worst, if most profitable bootleg beer in New York. His businesses were worth an annual $20 million but his fortunes declined after he had his top gunman, Jack 'Legs' Diamond (1896–1931) assassinated. Schultz' neanderthal style alienated the new 'businessmen' of the New York underworld who preferred more clandestine cash and less open warfare. He survived until 1935 when his response to crusading governor Thomas Dewey's anti-crime campaign was to order his execution. Subtler minds were appalled and Schultz, rather than Dewey, was gunned down on October 23rd by Charlie 'The Bug' Workman as he ate at supper at the Palace Chophouse in Newark, NJ. Schultz died in hospital as a confession-hungry police stenographer recorded a surreal stream of 'last words'.

SCHUMACHER, E.F. (1911–77) German economist and conservationist

Small is beautiful
book title, 1973

Schumacher gained a worldwide reputation for his book *Small Is Beautiful* in the early 1970s. Subtitled 'A Study of Economics as if

People Mattered', his book was the most accessible version yet of the theory that society should relinquish its dependence on industries that destroyed the world's ecology and environment. Unlike earlier campaigners, whose fringe status made it easy for governments to dismiss them as cranks, Schumacher's involvement with the highest levels of government planning meant that he commanded real attention. As he put it 'Any intelligent fool can make things bigger, more complex and more violent. It takes a touch of genius, and a lot of courage, to move in the opposite direction.'

SCHWEITZER, ALBERT (1875–1965) German theologian, physician and musician

Man is a clever animal who behaves like an imbecile.

Schweitzer gained three doctorates – in medicine, philosophy and theology – and all these disciplines can be seen in the contradictory life of a man categorised equally as an idealistic fool and one of the century's saints. In 1913 he abandoned what seemed like a glittering future to work as a doctor in Lambarene, an inhospitable village in French Equatorial Africa. There his main task was the provision of basic medical help to Africans who would otherwise have received none, although he continued to write and to travel abroad to exhibit his other talent, the playing of the organ. Schweitzer was awarded the Nobel Peace Prize in 1952 and while his critics disdained the choice, no-one could deny that he remained in every respect loyal to his central philosophy: 'reverence for life'.

SCORSESE, MARTIN (1942–) American film director

You don't make up for your sins in church. You do it at home and you do it in the streets. And the rest is bullshit and you know that.
Mean Streets (1973)

Pauline Kael called Scorsese's third film, *Mean Streets* 'a true original and a triumph of personal film-making' and in this story of growing up tough and crazy in New York's Little Italy, the director achieved a balance and a depth of feeling that he has never repeated. Apart from the script, the camerawork and the subtle interpolation of rock music, the film provided the first major role for Robert de Niro (1943–), who has since starred in a succession of Scorsese movies. This declaration serves as a preface to the film, delivered as a voice-over by Scorsese himself.

SCOTT, C.P.   (1846–1932) British journalist

Comment is free, but facts are sacred.
signed editiorial in *Manchester Guardian*, May 5 1921

Scott was appointed editor of the provincial *Manchester Guardian* in 1872, when the former weekly, founded in 1821, was still restricted very much to Mancunian affairs. Scott began writing editorials that came to the notice of influential London politicians, particularly those of the Liberal party, with whom he chose to identify the paper. By World War I the paper had gained a substantial reputation, recruiting major writers, influencing the prime minister Lloyd George and campaigning for a variety of issues – for Zionism, women's suffrage and Irish freedom and against the Boer war – dear to its editor's heart, but always governed strictly by his favourite dictum.

SCOTT, ROBERT FALCON   (1868–1912) British polar explorer

Had we lived, I should have had a tale to tell of the hardihood, endurance and courage of my companions which would have stirred the heart of every Englishman. These rough notes and our dead bodies must tell the tale.
diary entry March 1912

Scott's first journey to the Antarctic, as commander of the National Antarctic Expedition between 1901–04, penetrated further into the area than any previous exploration. He returned in 1910, determined to reach the Pole. He duly arrived on January 18, 1912, only to discover that the Norwegian Roald Amundsen had arrived there a month earlier, leaving his tent and his national flag. The return journey was plagued by exceptionally bad weather and the gradually deteriorating health of Scott's party. His diary traces their last desperate steps as one by one they died of exposure. The final entry reads 'It seems a pity but I do not think I can write more. R. SCOTT. For God's sake look after our people'.

SEEGER, PETE   (1919–) American folk singer

Do you know the difference between education and experience? Education is when you read the fine print; experience is what you get when you don't.
quoted in *Loose Talk*, ed. L. Botts (1980)

Pete Seeger is well-known as the composer of many modern folk music standards, beloved of the world's singalongs and hootenannies. The son of an ethnomusicologist, he dropped out of Harvard after he visited a North Carolina folk festival and determined to devote his life to the music. He picked up tips from such major figures as Woody Guthrie and Leadbelly before founding The Weavers in 1949 and then going solo in the Fifties. A pillar of modern folk music, Seeger has been a staple of most of the post-war protest movements, although the young people who joined him on the march tended to gravitate to harder-edged performers. He remains 'the Johnny Appleseed of folksong' and 'America's tuning-fork'.

SELLERS, PETER   (1925–980) British actor and comedian

There used to be a me, but I had it surgically removed.
in *Time magazine*, 1980

Sellers started his performing career as an impressionist, with a variety act called 'Speaking for the Stars'. He obtained his first BBC role by ringing up producer Roy Speer and pretending to be two of the corporation's then top stars Kenneth Horne and Richard Murdoch. His real breakthrough came with the *Goon Show*, a subversive barrage of crazy humour which starred Sellers, Harry Secombe, Spike Milligan and Michael Bentine (previously billed as 'The Happy Imbecile'). Sellers followed the Goons with a film career that in the Fifties amd Sixties made him one of Britain's best-loved comedians, but his career declined in the seventies: nobody seemed able to write a suitable script. Asked the inevitable 'Where's the real Peter Sellers?' he replied with a typical joke, but as critic John Simon mourned 'One regrets his inability to add to his list of impressions the Peter Sellers that was'.

SELLERS, PETER

People will swim through shit if you put a few bob in it.
after starring in *The Magic Christian* (1969).

Terry Southern, of *Candy* fame, had written *Dr. Strangelove*, Sellers' best film, and in 1968 Sellers starred in *The Magic Christian*, a film based on Southern's eponymous short novel. The plot revolves around the efforts of the multi-millionaire 'Guy Grand' to plumb the depths of human foolishness and greed. After exploiting the hapless public with a number of tricks and deceptions, Grand climaxes his vicious amusements by preparing an enormous vat, heated by vast gas burners and filled with thousands of gallons of slaughterhouse offal and animal excrement. Into this vile stew he stirs hundreds of thousands of dollars. The public, just as debased as Grand hoped, fight their way through boiling ordure to grab the free money. The film was a failure, a mismash of tacky psychedelia, a pop score and Ringo Starr. Sellers did himself no good and his comment was tinged with genuine bitterness.

SELZNICK, DAVID O. (1902-65) American film magnate

There are only two classes: first class and no class.'
in *Memo from David O. Selznick* (1972)

Selznick was born into Hollywood, the son of producer Lewis Selznick. He was a humourless figure, given to driving his employees hard, peppering them with extensive detailed memoranda and loath to relinquish his control of every aspect of a film. His strong point, epitomised in this comment, was his commitment to what he saw as right, notably his investment of enormous extra sums in *Gone With The Wind* (1939), a film that was already vastly over budget but which required even more money to attain Selznick's standards of perfection and, which, of course, duly justified his faith.

SEVENTY-SEVEN SUNSET STRIP

Kookie, lend me your comb.
American TV show, 1958–63

77 Sunset Strip was a television cop show which improved on the usual format by offering something, or rather someone for the teenagers, a consumer force to be indulged in advertising-dominated US television. Ed Byrnes (1933–) played the cleaned up juvenile delinquent 'Kookie', whose main role was to talk in yesterday's beatnik slang and comb his hair. It was all very hip, if slightly dated, and Kookie was a major role model for the less sophisticated. His hair, unlike his language, was right up to date, a luscious oil-encrusted pompadour, spilling creamily over his forehead and subject to the endless ministrations of his omnipresent comb. 'Kookie, lend me your comb' became the show's catchphrase and in 1960 Byrnes and singer Connie Stevens recorded a song that used the line for its title.

SHANE

A man's gotta do what a man's gotta do
screenplay by A.B. Guthrie, Jr. (1953)

The line should be big John Wayne's but in fact, as much as anyone said it, it was diminutive Alan Ladd, playing Shane, the eponymous hero of this Western that turns, as Pauline Kael puts it 'the Western stranger in town... into Galahad on the range'. Ladd rides into town to side with the 'little people' against their oppressor, Jack Palance. His good deeds done, Ladd rides off into the proverbial sunset, accompanied only by the child star Brandon de Wilde's plaintive cry of 'Shane!'. As far as the quoted line is concerned, the nearest Ladd approached it was to say 'A man has to be what he is, Joey'. A woman character gets nearer with 'Shane did what he had to do', but a perfect facsimile remains elusive.

SHANKLY, BILL   (1918–1981) British soccer manager

Some people think football is a matter of life and death. I don't like the attitude. I can assure them it is much more serious than that.
quoted in 1973

Shankly, generally known to the adoring fans of his phenomenally successful Liverpool Football Club as 'Shanks', was Britain's answer to such American sports coaches as Vince Lombardi or Woody Hayes, a hard-nosed, single-minded slave-driver, with the requisite heart of gold, for whom victory on the soccer pitch was the most important thing. The less committed might have assumed that Shankly's avowal was perhaps a joke, but those who knew better were under no such illusion.

SHAW, GEORGE BERNARD   Irish essayist, playwright and critic

Not bloody likely!
Pygmalion (1913)

Pygmalion concerns the turning of a sow's ear, the flower girl Eliza Doolittle into a silk purse, or at least an imitation English duchess, by the phonetician Henry Higgins. The play caused much concern on its London first night when the Daily Sketch asked its readers 'Mr. Shaw introduces a certain forbidden word. WILL MRS. PATRICK CAMPBELL SPEAK IT?' The word was 'bloody' and occurred when the remodelled Eliza, after a successful entry into Society, tells a young man who asks her whether she will be walking across the Park 'Not bloody likely! I'm going in a taxi.' The first performance was duly greeted with the hiss of indrawn breath, but subsequent audiences only laughed, often quite hysterically. The larger public veered between condescension and the usual fit of British morality. As Shaw said 'By making a fashionable actress use bad language in a fashionable theatre, I became overnight more famous than the Pope, the King, the Kaiser and the Archbishop of Canterbury'.

SHAW, GEORGE BERNARD

What is virtue but the Trades Unionism of the married?
Man and Superman (1903)

Man and Superman was Shaw's first theatrical hit. It tells how Ann Whitfield, respresenting Everywoman, pursues Jack Tanner, the personification of Anti-Marriage. Tanner does not even like her but unlike all the other characters he manages after a struggle to see through her mask of self-sacrifice and eventually succumbs to her and the 'life-force'. Shaw's polemic states that marriage is essential to produce the Superman and that the 'life-force' is the instrument of this end. At the end of the play Tanner announces that as soon as he and Ann are married they intend to sell their presents and use the profits to circulate copies of the 'Revolutionists' handbook'. Although the audience have to take this on trust, the handbook is included at the end of the published playscript. It combines a selection of Shaw's current political thought, and a collection of aphorisms: 'Maxims for Revolutionists'.

SHAW, GEORGE BERNARD

Comstockery
speaking in New York, 1905

Anthony Comstock (1844–1915) had been, since 1872, America's self-appointed anti-vice crusader. By 1905, when a New York theatre put on Shaw's play *Mrs. Warren's Profession*, Comstock was in his declining years and indeed, there seemed to be little 'vice' left unscourged. He seized on Shaw's work, condemning it roundly. Unlike Comstock's fellow-Americans, many of whom still seemed willing to take him seriously, Shaw found the whole topic hilarious and told the American press 'Comstockery is the world's standing joke, at the expense of the United States. Europe likes to hear of such things. It confirms the deep-seated conviction of the Old World that America is a provincial place, a second-rate country-town civilization after all.' Comstock was furious, but the play went on and Shaw had coined a new adjective.

SHAW, GEORGE BERNARD

England and America are two countries separated by the same language
attributed remark

As with a number of well-known remarks that enter the language with no particular provenance, quote collectors tend to compile a list of the best potential originators and plump for a possible candidate. This particular remark stresses the vast differences between the world's two major English-speaking countries, which goes far beyond the fact that Americans spell a-u-t-u-m-n as f-a-l-l. Some have chosen Oscar Wilde, but the vote seems on balance to go to Bernard Shaw. On the other hand, given that H.L. Mencken was the most vociferous proponent of the gulf between American and English English, it might equally well have been his line.

SHAW, GEORGE BERNARD

When a stupid man is doing something he is ashamed of, he always declares that it is his duty.
Caesar and Cleopatra (1907)

In this play, which might be seen as a preface to Shakespeare's *Antony and Cleopatra*, Shaw traces the story of the relationship between the young Egyptian queen and the Roman general. We see how he restores her to her throne; how, during the Egyptian revolt in Alexandria she went to him wrapped in a carpet; how she had her brother's guardian killed and how revenge was taken on her own servant; and finally, how as Caesar left he promised to send Mark Antony.

SHAW, GEORGE BERNARD

I'm only a beer teetotaller, not a champagne teetotaller.
Candida (1895)

Candida, one of Shaw's 'Pleasant Plays', concerns the Reverend James Morell, his wife Candida, and their young protégé the poet Eugene Marchbanks. Marchbanks is in love with Candida and, after telling the vicar of his feelings, challenges him to tell his wife and allow her to choose between the two men. Morell finds this idea terrifying, but in the end he does as the poet asks. Candida announces that 'I give myself to the weaker of the two'. Marchbanks, who has 'learnt to live without happiness', realises that he has lost his gamble and leaves the house.

SHAW, GEORGE BERNARD

The trouble, Mr Goldwyn, is that you are only interested in art and I am only interested in money.
declining to sell MGM the rights to his plays

Hollywood mogul Samuel Goldwyn, who once remarked that he would hire the Devil himself 'if he'd write me a good story', once attempted to obtain the film rights to Shaw's plays for his company MGM. He based his pitch on his belief that an intellectual such as Shaw would like to hear about MGM's cultural standards, the way in which his works would be transformed faithfully, and so on. Shaw, who had no desire to see his plays on film, teased Goldwyn by pretending to take him at his word but admitting, shame-facedly no doubt, that while the mogul was really a frustrated artist, he, the supposed intellectual, was actually desperate for wealth. Goldwyn retired defeated.

SHAW, GEORGE BERNARD

Martyrdom is the only way in which a man can become famous without ability.
Fabian Essays (1908)

Fabian Essays is the collection of Shaw's early political prose. 'Swept,' as he put it, 'into the great socialist revival' of the early 1880s, he was elected to the newly formed Fabian Society in 1884 and subsequently served on its committee and wrote its manifesto. The Society, named for the Roman Quintus Fabius Maximus, nicknamed Cunctator or 'delayer', embraced a form of socialism devoted to gradual reform from within the Establishment rather than instant, violent revolution.

SHAW, GEORGE BERNARD

Physically there is nothing to distinguish human society from the farm-yard except that children are more troublesome and costly than chickens and women are not so completely enslaved as farm stock.
Getting Married (1908)

Shaw uses this play to discuss the institution of marriage within a framework of farce. The bishop's daughter is getting married and friends and relations are gathering. However the young couple are reading through a pamphlet that sets out the law on marriage and when they have finished they announce that they flatly refuse to proceed with the wedding. The whole company plunges into a discussion of marriage and tries to draw up some form of private contract that will satisfy the young people. They, in turn, refuse to be satisfied by anything. A general realignment of relationships follows, after which the couple announce that after all they have been married, by the beadle, and their doubts have been resolved by the general discussion.

SHAW, GEORGE BERNARD

Alcohol is a very necessary article.... It enables Parliament to do things at eleven at night that no sane person would do at eleven in the morning.
Major Barbara (1907)

Major Barbara concerns the millionaire arms manufacturer Andrew Undershaft and his daughter Barbara, who has expressed her disapproval of his occupation by joining the Salvation Army. She is helped there by her fiancé, Adolphus Cusins, an impoverished but learned professor of Greek. Undershaft tells his daughter that he wishes her to take over the business, saying that the Salvationists' motto 'Blood and Fire' could well be his own. He agrees to visit her shelter and she to visit the factory. Barbara becomes disillusioned with the Army when the shelter accepts a large donation from a whiskey distiller and, in her view, sells out to 'Drunkenness and Murder'. Undershaft persuades her that by giving employment to poor men he too is a humanitarian, since no matter what the men produce poverty remains the greatest crime of all. Barbara and Cusins agree to take over the firm.

SHAW, GEORGE BERNARD

The word morality, if we met it in the Bible, would surprise us as much as the word telephone or motor-car.
preface to *Fanny's First Play* (1911)

Fanny's First Play uses the 'play within a play' device and is described by Shaw in its preface as a 'potboiler'. In this preface he puts forward the view that 'nowadays we do not seem to know that there is any other conduct except morality' and advises the young to go and do something bad so that in that way they can gain some first-hand knowledge of the difference between good and evil, as opposed to the morality that is simply passed down to them.

SHAW, GEORGE BERNARD

I have a technical objection to making sexual infatuation a tragic theme. Experience proves that it is only effective in the comic spirit.
preface to *Three Plays for Puritans* (1900)

Shaw is discussing the nature and content of the contemporary theatre. As in all his prefaces, which used to put forward his own polemics, he sets himself up as the playwright of the thinking, rather than the emotional man, writing plays that present the conflict of ideas rather than of love, passion or similar feelings. He uses the stage as an arena for his opinions and his plays are in the end dramatised discussions, hugely enlivened by his own wit.

SHAW, GEORGE BERNARD

Fashions, after all, are only induced epidemics.
The Doctor's Dilemma (1913)

In *The Doctor's Dilemma* Dr. Ridgeon is forced to choose which of two patients to save from death and which to let die. He has just been knighted for his discovery of a cure for consumption but has insufficient quantities of serum for all. The patients in question are an artist, Louis Dubedat, an amusing blackguard, and Blenkinsop, an insignificant but worthy East End doctor. Mrs Dubedat pleads her husband's case, and Ridgeon, who has fallen in love with her, is torn. His problems are solved when a fellow-surgeon agrees to treat the artist and Ridgeon duly cures Blenkinsop. Dubedat's treatment fails and he dies, but when Ridgeon declares his love for his widow she tells him that she has already remarried.

SHAW, GEORGE BERNARD

An Englishman does everything on principle: he fights you on patriotic principles; he robs you on business principles; he enslaves you on imperial principles.
The Man of Destiny (1907)

The Man of Destiny is Napoleon and the play concerns his encounter with a strange lady during the Italian campaign of 1796. It appears that the strange lady, after disguising herself as a boy, has stolen dispatches and letters from Napoleon's lieutenant, her reason being so to secure a love-letter that has been written by a woman friend of hers to an official whom Napoleon knows. What follows is a battle of wills and cunning over the possession of the letter, in which the balance of power shifts dramatically. This particular line is spoken by Napoleon, trying to work out the lady's nationality and assuming that she must be English because of the particular methods she is employing to get her way.

SHAW, GEORGE BERNARD

The fickleness of the women whom I love is only equalled by the infernal constancy of the women who love me.
The Philanderer (1893)

Shaw's play centres on the charming and attractive Leonard Charteris, the philanderer of the title, a character the author based on his own amatory adventuring of the period. Charteris is carrying on simultaneous affairs with two women, Grace and Julia, and they each discover the other's existence. Although Leonard has been behaving as if he intends to marry each of them, the truth is that he wishes to marry neither. Eventually Julia finds an alternative husband and Grace decides that she is far better off remaining single.

SHAW, GEORGE BERNARD

Assassination is the extreme form of censorship.
The Shewing Up of Blanco Posnet (1916)

Shaw called this one-act play 'a Sermon in Crude Melodrama'. It is set in the courtroom in the American 'Wild West' and concerns Blanco, a rogue, who runs off with his brother's horse in repayment for a debt but after meeting a woman with a dying child lends her the horse. Thus deprived of his mount, he is caught up with by a pursuing posse and arrested as a horse thief. The child dies. As the trial proceeds it appears that the 'bad guy' Blanco has been shown up as a 'goodie' who has gone soft. He then experiences a courtroom conversion and launches into a sermon on the nature of good and evil, claiming that the Lord made a job for him and 'I had to come along and do it'. The judge acquits him.

SHAW, GEORGE BERNARD

A pessimist is a man who thinks everybody is as nasty as himself and hates them for it.

SHAW, GEORGE BERNARD

Self-denial is not a virtue: it is only the effect of prudence on rascality.
Man and Superman (1903)

SHAW, GEORGE BERNARD

The more things a man is ashamed of, the more respectable he is.
Man and Superman (1903)

SHAW, GEORGE BERNARD

Revolutions have never lightened the burden of tyranny, they have only shifted it to another shoulder.
Man and Superman (1903)

SHAW, GEORGE BERNARD

Democracy substitutes election by the incompetent many for appointment by the corrupt few.
Man and Superman (1903)

SHAW, GEORGE BERNARD

Liberty means responsibility, that is why most men dread it.
Man and Superman (1903)

SHAW, GEORGE BERNARD

Do not unto others as they should do unto you – their tastes may not be the same.
Man and Superman: Maxims for Revolutionists (1903)

SHAW, GEORGE BERNARD

A drama critic is a man who leaves no turn unstoned.
quoted in the *New York Times*, 1950

SHAWCROSS, HARTLEY (1902–) British politician

We are the masters now.
challenging the defeated Tories, April 2 1946

Shawcross's comment came as he was winding up the debate of the third reading of the Trade Disputes and Trade Unions Bill. Noting that the Conservative opposition were attacking a measure that they once promised to institute themselves, he quoted Lewis Carroll's *Alice in Wonderland*: ' "When I use a word," said Humpty-Dumpty, "it means just what I intend it to mean, and neither more nor less." "But," said Alice, "the question is whether you can make a word mean different things." "Not so," said Humpty-Dumpty, "the question is which is to be the master. That's all." ' Shawcross then told the House 'We are the masters at the moment, and not only at the moment, but for a very long time to come, and as hon. members opposite are not prepared to implement the pledge which was given by their leader in regard to this matter at the General Election, we are going to implement it for them.' The bragging substitution of 'now' for 'at the moment' was not in fact Shawcross' own, but from Churchill who commented in 1950 after the Labour Party had lost much of their landslide majority of 1945 'No one will be able to boast "We are the masters now".'

SHELTON, GILBERT   American cartoonist

Dope can see you through times of no money better than money can see you through times of no dope.
the Fabulous Furry Freak Brothers motto

Still to be found on T-shirts and badges, twenty years after it was a popular hippie slogan, this marijuana-extolling line was coined by Gilbert Shelton, one of the most popular of America's 'underground' cartoonists. His strip *The Fabulous Furry Freak Brothers* (plus the indispensable sidebar *Fat Freddy's Cat*) brought domesticity to the alternative society with its regular delineation of the home life of three hippies: Fat Freddy, Phineas and Freewheelin' Franklin. Drugs, of all sorts, were their staple, and most of the strips concerned their attempts to obtain new varieties of mind-benders, but the strip in its own way was as homely as *Blondie* or *The Gambols*.

SHOR, TOOTS   (1903–197?) American saloon keeper

Anybody that can't get drunk by midnight ain't trying.
quoted in 1950

Shor was one of New York's legendary saloon keepers, whose tavern entertained everyone who saw themselves as a hard-drinking man about New York. In an era before New York succumbed to jogging, health foods and similar forms of narcissistic self-denial the idea of getting drunk was far from reprehensible and Shor encouraged his patrons enthusiastically.

SILONE, IGNAZIO   (1900–70) Italian radical and novelist

No one can ever write about anything that happened to him after he was twelve years old.
in 1963

Silone was among the founder members of the Italian Communist Party in 1921 and struggled constantly against Fascist attacks. In 1931, in temporary exile, he resigned from the Party, realising that it was not the easy cure-all for social injustices, and after his return to Italy in 1944 pursued his political ambitions as a Christian Socialist. Although Silone claims that twelve is a cutoff date for the novelist, his own experiences in losing both parents in an earthquake when he was aged 15, and in the social upheavals created by World War I and by Fascist rule, all bulk largely in his work.

SILONE, IGNAZIO

A dictatorship is a regime in which the people quote instead of thinking.
The School for Dictators (1939)

Silone's political consciousness was largely formed during the years of Fascist ascendancy in Italy. Totalitarian governments of left and right depend on sloganeering rather than on argument and as he points out, once such a government is in power, its constant use of easily assimilated lines means that the population soon begin coming out with them. That such slogans gradually erode the power of more reasoned political thought is Silone's contention. One slogan, irrespective of ideology, has much the same effect as another: the people forget to think for themselves.

SIMPSON, N.F.   (1919–) British dramatist

Life... a man trying to get a partially inflated rubber lilo into a suitcase slightly too small to take it even when uninflated.
quoted in *Contemporary Dramatists* (1977)

This satisfyingly absurd definition of the human condition comes from Britain's chief representative of the surreal imagery of the Theatre of the Absurd and one who has been compared with Ionesco. Simpson's plays, with their placing of inspired nonsense in a domestic setting, established him as a unique figure in the English theatre but he has not produced anything since these works enjoyed their original popularity.

SINGER, ISAAC BASHEVIS   (1904–) Polish-Jewish writer

You have to treat death like any other part of life.
The Family Moskat (1950)

Singer is the son and grandson of Polish rabbis and the younger brother of the novelists Israel Joshua Singer (1893–1944) and Esther Kreitman (1891–1954). Singer broke away from religious orthodoxy, although not from his deeply Jewish sensibility, and emigrated to New York in 1935. Here he worked for the Yiddish-language newspaper the *Daily Forward*, where he published most of his short stories. *The Family Moskat* is his first novel, and it highlights the concerns that echo throughout his work: the contrast of religious feeling and sceptical inquiry, of the instinctual and the intellectual, and the presence of the mystic and supernatural, all set against the Polish-Jewish background of his youth. He was awarded the Nobel Prize for Literature in 1978.

SINGER, ISAAC BASHEVIS

Every creator painfully experiences the chasm between his inner vision, and its ultimate expression. The chasm is never completely bridged. We all have the conviction, perhaps illusory, that we have much more to say than appears on the paper.
Esquire, 1974

Singer's own work mirrors his concern with the near-impossibility of making one's writing reveal everything that is in one's head. The extent to which the creator bridges the chasm between the brain and the blank sheet of paper is the extent to which he or she is considered a gifted artist. One needs the inner vision in the first place, but no-one who has read Singer's intensely vivid evocations of the spiritual and the strange would deny his ability in that area.

SINGER, ISAAC BASHEVIS

Yiddish is sick – but in our history between being sick and dying is a long, long way.
interviewed on BBC-TV, 1980

Yiddish, the colloquial language of European Jews, flourished for centuries as a spoken rather than a written language, before it began producing an impressive body of literature, all developing between the mid-19th century and the Nazi Holocaust. As Singer has also pointed out, it is the only language never to be spoken by those in power and, according to Leo Rosten, it is the 'Robin Hood of languages, stealing from the linguistically rich to give to the fledgling poor'. The decimation of European Jewry and the assimilation of many of their children has drastically reduced the number of Yiddish speakers, although the language itself can be found in substantial, if slightly adulterated quantities, in colloquial English and American. However, as its finest contemporary literary exponent makes clear, for the language as well as its speakers, there's a long way between illness and death.

SINYAVSKY, ANDREI   (1925–) Russian dissident author

How impossible to describe life! How shameless of literature to poke its nose in everywhere! How can you use a pen to describe – blood!
A Voice from the Chorus (1973)

Sinyavsky was one of Russia's better young writers in the Sixties, whose desire to put down what he felt rather than what ideology claimed that he ought led him to publish his book *Lubimov* outside Russia. The result of this was his arrest in September 1965, along with Yuli Daniel, another young author, whose own novels had also appeared abroad. The books only poked fun at the Moscow establishment and the press, but the two authors were charged with publishing anti-Soviet propaganda abroad. They were tried in February 1966, in the first literary show trial since Stalin's days. Despite petitions from inside Russia and from the West the two men were found guilty. Daniel and Sinyavsky received sentences of seven and five years in labour camps.

SITWELL, OSBERT (1892–1969) British man of letters

The greedy man has ever accomplished, I apprehend, more good in this world than all those sinister individuals put together who openly boast, lean and sallow men that they are, how they do not care what they eat so long as it comes out of a tin.
introduction to *Lady Sysonby's Cookbook* (1935)

Osbert Sitwell, the brother of Dame Edith (1887-1964) and Sacheverell Sitwell (1897–) was one of a gifted if sometimes eccentric trio of artistic, aristocratic children born to Sir George Sitwell of Renishaw Hall, Derbyshire. Like his brother and sister he wrote poetry, abandoning the traditionalist Georgians for stringent modernism. Although the critic F.R. Leavis disposed of the Sitwells as belonging to 'the history of publicity rather than that of poetry', Osbert wrote a number of volumes of poetry, a novel, some travel books and his crowning achievement, his autobiography, which appeared in six volumes between 1945–62.

SKELTON, RED (1910–) American comedian

It proves what they say, give the public what they want to see and they'll come out for it.
surveying the funeral of Hollywood mogul, Harry Cohn, 1958

The hatred that the average Hollywood magnate seems to have inspired in his employees is summed up by Skelton's comment on the funeral of one of the most loathed of all, Harry Cohn (1891–1958), the ex-song plugger who created his own studio, Columbia Pictures, allegedly after selling a picture called *Traffic in Souls* in 1924. Cohn revelled in his image, boasting 'I don't have ulcers, I give them' and 'If I wasn't head of a studio, who would talk to me?' Leslie Halliwell, compiler of many Hollywood quotations, gives the line to Skelton and the funeral to Cohn, but it has also been cited as the remark Samuel Goldwyn made, when attending his former partner Louis B. Mayer's well-attended obsequies in 1957.

SKINNER, B.F. (1904–) American psychologist

One of the advantages of education is simply coming to the end of it.
The Technology of Teaching

Burrhus Frederic Skinner taught at Harvard from 1948 to 1975. Skinner's version of psychology is to subordinate the discussion of internal feelings to his own theories of behaviourism, whereby human behaviour can be controlled by rewarding desired changes and failing to reinforce those that are not desired. In 1953 he began adapting his techniques to education, generating a systems of programmed learning. Skinner has been highly influential but simple control can never equal understanding and while his systems are useful, they may also threaten humanity's more subtle responses.

SKINNER, B.F.

Society attacks early when the individual is helpless.

SKINNER, B.F.

Education is what survives when what has been learnt has been forgotten.
quoted in *New Scientist* magazine, 1964

SKINNER, CORNELIA OTIS (1901–1979) American actress

Woman's virtue is man's greatest invention.
quoted in *The Wit of Women*, by L. and M. Cowan

Skinner, the daughter of the tragedian Otis Skinner, specialised in stage monologue, written by herself and involving a number of characters. Her comment reflects the double standard of male and female sexuality, as invented by men and still practised by many women. Men are almost expected to live a life of seductions and sexual adventuring; women are not, and are condemned if they do. Women's supposed virtue is convenient to men in that it permits them to indulge themselves, presumably with women who are not virtuous, while their 'better half' has no option but to sit demurely at home.

SLOGAN

Better Red than dead

During the era which combined anti-Communist witch-hunting with America's development of the atomic and then the nuclear bomb, one of the favourite slogans of the hard-right advocates of militant Americanism was 'Better dead than red'. Liberals simply reversed this to provide their own counter-slogan, which some authorities, notably Alexander Solzhenitsyn, think may have been coined by Bertrand Russell.

SLOGAN

Tinker to Evers to Chance

Tinker-to-Evers-to-Chance is a phrase synonymous with baseball's 'double play', a move whereby a combination of throws dismisses two of the batting team as they run around the bases. Joe Tinker (1880–1948), the shortstop, Johnny Evers (1881–1947), the second baseman, and Frank Chance (1877–1924), the first baseman played for the Chicago Cubs between 1906–10. So identified was the trio with the double play that many fans assumed they had invented it. In fact they only achieved 54 double-plays in their joint career. Ironically they could barely stand each other off the field and spoke on it as rarely as possible. The phrase was immortalised in columnist Franklin P. Adams' *Baseball's Sad Lexicon*, published 1910 and reflecting the Bears' regular trouncing of the New York Giants: 'These are the saddest of possible words, / Tinker to Evers to Chance. / Trio of bear cubs and fleeter than birds, / Tinker to Evers to Chance. / Ruthlessly pricking our gonfalon bubble, / Making a Giant hit into a double. / Words that are weighty with nothing but trouble, / Tinker to Evers to Chance.'

SLOGAN

Careless Talk Costs Lives
used in World War II

Careless Talk Costs Lives was one of the longest lasting of the slogans that the government put out in an attempt to persuade people not to betray the war effort through foolish, if innocent gossip. Illustrated by the popular *Punch* cartoonist Fougasse, posters portrayed people of all classes engaged in idle chatter while Hitler, disguised as a painting or as a wallpaper design, listened in. A similar slogan, 'Walls Have Ears', used a long-popular phrase to achieve the same effect.

SLOGAN

Beer is best

This slogan, originated for the general use of brewers in the Thirties, may, according Eric Partidge's *Dictionary of Catchphrases*, have come from G.K. Chesterton's poem *The Secret People*. One of Chesterton's impassioned evocations of things British, the poem suggests that 'It may be that we are meant to mark with our riot and our rest / God's scorn for all men governing. It may be beer is best'.

SLOGAN

Burn, baby, burn!

'Burn, baby, burn' started life as a joke, popularised circa 1964 by the black disk jockey Magnificient Montague and bearing sexual rather than revolutionary connotations. Fans shouted it at singers and musicians, encouraging them to put everything into their performances. As the Sixties moved on and America's cities exploded into racial violence and the black ghettos burnt in the 'long hot summers' of 1966–68, the phrase took on a more sinister meaning, with real, rather than metaphoric flames at its heart.

SLOGAN

Keep on truckin'

'Keep on trucking' originated in the American dance marathons of the Thirties when the contestants used the black slang word 'trucking' to imply continuous movement, analogous to that of the trucks that plied America's interstate highways. By the Sixties it had become a popular salutation among the hippies, even to the extent of signing their letters with it, a counterculture version of 'yours sincerely'. Its most abiding use was as the caption to underground cartoonist Robert Crumb's picture of monster-sneakered figures, striding endlessly into space.

SLOGAN

A funny thing happened to me...

Comedians have been using this as their entry line for decades and the precise origin remains shrouded in the theatre's past. The best known use of the phrase since World War II was in its revised version as '*A Funny Thing Happened To me On The Way To The Forum*', a popular musical first staged in 1962 and based on the farces of Plautus and Terence. The key figure, the slave

Lurcio, was played in New York by Zero Mostel and in London by Frankie Howerd.

Slogan

If it's Tuesday, this must be Belgium

This phrase originated as the title of a film comedy that appeared in 1969 and concerned the adventures of a group of American tourists as they hurtled on their culture grabbing way around too many European cities in too few days. The link with such tours remains, but it is used by touring rock bands, shuttling diplomats, self-promoting authors and similarly mobile figures.

Slogan

The Lost Generation

The Lost Generation referred both to those who had died in World War I and to those who, either through good fortune or simply being too young to fight, had survived the slaughter. When novelist Rose Macaulay used the phrase in *Staying With Relations* (1930), she was referring to the young men who died, especially those golden youths of the upper classes, whose apparently idyllic futures had been cut abruptly short. Conversely when Ernest Hemingway used the phrase 'You are all a lost generation' as an epigraph to *The Sun Also Rises* (1926), attributing it to 'Gertrude Stein in conversation', he was referring to those who had not fought but, utterly disillusioned by the War, were seen as having abandoned traditional values and failed to find any replacements, other than ceaseless, pointless hedonism.

Slogan

Daddy, what did you do in the Great War?
caption to poster in World War I

Among the most pernicious slogans used to seduce young, and not so young men to the trenches, was this line, which served as a caption to a poster of a small girl perching on the knee of her civilian-suited father who from the look on his face had probably rejoiced in a reserved occupation. The serving troops hated the poster, using its questioning moppet as the vehicle for a multitude of ribald replies.

Slogan

Up there, Cazaly!
in Australian Rules Football

SLOGAN

This popular Australian exhortation, encouraging its subject to greater effort, refers to Roy Cazaly (1893–1962), an Australian Rules footballer of the early 1920s whose high-marking for the South Melbourne team was especially noteworthy, despite the fact that Cazaly stood (short by his sport's standards) only 5'11" and weighed just 12.5 stone. The cry itself was first uttered by one of Cazaly's fellow players, 'Skeeter' Fleiter, and soon taken up by the crowd. The phrase entered the Australian language and even formed the key line of a song.

SLOGAN

If it moves, salute it; if it don't, paint it
in British and American forces

This summary of the private soldier's best policy when faced with any manifestation of army rules and regulations, was popular during World War II and afterwards, especially among British national servicemen. It had a number of variations, all of which boiled down to the same thing. They included 'If you can lift it, carry it; if you can't lift it, paint it; and if it moves by itself, salute it' and the extension of the basic phrase which adds 'if you can't paint it, fuck it!'

SLOGAN

The man you love to hate
on Eric von Stroheim in *'The Heart of Humanity'*, 1918

Eric von Stroheim (1885–1957) epitomised the stiff-necked, be-monocled Prussian stereotype, even though he was Austrian, not German. In Hollywood's devotedly anti-German propaganda picture The *Heart of Humanity*, Stroheim pulled out every stop, climaxing his affront to American values when, attempting to rape an innocent victim, he pauses only to snatch her squalling infant from its cot and toss it carelessly through an open window before returning, eyes glittering with lust, to his Hunnish beastliness. The studio, equally unrestrained, paraded these excesses with the slogan 'The man you love to hate'.

SLOGAN

Safety first
used by the Conservative Party, 1922–29

The use as a Tory party slogan of Safety First, hitherto best known for its popularisation of the policy of London's public transport firms, is possibly the first instance of an advertising agency being used to boost a party's image. The party chairman, J.C.C. Davidson, was offered the idea by the agency S.H. Benson, then London's largest. Davidson touted the phrase to his leader Stanley Baldwin, and in addition plastered the country with a poster of Baldwin, looking as avuncular as the camera could manage, to rub the slogan in. Baldwin loathed the whole campaign, and lost the election. Davidson was sacked.

SLOGAN

Today...Tomorrow the World!
used by the German National Socialist Press

For all its filmic popularity, this phrase was not merely a stereotype, but did originate in Nazi Germany. It began as a slogan for the Nazi press of the early Thirties, proclaiming 'Heute Presse der national-sozialisten, Morgen Presse der Nation' (Today the press of the Nazis, tomorrow the press of the nation). The idea caught on and climaxed with the Party's boast 'Heute gehort uns Deutschland – morgen die ganze Welt!' (Today Germany belongs to us, tomorrow the whole world). It remains in common use, though only in a mocking way and often delivered in a cod-Nazi accent.

SLOGAN

Be like dad, keep mum
used by the Ministry of Information, 1941

The use of 'mum' to mean silence, derived from the 'mmmmm' noise one might make through tightly closed lips, dates back to the mid-16th century, but this particular pun, exhorting British civilians to resist the temptation to gossip about the war, was first popularised by the Ministry of Information in 1941. It lasted longer than many such slogans, which were laughed to death before they achieved much of their purpose, and was still extant, mainly among ex-servicemen and their families, until the mid-Fifties.

SLOGAN

Happy days are here again
used in Franklin D. Roosevelt's campaign in 1932

To celebrate his acceptance of the Democratic nomination at the 1932 convention, Franklin Roosevelt, an ex-Navy man, had arranged for the band to strike up 'Anchors Aweigh', but the Bronx Democratic Boss Edward J. Flynn, listening to the broadcast on a hotel radio was appalled, considering that the music sounded like 'a funeral march'. He called up the convention hall and persuaded the floor manager to have the band play the popular tune '*Happy Days Are here Again*'. No-one bothered to tell Roosevelt that the song, written by Jack Yellen and Milton Agar for the musical *Chasing Rainbows*, had first appeared shortly before the Crash of 1929. The song became synonymous with Roosevelt and his plans for the New Deal and was even dragged out again in 1976 to confer some spurious appeal on Jimmy Carter.

SLOGAN

Business as usual
used in World War I

Created by British advertising copywriter H.E. Morgan, this optimistic slogan was written at the start of World War I. It spread widely, especially among those in whose interest the business was being conducted, notably the store owner Gordon Selfridge who announced on August 26, 1914 that ' "Business as usual" must be the order of the day'; and in November 1914, Winston Churchill told the Lord Mayor's Guildhall Banquet guests 'The British people have taken for themselves this motto "Business carried on as usual during alterations on the map of Europe" '.

SLOGAN

Britain Can Take It
used in World War II

This slogan was typical of those created by agencies far removed from the people who are supposed to be inspired by them. The ex-journalists of the Ministry of Information assumed wrongly that they were writing for a public who saw themselves in the same sterotypical way as they were portrayed in popular entertainment: Cockneys were chirpy, Yorkshiremen dour and so on. Britain Can Take It worked on this premise, positing an indomitable British bantam cock who could take whatever the Hun threw his way. The slogan was never popular, people disliked its implicit patronage, and it was dropped in December 1940.

SLOGAN

Kilroy was here

The origins of this elusive phrase, of which the only definite thing to be said is that it originated in the US Army immediately prior to World War II, and then spread to the UK where it became equally popular, are hard to pin down. Its meaning was simple enough:

the army (British or American) was here, but 'Kilroy'? Eric Partridge quotes the 'tolerably credible theory' of the *San Francisco Chronicle* in 1962: 'Two days before the Japanese attack on Pearl Harbor, an unimposing, bespectacled, 39-year-old man took a job with a Bethlehem Steel Company shipyard in Quincy, Mass. As an inspector..., James J. Kilroy (1900–62) began making his mark on equipment to show test gangs he had checked a job. The mark meant 'Kilroy was here'. Soon the words caught on at the shipyard, and Kilroy began finding the slogan written all over the installation. Before long the phrase spread far beyond of the yard.... When the war ended, a nation-wide contest to discover the real Kilroy found him still employed at the shipyard.'

SLOGAN

Women of Britain say GO!
used in World War I

This recruiting slogan adorned a picture in which two women, one blonde and presumably a wife, the other dark, a teenage daughter, and a skirt-clutching curly-headed androgyne (the youngest daughter?) gazed self-sacrificially through a window as the tail-end of a marching column disappeared across a rural landscape. It succeeded, as did that featuring a beckoning Kitchener, magnificently and while the Government had hoped for perhaps half a million volunteers in the first six months, a figure that in itself would stretch the capacity of the Army to clothe, feed and train them, they had that number within four weeks, and 100,000 more volunteered every month until 1916.

SLOGAN

I like Ike
used for General Eisenhower's campaign in 1952

General Dwight D. Eisenhower (1890-1972) had been the supreme commander of the allied forces that swept through Europe to finish World War II, and backed by the glory he had accumulated during his commmand he was spotted as early as 1947 as a potential Presidential nominee, although it was the Democrats rather than the Republicans who fancied his chances at this stage. The first buttons proclaiming the assonant slogan 'I Like Ike' appeared that year and in 1948 Irving Berlin composed a similarly titled song to help Eisenhower, now a Republican. He lost, to Thomas Dewey, in 1948, but the slogan and song were still around four years later when he defeated Adlai Stevenson to become America's 34th President.

SMITH, E.J. CAPTAIN (–1912) British merchant seaman

Be British boys, be British.
attributed last words, 1912

The S.S. Titanic, the 'unsinkable' pearl of Britain's White Star Line, set sail on its maiden voyage on Friday, April 12, 1912 on what was advertised as the world's fastest, most luxurious transatlantic crossing. At 11.59pm on Monday April 15th, some 1191 miles from New York, the Titanic struck an iceberg and within two hours she had sunk. 1493 passengers and crew died. Among the victims was the Captain, E.J. Smith. The exact circumstances of his death remain a mystery. Some survivors claim that he was calm, others that he lost control of the desperate situation. One version attributes him this last, rallying cry, another offers 'Let me go', spoken after he had swum with an abandoned child to a lifeboat, deposited the child and then declined his own rescue. A better attested set of last words were spoken by Mrs. Isadore Straus who refused to leave her husband and told those who wished her to enter a lifeboat 'We have been together now for forty years and we will not separate now.'

SMITH, H. ALLEN (1907–1976) American journalist

When there are two conflicting versions of the story, the wise course is to believe the one in which people appear at their worst.
Let the Crabgrass Grow (1960)

Smith was born in Illinois and followed a series of menial jobs with one as a reporter. By 1929 he was working in New York and wrote for a variety of papers, contributing his own brand of acerbic humour to their pages. Among his books are *Low Man on the Totem Pole* (1941), *Life in a Putty Knife Factory* (1943) and *Larks in the Popcorn* (1948).

SMITH, IAN (1919–) Rhodesian prime minister

We have struck a blow for the preservation of justice, civilisation and Christianity; and in the spirit of this belief we have this day assumed our sovereign independence.
making Rhodesia's unilateral declaration of independence, November 1965

When in 1964 the old Federation of Rhodesia and Nyasaland was broken up, Smith, the country's right-wing Prime Minister, determined not to allow the majority African population to gain the power that a policy of one man one vote would have ensured. Increasing friction between Smith and a succession of British-appointed Governors led to his unilateral declaration of independence in late 1965 and the sending home of Britain's representative Sir Roy Welensky. Smith stubbornly rejected all forms of peaceful change but the eight-year guerilla war that cost 20,000 black and white lives, forced his hand. The Marxist government of Robert Mugabe was elected in 1979. Rhodesia was renamed as Zimbabwe, but Smith has remained as the figurehead of those whites who yearn for the 'good old days'.

SMITH, LOGAN PEARSALL (1865–1946) American man of letters

What is more enchanting than the voices of young people when you can't hear what they say.
quoted in *The Faber Book of Aphorisms* (1964)

Smith was born into a wealthy Pennsylvania Quaker family. His sisters all married into the English intellectual aristocracy – one to Bertrand Russell, one to Bernard Berenson, another to Virgina Woolf's brother and a fourth to Lytton Strachey's. Smith followed to England, becoming a naturalised citizen in 1913, joining the chic intellectual and literary world. Relieved by family money from the necessity of earning a living, Smith collected first editions, gathered the aphorisms of others and composed a number of his own. He polished his bons mots religiously and as Gore Vidal has noted 'devoted his life to getting his sentences right'. Asked whether he had discovered any meaning in life, he replied 'Yes, there is a meaning, at least for me, there is one thing that matters – to set a chime of words tinkling in the minds of a few fastidious people'. His last words were to remark 'Thank heaven the sun has gone in, and I don't have to go out and enjoy it.'

SMITH, LOGAN PEARSALL

Those who set out to serve both God and Mammon soon discover that there is no God.

There are two things to aim at in life: first, to get what you want; and after that to enjoy it. Only the wisest of mankind achieve the second.

SMITH, LOGAN PEARSALL

There are few sorrows, however poignant, in which a good income is of no avail.
Afterthoughts (1931)

SMITH, LOGAN PEARSALL

A bestseller is the gilded tomb of a mediocre talent.
All Trivia (1933)

SMITH, LOGAN PEARSALL

How many of our daydreams would darken into nightmares were there any danger of their coming true.
All Trivia (1933)

SMITH, LOGAN PEARSALL

When they come downstairs from their ivory towers, idealists are apt to walk straight into the gutter.
All Trivia (1933)

SMITH, LOGAN PEARSALL

How awful to reflect that what people say of us is true.
All Trivia (1933)

SMITH, LOGAN PEARSALL

The denunciation of the young is a necessary part of the hygiene of older people, and greatly assists the circulation of their blood.
Last Words (1933)

SMITH, LOGAN PEARSALL

All reformers, however strict their social conscience, live in houses just as big as they can pay for.
More Trivia (1921)

SMITH, LOGAN PEARSALL

Few things are more shocking to those who practise the arts of success than the frank description of those arts.
Reperusals and Re-collections (1936)

SMITH, LOGAN PEARSALL

Those who are contemptuous of everyone are more than anyone terrified of contempt.
quoted in *The Faber Book of Aphorisms* (1964)

SMITH, STEVIE (1902–71) British poet and writer

I was much too far out all my life. And not waving but drowning.
Not Waving but Drowning (1957)

Florence Margaret 'Stevie' Smith combined a life of thirty years work as a publisher's secretary and a home with her aunt in suburban Palmer's Green with a career as one of Britain's more popular poets. She wrote three novels but she is best known for collections of poetry, the most popular of which was *Not Waving but Drowning*, from which this, the title poem originally published in *Punch*, is taken. Smith was an enthusiastic reader of her own work, and attended many poetry festivals in the Sixties. Glenda Jackson portrayed her in the film *Stevie* (1978).

SMITH, STEVIE

There you are you see, quite simply, if you cannot have your dear husband for a comfort and a delight, for a breadwinner and a crosspatch, for a sofa, a chair or a hotwater bottle, one can use him as a Cross to be borne.

Stevie Smith never married, and doubtless appeared to those who know no better, to be a gradually ageing spinster who commuted regularly between her suburban home and the office where she worked as secretary to a publisher. Her own variety of caustic wit, which is seen in many of her poems, deals neatly with the role of a man in many married women's lives, whereby if there's nothing good to be said for him, at least one can capitalise, if only as a martyr, on the bad.

SMITH, STEVIE

A Good Time Was Had By All
title of her poetry collection, 1937

So common is the phrase 'a good time was had by all' that it is hard to appreciate that it had a traceable origin. Stevie Smith called her first collection of poetry by the phrase and it soon became a common remark. Researching his dictionary of catchphrases, Eric Partridge requested her to explain where she had found the phrase, or had she actually coined it? 'Her explanation was startlingly simple: she took it from parish magazines, where a church picnic or outing or social evening or other sociable occasion, almost inevitably generated the comment "A good time was had by all".'

SNOW, C.P.   (1905–80) British novelist and adminstrator

The Two Cultures
title of article in the *New Statesman*, October 6, 1956

Charles Percy Snow, later Baron Snow of Leicester, was both a successful public administrator and a prolific novelist. His reputation rests on his Strangers and Brothers series, a sequence of ten volumes, appearing between 1940 and 1968. The books feature Lewis Eliot, who like his creator moves from his lower-middle class provincial origins to take his place within the British establishment. One title – *The Corridors of Power* (1964) – gave a new phrase to the language, denoting the worlds of Westminster and Whitehall. Apart from his novels, Snow is best known for his 1959 Rede Lecture entitled *The Two Cultures and the Scientific Revolution*. Snow's lecture talked of the gaps between arts and science and religion and suggested that for the good of the country these should be closed. His lecture opened a lengthy debate and simultaneously coined a phrase.

SNOWDEN, PHILIP   (1864–1937) British politician

It would be desirable if every government, when it comes to power, should have its old speeches burned.
quoted in *Philip Snowden*, by E.B. Roberts

Snowden was the Labour Chancellor of the Exchequer in 1924 and 1929–31, basing his policies squarely on the traditional virtues of thrift, hard work, self-denial, and economic prudence. Unfortunately this inflexibility took no heed of the current economic situation and proved to be exactly the opposite of what was required at the time. When, after 1931, the National Government attempted to combat the Depression with a very limited programme of expansion he condemned any such moves as 'Bolshevism run mad'. Snowden was enough of politician, however, to appreciate that however inflexible one might be when in power, there was no need for such measures to reflect in any way the promises or criticism that might have been made in opposition.

SOLZHENITSYN, ALEXANDER   (1918–) Russian novelist

There were three thousand six hundred and fifty-three days like that in his stretch. From the first clang of the rail to the last clang of the rail. The three extra days were for leap years.
One Day in the Life of Ivan Denisovich (1962)

Solzhenitsyn was arrested in 1945 for criticising Stalin in a letter to a friend and spent the next eight years in Siberian labour camps, followed by three more years in internal exile. After surviving a brush with cancer he began writing his first major novel, *The First Circle*, finally published in 1968. In 1960, while working as a teacher, he submitted his story *One Day in the Life of Ivan Denisovich* to Russia's leading literary magazine, *Novy Mir*. It coincided with Khrushchev's de-Stalinisation plans and he allowed this indictment of the camps to appear. Solzhenitsyn became an international celebrity, abandoned teaching and began amassing material for his factual exposure of the camps, the three-volume *Gulag Archipelago*. When in 1974 the first volume was seized by the KGB and Solzhenitsyn had it published abroad, he was deported from Russia. He has since lived and worked in America but his consistent denunciation of American excesses with the same crusading fervour as he once attacked Russian repression has disappointed those who hoped to capitalise on his emigration.

SONTAG, SUSAN (1933–) American writer

A photograph is not only an image (as a painting is an image), an interpretation of the real; it is also a trace, something directly stencilled off the real, like a footprint or a death mask.
On Photography (1979)

In this essay Sontag labels those who take or view photographs as junkies, rapists and murderers: art, at the least the art of the photographer, is now an amoral force, rather than one that enlivens human sensibilities and consciousness. 'By getting us used to what, formerly, we could not bear to see or hear, because it was too shocking, painful or embarrassing, art changes morals'. The assumption, of course, is that this change is for the worse. She also complains that the final effect of photography is to render the entire world a department store in which everything becomes one more consumer object. As she remarked in 1977: 'Reality has come to seem more and more like what we are shown by cameras.'

SONTAG, SUSAN

Camp is a vision of the world in terms of style, but a particular style. It is love of the exaggerated.
Against Interpretation (1961)

Against Interpretation and Other Essays is a brilliant expression of modern sensibility. Despite her title Sontag does interpret, making accessible the most striking experiments in avant-garde film and criticism. From her treatment of new-wave cinema to her famous 'Notes on Camp' (a concept that had hitherto been limited to describing the antics of more noticeably effeminate homosexuals) she is provocative and original. A small postscript to Sontag's Notes on Camp came when Mae West heard about it.

Interviewed in *Playboy* in 1971 she reinterpreted the interpreter: 'Camp is the kind of comedy where they imitate me.'

SONTAG, SUSAN

He who despises himself esteems himself as a great self-despiser.
Death Kit (1967)

In her novel *Death Kit*, Sontag wittily combines mythical, religious and philosophical elements within the structure of a who-done-it. As well as the detective fiction motif, the book used the traditional concept of the journey to hell. Her aphorism shows up the false modesty of those whose expertise in self-denigration has been honed as finely and is loved as intensely as the immodesty of others who prefer open self-promotion. The book owes a great deal to the influence of the 'nouveau roman' in France and Sontag has been described as America's principal link with European avant-garde literature.

SONTAG, SUSAN

The camera makes everyone a tourist in other people's reality, and eventually in one's own.
On Photography (1977)

This collection of six essays and '*A Brief Anthology of Quotations*' began as a study of 'some of the problems, aesthetic and moral, posed by the omnipresence of photographed images'. Subsequent essays developed as the initial study revealed the complexity of Sontag's basic considerations, but this quotation epitomises the complaint that underlies her analysis.

SONTAG, SUSAN

The truth is that Mozart, Pascal, Boolean algebra, Shakespeare, parliamentary democracy, baroque churches, Newton, the emancipation of women, Kant, Marx, and Balanchine ballets don't redeem what this particular civilisation has wrought upon the world. The white race is the cancer of human history.
What's Happening in America (1967)

This essay is Sontag's way of responding to a questionnaire which she was sent in summer 1966 by the editors of the literary magazine, *Partisan Review*. Sixteen celebrated people were asked what they felt about the state of American life and the direction in which they saw it as moving. Contributors were asked to frame their answers around a number of specified topics, including the presidency, inflation, racism, foreign policy, youth, and the future. All the answers were collated and published in the winter 1967 edition of the magazine. Sontag's absolute refusal to credit the white race with any virtues, setting the evils of racism above all else, is typical of the self-lacerating mood of many of the era's privileged white bourgeoisie.

SPENCE, BASIL (1907–76) British architect

Slums have their good points, they at least have a community spirit and solve the problem of loneliness.
speaking in 1966

Spence, a former assistant to Edward Lutyens (1869–1944), emerged as Britain's leading post-war architect, with his fresh approach to university buildings and to the conversion of older work. His pavilions for the 1951 Festival of Britain and prize-winning designs for housing estates were greatly admired. Spence, whose crusading zeal on behalf of modern architecture won him the nickname 'Saint Basil', rose through the architectural hierarchy to become President of the RIBA from 1958-60; he was knighted that same year and received the Order of Merit in 1962.

SPENDER, STEPHEN (1909–) British poet

**Pylons, those pillars
bare like nude giant girls that have no secret.**
The Pylons (1933)

After Oxford, where he met such future poets as Auden, Mac-Neice and Isherwood, Spender lived briefly in Weimar Germany, an experience which influenced his political attitudes, turning them leftwards. His first collection of poetry appeared in 1930. The poem 'Pylons' (1933) gave the nickname 'The Pylon School' to the work produced by Spender and his circle, all of whom regularly used industrial and technological imagery. He supported the Republicans during the Spanish Civil War, and worked in Spain as a propagandist. During the war he co-edited *Horizon* with Cyril Connolly and from 1953-67 co-edited *Encounter* and has worked extensively for the magazine *Index on Censorship* since 1972, as well as writing critical works, translations and an autobiography since then.

SPENDER, STEPHEN

In England, success is supposed to be kept within the bounds of decency... to bring to your friends credit for knowing you, but not pushed to that extent where they might become envious.
New York Review of Books, 1973

English reticence, or as less complimentary critics put it, English hypocrisy, is the subject of Spender's remark. The idea that, like an American, the nation traditionally brought up as the reverse of the English in this area, one might take pleasure in one's successes (or as a modest Englishman would put it, boast about them) is far beyond the pale. Spender also makes the human point that people, English or otherwise, don't mind a bit of glory for their friends, as long as it remains reflected.

SPENDER, STEPHEN

Politics without ideology, and with a strong tendency to autobiography, equals Liberalism
The Thirties and After (1978)

Spender's father E.H. Spender was a distinguished liberal journalist, but his own leanings were towards the left. Few young intellectuals of the era saw much point in liberalism, either with a large L, which was virtually defunct, or with a small, since that seemed to lead to appeasement and the condoning of dictatorship. What was required was an ideology with a specific direction and the chance to subsume one's tendency to autobiography in a collectivist stance. The aspirations of Spender and his peers were mocked in fellow-poet Roy Cambell's poem *Talking Bronco* (1946), in which he christened them collectively 'MacSpaunday' (MacNeice, Spender, Auden and Day-Lewis).

SPOCK, BENJAMIN   (1903–) American paediatrician

You know more than you think you do.
Common Sense Book of Baby and Child Care (1946)

Before Dr. Spock child care was a lottery, dictated over the centuries by a variety of fluctuating fashions. Spock told parents, as this, the first line of the book emphasises, that using their own judgement and their innate common sense was the best way of bringing up baby. He resisted laying down the law, confining himself to giving parents the information they needed to make these judgements, based on his own lengthy experience as a paediatrician. Twenty years later the right wing, watching young people reject orthodox society, claimed that Spock's 'liberal' principles had created a corrupt, 'permissive' generation. Spock's response was to ally himself with 'his' children in their condemnation of the war in Vietnam, earning himself an arrest for civil disobedience in 1967.

SQUIRE, J. C.   (1884–1958) British literary journalist and poet

I'm not so think as you drunk I am.

Sir John Collings Squire became literary editor of the *New Statesman,* writing under the name 'Solomon Eagle', in 1913 and soon established himself as one of Britain's leading literary journalists. He founded the *London Mercury* in 1919 and edited it until 1934, using it to attack modernism and publish such authors as Chesterton, Belloc and Yeats. He was loathed, inevitably, by the avant-garde, all of whom despised his traditional establishment stance. Squire was also a gifted parodist, rivalled only by Max Beerbohm, and his *Collected Parodies* appeared in 1921.

STALIN, JOSEPH   (1879–1953) Russian leader

The state is an instrument in the hands of the ruling class for suppressing the resistance of its class enemies.
on 'proletarian democracy'

Born Joseph Dzhugashvili, Stalin took his nom de guerre – Man of Steel – in 1901 when, after his expulsion from a theological seminary, he espoused Marxism and became leader of an underground Bolshevik cell. By 1929 he had assumed absolute power in Russia. His aim was to establish Russia as an industrial nation, a task achieved at an enormous social and cultural cost. Millions died as a result of his collectivization of agriculture, hundreds of thousands more in the labour camps of the 'Gulag archipelago', sent there for resisting reform, alleged counter-revolution, and similar supposed offences. The 'old Bolsheviks', leaders of the original revolution, were almost completely eliminated after a series of 'show' trials. Stalin's industrialisation paid off when Russia withstood the German invasion of 1941, although 25 million Russians died in the war. Stalin died in 1953. His legacy is both Russia's status as a superpower and the repression of individual freedoms that still typifies the system he worked so hard to perfect.

STALIN, JOSEPH

A single death is a tragedy, a million deaths is a statistic.
quoted in 1958

Stalin's disregard for human suffering has left him a reputation which, if not apparent at the time, is now that of an exemplary architect of human suffering. The 'personality cult' which he built around his own position was made even more grotesque by the carelessness with which he destroyed others. American commentator George Kennan has described his career as one of 'criminality without limits', but as 'Uncle Joe', as the allies schooled themselves to regard him during World War II, put it to the doubters 'You cannot make a revolution with silk gloves'. Stalin exhibited a similarly chilling turn of phrase when asked bluntly by the British MP Lady Astor 'When are you going to stop killing people?'. Replied Stalin: 'The undesirable classes never liquidate themselves'.

STALIN, JOSEPH

The Pope. How many divisions has he got?
talking to the French Prime Minister, May 13, 1935

In May 1935 the French Prime Minister, Pierre Laval, visited Moscow to back up the recently signed Franco-Soviet pact by talks with Stalin. Calling upon this new alliance, Laval allegedly asked Stalin whether, to help his own domestic relations with the French Catholics, who deplored this alliance with godless communism, he could not perhaps permit Russia's own Catholics to practise their religion unimpeded. Stalin, pragmatic as ever, replied 'Oh! The Pope! How many divisions has he got?'

STANLEY, AUGUSTUS OWSLEY   (1935–) American drug manufacturer

Chemistry is applied theology.
quoted in *The Electric Kool-Aid Acid Test* by Tom Wolfe (1969)

'Owsley', as he was universally known to the tens of thousands of hippies who owed their peeks at nirvana to LSD, was the most celebrated maker of mind-bending chemical hallucinogens in the 1960s. Grandson of a US senator, Owsley had dropped out of a variety of schools before, at the University of California's Berkeley campus, he found his niche: as a manufacturer of LSD, a drug that while uniquely powerful, remained quite legal until October 1966. By this time 'Owsley acid' was so popular that he simply moved his operation underground and continued to blow the collective hippie mind.

STANTON, CHARLES E.   (1859–1933) American soldier

Lafayette, we are here.
arriving in France, 1917

In 1777, a year after the American colonists declared their independence from England, the Marquis de Lafayette enlisted in the revolutionary army, thus creating an important bond between the American and French republican traditions. One hundred and forty years later, on July 4, nine days after arriving in France with the American Expeditionary Force in June 1917, Colonel Charles E. Stanton (1859–1933) stood at Lafayette's tomb in a Paris cemetery and announced to his gravestone 'Lafayette, we are here'. Ten days later, honouring France's Bastille Day, he repeated the ceremony.

STAR IS BORN, A

Hello everybody. This is Mrs Norman Maine.
Warner Bros, 1954

There are three versions of *A Star Is Born*; all date from the little-known *What Price Hollywood* (1930). The first appeared in 1937, starring Janet Gaynor as the self-sacrificing rising star and Frederic March as her husband, falling fast and drinking faster. The screenplay was written by Dorothy Parker and her husband Alan Campbell, based on director William Wellman's original story. The 1954 remake put Judy Garland and James Mason in the leads. It capitalised on Garland's natural neurotic intensity in what Pauline Kael termed 'a terrible, fascinating orgy of self-pity and cynicism and myth-making'. In 1976 a further remake replaced the movies with rock and roll, and featured Barbra Streisand and Kris Kristofferson. This line, delivered by the leading lady, sums up the whole movie. She is about to accept an Oscar, he is muttering drunkenly at her side, and rather than have him ejected, she acknowledges in the first line of her speech and the last of the film, that in the end she owes it all to him.

STAR TREK

These are the voyages of the Starship Enterprise... to boldly go where no man has gone before...
American TV series, 1960s

There were only three original seasons of *Star Trek*, from 1966–68, arguably television's most successful space opera. It was the brainchild of Gene Roddenberry, a TV writer and science fiction buff, who created this enduring series, screened continually ever since its launch on at least one network in the world, and focus of the dedicated attention of hundreds of thousands of fans, otherwise known as 'Trekkies'. This line, containing television's most celebrated split infinitive, comes from the regular introduction that prefaced each episode, before the Starship Enterprise and its multinational crew arrive like deep-space deities on a new planet, its civilisation often a convenient clone of a period in Earth's own history, for another episode of setting a world to rights.

STAR WARS

May the Force be with you.
script by George Lucas (1977)

Take the old Saturday morning sci-fi serials, especially those starring Flash Gordon, carefully extract every cliché, throw in a few robots, cute animals and Bad Guys possessed of Nameless Dread, toss in a bit of spurious mysticism and garnish the lot with state of the art special effects and you have *Star Wars*, one of the most successful pieces of science fantasy hokum yet screened. The movie was the brainchild of George Lucas (1945–). Most of the cast were relative unknowns, but he assigned the mystic element to Alec Guinness (1914–), playing the space samurai turned seer, Obi-Wan Kenobi, who many thought ought to have had better things to do than telling the goodies 'May the Force be with you', and assuming that anyone actually knew or cared what he meant.

STARR, RINGO   (1940–) British rock star

Q: Why do you wear all those rings on your fingers?
A: Because I can't get them through my nose.
quoted in *The Book of Rock Quotes* (1977) by Jonathon Green

In the era of Beatlemania, when the Press had decided that 'The Moptops' weren't ravaging barbarians, but just wacky Merseyside funsters, one of the party tricks the media most loved was the Beatles' press conference. In this ritual, flanked by a beaming Brian Epstein, the 'Fabs' as Fleet Street liked to abbreviate their other pet name 'The Fab Four', would take questions from the reporters and toss back 'irreverent' answers, usually a barely restrained synonym for 'Go to hell!' or 'Ask a silly question...'. The most celebrated of these, perhaps the only one worthy of celebration, was Ringo Starr's reply to the journalist who asked about the rings that were his trademark. Hallowed in the anthologies, it remains the drummer's monument.

STEFFENS, LINCOLN   (1866–1936) American journalist

I have seen the future and it works.
after a trip to Russia in 1919

For a man who was both celebrated and vilified as the doyen of America's muckraking journalism, Steffens showed himself remarkably suggestible in 1919 when he visited the newly established Soviet Union, as a member of an American diplomatic mission. Gazing on what must have been the very chaotic wonders of the new system of government, Steffens announced to his readers 'I have seen the future and it works'. The spontaneity of this line, which reflected the feelings of many starry-eyed visitors, was somewhat marred by the fact the Steffens, according to the mission's leader William C. Bullitt, had been perfecting his line even before they arrived in Russia. Fifty-five years later in 1974, the novelist, poet and critic Philip Toynbee (1916–81) visited America. He was unimpressed and wrote in the *Observer:* 'I have seen the future and it doesn't work.'

STEIN, GERTRUDE (1874–1946) American poet and literary doyenne

Rose is a rose is a rose is a rose.
'Sacred Emily'

Stein had little time for the aphorism: 'Remarks are not literature' she observed in 1933, but of all her writings, this line, usually misquoted, remains the best known. Stein studied psychology before moving to Paris in 1902 and establishing there an unrivalled salon where gathered for the next forty years the most celebrated exponents of the literary and artistic avant-garde. In her own work she stressed, in critic Edwin Morgan's words, her 'insistently repetitive, anti-associational style designed to render the precise movements of present consciousness...she applied to literature the equivalent of what Mondrian discovered in art and Wittgenstein in philosophy'. Her poem 'Sacred Emily' concerns the English painter Sir Francis Rose, whom she esteemed highly. Thus the lack of the indefinite article before the first 'Rose' is correct, for all that readers, striving for some reference as to the immutable reality of things, put one there.

STEINBECK, JOHN (1902–68) American writer

The profession of book writing makes horse racing seem like a solid, stable, business.
interviewed in *Writers at Work* 4th series (1977)

Steinbeck's realistic treatment of the disenfranchised poor of his native state of California made him into one of America's most popular novelists in the late Thirties and Forties. His chef d'oeuvre, *The Grapes of Wrath* (1939), revealed the plight of

America's 'Okies', poor sharecroppers evicted in the Depression years from their homes and forced to move to California, where they had no choice but to work, in even greater poverty, as exploited migratory farm workers. After *East of Eden* (1952) Steinbeck's work declined, often straying into sentimentality, but he was awarded a Nobel Prize in 1962.

STEINBERG, SAUL   (1914–) American illustrator and artist

The life of the creative man is led, directed and controlled by boredom. Avoiding boredom is one of our most important purposes. It is also one of the most difficult... in the end, working is good because it is the last refuge of the man who wants to be amused.
in *Time magazine*, 1978

Steinberg has made a reputation as an artist and a graphic satirist, noted for his precise line, his use of rubber stamps as a basis of some designs, and his wordless comments on people, architecture, contraptions and institutions, all treated with artistic wit to expose their basic pomposity, their fantastic nature and their grotesque appearance. His work frequently appears in the *New Yorker*, and has been collected in a variety of books. His most famous picture is probably the poster which centres the world on a view from midtown New York City, with such areas as California and Europe receding far into the distance.

STEVENSON, ADLAI   (1900–65) American politcian

My definition of a free society is a society where it is safe to be unpopular.
speech in Detroit, October 1952

Stevenson is best remembered as the liberal hope of the Fifties in America. He was chosen in 1948 by the Illinois political machine to stand as Governor and won with an unprecedented majority. His nomination as Democratic presidential candidate in 1952 made him the darkest of dark horses and he duly lost the election. A second attempt in 1956 failed badly and when President Kennedy was elected he noticeably passed over the Party's former leader, although Stevenson's public statements were invariably loyal to JFK. If, as some supporters claimed, Stevenson's wit undid his political ambitions, he proved incapable of restraining it. His propensity towards the epigram persisted throughout his life. Some of them are listed below:

Flattery is all right – if you don't inhale.

Power corrupts, but lack of power corrupts absolutely.

A politician is a statesman who approaches every question with an open mouth.

One man's cliché can be another man's conviction.

Nothing so dates a man as to decry the younger generation.

A lie is an abomination unto the Lord and a very present help in trouble.

The mainstays of diplomatic life are protocol, alcohol and Geritol.

STEVENSON, ADLAI

In America any boy may become President, and I suppose that's just the risk he takes.
campaigning in 1952

Stevenson's refusal to sacrifice his sense of humour to the pursuit of power may well have denied him the Presidency. Certainly his cultured urbanities had little chance in the fervently short-sighted atmosphere of the era. Ike's number two, Richard Nixon, attempted to smear Stevenson as 'Adlai the Appeaser – who got his PhD from Dean Acheson's College of Cowardly Communist Containment' but Stevenson hit back, calling Nixon 'the kind of politician who would cut down a redwood tree, then mount the stump for a speech on conservation.' Stevenson's greater error may have been in treating the electors as adults, telling them in a speech in Chicago on September 11, 1952 'that there are no gains without pain' and promising to 'talk sense to the American people'. America's war hero, campaigning against 'Korea, Communism and Corruption', took 442 electoral votes, Stevenson polled but 89.

STIMSON, HENRY   (1867–1950) American Secretary of War

Gentlemen do not read each other's mail.
on taking office in 1929

Stimson, who took office in 1929, had never been informed of the existence of his country's intelligence service. This was then a department known as 'the Black Chamber', which existed for the purpose of decoding and analysing the flood of telegrams that formed a constant traffic in and out of the various embassies in Washington. Although Stimson has been cited for his pragmatic approach to foreign affairs, he found it impossible to accept the necessity for an intelligence service. He was appalled to discover what he saw as a nest of sneaks and ordered the 'Black Chamber' abolished, justifying his move with the patrician remark 'Gentlemen do not read each other's mail.'

STINNETT, CASKIE   (1911–) American writer

A diplomat is a person who can tell you to go to hell in such a way that you actually look forward to the trip.
Out of the Red (1960)

Stinnett's definition is just one more way-station on the path of damnation that successive commentators have prepared for those who represent their countries in the embassies of the world. As the initiator of such attacks, the 17th century writer Sir Henry Wotton put it in 1604 'An ambassador is an honest man sent to lie abroad for the commonwealth.' Three hundred years later Ambrose Bierce defined 'Consul' as 'a person who having failed to secure an office from the people is given one by the Administration on condition that he leave the country.'

STOCKS, MARY   (1891–1975) British economist

We don't call it sin today, we call it self-expression.

Baroness Stocks, who was for many years a well-known educator and member of a variety of government committees, as well as appearing regularly on radio, was voicing a popular conservative view on the social revolution that was called 'the permissive society'. The concept of sin, usually implying some form of sexual self-indulgence and based in the precepts of religious dogma, was largely abandoned by the new credos. In the Sixties, less fixated on punishment and more on pleasure, those sexual peccadilloes that were once seen as leading straight to the Pit, were redefined by those who promoted the new libertarian world. They called them 'doing your own thing', 'letting it all hang out' or, when aiming for respectability 'self-expression'.

STONE, I. F.   (1907–) American political commentator

Every government is a device by which a few control the actions of many... on both sides at the moment complex human societies depend for the final decisions of war and peace on a group of elderly men any sensible plant personnel manager, whether under capitalism or Communism, would hesitate to hire.
in 1959

I.F. Stone is best known for his magazine *I.F. Stone's Weekly*, a four-page, double-column news-sheet, launched in 1953, that rose to a circulation of 75,000 and appeared regularly for 19 years, becoming the most influential political journal in America. Stone has been America's most perceptive political commentator, taking his ethics from Erasmus, More, Kropotkin and Milton and his topics from virtually anything that matters in Washington and the political world outside it. His sole ideology has been unshakeable liberalism, choosing no favourites, and subjecting all contenders to his sharp analyses to come to a conclusion that is drawn clearly and often painfully from the demonstrable facts.

STONE, I. F.

Those who set out nobly to be their brother's keeper sometimes end up by becoming his jailer. Every emancipation has in it the seeds of a new slavery, and every truth easily becomes a lie.
in 1969

Every government is run by liars and nothing they say should be believed.

STOPPARD, TOM   (1937–) British playwright

It's better to be quotable than to be honest.
quoted in the *Guardian*, 1973

Stoppard was born in Czechoslovakia, but took his English stepfather's surname after the war. He was working as a journalist when his first play was televised in 1963. His first real success, *Rosencrantz and Guildenstern are Dead*, a theatrical corollary of Shakespeare's *Hamlet*, was staged in 1966. Since then Stoppard has established himself as a highly popular yet uncompromisingly 'intellectual' playwright.

STOPPARD, TOM

The media. It sounds like a convention of spiritualists.
Jumpers (1972)

Stoppard's play deals with modern philosophy, based around the real-life professor of moral philosophy, George Moore. Moore's philosophy stated that since we really perceive nothing that is not filtered through the product of our own sensations, then affectionate interpersonal relations and the contemplation of beauty are the only perfectly good states of mind. Stoppard puns on his play's title to capitalise upon the 'verbal gymnastics' with which Moore's speeches brilliantly parody academic philosophy. Moore lived from 1873-1958, and not surprisingly found the modern, post-McLuhanite use of 'media' slightly confusing, although as a plural of the distinctly non-spiritualistic variety of medium it was well established in his time.

STOPPARD, TOM

I agree with everything you say, but I would attack to the death your right to say it.
Lord Malquist and Mr. Moon (1965)

Stoppard's novel is a fantasy set in a dream-like 'London' through which strange characters wander in a haze of despair. Like the plays that followed, Stoppard's novel is a complex of allusions, linguistic games, fantastic situations and similar mental exercises. Lord Malquist is an eighteenth century exquisite, marooned in modernity, offering such aphorisms as 'Of all forms of fiction, autobiography is the most gratuitous' and 'Nothing sounds more studied than a repeated spontaneity' to his Boswell Mr. Moon, who walks the streets with a bomb in his pocket. This line is a variation of that attributed to Malquist's spiritual contemporary Voltaire, who supposedly told an opponent 'I disagree with everything you say, but I would defend to the death your right to say it.'

STOPPARD, TOM

The House of Lords, an illusion to which I have never been able to subscribe – responsibility without power, the prerogative of the eunuch throughout the ages.
Lord Malquist and Mr. Moon (1965)

Lord Malquist is punning on Stanley Baldwin's famous attack on the press Lords Beaverbrook and Rothermere (qv). in which he used his cousin Rudyard Kipling's description of 'the prerogative of the harlot'. Malquist, accompanied by Moon's wife Jane, is riding in his carriage towards a state funeral, of which he remarks, en passant, that 'To see London on the morning of a state funeral is to see London at her best...provided one goes nowhere near the proceedings.'

STOPPARD, TOM

Life is a gamble at terrible odds, if it was a bet you wouldn't take it.
Rosencrantz and Guildenstern Are Dead (1967)

Travelling to England, where they are expecting to deliver Prince Hamlet into captivity but will instead, as they are beginning reluctantly to understand, meet their own deaths, Rosencrantz and Guildenstern find that on board their boat are the same players whom they have met earlier in the play. The Player-King counsels them: 'Life is a gamble at terrible odds, if it was a bet you wouldn't take it. Did you know that any number doubled is even?' Rosencrantz: Is it? Player: 'We learn something every day, to our cost.'

STOPPARD, TOM

Eternity's a terrible thought. I mean, where's it going to end.
Rosencrantz and Guildenstern Are Dead (1967)

Rosencrantz and Guildenstern are musing on death, and the way in which one has to accept, however long one puts the idea off, that living is a finite experience. In the end everyone dies. On the other hand, there is the alternative: eternity. Something that has the potential of going on for ever. In the end death, which at least has some kind of limit, is preferable.

STOPPARD, TOM

Every exit is an entrance somewhere.
Rosencrantz and Guildenstern Are Dead (1967)

In Shakespeare's *Hamlet* (1601) Rosencrantz and Guildenstern are 'attendant lords', old friends of Prince Hamlet who are killed when he sends them to England carrying a sealed letter ordering their immediate execution. The play's title is taken from Shakespeare's line, given to the Ambassador, who arrives in Denmark to be told of Hamlet's death and notes that 'the ears are senseless that should give us hearing / to tell him his commandment is fulfilled, / that Rosencrantz and Guildenstern are dead.' This speech, and that of Horatio that follows it also conclude Stoppard's play. In Stoppard's version, the two courtiers forsake their peripheral roles to take centre stage. Their actions take place while 'on stage' Shakespeare's play is proceeding elsewhere, and they suspend their conversations to blend as and when required into Shakespeare's text, thus exiting from '*Hamlet*' to enter into Stoppard's script. This line is taken from the pair's 'off-stage' meeting with the players, who will later perform the 'play within a play' before the court. One Player explains their art as 'We do on stage the things that are supposed to happen off. Which is a kind of integrity, if you look on every exit as being an entrance somewhere else.'

STOPPARD, TOM

The bad end unhappily, the good unluckily. That's what tragedy means.
Rosencrantz and Guildenstern are Dead (1967)

Running through Stoppard's play is the sense of impending death. Apart from the corpses that bestrew Shakespeare's play, which the audience for Stoppard's know is going on 'off-stage', there is the pervasive knowledge that the two lords are to die. Their conversations harp on the topic, and the other motif, of gambling and chance, refers back to the way life itself is subject to chances over which the liver has no real control. In the end, no-one can escape death, or even determine its manner. As Stoppard points out, the only difference between the good and the bad is that the bad have miserable, but deserved deaths, whereas while the good must die too, we see their demise as unfortunate.

STORY, JACK TREVOR   (1917–) British author

Live now, pay later
book title, 1962

The title of Jack Story's book became a phrase that defined a whole era. If, in 1957, Mr. Macmillan could tell the newly prosperous British consumer that they had never had it so good, then 'it', in the form of consumer durables, often came thanks to hire purchase, otherwise known as 'the never-never'. For many people, critics and consumers alike, the 'live now pay later' philosophy epitomised the materialist hedonism of the era. What exactly constituted 'living' and just how one managed to 'pay' varied as to the individual, but if the British had once deferred pleasure for payment in advance, now they were choosing to indulge at once, and pay some time in the unspecified future, if at all.

SUMMERS, DOROTHY   British actress

TTFN
catchphrase in *ITMA*, 1940s

Of the many catchphrases spawned by *ITMA*, Dorothy Summer's role as the charlady 'Mrs. Mopp' created one of the longest lasting. TTFN, otherwise known as Ta-Ta For Now, was her

invariable exit line, speedily providing *ITMA*'s many fans with one as well. The game soon became to cap her acronym with another longer one. Thus, as Eric Partridge cites in his *Dictionary of Catchphrases* (1985):
Mrs. Mopp: TTFN
Tommy Handley: NCAWWASBE
Mrs. Mopp: What's that?
Handley: Never clean a window with a soft-boiled egg.
The phrase is still used, particularly by BBC radio disk jockey Jimmy Young.

SUMMERSKILL, EDITH (1901–1980) British politician and physician
Nagging is the repetition of unpalatable truths.
in the *Observer*, 1960

As an MP (from 1938) and a life peeress (from 1961) Summerskill made her mark on public life as much by her very personal point of view as by her actual achievements and her name will always be associated with her campaign against professional boxing. In her opinion the prize ring was utterly barbaric and the damage inflicted upon each other by the fighters was ultimately deadly. What she saw as truth, the boxing establishment found quite unpalatable, and even though boxers continue to die in the ring, there has still been no real modification of the sport.

SUN, THE

Crisis, what crisis?

James Callaghan (1912–), Prime Minister from 1976–79, consistently pinned his hopes for governmental success on what he claimed was a special relationship with the unions. They were less enthusiastic. The winter of 1978–79 became 'The Winter of Discontent', with widespread industrial action causing the sort of chaos that the voters assumed only happened under the Conservatives. In January 1979 Callaghan attended a summit meeting in Guadaloupe. Returning to London Airport, he was asked by a *Sun* reporter 'What of the mounting chaos in the country at the moment?' The Prime Minister replied 'Please don't run down your country by talking about mounting chaos. If you look at it from the outside you can see that you are taking rather a parochial view. I do not feel there is mounting chaos'. The Sun sub-editors paraphrased this as 'Crisis? What crisis?'. Labour lost the May election and, coincidentally or otherwise, the *Sun's* editor, Larry Lamb, was knighted in the election honours.

SUNSET BOULEVARD

Holden: You used to be big in pictures'
Swanson: I am big. The films got smaller.
script for Billy Wilder with Charles Brackett & DM Marshman (1950)

William Holden plays a young scriptwriter, down on his luck, who chances on the mansion of the aged silent star 'Norma Desmond', played by Gloria Swanson, living out her days in solitary splendour, attended only by her equally veteran butler (Eric von Stroheim). All she has are mementos, and her endlessly rehearsed comeback, starring in her own version of Salome. Holden is persuaded to stay with her, ostensibly to help with the script, and becomes gigolo, gofer and victim. Many real-life Hollywood figures featured, including director Cecil B. De Mille and it is to him that Swanson gives her curtain line. Completely mad, she can only be lured from the mansion by indulging her fantasy that at last her script is to be shot. She sweeps from her bedroom to the stairs, posing momentarily to announce 'All right, Mr De Mille, I'm ready for my closeup.'

SUPERMAN

Faster than a speeding bullet! More powerful than a locomotive! Able to leap tall buildings at a single bound!
Look! Up in the sky!
It's a bird!
It's a plane!
It's Superman!. Yes, it's Superman! Strange visitor from another planet, who came to earth with powers and abilities far beyond those of mortal men. Superman! Who can change the course of mighty rivers, bend steel with his bare hands, and who – disguised as Clark Kent, mild-mannered reporter for a great metropolitan newspaper – fights a never ending battle for truth, justice and the American way!
introduction to the American radio and TV show, 1948 onwards

Superman was invented as a comic strip in 1933 by Jerry Siegel and Joe Shuster. It took them five years to find a publisher but once *Action Comics* took the *Man of Steel* in June 1938, he became a worldwide hit, a new American icon, benefitting everyone concerned, except his creators who had signed away their rights for a pittance. The strip was adapted for radio and TV. Both shows began with this stirring introduction, in which an announcer ran down the biography of the planet Krypton's mightiest expatriate, as 'onlookers' murmured 'Is it a bird?...is it a plane?'

SUTTON, WILLIE 'THE ACTOR' (1901–?) American thief

It is a rather pleasant experience to be alone in a bank at night.
in '*I, Willie Sutton*' (1953)

Willie Sutton was one of America's most successful thieves, an elite safecracker who, if his autobiography is to be believed, stole 50 cents from his mother's purse at the age of eight and never looked back. Tutored by one 'Doc' Tate, Sutton scorned explosives, preferring the delicate touch of his own fingers to tease open the complex locks. As his nickname shows, Sutton's speciality was disguise, appearing at one bank dressed as a messenger, at another as a window cleaner, and so on. He pulled fifteen straight robberies without detection until in 1931 a partner informed on him. Despite resisting the police 'third degree', and refusing to confess, he was duly tried and jailed for thirty years. Despite several escapes, between which he managed a few years more 'work', he effectively stayed in jail until his death.

SVEVO, ITALO (1861–1928) (Ettore Schmitz)Italian novelist, playwright and critic

One need only remind onself of all we expect from life to see how very strange it is, and to arrive at the conclusion that man has found his way into it by mistake and does not really belong there.
Confessions of Zeno (1923)

Svevo worked as a bank clerk in Trieste and his early work was ignored until in 1907 James Joyce, teaching in the city, met him and recognised his worth as a writer. Despite this encouragement, Svevo refused to write again until in 1923 he produced his most important work *La coscienza di Zeno* (*The Confessions of Zeno*). The novel is largely autobiographical, incorporating much ironic humour as its hero delivers a 'stream of consciousness' as he argues with his psychoanalyst over many aspects of his existence, concluding with the knowledge that he is a classical victim of the Oedipus complex. Svevo published one more novel and was working on a fifth when, in 1928, he died in a car crash.

SWOPE, HERBERT BAYARD (1882–1958) American journalist

The First Duty of a newspaper is to be Accurate. If it is Accurate, it follows that it is Fair.
quoted in 1958

Swope was a journalist on the *New York World* who, by the judicial application of the stock exchange tips that well-placed friends had offered to him, had parlayed his salary into a substantial fortune. He had a 28-room apartment on W. 58th Street in New York and an estate on Great Neck, Long Island where his lavish parties would not have disgraced Fitzgerald's Great Gatsby himself. He was a regular entertainer of the wits of the Algonquin Round Table, bartering their humour for his cash.

SZASZ, THOMAS   (1920–) American psychoanalyst

Two wrongs don't make a right, but they make a good excuse.
The Second Sin (1974)

Szasz is a psychoanalyst whose work in America parallelled and slightly pre-dated that of R.D. Laing (qv) in Britain, and as such he is credited as the founder of the 'anti-psychiatry' movement. He argued that if psychiatrists were still unable to agree on either a diagnosis of or prognosis for schizophrenia, then the malady must be a bogus one and the psychiatrists bogus doctors. Rather than curing people, as they claimed, they were in fact acting as agents of social control, treating their patients much as did earlier authorities treat their own anti-social misfits, whom they termed witches. While not denying that those otherwise termed schizophrenic certainly have problems, these problems are not madness, and he offers to treat anyone thus afflicted who wishes to approach him of their own free will. He is not interested in coercing the ill, and refuses to accept that such a concept as 'diminished responsibility' exists.

SZASZ, THOMAS

If you talk to God, you are praying; if God talks to you, you have schizophrenia.
The Second Sin (1974)

SZASZ, THOMAS

Happiness is an imaginary condition, formerly attributed by the living to the dead, now usually attributed by adults to children, and by children to adults.
The Second Sin (1974)

SZASZ, THOMAS

Masturbation: the primary sexual activity of mankind. In the nineteenth century it was a disease, in the twentieth, it's a cure.
The Second Sin (1974)

SZASZ, THOMAS

Men are rewarded and punished not for what they do, but rather for how their acts are defined. That is why men are more interested in better justifying themselves than in better behaving themselves.
The Second Sin (1974)

SZASZ, THOMAS

How men hate waiting while their wives shop for clothes and trinkets; how women hate waiting, often for much of their lives, while their husbands shop for fame and glory.
The Second Sin (1974)

SZASZ, THOMAS

Traditionally, sex has been a very private, secretive activity. Herein perhaps lies its powerful force for uniting people in a strong bond. As we make sex less secretive, we may rob it of its power to hold men and women together.
The Second Sin (1974)

SZASZ, THOMAS

Ours is an age in which partial truths are tirelessly transformed into total falsehoods and then acclaimed as revolutionary revelations.
The Second Sin (1974)

SZASZ, THOMAS

Formerly, when religion was strong and science weak, men mistook magic for medicine; now, when science is strong and religion weak, men mistake medicine for magic.
The Second Sin (1974)

SZENT-GYORGYI, ALBERT (1893–?) American biochemist

Discovery consists of seeing what everybody has seen and thinking what nobody has thought.
The Scientist Speculates (1962)

Born in Hungary, Szent-Gyorgyi fled eastern Europe in 1919, and worked in Holland and again in Hungary before moving to America in 1845. Szent-Gyorgyi made three important contributions to cell chemistry and respiratory physiology, for which in 1937 he received the Nobel Prize.

T

TAGORE, RABINDRANATH   (1861–1941) Indian writer

God is ashamed when the prosperous boast of his special favour.
Stray Birds (1916)

Tagore is still regarded by his fellow-countrymen as the greatest
Bengali of all time, and for a while was a fashionable figure in
Western intellectual circles as well, after he had been awarded
the Nobel Prize in 1913. Tagore combined writing with the
implementation of his own social theories, founding Santiniketan
University where the educational system was based on the
encouragement of rural values. As the leading exponent of
Bengali culture, Tagore was inevitably a nationalist, and
influenced Gandhi, although he took no part in activist politics.
In 1919 he renounced his knighthood as a protest against British
policy in the Punjab.

TAGORE, RABINDRANATH

Power takes as ingratitude the writhings of its victims.
Stray Birds (1916)

TARKINGTON, BOOTH   (1869–1946) American writer

**There are two things that will be believed of any man what-
soever, and one of them is that he has taken to drink.**
Penrod (1914)

Tarkington tried art and politics before settling to full-time
writing and establishing himself as one of America's most popular
novelists. His best-known works were *Monsieur Beaucaire*
(1900), *The Magnificent Ambersons* (1918), filmed as Orson
Welles' flawed masterpiece in 1942, *Alice Adams* (1921) and
Penrod (1914). This last, a story about the adventures of a gang of
boys in a mid-West city, was claimed by Scott Fitzgerald as one of
his major influences.

TARZAN THE APE-MAN

Me Tarzan, you Jane.
screen play by Ivor Novello, 1932

The first appearance of Tarzan the Ape-Man comes in Edgar Rice Burroughs' novel, published in 1914. His meeting with his future mate was simple. They say nothing and communicate only by notes. When Hollywood made the movie in 1932, the scene was embellished with dialogue, but not much. When Johnny Weismuller meets Maureen O'Sullivan, all he can offer by way of chat is 'Tarzan. Jane'. This badinage is helped by his pointing first to himself and then to her. The audience obviously found this overly minimal and it has read as quoted above ever since.

TAWNEY, R.H. (1880–1962) British economist

The certainties of one age are the problems of the next.
Religion and the Rise of Capitalism (1926)

Tawney taught at the Workers Educational Association, and served on the WEA committee from 1905–47. His economic theories were greatly influenced by his working-class pupils and he remained a socialist in principle and practice throughout his life. *Religion and the Rise of Capitalism* is Tawney's major work. In it he looked at the economic history of the years from 1558-1640, an era that became known as 'Tawney's century', pointing out the relations between economics, politics and contemporary morality. The lessons in social reform that he drew from this, combined with his own devout Christianity, helped offer the left a programme of socialist economic reforms that owed nothing to Marx, condemning privilege and demanding equality of education for all.

TAYLOR, A.J.P. (1906–) British historian

There is nothing more agreeable in life than to make peace with the Establishment – and nothing more corrupting.
Essays In English History

Taylor is England's best-known contemporary historian, whose extensive media exposure has brought him far greater public esteem than that accorded less conspicuous academics. His series on *The Russian Revolution of 1917* (1958) was one of the first attempts to use television for the teaching of history. Taylor stands consistently for the liberal view, and his work combines unorthodox method with brilliant exposition. The word 'Establishment', which he uses here, was coined by the writer Henry Fairlie when he defined it in a *Spectator* article in 1955 as 'not...only the centres of official power – though they are certainly part of it – but rather the whole matrix of official and social relations within which power is exercised.'

TEBBIT, NORMAN   (1931–) British politician

My father did not riot. He got on his bike and looked for work. And he kept on looking until he found it.
speech on October 15, 1981

Unemployment had yet to reach the heights it scaled during Mrs. Thatcher's second term in office when Tebbit, chairman of the Party until 1987, chose to counter the worries of those who had lost their jobs in a speech in October 1981. The rioting to which he referred had been widespread in Britain during the previous summer, when many young people expressed their desperation in the streets. His suggestion caused a furore. His supporters might have applauded, but for most people it was smug and insulting, the worst aspect of bully-boy Toryism. The 'on your bike' tag has stuck ever since, although his alleged comment in January 1987, 'Nobody with a conscience votes Tory anyway', dismissing fainthearts who feared that the party had alienated those with a social conscience, may last even longer.

TELLER, EDWARD   (1908–) American physicist

Very powerful nuclear weapons can be used in such a manner that they have negligible effects on civilian populations.
quoted in *A-Z of Nuclear Jargon* (1986) by Jonathon Green

Teller was one of the physicists who helped develop the hydrogen bomb. While many of his peers recognised the enormity of their discovery and began campaigning against it almost as soon as their researches were complete, Teller has remained the most ardent proponent of nuclear weaponry, pooh-poohing such reservations. Teller's suggestion that nuclear bombs need not hurt people comes from the early Fifties; later that decade he devised the 'neutron bomb', a weapon that would use its beefed-up fallout to kill off living tissue, but would leave buildings relatively unharmed. This idea was scrapped, but Teller remains among the most gung-ho of nuclear physicists.

TERRY-THOMAS   (1911–) British comedian

Do not assume that the other fellow has intelligence to match yours. He may have more.

Born Thomas Terry Hoar-Stevens Terry-Thomas has used his gap-teeth and unassailably upper-class manner to make himself into a popular comic actor in Britain and America, usually playing some form of comic villain. After serving from 1941-46 in the Royal Corps of Signals, he worked for BBC radio before making an early TV series, *How Do You View?* in 1951. Although T-T has worked consistently since the war, he has in recent years been suffering from a gradually debilitating disease from which it is unlikely he will recover.

THATCHER, MARGARET (1925–) British prime minister

To those waiting with baited breath for that favourite media catchphrase, the U-turn, I have only one thing to say: you turn if you want to. The lady's not for turning.
speech on government economic policy at Tory Conference, 1980

The policies of Prime Minister Margaret Thatcher have come to symbolise the materialistic rather than the paternalistic side of British Conservatism. Supporters see her as embodying the solid virtues of thrift, determination and self-reliance, others, not always of the left, have criticised her 'squalid regime'. Thatcher herself rejects all criticisms: if she is resolute, then she presumes that the party and the country must be too. Speaking at the 1980 Conference she summed up her defiant stance. In the face of media suggestions that she should moderate her economic policy, given its deleterious effect on much of the country, her reply gave no sign of weakness. Her last phrase puns on Christopher Fry's play *'The Lady's Not for Burning'* (1948), set in the year 1400. The 'lady' in question, Jennet Jourdemayne, is accused of turning the local rag and bone man into a dog.

THATCHER, MARGARET

I stand before you tonight in my green chiffon gown, my face softly made up, my fair hair gently waved...the Iron Lady of the Western World. Me? A cold war warrior? Well yes – if that is how they wish to interpret my defence of values and freedoms fundamental to our way of life.
speaking on January 31, 1976

Mrs. Thatcher has yet to rival President Reagan's condemnation of Russia as the 'evil empire' but she spares no love for the Soviets. In a speech on January 19, 1976 she branded Moscow with the Nazi image, saying 'The Russians are bent on world dominance...(they) put guns before butter.' A week later one Captain Y. Gavrilov counter-attacked. Writing in the Soviet Defence Ministry newspaper *Red Star*, he called her an 'Iron Lady' and accused her of aiming at a new Cold War. Undaunted Mrs. Thatcher deprecated prettily in this speech, as excerpted above. However in 1977, faced by a variety of crises, she changed her tune, suggesting that 'Maybe this country needs an Iron Lady' and during the Falklands Crisis, as well as much talk of 'our boys', simply revelled in the nickname.

THESIGER, ERNEST

My dear...the noise! And the people!
to a dinner party, 1919

Thesiger, who was related to the explorer Wilfred Thesiger, had managed to survive the horrors of World War I. At a dinner party given shortly after the war he was asked about his experiences, particularly at the battle of the Somme, during which the British suffered 60,000 casualties on the first day. Thesiger, ever the exquisite, replied 'My dear...the noise! And the people!' His sense of humour was further illustrated some years later when, on a visit to Moscow shortly after the defection of the two British diplomats in 1951, he claimed to have written on a public lavatory wall 'Burgess Loves Maclean'.

THIRD MAN, THE

In Italy, for 30 years under the Borgias, they had warfare, terror, murder and bloodshed, but they produced Michaelangelo, Leonardo da Vinci and the renaissance. In Switzerland they had brotherly love; they had 500 years of democracy and peace – and what did that produce? The cuckoo clock.
screenplay by Graham Greene (1949)

The Third Man is Harry Lime, played by Orson Welles with dialogue by Graham Greene. A naive American – Joseph Cotten – arrives in post-war, occupied Vienna searching for his friend Lime. Apparently Lime is dead but Cotten tracks him down, uncovering a sordid web of lies, deceit and corruption: Lime is a trafficker in bogus penicillin. As the two men gaze down from a fairground big wheel at the people below, reduced at this height to mere dots, Lime expounds his philosophy: why bother about insignificant individuals when all the matters is the greater issues; there is no progress without pain.

THIS IS THE ARMY

This is the Army, Mr Jones
No private baths and telephones

screenplay (1943)

This musical started off as a patriotic review, designed actually to be performed by serving soldiers. Irving Berlin wrote the score and the original cast of nonentities was embellished by a variety of stars. Berlin appeared to play himself and sing '*Oh, How I Hate to Get Up in the Morning*'. Gerald Murphy plays 'Jerry Jones', a First World War soldier who writes a show called 'Yip, Yip, Yaphank'. His son, 'Johnny Jones', is played by Ronald Reagan; the show he writes is called 'This Is the Army'.

THOMAS, DYLAN   (1914–1953) British poet

An alcoholic is someone you don't like who drinks as much as you do.

The self-styled 'Rimbaud of Cwmdonkin Drive' was born in Swansea and arrived in London in 1934, just as his first collection of poems was published. The success of these poems set him off on a peripatetic career that moved from London to Wales and America, making a living out of writing, broadcasting, scriptwriting for the Crown Film Unit and lecture tours and readings. As well as his poetry and prose his radio play, *Under Milk Wood*, remains very popular. Thomas played the romantic artist to the hilt, living fast and dying, a hopeless alcoholic, aged only 39, after a final spree in and around New York's notorious Chelsea Hotel. His descent into excess, while studied, was not wholly satisfying, and as he once put it sadly 'Somebody's boring me...I think it's me'.

THOMAS, DYLAN

**Do not go gentle into that good night
Rage, rage against the dying of the light**
Do Not Go Gentle (1951)

Thomas' poem was addressed to his father, whom he knew to be dying, and whose imminent decease filled him with dread. The burden of the poem is that one should not simply accept one's death, however inevitable it may be, but struggle against it with all one's being. The irony of the poem, as Thomas pointed out to a friend, was that since his father was not aware of his own terminal illness, he could not be shown the lines of which he was the subject.

THOMAS, DYLAN

A good poem is a contribution to reality. The world is never the same once a good poem has been added to it. A good poem helps to change the shape and significance of the universe, helps to extend everyone's knowledge of himself and the world around him.
Quite Early One Morning (1960)

Although Thomas was apparently happy to make his more general living in the worlds of broadcasting, documentary scriptwriting and in roistering his way around the lucrative American lecture circuit, his greatest talent, and his reputation, lies in his poetry. Its themes are sex, life and death, and the way they interact, shaping the individual who experiences them. His is not a particularly cheerful vision of humanity, and as he put it 'We are born in others' pain and perish in our own', but he undoubtedly captured the feelings of his many readers, and made it clear that in taking poetry seriously, he could communicate serious attitudes.

THOMAS, DYLAN

Isn't life a terrible thing, thank God.
Under Milk Wood (1954)

Dylan finished his *Under Milk Wood* only six weeks before his death. It was first broadcast by BBC radio on January 25, 1954, and subsequently adapted for the stage. Critics have cited it as the greatest radio play ever written, although others see that same success as grounded in sentiment and rhetoric. The action is set in the small Welsh village of Llareggub (the reverse of Bugger-all) and considers the villagers, exploring their lives, their dreams and memories in verse, ballads and highly poetic prose. This line, delighting in life's perversity, comes from Polly Garter, the local scarlet woman, mixing romantic dreams with a more lurid reality.

THOMAS, EDWARD   (1878–1917) British poet

Yes, I remember Adlestrop
Adlestrop (1915)

Unable to sustain himself by his first love, poetry, Thomas combined his celebration of the the English countryside and its denizens both human and animal, with journalism and biography. Praised by F.R. Leavis as 'an original poet of rare quality' Thomas published two collections of verse but died at Arras during World War I. Adlestrop is a small West Country village, near the Cotswold town of Stow on the Wold. The branch line on which it stands has long since returned to nature, but Thomas' poem commemorates his own passage through the station; his train stopped, no-one got off or got on and for a brief moment Thomas felt that Adlestrop represented the apotheosis of eternal, unworried peace and calm.

THOMPSON, E.P.   academic and anti-nuclear war campaigner

This 'going into Europe' will not turn out to be the thrilling mutual exchange supposed. I do not see the EEC as a great love affair. It was more like nine middle-aged couples with failing marriages meeting at a Brussels hotel for a group grope.
in the *Sunday Times*, April 27, 1975

After years of General de Gaulle telling successive governments 'Non', compounded by a native English insularity that has never really seen the charm of the European Community, the country voted in its first ever referendum and decided after all to join the Common Market. Thompson was right: since then, faced by butter mountains, wine lakes, a Common Agricultural Policy designed for the benefit of peasant smallholdings, the threat of a passport quite unlike the one beloved for years and the election of MPs to a Parliament that has no actual power, the nation has generally regretted its decision to help turn what was 'the Six' into 'the Nine'.

THOMPSON, HUNTER S.   (1939–) American journalist

When the going gets wierd, the wierd turn pro.
Fear and Loathing on the Campaign Trail (1972)

Hunter Thompson was the pioneer of what he called 'gonzo journalism'. Thompson was unique. In 1966 he had written his book *Hell's Angels*, a study of California's leading outlaw bike gang. In the rock magazine *Rolling Stone*, fuelled by fearsome drug cocktails, he offered personalised journalism in a high-speed stream of consciousness that would have been no more than hippie ramblings but for his incisive grasp of the issues at hand; whether covering presidential elections, major sports events or, in the piece that made his name and coined a phrase, suffering 'Fear and Loathing in Las Vegas'. His motto, usually attributed to his alter ego 'Raoul Duke', was the multiple drug abuser's version of the White House's more macho line.

THOMSON, ROY   (1894–1976) Canadian newspaper magnate

You know, it's like having a licence to print your own money.
referring to commercial television in 1957

Roy Thomson worked his way from relative poverty in Toronto to running an international media empire. Flagships of that empire were the *London Times* and *Sunday Times*, both of which flourished as Thomson resisted personal interference, taking care of business while the editors ran the news. This celebrated remark sums up the way in which commercial television stations, admittedly only for those rich enough to obtain a franchise, were indeed the most golden-egged of geese. Its date is debatable: either 1957, when Thomson set up Scottish TV; or possibly earlier in 1954.

THORPE, JEREMY (1929–) British politician

Greater love hath no man than this, that he lay down his friends for his life.
attacking Harold Macmillan, 1962

On July 13 1962 Harold Macmillan, showing the streak of ruthlessness that always lay beneath his much vaunted charm, fired at a single stroke one third of his Cabinet. Some felt these dismissals showed a loss of nerve in the old master, others saw it as the only way to give the Tory front bench a new look, better fitted to the Sixties. As showed by the popular nickname for the purge - the Night of the Long Knives (echoing Hitler's purge of the SA in 1935) – it was popularly seen as a savage betrayal of old allegiances. Jeremy Thorpe, speaking for the Liberals, summed it up by rephrasing John XV:13 for the occasion.

THORPE, JEREMY

Bunnies can (and will) go to France.
letter, February 13 1961

Jeremy Thorpe was the most charismatic leader the Liberal Party had managed to generate since Lloyd George. While he was unlikely to return his party to government, he had managed to drag them some way from their long years of absolute insignificance. This progress collapsed in 1976 when Norman Scott, a former male model, alleged that Thorpe had, fifteen years earlier, been his lover. In 1979 Thorpe was tried for his alleged plan to have Scott murdered. He was acquitted but in an attempt to calm the rumours, he had allowed the publication of a letter in which this embarrassing line was included. The reference 'bunnies' was to Thorpe's description of Scott as a frightened rabbit on the night he had seduced him.

THURBER, JAMES (1894–1961) American writer and cartoonist

Humour is emotional chaos remembered in tranquility.
New York Post, 1960

Thurber was one of the talented team assembled by editor Harold Ross to put together the *New Yorker*. His concern with stylistic perfection came from his model, Henry James, but his 'sure grasp

of confusion' came from his own mother. Thurber wrote prolifically, but his finest achievements were his cartoons. Hymning the
barely repressed desperation of bourgeois life, Thurber peopled
his suburban carnival with three stock characters – the miserable
man, the assertive woman and their dog. Among his best captions
were: 'It's Our Own Story Exactly! He Bold as a Hawk, She Soft
as the Dawn' or 'Well, I'm Disenchanted, Too. We're All
Disenchanted.' He fought unavailingly against gathering blindness and died in 1961. His last words were 'God bless, god
damn...'

THURBER, JAMES

**It's a naive, domestic burgundy, without any breeding. but I
think you'll be amused by its presumption.**
caption to *New Yorker* cartoon, 1943

Thurber's evisceration of the wine snob, touting his arcane
knowledge and his pretentious jargon, has transcended its original role as a cartoon caption and become a joke that identifies the
culinarily pompous in any sphere. Two couples sit around a
dinner table. The host, voluble, expansive and didactic is raising
his glass for inspection. His wife, smiling, follows suit, but their
guests, while humouring their host by duly gazing at their glasses
too, do not look even remotely convinced and if anything, are
extremely worried.

THURBER, JAMES

All right, have it your way – you heard a seal bark.
caption to *New Yorker* cartoon

This is the caption to a classic Thurber cartoon: a man and
woman, drawn in his inimitably sparse style, are lying in bed.
The man looks sceptical but resigned, the woman is refusing to
take no for answer. Above them, watching with detached amusement, a seal is leaning over the headboard of their bed, although
from the line of its mouth it does not appear to be barking.

THURBER, JAMES

That's my first wife up there and this is the present Mrs. Harris.
caption to *New Yorker* cartoon

One of Thurber's more wonderfully surreal cartoons: a man and
his wife are greeting a male friend. It is a conventional enough
room – lamp standard, landscape on the wall, shelves filled with
books. The hosts are smiling, but their guest looks nonplussed.

Could this hesitation be caused by the precise position of 'My First Wife' – crouching on all fours 'up there' on top of the bookcase.

THURBER, JAMES

Well, if I called the wrong number why did you answer the phone?.

cartoon caption in *Men, Women and Dogs*

Thurber's idea of infuriating, blasé womanhood at its devil-may-care worst. A middle-aged man, probably resting after a hard day in a New York office, looks up from his paper. On the floor a dog, also disturbed from his own reflections, looks around. Between them, reclining with legs crossed on their sofa, is a woman, presumably the wife. She is holding an old fashioned telephone and as she holds the earpiece in her right hand, the left holds the speaker at arm's length, all the better for her to upbraid the fool at the other end who had the temerity to answer his phone even though he should have known it wasn't him that she was ringing.

THURBER, JAMES

Then, with that faint fleeting smile playing about his lips, he faced the firing squad; erect and motionless, proud and disdainful, Walter Mitty, the undefeated, inscrutable to the last.

My World and Welcome to It (1932)

Like P.G. Wodehouse's Bertie Wooster, whose fantasies often see him 'flicking an invisible speck of dirt from the incomparable Mechlin lace at his wrist', Thurber's Walter Mitty draws his daydreams from the more lurid type of romantic and adventure fiction. Mitty is driving his wife on a mundane shopping expedition, the main purpose of which is her purchase of overshoes for him, telling him that 'You're not a young man any longer'. As he waits for her to shop, his 'secret life' runs the gamut of submarine captain, top-class surgeon, falsely accused murder trial defendant, World War I air ace and finally, as his wife's nagging reaches a crescendo, debonair target of a firing squad.

TIMERMAN, JACOBO (1923–) Argentine journalist

One point has already been proved. Everything that happened once can happen again.

Prisoner Without a Name, Cell Without a Number (1981)

Timerman was the editor of the main liberal paper in Buenos Aires during the worst period of right-wing terror in Argentina.

As a Jew, he came doubly under suspicion and in April 1977 was imprisoned and tortured. Released in September 1977, he was held under house arrest until 1979. His release was ordered by the Supreme Court but the ruling junta refused to allow him his freedom. Finally, after losing his citizenship and his possessions he was expelled from Argentina. He moved to Israel where he wrote this memoir of his experiences, in which he notes that even though a new government rules his country, the bad old days can always return.

TIMES, THE

It *Is* A Moral Issue
title of leader, June 11, 1963

The Profumo Affair, in which the Minister of Defence not only shared a call-girl with a member of the Russian embassy but also lied about his entanglements to the House of Commons, may have amused many of the public, but it appalled the Establishment. Nowhere was spluttering indignation more perfectly summed up than in *The Times*, which thundered its opinion: It *Is* A Moral Issue. What really irked editor Sir William Haley was not that Profumo had enjoyed his debauch, but that he had failed to tell his fellow MPs the truth. The leader equated the country's growing affluence with what it saw as moral decline: Conservative policies had brought the nation 'spiritually and psychologically to a low ebb'.

TIMES, THE

Who Breaks a Butterfly on a Wheel
title of leader, July 1, 1967

On February 12, 1967, tipped off by the *News of the World*, the police raided rock star Keith Richard's country home. Here they arrested Richard, Mick Jagger and art dealer Robert Fraser, charging them with possession of drugs. All three were found guilty: Richard was jailed for twelve months, Fraser for six and Jagger for three. The feeling that the establishment, eager to squash a couple of pop musicians whom they saw as spearheading the national decline, had gone too far was summed up on July 1, when *The Times* weighed in. Editor William Rees-Mogg took the headline of his leader from Pope's Epistle to Dr. Arbuthnot (1735): 'Satire or sense, alas! can Sporus feel? / Who breaks a butterfly upon a wheel?' and continues to deride fear of 'this bug with gilded wings − / This painted child of dirt, that stinks and stings'. He condemned Jagger's sentence, for four pep pills, as

absurd and suggested that had the star been 'any purely anonymous young man' things would have been very different. The
sentences were overturned on appeal.

TIZARD, HENRY   (1885–1959) British scientist

**The secret of science is to ask the right question, and it is the
choice of problem more than anything else that marks the man of
genius in the scientific world.**
quoted in C.P. Snow 'A Postscript to Science of Government' (1962)

In 1935 Sir Henry Tizard was chairman of the Committee for
Scientific Survey of Air Defence. He chose to adopt the still
fledgling invention that became known as 'radar' as the basis for
an early-warning coastal defence system; this undoubtedly
helped win the Battle of Britain and thus stave off Hitler's
invasion plans. Ironically, a quarrel with his old friend Linde-
mann, Churchill's favourite scientific adviser, meant that his
talents were ignored during the War. Afterwards he headed
committees on defence and on scientific policy, in both of which
he championed his scepticism of the usefulness of an independent British deterrent.

TO HAVE AND HAVE NOT

**You know you don't have to act with me, Steve. You don't have to
say anything and you don't have to do anything. Not a thing. Oh
maybe just whistle. You know how to whistle, don't you, Steve.
You just put your lips together and blow.**
screenplay by Jules Furthman and William Faulkner (1945)

Director Howard Hawks explained the genesis of this movie
thus: he and Hemingway were hunting together when he told
'Papa' that he could take his worst story and make a film out of it.
Hemingway suggested To Have and Have Not and Hawks duly
delivered. The hit of the film was not the plot, anyway, but the 19-
year-old model, Lauren Bacall. This particular scene, in which
she comes on strong to Bogart, inspired one writer to say 'Her
husky, underslung voice, which is ideal for the double-
entendres, makes even her simplest remarks seem like jungle
mating cries'. Nature then copied art and the two actually fell in
love during the shooting, living reasonably happily ever after
until Bogart's death in 1957.

TOFFLER, ALVIN   (1927–) American academic
Future Shock
book title, 1972

Toffler is one of America's most successful futurologists, who has made a career out of assessing the state of the world, especially as regards the cutting edge of technological progress, and prophesying what may happen. He defined his theory in the book of which it was the title: 'Future shock is the disorientation that effects an individual, a corporation or a country when he or it is overwhelmed by change and the prospect of change. It is the consequence of having to make too many decisions about too many new and unfamiliar problems in too short a time. Future shock is more than a metaphor. It is a form of personal and social breakdown.' Toffler was also responsible in his book *The Culture Consumers* (1964) for a concept known as The Law of Raspberry Jam, a theory that states 'The wider any culture is spread, the thinner it gets.'

TOKLAS, ALICE B. (1877–1967) American secretary and companion

As if a cookbook had anything to do with writing.
The Alice B. Toklas Cookbook (1954)

If *The Autobiography of Alice B. Toklas* (1933) was no more than a thinly disguised memoir of the life of its real author, Gertrude Stein, at least Ms. Stein's companion and secretary managed to write her own cookbook, itself as full of memoirs as of recipes. Although she dismisses the idea of 'writing' in a cookbook, her own effort creates a successful mix of literary quality and culinary knowledge, embellished by many anecdotes of the celebrities she knew. When Stein died she left everything to her companion but the Stein family ensured that Toklas received only a pittance.

TOLKIEN, J.R.R. (1892–1973) British philologist and writer

One Ring to rule them all,
One Ring to find them,
One Ring to bring them all
and in the darkness bind them.
Lord of the Rings (1954-55)

Neither in 1937 when J.R.R. Tolkien created the world and mythology of Middle Earth in *The Hobbit*, nor when he followed it in 1954 with his trilogy *Lord of the Rings* did the then Merton Professor of English language and literature at Oxford University envisage providing a literary fantasy land for half the world's hippies. Tolkien's primary aim had been to create a world that reflected his Christianity, his dislike of modernism in the arts and modernity in life. That Middle Earth was chosen as the name of the most LSD-drenched of London's hippie clubs appalled him and he eschewed any advances from the 'alternative society'.

TOMALIN, NICHOLAS   (–1973) British journalist

The only qualities for real success in journalism are ratlike cunning, a plausible manner and a little literary ability. The capacity to steal other people's ideas and phrases...is also invaluable.
Stop the Press, I Want to Get On

Nicholas Tomalin was among the most talented of the young journalists who were employed on the *Sunday Times* during the paper's heyday in the mid-Sixties and early Seventies. Tomalin, who was killed when his jeep went over a mine during the Yom Kippur war of October 1973, used this description of his own profession in a collection of his pieces. The phrase 'ratlike cunning' is particularly treasured by the more cynical of his colleagues.

TOMKINS, CALVIN   American writer

Living well is the best revenge
book title, 1971

Tomkins' book is the biography of Gerald Murphy (1888–1964) and his wife Sara (nee Wiborg). This rich, indolent young couple were among the first Americans to settle in the South of France, pioneering a flood of chic American expatriates who found it hot, cheap and satisfyingly distant from their less privileged compatriots. The Murphys had a wide social circle, but they are best known for their friendship with F. Scott Fitzgerald and his wife Zelda, a relationship best illustrated in Fitzgerald's book *Tender Is The Night* (1934).

TOWNSHEND, PETE   (1945–) British rock musician

I hope I die before I get old
'My Generation' (1965)

If rock'n'roll is nothing else it is teenage angst: lust and rebellion in equal measures, discovered anew by every fresh generation. Some bands give riot and some romance. For the teenagers of 1965 The Who served up the former, summed up in Pete Townshend's anthem 'My Generation', defying those who 'try to put us down / Just because we get around' and looking forward to an early death with all the insouciance of those who still believe in their own immortality. Townshend now combines music with publishing and has replaced early plaints with the charms of stability, saying that 'Nothing can really be better than waking up in the morning and everything is still the same as it was the day before. That's the best thing you can have in life – consistency of some kind.'

TOWNSHEND, ROBERT   (1920–) American writer

Getting there isn't half the fun – it's all the fun.
Up the Organisation (1970)

Townshend's guide to the corporate labyrinth was one of the successes of its year, a one-off publishing hit seized upon by a variety of young and not so young executives in the hope of solving their more pressing problems. His premise is that the real charm of playing office politics is the game, not the result. Once one has reached the top the fun is over, presumably because one finally has to take responsibility on oneself rather than merely manipulating that of others.

TOYNBEE, ARNOLD   (1889–1975) British historian

America is a large, friendly dog in a very small room. Every time it wags its tail it knocks over a chair.
broadcast on July 14, 1954

Toynbee was a specialist in Greek and Byzantine history and in international relations. His major work, *A Study of History* (10 vols. 1934–54), posits his theory of the way in which civilisations move in cycles. Drawing on studies of 21 different civilisations he shows the way in which they have all developed and then, after reaching their peak, duly declined. Professional historians were highly critical of Toynbee's method and his many errors in detail, but the public made a best-seller out of the book's abridged version, although few read it today. Toynbee's more important legacy was to break the mould of exclusively Western-orientated historiography and to open the way for the study of comparative history.

TOYNBEE, ARNOLD

The human race's prospects of survival were considerably better when we were defenceless against tigers than they are today when we have become defenceless against ourselves.
in the *Observer*, 1963

TRILLING, LIONEL   (1905–75) American literary critic

We who are liberal and progressive know that the poor are our equals in every sense except that of being equal to us.
The Liberal Imagination (1950)

TRILLING, LIONEL

Trilling was one of America's most influential critics, whose opinions were substantially conditioned by his admiration for Freud and his essentially liberal, humanist philosophies. He wrote his first book on Matthew Arnold and followed this with studies of a wide variety of literary figures. *The Liberal Imagination* is a collection of essays, in which he attempts to establish literary criticism as central to a more general culture, linking liberal ideas of both literature and society.

TRILLING, LIONEL

Immature artists imitate. Mature artists steal.
quoted in *Esquire* magazine, 1962

Trilling's remark, which is presumably less of an encouragement to plagiarism than the suggestion that one should take from one's expert predecessors their methods, rather than the content of their work, is hardly novel. T.S. Eliot suggested that 'Immature poets imitate, mature poets steal', and both Picasso and Stravinsky within their own disciplines have made much the same point.

TROTSKY, LEON   (1879–1940) Russian revolutionary leader

Insurrection is an art, and like all arts it has its laws.
History of the Russian Revolution (1932–33)

Trotsky, né Bronstein, was a leader of the Russian Revolution and the creator of the concept of 'permanent revolution', whereby Marx's theories were combined with Russian practice. His premise was that a revolution in one country should touch off another in a second, which would both sustain the first and encourage a third, and so on; he hoped that the Russian Revolution of 1917 would set this process in motion. As organiser of the Red Army, Trotsky ensured both a Bolshevik victory in the Civil War and his own rapid rise in the Party hierarchy. When Lenin fell ill in 1924 Trotsky, an intellectual but no politician, was easily outmanoeuvred in the power struggle by Stalin and in 1929 was actually banished from Russia. From his home in Mexico he continued to fulminate against Stalinist 'degeneration' until, in 1940, he was assassinated, presumably by Stalin's agents.

TRUMAN, HARRY S.   (1884–1972) American president

If you can't stand the heat, get out of the kitchen.
slogan

Truman succeeded Franklin D. Roosevelt who died suddenly, six weeks into his fourth term of office. Little was expected of him but he grew with the office and within four months was faced with giving the go-ahead to the first ever use of an atomic bomb. Re-elected narrowly in 1948, Truman pushed forward his 'Fair Deal' programme of social and educational reforms but failed to gain Congressional backing to make them law. Unabashed he moved to expand American influence, capitalising upon her superpower status to encourage her supporters in other, smaller countries and thus attempt to 'contain' Communism. Truman was a gutsy competitor, an image exemplified by the two mottoes that stood on his desk. One suggested that those who 'can't stand the heat should get out of the kitchen', the other declared 'The buck stops here'.

TRUMAN, HARRY S.

If you can't convince them, confuse them.

TRUMAN, HARRY S.

This is the greatest thing in history.
on the first A-bomb, 1945

Truman's decisive authorisation of the bombing of Japan was in part an attempt to confound his critics and show that despite his brief period in office he was the right man for the job; despite this many felt that his go-ahead was overly precipitous. Historians continue to argue whether Truman should in fact have warned the Japanese further and in greater detail, or whether by dropping the bomb he actually saved lives, both American and Japanese, by curtailing the war of attrition in the Pacific islands. Truman's own views were clear, when at a seminar at Columbia University in April 1958 he told his listeners 'The atom bomb was no "great decision"....It was merely another powerful weapon in the arsenal of righteousness', itself an envangelistic twist on Roosevelt's oft-quoted 'arsenal of democracy' (qv).

TRUMAN, HARRY S.

A leader is a man who has the ability to get other people to do what they don't want to do and like it.
quoted in *The People's Almanac* (1975)

By his own definition, Truman was a good leader. He resisted those who tried to sway him in directions he disliked, and managed to make others do what he wanted. His most celebrated run-in was with General Douglas MacArthur, who wanted a full-scale invasion of China and an extension of the Korean War. When MacArthur, an ex-war hero with plenty of public support, refused to accept the Presidential policy of moderation, Truman fired him, reminiscing in 1961 'I fired MacArthur because he wouldn't respect the authority of the President. I didn't fire him because he was a dumb son of a bitch, although he was, but that's not against the law for generals. If it was, half to three quarters of them would be in jail.'

TUCHMAN, BARBARA   (1912–) American historian

War is the unfolding of miscalculations.
The Guns of August (1962)

The further the study of history moves from the simple listings of kings and the battles they fought, the more apparent it becomes that the subject deals less in cool calculations than in the fortunate or not so fortunate outcome of sustained error: the conspiracy or the cock-up theory. Barbara Tuchman's Pulitzer Prize winning study of the battles of the first month of World War I produced a conclusion that stems very much from the latter style. A journalist and historian, her other works have included studies of the buildup to World War I, and of 14th century Europe.

TUCKER, SOPHIE   (1884–1966) American singer

From birth to age eighteen a girl needs good parents, from eighteen to thirty-five she needs good looks, from thirty-five she needs a good personality. From fifty-five on, she needs good cash.
quoted in 1953

Tucker was born in Russia as either Sonia Kalish or Sophie Abuza, depending on one's source. Once her family had moved to America she set about wowing vaudeville audiences with a brand of singing that had her nicknamed the 'red-hot momma', a heavyweight chanteuse who belted out the lyrics like no-one else. Her various essays into the movies have left little trace, but her single aphorism has the ring of experience.

TURNER, E.S.   (1909–) British writer

Advertising is the whip which hustles humanity up the road to the Better Mousetrap. It is the vision which reproaches man for the paucity of his desires.
The Shocking History of Advertising (1952)

Freelance writer Turner concentrated on the early history of advertising, leaving its post-World War II developments to other hands. As this comment makes clear, the difference between the modern version and its forbears, whether in Elizabethan broad-sides or Edwardian magazines, is only in chronology; the tech-niques, while increasingly sophisticated, have but a single aim: to part the consumer from his or her money. As George Orwell put it 'Advertising is the rattling of a stick inside a swill bucket.'

TWAIN, MARK   (1835–1910) American humourist

There are three kinds of lies – lies, damned lies, and statistics.
Autobiography (1924)

This line, which refers to the way in which all interested parties, especially governments, manipulate supposedly unimpeachable statistics in their own interest, is often attributed to Mark Twain. *The Autobiography,* in which he uses the line, shows that he is in fact quoting it, and gives his attribution to Disraeli (1804–81). Other claimants are Henry Labouchère (1798–1869) and Abram Hewitt (1822–1903). Its most recent use was as the title of *Lies, Damned Lies and Some Exclusives,* journalist Henry Porter's exposé of the way Fleet Street manufactures and manipulates some of its most notorious stories.

2001: A SPACE ODYSSEY

Open the pod door, Hal.
screenplay by Arthur C. Clarke (1968)

Clarke's obsession with space travel and his reputation as a leading writer of science fiction made him the ideal choice for scriptwriter on Stanley Kubrick's epochal film of human develop-ment and space exploration. Clarke's plot turns on man's encounter with a higher, alien intelligence, both at the earliest stage of evolution and in the year two thousand and one. The 'Hal' of this request is the massive computer that controls the spaceship and which attempts to take over from the humans who control it. The letters H A L are each a single alphabetical place back from IBM, the initials of the world's multinational computer purveyor.

TYNAN, KENNETH   (1927–80) British drama critic

A good drama critic is one who perceives what is happening in the theatre of his time. A great drama critic also perceives what is not happening.
Tynan Left and Right (1967)

Tynan was one of the most influential critics in Britain or America, a major force in the modern theatre whose own campaigning helped change the play-going habits of the century. He made it clear that while others might be satisfied with what was happening on the English stage, he was not. Thus, when John Osborne's play *Look Back In Anger* (1956), ushered in a potential revolution, he embraced it whole-heartedly. Tynan championed many young playwrights, as well as major European talents such as Ionesco and Beckett. He was instrumental in the founding of the National Theatre and a long-time supporter of the Royal Court's English Stage Company.

TYNAN, KENNETH

The liberal (on pornography)... is like a man who loathes whore-houses in practice, but doesn't mind them in principle, providing they are designed by Mies van der Rohe and staffed by social workers in Balenciaga dresses.
in *Esquire* magazine, 1968

Tynan's own views on pornography were decidedly less mealy-mouthed and to prove his point he staged *Oh Calcutta* or 'Oh quel cul tu as' or 'Oh what an arse you have'. 'Mr. Tynan's Nude Review' (*The Times*) appeared in New York in 1969 and in London in 1970. In essence a mix of a grubbier than usual undergraduate review and *Hair* with pubes, it called upon the talents of such as Joe Orton, John Lennon and Samuel Beckett. The anti-pornography lobby duly fulminated and Tynan deligh-tedly fanned the flames but in the end the authorities refused to sanction censorious demands for a prosecution and the show degenerated into coach party fodder.

TYNAN, KENNETH

I doubt if there are any rational people to whom the word 'fuck' would be particularly diabolical, revolting, or totally forbidden.
on BBC television, November 1966

As opposed to his accomplishments in the relatively exclusive world of the theatre, Tynan's fame in a wider arena may well attach to his dubious reputation as having been the first man to say 'fuck' on television. Given his propensity for self-advertise-ment, he probably engineered the situation, but in a supposedly 'permissive' world, he might genuinely have hoped that the 'rational people' would not be drowned out, as they were, by the bayings of the puritans. Tynan's best remark on the delights of hardcore, is his pun on the proverbial 'old habits die hard'. From his point of view, when it came to sexual turn-ons, 'old hards die habits.'

Tynan, Kenneth

Show me a congenital eavesdropper with the instincts of a Peeping Tom and I will show you the makings of a dramatist. ...Would you know the shortest way to good playwriting? Pause on the stairs.

Pausing on the Stairs (1957)

Tynan's piece concerns the best way to write a play. It begins by assuring the putative playwright that starting off with 'a great theme, a Grand Purpose' is the worst of errors and he condemns, without specifying, those who purvey uplifting political dramas. Instead 'the genesis of good plays...(is) something as concrete and casual as a glance intercepted, a remark overheard, or an insignificant news item...'. On those grounds he contends that curiosity about real people is the basis of good playwriting. It cannot provide everything one requires, but for Tynan the Peeping Tom wins out every time over the polemicist.

Tzara, Tristan (1896–1963) (Samuel Rosenstock) French artist

Any work of art than can be understood is the work of journalism.

In 1916 Tzara helped found the dadaist movement at Zurich's Café Voltaire. The movement exhibited its disillusion with the conventional art world by gestures of ostentatiously nihilistic flippancy. The name was plucked from a dictionary and meant nothing. The movement reached its peak in Paris between 1920-22, its gradual decline matching the growth of its successor, surrealism whose ranks Tzara eventually joined. In 1931 he wrote his masterpiece *L'homme approximatif (Approximate Man)*, a defiantly complex piece of writing that in no way even approached the category of 'journalism'. He joined the Communist Party in 1935 and the French resistance during World War II. After the war he continued to write poetry, but the intensity of earlier years had faded, even if the work was far easier to understand.

U

UPDIKE, JOHN (1932–) American novelist

Appealingness is inversely proportional to attainability.
in the *New Yorker*, 1975

Updike is a mainstay of the *New Yorker*, where much of his work
has originated, although he has not been a staff member since
1957. He is best known for his '*Rabbit*' trilogy featuring the
precarious adventures of the former basketball star turned subur-
banite Harry 'Rabbit' Angstrom. Updike's dictum, with its corollary 'Possession diminishes perception of value, immediately', is
in effect a slightly more elegant way of pointing out that not only
is the grass always greener, but once you're standing on it, what
was the road seems frustratingly to have turned into even more
verdant greenery.

USBORNE, RICHARD (1910–) British writer

**There is no suggestion that either clubman or girl would recog-
nize a double bed except as so much extra sweat to make an
apple-pie of.**
Wodehouse at Work (1961)

Richard Usborne is the best-known analyst of the works of
humourist P.G. Wodehouse. His first book was *Clubland Heroes*
(1953), a critical, but never over-serious study of the work of three
popular story-tellers: Sapper, Dornford Yates and John Buchan,
creators respectively of Bulldog Drummond, Berry, and Richard
Hannay. The clubmen to whom he is referring here may well
have read such writers, but they are of Wodehouse's world and as
such members of his fictional club, The Drones. Usborne is
making the point that despite the proliferation of pretty girls in
Wodehouse's stories, sex has yet to rear its serpentine head in this
unspoilt Eden.

V

Valéry, Paul (1871–1945) French writer

A man who is 'of sound mind' is one who keeps the inner madman under lock and key.
Mauvaises pensées et autres (1942)

Valéry studied mathematics and philosophy and both disciplines can be seen in the twin interests which dominated his life: the creation of a 'pure' poetry and his concern with the way the human mind works. The bulk of his work reflects the desire to create verse that minimised the presence of ideas or emotions, although his most celebrated poem *La Cimitière marin* (1922) is a disquisition on the difference between pagan and Christian attitudes to death. Valéry was elected to the French Academy in 1925 and until his death acted as an intellectual lodestone, to be produced and questioned as to his responses on a wide variety of topics.

Valéry, Paul

God created man, and finding him not sufficiently alone, gave him a companion to make him feel his solitude more.
Tel quel (1943)

Valéry, Paul

Politics is the art of preventing people from taking part in affairs which properly concern them.
Tel quel (1943)

Van Damm, Vivien British theatrical manager;

We Never Closed
slogan of the Windmill Theatre, 1939–45

The Windmill, described by stage historian John Fisher as 'disreputably innocent', was London's down-market answer to Paris' Folies Bergères. Apart from the difference in glamour and reputation, the Lord Chamberlain had only issued its manager Vivien Van Damm a license in 1932 on the grounds that his tableaux of naked girls should never, under any circumstances, move. Many future English comic stars played there, including

Alfred Marks, Tommy Cooper, Michael Bentine and Jimmy Edwards,but they were mere padding for the main attractions. The Windmill had only one real boast, underlined in this slogan: all through the Blitz, all through the War, Van Damm kept the doors open.

Vanzetti, Bartolomeo (–1927) American radical

If it had not been for these things, I might have lived out my life talking at street corners to scorning men. I might have died unmarked, unknown, a failure. Now we are not a failure. This is our career and our triumph. Never in our full life could we hope to do such work for tolerance, for justice, for man's understanding of man as we now do by accident. Our word – our lives – our pains – nothing! The taking of our lives – lives of a good shoemaker and a poor fish-pedlar – all! That last moment belongs to us – that agony is our triumph.
on receiving the death sentence, 1927

The Sacco-Vanzetti case, culminating in their execution in August 1927, was one of the great focal points of liberal opinion. Both avowed anarchists, they were arrested in 1920 for the killing of two men in a payroll robbery. To the world's liberals, who campaigned in vain against their death, it seemed that their trial had been a perversion of justice: they had been convicted in a surge of xenophobia, accentuated by the hysterical anti-Communism of Attorney-General Palmer. Before they were hanged both gave a statement, of which Vanzetti's, above, became one of America's required high school civics texts. Vanzetti has since been seen as innocent of murder while experts believe that Sacco probably did kill the two men. He too gave a last statement: 'I am so convinced to be right that if you execute me two times, and if I could be reborn those other two times, I would live again to do what I have already.'

VARIETY

Sticks Nix Hix Pix

Variety magazine was founded at the turn of the century by New York journalist Sime Silverman (1873-1933) and soon became recognised as the bible of American show business. As part of its regular reporting, the magazine developed a form of jargon that made it quite unique. Singers were 'terpers' or 'terps' (from the goddess Terpsichore), directors were 'meggers' and to direct a movie was to 'meg' (from the megaphone used in the silent era), shows were not just good, they were 'sock B.O.' (for box office) and so on. 'Variety-speak' reaches its apogee in its headlines. This one mixes slang and typical Variety spelling to explain that Sticks (rural movie theatres) Nix (do not like) Hix Pix (pictures about hicks, ie. those who live in the country). Other great Variety headlines include 'Wall Street Lays an Egg': the Wall Street Crash of Black Friday, October 1929; and 'Egghead Weds Hourglass': the marriage of playwright Arthur Miller to Marilyn Monroe.

VEECK, BILL (1914–) American sports entrepreneur

The only promotion rules I can think of are that a sense of shame is to be avoided at all costs and there is never any reason for a hustler to be less cunning than more virtuous men. Oh yes...whenever you think you've got something really great, add ten per cent more.
quoted in 1965

Bill Veeck (pronounced 'vek') is the king of American sporting ballyhoo; William L. (some say for Lunacy) Veeck has done more than any other to bring sport into the world of show business. His finest hour came on August 19, 1951 when he introduced into his baseball team, the St. Louis Browns, one Edward Gaedel. Gaedel, (1925-61), stood just 3' 7" tall. He popped out of an outsize birthday cake, waving a bat and displaying his number '1/8' on his uniform. The fans presumed this was just one more tasteless Veeck gimmick until halfway through the first innings Gaedel came up to bat. As pitcher Bobby Cain collapsed in laughter, and the umpire demanded to see (and was shown) Gaedel's contract, the diminutive hitter announced 'Throw it in there, fat, and I'll moider it!'. The next day his contract was declared invalid and baseball returned to normal proportions.

VICKY (1913–1966) British cartoonist

Introducing SuperMac
cartoon caption in the *Evening Standard*, November 6, 1958

Vicky (Victor Weiss) was one of Britain's best known political cartoonists, working on London's *Evening Standard*. In November 1958 he produced a cartoon titled 'Introducing Super-Mac' which featured the prime minister, Harold Macmillan, garbed in the distinctive uniform of the popular comic hero

Superman. It was perhaps ironic that Weiss, a founder member of CND, should be the instigator of this image of Macmillan, who was undoubtedly at the height of his success, poised between his 'Never had it so good' speech of 1957 and his general election victory of 1959. Another supposed critic, Aneurin Bevan, came up with his own nickname: 'MacWonder'.

VIDAL, GORE (1925–) American novelist, essayist, critic and dramatist

To the right wing 'law and order' is often just a code phrase, meaning 'get the niggers'. To the left wing it often means political oppression.
in 1975

Vidal was born into America's aristocracy, although he claims to have eschewed such connections, making his own reputation as a novelist, a scriptwriter and playwright and an essayist and critic. But when these last touch on the great and on their doings, he writes with an easy familiarity denied to less privileged men. Along with Truman Capote and Norman Mailer, Vidal was cited as one of the literary wunderkinder of the late 1940s. He blunted this approval in 1948, by offering in *The City and the Pillar* a portrait of a homosexual that was too sympathetic for contemporary tastes. Best known in the Fifties for his stage plays, as well as working for a while in Hollywood, Vidal has re-established his fiction with a mix of satires and historical novels. For many readers his strength lies in his essays, which consistently expose the pomposity, the pretension and the self-delusion of modern politics, culture and society, pricking a variety of inflated bubbles with impartial disdain.

VIDAL, GORE

Sex is. There is nothing more to be done about it. Sex builds no roads, writes no novels and sex certainly gives no meaning to anything in life but itself.
Norman Mailer's Self-Advertisements (1960)

VIDAL, GORE

The genius of our ruling class is that it has kept a majority of the people from ever questioning the inequity of a system where most people drudge along paying heavy taxes for which they get nothing in return.

VIDAL, GORE

Having no talent is no longer enough.

VIDAL, GORE

Commercialism is doing well that which should not be done at all.

VIDAL, GORE

What is there to say, finally, except that pain is bad and pleasure good, life all, death nothing.

in *Esquire* magazine, 1970

VIDAL, GORE

Each of us contains a private self and a public self. When the two have not met, their host tends to be average... amicable, self-deluding and given to sudden attacks of melancholy whose origin he does not suspect. When the two selves openly disdain each other, the host is apt to be a strong-minded opportunist...when the selves wrangle, the host is more a man of conscience than of action. When the two are in fierce and total conflict, the host is a lunatic – or a saint.

in *Esquire* magazine, 1968

VIDAL, GORE

It is not possible to regard our race with anything but alarm.... From primeval ooze to the stars, we killed anything that stood in our way, including each other.

in *Esquire* magazine, 1970

VIDAL, GORE

'After she was dead, I loved her.' That is the story of every life – and death.

in the *New York Review of Books*, 1980

VIDAL, GORE

The man and woman make love, attain climax, fall separate. Then she whispers 'I'll tell you who I was thinking of if you tell me who you were thinking of.' Like most sex jokes the origin of the pleasant exchange is obscure. But whatever the source, it seldom fails to evoke a certain awful recognition.

in the *New York Review of Books*, 1966

VIDAL, GORE

Style is knowing who you are, what you want to say, and not giving a damn.
in the *Daily Express*, 1973

VIDAL, GORE

Photography is the 'art form' of the untalented.
in the *New Statesman*, 1978

VIDAL, GORE

I can understand companionship. I can understand bought sex in the afternoon. I cannot understand the love affair.
in the *Sunday Times*, 1973

VIDAL, GORE

Wisdom is deepest platitude.
on London Weekend Television, 1981

VIDAL, GORE

Forcing the world to adjust to oneself has always seemed to me an honourable life work...that one fails in the end is irrelevant.
quoted in *Behind the Scenes*, ed. Joseph P. McCrindle

VON BRAUN, WERNHER (1912–77) German rocket scientist

It was very successful, but it fell on the wrong planet.

Von Braun, like many other German scientists who were involved in rocket research at the time, was conscripted into the German war effort by Hitler. This remark refers to the V2 rocket attacks on London during World War II. After the war he moved to America where he continued his work in civilian rocketry and played a major role in the development of the Apollo moon programme of the 1960s.

VON STROHEIM, ERICH (1885–1957) American film director

This isn't the worst – the worst is that they stole twenty-five years of my life.
last words, 1957

Von Stroheim's last words, a final despairing attack on the Hollywood which had exploited but never appreciated his talents. Although 'the man you love to hate' was popularly equated with the stereotype of Prussian Junkerdom, he was in fact an Austrian Jew who emigrated to America and then to Hollywood. He began directing in 1919 and created a series of pictures that were typified by his mordant critique of society, especially in its sexual habits. Lavish in his sets, leisurely in his direction and scandalous in conduct (rumour had it that the orgies he shot were real), von Stroheim terrified an increasingly puritan Hollywood. He made no major pictures after 1930, but continued to act, notably in *Sunset Boulevard* (1950), a role in which he displayed his contempt for a system in which mediocrity was invariably preferred over real talent.

VONNEGUT JR., KURT (1922–) American writer

It strikes me as gruesome and comical that in our culture we have an expectation that a man can always solve his problems. This is so untrue that it makes me want to cry – or laugh.
in *Playboy*, 1973

Vonnegut began his career with *Player Piano* (1952), an ostensible work of science fiction, but this novel, like its various successors, combined traditional sci-fi with realism, fantasy and satire, often directed at contemporary political targets. Vonnegut has created a unique style, in which he uses a simplicity reminiscent of a child's history primer, to put across usually complex facts. Typical is his summary of the Vietnam War in *Breakfast of Champions* (1973), which title derives from the advertising slogan used since 1950 to advertise the cereal Wheaties: 'Vietnam was a country where America was trying to make people stop being Communists by dropping things on them from airplanes.'

W

WALD, GEORGE (1906–) American biochemist

We are the products of editing, rather than authorship.
The Origin of Optical Activity (1957)

Wald is an American biochemist who in 1967 shared the Nobel Prize for his work on the chemistry of vision. In 1969 Wald left the laboratory and the classroom to establish himself as one of the most articulate spokesmen against American involvement in Vietnam, delivering a powerful speech entitled 'A World to Win' to a meeting at MIT and going on to address many such meetings, rallies, etc. In 1977 he became professor emeritus at Harvard and since 1980 has been vice-president of the Permanent People's Tribunal, a human rights organisation based in Rome.

WALESA, LECH (1943–) Polish trade unionist

The hungry hare has no frontiers and doesn't follow ideologies. The hungry hare goes where it finds the food. And the other hares don't block its passage with the tanks.
interviewed by Oriana Fallaci, 1981

Walesa was one of the leaders in the strike at the Gdansk shipyard in Poland in 1980 that led to the establishment in August of the Solidarity movement, the national confederation of trade unions. Walesa found himself the figurehead of 9.5 million Poles, and as such spotlighted by the authorities as the government (with Russia in the background) and the unions moved ever closer to a political confrontation. Walesa himself was a moderate and a devout Catholic, whose personality helped gain the approval of the powerful Polish church. Solidarity's bid to change Polish society ended when General Jaruzelski, appointed in September 1981 in the hope of finding some solution before Soviet troops moved in to quell the movement, broke off negotiations with Walesa in December 1981.

WALKER, SYD British comedian

What would you do, chums?
in *Band Wagon*, BBC radio 1939

Band Wagon, starring 'Big-Hearted' Arthur Askey and Richard 'Stinker' Murdoch, was BBC Light Entertainment's most popular show before World War II. Among the regular features were

'Chestnut Corner', a respository for appalling jokes, and 'Mr. Walker Wants to Know', featuring 'The Philosophic Dustman', cockney Syd Walker. Walker, posing as a rag-and-bone man and announcing himself as 'Your old china Syd Walker still seeing it through, chums', would tell a story of something that had happened to him last week and ask his audience for their opinion, prefacing his question with his catchphrase 'What would you do, chums?' and signing off the spot with a request to 'Drop me a postcard and tell me what you would have done'.

WALKER, JAMES J. (1881–1946) American politician

A reformer is a man who rides through a sewer in a glass-bottomed boat.
dictum

Walker epitomised Theodore H. White's maxim: 'People will forgive a politician they love almost any sin'. Elected with the backing of New York's Democratic political machine, Tammany Hall, Walker's career showed him to be a devoted follower of Tammany's founder, George Washington Plunkitt, who summed up his life: 'I seen my opportunities and I took them'. Despite charges of corruption against the man who liked to describe himself as 'New York's "night mayor" ', Walker held on through the Twenties until in 1932 further investigations proved massive municipal malfeasance. Walker resigned, and prudently took a trip to Europe, but never really forfeited the affection of the voters who loved his sparkling style.

WALLACE, EDGAR   (1875–1932) British novelist

What is a highbrow? It is a man who has found something more interesting than women.
interviewed in 1931

Wallace was born illegitimate and brought up in poverty in London. After selling papers in Fleet Street he went to South Africa as a soldier, but moved on to work as a war correspondent for Reuters. In 1905, back in England, he wrote the hugely successful *The Four Just Men* and followed it in 1911 with *Sanders of the River*. For the next twenty years Wallace made himself into the world's most prolific writer, penning 170 books totalling millions of words and 27 million sales, as well as 17 plays and a regular horse-racing column for the press. Many of his books were filmed. Wallace spent as fast, if not faster than he earned, a Big Spender of awesome dedication, who lived the

Good Life to the full and died, writing the script of *King Kong* for Hollywood, some £140,000 in debt.

WALLACE, GEORGE   (1919–) American politician

I draw the line in the dust and toss the gauntlet before the feet of tyranny and I say segregation now, segregation tomorrow and segregation forever!
inaugural address as Governor of Alabama, 1963

In the 1960s George Corley Wallace came to symbolise traditional Southern race relations, backing segregation and systematically denying black civil rights. On June 13 1963 Wallace literally drew his line, standing in the doorway of the University of Alabama to defy, as Governor, the efforts of federal officials to bring in two black students. Wallace scorned the efforts of 'pointed-headed professors' to change his views and based his own popularity on his flair for articulating the feelings of his white lower middle class supporters. He reached his peak in 1968, campaigning under the slogan 'Send Them a Message', and promising to take the opinions of the average American to Washington. Wallace's career was shattered when in 1972 he survived Arthur Bremer's assassination attempt, which left him confined to a wheelchair. Since then Wallace has vastly modified his stance on race, gaining much Black support in his state. He officially resigned from politics in 1987.

WALLACE, HENRY   (1888–1965) American vice-president

The century on which we are entering can be and must be the century of the common man.
speech, May 8 1942

Wallace, whose father had held the job, became Secretary of Agriculture in 1933. In office he used his researches into the development of higher yielding strains of maize to help US farmers increase their crops by 40-50%. Wallace was strong on agriculture but less astute in foreign affairs and his efforts inspired Clare Booth Luce's famous coinage of 'globaloney' (qv). Her attack was doubtless additionally prompted by the fact that Wallace's 'century of the common man' was directly opposed to the Luce papers' espousal of the 'American century'. Wallace served only one term as Vice-President and was rejected in favour of Harry S. Truman in 1944, although he formed his own progressive party in an effort to reinstate his own claims to the Presidency.

WALLIS, DUCHESS OF WINDSOR (1896–1986)

You can never be too rich or too thin.
quoted in *The Contemporary Dictionary of Quotations* by Jonathon Green (1982)

This maxim of economic and physical excellence is generally attributed to the late Duchess of Windsor, the former Wallis Simpson, a woman who was always as little burdened with surplus flesh as she was well-endowed with more than sufficient cash. Some collectors however, attribute the line to Truman Capote, a generally wittier if chubbier and poorer figure, who came out with it on American TV's David Susskind Show in 1958.

WALSH, RAOUL (1887–1980) American film director

Dammit, the sonofabitch looked like a man.
on seeing the young John Wayne

Walsh was one of Hollywood's veterans, a former assistant to D.W. Griffith. Among his many pictures the best may well have been *White Heat* (1949), and among his many achievements was his discovery of Marion Michael Morrison, otherwise known as John Wayne (1907-79). Wayne had played a few small parts before Walsh, already a distinguished director, recognised in him the macho characteristics that would endear him to millions of filmgoers. He put him into *The Trail* (1930) and launched a career that put Wayne forward as the embodiment of America's tough-guy myths for the next forty-six years.

WARHOL, ANDY (1927–1987) American artist

One's company, two's a crowd and three's a party.
Exposures (1979)

Warhol worked as a commercial artist until in 1962 his perfect representations of Coca-Cola bottles and Campbells Soup cans brought him enormous celebrity as one of the earliest exponents of 'Pop Art'. Warhol's art is dedicated to artificiality. Many so-called 'Warhols' have in fact been created completely by his assistants, and the artist never attempted to hide this. His social life continued to delight the gossip-writers, although he remained a determinedly opaque character until his death, consistently proclaiming his own superficiality even as the art critics searched for depth. Warhol's most celebrated line 'In the future everyone will be famous for 15 minutes' may well, in this era of instant celebrity and almost equally instant decline, have proved itself true. Its author, whose own fame lasted somewhat longer, modified the line in his book *Exposures* (1979), saying 'In fifteen minutes everybody will be famous.'

WARHOL, ANDY

Being born is like being kidnapped. And then sold into slavery.
From A to B and Back Again (1975)

WARHOL, ANDY

Everybody winds up kissing the wrong person goodnight.
From A to B and Back Again (1975)

WARHOL, ANDY

An artist is somebody who produces things that people don't need to have but that he – for some reason – thinks it would be a good idea to give them.
From A to B and Back Again (1975)

WARHOL, ANDY

What we're all looking for is someone who doesn't live there, just pays for it.
From A to B and Back Again (1975)

WARNER, JACK   (1894–1981) British actor

Mind my bike
catchphrase in *Garrison Theatre*, BBC radio 1939–45

Garrison Theatre was one of two variety shows which the BBC broadcast on Saturday nights. Created by Harry S. Pepper and Charles Shadwell, it was based on the actual Northern Command Garrison Theatre which both remembered from World War I and was enormously popular. Its format was of a show within a show, watched by a regular 'audience' composed of an irascible RSM, a soldier and his girlfriend. The soldier, who doubled as the compere, was Jack Warner, a former music hall comedian who specialised in genial folksiness. His catchphrase, 'Mind my bike', helped *Garrison Theatre* achieve a success that its quality barely deserved.

WARNER, JACK L.   (1894–1981) American film magnate

No – Jimmy Stewart for Governor, Reagan for best friend
on Ronald Reagan's first essay into politics, 1966

More idealistic sections of society may have found the election of an ageing Hollywood actor to the Presidency a little hard to stomach, but Hollywood always appreciated the potential of one of their own. The only clash was on the precise casting. Jack L. Warner was one of the celebrated Warner Brothers, working for whom the wit Wilson Mizner had observed was 'like fucking a porcupine: it's a hundred pricks against one'. When Warner heard that Reagan was campaigning to become Governor of California his movie-maker's instincts came to the fore. Looking at the two men's relative on-screen status, he delivered his judgement on the ideal roles for them both.

WARREN, EARL   (1891–1974) American lawyer

The sports page records people's accomplishments, the front page usually records nothing but man's failures.

Warren was a reforming, efficient Governor of California from 1940-52, before becoming Chief Justice of the US Supreme Court in 1953. As Chief Justice he managed to establish the Court as a more important element of American national life than it had been for 150 years. Warren led his fellow justices to liberal decisions on civil liberties, race relations, electoral reform and freedom of speech.

WATERGATE TAPES

Expletive deleted
transcription in 1973

Of the many crimes which were committed by the White House during the Watergate Affair, among the most heinous in average American eyes was the profligacy of the President's language. The public appeared to believe that their leaders, especially Nixon himself, should be as fair of tongue as they were supposed to be of deed. As the transcribed tapes made horribly clear, Nixon was devotedly foul-mouthed, spraying obscenities all over the Oval Office. To preserve the huddled sensibilities of America's masses, the published version of the Tapes religiously excluded such epithets, replacing each with the even more titillating disclaimer 'Expletive deleted'.

WATTS, ALAN   (1915–73) American philosopher, theologian and guru

If we live, we live; if we die, we die; if we suffer, we suffer; if we are terrified, we are terrified. There is no problem about it.
Beat Zen, Square Zen and Zen

Watts was one of the best known exponents of Zen Buddhism for the West, pushing his belief that the only solution for the hedonistic solipsism of Western civilisation was for the entire society to alter its consciousness and take up Buddhist principles. Rather than accentuating our individuality and indulging our egos, we should accept that way in which the whole of creation, including ourselves, is an inter-related, unified process. Watts appealed widely to the Sixties generation and was the inspiration of the Human Potential Movement, which embraced a variety of new therapies and varieties of consciousness.

WAUGH, EVELYN (1904–66) British novelist

An artist must be a reactionary. He has to stand out against the tenor of the age and not go flopping along.
in *Writers at Work*, 3rd series (1967)

Waugh's first novel, the highly successful *Decline and Fall*, appeared in 1928. This was followed by *Vile Bodies* (1930) which confirmed Waugh in everyone's opinion but his own (although he was willing to go along with the myth for professional reasons) as the representative of 'youth'. His first marriage collapsed in 1930 and he became a convert to Roman Catholicism, saying in later years to those who criticised his studied misanthropy 'You don't know how much nastier I would be if I hadn't become a Catholic'. Further novels followed, mixed with travel books and much freelance journalism. After the war, in which he proved a less than tractable Royal Marine, he wrote *Brideshead Revisited* (1945) and his '*Sword of Honour*' trilogy. His last novel was *The Ordeal of Gilbert Pinfold*, a thinly disguised piece of self-laceration, stemming from his own near nervous breakdown, accentuated by too much wine and too many barbiturates.

WAUGH, EVELYN

Sebastian had found a book on wine-tasting, and we followed its instructions in detail. We warmed the glass slightly at a candle, filled it a third high, swirled the wine around, nursed it in our hands, held it to the light, breathed it, sipped it, filled our mouths with it, and rolled it over the tongue, ringing it down the palate like a coin on a counter, tilted our heads back and let it trickle down the throat. Then we talked of it and nibbled Bath Oliver biscuits, and passed on to another wine; then back to the first, then onto another, until all three were in circulation and the order of glasses got confused, and we fell out over which was which, and we passed the glasses to and from between us until there were six glasses, some of them with mixed wines in them which we had filled from the wrong bottle, till we were obliged to

start again with three clean glasses each, and the bottles were empty and our praise of them wilder and more exotic.
Brideshead Revisited (1945)

In this episode of Waugh's first post-war book its narrator Charles Ryder and his Oxford friend Lord Sebastian Flyte indulge in an orgy of vintage wines in the latter's country home Brideshead. Waugh has deliberately set out to indulge the senses, explaining in the introduction that he had written such passages in a bleak period of present privation and threatening disaster '...and in consequence the book is infused with a kind of gluttony...'. The wine-tasting also seems to denote the end of Charles' idyll, contained in the novel's first section. From thereon he drifts apart from Sebastian, who wanders ever deeper into his own tragedy, while Charles has to deal with his own life.

WAUGH, EVELYN

I expect you'll be becoming a schoolmaster, sir. That's what most of the gentlemen does, sir, that gets sent down for indecent behaviour.
Decline and Fall (1928)

Decline and Fall begins with a prelude: at Scone College, Oxford, it is the night of the annual dinner of the Bollinger Club, an event dedicated to indulging the propensity of the English upper classes to drunken vandalism. As a pair of dons listen, they hear 'a shriller note...any who have heard that sound will shrink at the recollection of it; it is the sound of the English county families baying for broken glass'. After rampaging through the college they meet Paul Pennyfeather, an undistinguished theology student, whom they deprive of his trousers. Ignoring the Bollinger, the authorities seize Pennyfeather. He is sent down in disgrace and as he pauses in the porter's lodge he receives this advice as to a future career.

WAUGH, EVELYN

Anyone who has been to an English public school will always feel comparatively at home in prison. It is the people brought up in the gay intimacy of the slums...who find prison so soul-destroying.
Decline and Fall (1928)

After his ignominious expulsion from Oxford, his wretched months as a prep school master and his brief taste of happiness with the beautiful Margot Metroland, Paul Pennyfeather finds himself in prison, sentenced for his innocent involvement in Margot's white slave trading. His imprisonment is mitigated not only by the natural fitness for incarceration conferred upon him by a public school education, but by the fact that various old friends seem to have turned up in jail and that some unknown benefactor is substituting pâté de foie gras for his streaky bacon.

WAUGH, EVELYN

Manners are especially the need of the plain. The pretty can get away with anything.
in the *Observer*, 1962

WAUGH, EVELYN

Most of the world's troubles seem to come from people who are too busy. If only politicians and scientists were lazier, how much happier we should all be. The lazy man is preserved from the commission of almost all the nastier crimes and many of the motives which make us sacrifice to toil the innocent enjoyment of leisure are amongst the most ignoble: pride, avarice, emulation, vainglory and the appetite for power over others.
in the *Sunday Times*, 1962

WAUGH, EVELYN

Particularly against books the Home Secretary is. If we can't stamp out literature in the country, we can at least stop it being brought in from outside.
Vile Bodies (1930)

Waugh's reference is to William Joynson-Hicks (1865-1939) known generally to friends and foes as 'Jix', Britain's Home Secretary from 1924–9 and self-styled 'Policeman of the Lord'. A staunch Conservative, and President of the National Church League, Jix first deported a variety of aliens whose presence he did not require in Britain, before attacking a new target: sex, an unpleasant innovation, spawned in the aftermath of the First World War and threatening to overwhelm the country at large. Backed without question by an equally dedicated police force he prosecuted D.H. Lawrence for his paintings, Radclyffe Hall for her book *The Well of Loneliness* and, to general amusement, the drawings of William Blake. His policemen raided a number of bookshops with varying results.

WAUGH, EVELYN

Mr. Salter's side of the conversation was limited to expressions of assent. When Lord Copper was right he said 'Definitely, Lord Copper'; when he was wrong, 'Up to a point.' 'Let me see, what's the name of the place I mean? Capital of Japan? Yokohama isn't it?'

'Up to a point, Lord Copper.'

Scoop (1938)

Scoop is Waugh's satire on journalism, and particularly foreign correspondents, culled from his own expedition to Abyssinia for the Daily Mail in 1935. This conversation takes place between Lord Copper, owner of The Beast, and his hapless Foreign Editor Salter, a man far happier in 'those carefree days when he had edited the Women's Page, or, better still, when he had chosen the jokes for one of Lord Copper's comic weeklies'. Copper is modelled on Lord Beaverbrook (1879-1964) for whom Waugh, like many other smart young writers, had briefly worked.

WAUGH, EVELYN

What did your Loved One pass on from?

The Loved One (1948)

The Loved One is a satire on the burial practices of America's morticians, with their jargon and their posthumous manicures and make-up, and on the massive cemetery of Forest Lawns, on which Waugh modelled the fictitious Whispering Glades. The term 'loved one' is always used in place of 'corpse' and in this case it refers to a member of the expatriate English community, Sir Francis Hinsley who has hanged himself. The question is addressed to the book's hero, Dennis Barlow, himself a disgrace to the English community, since he has taken a job at the Happier Hunting Ground, an animal version of Whispering Glades, but who, since he is presumed to be familiar with death, has been deputed to arrange Sir Francis' funeral.

WAUGH, EVELYN

Creative Endeavour has lost her wings, Mrs Ape.

Vile Bodies (1930)

Waugh's second novel dealt with the fashionable world of which he had become a central figure after the success of its predecessor *Decline and Fall* (1928). Among the walk-ons who provide specific targets for his satire is Mrs. Melrose Ape, an American evangelist who is touring England with her band of 'angels' rejoicing in the names of Chastity, Faith, Charity, Fortitude,

Humility, Prudence, Divine Discontent, Mercy, Justice, and Creative Endeavour. Mrs. Ape is modelled on the real evangelist, Aimee Semple Macpherson (1890-1944), who at her peak in the Twenties was an international institution, but whose fake-suicide-cum-kidnap-scare, arranged in an attempt to pick up a £500,000 ransom and give her a few days with her married lover, went wildly wrong and exposed her not as a healer but merely as another all too human human.

WEBB, SIDNEY AND BEATRICE   (1858–1943; 1859–1947) British radicals

Old people are usually absorbed in something, usually themselves. We prefer to be absorbed in the Soviet Union.
quoted in Kingsley Martin, *The Webbs and Their Work*

The Webbs were partners not only in marriage but in their campaigning for a variety of socialist causes. They founded the London School of Economics in 1895 and launched the New Statesman in 1913. As Fabians, believing that reforms could be achieved by 'socialism from above', they were not part of the original Labour Party, although Sidney Webb, as Lord Passfield, held office under Ramsay MacDonald. Unlike more sceptical believers, who were unimpressed by socialism as practised in Russia, the Webbs were lifelong devotees, preferring blind obeisance to reasoned criticism of the system on which they based their whole existence. It was of the Webbs that Malcolm Muggeridge, himself a former advocate of Russian glories, remarked in his autobiography 'There is no snobbishness like that of professional egalitarians.'

WEIL, SIMONE   (1909–1943) French philosopher

Culture is an instrument wielded by professors to manufacture professors, who when their turn comes, will manufacture professors.
The Need for Roots (1952)

Weil was brought up in the finest liberal Jewish traditions, offering all the hallmarks of a top-flight academic career. Instead she chose to reject the enclosed world of self-perpetuating 'culture' and commit herself to the people, enlisting in the Spanish Civil War, working on the shop floor at Renault, and as a farm servant during World War II. This endless physical stress, coupled to her refusal to eat as long as the War went on, wore her out and she died aged only 34. Weil rejected all forms of established religion, preferring the mystical elements of Catholicism. Politically she preferred liberalism over socialism, and at her death was developing a philosophy that stemmed from her studies of the Greek classics and of modern industrial society and which envisaged the idea of an integrated whole human being.

WEIL, SIMONE

Whoever takes up the sword shall perish by the sword. And whoever does not take up the sword (or lets it drop) shall perish on the cross.
quoted in W.H. Auden, *The Dyer's Hand* (1962)

Auden chose Weil's comment as the epigraph to his discussion of the role of Shakespeare's Falstaff, 'The Prince's Dog'. With her sustained identification with victims rather than oppressors, which extended to virtually starving herself to death, Weil eschewed the sword and duly advanced towards the cross. She was not a pacifist, fighting in the International Brigade in Spain and later in the Resistance in France, but her own philosophy rejected the idea of a world dominated by its sword-bearers.

WELLES, ORSON (1915–1985) American film director and actor

I started at the top and worked my way down.
quoted in Leslie Halliwell, *The Filmgoers' Companion* (1985)

In 1941, when with a script by Herman J. Mankiewcz, he directed and starred in *Citizen Kane*, Welles was the boy wonder of the movies, who had already confirmed his own celebrity when he panicked America with a broadcast based on H.G. Wells' *War of the Worlds*. As he put it himself 'A movie studio is the best toy a boy ever had' but few boys, in or out of Hollywood, had Welles' genius and he seemed almost to threaten Hollywood with his prodigious abilities. He described himself as 'a man of the Middle Ages, with certain implications due to the barbarism of America' and although in 1941 he was indeed 'at the top', his subsequent career proceeded slowly but steadily downwards. Welles didn't enjoy this and remarked to the *New York Times* in 1962 'When you are down and out something always turns up – and it is usually the noses of your friends'.

WELLS, H.G. (1866–1946) British writer and visionary

Moral indignation is jealousy with a halo.

Wells began life as an impoverished draper's apprentice but worked his way first to teaching and then to studying science under T.H. Huxley. He mixed teaching with journalism until he gained literary recognition with his allegorical novel, *The Time*

Machine (1895). Wells was a highly prolific writer, using his scientific knowledge to create a number of bizarre fictional worlds, combining these books with several comedies, set in the lower middle-class world of his youth. He joined the Fabian Society but proved too independent for its ideological constraints. Wells' novels began to decline but he concentrated increasingly on non-ficton, producing his best-selling *Outline of History* in 1920, as well as various schemes for a better world, none of which, to his great and increasing sadness, would ever materialise.

WELLS, H.G.

The path of social advancement is, and must be, strewn with broken friendships.
Kipps (1905)

Kipps is the story of Arthur Kipps, an apprentice draper living in Folkestone, who is already on the path to self-improvement when he discovers that he has been left a fortune. His introduction to Folkestone society is complicated by such events as his finding himself a dinner guest in a house in which his erstwhile girl-friend, Ann Pornick, is a serving maid. It is suggested to him that his path upwards should by necessity leave behind such youthful infatuations and that such friendships must be broken, but Kipps is no snob and after further ups and downs marries Ann.

WELLS, H.G.

If the world does not please you, you can change it.
The History of Mr Polly (1910)

Ill-educated, unhappily married, enslaved to an unsatisfactory job as a provincial draper which has only led him to bankruptcy, Mr. Alfred Polly, aged 37 and a half, decides on suicide. The method he chooses is to set fire to his own house. But when he finds himself a hero after rescuing the old lady next door he opts instead for life, and, telling himself that he can change the world if he wants to, he leaves town and sets off for a new and more exciting career.

WELLS, H.G.

Human history becomes more and more a race between education and catastrophe.
The Outline of History (1921)

As a student at the Normal School of Science in South Kensington, Wells benefited from the teaching of T.H. Huxley (1825–

95). This scientific background made him one of the very few contemporary men of letters to have enjoyed any real grounding in science and his books are all marked by it. Although his popularity as a novelist had declined somewhat after World War I, he won a new and expanded audience with *The Outline of History*. Wells hoped, unsurprisingly, that education would win this life or death race, and envisaged a universe in which all men could find peace together and a new, rational civilisation take over. This utopian dream was finally dashed when World War II broke out, and he gave a bitter title to his final work: *Mind at the End of Its Tether* (1945).

WELLS, H.G.

The war to end wars
The War That Will End War (1914)

Wells believed firmly that with the judicious use of science it would be possible for man to divert what had seemed a grim destiny of struggle and war and create a truly utopian society. With awful irony Wells published a book called *The War That Will End War* in 1914. As he remarked later, when it was obvious that the legacy of World War I was anything but utopian, 'I launched the phrase "the war to end war" and that was not the least of my crimes'.

WEST, MAE (1892–1980) American film star

Give a man a free hand and he'll run it all over you.

West was and remains one of Hollywood's most original stars, mainly because although she was certainly in Hollywood she was never completely of it, coming to the studios as an experienced vaudeville performer of forty, rather than some malleable ingenue. No studio would have dared invent her anyway, and it was the producers' subservience to the censors of the Hays Office and Legion of Decency that muted her full glories. Although, as she pointed out 'I'm never dirty. I'm just interesting without being vulgar. I just...suggest.' On and off screen West was always quotable. A few of her better lines include:

Keep a diary and one day it'll keep you.

Beulah, peel me a grape. (in *I'm No Angel* (1933))

It's not the men in my life, it's the life in my men that counts.

When I'm good, I'm very good, but when I'm bad I'm better.

Whenever I'm caught between two evils, I take the one I've never tried. (in *Klondike Annie*, 1936)

Goodness, what beautiful diamonds!
West: Goodness had nothing to do with it.

West: How tall are you?
Man: I'm six feet seven inches.
West: Let's forget the six feet and talk about the seven inches.

Is that your sword, or are you just pleased to see me? (often rephrased as 'Is that a pistol in your pocket...')

It isn't what I do, but how I do it. It isn't what I say, but how I say it. And how I look when I do it and say it.

WEST, NATHANIEL (1903–40)(Nathaniel Weinstein)American writer

Are-you-in-trouble? – Do-you-need-advice? – Write-to-Miss-Lonelyhearts-and-she-will-help-you
Miss Lonelyhearts (1933)

Nathaniel West is best known for the two novels he wrote during a career that was cut short by his death in a car crash. These are his mordant satire on Hollywood, *The Day of the Locust* (1939), and *Miss Lonelyhearts*, the story of an advice columnist who becomes hopelessly entangled in the life of his lovelorn correspondents. This multi-hyphenated appeal is inserted in the (male) agony aunt's column in order to drum up trade.

WEST, REBECCA (1892–1982) (Cecily Fairfield) British writer

Just how difficult it is to write biography can be reckoned by anybody who sits down and considers just how many people know the real truth about his or her love affairs.
in *Vogue* magazine, 1952

West, who took her nom de plume from the heroine of Ibsen's *Rosmersholm* (1886), worked briefly as an actress but abandoned the stage for feminism and journalism. She soon became a noted writer and critic and her combative, incisive pieces included her review of H.G. Wells' *Marriage* (1912), the upshot of which was a decade-long affair and a son, the novelist Anthony West. Wells nicknamed her 'Panther' and later, writing the text for a book of David Low's caricatures, she took the pseudonym 'Lynx'. West's novels were often dismissed as overly difficult at the time, but are reassessed favourably by modern feminists.

WESTMINSTER GAZETTE

You are Mr. Lobby Lud, and I claim the Westminster Gazette prize.
newspaper publicity campaign, 1927

On August 1, 1927 the *Westminster Gazette* launched a new publicity stunt: a mystery man called Lobby Lud 'on the run' in a succession of seaside towns. Anyone carrying a copy of the paper and challenging him with the correct words would win £50.00. The name came from the *Gazette*'s telegraphic address: Lobby came from the Westminster and parliamentary lobbies, Lud was an abbreviation of the paper's address at Ludgate Circus. The game was put to a far grimmer fictional use by Graham Greene in *Brighton Rock* (1938) when the terrified Hale is forced to parade Brighton as 'Kolley Kibber' of the 'Daily Messenger'.

WEYGAND, GENERAL (1867–1965) French general

In three weeks England will have her neck wrung like a chicken.
speaking to the French Cabinet in 1940

After the Fall of France, many of those French generals whose incompetence had been at least in part responsible for their troops' defeat by the Germans, were eager to see the traditional enemy Britain suffer as they had done. Weygand made his feelings clear when he prophesied England's imminent demise. On hearing of this gloating prophecy Winston Churchill replied in Parliament on December 30, 1940 'When I warned them that Britain would fight on alone whatever they did, their Generals told their Prime Minister and their divided cabinet "In three weeks England will have her neck wrung like a chicken". Some chicken! Some neck!'

WHARTON, EDITH (1862–1937) American novelist

Blessed are the pure in heart for they have so much more to talk about.
quoted in *John O'London's Weekly*, April 10 1932

After her marriage failed Wharton devoted herself to a cosmopolitan social life, living after 1905 mainly in France and mixing with such literary grandees as Henry James. She produced her first major work, *The House of Mirth*, in 1900. The success of this story of a failed social climber was followed by much more writing, all of which, in a prolific output, deals in what she called the 'tribal behaviour' of various groups, taking a penetrating, witty and often satirical view of social, ethical, moral and cultural relationships.

WHITE, E.B.   (1899–) American writer

I say it's spinach and I say the hell with it!
cartoon caption in the *New Yorker*, December 8 1928

Elwyn Brooks White was one of the best of those writers whom Harold Ross enlisted for his magazine the *New Yorker*. Like many writers, White was called upon to compose captions for cartoons that the magazine's artists presented to Ross, leaving him to find suitable words. In this picture by Carl Rose a mother is sitting with her young daughter at a table. The mother promises 'It's broccoli, dear' but her daughter is unimpressed and replies 'I say it's spinach and I say the hell with it!'.

WHITE, EDMUND   (1940–) American writer

Someone once remarked that in adolescence pornography is a substitute for sex, whereas in adulthood sex is a substitute for pornography.
in *New Times* magazine, 1979

White is one of America's leading writers on the gay world, and his books *A Boy's Story* and *Travels in Gay America* have been best-sellers. His remark suggests that sex is much like any other commodity that seems all the more exciting the less accessible it is. As long as it remains tantalisingly out of reach, one is reduced to fantasising. Once it loses its mystique, one is reduced, for quite opposite reasons, to fantasising again.

WHITE, T.H.   (1906–64) British novelist

But I, unfortunately, was born at the wrong end of time, and I have to live backwards from the front.
The Sword in the Stone (1939)

Terence Hanbury White taught for some years before he chose to retire to a reclusive life, producing a series of novels, notably his idosyncratic rewriting of the Morte d'Arthur: *The Once and Future King* (1958). This trilogy followed King Arthur's life from his childhood to his death. While the birth of Mordred and the doomed love of Lancelot and Guinevere makes the later volumes increasingly tragic, the first, which deals with Arthur's childhood in the castle of his adoptive father, is much more cheerful. The story revolves around Arthur's education at the hands of the magician Merlin, who is living 'backwards from the front' and who prepares 'Wart' for his future kingship.

WHITE, WILLIAM ALLEN   (1868–1944) American journalist

Consistency is a paste jewel that only cheap men cherish.
Forty Years on Main Street (1937)

In 1895 White bought a small newspaper, *The Gazette*, published in his hometown of Emporia, Kansas. He remained its editor for life, making himself a nationwide reputation for his independent stance on many major issues. His first notable editorial came in 1896 when he launched an attack on Populism that indirectly swayed the nation towards the election of President McKinley. White involved himself prominently in Theodore Roosevelt's Progressive 'Bull Moose' party and became a leading Republican.

WHITE HEAT

Top of the world, Ma!
script by Ivan Goff and Ben Roberts(1949)

White Heat, directed by Raoul Walsh for Warner Brothers in 1949, is the perfect exemplar of the film noir, Hollywood's celluloid answer to the pulp magazine's hard-boiled dicks. It starred James Cagney in his most outrageous role, as the psychotic, mother-fixated and migraine-bedevilled Cody Jarrett. As the film ends Cagney makes his final stand. Betrayed by an FBI plant halfway through the 'big job', he shoots it out high among the storage vats of the chemical factory his gang had come to rob. As the monstrous vats explode around and under him, Cagney remains, as the biggest headache of all takes over, his mother's boy.

WHITEHEAD, ALFRED NORTH   (1861–1947) British philosopher and mathematician

Life is an offensive, directed against the repetitious mechanism of the Universe.
Adventures of Ideas (1933)

Whitehead was a tutor at Trinity College, Cambridge when with his former pupil Bertrand Russell (qv) he collaborated on the *Principia Mathematica* (1910-13), a book which revolutionised contemporary concepts of mathematics by proving that the entire discipline can be seen as a continuation of formal logic. After Cambridge Whitehead taught at Imperial College, London and later, as professor of philosophy at Harvard, began producing a series of metaphysical works based on his exposure of what he called the 'fallacy of misplaced concreteness'. By this he meant that the standard scientific picture of the world makes the mistake of presuming that it is the abstractions of the great scientific thinkers such as Descartes and Newton that form the real stuff of the world, rather than the data upon which those abstractions were based.

WHITEHEAD, ALFRED NORTH

Morality...is what the majority then and there happen to like and immorality is what they dislike.

WHITEHEAD, ALFRED NORTH

The major advances in civilisation are processes that all but wreck the societies in which they occur.

WHITEHEAD, ALFRED NORTH

'Necessity is the mother of invention' is a silly proverb. 'Necessity is the mother of futile dodges' is much nearer the truth.
quoted in *The Faber Book of Aphorisms*, ed. Auden & Kronenberger (1964)

WHITEHEAD, ALFRED NORTH

We think in generalities, but we live in detail.
quoted in *The Faber Book of Aphorisms*, ed. Auden & Kronenberger (1964)

WHITEHORN, KATHERINE   British journalist

In heaven they will bore you, in hell you will bore them.
in the *Observer*

Whitehorn worked variously as a publisher's reader and journalist before in 1960 she joined the Observer as a columnist. She has remained there ever since and is now an associate editor, still writing a column and producing regular books. Whitehorn has combined her journalism with a number of administrative jobs, notably membership of the Board of the British Airports Authority (1972) and the rectorship of St. Andrews University (1982–85).

WHITEHORN, KATHERINE

A food is not necessarily essential just because your child hates it.
How to Survive Children (1975)

Whitehorn, Katherine

The best careers advice to give to the young is 'Find out what you like doing best and get someone to pay you for doing it'.
in the *Observer*, 1975

Whiting, G. American songwriter

All dressed up and nowhere to go.
song, 1912

This popular catchphrase comes from the song *All Dressed Up and No Place to Go*. It runs, in mawkish part, 'When you're all dressed up and no place to go, / Life seems dreary, weary and slow. / My heart has ached as well as bled / For all the tears I've shed, / When I've had no place to go / Unless I went back to bed...' W.E. Collinson in his *Contemporary English* (1927) claims that the song was written by the American comedian Raymond Hitchock, but it is more likely that the comedian merely popularised it on the vaudeville stage.

Whiting, John (1917–63) British playwright

The tragedy of men is that they are men. And when there is food and drink, houses and clothing, peace, security and sanity for all, men will still be scared to death of death.
John Whiting on Theatre (1966)

Whiting was one of the British playwrights most responsible for breaking the cosy mould of West End drama in the mid-Fifties but unlike such peers as John Osborne he received less immediate acclaim for his work. Audiences and critics found it hard to deal with his 'personal vision of a dark world'. His best play is *The Devils* (1961). Taken from Aldous Huxley's *The Devils of Loudun* (1952) it is, like its inspiration, a study of sexual hysteria in a French nunnery.

Whyte, William H. (1917–) American writer

The Organization Man
book title, 1956

As Whyte explained in the first chapter of his book, which both coined a phrase and codified a concept that many people who worked in large organisations had already noted: 'This book is about the organisation man... I can think of no other way to describe the people I am talking about. They are not the workers, nor are they the white-collar people in the usual, clerk sense of the word. These people only work for the Organization. The ones I am talking about belong to it as well.'

WIENER, NORBERT (1894–1964) American mathematician

A conscience which has been bought once will be bought twice.
The Human Use of Human Beings (1954)

Wiener was a child prodigy who graduated at 14 and gained his PhD from Harvard at 18, before studying logic under Bertrand Russell at Cambridge. As a teacher at MIT he began by researching analytical and applied mathematics, before turning to what were still very basic computers. In 1948 he published his book *Cybernetics*, which he defined as 'the entire field of control and communication theory, whether in the machine or in the animal'. He considered the complete relationship between control, organisation and communication, a theory that has been used extensively in the subsequent study of the internal 'architecture' of computers. In *The Human Use of Human Beings* Wiener offered his opinions on the ethical, social and religious implications of cybernetics, written in a way that made his views accessible to most interested readers.

WILDER, BILLY (1906–) Austrian-American film director

Hindsight is always 20:20.
quoted in Leslie Halliwell, *The Filmgoers' Companion (1985)*

Wilder had started scriptwriting as a journalist in pre-World War II Vienna and moved to Hollywood when in 1934 he was forced to flee Austria. Here he has directed many successful films, often with his co-writers Charles Brackett (1892–1969) and I.A.L. Diamond (1915-). Wilder is among the very few Hollywood directors who have consistently demanded and obtained full artistic control of his work, a privilege he accepts as his due in his comment 'I have ten commandments. The first nine are, thou shalt not bore. The tenth is, thou shalt have right of final cut'.

WILDER, THORNTON (1897–1975) American novelist and dramatist

Literature is the orchestration of platitudes.
in *Time* magazine, 1953

Wilder was an extremely successful writer, who won three Pulitzer Prizes, for his novel *The Bridge of San Luis Rey* (1927) and for the plays *Our Town* (1938) and *The Skin of Our Teeth* (1942). Wilder was an essentially upbeat writer who refused to darken his themes despite the generally pessimistic atmosphere of the Depression era. His greatest commercial success was *The Matchmaker* (1954), which became the musical *Hello Dolly!* in 1965.

WILHELM II, KAISER (1859–1941) German monarch

A contemptible little army.
on the British Expeditionary Force, 1914

'Kaiser Bill' as the British he so disdained called him, was not in fact the Prussian brute of World War I propagandist claims, but a reasonably intelligent ruler who felt that his people expected him to act in an aggressive manner. After failing to find a suitable replacement for Bismarck, he was rendered prey to his own impetuous nature, taking Germany into a war in 1914 with only the dubious support of Austria-Hungary. Although the more vehement British jingoists still cried 'Hang the Kaiser' in 1918, he was allowed to flee Germany for Holland where he died. His dismissal of the BEF was taken up by its members, and the dwindling numbers who survive from that first autumn's campaign still call themselves 'The Old Contemptibles'.

WILKIE, WENDELL (1892–1944) American politician

Freedom is an indivisible word. If we want to enjoy it, and fight for it, we must be prepared to extend it to everyone, whether they are rich or poor, whether they agree with us or not, no matter what their race or the colour of the their skin.
One World (1943)

Wilkie, an Indiana-born New York lawyer, was the Republican challenger to Roosevelt in the election of 1940. During his campaign Wilkie made such obvious efforts to play up his 'Western' origins that Roosevelt's Secretary of the Interior, Harold Ickes, christened him 'the barefoot boy from Wall Street'. Wilkie led the internationalist wing of his party, setting out to popularise his concept of 'one world', the idea of which is further expounded in his book *One World*, based on a 49-day flight he made around the capitals of the world. His remarks, reminscent of Maxim Litvinov's comment that 'Peace is indivisible', bear out the premise of his book.

WILLANS AND RONALD SEARLE, GEOFFREY (1920–)
British writer and illustrator

Skool Food, or the Piece of Cod which Passeth Understanding.
The Compleet Molesworth (1958)

WILLIAM, LLOYD S.

The saga of Nigel Molesworth extended through four best-selling books which were collected in 'The Compleet Molesworth', charting the world of this supposedly typical British prep school boy, suffering the horrors of his alma mater, St. Custards, all deliciously familiar to those who were experiencing what is traditionally known as a 'first-rate English education'. This description of 'skool food' is a parody on Paul's Epistle to the Philippians IV:7 although one wonders whether the authors had ever heard of architect Sir Edwin Lutyens' breakfast-time remark, recorded in his biography, 'This piece of cod passes all understanding'.

WILLIAM, LLOYD S. American soldier

Retreat? Hell no, we just got here!
refusing to retreat from Belloar, June 5, 1918

Captain William had just brought his troops up to Belloar on the Western front when French troops, who were retreating under a German attack, advised him to retire with them. William, full of gung-ho enthusiasm, replied with this breezy line. A similar piece of bravado was exhibited during the Korean war by another American, General Oliver Prince Smith whose men were pinned down by eight divisions of Chinese Communist troops in autumn 1950. As he led his troops on a 70-mile breakout, which took thirteen days of bloody fighting, he answered those who suggested his men were retreating by saying 'Retreat, hell! We're just advancing from another direction'.

WILLIAMS, HEATHCOTE (1941–) British writer and playwright

You come out of a woman and you spend the rest of your life trying to get back inside.
The Speakers (1964)

Williams' book The Speakers is based on the lives of the regular orators who set up their soap boxes at London's Hyde Park Corner and harangue the crowds and each other with the virtues of their own views of life.

WILLIAMS, HEATHCOTE

Immortality is the only cause you can't die for. If you can't take it with you, don't go!
The Immortalist (1978)

The Immortalist is a 278 year-old man, known in the script simply as '278'. The play takes the form of an interview with 278 who proceeds to tie his sceptical interviewer into knots as he produces his vast store of arcane knowledge to dismantle our received notions of death. Williams brings in a multiplicity of sources to create a polemic on the nature of time, ageing and death that leaves the audience with a final thought: 'There are people alive now who are never going to die'.

WILLIAMS, KENNETH (1926–1988) British actor

The nicest thing about quotes is that they give us a nodding acquaintance with the originator which is often socially impressive.
Acid Drops (1980)

Williams was one of Britain's favourite comic actors, who graduated from Kenneth Horne's radio shows to film stardom as a regular of the 'Carry On...' team. He continued to work in film, radio and television, appearing on quiz shows, reading children's stories, providing all the voices for a regular animated cartoon and much more. This remark comes from one of his forays into the world of books, a collection of pithy witticisms and cynical put-downs which he suitably titled *Acid Drops*.

WILLIAMS, TENNESSEE (1911–83) American playwright

I learned that the heart of man, his body and his brain, are forged in a white-hot furnace for the purpose of conflict. That struggle for me is creation. I cannot live without it. Luxury is the wolf at the door and its fangs are the conceits and vanities germinated by success. When an artist knows this he knows where the dangers lie. Without deprivation and struggle there is no salvation, and I am just a sword cutting daisies.
quoted in 1972

Williams, born Thomas Lanier Williams in Columbus, Mississippi, followed his education by working as a clerk before he gained a Rockefeller Foundation Scholarship in 1940 and, after a variety of jobs, moved to Hollywood where he wrote his first play, *The Glass Menagerie* (1945). This play established most of the Williams stereotypes: the domineering elderly mother, the crippled daughter (physically or mentally) and the rebellious, artistic son, all drawn at least in part from his own life. Although Williams gained a reputation for the sexuality implicit in his work, his overriding theme was the essential unhappiness of being alive, an unhappiness he attempted to mask with binges of drink and drugs. He told *Playboy* in 1973 'All creative work, all life, in a sense, is a cri de coeur', but had always paradoxically

relished the pain since, as he pointed out in the *Observer* in 1958
'Don't look forward to the day when you stop suffering. Because
when it comes you'll know that you're dead.'

WILLIAMS, TENNESSEE

**We're all of us sentenced to solitary confinement inside our own
skins, for life.**
Orpheus Descending (1957)

Orpheus Descending was the first of Williams' plays to be given a
professional production, although it flopped after poor notices
and closed at the end of its tryout run in Boston. It is, as Williams
described it: 'the tale of a wild-spirited boy who wanders into a
conventional community of the South and creates the commotion
of a fox in a chicken coop. But beneath that now familiar surface it
is a play about the unanswered questions that haunt the hearts of
people and the difference between continuing to ask them... and
the acceptance of prescribed answers that are not answers at all,
but expedient explanations or surrender to a state of quandary'.

WILLIAMS, TENNESSEE

I have always depended on the kindness of strangers.
A Streetcar Named Desire (1947)

Stella and Stanley Kowalski live in a poor quarter of New Orleans
known as Elysian Fields. The local streetcar carries the destina-
tion marker 'Desire'. On it arrives Stella's sister Blanche DuBois,
allegedly on leave of absence from her job as a teacher. The play
deals with the way in which Blanche's southern belle fantasies
are systematically destroyed by the loutish Stanley, whose animal
magnetism she finds both repellent and irresistible. In the end
Stanley rapes her and her mind collapses. Blanche's line reflects
her pose as a delicate, dependent lady, but it also masks what she
calls her 'many intimacies with strangers': after her husband, a
homosexual, shot himself, she was dismissed from her job and
has since then been working as a prostitute.

WILLIAMS, TENNESSEE

**Mendacity is a system that we live in. Liquor is one way out, and
death's the other.**
Cat on a Hot Tin Roof (1955)

A typically bleak Williams line, declaring life so painful as to offer
only two escapes, one temporary and one permanent. The play
centres around a reunion of the Pollitt family, wealthy Southern

planters, to celebrate the 65th birthday of its head 'Big Daddy' Pollitt. His favourite son, Brick, is a drunkard, drug addict and latent homosexual; Brick's wife Maggie is determined to make sure that, for all his sins, he inherits the family money. Maggie fights both to save her marriage and to charm Big Daddy, announcing, mendaciously, that she is pregnant, and hoping that Brick will rouse himself sufficiently from his lethargy to help bring this about.

WILLIAMS, TENNESSEE

We have to distrust each other. It's our only defence against betrayal.
Camino Real (1953)

This play is about the crises that beset one's middle age. If one throws away the idealism and romantic nonsense of youth, with what does one replace it? If one chooses realism, the truth can prove too harsh to stomach. If one chooses to hold desperately on to youth, it makes one grotesque to those who really are young, and in the end to oneself. One can only hope to find some middle way, and if that fails, there is always death, sooner or later. Williams filled the play with symbols and images, all pointing to the central problem. Some critics dismissed it as a literary exercise, but as Williams said, 'symbols, when used respectfully, are the purest language of plays. Sometimes it would take page after page of tedious exposition to put across an idea that can be said with an object or a gesture...'.

WILSON, CHARLES E. (1890–1961) American secretary of defence

What's good for General Motors is good for the country.
in January 1953

Wilson was being grilled by the Senate Committee on Armed Services preparatory to his being appointed Eisenhower's Secretary of Defense. He was asked what would happen if, as head of General Motors and thus a major stockholder, he was forced to make a decision that might affect the company and its stocks adversely but benefit the nation as a whole. Wilson replied that he could make such a decision but 'I cannot conceive of one because for years I thought what was good for our country was good for General Motors and vice versa. The difference does not exist.' By the time this hit the headlines it had been rewritten as above and came to symbolise for liberals the way in which big business controlled the administration.

Wilson, Charles E.

A bigger bang for a buck.
on advances in military hardware, 1954

The importance of economic demands to military planning has always had a profound effect on the direction of that planning. The US started the 1950s as the sole possessors of the atomic bomb and for the early part of the decade believed that this superiority, as stated in John Foster Dulles' bullying policy of 'massive retaliation', would be maintained. Secretary Wilson called the policy 'The New Look', referring to Christian Dior's haute couture which featured lower hemlines and thus less 'exposure'. He added that with this policy, depending on a large stockpile of arms and a substantially expanded air force, the US would henceforth save on arms expenditure, maximise its defence capability, and deliver if necessary 'a bigger bang for a buck'.

Wilson, Harold   (1916–) British prime minister

The white heat of the technological revolution.
speech on October 1, 1963

Wilson's speech in October 1963, heralding the glorious future promised were the country to elect its first Labour government after 'thirteen years of Tory misrule', provided a keynote for the electoral campaign of 1964. Addressing that year's Labour Party conference he offered a vision that while alluring and headline-catching, seems in hindsight to nurture all the illusions of the Sixties: 'We are redefining and we are restating our socialism in terms of the scientific revolution... the Britain that is going to be forged in the white heat of this revolution will be no place for restrictive practices or outdated methods on either side of industry'.

Wilson, Harold

From now on the pound abroad is worth 14% or so less in terms of other currencies. That doesn't mean, of course, that the pound here in Britain, in your pocket or purse or in your bank, has been devalued. What it does mean is that she shall now be able to sell more goods abroad on a competitive basis.
announcing the devaluation of the pound, on November 19 1967

Wilson had been a superb economist at Oxford, so it was to be presumed that when talking of the economy he knew his subject.

Yet it seemed, in even the most charitable of views, that he had forgotten his basics when he announced the devaluation of the pound in November 1967. Writing in his memoirs in 1971 Wilson attempted to pass the blame for his less than lucid explanation of the facts on to the Treasury mandarins, who had redrafted the speech from his original notes. This may have been true, but it was too late to rescue his original broadcast, which was seized upon by a gleeful opposition as yet another example of prime ministerial duplicity. Wilson's ambiguous use of language brought him new problems in 1974, when he was accused of illicit land speculation involving an alleged slagheap. Countering his critics he explained 'If you buy land on which is a slagheap 120 feet high and it costs £100,000 to remove it, that is not speculation but land reclamation.' Few were very impressed, but the scandal died.

WILSON, HAROLD

If I had the choice between smoked salmon and tinned salmon, I'd have it tinned. With vinegar.
as opposition leader, 1962

Harold Wilson posed aggressively as a blunt, Northern member of the working class, and duly impressed the voters with his origins, but in fact he was the archetypical, middle-class meritocrat who, far from trudging to school in bare feet, could well have arrived there in the family Jowett, driven by his father, an industrial chemist. 'Dull, devious, diligent and deliberate' were the adjectives used of him by one enemy, and while he was rarely dull, this much-publicised flaunting of proletarian credentials was perhaps a little devious.

WILSON, HAROLD

Gnomes of Zurich
speaking on November 12, 1956

Wilson was speaking to Parliament on the economic problems that had plagued Britain in the wake of the Suez Crisis of earlier that year. He coined his phrase when describing the machinations of Swiss bankers and financiers, whose power was such that they could manipulate the economies of major nations seemingly at will. Eight years later, elected as a Labour Prime Minister, Wilson had to face the 'Gnomes' again when they assessed Britain's economy, found its credit rating to be low and forced austerity measures on Wilson's government.

WILSON, HAROLD

A week is a long time in politics.
speaking to Lobby correspondents in 1964

Wilson's line has usually been interpreted to mean that the fluid shift of national and international affairs means that the assumptions of a Monday may have become the fallacies of Friday and that a politician must therefore think on his feet, rather than set rigid timetables. However Wilson, according to an interview with broadcaster Nigel Rees in 1977, claimed 'It does not mean that I'm living from day to day', but was meant 'as a prescription for long-term strategic thinking and planning, ignoring the day-to-day issues and pressures which may hit the headlines but which must not be allowed to get out of focus while longer-term policies are taking effect'.

WILSON, WOODROW   (1856–1924) American president

The world must be safe for democracy.
address to Congress, April 2 1917

America resisted entry into World War I until increasing attacks by German U-boats on ostensibly neutral American shipping gradually eroded this isolationism. The Germans claimed that they were blockading Britain, but such events as the sinking of the Lusitania on May 7 1915, in which 128 Americans lost their lives, forced the President's hand. War was declared. In his speech Wilson disclaimed any 'selfish ends' but stressed that if America were to resume her neutrality, the world must first be made 'safe for democracy'. The phrase went unnoticed by most of the senators other than John Sharp Williams of Mississippi. Williams, who had to concentrate more than most on the speeches because of his own deafness, began clapping and gradually his fellows joined in. The newspapers picked up the line and immortalised it.

WINCHELL, WALTER   (1897–1972) American journalist

Good evening Mr. and Mrs. North America and all the ships at sea. Let's go to press!
introduction to his radio show

Winchell was the doyen of the Broadway gossip writers whose power to make and break, like that of their Hollywood sisters, made them into figures of far greater influence and authority than the tittle-tattle they purveyed remotely deserved. Winchell was the most powerful of them all, touting a loutish Americanism that brooked no dilution, toadying to and betraying by turn the celebrities, politicians, media personalities and an army of hangers on, who accorded him his phenomenal power. As well as his syndicated column, Winchell broadcast from 1932 a regular radio show which pulled in 20 million listeners, every one avid for his Sunday-night ralling-cry 'Good evening Mr. and Mrs. North America....' He retired in 1969, his column defunct, his only legacy the bizarre vocabulary that he liked to use in the columns.

WINNICOTT, D.W. (1896–1971) British child psychiatrist

The baby creates the object, but the object was there waiting to be created.
Playing and Reality (1971)

Winnicott worked for 40 years from 1923 at the Paddington Green Children's Hospital in London. A devotee of the theories of child analysis advocated by Anna Freud and Melanie Klein he underwent his own analysis and then began practising as a pyschoanalyst, specialising in children, in the mid-1930s. Winnicott established no specific 'school' but his influence on the subsequent methods of child analysis and therapy is immense. Child care experts and educationalists have also drawn on his work. He has been praised as 'unsurpassed in presenting both scientific and poetic truth about infants and children'.

WITTGENSTEIN, LUDWIG (1889–1951) Austrian philosopher

Wittgenstein studied at Cambridge as a pupil of Bertrand Russell, but was forced to discontinue his education to serve in World War I as an Austrian artilleryman. As a prisoner of war in Italy, he wrote his first major philosophical treatise, the *Tractatus Logico-Philosophicus* (1922). For the next ten years Wittgenstein abandoned philosophy, living simply and teaching in an Austrian elementary school. The interest his work aroused in other thinkers brought him back to Cambridge in 1929 and in 1939 he succeeded G.E. Moore as professor of mental philosophy and logic. During the war he worked in a variety of menial tasks, and resigned his professorship in 1947, already a seriously ill man. He died in 1951 and the results of his later views, which reject much of the *Tractatus*, were published as *Philosophical Investigations* (1953).

WITTGENSTEIN, LUDWIG

The world is a totality of facts, not things.
Tractatus Logico-Philosophicus (1922)

Wittgenstein's *Tractatus* takes the form of a series of aphorisms, which are presented to the reader with little supporting argument. It represents his early belief that 'philosophy is not a theory but an activity'. The work has a clear aim and a clear way of achieving it: the essential nature of language must be isolated and described so that its structure and its limits may be determined. He puts forward a theory of logic deduced, like his theory of the limits of language, from his early views of the nature of propositions, and he places religion and morality beyond the limits because they do not meet the requirements of what can be said. He argues in addition that all languages have a uniform logical structure which does not necessarily show on the surface but which can be disclosed by philosophical analysis.

WITTGENSTEIN, LUDWIG

Philosophy simply puts everything before us and neither explains nor deduces anything. Since everything lies open to view, there is nothing to explain. For what is hidden, for example, is of no interest to us.
quoted in *Esquire* magazine, 1970

WITTGENSTEIN, LUDWIG

That which mirrors itself in language, language cannot represent.
Tractatus Logico-Philosophicus (1922)

WITTGENSTEIN, LUDWIG

The limits of my language means the limits of my world.
Tractatus Logico-Philosophicus (1922)

WITTGENSTEIN, LUDWIG

What can be said can be said clearly, and what we cannot talk about we must consign to silence.
Tractatus Logico-Philosophicus (1922)

WITTGENSTEIN, LUDWIG

The totality of thought is a picture of the world.
Tractatus Logico-Philosophicus (1922)

WODEHOUSE, P.G. (1881–1975) British humourist

I can detach myself from the world. If there is a better world to detach oneself from than the one functioning at the moment I have yet to hear of it.
speaking on his 90th birthday, 1971

Wodehouse is the supreme British literary humourist of the

century. In a career that lasted seventy years he wrote nearly 100 books, and helped revolutionise the Broadway musical of the 1920s. Wodehouse's life was relatively uneventful. He began by writing serials about public school life for boys' magazines, and several became his earliest books. An early visit to America was followed by a more permanent stay there after World War I, and in alliance with Jerome Kern and Guy Bolton, he wrote many hit musicals. Wodehouse's greatest creation is his gallery of immortals: Bertie Wooster and his valet Jeeves, the impecunious Ukridge, the Earl of Emsworth and his pig the Empress of Blandings, Uncle Fred, Mr. Mulliner, and The Oldest Member. After his foolish broadcasts from Germany during the war, for which he was savaged by many 'patriots' but fully exonerated by the authorities, he never returned to England. He lived on Long Island, as workaholic as ever, writing continually, playing a little golf and watching the daytime soap operas.

WODEHOUSE, P. G.

Judges, as a class, display, in the matter of arranging alimony, that reckless generosity which is found only in men who are giving away someone else's cash.
Louder and Funnier (1932)

Louder and Funnier is one of Wodehouse's three 'autobiographical' books; the others are *Bring On the Girls* (1953) and *Over Seventy* (1953). The quotation marks are necessary since none of the three is strictly factual. Certainly the incidents that Wodehouse describes or, in the case of *Over Seventy* writes in a series of letters to his old friend the writer William Townend, happened, but few were quite as funny as Wodehouse made them after he had added the embellishments that he felt his readers would enjoy. As Lady Donaldson puts it, in her 1982 biography, Wodehouse 'believed that it is anecdotes that make a book'.

WODEHOUSE, P. G.

I had a private income – the young artist's best friend.
Quick Service (1940)

Quick Service is one of Wodehouse's light novels, a genre that he interspersed with the sagas of such major characters as Bertie Wooster and Lord Emsworth. There were thirty-six in all, almost invariably farces, with a rotating cast of characters who could have been, and sometimes actually were, plucked from the lightest of light comedies. By 1940 Wodehouse had not been a 'young artist' for many years and his income had been topping

WODEHOUSE, P.G.

£100,000 a year since the mid Twenties, but he had done his fair share of penny-a-line struggling. Among his perennial figures is that of a young man – an artist, writer, painter or actor – just waiting for the big break that Wodehouse found and which he invariably offers his fictional alter egos.

WODEHOUSE, P.G.

You would not enjoy Nietzsche, sir. He is fundamentally unsound.
Carry On Jeeves (1925)

Analysts of Wodehouse's books have shown that Jeeves is a positive polymath. Apart from this exchange, in which Jeeves, himself a professed admirer of Spinoza, warns his employer against the German's nihilism, he manages over the years to quote from Lucretius, Pliny the Younger, Whittier, Fitzgerald, Pater, Shelley, Kipling, Keats, Scott, Wordsworth, Emerson, Marcus Aurelius, Shakespeare, Browning, Moore, Virgil, Horace, Dickens, Tennyson, Milton, Henley, Stevenson, Gray, Burns, Byron and the Bible. Bertie quotes from a pretty wide selection of authors too; the difference is that he rarely gets his lines right.

WODEHOUSE, P.G.

I spent the afternoon musing on Life. If you come to think of it, what a queer thing Life is! So unlike anything else, don't you know, if you know what I mean
My Man Jeeves (1919)

In the story 'Rallying Round Old George' the reader can find the prototype Bertie Wooster. At this stage his name had yet to crystallize on Wodehouse's typewriter: the silly ass is called Reggie Pepper and his 'man' is Voules. However, as this particular piece of philsophising makes clear, the transformation of Pepper to Wooster is little more than a matter of typography. Indeed of the stories that are included in *My Man Jeeves*, several of those that feature Pepper were simply rewritten with the new nomenclature for *Carry On Jeeves*, a further collection of stories published in 1925.

WODEHOUSE, P.G.

I have had occasion, I fancy, to speak before now of these pick-me-ups of Jeeves's, and their effect on a fellow who is hanging to life by a thread on the morning after. What they consist of, I couldn't tell you. He says some kind of sauce, the yolk of a raw egg, and a dash of red pepper, but nothing will convince me that

the thing doesn't go much deeper than that. Be that as it may, however, the results of swallowing one are amazing. For perhaps the split part of a second nothing happens. It is as though all Nature waited breathless. Then suddenly, it is as if the Last Trump had sounded and Judgement set in with unusual severity. Bonfires burst out in all parts of the frame. The abdomen becomes heavily charged with lava. A great wind seems to blow through the world, and the subject is aware of something resembling a steam hammer striking the back of the head. During this phase, the ears ring loudly, the eyeballs rotate and there is a tingling about the brow. And then, just as you are feeling you ought to ring up your lawyer and see that your affairs are in order before it is too late, the whole situation seems to clarify. The wind drops. The ears cease to ring. Birds twitter. Brass bands start playing. The sun comes up over the horizon with a jerk. And a moment later all you are conscious of is a great peace.

Right Ho, Jeeves (1934)

Wodehouse's celebration of alcohol, its delights and dangers, runs through his books. Although Bertie Wooster claims a certain moderation in his own intake, his consumption of Jeeves' celebrated pick-me-ups, the effects of which are delineated lovingly above, gives the lie to his protestations. In *Thank You Jeeves*, Bertie's normally teetotal, newt-loving friend Gussie Fink-Nottle is persuaded to present the prizes to the star pupils of Market Snodsbury Grammar School. After imbibing vast quantities of Dutch courage, Gussie delivers a speech that has entered every Wodehouse anthology as a masterpiece of sustained humour. It is while attempting to alleviate Gussie's hangover that Bertie offers his readers this medico-gastronomic aside.

WODEHOUSE, P.G.

I could not restrain a wistful sigh. 'Jeeves is a wonder.' 'A marvel.' 'What a brain!' 'Size nine-and-a-quarter, I should say.' 'He eats a lot of fish.'

Thank You, Jeeves (1934)

Jeeves, the nonpareil of gentlemen's personal gentlemen, enters the Wodehouse canon in the short story *Extricating Young Gussie*, published in *The Man with Two Left Feet* (1917). Never amused and never rattled, a martinet of the wardrobe, especially when it threatens to extend to Old Etonian spats or soft silk shirts for evening wear, and a speaker of the most mandarin restraint, Jeeves is above all a deity who gazes fondly but firmly upon poor, blundering Everyman Wooster, managing his master, like so many fictional servants, with the motto 'Resource and tact'.

WODEHOUSE, P.G.

'Oh Bertie', she said in a low voice like beer trickling out of a jug, 'you ought not to be here.'
The Code of the Woosters (1938)

Throughout his many misadventures Bertie Wooster manages consistently to avoid one fate: long-term entanglement with any of the pretty, purposive girls who obviously have been set on the earth simply to wreak havoc on his life. One such is Madeline Bassett. Madeline is the daughter of the irascible Sir Watkyn Bassett but unlike her father she tends to the spiritual, murmering of the stars as God's daisy-chain and similar inanities. Although engaged in this book to Bertie's friend Gussie Fink-Nottle, she is obsessed with the belief that Bertie is himself devoted to her. When they meet at her house, Totleigh Towers, she draws him to one side and 'with a tender goggle which sent a thrill of dread creeping down the Wooster spine' starts to imitate the heroines of romantic fiction upon whom Wodehouse modelled her.

WODEHOUSE, P.G.

It is no use telling me that there are bad aunts and good aunts. At the core they are all alike. Sooner or later, out pops the cloven hoof.
The Code of the Woosters (1938)

Bertie Wooster has two aunts, who as he puts it in *The Inimitable Jeeves* (1923) are prone to call to each other 'like mastodons bellowing across primeval swamps...'. One is 'Aunt Agatha, who eats broken bottles and wears barbed wire next to the skin'; the other, less terrifying but equally aggressive, is Aunt Dahlia, brick red of face and bellowing of tone, who combines fox-hunting with the running of her magazine *Milady's Boudoir*. They, and a variety of other aunts, play a central role in Wodehouse's humour. As Richard Usborne puts it in his study *Wodehouse at Work to the End* (1977) 'Wodehouse...adopted aunts and aunthood as good comic business. The aunt represents authority and interference. The nephew owes her a duty. But there is no absolute necessity for love on either side. A monstrous aunt can be funny. A monstrous mother would be tragic'.

WODEHOUSE, P.G.

It's curious how, looking back, you can nearly always spot where you went wrong in any binge or enterprise. Take this little slab of community singing of ours, for instance. In order to give the thing zip, I stood on my chair and waved the decanter like a baton, and this, I see now, was a mistake. It helped the composition enormously , but it tended to create a false impression in the mind of the observer, conjuring up a picture of drunken revels.
The Mating Season (1949)

In this novel, Bertie's ability to convince the otherwise teetotal, in this case one Esmond Haddock, of the hitherto untasted charms of alcohol is once again brought into play. Forced, for the sake of a pal, to assume a false identity, and suffer not one but a whole dinner-table full of singularly unappealing aunts, Bertie's consumption of post-prandial port is understandable, but injudicious. As Haddock gives another chorus of 'A Hunting We Will Go' accompanied by Wooster on decanter, one of these aunts walks in and ruins the party, as Bertie puts it 'rather in the manner of the prudish Queen of a monarch of Babylon who has happened to wander into the banqueting hall just as the Babylonian orgy is beginning to go nicely'.

WODEHOUSE, P.G

It was my Uncle George who discovered that alcohol was a food well in advance of modern medical thought.
The Inimitable Jeeves (1923)

WOLFE, TOM (1931–) American writer

A cult is a religion with no political power.
In Our Time (1980)

In Our Time was Wolfe's memorial of the Sixties and their offspring the Seventies, an era that he had christened the 'Me Generation'. In a section entitled 'Entr'actes and canapes', in which he offered a quick run-down of passing events, he dealt with Jonestown, the Guyanese dystopia created by cult guru Jim Jones, where 900 people committed 'revolutionary suicide' (qv). Wolfe wrote 'Among other things, Jonestown was an example of a definition well known to sociologists of religion: a cult is a religion with no political power. Usually this is observed when the religion is in its ascendancy and is elevated from the status of "cult" to that of "church" or "denomination".' Wolfe's comment was parallelled by that of American philosopher James K. Feibleman (1904–) who wrote in *Understanding Philosophy* (1973) 'A myth is a religion in which no-one any longer believes.'

WOLFE, TOM

Mmmmmmmmmmmmmmmmmm. These are nice. Little Roquefort cheese morsels rolled in crushed nuts. Very tasty. Very subtle. It's the way the dry sackiness of the nuts tiptoes up against the dour savour of the cheese that is so nice, so subtle. Wonder what the Black Panthers eat here on the hors d'oeuvres trail? Do the Panthers like little Roquefort cheese morsels rolled in crushed nuts this way...?
Radical Chic (1970)

Radical Chic was first published in *New York Magazine* and latterly appeared in 1972 as one part of a book which included Wolfe's other essay into liberal guilt *Mau-Mauing the Flak-Catchers*. Apart from coining a phrase *Radical Chic* took a dispassionate look at the bizarre conjunction of rich white liberals, in this case conductor Leonard Bernstein and his friends, and the spokesmen of the revolution, the Black Panthers. Wolfe showed how such liberalism invariably preferred 'radicals who seem primitive, exotic and romantic', providing in their anger a thrilling reflection of how the smart and wealthy liked to envisage themselves vis-á-vis the more conservative elements of their privileged enclave, and how it is 'only radical in style... in its heart it is part of Society and its traditions.'

WOODROFFE, TOMMY   British radio commentator

I'll eat my hat!
commentating on the FA Cup, 1938

Lieutenant-Commander Tommy Woodroffe was one of the BBC's first commentators in an era when radio listeners followed the match on a map of the football field that had been divided into eight numbered squares, around which the commentator would guide them as the play ebbed and flowed. Covering the 1938 Cup Final he was so sure that there would be little further excitement in what was proving a tedious match, he told his audience 'If there's a goal now, I'll eat my hat'. Sure enough, a goal followed almost at once and to Woodroffe's credit, and to the amusement of the listeners, he duly consumed his hat.

WOOLCOTT, ALEXANDER   (1887–1943) American writer, critic and wit

I have no need of your God-damned sympathy. I only wish to be entertained by some of your grosser reminiscences.
remark during his last illness, 1943

This remark, offered to a visitor who had the temerity to wish him well during an illness that proved to be his last, is typical Woollcott: rude, gossipy and in the end, if one were not on the receiving end of the line, amusing. Woollcott died half way through a programme in which he was appearing as part of a group discussing the rise of Hitler. As the discussion continued he felt increasingly ill and wrote on a large sheet of paper, since the microphones were open, 'I Am Sick'. He then collapsed and was carried out of the studio. Playing the trouper he told Dr. Harry Gideonse, the panel's chairman and his rescuer 'Get back in there! Never mind me! Go back in there!'. He was rushed to hospital but never managed to revive.

WOOLCOTT, ALEXANDER

Anything you like is either illegal, immoral, or fattening
The Knock on the Stage Door

Woolcott was one of the best known members of the circle of wits and self-promoters, christened by the columnists The Algonquin Round Table. Nicknamed by James Thurber 'Old Vitriol and Violets' he was possibly the most self-obsessed of a coterie of egomaniacs. As his fame increased, both as a drama critic and as a radio broadcaster, the vitriol took the upper hand and Woolcott alienated more and more old friends with his gratuitous insults; the violets were reserved for his radio audience, who lapped up a regular ration of mawkish gush that hardly accorded with Woolcott's acid-tongued, off-microphone persona. Throughout his life Woolcott suffered from a weight problem. A series of 'fat doctors' did no good and Woolcott's cri-de-coeur is all too heartfelt.

WOOLF, VIRGINIA (1882–1941) British novelist and critic

The interest in life does not lie in what people do, nor even in their relations to each other, but largely in the power to communicate with a third party, antagonistic, enigmatic, yet perhaps persuadable, which one may call life in general.
The Common Reader (1925)

The Common Reader was the first volume of Woolf's *Collected Essays*. It was, as she said, an attempt to view literature with the eyes of the ordinary reader who is neither scholar nor critic. It contains a wide variety of essays and was received with high praise in many quarters. A further selection, under the same title, appeared in 1932. Many of her critics have suggested that it was in her non-fiction, discussing the work of others, that she was at her best, rather than in her introspective, bloodless novels.

WOOLF, VIRGINIA

More than... anything (life) calls for confidence in oneself. Without self-confidence we are babes in the cradle. And how can we generate this imponderable quality, which is yet so invaluable, most quickly? By thinking that other people are inferior to oneself.
A Room of One's Own (1929)

A *Rooom of One's Own* is an essay on women and creativity based largely on two papers Woolf had delivered in 1928. In this book she asserts that intellectual freedom depends upon material things, that in order to write one must have money and a room of one's own, and that neither women nor the the whole working class, irrespective of sex, have ever had these vital things and thus have never had intellectual freedom. She urges women to take advantage of the degree of educational freedom of opportunity which for the first time is becoming widely available to their sex.

WOOLF, VIRGINIA

It's not catastrophes, murders, deaths, diseases, that age and kill us; it's the way people look and laugh, and run up the steps of omnibuses.
Jacob's Room (1922)

In her novel *Jacob's Room* there is no plot and no attempt to preserve the outlines of chronological events. Jacob Flanders' life is presented in a collection of fragments - playing on the beach as a boy, at university, at dinner in Greece, in Paris and so on. Major facts, such as his death in World War I, are never mentioned and the reader is left to deduce them from their incidental effects, for instance as his friend Bonamy and his mother clear out his room and wonder what to do with his old shoes. Woolf probably had her brother Thoby in mind when she wrote the book: the bare bones of Flanders' life are much the same as his, including the premature death.

WRIGHT, FRANK LLOYD   (1867-1959) American architect

A doctor can bury his mistakes, but an architect can only advise his client to plant vines.
in the *Sunday Times*, 1957

Wright was one of the most prolific of twentieth century architects, extending his career over 74 years, and producing a large number of influential buildings as well as good deal of theoretical writing. The premise of his work was to create an architecture that was both close to nature and reflected new and specifically American values. His *Prairie House* (1910), with its interconnecting spaces, replacing the traditional compartmentalised rooms, can be seen as the forerunner of much modern design. Wright looked for what he defined as 'organic' architecture, a complex theory that attempted to free the building from influences imposed by external forces, that reflected nature and which unified both external and internal space.

WYATT, WOODROW (1919–) British politician and author

A man falls in love through his eyes. A woman through her ears.
To the Point (1981)

Wyatt is one of Britain's most celebrated political mavericks, who combined a dandy's lifestyle with the role of courtier to a succession of figures who have ranged from Bertrand Russell and Gandhi to Viscount Montgomery and Rupert Murdoch. Ennobled in 1987, he writes a column 'The Voice of Reason' in the *News of the World*. Wyatt's comment points up the traditional assumption of the difference in the way the sexes choose what they find attractive. Men tend to look first for physical attractions, worrying less about cerebral charms. Women, on the other hand, prefer some kind of emotional bond. While the male side of this thesis seems all too accurate, the exclusion of women from the ranks of those who find the purely physical appealing is surely an extension of a world in which women are not supposed to enjoy sex for its own sake.

Y

YEATS, W.B.   (1865–1939) Irish poet and playwright

The most fundamental of divisions is that between the intellect, which can only do its work by saying continually 'thou fool', and the religious genius which makes all equal.
Estrangement (1936)

Aged 21 Yeats abandoned his earlier study of art and turned instead to that of mystic religion and Irish legends of the supernatural. Inspired by his love for the beautiful revolutionary Maud Gonne he determined to use his talents in the cause of Irish nationalism, aiming to reawaken his people's consciousness of their own heritage, submerged beneath years of English domination. With the same intention, and helped by Lady Gregory, he created the Irish National Theatre Company and bought the Abbey Theatre. Politics and society gradually displaced mysticism from his work. After Home Rule, Yeats served as a senator of the Irish Free State from 1922-28, and was awarded a Nobel Prize in 1923.

YEVTUSHENKO, YEVGENY   (1933–) Russian poet

He who is conceived in a cage yearns for the cage.
quoted in 1968

Yevtushenko published his first collection of verse in 1942, but not until Khrushchev's cultural 'thaw' in the late Fifties did he become internationally celebrated. Yevtushenko appeared as the articulate, rebellious voice of his generation, leading literature from its Stalinist repression, but he was never more than a court rebel, who carefully sidestepped the real issues. Through the fluctuations of Soviet censorship, Yevtushenko has been notable for his apparent ability to drift with the current; for all his earlier 'outspokenness' he has never been numbered among Russia's dissidents and his aphorism seems to apply most ironically to himself.

YOUNG, MICHAEL   British writer

The Rise of the Meritocracy
book title, 1958

As defined by the Oxford English Dictionary a meritocracy is 'government by persons selected on the basis of merit in a competitive educational system; a society so governed; a ruling or influential class of educated people'. Young's book does not actually look at contemporary society but posits a 21st century Britain in which the evolving social revolution has thrown up a ruling elite who have been selected not by birth or wealth, but by intellectual ability as demonstrated in examinations. Judging by the speed with which the word was absorbed into the language, Young's concept has taken shape far sooner than he expected, although class-conscious Britain persists in maintaining at least some of the old hierarchies.

YOUNG, ANDREW (1932–) American politician

Nothing is illegal if 100 businessmen decide to do it.
quoted in 1976

Young began his career as an assistant to Martin Luther King and with the election of President Jimmy Carter in 1976 became America's best-known black politician. His remark reflects the way in which white collar crime differs so markedly from its less respectable peers. In most capitalist countries, the importance of the business community means that its relationship with the Establishment renders actions that would be crimes if ascribed to a working class perpetrator, mere peccadilloes in business terms. In parallel with this is the fact that in such areas as conservation or urban planning, if sufficient businessmen with sufficient clout decide to ride over a given law, then there is very little that can be done to stop them.

YULE, FRED British comedian

Lovely grub!
catchphrase in *ITMA*, 1940s

Yule played George Gorge 'the greediest man ever to have two ration books' in *ITMA*, wartime radio's favourite radio comedy show. In various episodes of the show Yule was also Norman the Doorman, who inevitably pronounced 'vice versa' as 'vicky verky', Johann Bull, the jovial, practical-joking friend of the jokey German agent Funf, and Big Chief Bigga Banga. In 1949 he moved to Ted Ray's show *Ray's A Laugh*, where he played Nelson, the star's supposed brother-in-law, a role that was later taken over by Kenneth Connor.

Z

ZANGWILL, ISRAEL (1864–1926) British writer

America is God's Crucible, the great Melting-Pot.
The Melting Pot (1908)

Zangwill was a noted Jewish writer and translator and spokesman for Jewish interests. He wrote a number of books, usually centred on the lives of the poor Jews of London's East End. His plays, like his books, mix social observations with pro-Jewish polemic. *The Melting Pot*, like the novel *Children of the Ghetto*, dealt with the topical subject of Jewish immigration, although turning from London to New York. David Quixano, a young Russian Jew, dreams of leaving the shtetl for America 'where all the races of Europe are melting and reforming'. The play deals with his attempts to fulfil his dream, and while it is no longer current, the phrase its title coined has been associated with America ever since.

ZANUCK, DARRYL F. (1902–79) American film magnate

Don't say yes until I finish talking!
quoted in Leslie Halliwell, *The Filmgoer's Companion* (1985)

Zanuck began his film career in 1924 as a scriptwriter for Warner Brothers. As an executive producer three years later he persuaded the Brothers to make *The Jazz Singer*, the first film to synchronise speech as well as music with the pictures and, for all its primitive nature, the harbinger of a Hollywood revolution. In 1933 he founded his own 20th Century Studio, merging it with Fox in 1935. Zanuck resigned from 20th Century Fox in 1956 but returned in 1962. Above all he was an authoritarian and a showman. His demand that his yes-men should at least make a pretence of considering what he said was used as the title of his biography. His attitude to the public was generally hard-nosed and he remarked on various occasions 'I know audiences feed on crap, but I cannot believe we are so lacking that we cannot dish it up to them with some trace of originality' and 'Public taste is an ascending spiral'. As far as quality was concerned his basic credo read 'Take a chance and spend a million dollars and hope you're right', and he was convinced that 'when you can get a sex story in biblical garb, you can open your own mint'.

ZAPPA, FRANK (1940–) American musician

Most rock journalism is people who can't write interviewing people who can't talk for people who can't read.
in *Rolling Stone* magazine, 1970

Zappa established himself as one of rock music's great innovators in the Sixties although his real stardom was postponed till the next decade, when his cult status expanded into the wider market. With his band the *Mother of Invention* he made an album that managed to satirise the world of middle-class American values and offer listeners some highly challenging music. In an era when recording studios were still primitive by today's standards Zappa showed himself to be a superb technician, whose tape editing was an integral part of his creativity. His mordant remark sums up his own views on the self-perpertuating monster into which rock 'n' roll has developed.

ZIEGLER, RONALD L. (1939–) American government spokesman

This is the operative statement. The others are inoperative.
statement to the press, April 17, 1973

Ronald Ziegler was official spokesman for the White House during the Watergate Scandal of 1973–74. Holding down government's least enviable job meant that Ziegler, a former guide to Disneyland's 'jungle', found himself the mouthpiece for a succession of evasions, contradictions and downright lies. Among his disclaimers had been 'The President is aware of what is going on. That is not to say that something is going on.' When, on April 17, 1973 the President, who had been steadfastly 'stonewalling' all enquiries up till then, suddenly announced that he would permit his aides to testify as the Senate Committee desired, the hapless Ziegler had to catch the reportorial flak. When R.W. 'Johnny' Apple Jr. of the *New York Times* asked him 'Would it be fair for us to infer, since what the President said today is now the operative statement, to quote you, that the other statement is no longer operative, that it is now inoperative?' Ziegler replied 'This is the operative statement. The others are inoperative.'

ZUCKERMAN, LORD (1904–) British zoologist and educationalist

We live as we live because of the decisions, however explicit or however indefined, that were taken yesterday about which technological developments to encourage to satisfy man's enduring urge for an ever better life.

ZUCKERMAN, LORD

in the *Sunday Times*, 1973

Zuckerman joined the zoological faculty of Oxford University in 1934 and during the war specialised in researching the biological effects of bomb blasts. From 1946–68 he was profesor of anatomy at Birmingham University and from 1955 secretary and from 1977 president of the Zoological Society. He has performed extensive work in the study of primates and published widely. In his collections of essays, *Man and Aggression* (1968) he criticised the view of Lorenz and Ardrey that claims that human aggression is instinctive, and he regularly voiced his own doubts as to the efficacy of the nuclear balance of terror.

Index

Belief

Culture

Cynicism

Critic

Critics

Death

Failure

Humanity

Illusion

lessons of history 404
Mr. Toad 346
old 529
prophet 401
young 529

Language
A thing of duty 595
America 660, 693
basic rule of bureaucracies 643
boys in the back room 254
businessmen 809
drunk 156
England 693
Evening, all 252
Fact 56
fuck 758
gin 557
ideology 660
ism 673
Judges 799
Judicial decrees 442
language 693, 798
law 567
law and order 764
lawyer 336
legislation 319
limits of my language 798
make my day 251
media 319
Not bloody likely 692
Nudge, nudge, wink, wink 405
point of principle 417
policeman 232
problem 459
See you later, alligator 364
sin 557
Slang 677
speaking 481
swearword 78
talk 459
truth 336
up to your ass in alligators 580
Voltaire 240
whiskey 557
world 798
Yiddish 702
'U and Non-U 661

Law
British Police Force 601

Leader
art of leadership 387
blood, toil, tears, and sweat 607
great and famous 604
History 604
leader 755
nation 187

Left
education 73
radical 73
young man 73

Liberalism
autobiography 720
Black Panthers 804
equal 753
ideology 720
liberal 68, 317
liberal and progressive 753
Liberalism 720
liberals 140
money 68
Politics 720
poor 753

Liberty
liberty is precious 476

Life
afraid 5
all life is six to five against 667
articulate 625
average man 309
barbarism 18
Being born is like being
  kidnapped 772
better life 811
born 90, 194
children 496
Civilisation 18
civilising 90
complex 383
concentration camp 22
death 792
destruction of this plane 458
disasters 457
disinterested 407
education 689
existance 59, 226
experience 109, 113, 289, 532,
  625

Literature

Love

credulity of love   311
deception of love   638
Emily I love you   237
fools   470
groans of love   502
hate   161
inexperienced years   352
life   41
love   41, 161, 167, 225, 353, 380,
   470, 529, 549
love affair   766
Love means   501
man   807
marriage   470
patriotism   470
proof of love   227
talking of Michelangelo   281
woman   807

Loyalty
all the President's men   447
fight and fight and fight
   again   320
walk over my grandmother   205

Luck
God   41
powerful   41
rich   41
whims of chance   537

Lying
act   14
all the President's men   447
art of leadership   387
autobiographer   380
Checkers   588
common people   339
Crisis, what crisis   733
De mortuis   463
demagogue   549
dinner-party   627
duty   694
Every government is run by liars
   729
fall for anything   365
fiction   379
fool all the people   484
Freedom   329
govern   397
government   426, 716

humanity   397
idiot   390
idiots   549
innacuracy   675
last territorial claim   388
late parrot   564
lawyer   336
leaders   427
liar   24
liars   379
liberty   333
lie   154
lies   604
lies, damned lies, and
   statistics   757
Lying   286
nice old gentleman   388
no whitewash at the White House
   591
official denial   438
philosophies   426
Political language   604
Political skill   188
politician 24,   240
politicians 2,   437
politics   489
propagandist reason   389
realism   89
realist   371
realistic decision   538
resign   324
revolution   427
revolutionary slogans   437
soap box   493
stark, staring bonkers   362
stupid man   694
swindling   322
The old Lie   611
Theatre   14
This is the operative
   statement   811
toothpaste   364
truth   151, 154, 336, 389
tyrannical   333
wait   48,
war   339
Well, he would, wouldn't
   he   650

Madness
A man ought to do   394

Planning

Pleasure

Power

Prison

Prizes

Promises

Propaganda

Prophecy

Race

Religion

Woman

Woman

Women

Work

World

Writer

Writing

Youth